FOOD PRODUCTS FORMULARY

VOLUME 1

MEATS, POULTRY, FISH, SHELLFISH

other AVI books with additional information on food processing

FOOD PRODUCTS FORMULARY

VOLUME 1

MEATS, POULTRY, FISH, SHELLFISH

by STEPHAN L. KOMARIK,
Consultant,
Coral Gables, Florida,
Formerly Director,
Food Product Development Research,
Griffith Laboratories, Inc.,
Chicago, Illinois

DONALD K. TRESSLER, Ph.D.,
President,
The Avi Publishing Company,
Westport, Connecticut

LUCY LONG,
Associate Editor,
The Avi Publishing Company,
Westport, Connecticut

WESTPORT, CONNECTICUT
THE AVI PUBLISHING COMPANY, INC.
1974

Preface

This is the first of a planned series covering commercial processing applications for a far-reaching range of food products. *Food Products Formulary, Volume 1*, herein presents formulas for meats (smoked and cured meats; sausages and bolognas; luncheon meats and loaves; miscellaneous canned products; frozen meat dishes; soups and gravies including mixes), poultry (frozen and canned chicken and turkey products, ducks, geese, guinea, and squab), and fish and shellfish (salted and pickled products, canned and frozen products, smoked products, and loaves, spreads, and salads).

Subsequent volumes in the series will cover cereal products (including baked goods) and dairy products in Volume 2, fruit and vegetable products in Volume 3, and beverages and snack foods in Volume 4.

The formulas presented in this volume are largely those developed and tested by the senior author during a lifetime of work in meat preservation. They include not only those used by American meat processors, but also formulas and procedures commonly employed for making sausages in Central Europe.

There is a special section in this Formulary devoted to the use of textured soy protein as a means of extending the protein value or partially replacing the meat or poultry content of many types of products: patties, loaves, casseroles, and other dishes. This is an area of commercial food processing which the authors believe will develop rapidly in the immediate future. Already, many of these products are presently included in school lunches and mass feeding programs where nutritional intake may be substandard. The authors are indebted to manufacturers of textured soy protein products who have supplied these formulas for publication in this Formulary.

The authors are also indebted to the U.S. Bureau of Commercial Fisheries and the U.S. Fish and Wildlife Service for many of the formulas in the sections on fish and shellfish. Many of the other formulas in these sections were first published in *Marine Products of Commerce, 1st and 2nd Editions* which were written by one of the junior authors of this work.

Although care has been taken to check the accuracy of the formulas and procedures included, the detailed methods should be tested further on a small scale before being adopted commercially. Also, the suggested processing times and temperatures for sterilization should be approved by a can manufacturer or the National Canners Association.

STEPHAN L. KOMARIK
DONALD K. TRESSLER
LUCY LONG

August 1973

Our Grateful Thanks to Numerous Contributors

It would not have been possible to publish the wide range of formulas contained in this book without the generous cooperation of manufacturers, industry associations, government agencies, publishers, and individuals. Even though acknowledgement of each of these contributions is given along with the formula which was contributed, we hereby gratefully extend our thanks to the following:

American Dry Milk Institute, Chicago, Illinois

Central Soya Company, Chemurgy Division, Chicago, Illinois

A Complete Course in Canning by Lopez and published by Canning Trade, Baltimore, Maryland

Cornell Hotel & Restaurant Administration Quarterly, Ithaca, New York

CPC International, Inc., Industrial Division, Englewood Cliffs, New Jersey

Far-Mar-Co, Research Division, Hutchinson, Kansas

Fish and Wildlife Service, U.S. Department of the Interior, Washington, D.C.

FMC Corp., Avicel Division of American Viscose Company, Marcus Hook, Pennsylvania

Food Dehydration, 2nd Edition, Vol. 2 by Van Arsdel, Copley, and Morgan and published by Avi Publishing Company, Westport, Connecticut

Food Flavorings, 2nd Edition by Merory and published by Avi Publishing Company, Westport, Connecticut

The Freezing Preservation of Foods, 3rd Edition, Vol. 1 and 2 by Tressler and Evers and published by Avi Publishing Company, Westport, Connecticut

The Freezing Preservation of Foods, 4th Edition, Vol. 3 and 4 by Tressler, Van Arsdel, and Copley and published by Avi Publishing Company, Westport, Connecticut

General Mills, Inc., Food Service and Protein Products Division, Minneapolis, Minnesota

Gentry International, Inc., Gilroy, California

Germantown Manufacturing Company, Broomall, Pennsylvania

Gold Kist, Inc., Atlanta, Georgia

Handbook of Food Manufacture by Fiene and Blumenthal and published by Chemical Publishing Company, New York, N.Y.

Henningsen Foods, Inc., New York, N.Y.

Industrial Fishery Technology by Stansby and published by Reinhold Publishing Company, New York, N.Y.

Kelco Company, Chicago, Illinois

Marine Products of Commerce by Tressler and published by Chemical Catalog Company, New York, N.Y.

Marine Products of Commerce, 2nd Edition by Tressler and Lemon and published by Reinhold Publishing Company, New York, N.Y.

Meat Merchandising, St. Louis, Missouri

Meat Processing, Chicago, Illinois

Merck Chemical Division, Merck & Company, Rahway, New Jersey

Miles Laboratories, Inc., Marschall Division, Elkhart, Indiana

George J. Mountney, Research Management Specialist, Food Science Programs, United States Department of Agriculture, Cooperative State Research Service, Washington, D.C.

National Marine Fisheries Service, Seattle, Washington

National Starch and Chemical Corp., Plainfield, New Jersey

Nestlé Company, Food Ingredients Division, White Plains, New York

Poultry Products Technology by Mountney and published by Avi Publishing Company, Westport, Connecticut

Ralston Purina Company, St. Louis, Missouri

A. E. Staley Manufacturing Company, Decatur, Illinois

Swift Edible Oil Company, Vegetable Protein Products Division, Swift & Company, Chicago, Illinois

U.S. Armed Services, U.S. Military Specifications, Washington, D.C.

U.S. Bureau of Commercial Fisheries, Washington, D.C.

Contents

CURED MEATS[1]

GENERAL RECOMMENDATIONS

During the last 30 yr, new methods for curing large pieces of meat, such as hams, picnics, etc., have been perfected yielding more desirable, more tender and flavorful products in greatly shortened curing periods.

Hams, picnics, and loins from hogs of 8-12 months of age should be used to obtain products of high quality. Older animals will result in products with less tenderness, drier texture, and darker color. Stags will not yield meat of good quality.

Carcasses should be chilled after slaughter to an internal temperature in the center of the hind leg to about 35°F before curing or freezing. Fresh frozen cuts can be used if properly defrosted.

Thawing Frozen Cuts.—When frozen meats are used, they should be thoroughly defrosted, preferably to 35°F. Thawing can be accomplished in large vats containing circulating 25° salinometer plain salt pickle. Use equal weights of brine and meat. Frozen meat will cool the brine, so brine should be circulated by pumping it from the top of the vat through a pipeline, reheated to a temperature of 45°F, then returned to the bottom of the vat, thus keeping the brine agitated and warmed during the defrosting period. Another method of defrosting is to circulate tap water through an inlet at the bottom of the vat with an overflow at the top. Low pressure compressed air is sometimes injected at the bottom of the vat to keep water in agitation. Pork bellies are usually defrosted with air circulated at room temperature until internal temperature reaches 36°-38°F.

Sanitation Is Important.—Sanitation in the curing cellars should be rigidly maintained. Careless hygiene (or cleanup) will contribute to contamination of the meats and may result in spoilage of the product. This results in serious loss to the processor.

Use approved cleaning agents containing one or more detergents which remove dirt and grease. Approved germicides should be used after the regular cleanup to kill microorganisms and produce sanitary conditions. Walls and ceilings should be sprayed with an approved germicide. All processing equipment and vats should be thoroughly cleaned. Floors should be hosed down or mopped. It is imperative that employees wash and sanitize their hands before handling meats.

Curing Cellar Temperature.—The recommended temperature of the curing cellar is 38°-40°F.

Curing Methods for Large Meat Cuts

Artery Pumping.—Artery pump pork products such as hams and picnics and beef products such as briskets, hams, and tongues.

Injecto Curing.—Inject curing pickle into boneless meat through a bank of perforated needles.

Sweet Pickle Cure.—Meats are cured in pickle through osmosis with or without pumping.

Dry Cure.—Meat is rubbed with dry salt, tightly packed, and cured by osmosis.

Curing Pickle Ingredients and Government Regulations

Use good quality materials: salt, sodium or potassium nitrite, sodium or potassium nitrate, sugars, food grade phosphates (or a combination of food grade phosphate with sodium hydroxide; see Table 1.1), sodium erythorbate, flavorings.

According to 1972 government regulations, the amount of sodium nitrite permitted is 2 lb per 100 gal. of pickle; the amount of sodium nitrate permitted is 7 lb per 100 gal. of pickle.

Sufficient sugar is used to obtain desired flavor.

Permitted Moisture Content.—According to government regulations for cured products such as hams, picnics, shoulder butts, and pork loins, the finished cooked meats shall not contain more moisture than the fresh, uncured product.

Phosphates.—Food grade phosphates must not result in more than 0.5% of phosphate in the finished product and not more than 5% of phosphate in the pickle solution based on 10% pumping pickle. Use of phosphates is permitted only in hams, pork shoulders, picnics, loins, and bacon.

---

[1] Data for this section by S. L. Komarik, Coral Gables, Florida.

Caution Regarding Use of Phosphates.—If disodium phosphate is used, it should be kept in mind that it is only slightly soluble in cold water. It should be dissolved in hot water. Therefore, the pickle must be heated and kept warm, otherwise it crystallizes out. Some phosphates (e.g., sodium acid pyrophosphate) dissolve easily in cold water; others are only slightly soluble and must be used in combination with other phosphates.

If the maximum amount of pohsphates is used in curing hams and picnics, it makes the finished product "slippery" when chewed in the mouth; therefore, somewhat less should be used.

Ascorbates.—Ascorbic acid, sodium erythorbate (or sodium ascorbate), sodium d-isoascorbic acid may be used in preparation of cured meat products, but the pickle used for curing meats shall not contain more than 5.5 lb per 100 gal. based on 10% pumping pickle.

Flavorings.—Spices, their extractives, monosodium glutamate, hydrolyzed plant protein, and smoke flavor may be used to flavor the meat.

Preparing Pickles for Curing

Salt is the basic ingredient of curing pickle. Curing pickle can be prepared by using a $100°$ salinometer salt brine or by adding salt directly to water to give curing pickle the desired salt content. Salt brine of $100°$ salinometer reading contains the maximum amount of salt that will dissolve in water at a temperature of $38°F$. Customarily, large operations use $100°$ salinometer salt brine in preparing curing solutions and then reduce its concentration by adding water to obtain a curing pickle of the desired concentration.

Sodium nitrite, sodium nitrate, phosphate, sugars, sodium erythorbate, and flavorings are added to the curing pickle; it is then agitated until all ingredients are in perfect solution. These added materials will increase salinometer readings of the pickle.

Phosphates do not increase the salt flavor in the finished product.

In using a dry curing mixture, it is very important that all ingredients are thoroughly mixed. If the sodium nitrite, sodium nitrate, sodium erythorbate (or sodium ascorbate), and sodium bicarbonate—even in the small amounts called for—are not evenly distributed in the salt, the cured meat will show "burned" spots (nitrite burn) in areas where too much nitrite is in contact with meat.

Pumping Pickles

Using Sodium Erythorbate (or Sodium Ascorbate).—The pickle temperature should not be over $40°F$ when sodium erythorbate and sodium bicarbonate are added. Air agitation should not be used to hasten solution of the dry ingredients. Hardwood paddles should be used. Keep pickle as cold as possible and prepare only a sufficient amount of this type of pickle for one day's operation.

Without Phosphate and Sodium Erythorbate.—Pumping pickle ingredients using salt and water or $100°$ salinometer brine are given in Table 1.1; just omit phosphate, erythorbate, and bicarbonate.

Cold water ($38°$-$40°F$) should be used in preparation of the pickle. Salt, sodium nitrite and sodium nitrate, sugar (cane or beet), and flavoring should be added to the water and agitated vigorously until all ingredients are dissolved and pickle is clear. The finished pickle should be kept at the cellar temperature of $38°$-$40°F$.

When Phosphates Are Used.—Ingredients are indicated in Table 1.1. Omit sodium erythorbate and bicarbonate.

Cold water ($38°$-$40°F$) should be used in preparation of the pickle. First step is to dissolve the phosphate in cold water, stirring vigorously until phosphate is dissolved with no sediment on the bottom of the tank. Then add salt or brine, cures, sugar, and flavorings; agitate until all ingredients are properly dissolved and pickle is crystal clear.

When Phosphate and Sodium Erythorbate Are Incorporated In the Pickle.—Ingredients are indicated in Table 1.1.

Cold water ($38°$-$40°F$) should be used. First step is to dissolve the phosphate in the cold water, stirring vigorously until phosphate is dissolved with no sediment on the bottom of the tank. Then add sodium erythorbate and sodium bicarbonate and stir until completely dissolved; then add salt or brine, cures, flavorings, and sugar. Agitate until all ingredients are dissolved and the pickle is crystal clear.

NOTE: Under no circumstances should the pickle be agitated with air or steam as this will oxidize the erythorbate.

When phosphates are used, the tank in which the pickle is prepared and stored *must* be stainless steel, glass-lined iron, or hardwood since phosphates will attack both galvanized and bare iron, which will discolor the product.

BRINE CONCENTRATIONS AND RELATED DATA

Degrees Salinometer	Degrees Baumé	Specific Gravity	Salt (%)	Weight (Lb)	Salt (Lb/Gal.)
20	—	—	5.305	—	0.427
21	—	—	5.570	—	0.453
22	—	—	5.835	—	0.479
23	—	—	6.100	—	0.505
24	—	—	6.365	—	0.531
25	—	—	6.630	—	0.557
26	—	—	6.895	—	0.583
27	—	—	7.160	—	0.609
28	—	—	7.425	—	0.635
29	—	—	7.690	—	0.661
30	—	—	7.955	—	0.687
31	—	—	8.220	—	0.713
32	—	—	8.485	—	0.739
33	—	—	8.745	—	0.765
34	—	—	9.010	—	0.791
35	—	—	9.275	—	0.817
36	—	—	9.540	—	0.843
37	—	—	9.805	—	0.869
38	—	—	10.070	—	0.895
39	—	—	10.335	—	0.921
40	10.40	1.073	10.600	8.939	0.947
41	10.66	1.075	10.865	8.955	0.973
42	10.92	1.077	11.130	8.972	0.998
43	11.18	1.079	11.395	8.989	1.024
44	11.44	1.081	11.660	9.005	1.050
45	11.70	1.083	11.925	9.022	1.075
46	11.96	1.085	12.190	9.039	1.101
47	12.22	1.087	12.455	9.055	1.127
48	12.48	1.089	12.720	9.072	1.154
49	12.74	1.091	12.985	9.089	1.180
50	13.00	1.093	13.250	9.105	1.206
51	13.26	1.095	13.515	9.122	1.232
52	13.52	1.097	13.780	9.139	1.259
53	13.78	1.100	14.045	9.164	1.287
54	14.04	1.102	14.310	9.180	1.313
55	14.30	1.104	14.575	9.197	1.340
56	14.56	1.106	14.840	9.214	1.367
57	14.82	1.108	15.105	9.230	1.394
58	15.08	1.110	15.370	9.247	1.421
59	15.34	1.112	15.635	9.264	1.448
60	15.60	1.114	15.900	9.280	1.475
61	16.86	1.116	16.165	9.297	1.502
62	16.12	1.118	16.430	9.314	1.530
63	16.38	1.121	16.695	9.339	1.559
64	16.64	1.123	16.960	9.355	1.586
65	16.90	1.125	17.225	9.372	1.614
66	17.16	1.127	17.490	9.389	1.642
67	17.42	1.129	17.755	9.405	1.670
68	17.68	1.131	18.020	9.422	1.697
69	17.94	1.133	18.285	9.439	1.725
70	18.20	1.136	18.550	9.464	1.755
71	18.46	1.138	18.815	9.480	1.783
72	18.72	1.140	19.080	9.497	1.812
73	18.98	1.142	19.345	9.514	1.840
74	19.24	1.144	19.610	9.530	1.868
75	19.50	1.147	19.875	9.555	1.899
76	19.76	1.149	20.140	9.572	1.927
77	20.02	1.151	20.405	9.580	1.956
78	20.28	1.154	20.670	9.614	1.987

BRINE CONCENTRATIONS AND RELATED DATA
(*Continued*)

Degrees Salinometer	Degrees Baumé	Specific Gravity	Salt (%)	Weight (Lb)	Salt (Lb/Gal.)
79	20.54	1.156	20.935	9.630	2.016
80	20.80	1.158	21.200	9.647	2.045
81	21.06	1.160	21.465	9.664	2.074
82	21.32	1.163	21.730	9.689	2.105
83	21.58	1.165	21.995	9.705	2.134
84	21.84	1.167	22.260	9.722	2.164
85	22.10	1.170	22.525	9.747	2.195
86	22.36	1.172	22.790	9.764	2.225
87	22.62	1.175	23.055	9.780	2.256
88	22.88	1.177	23.320	9.805	2.286
89	23.14	1.179	23.585	9.822	2.316
90	23.40	1.182	23.850	9.847	2.348
91	23.66	1.184	23.115	9.864	2.378
92	23.92	1.186	23.380	9.880	2.408
93	24.18	1.189	24.645	9.905	2.441
94	24.44	1.191	24.910	9.922	2.477
95	24.70	1.194	25.175	9.947	2.504
96	24.96	1.196	25.440	9.964	2.534
97	25.22	1.198	25.705	9.980	2.565
98	25.48	1.201	25.970	10.005	2.598
99	25.74	1.203	25.235	10.022	2.629
100	26.00	1.205	26.500	10.039	2.660

TABLE 1.1

LIQUID PICKLE FOR CURING LARGE PIECES OF MEATS USING
EITHER SALT OR BRINE

Ingredients	Quantity To Be Used When Various Percentages are To Be Pumped					
	10%	12%	14%	16%	18%	20%
When using salt (lb) Bring volume up to 100 gal. with water	167	140	130	111	95	83.50
or						
When using 100° salinometer brine (gal.) Bring volume up to 100 gal. with water	63	53	49	42	36	31.50
Make up pickle with these ingredients:						
Sodium nitrite (lb)	2.0	1.67	1.43	1.25	1.11	1.0
Sodium nitrate (lb)	2.0	1.67	1.43	1.25	1.11	1.0
Food grade phosphate (lb)[1]	50.0	41.66	35.71	31.25	27.78	25.0
Sodium erythorbate (lb)	5.51	4.55	3.90	3.42	3.04	2.75
Sodium carbonate or bicarbonate	Use sufficient amount to stabilize sodium erythorbate and sodium nitrite to pH of 7.6 at pickle temperature of 40°F					
Cane sugar (lb)	30.0	25.0	21.5	18.75	16.5	15.0
If flavoring ingredients are desired add:						
Monosodium glutamate (oz)	24.0	24.0	20.0	20.0	16.0	16.0
Plant protein hydrolyzate (oz)	15.0	12.50	10.75	9.50	8.25	7.50
Smoke flavor (optional)	Depending on the concentrate desired					

[1] It is now permissible to use sodium hydroxide in combination with food grade phosphate. It may be used only in combination with food grade phosphate in the ratio of 4 parts of phosphate to 1 part of sodium hydroxide. The combination should not exceed 5% pickle at 10% pump, or 0.5% to products. Instead of using the quantities indicated above of the food grade phosphate, the following combined percentages may be used:

	10%	12%	14%	16%	18%	20%
Food grade phosphate (lb)	40.0	33.33	28.57	25.00	22.23	20.0
Sodium hydroxide (lb)	10.0	8.33	7.14	6.25	5.55	5.0

TABLE 1.2

DRY CURE MIXTURE FOR RUBBING
LARGE PIECES OF MEAT AFTER
PUMPING WITH LIQUID PICKLE

Ingredients	Lb
Salt (free flowing)	94.00
Sodium nitrite	1.50
Sodium nitrate	1.50

NOTE: It is very important that all ingredients are thoroughly mixed. If small amounts of ingredients added to the salt are not evenly distributed in the salt, the cured meat will show "burned" spots (nitrite burn) where too much of an ingredient is in contact with the meat.

TABLE 1.3

COVER PICKLE[1] USED TO DEVELOP STABLE
COLOR AND IMPROVE FLAVOR AFTER PUMPING
WITH LIQUID PICKLE

Ingredients	Gal.	Lb
Water	100	
Salt		150
Sodium nitrite		1
Sodium nitrate		1

[1] No phosphate or sodium erythorbate is used in cover pickle.

Government Regulations Concerning Destruction of Trichinae

When fresh pork products are cured, the Meat Inspection Division (MID) of USDA is concerned that any live trichinae which the pork flesh may contain be destroyed during the processing procedure and subsequent cooking before being consumed. Humans consuming pork flesh containing the live trichinae parasites can be infected with the serious disease known as trichinosis.

For so-called uncooked cured pork products such as all forms of fresh pork, fresh unsmoked sausage containing pork, bacon, etc., that require further cooking before eating (usually to the well-done stage) destruction of the live trichinae is accomplished and provides a safe margin for the consumer.

However, when cured, smoked, and ready-to-eat products are processed which are consumed without further heating, the processing operation must bring pork products to an internal meat temperature of at least 137°F.

The above temperatures together with the preservative action of the salt in the cure and prolonged heating and cooking in the smokehouse gives protection which meets MID regulations.

Freezing also destroys the trichinosis parasite in pork flesh. To render pork products safe in this regard, USDA has prescribed the times and freezing temperatures given below.

Following is a summary of the USDA regulations governing meat inspection with regard to the destruction of trichinae in the curing processes for hams, butts, loins, and loin ends together with generalizations of the processor's responsibility in this regard to help ensure effective destruction of trichinae in all cured pork products which are not heat treated and which require no refrigeration.

Hams (Method No. 1).—Hams shall be cured by a dry-salt curing process not less than 40 days at a temperature not lower than 36°F. The hams shall be laid down in salt, not less than 4 lb per each 100 lb of hams, the salt being applied in a thorough manner to the lean meat of each ham. When placed in cure the hams may be pumped with pickle if desired. At least once during the curing process the hams shall be overhauled and additional salt applied, if necessary, so that the lean meat of each ham is thoroughly covered. After removal from cure the hams may be soaked in water at a temperature not higher than 70°F for not more than 15 hr, during which time the water may be changed once; but they shall not be subjected to any other treatment designed to remove salt from the meat, except that superficial washing may be allowed. The hams shall finally be dried or smoked not less than 10 days at a temperature not lower than 95°F.

Hams (Method No. 2).—Hams shall be cured by a dry-salt curing process at a temperature not lower than 36°F for a period of not less than 3 days for each pound of weight (green) of the individual hams. The time of cure of each lot of hams placed in cure should be calculated on a basis of the weight of the heaviest ham of the lot. Hams cured by this method, before they are placed in cure, shall be pumped with pickle solution of not less than 100° strength (salinometer) about 4 oz of the solution being injected into the shank and a like quantity along the flank side of the body bone (femur). The hams shall be laid down in salt, not less than 4 lb per each 100 lb of hams, the salt being applied in a thorough manner to the lean meat of each ham. At least once during the curing process the hams shall be overhauled and additional salt applied, if necessary, so that the lean meat of each ham is thoroughly covered. After removal from the cure, the hams may be soaked in water at a temperature not higher than 70°F for not more than 4 hr, but shall not be subjected to any other treatment designed to remove salt from the meat, except that superficial washing may be allowed. The hams shall then be dried or smoked not less than 48 hr at a temperature not lower than 80°F; and finally shall be held in a drying room not less than 20 days at a temperature not lower than 45°F.

Boneless Pork Loins and Loin Ends.—In lieu of heating or refrigerating (freezing) to destroy trichinae in boneless loins, the loins shall be cured for a period of not less than 25 days at a temperature not lower than 36°F by the use of one of the following methods:

(1) A dry-salt curing mixture containing not less than 5 lb of salt per each 100 lb of meat.

(2) A pickle solution of not less than 80° strength (salinometer) on the basis of not less than 60 lb of pickle to each 100 lb of meat.

(3) A pickle solution added to the approved dry-salt cure provided the pickle solution is not less than 80° strength (salinometer).

After removal from cure, the loins may be soaked in water for not more than 1 hr at a temperature not higher than 70°F, or washed under a spray but shall not be subjected, during or after the curing process, to any other treatment designed to remove salt.

Following curing, the loins shall be smoked for not less than 12 hr. The minimum temperature of the smokehouse during this period at no time shall be lower than 100°F, and for 4 hr of this period the smokehouse shall be maintained at a temperature not lower than 125°F.

Finally, the product shall be held in a drying room for a period of not less than 12 days at a temperature not lower than 45°F.

Capocollo (Capicola, Capacola).—Boneless pork butts for capocollo shall be cured in a dry-curing mixture containing not less than 4 1/2 lb of salt per 100 lb of meat for a period of not less than 25 days at a temperature no lower than 36°F. If curing materials are applied to the butts by the process known as churning, a small quantity of pickle may be added. During the curing period the butts may be overhauled according to any of the usual processes of overhauling, including the addition of pickle or dry salt if desired. The butts shall not be subjected during or after curing to any treatment designed to remove salt from the meat, except that superficial washing may be allowed. After being stuffed, the product shall be smoked for a period of not less than 30 hr at a temperature not lower than 80°F, and shall finally be held in a drying room not less than 20 days at a temperature not lower than 45°F.

Coppa.—Boneless pork butts for coppa shall be cured in a dry-curing mixture containing not less than 4 1/2 lb of salt per 100 lb of meat for a period of not less than 18 days at a temperature not lower than 36°F. If the curing mixture is applied to the butts by the process known as churning, a small quantity of pickle may be added. During the curing period the butts may be overhauled according to any of the usual processes of overhauling, including the addition of pickle or dry salt if desired. The butts shall not be subjected during or after curing to any treatment designed to remove salt from the meat, except that superficial washing may be allowed. After being stuffed, the product shall be held in a drying room not less than 35 days at a temperature not lower than 45°F.

Freezing To Destroy Trichinae.—At any stage of preparation and after preparatory chilling to a temperature of not above 40°F or preparatory freezing, all parts of the muscle tissue of pork or product containing such tissue shall be subjected continuously to a temperature not higher than one of those specified below, the duration of such refrigeration at the specified temperature being dependent on the thickness of the meat or inside dimensions of the container.

°F	No. of Days for Group 1	No. of Days for Group 2
5	20	30
-10	10	20
-20	6	12

Group 1 comprises product in separate pieces not exceeding 6 in. in thickness, or arranged on separate racks with the layers not exceeding 6 in. in depth, or stored in crates or boxes not exceeding 6 in. in depth, or stored as solidly frozen blocks not exceeding 6 in. in thickness.

Group 2 comprises product in pieces, layers, or within containers, the thickness of which exceeds 6 in. but not 27 in., and product in containers including tierces, barrels, kegs, and cartons having a thickness not exceeding 27 in.

The products undergoing such refrigeration or the containers thereof shall be so spaced while in the freezer as will ensure a free circulation of air between the pieces of meat, layers, blocks, boxes, barrels, kegs, and tierces in order that the temperature of the meat throughout will be promptly reduced to not higher than 5°, -10°, or -20°F, as the case may be.

Management Assistance in Safeguarding Processed Meats.—(1) Recognize the importance to the success of your operation in safeguarding the consumer's meat supply and adhere carefully to the regulations concerning the treatment of pork to destroy live trichinae. (2) All areas used in the treatment of pork for processing should be equipped with accurate recording thermometers which should be checked frequently for accuracy. Any found to be inaccurate and unreliable should be discarded and replaced. (3) Keep up-to-date time and temperature records in the handling, curing, drying, refrigerating, etc., of processed pork products for each lot processed.

HAMS AND PICNICS

CURING WHOLE SMOKED HAMS

Arterial Pumping of Pickle

Save Main Artery and Vein.—Workmen cutting hams from a carcass must be very careful to save the main artery and vein. Before the split carcass is disassembled, the leaf fat covering the main artery and vein has to be separated from the backbone and ribs. Remove leaf fat in such a manner that some of the fat will still remain on both artery and vein. This will prevent dehydration of the artery and vein until hams are pumped. Cut both about 5–6 in. distant from the point where they enter the ham.

The vein is thin and brittle, but the artery is larger and elastic; therefore, the artery is easy to find by the operator pumping the hams. The main artery branches in a Y form with the larger branch carrying pumping pickle to the shank part and the smaller branch carrying pickle into the cushion part of the ham.

If the main artery is left sufficiently long, the pumping needle can be inserted easily so that pickle will be carried throughout the whole body of the ham. This is the proper way to get an even distribution of the pickle.

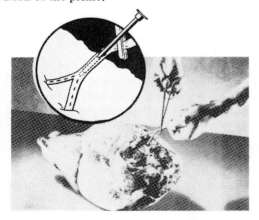

FIG. 1.1. THIS SHOWS THE WAY THE MAIN ARTERY IN A HAM BRANCHES INTO A Y AND HOW TO CUT IT SUFFICIENTLY LONG TO EASILY INSERT THE PUMPING NEEDLE (INSERT) SO THAT PICKLE WILL BE CARRIED THROUGHOUT THE WHOLE BODY OF THE HAM

In case the artery is cut too short, the pumping needle first has to be inserted in the larger artery to pump the shank part and then into the smaller artery to pump the cushion part. The shank part covers 60% of the ham area; the cushion part, 40%. Therefore, 60% of the pickle is injected in the shank part and 40% in the cushion part. Use the pickle ingredients given in Table 1.1 containing phosphate and with or without sodium erythorbate and bicarbonate.

Pumping Scales.—Pumping pickle should be metered on a percentage scale in order to get the right amount of pickle in each ham.

Pumping equipment, also, must be constructed of stainless steel.

Pumping.—Pump 10% by weight of the fresh ham. Pressure on the tank containing the pickle should be 50–60 lb. The pressure tank should be of stainless steel construction, particularly when phosphates are used in the pickle.

Fast Cure

After hams are pumped, they *can* be stockinetted and transferred to the smokehouse for further processing. But it is poor practice and will reduce quality of the finished product.

Full Cure

After hams are pumped, they should be rubbed with a dry curing mixture. Formula for dry curing mixture is given in Table 1.2.

After hams are rubbed, stack on racks 4–6 layers deep or in stainless steel trucks equipped with drain holes to discharge brine that otherwise would accumulate in the truck bottom.

Hold the hams at 38°–40°F for 4–6 days. Then soak in cold water no higher than 70°F just long enough to dissolve surface salt; scrub with a fiber brush or mechanical washer to remove surface salt.

Insert hams in stockinette and hang on smoke trees in such a manner that they do not touch one another.

Procedure for Smoking

Transfer hams to the smokehouse which has been preheated to a temperature of 125°–130°F with dampers wide open but without any smoke. Maintain this temperature for 4 hr to dry surface and warm the hams. Then raise temperature to 140°F and introduce smoke. Adjust dampers so they are ¼ open. Maintain the 140°F temperature for 8 hr, then raise temperature to 165°F and maintain this temperature until an internal meat temperature of 142°F is obtained.

Remove hams from the smokehouse and shower them with hot water to remove surface grease and coagulated gelatinous matter from the meat side of the hams. Transfer hams to chill room (45°F) for final chilling before putting the product into market channels. Product should be kept refrigerated throughout marketing.

Marketed as Uncooked Hams

Processed as outlined above, these hams are not cooked, but need further cooking prior to being served.

They may be marketed as whole hams which are oftentimes split in half by the retailer with center cuts removed and sold as ham steaks for frying or grilling. Also, the processor may split the hams before they go into market channels, putting the shank end and the butt end each in Cryovac or other moistureproof, tight-fitting wrapping. Product should be held under refrigeration.

READY-TO-EAT FULLY COOKED HAMS

This type of ham is more perishable than the smoked hams that are uncooked and should be marketed in a shorter period of time.

The procedures for pumping pickle, curing, smoking, washing, and chilling are identical with that just described for cured smoked hams with the exception: cooking time is extended to reach an internal temperature of 152°-155°F. To accomplish this, hams remain in the smokehouse at the 165°F temperature until internal temperature of the meat has reached 152°-155°F. They are then considered fully cooked and ready to eat.

These hams are usually wrapped for marketing channels without splitting. They should be kept under refrigeration until sold.

ARTERY-PUMPED SMOKED PICNICS (SHOULDERS)

The procedure follows that for curing whole smoked hams with the following exception: The amount of pickle pumped into a picnic may be as much as 16% of the weight of the fresh picnic. The reason for this is that during the curing period the picnic loses from 3 to 4% more pickle than does the ham.

Ready-To-Eat Fully Cooked Picnics

Treatment is identical to that of smoked picnics except that the internal temperature—like the fully cooked hams—should reach 152°-155°F in the smokehouse before removal, washing, chilling, and packaging for marketing. Keep under refrigeration until product is sold.

BONELESS OVAL-SHAPED AND ELONGATED READY-TO-EAT SMOKED HAMS IN FIBROUS CASINGS

No other smoked boneless hams have received such wide acceptance and popularity as the boneless, oblong-shaped hams. However, it was not until after these hams were processed in molds under pressure that they attained the great popularity they enjoy today.

Boneless, round-shaped smoked hams in fibrous casings were marketed many years ago but they had shortcomings. They were stuffed under pressure into casings, but during heat processing in the smokehouse they lost their pressure because of evaporation of moisture from the meat; and some moisture collected in the center of the ham. After processing, the finished product could not be sliced without falling apart.

Today, molds apply steady pressure during the cooking process in the smokehouse. These are constructed of a pear-shaped or oblong expanded metal base with springs attached and with a top fitted with eyelets so that when the springs from the base are attached to the eyelets on the top, the ham is kept under pressure during the cooking process. The resulting end product is very firm and easy to slice.

Processing Procedure

Green hams each weighing 12–14 lb give the best product. Follow procedure under Curing Whole Smoked Hams with regard to saving main artery and vein for injecting liquid pickle (see Fig. 1.1), using artery pumping method.

Use the pickle ingredients containing phosphate and with or without sodium erythorbate and sodium bicarbonate given in Table 1.1, may be used. Pump 10% of the weight of the green ham.

Curing.—After hams are pumped, rub with a dry

curing mixture. Ingredients in Table 1.2 may be used, omitting the erythorbate. Dry curing mixture must be thoroughly mixed before use to prevent nitrite burn; store mixture in a dry cool place.

Stack rubbed hams no deeper than 4–6 layers on racks or in stainless steel trucks equipped with drain holes to permit discharge of brine which would otherwise accumulate in the truck bottom. Keep hams in cure for 4–6 days at a temperature of 38°–40°F. The curing shrink will be approximately 2%.

Washing and Boning.—After curing, soak hams in cold water just long enough to dissolve surface salt; then scrub with a fiber brush. If a mechanical washer is available, hams may be conveyed through washer for scrubbing.

Hams are then boned. The boning operation should be carried out as carefully as possible. The boning operation is shown in Fig. 1.2 and 1.3 for regular oval hams.

In case a longer shaped ham is desired, follow description given in Fig. 1.4 for elongated hams.

Stuffing (Encasing).—A ham stuffing horn should be used with No. 10 fibrous "Easy Peel" casings for the regular oval shape and No. 7 casings for the elongated shape. Before using casings, soak in hot water (140°–150°F). Stuff the boneless hams in casings, then close under pressure. (Use of a pressure pack tying machine is recommended.) Pinprick casing when pressure is applied to let trapped air escape; then close casing.

Molding.—Oval-shaped ham molds should be used for the regular oval shape. Oblong-shaped molds (22 × 7 in.) should be used for the elongated shape. Place ham on base plate and attach springs in all four holes; put cover plate in place and fasten springs at top in their corresponding holes. An S-shaped hanger is placed on one of the narrow end springs and the hams are hung on a smoke tree, properly placed so they do not touch one another.

Smoking and Cooking.—Preheat the smokehouse to 130°F before transferring trees for smoking and cooking. Bring in loaded smoke trees, adjust dampers wide open to dry surface of hams without any smoke. Maintain 130°F temperature for 4 hr. Then adjust dampers to 1/4 open, introduce smoke and raise temperature to 150°F and hold for 4 hr more. Finally, temperature is raised to 165°F and smokehouse is kept at this temperature until internal meat temperature of 152°–155°F is ob-

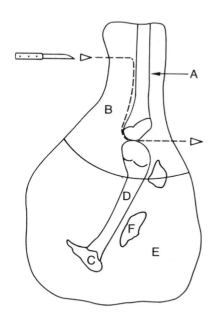

FIG. 1.2. SHOWING FIRST STEPS IN BONING A HAM

(A) Shank is partially removed. The part removed with the bone in can be smoked and sold separately. (B) Remove skin. (C) Remove aitch bone. (D) Remove femur. (E) Remove proper amount of fat (depending upon end use of ham). (F) Remove seam fat.

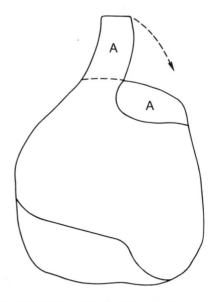

FIG. 1.3. FINISHING STEPS FOR REGULAR OVAL HAMS

(A) shows the portion of the shank which is still attached to the body of the ham after removing the shank bone portion. The attached portion is folded over the cushion of the ham and secured with a skewer to hold it in place until ham is stuffed into casing. Stuff regular oval hams into No. 10 "Easy Peel" fibrous casings.

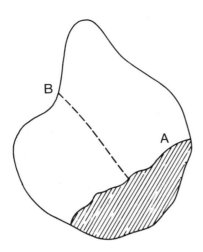 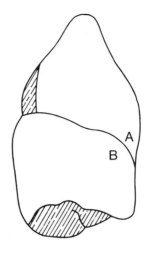

FIG. 1.4. SHAPING AN ELONGATED HAM

After ham is boned, lay ham face side up. Then cut in center so that ham can be opened up. Then, by holding shank part of ham (A) in its natural position, fold the cushion part (B) under (A) to elongate ham.

tained. If a strong smoked flavor is desired, smoke should be kept in the house during the entire smoking process.

Chilling.—When hams are removed from the smokehouse, shower them in the molds with cold water for 10 min. Then dry at room temperature for 4–5 hr. Transfer to chill room (45°F) and hold them at this temperature for 24 hr before removing molds.

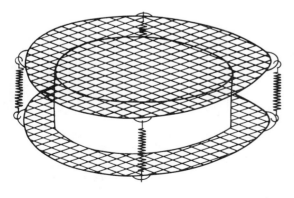

FIG. 1.5. HAM FORMING MOLD

Store at 45°F until they enter the marketing channels. Product should be marketed under refrigeration temperature.

BONELESS OR BONE-IN PEAR-SHAPED READY-TO-EAT SMOKED HAMS PROCESSED IN STOCKINETTE

Processing Procedure

Select green hams weighing 12–14 lb for best results and prepare for curing as described for Curing Whole Smoked Hams.

Curing Pickle.—Hams with bone in should be artery pumped. Use the ingredients given in Table 1.1 containing phosphate with or without erythorbate and bicarbonate. Pump the arteries with 10% of the weight of the green ham. Boneless hams should be spray pumped using the same pickle as for artery pumping. Inject 10% of the weight of the green ham.

Curing.—If pickle is pumped through arteries, hams should be rubbed after pumping with a dry curing mixture. Use dry curing mixture given in Table 1.2 being certain there is thorough mixing of ingredients. Injecto-cured hams should be cured in cover pickle (see Table 1.3). Hams should be cured 4–6 days at 38°–40°F.

If hams are cured in cover pickle, scrubbing and washing are all that is needed before the boning operation. If hams are rubbed with dry curing mixture, first soak hams in cold water just long enough to dissolve surface salt, then wash and scrub with a fiber brush (or put them through a mechanical washer).

Boning.—For bone-in hams, only the aitch bone is removed.

For boneless hams, collar skins can be removed or left on as indicated in Fig. 1.6. The seam fat from the center of the ham should be removed before stuffing and 1 tablespoon of 200 bloom gelatin placed in the cavity. Trimmings which are removed from the bones should never be put back into the cavity of the ham as they may cause discoloration.

Stuffing (Encasing).—Use of No. 9 FMS 30–36 in. long, heavy-ribbed stockinettes are recommended. Also, a ham stuffing horn is needed for this operation.

For Boneless Hams.—Pull stockinette over the ham stuffing horn; then the ham, butt end first, is pushed through the horn into the stockinette.

For Bone-In Hams.—Stuff ham through the horn shank end first; then shake the ham down into the stockinette.

After the ham is encased, pull stockinette tightly over the butt end in such a manner that it will fold over the area where the aitch bone was re-

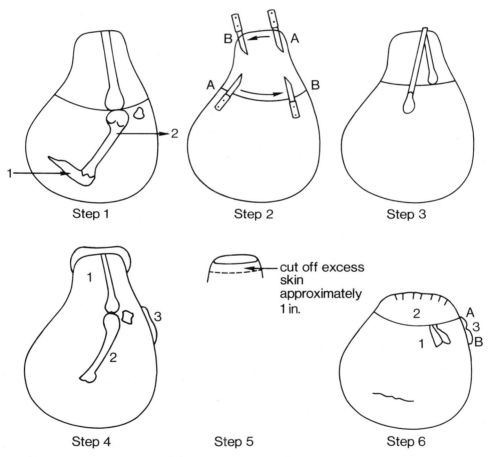

FIG. 1.6. BONING AND PREPARATION FOR PEAR-SHAPED HAMS

Step 1: Remove aitch bone (1); and chisel out leg bone (2). Step 2: Loosen up skin with knife from A to B. Leave skin untouched on the face side of the ham. Step 3: Anchor chisel on shank bone and lift skin over shank. Step 4: Remove shank bone (1); remove leg bone and cap bone (2); do not remove membrane over the knuckle bone and cap (3) as this creates a natural pocket for the shank. Step 5: Sew up shank skin from the inside, then fold skin back again over the tip of the ham. Step 6: Clean shank from connective tissue and turn shank into pocket left by removing leg bone (1). Turn skin back over top of ham (2). Make shank secure (3) with one stitch between A and B.

moved. Hold ham in the stockinette and twist ham to make stockinette as tight as is possible; then tie with twine.

Molding.—Oval-shaped ham molds should be used (see Fig. 1.4). Place ham on base plate and attach springs in all four holes; put cover plate in place and fasten springs at top in their corresponding holes. An S-shaped hanger is placed on one of the narrow end springs and the hams are hung on a smoke tree, properly placed so they do not touch one another.

Smoking and Cooking.—Preheat the smokehouse to 130°F before transferring trees for smoking and curing. Bring in loaded smoke trees and open dampers wide so as to dry the surface of the hams without any smoke. Maintain 130°F for 3–4 hr. Then adjust dampers to 1/4 open, raise temperature to 150°F and introduce smoke. Maintain these conditions until an internal temperature of 140°F is reached. Then raise smokehouse temperatures to 165°F until internal meat temperature reaches 152°–155°F.

Chilling.—Remove hams from smokehouse and hold at room temperature for 2 hr. Then transfer to chill room (38°–40°F) for final chilling. Hold at 45°F storage until product enters marketing channels. This product is perishable and should be kept under refrigeration until sold.

EXPORT HAMS AND PICNICS

Processing Procedure

Select green hams and picnics of uniform weight so processing will be uniform. Prepare for curing as described for **Curing Whole Smoked Hams**, saving main artery and vein so they can be artery pumped with pickle.

Pumping Pickle.—Use a pumping pickle of not less than 97°–100° salinometer strength. The following formula may be used for this: 100 gal. of 97° salinometer brine (50°F), 1 1/2 lb of sodium nitrite, 1 1/2 lb of sodium nitrate, 10 lb cane sugar.

Arterial Pumping.—Pump 8% of the weight of the green ham. In no instance should there be more than 9% of the green weight.

Curing.—Cure these hams a minimum of 18 hr per lb and no less than a minimum of 7 days nor more than 14 days in a cover pickle of not less than 80° salinometer strength. Move hams and picnics around (overhaul positions) at least once during cure.

Cover Pickle.—Use 100 gal. of 80° salinometer brine (50°F), 1 1/2 lb of sodium nitrite, 1 1/2 lb of sodium nitrate, 5 lb cane sugar.

Dry, Rub, Drain, and Wash.—Remove hams from cover pickle and rub with 2–3% salt per 100 lb of weight. Place on racks in chill room (38°–40°F)

and allow to drain for 4 days. After draining, do not soak but scrub with a fiber brush under shower of hot water or wash in a mechanical washer.

Smoking.—At no time should the temperature of the smokehouse exceed 142°F for these hams and picnics.

Procedure for Hams.—Start smoking at 120°F and maintain this temperature for 12 hr. Then raise temperature to 130°F and hold this temperature for 24 hr during which time the hams will reach an internal temperature of 122°F. Then raise the smokehouse temperature to 142°F and hold at this temperature for 12 hr so that hams will reach an internal temperature of 137°F. When this internal ham temperature has been reached, gradually reduce smokehouse temperature to 115°F and hold at this temperature for 48 hr. Hardwood-generated smoke should be used during the entire 96 hr of smoking. This will produce a dark-colored ham that need not be refrigerated for market channels. Hold product at room temperature for 24 hr before packaging for shipment. This product does not need any refrigeration through marketing channels.

Procedure for Picnics.—Picnics should be smoked continuously with hardwood sawdust for not less than 60 hr using the following smoking schedule:

Hr	Smokehouse Temp °F	Internal Meat Temp °F
12	120	
24	130	120
12	142	137
12	115	

This product also needs no refrigeration through marketing channels but hold for 24 hr at room temperature before shipment.

BOILED HAMS

Select green hams of uniform size (for uniform processing) and in weights of 12–14 lb or 14–16 lb depending upon the size of ham-cooking molds used. If arterial pumping is to be used for pickle, save main artery and vein as described for **Curing Whole Smoked Hams.** If spray pumping of pickle is to be used, hams should first be boned, skinned and the fat removed, leaving 1/4-in. of fat on the surface to give a nice appearance to the finished product.

Processing Procedure

Curing Pickles.—Use the formula ingredients given in Table 1.1 with or without sodium erythorbate and bicarbonate.

For cover pickle during curing use ingredients given in Table 1.3.

For Arterial Pumping.—If arterial pumping is used, pump 10% of the weight of the green ham. Follow this with rubbing hams with a dry curing mixture using ingredients given in Table 1.2. Make certain dry curing mixture is thoroughly mixed.

For Spray Pumping.—Using an injecto machine, a quantity equivalent to 10% of the weight of the green ham should be used after hams are boned, skinned, and fat removed.

Curing.—Hams should be cured in the cover pickle (Table 1.3) for 4–6 days. Then wash without soaking under a hot water shower and scrub with a fiber brush (or run through a mechanical washer).

Molding.—Before molding, remove seam fat in the center of the hams and place 1 tablespoon of 200 bloom gelatin in the cavity. Open-top cooking molds should be lined with parchment paper; 1 piece covering bottom and ends, and 1 piece overlapping the bottom and covering the sides with enough length to overlap on top of the ham. Hams are placed in the cooking molds, parchment overlapped over tops, lids put in place and springs locked under heavy pressure.

In case sandwich-sized hams are to be produced, hams should be cut by the seam, elongated to fit the 4 × 4 in. oblong molds, and closed under heavy pressure.

Cooking.—Place molds in cooking tanks with molds arranged so as to allow free circulation of hot water between molds. Fill tanks with hot water at 165°F. Agitate water with compressed air through a perforated pipe located at the bottom of the tank.

Cook hams approximately 30 min per lb or until an internal temperature of 155°F is reached.

In case hams of different sizes and weights are cooked in the same vat, the weight difference should not be more than 1 lb. Place the heavier hams on the bottom of the tank with the lighter hams in the layer on top separating the two layers with a wire screen. Remove lighter weight hams first after they reach an internal temperature of 155°F and chill in a separate tank. Cook lower layer (larger hams) 30 min longer to an internal temperature of 155°F; then drain hot water, introduce cold water and chill. Chill hams for 2 hr.

Repress and Chill.—Hams shrink during the cooking operation causing the springs on the mold to release some pressure. After removal from the cooking tank, springs should be retightened.

Transfer repressed molds to the chill room at 34°F overnight before stuffing into packaging.

Stuffing (Encasing).—Remove hams from molds after they have been properly chilled. This operation and the stuffing into casings which follows should be done as gently as possible because rough handling of the hams will cause damage which shows up when the ham is sliced and slices become broken. Stuff into Cryovac or Saran casings; place on shelf of a truck and transfer to the chill room (34°F) for 24 hr for further chilling before delivery into marketing channels. Keep under refrigeration until sold.

CANNED HAMS (PEAR-SHAPED AND PULLMAN)

The old method of canning boned hams is now virtually obsolete. The cured boneless hams were placed in a ham boiler and cooked in hot water, after which they were chilled and transferred to tin cans, vacuum-closed and reprocessed to an internal temperature of 155°F. This resulted in a double shrink, first in the ham boiler and then in the can. Valuable meat juices were lost in the cooking water and the double shrink made the canned hams dry because of the excessive loss of meat juices. The shrink from raw weight to the finished product amounted to as much as 25–30%. Not only was the product of poor quality, but was considered a very expensive item on a pound-per-dollar basis.

The invention of the hydraulic ham press and the perfection of improved manufacturing methods used today result in a much superior product both from the standpoint of quality and cost. With the ham press, cured hams are shaped right in the cans and the hams are processed without excessive shrinkage. With the savings on shrinkage and labor, cost of canned hams today is such that they are one of the best selling items all over the world.

The Ham Press

The ham press is equipped with inserts for all sizes of cans which are used for this product. The best method for fast operation of the press is to grade hams for their weights right at the end of the boning table.

Processing Procedure

The process for canning both pear-shaped and pullman hams is identical. The only difference is that the pullman hams are first formed in oblong shape by the ham press (not in the can as with the pear-shaped hams) and then stuffed through a stuffing horn into the oblong can. The following procedure is for both pear-shaped and pullman, except where noted.

Select good quality fresh hams. Prepare for curing as described for arterial pumping of pickle under **Curing Whole Smoked Hams,** saving the main artery and vein for pumping the pickle.

Pumping Pickle.—Use pickle formula given in Table 1.1 containing phosphate and with or without sodium erythorbate and sodium bicarbonate. Pump 10% of the weight of the green ham through the arterial system.

Curing.—After hams are pumped, rub with a dry curing mixture such as is given in Table 1.2. Make certain dry curing mixture is thoroughly mixed before applying to hams.

Stack rubbed hams no deeper than six layers on racks or in stainless steel trucks equipped with drain holes to discharge brine that otherwise would accumulate in the truck bottom. Or, hams may be stacked six deep in a stainless steel truck with a false bottom for brine drainage.

Cure hams 5–6 days in curing cellar at 38°–40°F. Curing shrink will be approximately 2% with a yield of 108% of the green weight (as required by government regulation).

Washing and Boning.—Remove hams from the curing cellar. Do not soak, but scrub under hot water shower using soft fiber brush; or, put hams through a mechanical washer.

Skin hams leaving approximately 1/4 in. fat on the skin side. Bone hams rejecting any found with blood clots and keeping intact the connecting tissue which covers the joints of femur and shank bones (this tissue forms a natural pocket into which the shank end is turned). Remove seam fat from center. Remove connecting tissues from shank; they will not bind with the body of the ham. Turn shank into pocket (described above) and make it secure with one or two stitches.

Smoke Is Optional.—Light smoking imparts an excellent flavor to the canned hams. If smoke is desired, place hams in stockinettes, hang on smoke trees and transfer to the smokehouse at a temperature of not over 80°F and smoke for 1 hr. Or, if a smoke precipitator tunnel is available, let hams move through the tunnel on the conveyor; for this type of smoking, stockinettes are not needed.

Filling and Pressing.—Hams should first be graded for weight and size of can required. (A grading scale is available for this which indicates weight and proper size of can to use.) Exact weight of ham is marked on each can with a tin marking ink stamp. This is a very important step since the exact weight of the ham must appear on the retail label.

Place 1 teaspoon of 200 bloom gelatin in the cavity of each ham where the seam fat was removed.

Place ham fat side down in the can with the shank side facing the narrow part of the can. Then fold butt end to cover and fill the cavity left by removal of the aitch bone. Place can on the platform of the ham press, close the locking device, and form the ham within the can under 270 lb pressure. (The ham press uses hydraulic pressure and this operation takes only 3 sec to perform.)

Remove can from the ham press. Put 1 teaspoon of 200 bloom gelatin around the edge of the ham in the can. Close cans in a vacuum closing machine under 27 in. vacuum.

Note—as stated earlier—that pullman hams are first formed into their oblong shape by the ham press before stuffing through a horn into the oblong cans.

After can closure, inspect each for faulty seams. If any are found, mark new can with weight of ham, insert ham, add another teaspoon of 200 bloom gelatin around edge of ham in can, and reseal under vacuum as above.

Cooking.—The cooking tank should be equipped with a perforated pipe on the bottom which is connected with an air pressure line with the pressure valve adjusted so as to give gentle agitation of the cooking water during cooking hams. There should be a false bottom above the steam lines in the cooking tank.

Place cans in the tank so as to allow proper circulation of water between cans.

Your can supplier (e.g., American Can Company, Continental Can Company) should be consulted to help determine accurate and safe cooking times and temperatures. The data in Tables 1.4, 1.5, and 1.6 may be used as guides. Final internal temperature of the hams should reach 155°F.

Cooling.—Remove canned hams from cooking tank and thoroughly chill in cold running water for at least 2 hr. Upon completion of the chilling, transfer to chill room (38°–40°F) for at least 24 hr before final inspection, labeling, and casing for shipment.

Keep Under Refrigeration.—These canned hams must be kept under refrigeration at all times, including storage and through the marketing channels.

PROSCUITTI (ITALIAN-STYLE HAMS)

Italian-style hams require a good deal of care in their preparation. They must conform to certain government regulations concerning trichinae that must be destroyed during the curing procedure because these hams are eaten uncooked.

Hams for proscuitti should be carefully selected in the weight range of 12–15 lb. They should be free from all bruises and with good conformation.

TABLE 1.4

COOKING SCHEDULE FOR PEAR-SHAPED HAMS IN SMALL BASE (NO. 2) CONTAINERS IN
CAN SIZES 904 X 606 FROM 3$\frac{1}{4}$ TO 5$\frac{1}{2}$ IN. IN DEPTH

Depth of Can (In.)	Weight of Meat in Can	Cooking Temperature and Time		
		at 120° F (Min)	at 176° F (Min)	at 165° F (Min)
3$\frac{1}{4}$	4 lb 8 oz to 4 lb 15 oz	150	90	55
3$\frac{1}{2}$	4 lb 15 oz to 5 lb 6 oz	150	90	60
3$\frac{3}{4}$	5 lb 6 oz to 5 lb 12 oz	150	90	65
4	5 lb 12 oz to 6 lb 2 oz	150	90	70
4$\frac{1}{4}$	6 lb 2 oz to 6 lb 10 oz	150	90	80
4$\frac{1}{2}$	6 lb 10 oz to 7 lb	150	90	90
4$\frac{3}{4}$	7 lb to 7 lb 7 oz	150	90	100
5	7 lb 7 oz to 7 lb 14 oz	150	90	110
5$\frac{1}{4}$	7 lb 14 oz to 8 lb 4 oz	150	90	120
5$\frac{1}{2}$	8 lb 4 oz to 8 lb 11 oz	150	90	130

TABLE 1.5

COOKING SCHEDULE FOR PEAR-SHAPED HAMS IN MEDIUM BASE (NO. 4) CONTAINERS IN
CAN SIZES 1010 X 709 FROM 4 TO 6$\frac{1}{4}$ IN. IN DEPTH

Depth of Can (In.)	Weight of Meat in Can	Cooking Temperature and Time		
		at 120° F (Hr)	at 176° F (Hr)	at 165° F (Hr)
4	8 lb 1 oz to 8 lb 12 oz	3$\frac{1}{2}$	1–1$\frac{1}{2}$	1–1$\frac{1}{4}$
4$\frac{1}{4}$	8 lb 12 oz to 9 lb 6 oz	3$\frac{1}{2}$	1–1$\frac{1}{2}$	1$\frac{3}{4}$
4$\frac{1}{2}$	9 lb 6 oz to 10 lb	3$\frac{1}{2}$	1–1$\frac{1}{2}$	2
4$\frac{3}{4}$	10 lb to 10 lb 9 oz	3$\frac{1}{2}$	1–1$\frac{1}{2}$	2$\frac{1}{4}$
5	10 lb 9 oz to 11 lb 4 oz	3$\frac{1}{2}$	1–1$\frac{1}{2}$	2$\frac{1}{2}$
5$\frac{1}{4}$	11 lb 4 oz to 11 lb 13 oz	3$\frac{1}{2}$	1–1$\frac{1}{2}$	2$\frac{3}{4}$
5$\frac{1}{2}$	11 lb 13 oz to 12 lb 6 oz	3$\frac{1}{2}$	1–1$\frac{1}{2}$	3
5$\frac{3}{4}$	12 lb 6 oz to 12 lb 15 oz	3$\frac{1}{2}$	1–1$\frac{1}{2}$	3$\frac{1}{4}$
6	12 lb 15 oz to 13 lb 9 oz	3$\frac{1}{2}$	1–1$\frac{1}{2}$	3$\frac{1}{2}$
6$\frac{1}{4}$	13 lb 9 oz to 14 lb 5 oz	3$\frac{1}{2}$	1–1$\frac{1}{2}$	3$\frac{3}{4}$

TABLE 1.6

COOKING SCHEDULE FOR OBLONG-SHAPED HAMS IN PULLMAN BASE CONTAINERS
410 X 414 FROM 8$\frac{1}{2}$ TO 12$\frac{1}{4}$ IN. IN LENGTH

Length of Can (In.)	Weight of Meat in Can	Cooking Temperature and Time
8$\frac{1}{2}$	5 lb 6 oz to 5 lb 9 oz	All pullman base containers are the
9$\frac{1}{2}$	5 lb 9 oz to 6 lb 14 oz	same thickness; they differ only in
9$\frac{3}{4}$	6 lb 14 oz to 7 lb 5 oz	length. So all lengths are given the
10$\frac{1}{4}$	7 lb 5 oz to 7 lb 12 oz	same cook: 2$\frac{1}{2}$ hr at 125° F followed
10$\frac{3}{4}$	7 lb 12 oz to 8 lb 3 oz	by 3 hr at 165° F (based on an initial
11$\frac{1}{4}$	8 lb 3 oz to 8 lb 10 oz	meat temperature of 42°–45° F). Final
11$\frac{3}{4}$	8 lb 10 oz to 9 lb 1 oz	internal temperature should reach
12$\frac{1}{4}$	9 lb 1 oz to 9 lb 8 oz	155° F.

Fat layer under the skin should not be over $1\frac{1}{2}$-2 in. thick.

Processing Procedure

Skin is left on the whole ham. The foot is cut off just below the dew claws. Remove only the aitch bone at the joint of the femur; take care to leave meat smooth without any incisions.

Curing.—Hams for proscuitti are rubbed with curing salt. For this operation, they should have an initial internal temperature of 34°-36°F.

Mix together thoroughly the following spice-cure mixture using only purified sterilized spices:

Ingredient	Lb	Oz
White pepper, ground	3	
Black pepper, ground	1	
Allspice, ground	5	
Nutmeg, ground	1	
Mustard seed, ground		3
Coriander		3
Sodium nitrate	5	8
Sodium nitrite		2
Cane sugar	4	

Use $6\frac{1}{2}$ oz of the spice-cure mixture with each 4 lb of salt. Spice-cure mixture should be thoroughly mixed with the salt before use. For each 100 lb of hams, use 4 lb $6\frac{1}{2}$ oz of the salt cure.

After rubbing with the cure, stack hams on a platform 12 in. above the floor. Hams may be stacked four layers deep. Always stack with skin side down. Sprinkle some of the dry curing mixture between each layer as they are stacked on the platform. Chill room temperature for curing should be 36°-38°F and never lower than 36°F. Cure for 10 days. Then overhaul position of hams so that the top layer is placed on the bottom. Cure for an additional 10 days when each ham is rubbed again with the dry curing mixture. Cure hams for a total of 40-45 days.

During this time, hams should be kept under canvas cover to exclude as much air as possible.

To Flatten Shape.—If hams are properly handled, they will emerge from the curing room in a nearly flat shape. But if a perfect flat shape is desired, lay hams—skin side down—in a single layer on planks, cover with top planks and sufficient weights to give hams the perfect proscuitti shape.

Postcure Treatment.—Remove hams from cure and soak in water at a temperature not higher than 70°F for not more than 15 hr; change water once during this period of soaking. Then scrub on the skin side with a soft fiber brush so there will be no visible salt after drying.

Do not string the hams for hanging on the smoke tree by spearing the stringing needle through the ham skin. Instead, make a double loop circle around the shank and tie. Hang on smoke trees spaced so they do not touch one another.

Smokehouse Treatment.—Preheat smokehouse to 130°F before transferring hams to dry. With dampers $\frac{1}{4}$ open, hold them at this temperature for 48 hr. If the trade demands a smoked product, introduce light smoke in the house after the first 24 hr of drying and smoke just long enough to obtain the desired color. After hams have been at 130°F for 48 hr, gradually raise temperature to 140°F and hold for 2 hr; then let it drop to 120°F and hold for 8 hr. Discontinue heat and let hams hang in the smokehouse until internal temperature of the hams is reduced to 100°F.

Postsmokehouse Treatment.—Remove hams from smokehouse and let hang at room temperature for 6-8 hr. Then rub meat side of the hams with a mixture of equal parts of ground black and ground white peppers. Take care not to scratch the skin side while doing this and wipe off any specks of pepper which may adhere to the skin.

Transfer properly spaced hams on trees to the drying room; maintain 70°-75°F temperature with relative humidity of 65-75%. Hold for 30 days before shipment.

PORK BUTTS AND LOINS

CAPOCOLLO (ITALIAN-STYLE CURED BUTTS) (ALSO CAPICOLA, CAPACOLA)

Dry Cure Procedure

Use trimmed Boston butts with an average weight of 3-4 lb for uniform processing.

Curing.—A dry curing mixture is used made up of the following ingredients:

	Lb	Oz
Salt	4	8
Cane sugar		$12\frac{1}{2}$
Sodium nitrate		$3\frac{1}{2}$
Total weight	5	8

Use this amount (5 lb 8 oz) of dry curing mixture for each 100 lb of meat.

Butts should be at a temperature of 34°–36°F. Rub evenly and thoroughly with the dry cure mixture. Pack in vats, spreading leftover curing mixture between layers. Next day, press butts down tightly in the vats; if the dissolved pickle does not entirely cover the meat, add enough 80° salinometer brine to cover.

Hold curing room temperature at not less than 36°F and not over 48°F and cure butts for not less than 25 days. After the first 10 days of this curing period, overhaul position of butts so top layers are transferred to bottom layers. While doing this, additional dry curing mixture should be spread between each layer.

After-Cure Treatment.—Do not soak butts; wash lightly, then drain. Follow this with rubbing each butt with a spice mixture of ground Spanish paprika and ground red pepper. (Commercial products are available for this.) The amount of red pepper used in this mixture is dependent upon customers' preferences.

Stuff butts in beef bungs and tie securely. Wash off casings; then perforate with a needle to let out entrapped air. Hang butts on smoke trees properly spaced so they do not touch one another.

Smoking.—Preheat smokehouse to 90°F. Transfer butts to smokehouse; open dampers wide to dry casings and hold at this temperature for 10 hr. Then adjust dampers to 1/4 open and introduce light smoke. Smoke butts for 20 hr at 90°F.

Final Treatment.—Remove butts from the smokehouse. Dip each momentarily in boiling water to shrink the casing. Let butts hang at room temperature until casings are dry. Transfer to the drying room at a temperature of 70°–75°F with relative humidity of 65–75% and hold butts for not less than 20 days under these conditions before shipment.

Twine Wrapping.—Wrap casings tightly with three-ply twine in the following manner: Wrap twine once around butt lengthwise; then wrap twine around circumference in loops 1/2-in. apart, tieing each loop securely to the lengthwise twine.

FULLY COOKED READY-TO-EAT CAPOCOLLO

Some of the processing procedures are identical to those given above for dry cured Capocollo and will be referred to in the procedures given here. However, fully cooked, ready-to-eat Capocollo is injected with a liquid curing pickle and smoking-drying conditions are different.

Curing.—Use trimmed Boston butts with an average weight of 3–4 lb for uniform processing. For the curing pickle, use formula ingredients given in Table 1.1 with or without sodium erythorbate.

Injecto pump brine into butts using an injecto machine and metering brine to 10% of the weight of the green butt. Pack into vats and for cover pickle use formula ingredients given in Table 1.3. Cure for 4–6 days.

After-Cure Treatment.—Follow procedure given above for dry cure of Capocollo.

Smoking.—Preheat smokehouse to 130°F and transfer stuffed butts. Hold at this temperature with dampers wide open until casings are dry. Then elevate temperature to 140°F, adjust dampers to 1/4 open position, introduce smoke and hold for 2 hr. Then raise temperature to 165°F and hold until an internal temperature of 152°F is reached.

Final Treatment.—Dip butts in boiling water momentarily to shrink casings; then let hang at room temperature until an internal temperature of 110°F is reached. Then transfer to chill room (45°F) for overnight chilling before shipment or storage. This product is perishable and should be kept refrigerated throughout storage and marketing channels.

Twine Wrapping.—Same as for dry cured Capocollo.

SMOKED BONELESS BUTTS

Processing Procedure

Select trimmed Boston butts of 3–4 lb average weight for uniform processing.

Curing.—Injecto curing is used for smoked boneless butts. For curing pickle, ingredients given in Table 1.1 with or without sodium erythorbate and sodium bicarbonate. Through an injecto machine, inject 10% of the weight of the green butts.

Butts are kept in a cover pickle during the curing period. The same pickle that is used for pumping may be used for the cover pickle; use formula ingredients given in Table 1.3.

Cure butts 4–6 days in curing cellar held at 38°–40°F.

After-Cure Treatment.—Remove butts from cover cure and wash lightly with a soft fiber brush. Do not soak.

Stuff butts through forming machine into stockinettes. Pull stockinettes very tight around butts and tie. Hang on smoke trees so they do not touch one another.

Smoking.—Preheat smokehouse to 130°F. Transfer trees to smokehouse and hold at this temperature (130°F) for 2 hr with dampers wide open. Set dampers 1/4 open and raise temperature to 140°F and introduce smoke for 1 hr. Then raise temperature to 160°F and hold until an internal temperature of the meat reaches 142°F.

After-Smoke Treatment.—Remove butts from smokehouse and shower with hot water for 2 min.

Then cool at room temperature to an internal meat temperature of 110°F.

Transfer butts to chill room (36°-38°F) and hold overnight. Then remove stockinettes and stuff butts in Cellophane casings. (Red color Cellophane is usually used.) Encased butts are then ready for shipment and need refrigeration throughout the marketing channels.

DEWEY HAMS (LOINS)

Dewey hams are boned, trimmed pork loins, cut in half with the two halves put together with a gelatin binder which sets in the casing during smoking-cooking to a ready-to-eat temperature of 152°-155°F. They are a perishable product and should be kept refrigerated throughout storage and the marketing channels.

Processing Procedure

Select quality pork loins of either 12-14 lb or 14-16 lb average weight for uniform processing. Remove bones carefully so as not to damage meat. Trim surface fat down to the lean meat.

Curing.—Loins are injected with liquid pickle using an injecto machine.

Chill boned loins to 36°-38°F before injecting pickle. Use ingredients given in Table 1.1 with or without erythorbate and bicarbonate. Inject 10% of the weight of the trimmed, green loin. Place loins in vats and cover with pickle using ingredients given in Table 1.3. Cure for 4-6 days.

After-Cure Treatment.—Remove loins from pickle. Wash under a shower of hot water, scrubbing with a fiber brush; or, run loins through a mechanical washer.

Cut loins in center.

Rub lean sides of both pieces with 200 bloom, fine, granulated gelatin to bind the pieces together. Put together by joining large ends with narrow ends as shown.

Easy-Peel fibrous casings are used to encase the finished loins. The required size of casing will depend on the dimensions of the finished, joined

loin. Before using casings, soak in hot water (140°-150°F). Stuff loins into casings and close under pressure. Pinprick casing when pressure is applied to let entrapped air escape, then tie end of casing securely.

Hang stuffed loins on smoke trees spaced so they do not touch one another.

Smoking.—Preheat smokehouse to 130°F with draft wide open. Transfer loins to smokehouse and hold for ½-¾ hr to dry casings. Then adjust dampers to ¼ open, raise temperature to 140°F, introduce smoke and hold for 4-5 hr. Cut off smoke and raise temperature to 165°F. Hold until an internal meat temperature of 152°-155°F is obtained.

After-Smoke Treatment.—Remove loins from smokehouse and chill under shower of cold water to an internal temperature of 110°F. Then hang at room temperature for approximately 1 hr to dry casings.

Transfer to cooler (45°F) overnight to chill before shipment. As noted previously, this is a perishable product and should be kept refrigerated throughout storage and marketing.

CANADIAN-STYLE BACON

Select quality pork loins of average weight (12-14 lb) for uniform processing.

Remove bones carefully so as not to damage meat. Trim surface fat down to the lean meat.

Curing.—Follow procedure given for Dewey Hams (above).

Stuffing (Encasing).—No-stretch cellulose casings are used for Canadian-style bacon. A stuffing machine is used which forms the loins into uniform diameter with air pressure; the piston pushes the loin into the casing. Casings should be stuffed very tight. The casing is tied with a cord and the loins are hung on smoke trees so they are not touching one another.

Smoking.—Preheat smokehouse to 130°F. Transfer loins to smokehouse and hold for 4 hr with draft open and without smoke. Raise smokehouse temperature to 150°F, adjust damper to ¼ open, introduce smoke, and hold for 3 hr after which raise temperature to 160°F and hold until internal meat temperature reaches 142°F.

After-Smoke Treatment.—Remove loins from smokehouse and chill under shower of cold water to an internal temperature of 110°F. Then hang at room temperature until casings are dry. Transfer to cooler (45°F) for overnight chilling before shipping. This is a perishable product and should be kept refrigerated throughout storage and marketing.

BACON (BELLIES)

Bacon is one of the most popular cured meats in the United States. Newer processing procedures have steadily improved this product during the last 30 yr and science continues to improve curing methods which save labor costs and improve quality of the finished product as well.

The penetronic-curing process is a big improvement over the box-curing method (processing procedures for both are given below). The box-curing process takes 13 days to cure 12–14 lb bellies and 15 days for 14–16 lb bellies. Because of the long time required to get the cure into the center of the bellies, the thin layer of lean meat on the surface of the bellies may be overcured, the color of the cured meat is dark, and the salt content is variable. The penetronic process reduces the curing time to 4–5 days and, at the same time, improves quality of the end product. The lean of the bacon is brighter and the salt content uniform.

When the injecto process is used (also given below), the curing time is also reduced over the box-curing process and the color of the lean is brighter, but the quality of the end product is not improved (as described below under penetronic dry curing).

It may not be long before pork bellies will be sliced, cured, and packaged in one continuous operation and will be ready for marketing channels overnight. The principles of this new continuous process are herewith described.

Continuous Process with Overnight Cure

Rinds are removed from the green bellies and they are chilled to an internal temperature of $24°-26°F$ at the start of processing. They are formed in a bacon-forming machine, after which they are sliced. The curing solution is then applied through spray nozzles in a protective housing of the slicing machine. The spray of the curing solution is directed at the end of the belly to be sliced and upon the face of the last slice. The orifice of the nozzles are adjusted so that they will eject 5 parts of cure solution to 100 parts of bellies. The curing solution contains salt, sodium nitrite, sodium nitrate, sodium erythorbate, and sodium bicarbonate.

Slices are Dried, Smoked, and Packaged.—After slices have been sprayed with cure and shingled automatically on the conveyor belt, they enter a drying zone where moisture from both top and bottom of the shingled slices is removed. Temperature of the drying zone is well under the rendering temperature of the sliced bacon. From the drying zone, the conveyor takes the bacon through a smoke tunnel. As it leaves the smoke tunnel, slices are sprayed with a concentrated solution of glucono delta lactone or sodium acid pyrophosphate which does not add extra weight to the bacon. Then the bacon enters the packaging department where the slices are weighed and packaged under vacuum.

Overnight Curing.—Because of the short time required for the continuous process up to this point, color of the lean meat is not fully developed. However, the full color develops overnight in a chill room right in the package after boxing and storage. When the glucono delta lactone reacts with the sodium nitrite, it produces nitrous oxide and nitrogen dioxide which have germicidal prop-

erties. The sodium erythorbate causes fast color development; and because of the acid reaction of glucona delta lactone on the nitrite, the product has excellent storage and flavor stability.

Research and development, engineering, and installation of new equipment for a new process is always time-consuming and costly. But when this new method comes into general use for processing, there will be great savings in time and labor as well as improvement in quality of the cured bacon that reaches the American breakfast table.

BOX DRY-CURED BACON

This method of curing bacon is not generally used at present although it produces a good quality product. It has two disadvantages: The method requires a long curing time; and much costly labor is involved.

The box used for this method of curing is a galvanized iron box with a capacity of 625 lb of trimmed bellies. In case phosphate is used stainless steel boxes are necessary.

Processing Procedure

Select fresh green bellies, properly trimmed, with an average weight of 10–16 lb each.

Curing.—Bellies are first rubbed with a dry curing mixture usually of the following composition:

	Lb	Oz
Salt	70	
Cane sugar	22	
Sodium nitrite	1	4
Sodium nitrate	1	4
Food grade phosphate		6

Mix ingredients thoroughly before using. Use 4 lb of the dry cure per 100 lb of bellies.

Pack rubbed bellies tightly in curing boxes; always pack bellies meat side up. Each box should be filled with bellies averaging only 2 lb difference in weight, such as 10-12, 12-14, or 14-16, because of the difference in the curing time. Avoid air pockets between layers and sides of box by filling open spaces with square-cut hog jowls which can be cured at the same time. (First rub the pieces of hog jowls with the dry cure mixture.) When box is completely filled, press down cover tightly with the attached springs. Allow 1 day of curing for each pound of the average weight of the bellies; e.g., curing time of 11 days for 10-12 lb, 13 days for 12-14 lb, 15 days for 14-16 lb. If, after 2 days in cure the bellies are not covered with pickle, make additional pickle to cover the top layer of bellies, using 1 1/4 lb of dry curing mixture per 1 gal. water. Bellies should not be left in cure for more than 3 days after the curing time indicated above.

Washing.—Never soak cured bellies. Remove from curing box and wash under shower of hot water scrubbing with a soft fiber brush; or, pass bellies through a mechanical washer.

Smoking.—Hang bellies on bacon combs on properly spaced smoke trees. Preheat smokehouse to 135°F and transfer bellies. Hold at this temperature with damper wide open until surface of bellies is dry. Then adjust dampers to 1/4 open, introduce smoke, and hold at the same temperature (135°F) until an internal meat temperature of 127°-128°F is reached. Reduce smokehouse temperature to 120°F and smoke until the desired color is obtained.

After-Smoke Treatment.—Remove rind from bellies as soon as possible after they are taken from the smokehouse. A derinding machine is usually used for this. Then again hang the bellies on trees, properly spaced, and transfer them to a freezer at a temperature of 22°-24°F. Hold at this temperature until the internal meat temperature reaches 26°-27°F.

Forming and Slicing.—Use a bacon forming machine to form the bacon slabs. Then slice and package. It is very important that these operations are performed in a special room maintained at a temperature of 36°-38°F.

Product is perishable and should be kept refrigerated for storage and through marketing channels.

DRY PENETRONIC-CURED BACON

In this method of curing, boneless meat is penetrated with a bank of solid needles after which a dry cure mixture is spread over the meat surface. The perforations made by the needles hasten penetration of the cure into the meat and the bellies can be cured in from 4 to 5 days.

The Penetronic Machine

This perforating machine has 2 rows of solid stainless steel needles each 1/8-in. in diameter and spaced 3/4 in. apart. It is so constructed that it carries the bellies under the penetronic needles automatically and discharges them on a conveyor where the dry curing mixture is spread over the surface of each belly.

Instead of the penetronic machines, injecto curing equipment may be used. Usually, hollow needles are used when injecto-curing meats; but in this case, replace the hollow needles with solid ones. Needles in the injecto curing equipment are not farther apart than 1 in. Use the injecto equipment only for perforations and not with any injection pickle.

Perforations of needles, using either equipment, should penetrate bellies to within 1/4-in. of the other side of the slab.

At present, this method is the most efficient procedure for curing bacon. The main reason that bacon can be cured in such a short time and with such excellent results is due to the rapid penetration of the cure mixture and diffusion between the perforated holes. Also, during the heating process the small holes disappear, the resulting end product will not splatter in the skillet or on the grill, and there is no excessive shrink.

This method assures a uniform predetermined cure content and, thus, better keeping quality.

By contrast, the injecto method of curing bacon uses hollow needles that penetrate the fat of the bellies and liquid pickle is injected through them under pressure. This produces pockets of pickle in the fat tissues and it takes more time to absorb the pickle by osmosis. Also, the disrupted fat tissues will not hold the moisture when the bacon is processed and ultimately fried or grilled. It releases moisture during frying or grilling causing sputtering and fat rendering.

Processing Procedure

Use properly trimmed fresh green bellies with uniform weights: 10-12 lb, 12-14 lb, 14-16 lb, or 16-18 lb.

Remove rinds and chill bellies to an internal temperature of 26°-27°F. Shape them in a forming machine before putting them in cure.

Dry Curing Mixture.—Thoroughly mix together the following ingredients:

	Lb
Salt	70
Cane sugar	22
Sodium nitrite	1
Sodium nitrate	1
Food grade phosphate	6

Use 3–5 lb of curing mixture per 100 lb of bellies, depending on desired salt content of the finished product.

Curing.—Perforate bellies with the penetronic machine. As the bellies come through on the conveyor, spread the dry curing mixture evenly over the top of each piece. Use a measured amount of cure on each piece, as given in the following examples:

Belly Weight Lb	Cure Mixture Oz
10–12	7
12–14	8
14–16	9
16–18	10

Do not rub the cure into the bellies; just spread it evenly over the top surface of each belly as it comes through the penetronic machine.

Curing is done on pallets which should be at least 8 in. above the floor or on racks on rollers. Spread curing mixture evenly over pallets or shelves of racks, then stack bellies 8–10 layers high in a crisscross pattern to prevent shifting during curing; and always stack bellies with perforated side up. Also, pack bellies as closely together as possible to eliminate air pockets. Cover stacked bellies with waxed paper topped with a canvas sheet to exclude as much air as possible during curing. Cure for 4–5 days at cellar temperature of 38°–40°F.

After-Cure Treatment.—Never soak bellies in water. Wash them under a shower of hot water and scrub with a soft fiber brush or pass them through a mechanical washer.

Hang bellies on bacon combs spaced on smoke trees so they do not touch one another.

Smoking.—Preheat smokehouse to 135°F before bringing in smoke trees. Adjust dampers wide open to dry surface of the bacon, after which adjust dampers to 1/4 open and introduce smoke. Hold at the 135°F temperature until the internal meat temperature reaches 127°–128°F. Then reduce smokehouse temperature to 120°F and continue smoking until the desired bacon color is obtained.

After-Smoke Treatment.—Transfer trees to a freezer room at a temperature of 22°–24°F and hold at this temperature until bacon reaches an internal temperature of 26°–27°F. Then put slabs

through a bacon forming machine, slice and package. It is very important that the forming and slicing operation is conducted in a special sanitary, hygienic room at a temperature of 38°–40°F.

For a More Stable Color.—As the bacon slices come through the slicing machine on the conveyor, they may be sprayed with a 5% solution of sodium erythorbate or ascorbic acid in water or in a 30° salinometer plain salt brine. The use of such a spray solution will not result in the addition of a significant amount of moisture to the product.

INJECTO-CURED BACON

Except for the method of applying the cure to bellies, the processing procedure follows closely that of penetronic cured bacon (preceding formula) and should be referred to for detailed directions.

Injecto Process.—As described above in outlining the differences between penetronic and injecto curing, the perforating needles in the injecto equipment are hollow and carry a liquid cure under pressure through the needles into the bellies.

Bellies should be chilled to 38°–40°F before being injected. Curing pickle temperature also should be 38°–40°F. Either of the curing pickles given below may be used:

	Gal.	Lb	Oz
Water	100		
Salt		167	
Cane sugar		40	
Sodium nitrite		1	4
Sodium nitrate		1	4
Food grade phosphate		20	

or

	Gal.	Lb	Oz
100° salinometer brine	63		
Water	37		
Cane sugar		40	
Sodium nitrite		1	4
Sodium nitrate		1	4
Food grade phosphate		20	

Salt content in the above formulas can be lowered if a less salty finished product is desired.

Inject 8–10% of the green weight of the fresh bellies with the liquid cure.

Curing.—Pack pumped bellies in stainless steel meat trucks with a drainage hole on the bottom to remove excess curing solution draining out of the pumped bellies. Transfer to the curing room at 38°–40°F for 3–4 days' cure.

After curing, do not soak, but wash cured bellies under a hot water shower using a soft fiber brush, or pass them through a mechanical washer.

Smoking.—Follow directions given above for penetronic cure.

After-Cure Treatment.—Same as for penetronic cure.

CURED BEEF PRODUCTS

BEEF BACON

In general, sliced beef bacon is processed the same as bacon from pork bellies. Use properly trimmed beef plates of choice quality and follow any of the curing processes given above in the previous section for bacon from pork bellies but omit phosphate from curing pickle. Curing time and after-cure treatment are identical with the way pork bellies are handled.

Smoking Schedule.—When beef plates are properly hung on smoke trees, preheat smokehouse to 135°F with dampers wide open. Transfer trees to the smokehouse and hold beef plates at this temperature with dampers open until surface of plates is dry. Then introduce smoke, adjust dampers to 1/4 open, and maintain this temperature until the desired color is obtained. Then shut off smoke, close dampers, and raise temperature to 155°-160°F and hold until an internal meat temperature of 135°F is reached.

After-Smoke Treatment.—Remove beef plates from the smokehouse and hold at room temperature until internal meat temperature is reduced to 100°-110°F. Then transfer bacon slabs to a chill room (34°-36°F) for final chilling before slicing and packaging.

DRIED BEEF FOR SLICING

Bone, defat (if any), and trim canner grade beef rounds. Then section into insides, outsides, and knuckles.

Curing pickle ingredients:

	Gal.	Lb
Water	100	
Salt		200
Cane sugar		44
Sodium nitrite		1.50
Sodium nitrate		1.50

Use 5 1/2 –6 gal. of pickle per 100 lb of meat. Both the pickle and the meat pieces should be chilled to 38°F before use and the curing cellar temperature should not be higher than 34°-36°F. This cellar temperature slows down the cure somewhat, but it lessens the danger of spoilage during the long curing time required. Because of the difference in weight and thickness of the meat pieces, insides, outsides, and knuckles should each be cured in separate vessels.

Cure.—Curing time is approximately 7 days per pound. It takes approximately 75–85 days to cure heavy insides and 65–70 days to cure outsides and knuckles.

Soak.—Remove meats from curing pickle and soak in tap water for 24 hr in the curing cellar holding temperature at 34°-36°F. For uniform results, change the water 3 or 4 times during the soaking period.

Dry and Smoke.—Remove cured meats from the soaking water and hang on smoke trees. Allow meat to dry thoroughly before transferring pieces to the smokehouse. The following smoking and drying schedule is recommended:

Hr	Temp °F	
12	100–110	No smoke
24	100–110	With smoke
8	125	With smoke
8	130	No smoke

Then drop temperature to 120°F and hold at this temperature until a 35% shrink from the cured weight is obtained.

The finished dried beef for slicing averages about 50% moisture.

Slice and Package.—Slice dried beef paper thin, using a dried beef slicing machine. Package in glass jars and close under 27 in. of vacuum. No sterilization processing is necessary.

DRIED BEEF FOR SLICING (FAST METHOD)[2]

Ingredients	Lb	Oz
Beef rounds	100	
Salt	3	
Sodium nitrite		1/4
Sodium nitrate		1
Sodium erythorbate		7/8
Corn sugar		1

Processing Procedure

It is imperative that sinews, gristle, connective tissues, and fat (if any) be removed from the beef

[2] U.S. Pat. 2,224,397, Dec. 10, 1940, Manufacture of Dried Beef; 3,238,046, Mar. 1, 1966, Production of Integrated Meat Products. Issued to S. L. Komarik and assigned to Griffith Laboratories.

rounds. Meat should be chilled to 32°-34°F before processing.

Grinding.—Grind 10% of the knuckle part of the round through the $1/4$-in. plate of the grinder; then mix it with 3% of chipped ice and regrind through the $1/16$-in. plate of the grinder. Grind the remainder of the meat through the $1\frac{1}{2}$-in. plate.

Mixing.—Transfer ground meats to a mechanical mixer, add salt previously mixed with the dry ingredients and mix until a uniform mixture is obtained (approximately 2 min).

Curing.—Pack meat mixture tightly without any air pockets into meat truck or tub. Transfer to cooler at a temperature of 36°-40°F. Hold for 3-4 days for curing. Then transfer meat to the vacuum mixer, and, under 25 in. vacuum, mix meat for 3 min.

Stuffing.—Stuff meat material in $4\frac{1}{2}$-in. diameter Easy-Peel fibrous casings. Press each filled casing between two oblong perforated side-molds and lock the attached springs tightly.

Cooking.—Transfer stuffed molds to a cooking tank. Have water in the tank preheated to 160°F. Cook at this temperature until an internal meat temperature of 150°F is reached. This will take approximately 3-3½ hr.

Drying and Smoking.—Remove cooked meats from the molds and encase them in stockinettes. Have smokehouse preheated to 150°F and transfer meat immediately to smokehouse. Keep dampers wide open and maintain this temperature for 4-5 hr. Smoke can be introduced during this time if so desired.

Chilling.—Remove dried beef from smokehouse and let it cool for 4-5 hr at room temperature to reduce internal meat temperature to that of the room. Then transfer beef to cooler (40°-45°F). The chill room should have a very low humidity.

The process given above should produce a finished product with a yield of 50% of the green weight. It may be sold in blocks (in the form in which it was processed); or it may be sliced paper thin through a dried beef slicing machine and packaged in pouches under inert gas, sealed, and sold as chipped beef.

KOSHER-STYLE CORNED BEEF BRISKET

Use good or a better grade of beef briskets for the best results. Select uniform weights for uniform processing. Remove deckle fat from the briskets. Bone carefully so as not to damage the meat.

Curing Pickle.—Briskets may be artery or injecto pumped. Use Table 1.1 for pickle formula with or without erythorbate and bicarbonate. In case a saltier finished product is desired, bring up the pickle with added salt or salt brine. Emulsified

seasonings and also garlic juice may be added to the pickle if desired.

Curing.—Government regulation permits pumping 20% of the weight of the green brisket. After briskets are pumped (either artery or injecto), place them in vats or tierces in such manner that one flesh side always faces another. Sprinkle commercial pickling spice mix between each layer. After the vat or tierce is filled, press meat down tightly with a laced hardwood cover. Then add enough of the same pumping pickle to cover the meat. Cure artery-pumped briskets for 2-3 days; injecto-pumped briskets, 4-5 days.

Packaging.—Briskets can be sold in bulk as soon as they are removed from cure. Or, they may be cut into pieces, packaged, and held in refrigerated storage in the following manner: Cut pieces should be dipped into a 30° salinometer brine in which 5% sodium erythorbate is dissolved. They are then stuffed into Cryovac bags and heat sealed. The finished product should be kept at 36°-38°F through storage and kept under refrigeration until sold.

COOKED CORNED BEEF ROUNDS

For best results select beef round graded good or better than average 65-70 lb in weight. Save main artery and vein for pumping the pickle as described under **Curing Whole Smoked Hams.**

Curing Pickle.—To prepare pumping pickle, use formula given in Table 1.1 with or without erythorbate and bicarbonate. If a saltier finished product is desired, bring salinometer reading up with added salt or salt brine. Emulsified seasonings and garlic juice may be added to pickle if desired.

Curing.—Use artery pumping in the same way it is done with hams (see **Curing Whole Smoked Hams).** Pump 10% of the weight of the green beef round. After rounds are pumped, transfer them to the curing cellar at a temperature of 38°-40°F for overnight cure. No cover pickle or dry cure rubbing is necessary at this point of processing.

Boning.—Remove rounds from curing cellar. Remove all surface fat and skin tissues. Then remove shank and hip bones and make an incision right through the seam in direct line with the femur; remove femur without damaging surrounding meat. Next cut away shank and knuckles and open up the round to remove seam fat and connective tissues. The meat is then cut into four equal pieces.

Aging and Flavor Development.—Place the sectioned beef rounds in the same cover pickle used for pumping and transfer to the curing cellar (38°-40°F) for an additional 4-5 days for flavor development.

Molding and Cooking.—Remove the cured pieces of rounds from the pickle, wash them under a shower of hot water; and drain. Then press them tightly into parchment paper-lined oblong ham molds. Place molds in cooking vats so there will be free circulation of water around each. Introduce hot water (175°F) and maintain this temperature until internal meat temperature reaches 165°F. Allow approximately 50 min per pound of the average weight of each mold.

Chilling and Stuffing.—Drain cooking water from vats, introduce cold water and chill molds for 2 hr. Then remove molds from vats and repress and tighten molds. Transfer molds to cooler (36°-38°F) for final chilling.

Remove meat from molds; dip into gelatin solution and stuff into Cellophane casings.

Store in a cold room (36°-38°F) until product is shipped. This product should be kept refrigerated throughout the marketing channels.

PEPPERED BEEF ROUNDS

Follow procedure given above for **Cooked Corned Beef Rounds** for selection of meat, curing pickle and pumping, and curing the rounds.

Whole pieces of boneless top and bottom round of uniform thickness may also be peppered. In this case, use injecto pumping of the pickle, using the same curing pickle used for artery pumping the whole rounds. Inject 10% of the weight of each piece.

Boning.—Remove rounds from curing cellar. Remove all surface fat and skin tissues. Remove shank and hip bones and separate knuckle and shank from rounds. Then cut the rounds into desired pieces of uniform thickness for uniform aging and cooking in the smokehouse.

Aging.—Immediately after pumping or injecting curing pickle, rub the cut pieces generously with cracked black pepper. Then pack pieces tightly into tierces or vats equipped with laced wooden covers to press down meat. Press meat down tightly with the cover and then add enough of the curing pickle (same as was used to artery pump or injecto pump) to cover the meat. Age peppered pieces for 6-7 days in the curing cellar at a temperature of 36°-38°F for pieces and 38°-40°F for top and bottom round slabs.

Remove meat from cure and place each piece in stockinette. Small pieces may be hung on smoke trees. Large pieces should be laid on expanded stainless steel screening. Allow about 2 in. between pieces for good air circulation.

Smoking and Cooking.—Preheat smokehouse to 130°F. Bring in peppered meat pieces and, with dampers wide open, hold until meat surface is dry. Then raise temperature to 150°F, adjust dampers to 1/4 open, introduce smoke and hold for 3 hr. At the end of this time, shut off smoke and raise

temperature to 212°F. Hold at this temperature until internal meat temperature reaches 165°F.

Remove from smokehouse and hold at room temperature until internal meat temperature reaches 120°F. Then transfer to chill room (24°-26°F) until internal meat temperature is reduced to 28°-30°F.

Packaging.—At a temperature of 28°-30°F, the product can be sliced efficiently. Pack slices in polyethylene or Mylar bags and close under vacuum. Pack large pieces in Cryovac bags and close under vacuum.

Product should be held at refrigerated temperature through storage and marketing channels.

PASTRAMI

Use navel ends of beef plates or briskets. Select good or a better grade. Remove deckel fat.

Curing Pickle.—Use injecto method to pump plates or briskets, allowing 10% of the green weight of each meat piece. Use formula in Table 1.1 with or without erythorbate and bicarbonate and omitting phosphate (phosphates are allowed only in hams, picnics and bacon). Garlic juice may be added to the pickle if desired to give this flavor to the pastrami.

Curing.—After meats are injected with pickle, pack them tightly in tierces or vats with a laced hardwood cover and press meat down with cover. Add sufficient pickle of the same formula and strength used for pumping to cover meat. Cure 4-5 days in cellar at a temperature of 38°-40°F.

Rubbing.—Remove meat pieces from cure and drain. Then rub generously with cracked black pepper or a combination of cracked black pepper and whole coriander. (Some processors prefer using coarsely chopped pickling spices.) A light sprinkling of Spanish paprika over the top will give the finished product an attractive appearance.

Hang rubbed pieces on bacon combs on smoke trees properly spaced so they are not touching one another.

Smoking and Cooking.—Pastramis of high quality can be produced when temperature is high, cooking time short, and smoke is light. Preheat smokehouse temperature to 140°F. Transfer pastramis to smokehouse and, with dampers wide open, hold at this temperature until meat surface is dry. Then adjust dampers to 1/4 open, introduce light smoke and smoke at 140°F for 1 hr. Shut off smoke, close dampers, and raise temperature to the highest temperature setting and cook pastramis until an internal meat temperature of 165°F is reached.

Chill and Package.—Remove pastramis from smokehouse and allow to hang at room temperature until internal meat temperature is reduced to 110°-120°F. Then transfer to chill room at 36°-

38°F for final chilling. At this temperature the pastramis can be sliced efficiently and packaged in Mylar or polyethylene bags and closed under vacuum. Or, large pieces can be packaged in Cryovac bags and sealed under vacuum.

Product should be held under refrigeration through storage and marketing channels.

CURED AND SMOKED BEEF TONGUES

Tongues coming from the killing floor should be thoroughly cleaned to rid them of slime. This is best accomplished by washing them in a vat equipped with a perforated compressed air line on the bottom to keep water agitated. Fill tank with fresh tongues, then introduce cold water and open air-line valve. Let water overflow during washing to carry away slime. Wash until overflow water runs crystal clear.

Artery Pumping and Curing.—The better curing procedure to use is artery pumping of the pickle, although some processors prefer to cure tongues using only a cover pickle (see below).

The following formula may be used:

	Gal.	Lb
Water	100	
Salt		100
Sodium nitrite		1½
Sodium nitrate		1½
Sodium erythorbate		5½

Sodium bicarbonate to adjust pH
to 7.6 at pickle temp of 40°F
(optional)

No phosphate is allowed; phosphate is permitted only in hams, picnics, and bacon.

Using the 2 arteries located at the base of the tongue, pump 5% of the weight of each tongue into each artery. Place tongues in vats or tierces and cover with the same pickle used for pumping. Cure for 2-3 days in curing cellar at 38°-40°F.

Cover Pickle Curing.—Use ingredients given above for artery pumping pickle omitting the sodium erythorbate and bicarbonate and using no phosphate. Place tongues in vats or tierces and cover with pickle. Hold in the curing cellar at 38°-40°F for 5 days. Overhaul position of tongues in the cover pickle on the 5th day, then cure for 2-3 more days. Maximum curing time is 8 days.

Smoking.—Remove tongues from cure, wash them thoroughly, encase each in a stockinette, and hang on smoke trees spaced so there is good air circulation between tongues. Before transfer to smokehouse, hold tongues at room temperature for 5-6 hr to warm up before smoking.

Preheat smokehouse to 140°F. Transfer tongues to smokehouse and, with dampers wide open, allow meat surface to dry (approximately 1-1½ hr). Then adjust dampers to ¼ open, introduce smoke, and raise temperature of smokehouse to 180°F.

Hold at this temperature for 5-6 hr, depending upon size of the tongues. Tongues should be firm to the touch before removal from the smokehouse.

Transfer tongues to room temperature and hold until an internal meat temperature of 110°F is reached. Then transfer tongues to chill room (36°-38°F) for final chill.

Smoked tongues should be held at refrigerated temperature during storage and marketing.

CURED AND COOKED BEEF TONGUES CANNED IN TIN OR GLASS CONTAINERS

Follow procedure given above for **Cured and Smoked Beef Tongues** in cleaning, pumping pickle, and curing tongues that are to be cooked and canned.

After-Cure Treatment.—Remove tongues from cure and wash thoroughly. Place in cooking vats and cook in boiling water until tongues are tender. As they are removed from the cooking vats and without appreciable cooling, skin, remove gullet bone, and trim tongues, and press into tin or glass containers of suitable size. This operation should be carried out very rapidly because tongues should still be hot when they are pressed into their containers; they lose their elasticity upon cooling and will not fit properly into the containers. (Trimmings can be utilized to process deviled tongue spread.)

Packaging.—Prepare an agar solution by dissolving 5% of agar in 95% of boiling water; heat until the agar is in solution and keep hot during the canning operation.

Pour a small quantity of the agar solution in the bottom of each can or glass container, fit in hot tongue, press down, fill container with agar solution, and close under 27 in. of vacuum.

Processing.—It is imperative when processing canned foods to check either with your can supplier or the National Canners Association for accurate and safe processing times and temperatures. The following may be used as a guide.

For Tin Containers.—Process 48-oz (net) cans 2 hr 30 min at 230°F followed by cooling under 10 lb air pressure for at least 30 min with final cooling under atmospheric pressure.

For Glass Containers.—Glass containers should be processed in retorts filled with water under 10 lb air pressure over the recommended steam pressure for the following times and temperature:

Container Size	
Oz	Hr at 240°F
12	1½
16	1½
22	2

Chill under 15 lb air pressure.

SAUSAGES

FRESH SAUSAGES

Fresh sausages are one of the most popular, best selling items at the meat counter. The processing procedure is very simple and, with proper observation of certain rules, the making of fresh sausage can be a very profitable part of a meat processor's operation.

Material used is fresh pork trimmings, usually with a ratio of 50% lean to 50% fat meat. However, a more desirable sausage—both in appearance and flavor—can be made by adding 10–25% additional lean meat, although one government regulation specifies that the ratio of lean and trimmable fat should be 50/50.

Low Temperatures Are Important

Fresh sausage is a very perishable item; the fat part of the pork trimmings may turn rancid very rapidly with too high temperatures during both the processing procedure and through the marketing channels. Even at $40°F$, development of rancidity and bacterial growth in fresh pork is much more rapid than at $32°F$. So trimmings should be as fresh as possible. Use them right from the cutting floor, if this is possible, and promptly chill to $30°$-$32°F$; or, use freshly frozen thawed trimmings.

Cause of the development of rancidity in pork is the chemical reaction of oxygen in the air with the unsaturated fatty acids present in pork fat. The lower the temperature, the slower the development of this rancidity. Therefore, the temperature of the pork and the sausage made from it should never go much above $32°F$ for any length of time. After sausages have been made they can be held in cold storage and through shipment to the grocer at low temperatures.

Dry Ice may be used to keep pork at low temperature during the chopping and mixing operations.

Practice Strict Sanitation

Contact of the pork fat with certain metals, such as iron or copper, also increases the rate of development of rancidity. So use only stainless steel utensils and equipment in handling pork. Furthermore, strict sanitation must be practiced with regard to utensils, equipment, and the entire sausage making area. If equipment is used that has been used for curing meats, even a trace of sodium nitrite coming in contact with the pork could affect the flavor and bloom of the sausage reaching the customer. Bloom is that fresh pink color of the finished product which some customers look for at the meat counter. In some cases, traces of sodium nitrite in the finished sausages have caused them to turn red when fried.

Destruction of Trichinae

The Meat Inspection Division (MID) of USDA is concerned with protecting public health by setting up regulations that assure destruction of live trichinae in pork flesh when pork products are processed for the consumer. Trichinae are the live parasites that can invade pork flesh and, if not destroyed before being consumed, can cause the serious disease known as trichinosis in humans. However, in the case of fresh pork sausage which MID classifies as a product which is customarily well cooked in the home or elsewhere before being served to the consumer, MID requires no treatment of such products for the destruction of trichinae.

Avoid Smeary Texture

Pork sausage is made by using either a meat grinder or a rapid high speed meat chopper. In order to produce the best product and to avoid a smeary texture, the meat grinder should have sharp blades and be in good working condition and the high speed meat chopper should not be overloaded when chopping pork for sausage. If a badly worn meat grinder with dull blades is used, it breaks up the fat cells and crushes rather than grinds the lean meat portion so that smeariness results.

Use of Spices

There are three options to the sausage maker in the type of spices he may use: Dry soluble spices, natural spices, or strongly-flavored southern-style spices.

Dry soluble spices are a mixture of extracted oils and oleoresins of the natural spices with sugar or salt as the carrier. These will help preserve the bloom in sausage and are the best type of spices for sausages packaged in window-type containers where the consumer can see the product.

Natural spices, especially the herb-type, may discolor the meat giving it a grayish cast; but many consumers prefer this kind of spice flavoring regardless of color because of its rich flavor. If natural spices are used, they must be purified and sterilized to avoid contamination of the meat.

Southern-style seasoning is hot and very strongly flavored with red pepper and paprika imparting a reddish color to the mixture. Again, the hot, strong flavor and the reddish color in fresh sausage are preferred by some consumers.

Standard spice formulas are given in Table 2.1 for the three kinds of sausage seasoning mentioned above.

TABLE 2.1

FRESH SAUSAGE SEASONING FORMULAS FOR 500-LB BATCHES OF SAUSAGE[1]

Dry Soluble Spices[2]	Cc	Natural Spices[3]	Oz	Southern-Style[3]	Oz
Oleoresin capsicum	17.00	White pepper	15.00	Ground red pepper	10.00
Oleoresin ginger	7.25	Ground nutmeg	3.75	Cracked red pepper	5.00
Oil of nutmeg	7.50	Ground ginger	5.00	Ground ginger	5.00
Oil of thyme	7.50	Ground thyme	5.00	Ground thyme	5.00
Oil of Dalmatian sage	10.50	Rubbed sage	10.00	Rubbed sage	15.00
				Paprika	10.00

SOURCE: Stephan L. Komarik, 4810 Ronda, Coral Gables, Florida.
[1] Use a percentage of the ingredient amounts given for smaller batches.
[2] Mix with 1 lb 4 oz of corn sugar as the carrier ingredient.
[3] Use only purified and sterilized natural spices to avoid contamination of meat product.

Shelf-Life

As stated above, fresh pork sausage is very perishable. The keeping quality of freshly-made sausage is 5–6 days. Certain natural spices, e.g., rosemary and sage, have some antioxidant properties and will help extend the shelf-life of sausages longer than those made only with dry soluble seasonings. An extract of herbs such as sage and rosemary is permissible and is commonly used; it is available as a patented, proprietary product. It is claimed that using this extract increases the shelf-life of fresh sausages 16–20 days, extending its keeping quality from 5–6 days to up to 30 days with proper handling in making the sausage and if kept under proper refrigeration.

Antioxidants are permitted in fresh pork sausages. If used, shelf-life can be extended from 5–6 days to 16–20 days.

Casings and Stuffing

Fresh pork sausage is stuffed into sheep, hog, or artificial casings. Small casings (20/22 sheep or 28/32 hog) are used for links with the links usually made in $3^1/2$-in. lengths. For larger casings for sausage of 1-lb weight, artificial cellulose casings are well liked for their uniformity; however, hog or sheep casings are still used by many for the larger 1-lb links (or rings). Bulk sausage may be packaged in cloth bags, in larger sized hog or sheep casings, or in cellulose casings. For consumer use, these are usually 1 lb in weight; for institutional use, they are the same diameter but are longer and of larger weight.

FINEST QUALITY FRESH PORK SAUSAGE

Ingredients	Lb	Oz
Regular pork trimmings 50/50	350	
Lean pork trimmings 85/15	150	
Salt	8	12
Ice, chopped	15	
Corn sugar	1	4
(used as carrier for dry soluble seasonings)		
Seasoning formula ingredients (see Table 2.1)		

Processing Procedure

Check condition of meat grinder for sharpness and cleanliness and meat mixer for cleanliness (particularly if it has been used in curing meats).

Trimmings should be free of bones, sinews, blood clots, and skins. Trimmings should also be chilled to about 33°F at start of processing.

Mix together salt, corn sugar, and seasonings (from Table 2.1).

Grinding Method.—Grind chilled trimmings through the $1–1^1/2$-in. plate of the grinder. Then transfer to mechanical mixer, add salt mixture and ice and mix for 2 min. Remove from mixer and grind again using either the $1/8$- or $3/36$-in. plate of the grinder.

Rapid Meat Chopper Method.—A rapid meat chopper operates at speeds up to 3000 rpm and will reduce meat pieces to particle size very rapidly. Use well-chilled meat pieces or trimmings. Fill chopper bowl only half full, add salt mixture and ice and let machine run until meat is reduced to desired size. Pulverized Dry Ice may be added to the chopped ingredients along with chopped ice to keep meat temperature down to 28°–32°F. Transfer meat mixture to mechanical mixer and mix approximately 1–2 min to assure proper distribution of salt and flavorings and also to increase the binding capacity of the soluble proteins in the meat.

Stuffing.—Keep the stuffing table well iced to keep sausages cold. Immediately after mixing and grinding, stuff into casings using casings as described above suitable for the end product. Link and hang on sausage trees. Carry immediately to chill room (under 32°F) to dry casings and chill sausages. Casings should be dry before packaging; fans may be used to help dry them. Chill sausages to 32°F before packaging when they are ready for shipment.

The best way to hold the bloom and prevent development of rancidity is to transfer them to a freezing temperature of 0°F after they are chilled and the casings dry.

SOURCE: Stephan L. Komarik, 4810 Ronda, Coral Gables, Florida.

HOT WHOLE HOG SAUSAGE

This product is processed from hogs weighing approximately 300–350 lb live weight. Processing should be undertaken immediately after slaughter. If this is prompt and without delay, the finished sausage will have a very low bacterial count which will extend its shelf-life considerably, especially if the product is kept at 0°F temperature or below during storage. Average yield is about 70% as finished sausage.

It is common knowledge that the carcass of a hog immediately after slaughter is virtually bacteria-free. To retard bacterial growth during processing (1) avoid contamination, (2) add salt, (3) chill rapidly, and (4) work rapidly.

Processing Procedure

As soon as the hog is dressed, transfer carcass to a well-ventilated room close to the killing floor. Remove outside fat of the carcass in 3–4-in. strips with the skin on. Collect fat in tubs or a meat truck. Bone out lean part of the carcass, removing blood clots and sinews. Adjust ratio of lean meat to fat to about 55/45%. Weigh meat and transfer to a meat truck. To each 100 lb of meat add and thoroughly mix the following ingredients: Mix together 1 lb 12 oz salt, 4 oz corn sugar or corn syrup solids, and natural spice seasonings as given in Table 2.1. Grind the meat mixture through the $3/16$-in. plate of the grinder.

If all the processing steps up to this point are followed immediately after slaughter, temperature of the meat may not drop to below 85°F. At this temperature the muscle protein (myosin) is still in fluid state and will combine readily with the salt and the fat is still warm enough to dissolve the essential oils of the ground natural spices which, because of their anitoxidant properties, will retard the development of rancidity.

Place the ground meat mixture in pans not over 6 in. deep and hold in a cooler (30°–32°F) overnight to thoroughly chill. Stuff sausages next day. Use polyethylene casings or cloth bags (as trade demands) and pack in boxes for storage at 32°F until shipment if product is sold soon after processing. Otherwise, hold at 0°F temperature to extend shelf-life of product.

SOURCE: Stephan L. Komarik, 4810 Ronda, Coral Gables, Florida.

SAUSAGE WITH ADDED $3\frac{1}{2}$% CEREAL AND NONFAT DRY MILK

Use either of these meat combinations:

Ingredients	No. 1 Lb	No. 2 Lb
Regular pork trimmings 50/50	350	150
Beef tripe (white) treated	150	150
Beef plates or flanks (fresh)		200

with the following ingredients:

	Lb	Oz
Semolina flour	10	
Nonfat dry milk	7	8
Salt	10	
Corn sugar	1	4
Ice, chopped	48	
Seasoning mixture from Table 2.1		

Processing Procedure

Have all meat products well chilled. Grind beef plates or flanks and tripe through the 1-in. plate of the grinder. Pork trimmings are used without grinding to avoid smearing the fat. Transfer meat items to mechanical mixer. Mix together salt, corn sugar, and seasonings and add to meat items along with the ice. Put mixer in operation and while mixing, evenly distribute over contents the flour and nonfat dry milk. Mix approximately 2 min. After mixing is completed, grind mixture through the $1/8$- or $3/16$-in. plate of the grinder.

Immediately stuff into hog or sheep casings and link. Keep stuffing table well iced to help keep sausages cold during stuffing.

Hang linked sausages on trees and transfer immediately to chill room (under 32°F) to dry casings and chill sausages. Casings must be dry before packaging sausages; a fan may be used to help dry casings. Never package warm sausages.

Product is ready for shipment; for extended shelf-life hold at 0°F while in storage until shipped.

SOURCE: Stephan L. Komarik, 4810 Ronda, Coral Gables, Florida.

BULK PORK AND TOMATO SAUSAGE USING NONFAT DRY MILK

Ingredients	Lb	Oz
Pork trimmings	85	
Canned tomatoes	15	
Nonfat dry milk	3	
Salt	$2^{1}/_{2}$	
Ground white pepper		7
Ground sage		2

Procedure

Grind pork through $3/8$-in. plate.

Place pork in mixer, add tomatoes, nonfat dry milk, and seasoning. Mix well. Then grind all through $1/8$-in. plate.

Place in suitable size bulk cartons, or stuff in 1-lb cellulose casings.

Product is perishable and should be kept under refrigeration at all times. Shelf-life will be extended if storage temperature is maintained at 0°F or below.

SOURCE: American Dry Milk Institute, 130 N. Franklin, Chicago, Ill.

FRESH KOSHER-STYLE BEEF SAUSAGE

Ingredients	Lb	Oz
Beef plates	33	
Beef flanks	33	
Beef navels	33	
Salt	1	12
Ice, chopped	3	
Corn sugar	1	4
Seasonings (selected from below)		

Seasoning Formulas

Optional seasoning formulas are given for use of dry soluble spices which help hold the fresh pink color of the sausage, natural spices which should be purified and sterilized and which will give a grayish color to the finished product, and a hot, strongly-flavored southern-style seasoning mixture.

Dry Soluble Spice Formula.—Oleoresin capsicum, 4 cc; oleoresin ginger, 1.5 cc; Oil of nutmeg, 1.5 cc; oil of thyme, 1.5 cc; oil of Dalmatian sage, 2 cc. Mix thoroughly with the corn sugar and salt before using.

Natural Spice Formula.—Ground white pepper, 3 oz; ground nutmeg, 0.75 oz; ground ginger, 1 oz; ground thyme, 1 oz; rubbed sage, 2 oz.

Southern-Style Formula.—Ground red pepper, 2 oz; cracked red pepper, 1 oz; ground ginger, 1 oz; ground thyme, 1 oz; rubbed sage, 3 oz; Spanish paprika, 2 oz.

Meat Selection

Use only beef of choice or prime grade which has bright color, white fat, and tender texture. Meat should be free of blood clots, sinews, and gristle. Fat content of the finished sausage should not be over 50%.

Grinding and Mixing

Have meat thoroughly chilled to 32°-34°F at start of procedure and be certain mixing and grinding equipment are thoroughly clean and free of any trace of sodium nitrite which will react with the meat and turn it gray. Also, prechill mixer and grinder with chopped ice.

Premix dry ingredients (salt, corn sugar, seasonings). Grind meat items through the 1-$1^{1}/_{2}$-in. plate of the grinder; then transfer to mechanical mixer; add dry ingredients and ice; mix just long enough to evenly distribute all ingredients (approximately 1 min). Dry Ice may be added to the mixture to keep meat temperature down to as near 32°F as possible. Transfer sausage ingredients from mixer to grinder and regrind through the $1/8$-in. plate.

Stuff immediately into hog or sheep casings and link. Or, stuff into 1-lb size artificial casings. Hang sausages on trees and immediately transfer to chill room (under 32°F) to dry casings and chill sausages. Never package sausages before meat is thoroughly chilled and casings are dry; use a fan to help dry casings, if necessary. Then transfer to 0°F storage until shipped and should be kept refrigerated until sold.

SOURCE: Stephan L. Komarik, 4810 Ronda, Coral Gables, Florida.

ITALIAN-STYLE SAUSAGE

With the exception of a different formula for hot Italian-style and mild Italian-style seasonings, processing procedure is identical.

Use either of these meat combinations:

Ingredients	No. 1 Lb	No. 2 Lb
Regular pork trimmings 50/50	75	75
Lean beef trimmings		25
Lean pork trimmings	25	

with these ingredients:

	Lb	Oz
Salt	1	12
Ice, chopped	3	
Cane sugar		8
Garlic powder (optional)		$1/8$
Hot or mild seasonings (see below)		

For Hot Italian-Style.—Use the following purified and sterilized seasoning ingredients:

	Oz
Ground red pepper	2
Ground caraway seed	$1/2$
Ground coriander	1
Ground nutmeg	$1/2$
Ground fennel seeds	1
Crushed red pepper	2
Cracked black pepper	1

For Mild Italian-Style.—Use the following purified and sterilized seasoning ingredients:

	Oz
Ground fennel seeds	$3/4$
Whole fennel seeds	1
Spanish paprika	1
Coarse ground black pepper	$2^1/2$

Processing Procedure

Be sure all trimmings are fresh and free of bones, sinews, blood clots, and skin and are well chilled to 32°-34°F.

Grinding Method.—Meat grinder should be scrupulously clean and in good condition with sharp knives and plate. Grind regular pork trimmings through the $3/8$- or $1/2$-in. plate (as trade demands). Grind lean beef trimmings or lean pork trimmings through the $1/8$-in. plate. Prechill mechanical mixer with crushed ice. Transfer ground meats to mixer. Mix together salt, sugar, garlic powder (if used), and hot or mild seasonings. Distribute dry ingredients over meat and add chopped ice. Start mixer and mix just long enough to evenly distribute all ingredients.

Rapid Meat Chopper Method.—If rapid meat chopper is used there is no need to pregrind meats. Remember to fill chopper only about half full. First, put the lean pork or beef in the chopper and reduce meat particles to approximately $1/4$-in. size.

Then add pork trimmings, premixed dry ingredients, and ice. Let machine run until the fat particles are reduced to the desired size ($1/4$-$1/2$ in.). Pulverized Dry Ice may be used with the chopped ice to keep meat temperature down to 28°-32°F. Transfer sausage mixture to mechanical mixer and mix for 1-2 min to ensure proper distribution of dry ingredients and to increase the binding action of the soluble proteins (myosin).

Stuffing.—Immediately stuff mixture into wide hog casings and link to desired length. Keep the sausage stuffing table as cold as possible with crushed ice. Hang linked sausages on trees and transfer immediately to chill room (32°-34°F) to dry casings and thoroughly chill sausage meat. Use of a fan will help dry sausage casings. Do not package sausages before they are thoroughly chilled and the casings are dry.

Storing and shipping to market is best if done at a freezing temperature (0°F or below). This product has to be kept refrigerated until sold.

SOURCE: Stephan L. Komarik, 4810 Ronda, Coral Gables, Florida.

FRESH CHORIZOS

Use any of these meat combinations:

Ingredients	No. 1 Lb	No. 2 Lb	No. 3 Lb
Lean pork trimmings 85/15	175		
Neck bone trimmings	175		
Regular pork trimmings	150	200	175
Lean beef trimmings		300	150
Beef cheeks, trimmed			100
Beef or pork hearts			75

with these ingredients, using purified and sterilized spices:

	Lb	Oz	Pt
Salt	15		
Corn syrup solids	5		
Sodium nitrite		$1^1/4$	
Sodium nitrate		10	
Sodium erythorbate		$4^1/3$	
Spanish paprika	15		
Ground black pepper	1	4	
Ground red pepper		$2^1/2$	
Ground coriander		5	
Ground oregano		1	
Ground Jamaica ginger		5	
Iced water	50		
White wine vinegar (45 grain)			$2^1/2$

Procedure

Have all meat items well chilled. Grind pork trimmings through the $1/2$ in. plate of the grinder.

Grind beef items and pork hearts (if used) through the 1/8-in. plate. Mix together salt and other dry ingredients except the vinegar; add vinegar to the ice water. Transfer meats to mechanical mixer. Start mixing operation and add, first, ice water-vinegar mixture and, then, the dry ingredients spreading dry ingredients evenly over meat mixture. Mix until all ingredients are properly distributed. Then regrind through the 1/4- or 3/8-in. plate of the grinder.

Stuffing.—Immediately stuff mixture into medium or wide hog casings and link or tie (as trade demands). Hang sausages on smokehouse trees, properly spaced so air circulates around each freely, and transfer to cooler (36°-38°F) for overnight cure and to dry casings.

If sausages are not to be smoked, they are ready for packaging and distribution to retail channels.

Smoking.—Chorizos are often given a light smoking to enhance flavor. If smoking is desired, take chorizos from cooler after they have cured for overnight and let them hang at room temperature to warm a couple of hours before taking them into the smokehouse. Maintain smokehouse temperature no higher than 120°F; keep dampers wide open until casings are dry; then introduce light smoke until desired color is obtained. Remove from smokehouse and transfer to cooler and hold until internal meat temperature is reduced at least 55°F.

Hold Refrigerated or Frozen.—After packaging, this product must be stored and marketed under refrigerated temperatures. For longer storage, lower temperatures (0°F or below) are recommended.

SOURCE: Stephan L. Komarik, 4810 Ronda, Coral Gables, Florida.

BOCKWURST (WHITE SAUSAGE)

In Germany, this sausage is also called Munchener Weizwurst. It is made with lean pork and veal and is a white sausage with whole milk and eggs in the formula and is delicately seasoned.

Use these meat ingredients:

	Lb
Lean pork shoulder and neck top	250
Boneless veal	150
Backfat	100

with these ingredients, using purified and sterilized spices:

	Lb	Oz	Gal.
Salt	16		
Sodium erythorbate		4 1/3	
Ice-cold whole milk			5

Whole eggs, frozen	16
Fresh parsley	10
Fresh chives (20 bunches) or onion powder	1 1/2
Ground white pepper	4 1/2
Ground mace	2 1/4
Ground Jamaica ginger	4 1/2
Grated lemon peel (optional)	5

Procedure

Have meat items well chilled (32°-34°F). Before grinding, premix 15 lb of the salt with the sodium erythorbate and mix together thoroughly. Also premix remaining 1 lb of salt with the dry seasonings and grated lemon peel.

Grind meat items through the 1/8-in. plate of the grinder and transfer to prechilled mixer; add salt-erythorbate mixture and mix thoroughly. Dump meat mixture into truck and transfer to cooler (34°F); hold overnight to precondition meats.

Frozen eggs may be defrosted ahead of time by holding in a cooler (40°-45°F) or the frozen product may be chopped up with a cleaver and then ground through the 1-in. plate of the grinder for immediate use.

Transfer chilled, preconditioned meat to a chopper and start machine. Add frozen eggs, washed parsley and chives (or onion powder), and premixed salt-seasoning mixture evenly over top of meat. Then slowly add the ice-cold milk. Chop materials until parsley particles are reduced to about 1/8 in. in size.

Stuff immediately into 22/24 mm or 28/30 mm hog casings and link sausages 4 in. long. Hang on smoke sticks and give finished sausages a brief cold water shower; transfer to a cooler at 26°F temperature until casings are dry. Then package.

Bockwurst is sold as a fresh sausage. It is best to hold packaged sausages at 26°F or below through short storage until shipped. The product should be held under refrigeration until sold; it is a perishable product.

SOURCE: Stephan L. Komarik, 4810 Ronda, Coral Gables, Florida.

BOCKWURST USING NONFAT DRY MILK

Make up this cure:

	Lb	Oz
Sodium nitrate	3	7
Sodium nitrite		5
Dextrose (corn sugar)	10	

Place ingredients in a 5-gal. glass container. Fill with water and dissolve. Use 1 qt (2 3/4 lb) of solution for each 100 lb of meat.

Ingredients	Lb	Oz
Veal trimmings	40	
Beef trimmings	25	
Regular pork trimmings	20	
Lean pork trimmings	15	
Nonfat dry milk	4³/₄	
Salt	3¹/₄	
Ground white pepper		7
Ground sage		1
Angostura bitters		2
Fresh whole eggs (about 2 doz)	3	
Parsley		12
Cure	2³/₄	
Chopped ice		

Procedure

Grind meats through ³/₈-in. plate. Beat eggs well. Chop parsley fine.

Place beef in silent cutter; add some chopped ice, salt, and cure. After a few revolutions add nonfat dry milk and chopped ice alternately until all nonfat dry milk is used. Then add veal, pork, parsley, and seasoning. When nearly fine enough, add beaten eggs. Chop well. Stuff into wide hog casings; can also be stuffed into 1-lb size cellulose casings.

This sausage must be handled in the same manner as fresh pork sausage.

SOURCE: American Dry Milk Institute, 130 N. Franklin, Chicago, Ill.

PORK SAUSAGE FOR PATTIES OR BULK (WITH SWIFT'S FOOD PROTEIN)

Ingredients	Lb
Lean pork trimmings	100
Regular pork trimmings	100
Pure pork sausage seasoning (such as Uncle Bemis)	4
Swift's food protein (S.F.P.)	6
Water, chilled	9
Chopped or shaved ice per 200-lb batch	10

Procedure

1. Weigh out 6 lb of S.F.P. into container.
2. Add four 1-lb bags of spice to dry S.F.P.; blend well by hand.
3. Add 9 lb of chilled (35°–40°F) water to S.F.P. and spice mixture.
4. Allow mixture to set while pork trimmings are weighed out.
5. Weigh out 100 lb of regular and 100 lb of lean pork trimmings.

6. Grind through ³/₈-in. plate adding shaved ice as grinding process continues. (Use 10 lb of ice per 200-lb batch.)
7. As grinding process continues, sprinkle S.F.P.-spice mix throughout meat. Mix 2.5–3.5 min.
8. Grind through ¹/₈-in. plate.
9. Hollymatic through 8-S plate for patties; or pack into containers for bulk sausage.

This is a perishable product and should be kept refrigerated.

SOURCE: Swift Edible Oil Co., Vegetable Protein Products Div., 115 W. Jackson Blvd., Chicago, Ill.

PORK SAUSAGE EXTENDED WITH TEXTURED VEGETABLE PROTEIN

Ingredients	A %	B %
Fresh pork, 40% fat	80.0	70.0
Textured vegetable protein (Supro 50₸ₘ, regular)	6.60	10.0
Water	10.65	17.25
Red pepper, ground	0.20	0.20
Salt	2.50	2.50
Sage, ground	0.05	0.05
	100.00	100.00

Formula A replaces 20% of the pork with Supro 50₸ₘ
Formula B replaces 30% of the pork with Supro 50₸ₘ

Procedure

1. Hydrate the textured vegetable protein (Supro 50₸ₘ) with water.
2. Mix the pork with the hydrated textured vegetable protein, and grind the mixture through a ³/₁₆-in. plate.
3. Place all ingredients in a Hobart mixer and mix at low speed 5 min.

Note: The meat should be kept at 32°–35°F during processing.

SOURCE: Ralston Purina Company, Checkerboard Square, St. Louis, Mo.

FONDWURST (BRATWURST) (WITH SWIFT'S FOOD PROTEIN)

Ingredients	Lb	Oz
Boston pork butts	50	
Swift's food protein (S.F.P.)	4	
Water	17	
Salt	1¹/₂	
Black pepper		1
Mace		1

Procedure

1. Weigh out 4 lb of Swift's food protein (S.F.P.) into container and add 12 lb of chilled (35°–40°F) water.

2. Weigh out 5 lb of chilled (35°–40°F) water into separate container and add salt, black pepper, and mace. Stir slightly until salt has dissolved.

3. Allow the food protein-water and salt-water mixture to stand for 10–15 min.

4. Weigh out 50 lb of pork and put on grinder hopper.

5. Add water-salt mixture to food protein-water mixture and blend slightly by hand.

6. Spread food protein mixture over rough cuts in hopper and grind through 3/8-in. plate. Grind into mixer or transfer to mixer and mix for 1.5–2.5 min.

7. Stuff into natural casings and refrigerate.

Note: Alternative for Step 5: Instead of adding water and salt mixture to S.F.P., pour it very slowly into mixing process and mix 2–3 min.

This is a perishable product and should be kept refrigerated.

SOURCE: Swift Edible Oil Co., Vegetable Protein Products Div., 115 W. Jackson Blvd., Chicago, Ill.

SWEDISH POTATO SAUSAGE (POTATIS KORV) USING NONFAT DRY MILK

Ingredients	Lb	Oz
Pork trimmings	65	
Beef trimmings	35	
Potato flour	8	
Nonfat dry milk	8	
Fresh onions	4	
Salt	3½	
Ground white pepper		9
Ground marjoram		2½
Ground ginger		2
Ground nutmeg		2
Ground allspice		1¼
Ground cloves		1½
Ground cardamom		1
Water	24	

Procedure

Grind onions and meat through a large lard cutting plate and place in mixer. Add about half of the water and sprinkle potato flour, nonfat dry milk, and seasoning, mixing well. Then run all through 3/8-in. plate. Place in mixer again; add balance of water and mix well. Then run again through 3/8-in. plate. Stuff into beef rounds or large pork casings making sausages about 1 lb each.

This sausage must be cooked, roasted, or fried before serving.

This is a perishable product and must be kept under refrigeration. Shelf-life will be extended if stored at frozen temperature.

SOURCE: American Dry Milk Institute, 130 N. Franklin, Chicago, Ill.

DRY AND SEMIDRY SAUSAGES

As with other pork products, certain procedures (including government regulations) and precautions are necessary for the processing of dry and semidry sausages. These include, as described earlier under fresh sausage formulas, working with meats that are properly chilled, having equipment in the best possible working condition (sharp knives and grinder blades), maintenance of scrupulous sanitation throughout the sausage-making area, use of purified and sterilized spices when the natural spices are used so as not to contaminate the sausage mixture, and general practice of good processing principles so as to ensure a quality product.

Government Regulations

Dry and semidry sausages are usually eaten by the consumer without further cooking; yet they are not heated during processing to an internal temperature which assures destruction of live trichinae in pork flesh, the parasite that causes trichinosis in humans. As a safety measure to guard against trichinosis, the Meat Inspection Division (MID) of USDA has established processing regulations in the treatment of pork with regard to sausage making, as described below.

Sausage may be stuffed in animal casings, hydrocellulose casings, or cloth bags. If animal casings are used, according to government regulation it is permissible to use potassium sorbate only to retard mold on dry sausages (salami type). Use a water solution containing 2.5% potassium sorbate; it may be applied to casings after stuffing or casings may be dipped in the solution prior to stuffing.

In the preparation of sausage, one of the following methods may be used.

Method No. 1.—The meat shall be ground or chopped into pieces not exceeding $3/4$ in. in diameter. A dry-curing mixture containing not less than $3^1/_3$ lb of salt per each 100 lb of the unstuffed sausage shall be thoroughly mixed with the ground or chopped meat. After being stuffed, sausage having a diameter not exceeding $3^1/_2$ in., measured at the time of stuffing, shall be held in a drying room not less than 20 days at a temperature not lower than 45°F, except that in sausage of the variety known as pepperoni, if in casings not exceeding $1^3/_8$ in. in diameter at time of stuffing, the period of drying may be reduced to 15 days. In no case, however, shall the sausage be released from the drying room in less than 25 days from the time the curing materials are added, except that sausage of the variety known as pepperoni, if in casings not exceeding the size specified, may be released at the expiration of 20 days from the time the curing materials are added. Sausage in casings exceeding $3^1/_2$ in., but not exceeding 4 in., in diameter at time of stuffing, shall be held in a drying room not less than 35 days at a temperature not lower than 45°F, and in no case shall the sausage be released from the drying room in less than 40 days from the time the curing materials are added to the meat.

Method No. 2.—The meat shall be ground or chopped into pieces not exceeding $3/4$ in. in diameter. A dry-curing mixture containing not less than $3^1/_3$ lb of salt per 100 lb of unstuffed sausage shall be thoroughly mixed with the ground or chopped meat. After being stuffed, the sausage having a diameter not exceeding $3^1/_2$ in., measured at the time of stuffing, shall be smoked not less than 40 hr at a temperature not lower than 80°F, and finally held in a drying room not less than 10 days at a temperature not lower than 45°F. In no case, however, shall the sausage be released from the drying room in less than 18 days from the time the curing materials are added to the meat. Sausage exceeding $3^1/_2$ in., but not exceeding 4 in., in diameter at the time of stuffing, shall be held in a drying room, following smoking as above indicated, not less than 25 days at a temperature not lower than 45°F, and in no case shall the sausage be released from the drying room in less than 33 days from the time the curing materials are added to the meat.

Method No. 3.—The meat shall be ground or chopped into pieces not exceeding $3/4$ in. in diameter. A dry-curing mixture containing not less than $3^1/_3$ lb of salt per each 100 lb of the unstuffed sausage shall be thoroughly mixed with the ground or chopped meat. After admixture with the salt and other curing materials and before stuffing, the ground or chopped meat shall be held at a temperature not lower than 34°F for not less than 36 hr. After being stuffed the sausage shall be held at a temperature not lower than 34°F for an additional period of time sufficient to make a total of not less than 144 hr from the time the curing materials are added to the meat, or the sausage shall be held for the time specified in a pickle-curing medium of not less than 50° strength (salinometer reading) at a temperature not lower than 44°F. Finally, the sausage having a diameter not exceeding $3^1/_2$ in., measured at the time of stuffing, shall be smoked for not less than 12 hr. The temperature of the smokehouse during this period at no time shall be lower than 90°F; and for 4 consecutive hours of this period the smokehouse shall be maintained at a temperature not lower than 128°F. Sausage exceeding $3^1/_2$ in., but not exceeding 4 in., in diameter at the time of stuffing shall be smoked, following the prescribed curing, for not less than 15 hr. The temperature of the smokehouse during the 15-hr period shall at no time be lower than 90°F, and for 7 consecutive hours of this period the smokehouse shall be maintained at a temperature not lower than 128°F. In regulating the temperature of the smokehouse for the treatment of sausage under this method, the temperature of 128°F shall be attained gradually during a period not less than 4 hr.

Method No. 4.—The meat shall be ground or chopped into pieces not exceeding $1/4$ in. in diameter. A dry-curing mixture containing not less than $2^1/_2$ lb of salt per each 100 lb of the unstuffed sausage shall be thoroughly mixed with the ground or chopped meat. After admixture with the salt and other curing materials and before stuffing, the ground or chopped sausage shall be held as a compact mass, not more than 6 in. in depth, at a temperature not lower than 36°F for not less than 10 days. At the termination of the holding period, the sausage shall be stuffed in casings or cloth bags not exceeding $3^1/_2$ in. in diameter, measured at the time of stuffing. After being stuffed, the sausage shall be held in a drying room at a temperature not lower than 45°F for the remainder of a 35-day period, measured from the time the curing materials are added to the meat. At any time after stuffing, if a concern deems it desirable, the product may be heated in a water bath for a period not to exceed 3 hr at a temperature not lower than 85°F, or subjected to smoking at a temperature not lower than 80°F, or the product may be both heated and smoked as specified. The time consumed in heating and smoking, however, shall be addition to the 35-day holding period specified.

Method No. 5.—The meat shall be ground or chopped into pieces not exceeding $3/4$ in. in diameter. A dry-curing mixture containing not less than $3^1/_3$ lb of salt per each 100 lb of the unstuffed sausage shall be thoroughly mixed with the ground or chopped meat. After being stuffed the sausage shall be held for not less than 65 days at a temperature not lower than 45°F. The coverings for sausage prepared according to this method may be coated at any stage of the preparation before or during the holding period with paraffin or other substance approved by the Director of the Meat Inspection Division, USDA.

Freezing.—Freezing under specified conditions for times and temperatures will also destroy live trichinae in pork tissue. See the MID regulations for freezing pork given in the introduction of Section 1 on Cured Meats.

Selection of Meats

Freshly slaughtered meats should be selected for dry and semidry sausage making. The pH value of the meat should be between 5.4 and 5.8 but never over 6.0. Meat should be from mature animals and should have a dry, firm texture. Beef from grass fed cattle is likely to be watery and should be rejected. Because the binding quality of the meat used is most important in dry and semidry sausage making, the selection of meat cuts is of great importance. Tables 2.2 and 2.3 show the binding capacity of various carcass parts of pork, beef, veal, and mutton along with other characteristics of these meats for use in sausage making.

TABLE 2.2

PORK: CHARACTERISTICS OF SAUSAGE INGREDIENTS

Carcass Part	Level of Fat (%)	Color Rating[1]	Binding Property[1]	Protein Content (%)	Ratio of Moisture to Protein	Added Water (%)
Blade meat	8	80	95	19.2	3.76	16.2
Liver	8	80	—	20.6	3.47	23.1
Jaw meat	8	80	80	20.9	3.40	24.9
Ears	10	10	20	22.5	3.00	36.0
95% trimmings	10	70	90	18.9	3.73	16.8
Picnic hearts	12	80	90	18.6	3.73	16.6
Stomachs, scalded	13	20	5	16.7	4.20	7.3
Spleens	15	60	—	15.9	4.33	5.2
Nose meat	15	45	70	17.9	3.74	16.2
Cheeks, trimmed	15	65	75	17.8	3.79	15.2
Weasand meat	17	80	80	16.4	4.05	10.1
Giblets	17	75	75	16.9	3.91	12.4
Hearts	17	85	30	15.3	4.40	4.2
Boneless ham	19	60	80	16.9	3.80	15.2
Tongues	19	15	20	16.3	3.95	11.9
Partially defatted chopped pork	21	50	50	17.4	3.54	19.9
80% trimmings	25	50	80	15.8	3.72	16.0
Head meat	25	50	80	16.1	3.60	11.8
Picnic trimmings	25	60	80	15.6	3.80	14.4
Neckbone trimmings	25	60	70	15.9	3.55	19.0
Skirts	30	50	45	14.2	3.90	12.6
Lips	31	5	10	20.1	3.42	23.8
Skin	32	5	20	28.3	1.40	92.6
Tongue trimmings	32	15	10	15.6	4.34	5.1
Snouts	35	5	10	14.6	3.45	19.9
Partially defatted tissue	35	15	20	14.0	3.63	16.8
50% trimmings	55	35	55	9.7	3.64	15.0
Head skin trimmings	55	15	50	9.2	3.90	12.0
Regular trimmings	60	30	35	8.4	3.77	13.1
Backfat trimmings	62	25	15	8.1	3.71	13.6
Skinned jowls	70	20	35	6.3	3.72	13.1
Belly trimmings	70	20	30	6.3	3.75	12.8
Bacon ends	70	10	5	8.8	2.40	26.5
Backfat, untrimmed	80	20	30	4.2	3.83	11.9

SOURCE: The Anderson–Clifton Company, Chicago, Ill.

[1] Based upon 100.

TABLE 2.3

BEEF, VEAL, MUTTON: CHARACTERISTICS OF SAUSAGE INGREDIENTS

Carcass Part	Level of Fat (%)	Color Rating[1]	Binding Property[1]	Protein Content (%)	Ratio of Moisture to Protein	Added Water (%)
Beef						
Wesand meat	6	75	80	17.8	4.20	7.1
Bull meat	8	100	100	20.8	3.40	24.8
Liver	9	80	—	20.7	3.40	23.6
Imported cow meat	10	95	100	19.0	3.65	18.6
Boneless chucks	10	85	85	19.5	3.57	20.4
Tripe	11	5	10	12.8	5.90	(16.2)[2]
Melts	12	95	20	16.9	4.20	7.2
Lungs	12	75	5	17.5	4.00	11.0
Shank meat	12	90	80	16.8	4.20	7.2
Domestic cow meat	12	95	100	18.8	3.65	18.4
85/90 trimmings	15	90	85	18.9	3.45	22.7
Cheeks	15	90	85	18.3	3.59	19.4
Tongues	20	25	20	15.5	4.15	8.4
Tongue trimmings	40	15	15	12.6	3.75	14.6
Lips	20	5	20	15.9	4.00	11.0
Partially defatted chopped beef	20	50	45	20.0	3.00	33.2
Hearts	21	90	30	14.9	4.30	6.0
Head meat	25	60	85	16.4	3.54	19.4
Partially defatted tissue	25	30	25	18.9	3.20	15.2
75/85 trimmings	25	85	80	16.9	3.41	22.2
Boneless navels	52	65	55	10.5	3.55	16.3
Boneless flanks	55	55	50	9.9	3.54	16.2
Cooler trimmings	65	20	15	8.0	3.40	16.3
Beef fat	85	10	5	3.3	3.55	11.3
Beef clods	10	95	100	20.0	3.50	19.9
Veal						
Trimmings	10	70	80	19.4	3.62	19.3
Mutton						
Boneless mutton	15	85	85	18.1	3.70	17.1

SOURCE: The Anderson–Clifton Company, Chicago, Ill.

[1] Based upon 100.
[2] Water must be subtracted.

Pork also should be selected from mature hogs with solid fat and marbled lean. Peanut-fed hogs that produce a soft pork are not desirable for dry sausage making.

Bruised meats should not be used. Sinews, bones, large connective tissues, and watery gelatinous pockets should be removed.

No skin should adhere to backfat. So rinds should not be removed too closely. Also, use only the solid skin side of backfat for dry sausage; utilize the soft side for other sausage products. There will be less smearing when backfat is used if it is first frozen and added to the meat mixture in the frozen state (as nearly to $17°F$ as possible but never lower than $4°F$). If only a grinder and a mixer are used, cut the backfat in small dice; if a high speed meat chopper is used, just cut the backfat in small pieces before freezing.

Meats for sausage making should be kept under refrigeration both prior to and during the curing operation to obtain proper reaction of salts, cure, and flavoring materials.

Cleanliness of Kitchen and Equipment

It is imperative not only to keep equipment in first class condition with sharp and well-adjusted knives and blades, but to also practice strict sanitation with regard to the grinder, the rapid meat chopper, and the mixer. Knives in the high speed (3000 rpm) meat chopper should be very sharp and adjusted very close to the bowl so meat and fat are cut straight through without smearing and mashing. Bowl speed should be synchronized to knife speed so there is no drag on the meat which would cause smearing and heating of the product. A worn-out auger, dull knives, and plates of a grinder will also heat and smear the sausage product.

The processing of meats for sausage should be in an air-conditioned room with temperature of 58°–60°F for best results. Careless hygiene and neglected cleanup are too often causes of contamination which escapes detection until too late and spoilage becomes a serious threat to the processor. Scientifically-prepared detergents and germicides are available from reputable manufacturers for sanitizing kitchen and equipment. A regular and thorough daily cleanup of the sausage kitchen should be routine.

The Sausage Making Procedure

Dry and semidry sausage can be made successfully with a grinder and either a high speed (3000 rpm) or a regular low speed (400–600 rpm) meat chopper. It is best to use only 2 or 3 knives with the meat chopper. However, sausages can be made using only a grinder and a mixer. But the most efficient method with best results is obtained by using a combination of first grinding then chopping in a high speed chopper.

Curing Materials and Seasonings.—Federal regulations specify that meat mixture for dry and semidry sausages contain not less than $3\frac{1}{3}$ lb of salt and not over $2\frac{3}{4}$ oz of sodium nitrate per 100 lb of meat mixture.

Also, to avoid contamination of the mixture, only purified and sterilized spices should be used.

Curing.—After the meat mixture has been prepared, it is tightly packed to eliminate air pockets in meat pans not deeper than 6 in. This depth of the meat mixture in pans should be reduced with the finer granulated meat particles so as to facilitate rapid chilling of the mixture in the chill room. Cover with parchment or wax paper to avoid oxidation of the top layer of mixture in the pans.

Curing room temperature should be kept at 36°–38°F and the meat mixture held there for 2–3 days depending upon the granulation of the mixture. Curing room must have proper air circulation to keep walls and ceilings dry.

Stuffing.—Preparatory to stuffing, the sausage mixture is removed from the curing room and placed in a vacuum mixer and mixed under 25 in. of vacuum just long enough to make it pliable for stuffing. This takes approximately 1–2 min. Do not start the mixer until the air has been evacuated.

When mixture is pliable, it is packed tightly in the stuffer so as to avoid air pockets. The size and type of casings and tying for different sausages are given with each formula that follows. After stuffing, casings are punctured to allow entrapped air to escape.

Green Sausage Room.—Sausages are held in a green room for 3–4 days to lose some of their moisture and to develop further cure and flavor before transferring them either to the drying room or to the smokehouse if they are to be smoked. The green room should be maintained at a temperature of 70°–75°F with a relative humidity of 75–80%. Under these conditions, the pores of the casings are kept open so sausages can lose moisture. Hang sausages on sticks 4–6 in. apart for good air circulation.

Smoking.—Smoking is usually more necessary for sausages stuffed in beef casings than in hog casings. Beef casings are hard to dry without development of slime unless they are smoked.

Successful smoking is dependent upon proper temperature, proper humidity control, and proper air movement in the smokehouse. Under no circumstances should the smokehouse temperature be higher than 90°F as this might sour the sausages. The recommended temperature is between 75° and 76°F with relative humidity of 70%.

Case hardening of the sausages results from rapid lowering of the humidity; this causes a gray ring in the mixture just under the casing and slows moisture removal from the interior of the sausage.

Too high humidity causes condensation of moisture on the casings resulting in poor color of the sausages and loss of the desired firm texture.

The length of smoking depends upon the type and size of the sausages. They should be smoked until the desired color is obtained.

Drying.—If the sausages are smoked, they are transferred to the drying room without any delay.

Drying room temperature should range from 52° to 56°F with relative humidity from 65 to 75% depending upon the character of the product. Circulation of the air conditioned to the above temperature and relative humidity is most important. Improperly designed air-conditioning can be the source of many troubles. Different grades of sausages require different rates of air circulation. Sausages stuffed in hog casings need more air movement than sausages in beef casings. Finely chopped sausage mixtures dry slower than coarsely chopped mixtures. So temperature, humidity, and air circulation should be closely controlled during drying.

Since the sausage mixture must dry from the inside out, any attempt to speed up the drying procedure results in case hardening. This closes the pores of the casings and stops the escape of moisture from the interior of the sausage. On the other hand, if sausages dry too slowly, molding may occur. But sausages should dry slowly under proper conditions in the drying room.

When transferring sausages from the green room to the drying room, they should not be hung too closely to sausages already in the room that are partially dried. Plenty of space should be left between different lots of sausages for proper air circulation. It is even better to place them in a different room.

Sausages will dry too slowly if fat accumulates on the surface of the casings. If this happens, wash sausages with warm water to remove grease and facilitate drying.

The drying time under proper conditions depends upon the type of sausages being produced. Semidry sausages require from 10 to 25 days with an approximate shrinkage of 20% from the green weight. Medium-dry sausages require from 30 to 60 days with approximately 32% shrinkage. Fully dried sausages require from 60–90 days with approximately 40% shrinkage after smoking.

DRY SALAMI

Use any of these meat combinations:

	No. 1 Lb	No. 2 Lb	No. 3 Lb	No. 4 Lb
Beef chucks, trimmed	125	200	325	250
Lean pork trimmings 85/15	225	150		
Backfat	150	150	175	
Regular pork trimmings 50/50				250

with these ingredients, using purified and sterilized spices:

	Lb	Oz
Salt	16	14
Sodium nitrate		$12\frac{1}{2}$
Sodium erythorbate		$4\frac{1}{3}$
Corn syrup solids	5	
Ground white pepper		15
Ground ginger		8
Garlic powder (optional)		1

Processing Procedure

Use chilled meat items ($32°$–$34°$F). Use firm portion of backfat (rinds fully removed) either diced or cut into small pieces and chilled.

Using a Grinder and Mixer.—Grind beef through the $1/16$-in. plate and pork through the $3/8$-in. plate. Mix together the salt with the cure and other dry ingredients. Transfer ground beef to mechanical mixer and add salt-cure mixture; while mixer is in operation, add ground pork and frozen backfat dice. Mix until a uniform mixture is obtained. Then regrind through the $1/8$-in. plate.

Using Grinder and High Speed Chopper.—Use 3 knives with the chopper; fill bowl only $1/2$ full to operate.

First grind beef through the $3/16$-in. plate of grinder. Then transfer operation to chopper. Mix together salt, cure, and the other dry ingredients. Fill chopper bowl with beef, pork, and frozen backfat (if used) and add salt-cure mixture. Run chopper until fat particles are reduced to desired size (approximately $1/8$ in.).

Curing.—Pack mixtures tightly in pans (6 in. deep). Hold in curing room ($36°$–$38°$F) for 3 days.

Stuffing.—To make meat pliable for stuffing, put mixture in vacuum mixer under 25 in. vacuum and mix approximately 1 min.

Maintain stuffing room temperature at $58°$–$60°$F. Load meat mixture into stuffer compactly to avoid air pockets. Use either sewed beef middles or de-fatted hog bungs 20 in. long and measuring $3\frac{1}{2}$ in. in diameter at the time of stuffing. Wrap with twine looped once every 2 in. and slightly drawn in to the casing to give sausages a "scalloped" appearance.

Ripening (Green Room).—Maintain temperature of $70°$–$75°$F with 70–80% RH. Hold in green room 3–4 days.

Smoking.—Smoking is necessary only for sausages stuffed in beef casings. Temperature of smokehouse should never be over $90°$F during the smoking period. Best temperature is $75°$–$76°$F with 70% RH. Smoke until desired color is obtained.

Drying.—Temperature range for unsmoked sausages is from $45°$ to $55°$F with 70–72% RH; for smoked sausages, from $50°$ to $55°$F with 70–72% RH.

Fully dried sausages lose 35% moisture during drying period which takes approximately 90 days.

SOURCE: Stephan L. Komarik, 4810 Ronda, Coral Gables, Florida.

GENOA SALAMI

Use any of these meat combinations:

	No. 1 Lb	No. 2 Lb	No. 3 Lb
Lean pork and trimmings	350	250	175
Boneless beef chucks or rounds		100	175
Backfat	150	150	150

with these ingredients; use purified and sterilized spices:

	Lb	Oz	Qt
Salt	16	14	
Sodium nitrate		5	
Sodium erythorbate		4⅓	
Cane sugar or corn syrup solids	1	4	
Whole black pepper		5	
Ground white pepper		10	
Garlic powder		2½	
Good quality Chianti wine			2

Processing Procedure

Meat Selection and Preparation.—Use well-chilled meats (32°-34°F).

Trim beef of sinews, cords, and connective tissues and grind through the ⅛-in. plate of the grinder.

Select lean pork from hams and shoulders of older hogs having darker meat. Use trimmings from bellies, shoulders, and hams; use 85% lean to 15% fat ratio. Use backfat with rinds fully removed and use firm skin side portion; thinly slice or dice. Cut lean pork into 1-lb chunks. Freeze both lean pork and backfat before use. Pork trimmings are used as they are collected without further cutting and freezing.

Sausages Made Only with Pork.—Fit high speed chopper with 3 knives and load chopper bowl only ½ full for each operation of mixing.

Premix salt, cure, and all other ingredients except the whole black pepper.

Put lean pork in the chopper and reduce particles to approximately ½ in. in size. Stop machine and add salt-cure mixture evenly over top of meat. Start machine and add trimmings and backfat; then pour in the wine. Run chopper until fat particles are reduced to desired size.

Sausages Made with Beef and Pork.—Premix salt, cure, and other seasoning ingredients except the whole black pepper.

Fit chopper with three knives and put ground beef into chopper. Start machine and add trimmings, frozen pork and backfat, and salt-cure mixture; then add wine. Run chopper until desired particle size is obtained.

Curing.—Pack mixture tightly in 6-in. deep pans. Cure for 3 days at 36°-38°F.

Stuffing.—First put cured sausage mixture in vacuum mixer and spread the whole black pepper evenly over top of mixture before closing and running under 25 in. vacuum 1-2 min.

Pack stuffer tightly to avoid air pockets. Use export hog bungs entirely free from fat and approximately 20 in. long and 3½ in. in diameter when stuffed. Stuffing room temperature should be maintained at 58°-60°F.

NOTE: After stuffing, some processors prefer to put the sausages in a 50° salinometer brine at a temperature not lower than 34°F for 2 days; and after removal of the sausages from the brine, they are then dipped in simmering water for 3 sec. They claim this removes surface salt and fat and opens the pores of the casings for more efficient drying.

Ripening (Green Room).—Maintain temperature at 70°-75°F with 70-80% RH. Hold for 2 days.

Wrap with Twine.—Use 4-lb weight flax twine. Start from small end and make a hitch of twine every ½ in. to end of sausage.

Drying.—Maintain drying room temperature at 45°-55°F with 75% RH. Dry for 70-80 days.

SOURCE: Stephan L. Komarik, 4810 Ronda, Coral Gables, Florida.

SALAMI DE MILANO

Milano salami is virtually identical to Genoa Salami; the major difference is that it is chopped somewhat finer. Use meat combination No. 2 with salt, cure, and seasonings as given above for Genoa salami and follow same processing procedure. Stuff Milano salami in casings approximately 25 in. long and 3½ in. in diameter when stuffed, using either export hog bungs or sewed hog casings. Wrap with twine same as for Genoa salami.

SOURCE: Stephan L. Komarik, 4810 Ronda, Coral Gables, Florida.

SALAMI D'ARLES

This salami, too, is identical with Genoa Salami. Follow Genoa salami formula given above, using meat combination No. 2. Stuff sausages in export hog bungs or beef middles and wrap with 4-lb weight flax twine in criss-cross pattern.

SOURCE: Stephan L. Komarik, 4810 Ronda, Coral Gables, Florida.

HOLSTEINER DRY SAUSAGE

Ingredients	Lb	Oz
Boneless lean beef	300	
60% lean pork trimmings	150	
Backfat trimmings	50	
Salt	16	14
Sodium nitrate		12½
Sodium erythorbate		4⅓
Corn syrup solids	5	
Ground black pepper (purified and sterilized)		2
(Some trade demands as high a pepper content as 10 oz per 100 lb of meat)		

Processing Procedure

Use prechilled meats (32°–34°F).

Grinding, Chopping, Mixing.—Premix salt and other dry ingredients. Grind beef through 1/8-in. plate. Put pork trimmings in rapid chopper (using 3 knives); chop until pork is reduced to approximately 1/2-in. pieces. Transfer beef and pork to mechanical mixer; add salt mixture; mix thoroughly (2–3 min).

Curing.—Maintain curing room temperature at 36°–38°F. Pack tightly in 6-in. deep pans. Cure for 3 days.

Stuffing.—To make sausage mixture pliable for stuffing, mix in vacuum mixer under 25 in. vacuum for 1–2 min. Avoid air pockets in loading stuffer. Stuff into wide beef middles 3 1/2 in. in diameter and 19–20 in. in length.

Ripening (Green Room).—Maintain temperature at 75°F with 75–80% RH. Hold 12 hr before smoking.

Smoking.—Maintain smokehouse temperature at 75°–76°F with 75–80% RH. Smoke with heavy smudge for 3–4 days.

Drying.—Maintain temperature of 52°–56°F with 65% RH and dry at least 26 days.

Shelf-life of product will be extended if kept under refrigeration through storage and marketing.

SOURCE: Stephan L. Komarik, 4810 Ronda, Coral Gables, Florida.

DRIED FARM SAUSAGE

With minor exceptions, pointed out here, Dried Farm Sausage is identical to the formula given above for Holsteiner Dry Sausage. Follow Holsteiner Dry Sausage formula except: Dried Farm Sausage is a leaner sausage; no backfat trimmings are used. Use 300 lb of boneless lean beef and 200 lb of 60% lean pork trimmings. Stuff Dried Farm Sausage in 2–2 1/4 in. diameter beef middles 19–20 in. long.

SOURCE: Stephan L. Komarik, 4810 Ronda, Coral Gables, Florida.

ITALIAN-STYLE PEPPERONI

Ingredients	Lb	Oz
Lean pork trimmings	250	
Regular pork trimmings 50/50	100	
Beef chucks	150	
Salt	16	14
Cane sugar	1	4
Sodium nitrate		10
Sodium nitrite		1/2
Ground red pepper		10
Ground allspice		10
Ground anise seed		5

Pepperoni pepper	1	4
Garlic powder		1 1/2
(Use purified and sterilized spices)		

Processing Procedure

Use prechilled meats (32°–34°F) and premix salt, cures, and other dry ingredients.

Using Grinder and Mixer.—Grind beef through the 1/8-in. plate and pork trimmings through the 3/16-in. plate. Transfer to mechanical mixer, add salt-cure mixture; mix approximately 3 min, just long enough to make a uniform mixture.

Using High Speed Chopper.—Use 3 knives with chopper and in operating fill bowl only 1/2 full.

First grind beef through 1/8-in. plate and pork through 1-in. plate of a grinder. Transfer meats to chopper; add salt-cure mixture and run machine until fat particles are reduced to desired size.

Curing.—Maintain temperature at 38°–40°F and cure for 48 hr.

Stuffing.—First mix sausage mixture in vacuum mixer (25 in. vacuum) 1–2 min. Avoid air pockets in stuffer. Use hog casings of the desired caliber and link sausages in pairs 10–12 in. long. Squeeze a little meat out of open ends of links and fold over end of casing.

Ripening (Green Room).—Maintain temperature of 70°F with 75% RH and hold for 48 hr.

Drying.—Maintain temperature at 50°–55°F with 70–72% RH. If diameter of stuffed sausages does not exceed 1 3/8 in., drying period may be reduced to 15 days. In no case, however, should the sausages be released from the drying room in less than 20 days from the time curing materials were added to meat.

Shelf-life of product is improved if kept under refrigeration through storage and marketing.

SOURCE: Stephan L. Komarik, 4810 Ronda, Coral Gables, Florida.

PEPPERONI STICKS

Use either of these meat combinations:

	No. 1 Lb	No. 2 Lb
Boneless cow meat	250	200
Beef cheeks (trimmed)	100	200
Beef flanks or plates	150	100

with these ingredients using purified (sterilized) spices:

	Lb	Oz
Salt	16	14
Cane sugar	1	4
Sodium nitrite		4 1/4
Sodium nitrate		5
Ground black pepper	1	4

Garlic powder (optional)	1
Ice water	50

Ice water	25
White wine vinegar (45 grain)	2½

Processing Procedure

Use prechilled meats (32°–34°F). Premix salt, cures, and other dry ingredients.

Use Grinder and Mixer.—Grind meats through ³/₁₆-in. plate. Transfer to mechanical mixer, start machine and immediately add ice water and salt-cure mixture. Mix 3 min. Then regrind mixture through ⅛-in. plate.

Stuffing.—Use 16–18 mm sheep casings with a short stuffing horn to avoid smearing; link into 6-in. lengths.

Curing.—Maintain temperature at 45°F. Cure sticks overnight.

Smoking.—Preheat smokehouse to 100°–110°F. Transfer sticks and keep sausages at this temperature with dampers wide open until casings are dry. Then adjust dampers partly open, apply heavy smudge, and maintain same temperature during smoking for 12 hr.

Drying.—Maintain temperature at 50°–55°F with 70–75% RH and hold sausages until a 50–55% yield from the green weight is obtained.

Shelf-life of product is improved if kept under refrigeration through storage and marketing.

SOURCE: Stephan L. Komarik, 4810 Ronda, Coral
      Gables, Florida.

DRIED CHORIZOS

Use any of these meat combinations:

	No. 1 Lb	No. 2 Lb	No. 3 Lb
Lean pork trimmings 85/15	175		
Neck bone trimmings	175		
Regular pork trimmings 50/50	150	200	175
Lean beef trimmings		300	150
Beef cheeks, trimmed			100
Beef or pork hearts			75

with these ingredients, using purified and sterilized spices:

	Pt	Lb	Oz
Salt		16	14
Corn syrup solids		5	
Sodium nitrate			12
Sodium erythorbate			4⅓
Spanish paprika		15	
Ground black pepper		1	4
Ground red pepper			2½
Ground coriander			5
Ground oregano			1
Ground Jamaica ginger			5

Processing Procedure

Prechill meats (32°–34°F). Premix salt, cure, and other dry ingredients.

Preparation.—Grind pork trimmings through the ½-in. plate of the grinder; grind beef items and pork hearts (if used) through the ⅛-in. plate. Transfer ground meats to mechanical mixer; add ice water and vinegar; and, while mixer is in operation, add salt-cure mixture. Pack tightly in meat trucks; avoid air pockets.

Curing.—Maintain temperature at 34°–36°F for overnight to cure.

Stuffing.—Before stuffing, grind meat mixture again through the ¼- or ⅜-in. plate of the grinder and remix sausage mixture just long enough to make it pliable for stuffing. Stuff in narrow or medium wide hog casings; link into 3- or 4-in. lengths. Links are not twisted, but are tied with string.

Do not stuff casings too tightly; just enough to make a plump filling after the links are tied. Shower sausages with cold water to wash casings.

Ripening (Green Room).—Maintain temperature of 70°–75°F with 75–80% RH. Hold for 3 days.

Smoking.—If smoking is desired, maintain temperature at 70°–75°F with 75–80% RH and smoke lightly with drafts ¼ open.

Drying.—Maintain temperature at 52°–56°F with 65–70% RH. Space sausages closely for 24 hr; then separate them 3 in. apart and dry for 15 days.

Shelf-life of product will be improved if kept under refrigeration through storage and marketing.

For Export Packaging.—Pack chorizos dry for export in vacuumized cans or in lard, as the trade demands.

SOURCE: Stephan L. Komarik, 4810 Ronda, Coral
      Gables, Florida.

TIROLER LANDJAGER SAUSAGE

Use either of these meat combinations:

	No. 1 Lb	No. 2 Lb
Lean beef	125	375
Certified pork trimmings[2]	375	
Backfat		125

---

[2] Certified pork are those fresh pork meats certified by the USDA Meat Inspection Division as being free of live trichinae. Only certified pork trimmings should be used in processing this sausage since the processing procedure does not conform otherwise to government regulations concerning destruction of live trichinae.

with these ingredients, using purified and sterilized spices:

	Lb	Oz
Salt	16	14
Sodium nitrate		12$\frac{1}{2}$
Sodium erythorbate		4$\frac{3}{4}$
Corn syrup solids	5	
Ground white pepper		12
Ground caraway seed		2$\frac{1}{2}$
Ground coriander		2
Ground cardamom		$\frac{1}{2}$

Processing Procedure

Prechill meats (32°-34°F) before use. Premix salt, cure and other dry ingredients. Dice and freeze backfat before use.

Grinding, Mixing, Chopping.—Pork trimmings are used without grinding. Grind beef through the $\frac{1}{8}$-in. plate of the grinder. Put ground beef, pork trimmings, and frozen backfat (if used) into mechanical mixer; start mixer and add the salt-cure mixture evenly over top; mix until ingredients are thoroughly distributed. Transfer to rapid meat chopper and chop until fat particles are reduced to $\frac{1}{4}$-in. size.

Curing.—Pack sausage mixture in a truck tightly to avoid air pockets. Maintain 34°-36°F temperature; hold overnight for curing.

Stuffing.—Before stuffing, mix 1–2 min under 25 in. vacuum to make mixture pliable for stuffing. Stuff loosely in 35 mm hog casings; link into sausages weighing approximately 5 oz. Link in pairs and place each pair of sausages in a specially constructed wooden mold board. As boards are filled, they are placed in a stainless steel truck and one board is placed on top of another. This presses the sausages into their unique flat, oblong shape. Boards are piled on top of one another until the truck is filled.

Ripening (Green Room).—Maintain temperature at 70°-75°F with 70-80% RH. Hold for 3 days.

Drying.—Remove sausages from molding boards and hang on smoke trees. Maintain temperature of 52°-56°F with 65-75% RH. Hold in drying room for 2 days.

Smokehouse temperature should never be higher than 90°F. Best temperature to use is 75°-76°F with 70% RH. Use light smoke until desired color is obtained.

Keep Refrigerated.—This sausage should be kept refrigerated (45°-50°F) after smoking, through storage, and through the marketing channels.

SOURCE: Stephan L. Komarik, 4810 Ronda, Coral Gables, Florida.

MORTADELLA (DRY PROCESS)

Use either of these meat combinations:

	No. 1 Lb	No. 2 Lb
Lean pork	450	
Lean beef		250
Treated beef tripe		100
Beef hearts or pork hearts		75
Backfat or jowls	50	75

with these ingredients using purified and sterilized spices:

	Lb	Oz
Salt	16	14
Corn syrup solids	5	
Sodium nitrate		10
Sodium nitrite		1$\frac{1}{4}$
Sodium erythorbate		4$\frac{1}{3}$
Ground black pepper		10
Ground coriander		5
Ground cinnamon		2
Rum		10
Ice, chopped	50	

Processing Procedure

Finished Mortadella sausage should be a light red-colored product. Therefore, when beef is used it should be selected from young steers or bulls; and lean pork should be selected from fully matured hogs, shoulders and hams, with fat removed to 85% lean. Use solid skin side of backfat, if used. Both backfat and jowls should be semifrozen and then diced in $\frac{1}{4}$-in. dice. After dicing, mix with 2% salt and keep at cooler temperature (34°-36°F). Just before adding to the mixer with other meats, wash in lukewarm water and drain.

Use all meats well chilled (32°-34°F). Premix salt, cures, and all other dry ingredients.

Making the Emulsion.—Grind pork through the $\frac{3}{16}$-in. plate of the grinder; grind beef tripe and hearts through the $\frac{1}{8}$-in. plate. Transfer meats to conventional chopper; add 50 lb chopped ice and Dry Ice as needed to keep meat cold; chop for 2 min. Then add salt-cure mixture and rum; continue to chop until a fine emulsion is obtained.

In case an emulsifier is used, remove meat mixture from chopper immediately after seasonings are added and well distributed in sausage meat. Put through the finest plate of the emulsifier.

Under no circumstances should the meat emulsion temperature go higher than 45°-50°F.

Curing.—Pack emulsion tightly in a truck and hold at 34°-36°F overnight for cure.

Next day transfer meat to the vacuum mixer, add diced and washed fat evenly over top of meat; close mixer and draw 25 in. vacuum; mix just long enough for proper distribution of the fat (approximately 2 min).

Stuffing.—Pack stuffer tightly without air pockets. Beef bladders of as uniform size as possible are used. Before using, turn bladders inside out and soak overnight in water at a temperature of 40°-45°F and hold in the cooler. Remove them from cooler and soak them for 2-3 hr in lukewarm water (100°-110°F) before using. Turn bladders right side out for stuffing. Stuff bladders as firmly as possible; prick with needle pad to let entrapped air escape from under the casing. Use heavy twine and wrap sausages lengthwise and then crosswise forming a loop at top on which to hang the sausages for ripening and cooking.

Ripening (Green Room).—Properly space sausages on smoke sticks. Hold in green room for 24-48 hr at 70°-75°F with 75-80% RH. This will dry casings.

Smokehouse Cooking.—Mortadella are not smoked. They are cooked in the smokehouse. Use this cooking schedule: Preheat smokehouse to 120°F with 65-70% RH and with drafts ¼ open. Hold sausages for 12 hr; then gradually raise temperature to 150°F maintaining 65-70% RH. Hold at this temperature until an internal sausage temperature of 138°F is obtained.

Remove sausages from smokehouse and hang at room temperature until internal sausage temperature is reduced to room temperature. Then dip momentarily into simmering water to tighten casings and wrap each in cheesecloth bag. Transfer to drying room.

Drying.—Maintain temperature at 52°-56°F with 65-75% RH. Hold sausages until the desired moisture loss is obtained. A fully dried Mortadella should have a moisture content of 55%.

Shelf-life of product will be improved if held under refrigeration through storage and marketing.

SOURCE: Stephan L. Komarik, 4810 Ronda, Coral Gables, Florida.

MORTADELLA-STYLE SAUSAGE USING NONFAT DRY MILK

Make up this cure:

	Lb	Oz
Sodium nitrate	3	7
Sodium nitrite		5
Dextrose (corn sugar)	10	

Place ingredients in a 5-gal. glass container. Fill with water and dissolve. Use 1 qt (2¾ lb) of solution for each 100 lb of meat.

Ingredients	Lb	Oz
Boneless chuck	70	
Beef fat off of brisket	10	
Lean pork trimmings	20	
Nonfat dry milk	4	
Salt	3	
Gelatin		4
Fresh garlic		1
Whole cloves		2
Ground white pepper		7
Ground coriander		2
Ground bay leaves		4
Ground cinnamon		3
Ground mace		4
Red wine	8	
Ice water	7	
Cure	2¾	

Procedure

Grind meats separately through ½-in. plate. Chop garlic fine and mix with cure. Place spices (except pepper and garlic) in muslin bag and add to wine. Heat together for 20 min at 200°F. Remove spice bag and press bag free of wine. Cool wine. Soak gelatin in ice water and add cure to it.

Place meat in mixer. Sprinkle dissolved gelatin, water, cure, nonfat dry milk, salt, pepper, and wine (in the order named) over meat while mixer is revolving. Mix well. Run mixture through a ⅛-in. plate and spread in pans 5-6 inches deep. Cure for 12-15 hr. Stuff into beef bung cap ends, bladders, or corresponding size cellulose casings.

Place in smokehouse at 120°F, gradually increasing temperature so that after 8 hr it is 170°F. Maintain this heat until internal temperature reaches 155°F. Rinse with very hot water to remove greasy film on casings. Put under cold shower. When cool and dry, store in cooler at 55°-60°F.

SOURCE: American Dry Milk Institute, 130 N. Franklin, Chicago, Ill.

KRAKAUER DRY SAUSAGE

Use either of these meat combinations:

	No. 1 Lb	No. 2 Lb
Lean beef	250	325
Lean pork trimmings 85/15	75	
Backfat	175	100
Beef fat		75

with these ingredients, using purified and sterilized spices:

	Lb	Oz	Pt
Salt	16	14	
Sodium nitrate		12$\frac{1}{2}$	
Sodium erythorbate		4$\frac{1}{3}$	
Corn syrup solids	5		
Ground white pepper		15	
Ground coriander		2$\frac{1}{4}$	
Spanish paprika		4	
Rum			2

Processing Procedure

Premix salt, cures and other dry ingredients. Use only well-chilled meats (32°-34°F). Backfat should have no portions of skin left on; use only firm skin side of backfat. For grinding and mixing, backfat should be diced and frozen; for using high speed chopper, backfat can be cut into larger pieces but it, too, should be frozen when added to other meats.

Using Grinder and Mixer.—Grind beef through the $\frac{1}{8}$-in. plate; grind pork through the 1-in. plate. Transfer meats to mechanical mixer; add salt-cure mixture, frozen backfat dice, and rum. Mix to a uniform mixture and regrind through the $\frac{3}{8}$-in. plate of the grinder.

Using High Speed Chopper.—Grind beef through the $\frac{1}{8}$-in. plate of grinder and pork through the 1-in. plate. Transfer to mixer; add salt-cure mixture, frozen backfat pieces, and rum; mix thoroughly. Then transfer ingredients to rapid chopper using only 3 knives and filling bowl only $\frac{1}{2}$ full. Run chopper until particles are reduced to approximately $\frac{3}{8}$ in.

Curing.—Pack mixture tightly (avoid air pockets) in 6-in. deep pans. Hold at 36°-38°F for 3 days.

Stuffing.—First put meat in vacuum mixer and, under 25 in. vacuum, mix just long enough to make meat pliable for stuffing. Avoid air pockets when filling stuffer. Use beef middles 2-2$\frac{1}{2}$ in. (55-60 mm) in diameter measured at the time of stuffing. Stuff to desired length (15-20 in. long). Hang on smoke trees.

Ripening (Green Room).—Maintain temperature at 70°-75°F with 70-80% RH. Hold sausages for 3-4 days to lose some moisture and develop color and flavor.

Smoking.—Temperature of the smokehouse should never be above 90°F. Best temperature to use is 75°-76°F with 70% RH. Rapid lowering of the humidity may cause a gray crust under casings and retard loss of moisture from sausages. Smoke until desired color is obtained.

Drying.—Transfer immediately to drying room. Maintain temperature at 50°-55°F with 75% RH.

Dry sausages until the desired moisture loss is obtained.

Shelf-life of product will be improved if held under refrigeration through storage and marketing.

SOURCE: Stephan L. Komarik, 4810 Ronda, Coral Gables, Florida.

LONGANIZA TIPO PURO (SEMIDRY) (SPANISH OR PORTUGESE SAUSAGE WITH CERTIFIED PORK[3])

Meat Ingredients	Lb
Certified extra lean pork trimmings	80
Certified belly trimmings	20

Cure and Purified Spice Ingredients

	Lb	Oz	Pt
Salt	3		
Corn syrup solids	2		
Spanish paprika (part of this could be the hot variety)	3		
Ground black pepper		1	
Ground fresh garlic		10	
Ground marjoram		2	
Sodium nitrite		$\frac{1}{4}$	
Sodium nitrate		1	
Sodium erythorbate		$\frac{7}{8}$	
Good quality red wine			1
Ice water	5		

Processing Procedure

Freeze pork and belly trimmings. Premix salt, cure, and other dry ingredients. Chop or grind fresh garlic very fine.

Chopping and Mixing.—Use frozen meat cutter to cut pork and belly trimmings into approximately 2 in. slices. Then put into high speed chopper using only 3 knives and filling bowl only $\frac{1}{2}$ full. Run chopper until meat particles are reduced to pieces of $\frac{1}{2}$ or $\frac{3}{4}$ in.

Transfer meat to mechanical mixer. Start machine and add salt-cure mixture and chopped garlic. Mix only until ingredients are uniformly distributed.

Curing.—Tightly pack meat (avoid air pockets) in 6-in. deep pans. Hold in cooler (36°-38°F) for 3 days to cure.

[3] Certified pork are those fresh pork meats certified by the USDA Meat Inspection Division as being free of live trichinae. Only certified pork trimmings should be used in processing this sausage since the processing procedure does not conform otherwise to government regulations concerning destruction of live trichinae.

Stuffing.—Transfer meats from curing room to vacuum mixer. Start machine, add ice water and wine and mix under 25 in. vacuum just long enough to make mixture pliable for stuffing. Pack stuffing machine tightly to avoid air pockets. Use medium hog casings or medium beef rounds. Link and tie into 12-in. long pairs or rings and hang on smoke sticks 4 in. apart.

Ripening (Green Room).—Maintain temperature at 75°F with relative humidity of 75-80%. Hold for 12 hr.

Smoking.—Maintain smokehouse temperature at 70°-75°F with 65% RH and cold smoke for 12-14 hr (as desired).

Drying.—Maintain temperature at 50°-55°F with 70-72% RH. If the diameter of the casings does not exceed 1 3/8 in. after stuffing, the drying period can be reduced to 15 days. In no case, however, should the sausage be released from the drying room in less than 20 days from the time curing materials are added to the meat.

Shelf-life of product will be extended if held under refrigeration through storage and marketing.

SOURCE: Stephan L. Komarik, 4810 Ronda, Coral Gables, Florida.

CERVELAT SUMMER SAUSAGE

Use any of these meat combinations:

	No. 1 Lb	No. 2 Lb	No. 3 Lb
Lean beef trimmings	150	150	100
Pork hearts, trimmed	125		
Beef hearts, trimmed	125		100
Backfat	100		
Pork trimmings 50/50		125	125
Beef tripe, treated		100	
Pork stomachs			175
Beef cheeks, trimmed		125	

with these ingredients, using purified and sterilized spices:

	Lb	Oz
Salt	15	
Corn syrup solids	5	
Sodium nitrite		3/4
Sodium nitrate		12 1/2
Sodium erythorbate		4 1/3
Ground black pepper	1	4
Ground coriander		4
Ground ginger		4
Ground mustard		4
Garlic powder (optional)		1

Processing Procedure

Premix salt, cures, and other dry ingredients. Have all meats well chilled (32°-34°F) before use.

Grind through the 3/16-in. plate of the grinder the following meats: beef trimmings, pork and beef hearts, beef cheeks, tripe, and stomachs.

Grind through the 1-in. plate the following: pork trimmings and backfat.

Mix and Cure.—Put ground meats in mechanical mixer. Start machine and add salt-cure mixture; mix only until all ingredients are uniformly distributed. Tightly pack in truck (avoid air pockets) and hold at 36°-38°F for 2 days for curing.

Regrind and Stuff.—Regrind meat mixture through the 1/8-in. plate of the grinder; transfer to vacuum mixer and mix under 25 in. vacuum approximately 2 min.

Tightly pack stuffer (avoid air pockets). Use beef middles or cellulose casings of same diameter. Stuff casings as tightly as possible and prick natural casings with needle pad to let entrapped air escape.

Ripening (Green Room).—Hang sausages on smoke trees properly spaced and rinse under cold water; let drain before transferring sausages to green room. Hold in green room at 45°F for 24 hr.

Smoking.—Bring sausages to room temperature before putting them in the smokehouse. Temperature and smoking schedule is dependent upon type of sausage desired.

For Semisoft Sausage.—Preheat smokehouse to 120°F with dampers wide open and hold until casings are dry. Close dampers to 1/4 open, introduce light smoke, raise temperature to 140°F and smoke for 4 hr. Then gradually raise temperature to 165°F and hold until an internal meat temperature of 152°F is obtained.

Remove sausages from smokehouse and hold under cold water shower until internal meat temperature is reduced to 110°F. Let casings dry at room temperature; then transfer to a holding cooler (45°F) for final chilling.

For Firmer Sausage.—After removing sausages from green room, hold at room temperature to warm to room temperature. Transfer sausages to smokehouse at 75°F and with dampers wide open hold for 24 hr at this temperature. Then rapidly raise temperature to 120°F, introduce light smoke, and hold for another 24 hr. Then raise temperature to 160°F and hold until an internal meat temperature of 142°F is reached.

Remove sausages from smokehouse and hold at room temperature until internal meat temperature is reduced to room temperature. Then dip sausages momentarily in simmering water to tighten casings. Hold in cooler (45°F) for final chilling.

Shelf-life of product will be improved if held under refrigeration through storage and marketing.

SOURCE: Stephan L. Komarik, 4810 Ronda, Coral Gables, Florida.

CERVELAT SAUSAGE USING NONFAT DRY MILK

Make up this cure:

	Lb	Oz
Sodium nitrate	3	7
Sodium nitrite		5
Dextrose (corn sugar)	10	

Place ingredients in a 5-gal. glass container. Fill with water and dissolve. Use 1 qt (2¾ lb) of solution for each 100 lb of meat.

Ingredients	Lb	Oz
Beef trimmings	35	
Pork cheek meat	35	
Regular pork trimmings	20	
Lean pork trimmings	10	
Nonfat dry milk	4½	
Salt	2¾	
Fresh onions	1	
Ground white pepper		6
Fresh garlic		1
Cold water	6	
Cure	2¾	

Procedure

Chop garlic fine and mix with cure. Grind beef and onions through ⅛-in. plate. Grind pork cheeks separately through ⅛-in. plate, and pork trimmings through ¼-in. plate. Place all meat in mixer. Add water, salt, cure, nonfat dry milk, and seasoning. Mix thoroughly. Place not more than 6 in. deep in pans. Cure overnight at 38°–40°F. Run through ⅜-in. plate. Stuff into wide beef middles or corresponding size cellulose casings.

Start smoking with 120°F temperature, gradually increasing heat so that at end of 6 hr the thermometer will register 170°F. Maintain this heat until an internal temperature of 155°F is obtained. Place under hot shower for a few minutes to rinse off grease. Sausage should be cool and dry before placing in storage. Store at 60°-65°F.

SOURCE: American Dry Milk Institute, 130 N. Franklin, Chicago, Ill.

THURINGER-STYLE SAUSAGE USING NONFAT DRY MILK

Make up this cure:

	Lb	Oz
Sodium nitrate	3	7
Sodium nitrite		5
Dextrose (corn sugar)	10	

Place ingredients in a 5-gal. glass container. Fill with water and dissolve. Use 1 qt (2¾ lb) of solution for each 100 lb of meat.

Ingredients	Lb	Oz
Boneless chuck	60	
Regular pork trimmings	40	
Nonfat dry milk	4	
Cold water	6	
Salt	3	
Cure	2¾	
Sugar	1½	
Ground white pepper		6
Ground mustard		3
Whole mustard seed		2
Fresh garlic		1

Procedure

Grind chuck through ⅜-in. plate, and pork trimmings through 1-in. plate. Chop garlic fine and mix with cure.

Place all meats in mixer. Add nonfat dry milk, salt, cure, sugar, and seasoning. Mix well. Run all through ⅛-in. plate. Put mixture in pans not over 7 in. deep. Store in 38°-40°F cooler for 24 hr.

Place in smokehouse at low temperature for 6 hr. Then gradually raise temperature so that at 8 hr the temperature is 170°F. Maintain this heat for 1 hr. Place under hot shower for a few seconds to rinse off any foreign matter adhering to casings. Keep at sausage room temperature, protected from draft, until cold. Store at 55°-65°F.

SOURCE: American Dry Milk Institute, 130 N. Franklin, Chicago, Ill.

SEMIDRY SAUSAGES USING LACTIC ACID STARTER CULTURE

A lactic acid starter culture, such as Lactacel® (a Merck product) and Accel® (a Pfizer product) may be used in processing a number of sausages: thuringer, summer sausage, cervelat, Lebanon bologna, pork roll, pepperoni, hot bar sausage, etc. Merck Chemical Division of Merck & Co. gives the following information about sausage making using their lactic acid starter culture.

SUGGESTIONS FOR PRODUCING A SEMIDRY SAUSAGE WITH LACTACEL® LACTIC ACID STARTER CULTURE

Meat Formulation

High quality, fresh or frozen, beef, beef trimmings, pork trimmings, pork fat, or any combination may be used to make a semidry sausage with a lactic acid starter culture (Lactacel®). Low bacterial counts (high quality) are essential to avoid off-flavors due to undesirable organisms. As with any comminuted product, the meat formulation must be selected to yield the optimum fat level in the finished product.

Spice Formulation

The choice of spice remains at the discretion of the sausage producer. Either a preblended spice mixture or the individual spices may be used. In any case, it is important that the nitrite level not exceed $\frac{1}{8}$ oz per 100 lb; the nitrate level should not exceed $\frac{1}{4}$ oz per 100 lb; the dextrose level should be at least 12 oz per 100 lb; and, especially for products which will be presliced, the use of $\frac{7}{8}$ oz of erythorbate (Neo-cebitate®) or $\frac{3}{4}$ oz of erythorbic acid (Neo-cebicure®) per 100 lb is essential.

Grinding and Mixing

The meats may be coarse ground, all of the ingredients mixed in, the thawed and diluted lactic acid starter culture mixed in, and the mixture fine ground. Where the silent cutter is used, the cure, salt, and spices should be added at the beginning of the chop and the thawed, diluted lactic acid starter culture added long enough before the end of the chop to ensure uniform distribution.

Addition of Starter Culture

The starter culture (Lactacel®) may be thawed while the meats are being ground by immersing the unopened can in water at 70°–75°F. The thawed starter culture should be diluted with water and added to the sausage batch at the rate of 2 oz per 100 lb. Thorough distribution is essential for uniform flavor development.

Stuffing

When mixing or chopping operation is completed, no holding period is required for Lactacel® and the sausage may be promptly stuffed and hung on smoke trees. Any type of casing may be used, although the choice will be somewhat limited by the specific product involved and whether it is to be presliced or sold in bulk.

Smoking Schedule

The product should be moved to the smokehouse as soon after stuffing as smokehouse space is available. If a lengthy delay will occur, the stuffed product should be held in a warm, humid location. When the smokehouse is loaded, the temperature should be raised to 110°–115°F dry bulb, 105°–110°F wet bulb as quickly as the product and the equipment will permit. For some products, the temperature has to be increased relatively slowly, particularly at higher humidities to avoid a breakdown of the texture. For most products, the use of Lactacel® permits the added convenience of moving the sausage directly into a smokehouse preheated to the above temperature.

The product should be smoked to the desired level during this fermentation period. Some products in the semidry class are typically heavily smoked, while others may receive little, if any, smoke flavoring. The 110°–115°F dry bulb, 105°–110°F wet bulb should be maintained until the desired tang of pH is approached. The graph below will give a good estimate of the fermentation time to reach a specific pH level. Since the time required for the internal temperature to reach the point for optimum growth of the starter culture organism will vary widely depending upon the specific product and the type of smokehouse, the times shown on the graph are the hours after the internal temperature reaches 100°F.

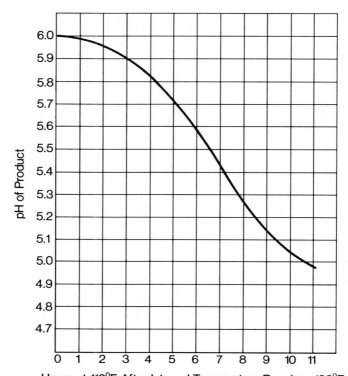

FIG. 2.1. RELATIONSHIP OF LACTACEL FERMENTATION TIME TO PH

SOURCE: Merck Chemical Division, Merck & Co., Rahway, N.J.

CERVELAT SUMMER SAUSAGE WITH LACTIC ACID STARTER FERMENTATION

Use either of these meat combinations:

	No. 1 Lb	No. 2 Lb
Lean beef	300	
Certified[4] lean pork 80/20		360
Backfat	200	140

with these ingredients, using purified and sterilized spices:

	Lb	Oz
Salt	15	
Sodium nitrite		5/8
Sodium nitrate		5/8
Corn sugar (dextrose)	5	
Sodium erythorbate		4 3/8
Ground white pepper	1	4
Ground cardamom		3/4
Ground Spanish paprika		4
Ground Jamaica ginger		2
Ground coriander		2
Chopped ice	25	

and use either

Accel®		5
or		
Lactacel®		10

[4] Certified pork are those fresh pork meats certified by the USDA Meat Inspection Division as being free of live trichinae. Only certified pork should be used in processing this sausage since the processing procedure does not conform otherwise to government regulations concerning destruction of live trichinae.

Processing Procedure

Premix salt, cures, and other dry ingredients. Prechill mechanical mixer. Use only well-chilled meats (32°–34°F); backfat should be frozen when used. First freeze (26°–27°F) the backfat (without any traces of rind) and cut into 2-in. strips; then slice 1/4-in. thick and return to freezer until used.

Processing with Accel®.—Grind chilled beef or pork through the 3/16-in. plate of the grinder.

Suspend Accel® in 2 lb of tepid water (70°–75°F) and use within $1/2$ hr after preparation.

Put ground meat into mixer; start machine and add frozen backfat slices, the Accel® suspension, the salt-cure mixture, and the chopped ice. Run machine until ingredients are uniformly distributed (approximately 2 min).

At this point if a grinder is used, regrind meat mixture through either the $1/8$- or $3/16$-in. plate. But it is preferable to transfer meat mixture to a rapid chopper (use 2 or 3 knives). Fill the bowl just $1/2$ full and chop until fat particles are reduced to $1/4$-in. or to the desired size. In either of these operations it is important that the meat temperature should never rise above 55°F.

Stuff in No. 6 fibrous casings 30 in. long or in 55–60 mm beef middles of the same length. Hang sausages on smoke trees and transfer to a warm, humid room (temperature, 80°–85°F; with 90% RH) and cure overnight. They are then ready for smoking.

Processing with Lactacel®.—Grind well-chilled beef through the $3/16$-in. plate of the grinder.

Thaw unopened cans of Lactacel® in tepid water (70°–75°F) for 15 min; then suspend Lactacel® in 2 lb of ice water. This suspension should be used within $1/2$ hr after preparation.

Transfer ground meat to prechilled mechanical mixer; start machine and add salt-cure mixture and the chopped ice. Then add frozen backfat slices and the Lactacel® suspension and run machine until all ingredients are uniformly distributed (approximately 2 min).

If a grinder is used at this point, regrind meat mixture through the $1/8$- or $3/16$-in. plate. But it is preferable to transfer mixture to a rapid chopper (use 2 or 3 knives); fill the bowl just $1/2$ full and chop until fat particles are reduced to $1/4$-in. or the desired size.

Stuff in No. 6 fibrous casings 30 in. long or 55–60 mm beef middles of the same length.

This method using Lactacel® needs no overnight cure. After stuffing, sausages are transferred directly to the smokehouse.

Smoking Procedure for Both Methods

Maintain smokehouse temperature at 100°–110°F with 85–90% RH and hold sausages for 12 hr to encourage growth of lactic acid bacteria. Introduce smoke in the house during all or part of the fermentation period. Smoke may be continued for 24 hr or until the desired smoke color and flavor are obtained. Gradually raise smokehouse temperature of 150°F until an internal meat temperature of 137°F is obtained.

After the smoking process, shower sausages very briefly with hot water (180°F) and hold at room temperature until casings are dry and internal meat is reduced to 110°F. Then transfer to chill room (45°F) for final chilling and hold at least 24 hr before packaging and shipping.

Shelf-life of product will be improved if held under refrigeration through storage and marketing.

SOURCE: Stephan L. Komarik, 4810 Ronda, Coral Gables, Florida.

THURINGER SUMMER SAUSAGE WITH LACTIC ACID STARTER FERMENTATION

Use any of these meat combinations:

	No. 1 Lb	No. 2 Lb	No. 3 Lb
Cow meat, lean	400	350	200
Beef cheeks, trimmed			100
Beef hearts, trimmed			100
Backfat	100		100
Beef flanks, trimmed		150	

with these ingredients, using purified and sterilized spices:

	Lb	Oz
Salt	15	
Sodium nitrite		$5/8$
Sodium nitrate		$1 1/4$
Sodium erythorbate		$4 3/8$
Corn sugar (dextrose)	3	12
Ground black pepper	1	8
Ground ginger		5
Whole or cracked black pepper (optional)		5
Chopped ice	25	

and use either

Accel®		5

or

Lactacel®		10

Processing Procedure

Use dry, solid pieces of cow meat; beef hearts without blood clots and with surface fat removed; flanks from good quality steers with plenty of hard fat between the layers of meat. Chill (32°–34°F) meats before use. Backfat should be diced in $1/2$-in. cubes and solidly frozen.

Processing with Accel®.—Grind cow meat and beef hearts and cheeks through the $3/16$-in. plate of the grinder; beef flanks (if used) through the $1/2$-in. plate.

Suspend Accel® in 2 lb of tepid water (70°–75°F) and use within $1/2$ hr after preparation.

Put the lean ground meats into mechanical mixer; start machine and add salt-cure mixture and the chopped ice; mix until all ingredients are uniformly distributed (approximately 2 min). Then add ground flanks or frozen backfat dice and the Accel® suspension. Mix thoroughly.

At this point if a grinder is used, regrind meat mixture through $1/8$- or $3/16$-in. plate. But it is preferable to transfer meat mixture to a rapid chopper (using 3 knives and filling bowl only $1/2$ full) and chop until fat particles are reduced to $1/8$-$3/16$ in. in size.

Use casings that are $2\,3/4$ in. in diameter when stuffed; either sewed single wall beef middles, sewed defatted hog bungs, or fibrous casings; all 30 in. long.

After stuffing, hang on smoke trees and transfer to warm, humid room for short cure. Smokehouse may be used for this period. Preheat smokehouse to 80°F with 80–85% RH and hold sausages for 12–16 hr to encourage growth of the lactic acid bacteria. They are then ready for smoking.

Processing with Lactacel®.—Grind cow meat and beef hearts and cheeks through the $3/16$-in. plate of the grinder; beef flanks, is used, through the $1/2$-in. plate. Backfat should be diced in $1/2$-in. cubes and solidly frozen.

Thaw unopened cans of Lactacel® in tepid water (70°–75°F). Suspend Lactacel® in 2 lb of 70°–75°F water. This suspension should be used within $1/2$ hr after preparation.

Transfer the lean ground meats to a mechanical mixer; start machine and add salt-cure mixture and chopped ice, mix until ingredients are uniformly dispersed (approximately 2 min). Then add ground flanks or frozen backfat dice and the Lactacel® suspension. Mix thoroughly.

If a grinder is used at this point in processing, regrind meat mixture through the $1/8$- or $3/16$-in. plate. But it is preferable to transfer meat mixture to a rapid chopper (using 3 knives and filling bowl only $1/2$ full) and chop until fat particles are reduced to $1/8$-$3/16$ in. in size.

Use 30-in. long casings that are $2\,3/4$ in. in diameter when stuffed; either sewed single wall beef middles, sewed defatted hog bungs, or fibrous casings. Hang sausages on smoke trees, properly spaced for good air circulation, and transfer to the smokehouse. They are ready for smoking. This method using Lactacel® needs no overnight cure.

Smoking Procedure for Both Methods.—Maintain smokehouse temperature at 100°–110°F and 85–90% RH, introduce smoke and smoke sausages (16–20 hr) until desired tang and smoke flavor are developed. Then raise temperature to 120°F with 75% RH and raise temperature 10° higher every 2 hr until internal meat temperature of 137°F is obtained.

Transfer sausages to a holding cooler (45°F) and chill at least 24 hr before packaging and shipping.

Product should be held under refrigeration through storage and marketing.

SOURCE: Stephan L. Komarik, 4810 Ronda, Coral Gables, Florida.

THURINGER SAUSAGE USING LACTIC ACID STARTER CULTURE

Meat Formulation

Ingredients	Lb
Beef chuck	60
Beef plates	20
Regular (50%) pork trimmings	20

Spice Formulation

Ingredients	Lb	Oz
Salt	2	8
Nitrite (with $1/2$ pt water)		$1/8$
Nitrate (with $1/2$ pt water)		$1/4$
Dextrose		12
Ground black pepper		6
Whole black pepper		1
Mustard		$1/2$
Nutmeg		$1/2$
Sodium erythorbate (Neo-Cebitate®) (with 2 qt water)		$7/8$
Lactic acid starter culture, *Pedioccocus Cerevisiae* (Lactacel®) (with 1 pt water)		2

Process

Grind meat through a $1/2$-in. plate, mix and add with mixing salt, cure in solution, and all spices except whole black pepper. Add sodium erythorbate (Neo-Cebitate®) solution, mix thoroughly; add starter culture (Lactacel®) which has been thawed and suspended in designated amount of water, and mix thoroughly. Regrind mixture through fine plate ($3/16$ in.); add whole black pepper, mix; stuff into appropriate casings.

Immediately move to smokehouse and bring house to 110°F dry bulb, 105°F wet bulb temperature as quickly as equipment and product will permit. After the internal temperature of the product reaches 100°F, maintain this temperature and humidity for 8 hr. Advance temperature to 140°F dry bulb, 130°F wet bulb for $1/2$ hr and then to 160°F dry bulb, 150°F wet bulb until internal temperature reaches 137°F.

Smoke may be applied during any part or all of this process time after the sausage has reached the 100°F temperature and the surface has dried.

Remove to cooler. Allow 2–3 days for flavor to mellow before taste evaluation.

Hold product in refrigeration through storage and marketing.

Analysis

Typical analysis of sausage made with this formulation and process will be approximately: moisture, 55%; fat, 21%; salt, 2.9%; sodium erythorbate 400 ppm; pH, 5.2.

SOURCE: Merck Chemical Division, Merck & Co., Rahway, N.J.

HOT BAR SAUSAGE USING LACTIC ACID STARTER CULTURE

Ingredients	Lb	Oz
Beef chuck	28	
Beef plates	12	
Salt	1	3
Dextrose		4
Ground black pepper		1.75
Cayenne pepper		3.5
Mustard		0.25
Garlic powder		0.05
Sodium nitrite (dissolved in 60 ml water)		0.05
Sodium erythorbate (Neo-Cebitate®) (dissolved in 300 ml water)		0.3
Starter culture of lactic acid bacteria (Lactacel® suspended in 200 ml water)		0.9

Procedure

Grind chuck through coarse plate (³⁄₈ in.); add salt and mix thoroughly. Grind plates through coarse plate, add to above mixture along with all other ingredients except sodium erythorbate (Neo-Cebitate®) and starter culture (Lactacel®) and mix thoroughly. Add sodium erythorbate solution and mix thoroughly. Thaw starter culture, suspend in water; add to mixture and mix thoroughly. Grind through fine plate (¹⁄₈ in.) and stuff into edible casings, such as Devro 140 collagen casings. Hang stuffed sausage; move directly to smokehouse. Process according to the following schedule (low fan speed):

Time Hr	Dry Bulb Temp °F	Wet Bulb Temp °F
1		90 ⎫ No sock
8		110 ⎭
2½	130	122
2½	135	125
2½	135	120
2½	140	120
2½	130	105

During last setting, increase fan speed to accelerate drying.

Critical Factors Related to the Use of Starter Culture (Lactacel®)

1. To ensure controlled fermentation, fresh or frozen meats of high quality (low bacterial population) should be used.

2. Pork and pork trimmings must be handled in compliance with the MID regulations covering the destruction of trichinae.

3. For best results, straight sodium nitrite should be used at the level of ¹⁄₈ oz per 100 lb. A mixed cure may be used, but the nitrite should not exceed ¹⁄₈ oz per 100 lb and the nitrate should not exceed ¹⁄₄ oz per 100 lb.

4. At least 12 oz dextrose per 100 lb must be used with Lactacel®. The lactic acid organism requires this level of dextrose for optimum growth. Additional dextrose, cane or other sugar or corn syrup solids may be used if desired. (Note: the dextrose equivalent of corn syrup solids cannot be used in lieu of dextrose; the actual dextrose content may be calculated and serve as part or all of the dextrose requirement.)

5. Humidity is very important in the production of semidry sausage. The proper level of humidity will serve to maintain the proper moisture balance required for optimum growth of the lactic acid organism and help prevent excessive shriveling or wrinkling and formation of an undesirable rind.

6. The addition of sodium erythorbate (Neo-Cebitate®) or erythorbic acid (Neo-Cebicure®) assists the development and stability of the internal color of the sausage. For products which will be sliced, prepackaged, and displayed in the retail store, the use of one of the ascorbates is essential.

7. Hold product at refrigerated temperatures through storage and marketing.

SOURCE: Merck Chemical Division, Merck & Co., Rahway, N.J.

COOKED SMOKED AND UNSMOKED SAUSAGES (FRANKFURTERS, WEINERS, BOLOGNA TYPES)

These types of sausages are the largest volume of sausages consumed in America. The application of modern food technology and the development of high-speed and continuous processing and packaging equipment have made this great volume possible. Today, cooked smoked and unsmoked sausages are produced at great speed and effecting great labor-saving costs as well.

Some of the important advances over the past 30 yr making this possible include the following: Use of new chemicals making possible the curing of meats in a matter of minutes; high-speed meat choppers; meat emulsifiers; vacuum mixers; air-conditioned stationary and continuous smokehouses; continuous stuffing, linking, and peeling machines; continuous packaging equipment; and, more recently, the continuous conveyor-type assembly machinery which produces vacuum-packaged frankfurters in less than 1 hr.

MID Regulations Concerning Added Materials In Sausage Products

When cereals, vegetable starch, starchy vegetable flour, soy flour, isolated or concentrated soy protein, or dry milk (either whole or nonfat) is added to the sausage emulsion, the limits of such additions are regulated by the USDA Meat Inspection Division and their use shall appear on the label of the product in a prominent manner contiguous to the name of the product; e.g., Bologna Sausage—Cereal Added, Bologna Sausage—Cereal and Nonfat Dry Milk Added, Bologna Sausage—Soy Flour Added, Bologna Sausage—Soy Protein Added, etc.

Sausage may contain not more than $3^1/_2\%$ individually or collectively of cereal, vegetable starch, starchy vegetable flour, soy flour, nonfat dry milk, or whole dry milk.

The permissible use of isolated soy protein containing 90% protein is 2%. The permissible use of soy protein concentrate containing 70% protein is 3%.

NEW FDA BAN ON PREMIXED COMMERCIAL SEASONINGS CONTAINING SODIUM NITRITE

Premixed spice and flavoring ingredients from commercial suppliers are widely used in the manufacture of products such as luncheon meats and weiners. In the past, some of these premixed products also contained the recommended amount of allowable sodium nitrite. Because test data from USDA showed that an undesirable chemical (nitrosamine, a causative of cancer in test animals) may form when the nitrite preservative combined with the amines in the seasonings, the Food and Drug Administration on July 19, 1973 ordered manufacturers of meat curing premixes which combine nitrite curing agents with seasonings to package the nitrite and seasonings separately. The FDA action does not affect manufacturers of premixed seasoning ingredients who use a chemical "buffer" to separate the nitrite and the seasoning in a premix.

OUTLINE OF RAPID PROCESSING PROCEDURE FOR SKINLESS FRANKFURTERS THROUGH CONVEYOR SYSTEM

Formerly, it took nearly 2 hr just to cure and cook frankfurters from raw meat to the finished product, not including the time required for chilling, peeling, and packaging. With the continuous system used today, frankfurters can be produced in 30–40 min and a proper assembly line can produce up to 12,000 lb of finished frankfurters per hour ready for shipment.

The slow curing reaction of sodium nitrite on the meat emulsion to develop a cured meat color was the biggest stumbling block in attempting to speed up frankfurter production. Coauthor Stephen L. Komarik and co-workers invested a great amount of work on the problem attempting to reduce curing time. Their biggest breakthrough came with the invention (U.S. Patent 3,391,006, July 2, 1960) of the use of sodium erythorbate or sodium isoascorbate in combination with sodium acid pyrophosphate or glucono delta lactone. Using these materials, the curing time during the cooking procedure was reduced to a matter of minutes making it possible for continuous processing of skinless frankfurters.

Following is an outline of this rapid processing procedure.

Step No. 1.—After sausages are stuffed in casings and linked to the desired size, they go through an acid bath to coagulate the surface of the sausage emulsion under the casing. This makes the peeling of the sausages possible with high-speed peeling machines after sausages are cooked and chilled at the end of the process. If liquid smoke is used in combination with acids such as vinegar, citric, or malic acid, it gives a smoke flavor to the sausages and eliminates the step of putting the sausages through a smoke chamber.

Step No. 2.—If no smoke flavor is used, the sausages are conveyed through the smoke chamber where air current, temperature, and relative humidity are rigidly controlled.

Step No. 3.—From the smoke chamber sausages are conveyed to the cooking chamber, again rigidly controlled, to raise the internal temperature of the sausages to 155°F.

Step No. 4.—The cooked sausages are then conveyed through a cold water shower and into a refrigerated 6% brine solution with a temperature of 20°–24°F to chill frankfurters to an internal temperature of 38°–40°F. They are then conveyed directly to high-speed peelers to be peeled and packaged.

Elapsed time from start to the packaged product depends upon the machines used and cooking temperatures (200°F or over). Elapsed time will vary from 30 to 40 min.

BOLOGNA-TYPE SAUSAGES: JUMBO, LONG, AND RING

Use any of these meat combinations:

	No. 1 Lb	No. 2 Lb	No. 3 Lb	No. 4 Lb	Kosher Lb
Bull or cow meat	300	150	200	150	300
Regular pork trimmings 50/50	200		125		
Beef trimmings 50/50		200	100		
Pork cheeks, trimmed			75		
Beef hearts				100	
Pork hearts				100	
Beef flanks, trimmed					200
Pork jowls, skinned		150		150	

with these ingredients:

	Lb	Oz	Cc
Salt	15		
Corn syrup solids	10		
Dry soluble pepper[1]	1	4	
or oleoresin capsicum			15.00
Sodium nitrate		5	
Sodium nitrite		1¼	
Sodium erythorbate		4³⁄₈	
Oil of nutmeg			14.00
Oil of coriander			4.50
Oil of allspice			2.00
Oil of caraway			0.25
Oleoresin ginger			0.50
Garlic powder (optional)		¼	
Chopped ice or ice water[2] or			
a combination of both (approx)	150		

[1] If dry soluble pepper is used, mix oils with the dry soluble pepper. If oleoresin capsicum is used, omit dry soluble pepper and mix oleoresins and oils with 1 lb of the 15 lb of salt called for.

[2] Add approximately 150 lb of ice or ice water, or a combination of the two, per 500-lb batch of meat. The exact moment of water and/or ice will depend upon the moisture/protein ratio of the meat (see Tables 2.2 and 2.3).

METHOD NO. 1
CHOPPING OPERATION USING GRINDER AND CONVENTIONAL CHOPPER

Be sure that all meats are chilled (32°–34°F). Grind all beef items and pork hearts through ⅛-in. plate. Cut skinned jowls into strips and pork trimmings through ³⁄₁₆-in. plate. Transfer ground beef to a chopper. Add salt mixture (previously mixed with the curing ingredients, corn syrup solids, sodium erythorbate and seasonings) evenly on the top of the meat while chopper is running; add ⅓ of the ice. Then slowly add remaining ice. The purpose of slowly adding ice is to keep meat cool (at about 40°F) during the chopping. When the last of the ice has been added (it takes about 5 min to chop the beef to a good emulsion), add ground pork trimmings or pork jowls strips and chop meat until the emulsion reaches 58°–60°F but never over 65°F.

In case fat beef trimmings such as navel or plates are used, then after 2 min chopping, add the salt and the rest of the ingredients, including ⅓ of the ice. Then add ground fat trimmings and with slow addition of ice. Chop meat until the emulsion temperature reaches 58°-60°F. During the chopping operation, air is unavoidably mixed in; therefore, it is suggested that the chopped emulsion be transferred to a prechilled vacuum mixer (if available) and mixed for 3 min under 25 in. vacuum. Then the emulsion is ready for stuffing.

METHOD NO. 2
CHOPPING OPERATION WHEN HIGH-SPEED CHOPPER IS USED

In case fresh meats are used, chill to 32°-34°F with chopped ice. If frozen meat is used, put it through the frozen meat slicer and then directly into the high-speed meat chopper. Instead of ice, use water (even warm water), but water temperature should never be over 120°F. Hot water over 134°F will coagulate the protein and ruin the emulsion.

Chopping.—Place lean beef and pork in the chopper, start the machine, then add salt mixture (previously mixed with the other seasoning and curing ingredients) evenly over the top of the meat, add $^1/_3$ of the ice or water. After mixing for 2 min, add the fat beef material and another $^1/_3$ of the water; let machine run an additional 1 min. Add the remaining $^1/_3$ of water or ice and add fat pork if it is used instead of fat beef. Let machine run until temperature reaches 62°-65°F. The emulsion is ready for vacuum mixing and stuffing.

METHOD NO. 3
CHOPPING OPERATION WHEN GRINDER, CONVENTIONAL CHOPPER, AND AN EMULSIFIER ARE USED

Grind meat as described in No. 1 method, but instead of finishing the emulsion in the chopper, it should be finished in the emulsifier. Place all ground meats and pork in the chopper, add salt mixture (previously mixed with cures and other seasoning ingredients) and chop for 2 min with $^1/_2$ of the ice. Then add remaining ice and chop for 1 min. Temperature of the emulsion at this time should be approximately 40°F. Remove partially finished emulsion from the chopper and put it through the fine, then the superfine plate of an emulsifier. The temperature of the finished emulsion should not be over 65°F.

The latest type of Mince Master emulsifier is equipped with a dual chopping head arrangement which puts the emulsion first through the fine, then through the superfine plate in a continuous operation. The advantage of this type of emulsifier is that all the trapped air is removed from the emulsion and no vacuum mixing is necessary; also, no sinew, gristle, or bones can pass through the superfine plate.

METHOD NO. 4
CHOPPING OPERATION WHEN HIGH-SPEED CHOPPER AND AN EMULSIFIER ARE USED

In this case, follow the directions given for Method No. 2. But instead of finishing the product in the chopper, remove meat from the chopper $^1/_2$ min after the pork fat and ice or water have been added to the chopper. At this time the temperature of the semifinished emulsion will be approximately 40°F. Remove meat from chopper and put it through the emulsifier. Meat temperature should not go over 65°F.

METHOD 5
CHOPPING OPERATION USING GRINDER, MIXER, AND AN EMULSIFIER

Grind all well-chilled meats, both red and fat, through the $^3/_{16}$-in plate. Transfer meats to mixer and add $^1/_2$ the amount of ice or a mixture of ice and water (the amount depending on the batch size and meats used) and all the dry ingredients and mix for 2 min; then add the other $^1/_2$ of the water or ice and let the mixer run an additional 1 min. Put mixed material through the fine, then through the finest plate of the emulsifier. The finished emulsion temperature should be not over 65°F.

Other Added Materials

If added materials, such as nonfat dry milk or cereals are used, it is suggested that they be added to the emulsion immediately after the addition of fat pork trimmings. When such materials are added to the sausage meat, it cannot be labeled "all meat product." (See MID regulations given above.)

Stuffing

Special care should be taken packing emulsions into the stuffer so as not to create air pockets. Stuff material in long beef bungs, or jumbo or smaller diameter artificial casings, to the maximum of their capacity. For ring bologna stuff in export wide beef round or artificial casings.

Smoking and Cooking

Hang properly spaced stuffed sausages on smoke trees. It is suggested that stockinettes be used for jumbo bologna to reduce breakage, sausages stuffed in beef bungs should be wrapped with twine for the same reason. Shower sausages with cold water to remove meat particles after stuffing. Jumbo bologna should be placed in a chill room at a temperature of 40°-45°F until they are smoked. Long bolognas of smaller diameter should be placed immediately in a preheated smokehouse at a temperature of 130°-135°F. After sausages are placed in the smokehouse, adjust dampers wide open to dry casings for $1/2$-$3/4$ hr, then apply heavy smoke for $1^1/2$ hr for 3-$3^1/2$ in. diameter sausages, and 3 hr for 5 $3/4$ jumbos. Cut off smoke, adjust dampers $1/4$ open and gradually raise temperature 10° every hour to 175°-180°F until an internal meat temperature of 155°F is obtained. Remove sausages from the house and shower them with a fine spray of water until internal meat temperature is reduced to 110°F. Keep the smallest size sausages at room temperature at least 30 min and 60 min for jumbo before transferring them to the chill room (45°F) for further chilling to an internal meat temperature of 50°F before packaging.

Bologna in natural casings is smoked according to the following schedule: Preheat house to 130°-135°F with dampers wide open until the casings are dry; this takes approximately 30-45 min. Apply heavy smoke for about $1^1/2$ hr for ring bologna and 3 hr for the beef jumbos. Then cut off smoke, adjust dampers $1/4$ open, and gradually raise the temperature of the house to 160°-165°F and keep sausages in the house until an internal meat temperature of 135°F is obtained. Transfer sausages immediately to a steam house or Jordan cooker and maintained temperature at 165°F until an internal meat temperature of 150°F is obtained. Then remove sausages from the cooker and shower them with a fine spray of cold water until the internal meat temperature is reduced to 110°F. Keep sausages at room temperature until casings

are dry, then transfer them to the chill room (45°F) and keep them there until internal meat temperature of 50°F is obtained. The sausages are then ready for shipment.

Fast Process Using Combination of Glucono Delta Lactone or Sodium Acid Pyrophosphate and Sodium Erythorbate

The smoking and cooking operation can be accelerated by the addition of glucono delta lactone or sodium acid pyrophosphate. Because larger size products, such as bologna sausages, take considerably longer to heat to 155°F than do frankfurter-type sausages, the amount of glucono delta lactone or sodium acid pyrophosphate added to the emulsion in combination with sodium erythorbate should be considerably reduced. The recommended amount is 4 oz of sodium acid pyrophosphate or glucono delta lactone per 100 lb of sausages with a diameter of $3^1/2$ in. or less and 2 oz for jumbo bologna in Cellophane casings.

Smoking-Cooking Schedule.—The recommended smoking and cooking schedule for jumbo bologna $5^3/4$ in. in diameter is as follows:

60 min at 160°F db temp and 128°F wb temp with 40% RH and damper wide open; apply smoke

60 min at 180°F db temp and 152°F wb temp with 53% RH and damper $1/4$ open; continue smoke

60 min at 200°F db temp and 172°F wb temp with 52% RH; stop smoking

Maintain 200°F db temp but raise wb temp to 190°F with 80% RH and hold until internal meat temp reaches 155°F

The recommended smoking and cooking schedule for bolognas $3^1/2$ in. in diameter:

60 min at 160°F db temp and 128°F wb temp with 40% RH and damper wide open; apply smoke

60 min at 180°F db temp and 152°F wb temp with 53% RH; adjust damper $1/4$ open

Raise db temp to 200°F and wb temp to 190°F with 80% RH and hold until internal 155°F

Further chilling and handling of the sausages are identical with those handled the conventional way. Product should be kept refrigerated through storage and marketing.

SOURCE: Stephan L. Komarik, 4810 Ronda, Coral Gables, Florida.

FRANKFURTER SAUSAGES (WIENERS)

Use any of these meat combinations:

	No. 1 Lb	No. 2 Lb	No. 3 Lb
Boneless cow meat	275	300	350
Regular pork trimmings	225		
Pork jowls, skinned		200	
Backfat			150

with these ingredients:

	Lb	Oz	Cc
Salt	15		
Corn syrup solids	10		
Sodium nitrite		$1^{1}/_{4}$	
Sodium nitrate		5	
Sodium erythorbate		$4^{3}/_{8}$	
(If used) glucono delta lactone or			
or sodium acid pyrophosphate	2	8	
Mustard flour (enzyme free)	5		
Dry soluble pepper	1	4	
Oil of nutmeg			7.50
Oil of allspice			1.50
Oil of cardamom			1.50
Oil of coriander			1.50
Oil of cassia			0.075

(Thoroughly mix oils with dry soluble pepper)
Chopped ice or water or a combination of the two
(approx) 30–35% per 100 lb of meat
(Amount depends on moisture/protein ratio of
the meats; see Tables 2.2 and 2.3 pp. 35–36)

METHOD NO. 1
CHOPPING OPERATION USING GRINDER AND CONVENTIONAL CHOPPER

Use well-chilled meats (32°–34°F). Premix salt with the dry seasoning and curing ingredients (spice oils are thoroughly mixed with the dry soluble pepper).

Grind chilled beef through the $1/8$-in. plate, pork trimmings through the $3/8$-in. plate. Jowls and backfat are not ground. Transfer ground beef to chopper and distribute the salt-cure mixture evenly over top of the meat while the chopper is running. Add $1/3$ of the chopped ice; then slowly add remainder of the ice. By slowly adding the ice, it keeps the meat temperature near 40°F during chopping. When the last of the ice is added (it takes about 5 min to chop beef to a good emulsion), add ground pork and pork fat and chop until meat emulsion temperature reaches 58°–60°F, never over 68°F. Air is unavoidably mixed into the emulsion during chopping, so it is recommended that the emulsion be transferred to a prechilled vacuum mixer and mixed for 3 min under 25 in. vacuum. Then the emulsion is ready for stuffing.

METHOD NO. 2
CHOPPING OPERATION WHEN HIGH SPEED CHOPPER IS USED

In case fresh meat is used, it should be chilled to 32°–34°F; use chopped ice in making the emulsion. If frozen meat is used, it should be put through the frozen meat slicer and then directly into the high speed chopper; instead of ice, use water or even warm water, but never over 120°F temperature. Hot water over 134°F will coagulate protein and ruin the emulsion.

Place lean beef (or veal, if used in place of beef) and pork trimmings in the chopper. Start machine and distribute salt mixture (previously mixed with cures and other seasoning ingredients) evenly over the top of the meat; then add $1/3$ of the ice or water (whichever is used) and run chopper for 1 min. Then add another $1/3$ of the ice (or water) and let machine run 1 min. Next add final $1/3$ of the ice or water and pork fat (is used). Let machine run until temperature reaches 62°-65°F. The emulsion is ready for stuffing.

METHOD NO. 3
CHOPPING OPERATION WHEN GRINDER, CONVENTIONAL CHOPPER AND EMULSIFIER ARE USED

Grind meat as described in method No. 1, but instead of finishing emulsion in the chopper it will be finished in the emulsifier. Place all ground meat (beef and pork) in the chopper, add salt, previously mixed with cures and the remainder of the dry ingredients, and chop for 2 min with $1/2$ of the ice. Then add remaining ice and chop for 1 min. Temperature of meat at this time should be approximately 40°F.

Remove partially finished emulsion from the chopper and put it first through the fine, then the super-fine plate of the emulsifier. The temperature of the finished emulsion should not be over 65°F. The latest type of Mince Master emulsifier is equipped with a dual chopping head arrangement which permits the emulsion to go first through the fine, then through the superfine plate, in a continuous operation. The advantage of this type of emulsifier is that all trapped air is removed from the emulsion so no vacuum mixing is necessary, and no sinews, gristle, or bone can go through the superfine plate.

METHOD NO. 4
CHOPPING OPERATION WHEN HIGH SPEED CHOPPER AND EMULSIFIER ARE USED

In this case, follow the instructions given for Method No. 2. But instead of finishing the product in the chopper, remove meat from the chopper $1/2$ min after the pork fat and last portion ice or water are added to the chopper. At this time, the temperature of the semifinished emulsion will be approximately 40°F. Dump meat from the chopper and put it through the emulsifier. The finished emulsion temperature should not be over 65°F.

METHOD NO. 5
CHOPPING OPERATION USING GRINDER, MIXER, AND EMULSIFIER

Grind all meats (well chilled to 32°-34°F), both red and fat through the $3/16$-in. plate of the grinder. Put $1/2$ of the ice or a mixture of ice and water in the mixer, the amount depending on the batch size and meats used; start mixer and add all the dry ingredients. Then add ground meat and mix for 2 min, then add the other $1/2$ of the ice or water and let mixer run 1 min. Let mixed material go first through the fine, then the finest plate of the emulsifier. Finished emulsion temperature should not be over 65°F. No vacuum mixing is necessary.

Added Materials

If added material such as nonfat dry milk or cereal is used, it is recommended that it be added immediately after the addition of the pork trimmings and pork fat (if used).

Stuff

Pack sausage emulsion tightly into the stuffers without any air pockets. It can be stuffed in artificial casings for skinless, sheep casings, or hog casings depending on the trade demand. Link sausages in a linking machine, hang on properly spaced smokehouse trees, then rinse frankfurters in animal casings with cold water.

Smoke and Cook

As indicated previously, the permissible use of sodium ascorbates has made it possible to cook sausages in a relatively short time (by reducing the curing and color development time of the sausages) and produce a product with longer keeping quality. An exact smokehouse schedule cannot be recommended because different types of smokehouses are used; some are larger, others smaller, and with different air circulation.

The following suggestions are for modern air-conditioned houses with high heat capacity and with humidity controls so that frankfurters can be processed uniformly and in the shortest possible time.

Smoking and Cooking in Artificial Casings.—Preheat house to temperature of 140°F with dampers closed to equalize temperature in all sections of the house for 15 min. This should be done if the houses are cold when the smoking operation starts. Then open dampers and place frankfurters in the house; introduce heavy smoke and keep sausages at 140°F and ½ hr or until casings are dry.

Raise temperature to 160°F and keep them at this temperature for another ½ hr and keep on smoking, then raise temperature to 175°F for 15 min or until the frankfurters reach an internal temperature of 145°F.

Steam Cook.—This operation can be done either in the smokehouse or in a steam cooker. If it is done in the house, adjust dry bulb temperature to 165°F and temperature to wet bulb 162°F, and hold sausages for 3–4 min (until sausages reach an internal temperature of 152°–155°F).

If sausages are cooked in a steam cooker, after sausages reach an internal temperature of 145°F in the house, transfer them to the steam cooker at a temperature of 165°F for 5–8 min or until an internal temperature of 152°–155°F is obtained.

In both cases, after cooking shut off steam and spray sausages with cold water until internal temperature of the frankfurters is reduced to 100°–105°F. After chilling, let sausages hang at room temperature just long enough for the casings to dry.

Chill and Peel.—Fast method: After casings are dry, transfer sausages to a blast-type chill unit to cool sausages to an internal temperature of 38°F; then remove sausages from the cooler and hold them at room temperature for 10 min to let sausages sweat; then transfer them to an air-conditioned peeling room for peeling and packaging.

If the sausage kitchens are not equipped with a rapid chilling unit then, after casings are dry, transfer them to a chill room at a temperature of 40°–45°F until the internal sausage temperature is 50°F or lower before peeling and packaging.

Whatever method is used, be sure that the sausages do not dehydrate in the blast chill or in the cooler. When this happens the sausages will not peel. If the sausages sweat, peeling will be very easy.

Smoking and Cooking in Animal Casings.—Let sausages hang at room temperature for 1 hr before transferring them to the house. Preheat house to temperature of 130°F with dampers wide open to dry sausages for ½ hr. Close dampers ¼ open, introduce heavy smoke, and raise temperature gradually to 165°F until proper color is obtained and an internal sausage temperature of 132°F is reached. Remove from the house, transfer to a steam cabinet or Jordan cooker at a temperature of 165°F, and cook sausages until an internal temperature of 152°–155°F is reached. Shut off steam, shower frankfurters with cold water until internal temperature is reduced to 95°–100°F. Allow them to hang at room temperature until casings are dry, then transfer to a cooler (40°–

45°F) until an internal sausage temperature of at least 50°F is reached before packaging.

Package

Frankfurters are usually vacuum packaged in polyethylene or Saran films.

Fast Process Using Combination of Glucono Delta Lactone With or Without Sodium Acid Pyrophosphate and Sodium Erythorbate

As mentioned previously, the addition of glucono delta lactone or preferably sodium acid pyrophosphate makes it possible to cure and cook frankfurters in from 16–30 min. Due to the fast short period of cooking time the moisture loss is lower during the heat cycle than the conventionally smoked and cooked sausages. The added moisture has to be adjusted to that the MID standard of $4 \times P + 10$ will be met in the finished product.

Cooking Schedule in Stationary Air-Conditioned Houses.—Whatever temperature given below is used to process the sausages the house should be preheated to the temperature given.

Due to the short time of cooking in stationary houses, no smoke is applied during the cooking period. After the stuffing and linking operation, sausages are sprayed with liquid smoke before entering the house. Using liquid smoke is permitted by MID regulations.

Two smokehouse temperatures with cooking times are given below for the fast process using sodium acid pyrophosphate or glucono delta lactone:

Schedule No. 1

Min	Smokehouse Temperature
20	db temp 200°F, wb temp 170°F, 49% RH
	db temp 200°F, wb temp 190°F, 80% RH
5	
25	Total cooking cycle to reach 155°F internal temperature of sausages

Schedule No. 2

Min	
17	db temp 220°F, wb temp 190°F
	Then
3	Introduce live steam
20	Total cooking cycle to reach 155°F internal temperature of sausages

After cooking sausages to an internal temperature of 155°F, shower, blast chill, or cold water chill; follow by peeling and packaging.

Procedure in Continuous Smokehouses.—The use of sodium acid pyrophosphate or glucono delta lactone in combination with ascorbates makes it possible to continuously produce frankfurters from a fresh emulsion to fully precooked products ready for packaging. This type of machinery is a combination of equipment which includes continuous stuffers, linkers, moving the stuffed links on conveyors through the heat chambers where the sausages are cooked, then through chill chambers where the sausages are chilled to 44°–46°F, to peeling machines, and then to the packaging conveyors.

Much technical study is still needed to perfect the efficiency of this kind of installation but many are already in service and it is just a matter of time before they will be in general use.

All frankfurter products should be kept refrigerated through storage and marketing.

SOURCE: Stephan L. Komarik, 4810 Ronda, Coral Gables, Florida.

OIL SPICE FOR SMOKED MEAT FLAVOR

Mix together the following and use as much as suffices:

	Gm
Oil of cade	687.5
Oleoresin capsicum	187.5
Oil of black pepper	125.0
Total	1000.0

Shake well before using to thoroughly mix ingredients.

SOURCE: *Food Flavorings, 2nd Edition* by J. Merory, published by Avi Publishing Co., Westport, Conn.

RING BOLOGNA
USING NONFAT DRY MILK

Make up this cure:

	Lb	Oz
Sodium nitrate	3	7
Sodium nitrite		5
Dextrose (corn sugar)	10	

Place ingredients in a 5-gal. glass container. Fill with water and dissolve. Use 1 qt (2¾ lb) of solution for each 100 lb of meat.

Ingredients	Lb	Oz
Boneless chuck	65	
Regular pork trimmings	35	
Nonfat dry milk	5	
Salt	3	

Fresh onions	2	
Ground white pepper		7
Ground mustard		2
Ground caraway seed		2
Fresh garlic		2
Cure	2¾	
Chopped ice		

Procedure

Chop garlic fine and mix with cure. Grind boneless chuck and onions through ⅜-in. plate. Grind pork trimmings separately, also through ⅜-in. plate.

Place chuck in silent cutter. Add some chopped ice, salt, and cure. After a few revolutions, add nonfat dry milk and chopped ice alternately a little at a time until all nonfat dry milk is used. When nearly fine enough, add pork and seasoning, and chop fine. During chopping, add enough shaved ice to have mixture of fairly stiff consistency.

Stuff into beef rounds. Place in smokehouse at about 120°F. Gradually increase temperature to 165°–170°F, until the desired color appears. Cook at 160°–165°F for 30–45 min depending upon diameter of casing. Internal temperature should reach 155°F. Place under cold shower. Enough heat should be left in sausage to dry it.

SOURCE: American Dry Milk Institute, 130 N. Franklin, Chicago, Ill.

LARGE BOLOGNA
USING NONFAT DRY MILK

Make up this cure:

	Lb	Oz
Sodium nitrate	3	7
Sodium nitrite		5
Dextrose (corn sugar)	10	

Place ingredients in a 5-gal. glass container. Fill with water and dissolve. Use 1 qt (2¾ lb) of solution for each 100 lb of meat.

Ingredients	Lb	Oz
Bullmeat	30	
Beef trimmings	30	
Regular pork trimmings	40	
Nonfat dry milk	4¾	
Salt	3	
Fresh onions	2½	
Ground white pepper		6
Ground coriander		2
Ground allspice		1
Ground sage		1
Fresh garlic		1

Cure   2¾
Chopped ice

Procedure

Chop garlic fine and mix with cure. Grind meats separately through ³⁄₈-in. plate. Place bullmeat and beef trimmings with chopped ice in silent cutter. After a few revolutions add salt and cure. Then add nonfat dry milk and chopped ice alternately until all nonfat dry milk has been used. Then add seasoning, pork trimmings and shaved ice until the proper consistency is obtained. Chop fine. Stuff into beef bungs or corresponding size of cellulose casings.

Place in smokehouse. Start at 120°F gradually raising temperature to 165°F until the desired color appears. This will be in 2½–3 hr. During hot summer months cook at 160°F until internal temperature reaches 155°F. In cold weather, 148°F will be sufficient. Then place under cold water shower for about 10 min.

SOURCE: American Dry Milk Institute, 130 N. Franklin, Chicago, Ill.

BOLOGNA FORMULAS USING SOY PROTEIN

Formula No. 1	Using Soy Protein Concentrate	Using Isolated Soy Protein
Ingredients	Lb	Lb
Lean beef (90% lean)	55.0	55.0
Pork jowls	45.0	45.0
Soy protein concentrate (Promosoy-100)	4.0	
Isolated soy protein (Promine-D)		2.5
Corn syrup	2.0	2.0
Dextrose	2.0	2.0
Salt	2.5	2.5
Water	30.0	30.0
Spice, cure, seasonings to suit		

Formula No. 2		
Ingredients		
Beef plates	35.0	35.0
Pork stomachs	28.0	28.0
Pork hearts or beef hearts	27.0	27.0
Pork backfat	10.0	10.0
Soy protein concentrate (Promosoy-100)	4.0	
Isolated soy protein (Promine-D)		2.5
Corn syrup	2.0	2.0
Dextrose	2.0	2.0
Salt	2.5	2.5
Water	25.0	25.0
Spice, cure, seasonings to suit		

Imitation Bologna Formula

Ingredients		
Lean beef (90% lean)	100.0	100.0
Beef plates	80.0	80.0
Pork jowls	50.0	50.0
Beef hearts	20.0	20.0
Beef tongue trimmings	100.0	100.0
Soy protein concentrate (Promosoy-100)	17.0	
Isolated soy protein (Promine-D)		15.0
Corn syrup	10.0	10.0
Dextrose	10.0	10.0
Salt	12.0	12.0
Water	125.0	130.0
Spice, cure, seasonings to suit		

Procedure

1. Chop lean meats with moisture, salt, cure, and spices for about 2 min.
2. Add soy protein concentrate (Promosoy-100) or isolated soy protein (Promine-D) and chop for an additional 3 min.
3. Add fat meats and complete chop.
4. Stuff and cook using usual cooking procedures.
5. Product should be chilled and held under refrigeration through storage and marketing.

SOURCE: Central Soya Co., Chemurgy Division, 1825 N. Laramie St., Chicago, Ill.

HIGH GRADE FRANKFURTER USING NONFAT DRY MILK

Make up this cure:

	Lb	Oz
Sodium nitrate	3	7
Sodium nitrite		5
Dextrose (corn sugar)	10	

Place ingredients in a 5-gal. glass container. Fill with water and dissolve. Use 1 qt (2¾ lb) of solution with each 100 lb of meat.

Ingredients	Lb	Oz
Veal trimmings	45	
Bullmeat	20	
Regular pork trimmings	35	

Nonfat dry milk	4½	
Salt	3	
Cure	2¾	
White pepper		7
Mace		2
Ground Mustard		4
Onion powder		1
Garlic		¼
Paprika		2
Moisture	36	

Stuff into cellulose casings.

Processing Data

144	lb:	Weight in smoke (1¾ hr; 130°–175°F)
134½	lb:	Weight out smoke in cook
6½	%	of smoke loss
137¼	lb:	Weight out cook
2	%	cook gain
131	lb:	Weight next morning
9	%	of processing and cooler loss

SOURCE: American Dry Milk Institute, 130 N. Franklin, Chicago, Ill.

FRANKFURTER
USING SOY PROTEIN CONCENTRATE

	Formulations		
	No. 1	No. 2	No. 3 (Imitation)
Ingredients	Lb	Lb	Lb
Lean beef (90% lean)	55.0		100.0
Beef plates		35.0	80.0
Pork jowls	45.0		50.0
Pork stomachs		28.0	
Pork or beef hearts		27.0	
Beef hearts			20.0
Pork backfat		10.0	
Beef tongue trimmings			100.0
Soy protein concentrate (Promosoy-100)	4.0	4.0	17.0
Corn syrup	2.0	2.0	10.0
Dextrose	2.0	2.0	10.0
Salt	2.5	2.5	12.0
Water	35.0	30.0	135.0

Spice, cure, seasonings to suit

Procedure

1. Chop lean meats with moisture, salt, cure, and spices for about 2 min.

2. Add soy protein concentrate (Promosoy-100) and chop for an additional 3 min.

3. Add fat meats and complete chop.

4. Stuff and cook using usual cooking procedures.

5. Product should be chilled and held under refrigeration through storage and marketing.

SOURCE: Central Soya Co., Chemurgy Division, 1825 N. Laramie St., Chicago, Ill.

HOT DOGS EXTENDED WITH TEXTURED VEGETABLE PROTEIN

Ingredients	%
Beef chuck (12% fat)	19.33
Pork trimmings (50% fat)	34.00
Ice	13.00
Water	23.00
Textured vegetable protein (Supro 50$_{TM}$, minced)	5.00
Savortex (available from Western Dairy Products, San Francisco)	3.50
Salt	1.90
Wiener spice No. 2553 (available from Stange Co., Chicago)	0.02
Prague Powder (available from Griffith Laboratories, Chicago)	0.25
	100.00

Procedure

1. Hydrate the textured vegetable protein (Supro 50$_{TM}$) with 50% of the water.

2. Disperse all ingredients except for the pork trimmings and remaining 50% of the water as evenly as possible around the bowl of the silent cutter.

3. Chop for 5 revolutions.

4. Add the remainder of the ingredients and chop an additional 30 revolutions. Final product temperature 50°–55°F.

5. Stuff, link, and smoke the hot dogs using a 1¾ hr cycle in the smokehouse.

Note: Final product: 13% protein, 24% fat.

SOURCE: Ralston Purina Company, Checkerboard Square, St. Louis, Mo.

SKINLESS FRANKFURTERS USING NONFAT DRY MILK

Make up this cure:

	Lb	Oz
Sodium nitrate	3	7
Sodium nitrite		5
Dextrose (corn sugar)	10	

Place ingredients in a 5-gal. glass container. Fill with water and dissolve. Use 1 qt (2¾ lb) of solution for each 100 lb of meat.

Ingredients	Lb	Oz
Veal trimmings	20	
Beef trimmings	15	
Bullmeat	30	
Pork cheeks	35	
Nonfat dry milk	5	
Salt	3	
Cure	$2^3/4$	
Pepper		7
Mace		2
Ground mustard		3
Onion powder		1
Garlic powder		$^1/4$

Procedure

This formula will give approximately 141 lb of finished, skinned product. It may vary a pound either way, depending upon the condition of the meats and the amount of moisture added.

This formula can be used for sheep casing frankfurters with good results.

SOURCE: American Dry Milk Institute, 130 N. Franklin, Chicago, Ill.

SKINLESS CHEESEFURTERS USING NONFAT DRY MILK

Make up this cure:

	Lb	Oz
Sodium nitrate	3	7
Sodium nitrite		5
Dextrose (corn sugar)	10	

Place ingredients in a 5-gal. glass container. Fill with water and dissolve. Use 1 qt ($2^3/4$ lb) of solution for each 100 lb of meat.

Ingredients	Lb	Oz
Beef trimmings	35	
Veal trimmings	25	
Regular pork trimmings	25	
American process cheese	15	
Nonfat dry milk	5	
Salt	$2^1/2$	
Fresh onions	3	
Ground white pepper		6
Ground mustard		3
Fresh garlic		2
Cure	$2^3/4$	
Chopped ice		

Procedure

Grind beef, onions and veal through $^1/8$-in. plate, pork through $^3/8$-in. plate, and cut cheese into 1-in. pieces. Chop garlic fine and mix with cure.

Place beef in silent cutter. Add a little ice, salt,

and cure. Chop a few revolutions. Add ice and nonfat dry milk alternately a little at a time until all nonfat dry milk is used. Then add veal, cheese, pork, seasoning, and enough chopped ice to make emulsion of the same consistency as for frankfurters. Stuff into 29–32 in. cellulose casings, making 5-in. links.

Smoke and cook same as frankfurters.

SOURCE: American Dry Milk Institute, 130 N. Franklin, Chicago, Ill.

COOKED SALAMI (SALAMI COTTO)

Use any of these meat combinations:

	No. 1 Lb	No. 2 Lb	No. 3 Lb
Lean beef (carcass)	150	300	150
Extra lean pork trimmings	175		
Regular pork trimmings 50/50	175	200	
Pork cheeks, trimmed			100
Beef cheeks, trimmed			150
Backfat			100

with these ingredients

	Lb	Oz
Salt	15	
Sodium nitrite		$1^1/4$
Sodium nitrate		5
Sodium erythorbate		$4^1/3$
Black pepper, 60 mesh	1	4
Cane sugar	1	4
Ground nutmeg		5
Ground allspice		$2^1/2$
Ground Jamaica ginger		$2^1/2$
Ground caraway seed		1
Garlic powder (optional)		$2^1/2$–5
Cracked black pepper		7
Ice, chopped		10–15

Processing Procedure

Grind chilled beef items through the $^3/16$-in. plate of the grinder, all pork items except backfat through the $^1/4$ in. plate. Take 75 lb of ground beef (or 35 lb of beef and 45 lb of beef cheeks if used), transfer to the chopper, add 10–15% of the ice and 3 lb of salt and chop to obtain a fine emulsion.

If backfat is used chill it to 27°F in the freezer, then cut into 3-in. wide strips and slice strips $^1/4$-in. thick on a slicing machine; just before finishing the emulsion in the chopper, add sliced backfat and let machine run until the fat is chopped up to $^1/4$-in. size particles.

Transfer meat emulsion to the mixer, add ground

pork, the remaining ground beef, salt (minus the 3 lb used for the emulsion) previously mixed with the remainder of the ingredients and mix for 3 min.

Dump meat in a meat truck and transfer to cooler at 38°–40°F for overnight cure.

Remove meat from cooler and remix in the vacuum mixer under 27 in. of vacuum just long enough to make the meat pliable for stuffing (this takes approximately 1–1½ min).

Stuff material into 2¾–3 × 20 in. or 1⅞ × 11 high-stretch cellulose casings as desired. Hang sausages on smokehouse trees and transfer to the smokehouse.

Smoking.—Preheat house to a temperature of 135°F with dampers wide open until casings are dry, then apply smoke, adjust dampers ¼ open and gradually raise temperature to 150°F. Keep sausages at this temperature until fully cured and the desired color is developed.

Cut off smoke, raise temperature to 175°–180°F and keep at this temperature until an internal sausage temperature of 155°F is obtained.

Remove sausages from the house and shower with cold water until an internal sausage temperature of 120°F is obtained.

Keep sausages at room temperature until casings dry, then transfer to holding cooler (45°F) until internal temperature of sausages drops to 50°F before packaging and shipping. Product should be kept refrigerated through storage and marketing.

SOURCE: Stephan L. Komarik, 4810 Ronda, Coral Gables, Florida.

COOKED SALAMI COTTO (PERISHABLE)
FINEST QUALITY COOKED SALAMI IN 3- OR 6-LB CANS

Ingredients	Lb	Oz
Lean boneless beef (canner cutter grade)	150	
Extra lean pork trimmings	175	
Regular pork trimmings	175	
Salt	15	
Cane sugar	1	4
Sodium nitrite		1¼
Sodium nitrate		5
Sodium erythorbate		4⅓
Black pepper, 60 mesh	1	4
Ground nutmeg		5
Ground allspice		2½
Ground Jamaica ginger		2½
Ground caraway seed		1
Garlic powder (optional)		5–10
Cracked black pepper (optional)		7
Ice, chopped	60	

Processing Procedure

Grind 75 lb of chilled beef through the 3/16-in. plate, and remaining 75 lb of beef and pork through ¼-in. plate. Transfer the 3/16-in. ground beef to the chopper, and add 30 lb of ice, 3 lb salt, ¼ oz sodium nitrite, 1 oz sodium nitrate, ⅞ oz sodium erythorbate, previously mixed, and chop for 3 min. Add remaining ice and chop 3 min. Transfer emulsion to the mixer; add ground pork and the rest of the ingredients (part of it used in the emulsion) and mix for 2–3 min. Dump mixture into meat truck and transfer to cooler at a temperature of 38°–40°F for overnight cure.

Next day, remove from cooler, place in the vacuum mixer and, under 27 in. vacuum, mix for 1 min to make meat pliable for stuffing.

Stuffing.—Stuff meat in 3- or 6-lb oblong parchment-lined cans and close under 27 in. vacuum.

Process.—3½ hr at 160°F water temperature.

Chill.—2 hr in iced water before transferring to chill room at 34°–36°F for final chilling.

Hold product under refrigerated temperatures through storage and marketing.

SOURCE: Stephan L. Komarik, 4810 Ronda, Coral Gables, Florida.

SALAMI COTTO
USING NONFAT DRY MILK

Make up this cure:

	Lb	Oz
Sodium nitrate	3	7
Sodium nitrite		5
Dextrose (corn sugar)	10	

Place ingredients in a 5-gal. glass container. Fill with water and dissolve. Use 1 qt (2¾ lb) of solution for each 100 lb of meat.

Ingredients	Lb	Oz
Boneless chuck	60	
Pork cheek meat	25	
Regular pork trimmings	15	
Nonfat dry milk	4¾	
Salt	3	
Fresh garlic		3
Ground black pepper		7
Ground cardamom		2
Cold water	6	
Cure	2¾	

Procedure

Grind chucks through ⅛-in. plate and pork through ⅜-in. plate. Chop garlic fine and mix with cure.

Place all meats in mixer. Add salt, cure, and water. Sprinkle with nonfat dry milk and seasoning and mix well.

Stuff into beef cap ends or corresponding size cellulose casings. Hang in cooler at 38°–40°F for 48 hr. Place in smokehouse. Start at 120°F and gradually increase heat to 170°F at the end of 7 hr. Maintain this heat for 30 min. Then place under hot shower to rinse off grease. Give cold shower and keep in sausage room temperature until dry.

SOURCE: American Dry Milk Institute, 130 N. Franklin, Chicago, Ill.

KOSHER AND KOSHER-STYLE SALAMI

Use any of these meat combinations:

	Kosher	Kosher-Style	
		No. 1	No. 2
	Lb	Lb	Lb
Kosher beef chucks	300		
Kosher steer plates	200		
Cow meat		300	200
Steer plates		200	200
Beef cheeks, trimmed			100

with these ingredients

	Lb	Oz
Salt	15	
Cane sugar	1	4
Sodium nitrite		1¼
Sodium nitrate		5
Sodium erythorbate		4³⁄₈
Ground black pepper, 60 mesh		4
Ground Jamaica ginger		8
Ground Spanish paprika		10
Ground nutmeg		8
Ground allspice		2½
Garlic powder		1³⁄₄

Processing Procedure

Use well-chilled meats (32°–34°F). Premix salt with cures and other dry ingredients. Grind beef and beef cheeks through ⅛-in. plate and steer plates through 1-in. plate of the grinder.

Transfer ground meats to the mixer, add salt-cure mixture and mix for 2–3 min. Dump into truck and transfer to cooler at 38°–40°F for overnight cure. Remove from cooler, regrind meat through ³⁄₁₆-in. plate of the grinder.

If a rapid meat chopper is used, first grind meats as indicated above and fill chopper bowl ½ full; add salt-cure mixture and chop until fat particles are reduced to the desired size.

Dump meat in truck and transfer to cooler at 38°–40°F for overnight cure. Next day remix meat under 25 in. of vacuum just long enough

to make meat pliable for stuffing. Stuff into 3 × 24 in. fibrous casings or no-stretch Cellophane casings for chubs.

Smoking.—Transfer sausages to a preheated house at a temperature of 130°–135°F with dampers wide open and hold at this temperature until the casings are dry. Adjust dampers to ¼ open and introduce heavy smudge. Raise temperature to 140°F for 1 hr, then gradually to 160°F for another hour. Cut off smoke, then raise temperature to 175°F and hold until an internal meat temperature of 152°F is obtained.

Remove sausages from the house and shower under cold water to an internal meat temperature of 110°F. Hold sausages at room temperature until casings are dry. Then transfer to cooler (45°F) until internal meat temperature is reduced to 50°F before packaging and shipping.

Keep this product at refrigerated temperatures through storage and marketing.

SOURCE: Stephan L. Komarik, 4810 Ronda, Coral Gables, Florida.

MINCED HAM

Ingredients	Lb	Oz
Lean boneless beef	125	
Regular pork trimmings 50/50	100	
Pork hearts, trimmed	100	
Pork tongues, trimmed	75	
Pork cheek meat, trimmed	100	
Salt	15	
Cane sugar	5	
Ground black pepper or dry soluble pepper		1
Sodium erythorbate		4¹⁄₃
Sodium nitrate		5
Sodium nitrite		1¼
Ground nutmeg or mace		5
Ground allspice		2½
Ground Jamaica ginger		2½
Ground caraway seed		1
Ice, chopped	25	

Processing Procedure

Remove sinews and blood clots and chill all meats (32°–34°F) before processing.

Grinding and Chopping.—Grind lean beef through ⅛-in. plate of the grinder, regular pork trimmings and pork cheeks through the ¼-in. plate, and pork hearts and trimmed boneless pork tongues through the ⅛-in. plate. Transfer 100 lb of the ground beef to the chopper; add 3 lb salt previously mixed with ¼ oz sodium nitrite, 1 oz sodium nitrate, ⅞ oz sodium erythorbate, and 1 lb of cane sugar evenly over top of meat. Start chopper and after a few revolutions of the bowl, add 25 lb of chopped ice and chop 5 min. Transfer meat emulsion to the vacuum mixer, add the remaining beef and other ingredients, including the seasonings; mix under 25 in. vacuum for 3 min. Dump mixed meats into truck and transfer to chill room at 34°–36°F for overnight cure. Next day remix meat under 25 in. vacuum, just long enough (1 min) to make meat pliable for stuffing.

Stuff, Smoke, and Cook.—Stuff material in beef bungs, bladders, or jumbo or smaller diameter artificial casings; fill to the maximum of their capacity. Minced ham also can be stuffed in 4 × 4 × 24 in. or 2 DS molds equipped with pressure springs. In this case, follow the stuffing and cooking instructions outlined for **New England Pressed Ham** formula in Section 3.

For Artificial Casings.—Hang properly spaced sausages on smoke trees. Stockinettes should be used for jumbo minced hams to reduce breakage. Sausages stuffed in beef bungs should be wrapped with twine. Sausages stuffed in beef bladders are usually processed in wire molds before the smoking and cooking treatment. Shower sausages with cold water to remove meat particles. Those stuffed in large size casings should be placed in the chill room at a temperature of 40°–45°F until they are to be smoked. Smaller diameter sausages can be placed immediately after stuffing in the preheated smokehouse at 130°–135°F. After sausages are placed in the smokehouse, adjust dampers wide open to dry casings for 1/2–3/4 hr, then apply heavy smoke for 1 1/2 hr for 3–3 1/2 in. diameter sausages and 3 hr for 5–3/4 for jumbos. Cut off smoke, close dampers to 1/4 open position, gradually raise temperature 10° every hour to 175°–180°F until an internal meat temperature of 155°F is obtained. Remove sausages from the house and shower with fine spray of water until the internal meat temperature is reduced to 110°F. Keep sausages at this temperature at least 30 min for the smaller size and 60 min for jumbos before transferring them to chill room at 45°F for final chilling to an internal meat temperature of 50°F before packaging.

For Natural Casings.—Minced hams in natural casings should be smoked according to the following schedule, and cooked in the Jordan cooker or in a steam chamber: Preheat house to 130°–135°F with dampers wide open, until casings are dry. This takes approximately 30–45 min. Apply heavy smoke for 3 hr at 135°F. Cut off smoke, adjust dampers 1/4 open, and gradually raise temperature to 160°–165°F until an internal meat temperature of 135°F is obtained. Transfer sausages immediately to a steam house or Jordan cooker at 165°F until an internal meat temperature of 150°F is obtained. Remove sausages from the cookers and

shower them with a spray of cold water until the internal temperature is reduced to 110°F. Keep sausages at room temperature until casings are dry, then transfer them to the chill room (45°F) for final chilling before packaging and shipping.

Hold product under refrigeration through storage and marketing.

SOURCE: Stephan L. Komarik, 4810 Ronda, Coral Gables, Florida.

ALL MEAT SMOKED SAUSAGE

Use any of these meat combinations:

	No. 1 Lb	No. 2 Lb	No. 3 Lb
Lean beef trimmings	150	150	150
Regular pork trimmings	200	200	200
Pork cheek meat, trimmed	150		
Pork hearts, trimmed		150	
Pork tongues, trimmed			150

with these ingredients:

	Lb	Oz
Ice, chopped	50	
Salt	12	8
Corn sugar	1	4
Sodium nitrite		1 1/4
Sodium erythorbate		4 1/3
Select type of seasoning formula given in Table 2.1		

Processing Procedure

Hearts should be free of blood clots; remove arteries, gullets, and bones from tongues.

Grind chilled beef trimmings through 1/8-in. plate of the grinder, then transfer to the chopper; add salt, previously mixed with cure and other dry ingredients, followed by the ice; chop to an emulsion (for approximately 2 min).

Grind remainder of the meat through 3/16-in. plate of the grinder. Transfer chopped and ground meats to the mechanical mixer and mix for 2–3 min.

Dump meat into a meat truck and transfer to cooler at 35°–36°F for overnight cure.

Next day, put meat in a vacuum mixer and, under 27 in. of vacuum, mix for 1 min, just long enough to make meat pliable for stuffing. Stuff in 28–32 mm hog casings and link to the desired length. Hang links, properly spaced, on smokehouse trees.

Smoking Procedure.—Transfer sausages to a preheated house at 110°–115°F with vent wide open to dry surface of the sausages. This takes approximately 20 min in a well-ventilated house. Then adjust vents to 1/4 open, introduce heavy smudge, and gradually raise temperature to 140°F. Hold at this temperature until the proper cured color is obtained in the center of the sausages. Stop smoking. Raise temperature to 160°–165°F and maintain this temperature until an internal meat temperature of 135°F is obtained. Introduce live steam in the house until an internal meat temperature of 152°F is reached. In case a steam cooker is used: then, transfer sausages immediately from the smokehouse to the steam cooker; cook sausages to an internal temperature of 152°F. After cooking, shower sausages with cold water until internal meat temperature is reduced to 110°F. Hold sausages at room temperature until the casings are dry. Transfer trees to a chill room (45°F) and do not package sausages until the internal meat temperature is 50°F or lower.

Product should be held under refrigeration through storage and marketing.

SOURCE: Stephan L. Komarik, 4810 Ronda, Coral Gables, Florida.

SMOKED LINK SAUSAGE WITH 3½% CEREAL AND NONFAT DRY MILK ADDED

Use any of these meat combinations:

	No. 1 Lb	No. 2 Lb	No. 3 Lb
Lean beef trimmings	125	125	125
Regular pork trimmings 50/50	125	125	125
Beef tripe, white, treated	125	125	125
Pork cheek meat	125		
Pork hearts		125	
Pork tongues			125

with these ingredients:

	Lb	Oz
Semolina flour	10	
Nonfat dry milk	10	
Salt	12	8
Corn sugar	1	4
Sodium nitrite		1¼
Sodium erythorbate		4⅓
Ice, chopped	75	

Select type of seasoning formula given in Table 2.1

Processing Procedure

Hearts should be free of blood clots, with arteries removed and gullets and bones removed from the tongue. Grind chilled beef trimmings through the ⅛-in. plate of the grinder; transfer to the meat chopper, add salt (previously mixed with the seasonings), sugar, sodium nitrite and sodium erythorbate followed by ice, flour, and nonfat dry milk. Chop material to an emulsion. This takes approximately 2 min. Grind remainder of the meats through 3/16-in. plate of the grinder. Transfer beef emulsion and ground meat to the mechanical mixer and mix for 2 min. Dump mixture into meat truck, transfer to cooler at 35°–36°F for overnight cure. Next morning, put cured meat in a vacuum mixer and, under 27 in. of vacuum, mix for 1 min, just long enough to make the meat pliable for stuffing.

Stuff in 28–32 min hog casings and link to the desired length. Hang on properly spaced smokehouse trees.

Smoking Procedure.—Transfer sausages to a preheated house at a temperature of 110°–115°F with vents wide open to dry the surface of the sausages which takes about 20 min in a well-ventilated house. Then adjust vents partially open, introduce heavy smudge, and gradually raise temperature of the house to 140°F. Hold at this temperature until the proper cured color is obtained in the center of the sausages. Stop smoking. Raise temperature to 160°–165°F and maintain temperature until an internal meat temperature of 135°F is obtained. Introduce live steam in the house and keep sausages in the house until an internal meat temperature of 152°F is reached. In case a steam cooker is used: transfer sausages immediately from the smokehouse to the steam cooker and cook to an internal temperature of 152°F.

After the cooking process, shower sausages with cold water until internal meat temperature is reduced to 110°F. Hold sausages at room temperature until the casings are dry. Transfer trees to a chill room (45°F). Do not package sausages until an internal meat temperature of at least 50°F is obtained.

Product should be held under refrigeration through storage and marketing.

SOURCE: Stephan L. Komarik, 4810 Ronda, Coral Gables, Florida.

"SMOKIES" PORK SAUSAGE

Ingredients	Lb	Oz
Pork shank meat or picnics (trimmed)	150	
Lean pork trimmings	100	
Regular pork trimmings 50/50	200	
Ice, crushed	50	
Salt	12	8
Dry soluble pepper	1	4
Monosodium glutamate		5
Sodium nitrate		5

Sodium nitrite		$1\frac{1}{4}$
Sodium erythorbate		$4\frac{1}{3}$
Corn syrup solids	5	

Processing Procedure

All trimmings must be free of blood clots, sinews and skins.

Grind well-chilled, shank meat through the $\frac{1}{8}$-in. plate of the grinder, and the trimmings through the $\frac{3}{16}$-in. plate.

Place ground shank meat into the meat chopper and with three pounds of the salt, $\frac{1}{4}$ oz sodium nitrite, 1 oz sodium nitrate, and 50 lb of crushed ice, chop into a fine emulsion. Transfer emulsion to the mechanical mixer, add ground pork trimmings, and remaining salt, previously mixed with the remainder of the ingredients. Mix for 3 min. Dump mixed meat into a truck and transfer to the cooler at 36°-38°F for overnight cure. Next day, remix meat in a vacuum mixer under 27 in. vacuum just long enough to make meat pliable for stuffing (approximately 1-2 min).

Pack tightly in the stuffer (avoid air pockets) and stuff into Cellophane casings, size 22-32 mm, and link in 4-in. lengths.

Smoking.—After stuffing, hang sausages on smokehouse trees (properly spaced) and keep them at room temperature until casings are dry. Transfer to preheated house at a temperature of 120°F with 90% RH. Apply heavy smudge and smoke sausages for 1 hr.

Raise temperature to 130°F with 70% RH for $1\frac{1}{2}$ hr; then increase temperature to 150°F for $\frac{1}{2}$ hour. Raise house temperature to 170°F until an internal meat temperature of 152°F is obtained. Introduce live steam in the house for 1-2 min. Remove sausages from the house. Heavy smudge should be applied all during the smoking operation. Remove sausages from the house and shower with cold water until internal meat temperature is reduced to 110°F. Keep at room temperature until casings are dry, then transfer to cooler (45°F) until an internal meat temperature of 50°F is reached. Peel and package.

Keep product refrigerated through storage and marketing.

SOURCE: Stephan L. Komarik, 4810 Ronda, Coral Gables, Florida.

NEW ENGLAND STYLE SMOKED SAUSAGES

Ingredients	Lb	Oz
Boneless, skinless, defatted picnics	375	
Lean beef trimmings (cow meat)	125	
Salt	12	8
Corn syrup solids	5	
Sodium nitrate	5	
Sodium nitrite	$1\frac{1}{4}$	
Sodium erythorbate	$4\frac{1}{3}$	
Dry soluble pepper or ground white pepper	10	
Ground Jamaica ginger	1	
Ground nutmeg or mace	1	
Ground allspice	$\frac{1}{2}$	
Ice, chopped	35	

Processing Procedure

All meats should be chilled to 32°-34°F before processing. Remove sinews and blood clots.

Grinding and Chopping.—Grind lean beef through $\frac{1}{8}$-in. plate of the grinder, lean defatted picnics through the 1- or $1\frac{1}{2}$-in. plate. Place ground beef in the chopper and add $2\frac{1}{2}$ lb salt, $\frac{1}{4}$ oz sodium nitrate, 1 lb of corn syrup solids, and $\frac{7}{8}$ oz erythorbate, then add chopped ice and chop for 5 min. Transfer meat emulsion to the vacuum mixer, add ground pork along with the remaining dry ingredients and seasoning, and mix for 3 min under 25 in. vacuum. Dump mixed meat into a meat truck and transfer to the cooler at 34°-36°F for 24 hr cure. Next day transfer cured meat to the vacuum mixer and mix for 3 min under 25 in. vacuum.

Stuff, Smoke, and Cook.—Avoid creating air pockets when loading stuffer. Stuff material tightly into artificial casings or beef bungs to the maximum of their capacity.

The use of stockinettes for jumbo size sausages is suggested in order to reduce breakage, sausages stuffed in beef bungs should be wrapped with twine. Shower sausages to remove meat particles, then place in the chill room at a temperature of 40°-45°F until they are smoked.

Transfer Cellophane-encased sausages to a preheated house at a temperature of 130°-135°F, adjust dampers wide open, to dry casings for $\frac{1}{2}$-$\frac{3}{4}$ hr, then smoke 3-$3\frac{1}{2}$ in. sausages for $1\frac{1}{2}$ hr and 5-$\frac{3}{4}$ in. jumbos for 3 hr. Discontinue smoking, close dampers to $\frac{1}{4}$ open, and gradually raise temperature 10° every hour to 175°-180°F, until an internal meat temperature of 155°F is obtained. Remove sausages from the smokehouse, and shower with a fine spray of cold water until the internal meat temperature is reduced to 110°F.

Keep smaller sausages at room temperature for at least 30 min and jumbos for 60 min before transferring to chill room (45°F) for final chilling to an internal meat temperature of 50°F before shipping.

Sausages stuffed in beef bungs should be smoked on the following schedule: Preheat smokehouse to 130°-135°F, with dampers wide open, for 45 min in order to dry casings, then apply heavy smoke for 3 hr at 135°F. Cut off smoke, adjust dampers ¼ open, and gradually raise temperature to 165°F until internal meat temperature of 135°F is obtained. Transfer sausages immediately to a steam house or Jordan cooker at 165°F and cook until an internal meat temperature of 150°F is obtained. After removing the sausages from the cooker, spray, prechill, and dry as described above.

Product should be kept refrigerated through storage and marketing.

SOURCE: Stephan L. Komarik, 4810 Ronda, Coral Gables, Florida.

SMOKED ITALIAN-STYLE HOT OR MILD SAUSAGE

Use either of these meat combinations:

	No. 1 Lb	No. 2 Lb
Regular pork trimmings 50/50	75	75
Lean beef trimmings		25
Extra lean pork trimmings	25	

with these ingredients:

	Lb	Oz
Salt	2	8
Corn syrup solids	2	
Ice, chopped	15	
Sodium nitrite		¼
Sodium nitrate		1
Sodium erythorbate		⅞
Garlic powder (optional)		⅛

For Hot Italian-Style.—Use the following seasoning ingredients:

	Oz
Ground red pepper	2
Ground caraway seed	½
Ground coriander	1
Ground nutmeg	½
Whole fennel seeds	1
Cracked black pepper	2½

For Mild Italian-Style.—Use the following seasoning ingredients:

	Oz
Spanish paprika	1
Ground fennel seeds	¾
Whole fennel seeds	1
Ground black pepper, 14 mesh	2½

Processing Procedure

Grind beef trimmings or extra lean pork trimmings (blade meat, shanks, or defatted picnics), chilled to 32°–34°F, through the ⅛-in. plate, and grind regular pork trimmings through the ¾-in. plate of the grinder.

Chopping.—Put lean beef or pork in the chopper; add salt (previously mixed with cure and rest of the dry ingredients) and chopped ice; chop approximately 2 min for a medium fine emulsion.

Mixing.—Transfer chopped and other ground meats to a vacuum mixer; mix for 2–3 min under 27 in. vacuum.

Stuffing.—Stuff material in wide hog casings and link to the desired length. Hang properly spaced sausages on smoke trees.

Smoking Procedure.—Put sausages for approximately 30 min in a preheated smokehouse at 110°–115°F, with vents wide open to dry surface of the sausages. Then adjust vents ¼ open and introduce heavy smoke. Gradually raise the temperature to 140°F and keep at this temperature until proper color is obtained in the center of the sausages. This will take 2–3 hr. Raise temperature to 165°–170°F and maintain this temperature until an internal meat temperature of 152°F is reached. Introduce live steam in the smokehouse and keep sausages under steam for 1–2 min.

Cooking in Steam House or Jordan Cooker.—If sausages are cooked in steam house or Jordan cooker: remove sausages from the smokehouse when they reach an internal temperature of 135°F. Transfer sausages to the steam house or Jordan cooker at 160°F and maintain this temperature until an internal meat temperature of 152°F is obtained. In either case (finishing sausages in the smokehouse or cooking them with steam), shower sausages with cold water until internal meat temperature is reduced to 110°F. Hold sausages at room temperature until casings are dry. Transfer smoke trees to chill room (45°F) and do not package sausage until an internal meat temperature of 50°F or lower is obtained.

Product should be kept refrigerated through storage and marketing.

SOURCE: Stephan L. Komarik, 4810 Ronda, Coral Gables, Florida.

ALL MEAT POLISH SAUSAGE

Use either of these meat combinations:

	No. 1 Lb	No. 2 Lb
Regular pork trimmings 50/50	150	150
Pork cheeks, trimmed	200	100

Pork head meat		50
Beef trimmings, lean	75	125
Beef cheeks, trimmed	75	75

with these ingredients:

	Lb	Oz
Salt	12	8
Corn syrup solids	10	
Sodium nitrite		$1^1/_4$
Sodium erythorbate		$4^1/_3$
Ice, chopped	45	

and either of these seasonings:

	Lb	Oz	Cc
Ground black pepper	1	4	
Ground nutmeg		10	
Ground coriander		10	
Ground Jamaica ginger		15	
Ground caraway seed		10	
Garlic powder		10	

or

	Lb	Oz	Cc
Dry soluble pepper	1	4	
Oil of nutmeg			3.40
Oil of coriander			0.44
Oil of caraway			1.84
Oil of ginger			3.45
Garlic powder		10	

Processing Procedure

Grind chilled beef trimmings and beef cheeks through the $^1/_8$-in. plate of the grinder and grind pork items through the $^3/_8$-in. plate.

Transfer ground beef to the chopper, add salt (previously mixed with the seasonings, cure, sodium erythorbate, and corn syrup solids) and ice; chop to a medium fine emulsion. Transfer beef emulsion and ground pork to a vacuum mixer, and, under 27 in. vacuum, mix for 3 min. Transfer mixture to the stuffer. For ring Polish sausage, stuff into "export" wide beef rounds. For link sausage stuff in 32-35 mm hog casings and link to the desired length.

Smoking Procedure.—After stuffing, hang sausages on properly spaced smokehouse trees and place in a preheated house at 110°-115°F with vents wide open to dry surface of the sausages. This will take approximately 15-20 min for the link and 30 min for beef round-encased sausages; then adjust vents partially open and introduce heavy smudge.

Gradually raise the temperature of the house to 140°F. Hold at this temperature until the proper cured color is obtained in the center of the sausages. Raise temperature to 165°-170°F and maintain this temperature until an internal meat temper-

ature of 152°F is obtained. Introduce live steam in the house and keep sausages under steam for 1-2 min.

In case a steam cooker is used: after sausages are removed from the smokehouse, transfer immediately to the steam cooker and steam for 1-2 min.

After the cooking process, shower sausages with cold water until internal meat temperature is reduced to at least 110°F. Hold sausages at room temperature until casings are dry. Transfer trees to chill room (45°F) and do not package sausages until an internal meat temperature of 50°F or lower is reached.

Sausages should be kept refrigerated through storage and marketing.

SOURCE: Stephan L. Komarik, 4810 Ronda, Coral Gables, Florida.

POLISH SAUSAGE IN VINEGAR PICKLE

All meat Polish Sausages in links as prepared in the above formula may be used for this unusual version of a popular European-type sausage product.

Sausages must be thoroughly smoked and dried before pickling. Also, be sure that sausages are not exposed too long to a humid atmosphere during filling of the jars and that no air pockets are left between the sausages after the jars are filled with vinegar pickle.

Place thoroughly smoked and dried sausages in wood or stainless steel containers and cover them with a 35-grain vinegar; let stand overnight. This first step is very important. Sausages will release some water-soluble materials during this immersion in vinegar which otherwise would be released in the vinegar pickle in the jars causing cloudiness and bottom sediment which would be undesirable when the product is displayed for sale.

After overnight immersion in the vinegar, remove sausages and pack them in jars of suitable size. Fill jars to capacity with the following 45-grain vinegar pickle:

To each 100 gal. of 45-grain vinegar add 10 lb salt, 5 oz ascorbic acid, and 5 cc oil of tarragon (optional).

Fill jars to capacity with the vinegar pickle and close. Hold under refrigeration.

SOURCE: Stephan L. Komarik, 4810 Ronda, Coral Gables, Florida.

POLISH SAUSAGE CONTAINING $3^1/_2$% CEREAL AND NONFAT DRY MILK

Use the same formula and procedure as outlined above for **All Meat Polish Sausage** with the following exceptions:

When making the beef emuslion, add to the

chopper 10 lb of semolina flour and 10 lb of non-fat dry milk. Instead of using 45 lb of chopped ice in the formula, increase the amount of ice to 65 lb. The smoking procedure is identical.

SOURCE: Stephan L. Komarik, 4810 Ronda, Coral Gables, Florida.

POLISH STYLE SAUSAGE WITH TEXTURED SOY PROTEIN

Ingredients		Lb	Oz
Boneless chuck	⎫	30	
Pork cheeks	⎪	20	
Lean pork trimmings	⎬ Cured	20	
Regular pork trimmings	⎪	20	
Lean boneless picnics	⎭	10	
Swift's food Protein (S.F.P.)		3½	
Fresh onions		2	
Salt			8
Ground black pepper			7
Ground mace			2
Ground coriander			2
Fresh garlic			5
Chopped ice		23	

Procedure

Grind chucks and onions through ⅛-in. plate. Grind other meat products separately through ⅜-in. plate. Chop garlic fine and mix with salt. Place boneless chucks in silent cutter, add food protein (S.F.P.), and chopped ice alternately until all the S.F.P. is used and all of the chopped ice is incorporated in the emulsion.

Put pork meats into mixer. Add beef emulsion and seasonings; mix thoroughly. Stuff into appropriate cellulose casings or beef middles.

Place in smokehouse, starting at 125°F, gradually raising temperature to 170°F. Smoke to desired color. Cook to internal meat temperature of 152°–155°F. Shower with cold water to internal meat temperature of 90°F. When dry, store in cooler at 26°–38°F. Keep refrigerated through marketing channels.

SOURCE: Swift Edible Oil Co., Vegetable Protein Products Div., 115 W. Jackson Blvd., Chicago, Ill.

POLISH-STYLE SAUSAGE USING NONFAT DRY MILK

The following cured meat products will be needed:

	Lb
Boneless chuck	40
Lean pork trimmings	20
Pork cheek meat	20
Regular pork trimmings	20

with these ingredients:

	Lb	Oz
Nonfat dry milk	4½	
Fresh onions	2	
Salt		8
Ground black pepper		7
Ground mace		2
Ground coriander		2
Fresh garlic		5
Chopped ice	20	

Procedure

Grind chucks and onions through ⅛-in. plate. Grind the other meat products separately through ⅜-in. plate. Chop garlic fine and mix with salt.

Place boneless chuck in silent cutter, add chopped ice and nonfat dry milk alternately, a little at a time, until all nonfat dry milk is used. Approximately 20 lb of chopped ice may be incorporated.

Put pork meats into mixer. Add beef emulsion and seasoning and mix thoroughly. Stuff into beef middles or corresponding size cellulose casings.

Place in smokehouse; start with 120°F and gradually raise temperature to 170°F. Smoke until desired color appears. Cook at 160°–165°F. The internal temperature should reach 155°F. Spray with or immerse in cold water. Enough heat should be left in sausage so that it will dry. When dry and cool, place in cooler.

SOURCE: American Dry Milk Institute, 130 N. Franklin, Chicago, Ill.

BLOOD SAUSAGE

Use any of these precooked meat combinations:

	No. 1 Lb	No. 2 Lb	No. 3 Lb	No. 4 Lb
Pigskins, closely defatted	125	75	100	75
Pork tongues, cured	100	150	200	
Pork jowls, cured	100		100	100
Pork snouts, cured	125	150		100
Backfat, cured		50		
Beef shank meat, cured				125
Beef blood, cured	50	75	100	100

with these ingredients:

	Lb	Oz
Salt	7	8
Fresh onions	5	
Sodium nitrate		2½
Sodium nitrite		½
Sodium erythorbate		4⅓
Dry soluble pepper	1	

Ground marjoram	8
Ground cloves	2
Ground mace	2
Ground thyme	2
Ground caraway seed	1

Cure Pork Tongues

Trim and carefully wash tongues.

Prepare the following curing solution: 50 gal. water, 68 lb salt, 12 oz sodium nitrite, and 15 lb sugar.

Put pork tongues in a barrel, cover with the above pickle and cure for 3-4 days. Remove tongues from pickle and wash thoroughly.

Cure Beef Blood

Use only defibrinated red beef blood. (Pork blood is not permitted by U.S. regulations.) To each gallon of blood, add 2 oz salt and $\frac{1}{4}$ oz sodium nitrate. Stir thoroughly. Then transfer to cooler at $34°-36°F$ and cure for 1-2 days. Occasional stirring during this time is advisable. Strain cured blood before use in sausages.

Cure Beef Shank Meat

Remove connective tissues and tendons; dice into 2-in. cubes and transfer to a mechanical mixer. To each 100 lb of meat add 3 lb of salt thoroughly mixed with 1 oz of sodium nitrate and $\frac{1}{4}$ oz of sodium nitrite. Thoroughly mix salt mixture with the meat. Dump mixture into tubs or trays and cure for 24 hr in a cooler at $34°-36°F$.

Cure Pork Snouts

Carefully wash snouts; then dice into 2-in. cubes and transfer to a mechanical mixer. To each 100 lb of meat add 3 lb of salt thoroughly mixed with 1 oz sodium nitrate and $\frac{1}{4}$ oz sodium nitrite. Mix salt mixture thoroughly with meat. Dump into tubs or trays and cure for 24 hr in a cooler at $34°-36°F$.

Cure Pork Jowls or Backfat

Skin jowls or backfat (whichever is used). Use only the skin side of the backfat which has a hard texture. Chill to a temperature of $27°F$ and put through the dicing machine, cutting into $\frac{1}{4}$- or $\frac{1}{2}$-in. cubes, as trade demands. To each 100 lb of diced fat, add 3 lb of salt. Mix in salt thoroughly and transfer to cooler at $34°-36°F$. Cure for 24 hr.

Precook Meats

In steam-jacketed kettle, cook pork tongues in simmering water for 2-2$\frac{1}{2}$ hr; remove from cooking water; skin and remove gullet bones. Then cut

tongues into 4 or 5 pieces. Rinse with hot water and drain.

Cook cured beef cubes for 2 hr or until tender in simmering water.

Blanch jowl or backfat cubes in simmering water for a few minutes. (Use small mesh net wire or perforated baskets to enclose cubes.) Then rinse with hot water and drain to remove any loose fat from the surface of the cubes.

Cook pigskin (entirely clean of fat) in boiling water. Do not overcook. Skins should be tender but not mushy. If pigskin is overcooked it loses its binding ability.

Cook pork snouts until tender.

Grind, Chop, and Mix

Grind cooked pork snouts through the $\frac{1}{2}$- or 1-in. plate of the grinder.

Grind fresh onions through the $\frac{1}{4}$-in. plate.

Grind cooked pigskins through the $\frac{1}{8}$-in. plate and transfer pigskins—while still hot—to the chopper. Add onions and cured beef blood. Continue chopping until a creamy emulsion is obtained.

Transfer all prepared meat items to a meat truck and add salt which has been previously mixed with the cures and seasonings; mix thoroughly with a meat paddle. Finally, add the pigskin-blood emulsion and again mix thoroughly.

Stuff and Tie

Stuffing is done with hand scoops. Agitate meat mixture during stuffing operation so that the right proportion of ingredients goes into each sausage. Stuff into beef bungs or $4 \times 4 \times 24$ in. polyethylene-lined molds.

Tie beef bungs with twine. Also tie bags with twine that is used in the molds before molds are closed.

Cook

Transfer sausages stuffed in beef bungs to cooking vat with a water temperature of $200°-205°F$. Lower water temperature gradually to $180°F$ and maintain this temperature until an internal meat temperature of $170°F$ is obtained. This will take approximately 3$\frac{1}{2}$ hr.

The same cooking procedure is followed for sausages in molds, but cooking time will be somewhat less. Cook approximately 3 hr until an internal meat temperature of $170°F$ is obtained.

Chill

Cooling is identical for both sausages in bungs and sausages in molds.

Remove sausages from the cooking vat and chill in cold water for 2 hr. Proper circulation of the cold water is necessary in order to chill uniformly. Product in molds is transferred immediately to the chill room at 36°–38°F. But that in beef bungs is first placed horizontally (without touching one another) on rack trucks and inspected for air pockets under the casing. Prick air pockets to let entrapped air escape. Then immediately transfer trucks to chill room at 36°–38°F for at least 24 hr chilling.

Smoke Bung-Encased Sausages

Sausages encased in beef bungs are normally smoked for better appearance and keeping quality.

Place chilled sausages on wire screens and give them a cold smoke with smokehouse temperature not over 80°F and with dampers wide open. Smoke until the desired color is obtained.

After smoking, return sausages to chill room (36°–38°F) to finish chilling before shipment.

Keep Product Refrigerated

Product should be held under refrigeration through storage and marketing.

SOURCE: Stephan L. Komarik, 4810 Ronda, Coral Gables, Florida.

LIVER SAUSAGE SMOKED OR UNSMOKED

Use these precooked meat ingredients:

	Lb
Pork livers	175
Pork snouts	175
Beef tripe, treated or hog stomachs	150

with these ingredients:

	Lb	Oz
Salt	12	8
Onion powder	1	
Corn sugar	1	4
Sodium nitrite		¾

and either of these seasoning combinations:

	Lb	Oz	Cc
Ground white pepper	1	14	
Ground sage		2½	
Ground marjoram		2½	
Ground nutmeg		2½	
Ground ginger		2½	

or

	Lb	Oz	Cc
Dry soluble pepper[1]	1	14	
Oil of cloves			10.00
Oil of sage			3.00
Oil of marjoram			2.50
Oil of nutmeg			5.00
Oleoresin ginger			2.50

[1] Oils and oleoresin should be thoroughly mixed with the dry soluble pepper.

Processing Procedure

Cut 1-in. slashes in pork livers, then scald in hot water (160°F) for 3 min. Uniform size pork snouts should be selected for uniform cooking; cook approximately 1–1½ hr.

In case treated but not precooked beef tripe is used, then cook until tender.

If hog stomachs are used, after cooking until tender, remove black inside lining of the stomachs.

Without any prechill, grind all the meat items through the ⅛-in. plate of the grinder.

Transfer ground meats to the chopper add enough broth from the pork snouts to bring up weight of the raw material to 500 lb; add salt, previously mixed with sugar, cure and seasonings; chop into a fine emulsion.

In case a meat emulsifier is used, first grind the meats, then mix all ingredients in a mechanical mixer and put mixture through the finest plate of the emulsifier.

Stuff emulsion in artificial casings or prime hog bungs. After stuffing place sausages immediately in a meat truck filled with cold water to avoid breakage and carry sausages in the truck to the cooking vats.

Cooking water should be preheated to 165°F and maintained at this temperature until an internal meat temperature of 150°–152°F is reached.

After cooking, transfer immediately to chill truck containing ice water for fast chill of the sausages, then during chilling add more chopped ice to the truck. Internal temperature of the sausages should be reduced to 110°F.

If sausages are stuffed in natural casings, then, after the chilling operation, they should be hung on smoke sticks on a smoke tree. To remove surface fat from the sausages, put under a hot water shower (180°F) for a few seconds. (Sausages in artificial casings do not need to be showered with hot water.)

If sausages are sold without smoking, transfer them to chill room (45°F) and keep them there at least 24 hr before packaging and shipping.

Smoking.—Sausages to be smoked after cooking should be left at room temperature just long enough to dry casings; then place them in a preheated house at a temperature not over 110°F; introduce smoke and smoke until the desired smoked color is obtained. This takes approximately 3–4 hr to give the best results.

Remove sausages from the house, shower them in hot water (180°F) for a few seconds to remove any remaining fat, then transfer to cooler (45°F) for at least 24 hr before packaging and shipping.

Keep Product Refrigerated

Product should be held under refrigeration through storage and marketing.

SOURCE: Stephan L. Komarik, 4810 Ronda, Coral Gables, Florida.

BRAUNSCHWEIGER LIVER SAUSAGE

Use any of these meat combinations:

	No. 1 Lb	No. 2 Lb	No. 3 Lb
Pork livers	250	250	250
Pork jowls	250		200
Smoked pork jowls			50
Pork trimmings 50/50		250	

with these ingredients:

	Lb	Oz
Salt	12	8
Onion powder	1	8
Corn sugar	1	4
Sodium nitrite		3/4
Sodium erythorbate		4 1/3

and either of these seasoning combinations:

	Lb	Oz	Cc
Ground white pepper	1	4	
Ground allspice		2 1/2	
Ground cloves		2 1/2	
Ground sage		2 1/2	
Ground marjoram		2 1/2	
Ground nutmeg		2 1/2	
Ground ginger		2 1/2	

or

	Lb	Oz	Cc
Dry soluble pepper[1]	1	4	
Oil of allspice			3.00
Oil of cloves			5.00
Oil of sage			3.00
Oil of marjoram			2.50
Oil of nutmeg			5.00
Oleoresin ginger			2.50

[1] Oils and oleoresin should be thoroughly mixed with the dry soluble pepper.

Processing Procedure

Grind chilled jowls and regular pork trimmings through the 1/4-in. plate of the grinder. Place hog livers in the meat chopper; chop until bubbles appear on the surface of the emulsion (approximately 10 min). Then add ground jowls or trimmings and salt, previously mixed with cure, flavorings and corn sugar, and let the chopper run until the fat specks are not visible in the emulsion.

In case an emulsifier is used put liver through the 1/8-in. plate of the grinder, and pork trimmings or jowls through the 1/4-in. plate. Transfer ground meat into mechanical mixer, add remainder of the ingredients, premixed, and without any delay, put mixed product through the finest plate of the emulsifier.

Stuff immediately in sewed hog bungs 2 3/4–3 in. in diameter. After stuffing, place sausages in a meat truck filled with cold water to avoid breakage and transfer sausages in the truck to the cooking vats.

Preheat cooking water (180°F) and place a wooden laced cover over the sausages in such manner that all the sausages will be submerged in the cooking water.

Let water temperature drop to 160°F and maintain this temperature during the cooking process. Cook sausages to an internal temperature of 152°F. Then transfer sausages very carefully to a truck containing chopped ice and water for fast chilling and during chilling add more chopped ice to the truck. Internal meat temperature should be reduced to 110°F. Remove sausages from the chilled water, hang on smoke sticks properly spaced on a smokehouse tree and hold under a hot shower (180°F) for a few seconds to remove surface fat from the casings.

Let sausages hang at room temperature to dry casings, then transfer to smokehouse at a temperature not higher than 110°F. Apply heavy smudge, maintaining 110°F and proper air circulation; smoke sausages until the desired smoked color is obtained (approximately 3–4 hr).

Remove sausages from the house, shower with hot water (180°F) a few seconds to remove any remaining fat. Let casings dry at room temperature before transferring to chill room (45°F) for final chilling.

Chill sausages at least 24 hr before packaging and shipping. Keep product at refrigeration temperatures through storage and marketing.

SOURCE: Stephan L. Komarik, 4810 Ronda, Coral Gables, Florida.

BRAUNSCHWEIGER-STYLE LIVER SAUSAGE WITH SOY PROTEIN

Ingredients	Lb	Oz
Pork livers	55	
Skinned pork jowls	45	

Swift's food protein (S.F.P.)	4	
Salt	3	
Onion powder		4
Ground white pepper		6
Ground ginger		2
Ground marjoram		1
Fresh garlic		$1/2$
Chopped ice	4	
Nitrite		$1/4$
Nitrate		$3/4$

Processing Procedure

Grind pork livers through $1/8$-in. plate. Grind jowls through $1/4$-in. plate. Chop garlic fine and mix with cure.

Place ground livers in silent cutter. Add salt, cure, food protein (S.F.P.), and chopped ice. When bubbles appear on surface, add ground jowls and seasonings. Chop fine. Stuff into hog bungs or opaque cellulose casings of appropriate size.

Cook at 160°–165°F for 1–1$1/2$ hr. Chill quickly in ice water until firmly set. Smoke at 90°–120°F until an even golden color appears.

Chill product and hold under refrigeration through storage and marketing.

SOURCE: Swift Edible Oil Co., Vegetable Protein Products Div., 115 W. Jackson Blvd., Chicago, Ill.

BRAUNSCHWEIGER WITH ISOLATED SOY PROTEIN

Ingredients	Lb
Pork livers	50.0
Pork jowls	50.0
Corn syrup	2.0
Salt	2.5
Isolated soy protein (Promine-D)	2.0
Fresh onion	2.5
Moisture	2.5
Spice, cure, seasonings to suit	

Processing Procedure

1. Chop lean meats with moisture, salt, cure, and spices for about 2 min.
2. Add isolated soy protein (Promine-D) and chop for an additional 3 min.
3. Add fat meats and complete chop.
4. Stuff and cook using usual cooking procedures.
5. Chill product and keep under refrigeration through storage and marketing.

SOURCE: Central Soya Co., Chemurgy Division, 1825 N. Laramie St., Chicago, Ill.

BRAUNSCHWEIGER-STYLE LIVER SAUSAGE USING NONFAT DRY MILK

Make up this cure:

	Lb	Oz
Sodium nitrate	3	7
Sodium nitrite		5
Dextrose (corn sugar)	10	

Place ingredients in a 5-gal. glass container. Fill with water and dissolve. Use 1 qt ($2^3/4$ lb) of solution for each 100 lb of meat.

Ingredients	Lb	Oz
Pork livers	55	
Skinned pork jowls	45	
Nonfat dry milk	4	
Salt	3	
Fresh onions	2	
Ground white pepper		6
Ground ginger		2
Ground marjoram		2
Fresh garlic		$1/2$
Chopped ice	4	
Cure	$2^3/4$	

Processing Procedure

Grind pork livers and onions through $1/8$-in. plate. Grind pork jowls through $1/4$-in. plate. Chop garlic fine and mix with cure.

Place ground livers in silent cutter. Add salt, cure, nonfat dry milk, and chopped ice. When bubbles appear on surface of mixture, add seasoning and ground jowls. Chop fine. Stuff into hog bungs, sewed hog bungs, or opaque cellulose casings of corresponding size.

Cook at 160°–165°F for 1–1$1/2$ hr, depending upon diameter of casings. Chill quickly in ice water until firmly set. Smoke at 90°–120°F until even golden color appears.

SOURCE: American Dry Milk Institute, 130 N. Franklin, Chicago, Ill.

KOSHER-STYLE LIVER SAUSAGE

Ingredients	Lb	Oz	Gm	Cc
Beef liver	30			
Veal trimmings	40			
Beef plate or flanks	30			
Salt	2	8		
Sodium erythorbate		$7/8$		
Sodium nitrite		$1/8$		
Ground white pepper		3		
Ground nutmeg		$3/4$		
Ground Jamaica ginger		$3/4$		

Ground allspice	10	Onion powder	1
Ground cloves	10	Corn syrup solids	2 8
Ground thyme	10	Ground black pepper	10
Ground marjoram	3/4	Ground marjoram	8
Onion powder	4	Ground cloves	2
Garlic powder	2	Ground ginger	2 1/2
Natural wood smoke flavor	1.00		

Processing Procedure

Precautions.—Be sure that trimmings are chilled to 32°-34°F. Cut slashes in properly trimmed beef liver 3/4-1 in. apart, then dip into simmering water just long enough to coagulate surface blood.

Grinding.—Grind all meat items through the 1/8-in. plate of the grinder.

Chopping.—Transfer ground meats to the chopper. Add salt, previously mixed with the rest of the dry ingredients, add smoke flavor diluted with 1 pt of water. Add approximately 10 lb of pulverized Dry Ice to reduce temperature, then chop into a fine emulsion. If temperature goes higher than 55°F, add more Dry Ice. The product is ready for stuffing.

If Meat Emulsifier Used.—If meat emulsifier is used after grinding transfer meat to the mechanical mixer. Add salt previously mixed with the dry ingredients and smoke flavor diluted with 1 pt of water, and mix just long enough to distribute all ingredients uniformly. This takes approximately 2 min. Put mixed material first through the fine, then the superfine plate of the emulsifier.

Stuffing.—Stuff sausage in artificial casings of desired size and length.

Cooking.—Transfer sausages to the cooking vat with water temperature at 160°F or a steam cabinet at a temperature of 165°F. Cook sausages until an internal meat temperature of 152°F is obtained.

Chilling.—Chill sausages in iced water as rapidly as possible to an internal temperature of 80°F then transfer to chill room at 34°-36°F overnight before packaging and shipping.

Product should be held under refrigeration through storage and marketing.

SOURCE: Stephan L. Komarik, 4810 Ronda, Coral Gables, Florida.

FARMER-STYLE LIVER SAUSAGE

Ingredients	Lb	Oz
Pork livers (light colored)	150	
Lean pork trimmings, precooked	100	
Pork head meat	100	
Pork belly trimmings, precooked	150	
Salt	12	8

Processing Procedure

Preparation of the Ingredients.—Grind 75 lb of pork liver (chilled to 34°F) through the 1/8-in. plate of the grinder. Slash the other 75 lb of liver, and cook in simmering water just long enough to coagulate the blood in the center of the slices, then grind through the 1/2-in. plate of the grinder. Cook lean pork trimmings for 30 min in simmering water, then grind through the 1/2-in. plate. Cook belly trimmings 30 min then dice into 1/2-in. dice. Grind well-chilled pork head meat through the 1/8-in. plate. Premix salt with the dry ingredients.

Mixing.—Place all meats in the mechanical mixer and mix for 2 min with the salt mixture.

Chopping.—A regular or rapid chopper could be used. Do not overfill chopper. Chop material until the fat particles are reduced to 3/8-in. size.

Stuffing.—Stuff material in beef middles, sewed hog bungs, or artificial casings. After stuffing, place sausages in cold water in a meat truck and move sausages in the truck to the cooking vats to avoid breakage.

Cooking.—The cooking water should be preheated to 175°-180°F. Let temperature drop to 165°F and maintain this temperature until an internal meat temperature of 152°F is reached.

Chilling.—After cooking, transfer sausages immediately to chill truck containing ice water for fast chilling. During chilling add more ice to the water. The internal meat temperature should be reduced to 110°F. Hang sausages on smoke trees. Those stuffed in natural casings should be showered with hot water at 180°F for a few seconds to remove any grease from casings. Sausages in Cellophane casings can be smoked immediately after chilling.

Smoking.—Let sausages hang at room temperature to dry casings, then place in a preheated house at a temperature not over 110°F and smoke until the desired color is obtained. Remove sausages from the house, shower with hot water at 180°F for a few seconds to remove any remaining fat; then transfer to holding cooler at 45°F for at least 24 hr before shipping.

Product should be kept refrigerated throughout storage and marketing channels.

SOURCE: Stephan L. Komarik, 4810 Ronda, Coral Gables, Florida.

BOHEMIAN LIVER SAUSAGE

Ingredients	Lb	Oz
Pork snouts, precooked	30	
Beef lungs, precooked	15	
Pork livers	10	
Pork jowls, precooked	5	
Stale white bread	20	
Broth (from cooking snouts and jowls)	20	
Salt	2	
Fresh onions, sliced	2	
Ground black pepper		4
Ground marjoram		2
Spanish paprika		1

Processing Procedure

Cook pork snouts with the pork jowls until tender. Use broth of these products only. Remove tubes from lungs, cut into large pieces and cook thoroughly. Do not cook livers. Fry onions in lard until golden yellow.

Grinding.—After meats are prepared as above, add broth to the stale bread and add fried onions. Grind meats and bread mixture through the $3/16$-in. plate of the grinder. Transfer ground mixture to the mechanical mixer, add salt mixed with the seasonings, and mix for 3 min.

Stuffing.—Stuff immediately in medium or large hog casings (as trade demands) and tie casings to the desired length with skewers.

Cooking.—Cook sausages in preheated water at 165°F for 40–50 min, depending on the diameter of the casings. Remove sausages from cooking vat and chill in iced water to an internal temperature of 40°F.

NOTE. This product is very perishable, and should be sold within 24 hr or held in a cooler in 40° salinometer brine to prevent casings from drying out and darkening.

SOURCE: Stephan L. Komarik, 4810 Ronda, Coral Gables, Florida.

HOMEMADE GERMAN-STYLE LIVER SAUSAGE (HOUSMACHER LEBERWURST)

Use any of these meat combinations:

	No. 1 Lb	No. 2 Lb	No. 3 Lb
Pork liver	40	35	30
Lean pork trimmings	50	45	45
Pork jowls or backfat	10	20	25

with these ingredients:

	Lb	Oz	Gm
Salt	2	8	
Sodium nitrite			$1/4$
Sodium erythorbate		$7/8$	
Onion powder		4	
Ground white pepper		3	
Ground mace or nutmeg		$3/4$	
Ground Jamaica ginger		$3/4$	
Ground marjoram		$3/4$	
Ground allspice			10
Ground cloves			10
Ground thyme			10

Processing Procedure

Lean pork trimmings are cooked in simmering water just long enough to permit dicing into $3/8$-in. cubes or ground through the $1/2$-in. plate of the grinder. Grind pork jowls or backfat (chilled to 32°–34°F) through the $1/4$-in. plate of the grinder.

Chopping.—Place hog livers in the meat chopper and chop until bubbles appear on the surface of the emulsion (approximately 10 min). Then add the ground jowls along with the salt, which has been previously mixed with sodium nitrite and the rest of the ingredients. Let the chopper run until the fat particles are not visible in the emulsion.

In case an emulsifier is used put the liver through the $1/8$-in. plate of the grinder, and the jowls or backfat through the $1/4$-in. plate. Transfer the ground meat to the mechanical mixer; add the dry ingredients premixed with the salt, and mix thoroughly. Without delay, put mixture through the fine plate, then again through the superfine plate of the emulsifier.

Mixing.—In both cases, the liver emulsion is finally mixed with the diced cooked pork. It should be mixed until the cubes are thoroughly coated and are evenly distributed in the emulsion.

Stuffing.—Stuff material into sewed hog bungs $2^3/4$–3 in. in diameter, or 30-in. long beef middles or artificial casings of the same size. After stuffing, to avoid breakage, place sausages in a meat truck filled with cold water for transport to the cooking vat.

Cooking.—Preheat cooking water to 180°F and place a wooden laced cover over the cooker so that all the sausages will be submerged in the cooking water. Let water temperature drop to 160°F and maintain this temperature during cooking process. Cook sausages to an internal temperature of 152°F. This will take approximately 2–$2^1/2$ hr.

Chilling.—After cooking, carefully transfer sausages to a truck containing chipped ice and water for a fast chill; during chilling add more ice to the truck. Internal meat temperature should be reduced to 110°F. Remove sausages from the chill water; hang them on properly spaced smoke sticks on a smokehouse tree, and hold under a hot shower (180°F) for a few seconds to remove surface fat from the casings. Then hold sausages at room temperature to dry casings.

Smoking.—After casings are dry, transfer sausages to a preheated smokehouse at a temperature not higher than 110°F. Apply heavy smoke and maintain 110°F and proper air circulation. Smoke sausages until the desired color is obtained (approximately 3–4 hr). Remove sausages from the house, shower with water at 180°F for just a few seconds to remove any remaining fat; then let dry at room temperature, before transferring them to chill room at 45°F for final chilling. Chill sausages at least 24 hr before packaging and shipping.

Hold product under refrigerated temperatures throughout storage and marketing channels.

SOURCE: Stephan L. Komarik, 4810 Ronda, Coral Gables, Florida.

HUNGARIAN-STYLE RICE LIVER SAUSAGE

Ingredients	Lb	Oz
Pork head meat, precooked	50	
Pork livers, precooked	25	
Rice	8	
Fresh onions, sliced	2	
Salt	2	
Broth (from cooking head meat)	10	
Ground black pepper		4
Ground marjoram		2
Spanish paprika		1

Processing Procedure

Cook head meat in simmering water until tender and reserve broth. Cut slashes in liver 1 in. apart and blanch in simmering water just long enough to coagulate blood in the center of the slices. Slice onions, then fry in lard until golden yellow. Cook approximately 8 lb of rice until tender (do not overcook), then rinse in cold water and drain.

Grinding.—Grind cooked head meat with the fried onions through the 1/8-in. plate of the grinder. Grind blanched liver through the 1/4-in. plate.

Mixing.—Transfer all the ground items to a mechanical mixer, add salt mixed with the seasonings, and drained rice; then add 10 lb of hot broth, in which the head meat was cooked, and mix for 3 min.

Stuffing.—Stuff immediately in medium or large hog casings as trade demands, and tie with skewers into the desired sizes.

Cooking.—Cook sausages in preheated water at 165°F for 40–50 min, depending on the diameter of the casings. Remove sausages from the cooking vat and chill in iced water to an internal meat temperature of 40°F.

NOTE. This product is very perishable and should be sold within 24 hr or kept in a cooler immersed in a 40° salinometer brine to keep casings from drying out and darkening.

SOURCE: Stephan L. Komarik, 4810 Ronda, Coral Gables, Florida.

RING LIVER PUDDING

Ingredients	Lb	Oz
Pork livers	30	
Beef tripe or hog stomachs	20	
Pork jowls or regular pork trimmings 50/50	20	
Pork snouts or pork skins	30	
Rye flour	10	
Broth (from cooking snouts or skins)	25	
Salt	3	4
Onion powder		5
Ground black pepper		4
Ground ginger		1
Ground cloves		1
Ground marjoram		1 1/2

Processing Procedure

Cook all meat items in simmering water at 200°F until well done. (Weights given above are precooked weights.) Reserve broth from snouts or skins.

Grinding.—Grind cooked liver, jowls or pork trimmings, snouts or skins through the 1/8-in. plate.

Mixing.—Put all the ground meat items in a mechanical mixer, add premixed salt, flour, and the remainder of the dry ingredients to the meats while the machine is running, then slowly add the hot broth. Run mixer until everything is thoroughly mixed.

Stuffing.—Stuff material immediately into beef rounds.

Cooking.—Cook sausages in preheated water at 165°F for 40–50 min, depending on the diameter of the casings. Remove sausages from the cooking vat and chill in iced water to an internal meat temperature of 40°F.

NOTE. This product is very perishable and should be sold within 24 hr or kept in a cooler in 40° salinometer brine in order to prevent casings from drying out and darkening.

SOURCE: Stephan L. Komarik, 4810 Ronda, Coral Gables, Florida.

COOKED KRAKAUER SAUSAGE

Ingredients	Lb	Oz
Lean beef	250	
Regular pork trimmings 50/50	250	
Salt	13	

Sodium nitrate	5
Sodium nitrite	1¼
Sodium erythorbate	4⅓
Corn syrup solids	5
Ground black pepper	8
Ground mace or nutmeg	2
Ground coriander	2
Ground ginger	2
Garlic powder	½–1
Ice, chopped (approximately; only sufficient amount to make emulsion)	75

Processing Procedure

Grinding.—Grind chilled lean beef through the ¼-in. plate of the grinder and regular pork trimmings through the 1-in. plate.

Chopping.—Regardless of the size of chopper used, fill the hopper only ½ full. Transfer the ground beef to the chopper, add 50 lb of ice; then salt previously mixed with the remainder of the dry ingredients; chop sufficiently to make a medium emulsion; add 25 lb ice; then add ground pork evenly over the top of the emulsion; and run machine until the fat particles of the pork trimmings are reduced to ¼ to ⅜ in. in size. Transfer meat from the chopper to a vacuum mixer, and, under 25 in. vacuum, mix for 2 min.

Stuffing.—Stuff emulsion into wide beef rounds; hang on smokehouse trees, and transfer to cooler at 40°–45°F until a smokehouse is available for the sausages.

Smoking.—Allow sausages to warm slightly (1 hr) at room temperature before placing them in a preheated house at 130°–135°F, with dampers wide open, until casings are dry.

Then apply heavy smoke, adjust dampers ¼ open and keep sausages at 140°F for about 2½–3 hr. Stop smoking and raise temperature gradually to 165°F until an internal meat temperature of 135°F is obtained. Introduce live steam in the house keeping house temperature at 165°F and cook sausages until an internal meat temperature of 152°–155°F is reached. Open cold shower system and keep sausages under the shower until internal meat temperature is reduced to 120°F. Dry sausages at room temperature before they are transferred to a cooler at 40°–45°F for final chilling. Internal meat temperature should be reduced to 50°F before stuffing.

In case a cabinet with hot water circulation is used for cooking the sausages, after bringing sausages to an internal temperature of 135°F, transfer sausages to the cooking cabinet. Have the water temperature at 165°F until an internal meat temperature of 152°–155°F is reached. Chill under cold shower until internal meat temperature is reduced

to 120°F. Dry sausages at room temperature before transferring them to a cooler at 40°–45°F for final chilling. Internal meat temperature also should be reduced to 50°F before shipping.

Product is perishable and should be kept refrigerated throughout storage and marketing.

SOURCE: Stephan L. Komarik, 4810 Ronda, Coral Gables, Florida.

BERLINER SAUSAGE USING NONFAT DRY MILK

Make up this cure:

	Lb	Oz
Sodium nitrate	3	7
Sodium nitrite		5
Dextrose (corn sugar)	10	

Place ingredients in a 5-gal. glass container. Fill with water and dissolve. Use 1 qt (2¾ lb) of solution for each 100 lb of meat.

Ingredients	Lb	Oz
Lean pork trimmings	30	
Trimmed pork cheek meat	30	
Boneless chuck	20	
Veal trimmings	20	
Nonfat dry milk	4	
Salt	3	
Fresh onions	1½	
Mapleine		2
Ground white pepper		7
Fresh garlic		1
Ice water	8	
Cure	2¾	

Procedure

Grind pork trimmings through ¼-in. plate. Grind pork cheeks, chucks, and onions through ⅛-in. plate, and veal trimmings through 3/16-in. plate. Chop garlic fine and mix it and Mapleine with cure.

Place all meats in mixer. Add water, salt, cure, and pepper. Scatter nonfat dry milk, mix well. Stuff into extra wide beef middles or corresponding size cellulose or fibrous casings.

Hang in 38°–40°F cooler for 48 hr. Remove from cooler and leave in sausage room for 2½–3 hr before placing in smokehouse. If stuffed in cellulose casings, spray with hot water shortly before putting in smokehouse. Start smoking at 120°F. Gradually raise temperature to 165°F. When desired color appears, remove from smokehouse and cook at 160°–165°F until internal meat center reaches 155°F. Place under cold shower or immerse in cold water. Sausage should be lukewarm when removed from cold water. There is enough heat left to dry it.

SOURCE: American Dry Milk Institute, 130 N. Franklin, Chicago, Ill.

KNOCKWURST

Use either of these meat combinations:

	No. 1 Lb	No. 2 Lb
Lean beef, bull or cow meat	300	350
Regular pork trimmings 50/50	200	
Backfat		150

with these ingredients:

	Lb	Oz
Ice, chopped	150-175	
Salt	13	
Corn syrup solids	5	
Sodium nitrite		$1\frac{1}{4}$
Sodium nitrate		5
Sodium erythorbate		$4\frac{1}{3}$
Dry soluble pepper or ground white pepper	1	4
Ground mace		4
Ground allspice		4
Ground coriander		2
Garlic or onion powder (optional)		1

Processing Procedure

Grinding and Chopping.—Grind chilled beef through the $\frac{1}{8}$-in. plate, pork trimmings and backfat through the $\frac{1}{4}$-in. plate of the grinder. Transfer ground beef to the chopper add $\frac{1}{2}$ of the ice and start machine. Add salt, previously mixed with the remainder of the ingredients, and chop until fine emulsion is obtained; add ground regular pork trimmings or backfat; add remaining ice; and chop until the all fat particles disappear.

Using an Emulsifier.—Grind meats as described above. Transfer ground meat to a mechanical mixer. Instead of ice use iced water (at 32°F). Add $\frac{1}{2}$ the water; start machine; and add the salt (previously mixed with the remainder of the ingredients) evenly on the top of the meat. Gradually add the remainder of the iced water. Mix until all ingredients are uniformly distributed (approximately 3 min). Put mixed meat through the finest plate of the emulsifier. The temperature of the emulsion should not be over 55°F.

Stuffing.—Stuff emulsion into medium or narrow beef rounds, and tie into approximately $2\frac{1}{2}$-oz (net weight) links. Hang on smokehouse trees (properly spaced) and transfer to cooler at 38°-

40°F for overnight cure. Next day remove sausages from the cooler and predry casings for a couple of hours at room temperature before placing them in the smokehouse.

Smoking.—Preheat house to 140°F with dampers wide open. Place smoke trees in the house. Do not introduce smoke in the house before casings are dry. If there is good air circulation, it takes approximately 30 min to dry casings. Close damper to $\frac{1}{4}$ open and introduce heavy smoke; raise temperature gradually to 160°F and keep sausages at this temperature until an internal meat temperature of 135°F is obtained. Stop smoking and introduce live steam in the house and hold sausages until an internal meat temperature of 152°F is reached. Shut off steam, open shower system, and keep sausages under shower until internal temperature is reduced to 95°F.

Cooking in Hot Water Cabinet.—In this case, remove sausages from the smokehouse after an internal temperature of 135°-140°F is obtained. Immediately transfer the trees to the cooking cabinet at 160°F. Cook sausages until an internal temperature of 152°F is reached. Remove trees from the cabinet and keep sausages under cold shower until the internal temperature is reduced to 95°F.

In both cases (smokehouse cooking or cabinet cooking) let sausages hang at room temperature until casings dry; then transfer to holding cooler at 38°-40°F until the internal temperature is reduced to the cooling room temperature.

Keep product under refrigeration throughout storage and marketing.

SOURCE: Stephan L. Komarik, 4810 Ronda, Coral Gables, Florida.

THURINGER KNOCKWURST

Use any of these meat combinations:

	No. 1 Lb	No. 2 Lb	No. 3 Lb
Lean pork (80% lean)	200	300	250
Regular pork trimmings 50/50	200	75	100
Lean beef	100	125	150

with these ingredients:

	Lb	Oz
Salt	13	
Corn syrup solids	5	
Sodium nitrite		$1\frac{1}{4}$
Sodium nitrate		5
Sodium erythorbate		$4\frac{1}{3}$
Ground white pepper or dry soluble pepper	1	4

Ground marjoram	2
Ground caraway seed	4
Ground coriander	2
Ice, chopped	25

Processing Procedure

All meats should be free from sinews, connective tissues, and slivers of bones.

Grinding.—Grind chilled beef through the $1/8$-in. plate, lean and regular pork trimmings through the 1-in. plate.

Chopping.—Whatever size chopper is used, fill it only half full.

Transfer 100 lb of ground beef (regardless of the formula selected) to a conventional or rapid chopper and with 25 lb of ice and 3 lb of salt chop for a medium emulsion. Stop chopper, add ground pork and remaining ground beef. Start machine and immediately add remaining salt, previously mixed with the remainder of the dry ingredients; run machine until pork particles are reduced to approximately $1/4$ in.

Stuffing.—Stuff material into 30–32 mm hog casings and tie into desired length and weight. They are usually sold in pairs weighing approximately 4–6 oz per pair. Hang sausages on smokehouse trees then transfer to chill room at 38°–40°F for overnight cure. Next day remove sausages from cooler and predry casings for a couple of hours at room temperature before placing them in the smokehouse.

Smoking.—Preheat house to 140°F with dampers wide open. Place smoke trees in the house. Do not introduce smoke in the house before casings are dry; with good air circulation this will take approximately 30 min. Close damper to $1/4$ open, introduce heavy smoke, and raise temperature gradually to 160°F. Keep sausages at this temperature until an internal meat temperature of 135°F is obtained. Stop smoking, introduce live steam in the house and keep sausages at 160°F until an internal meat temperature of 152°F is reached.

Shut off steam, open shower system, and keep sausages under shower until internal meat temperature is reduced to 95°F.

Cooking in Hot Water Cabinet.—In this case, remove sausages from the smokehouse after an internal meat temperature of 135°–140°F is obtained. Immediately transfer trees to the cooking cabinet at 160°F and cook sausages until an internal temperature of 152° is reached.

Remove trees from the cabinet and keep sausages under cold shower until internal meat temperature is reduced to 95°F.

In both cases, let sausages hang at room temperature after shower until casings are dry, then transfer to holding cooler at 38°–40°F until internal meat temperature is reduced to the cooling room temperature.

Keep product refrigerated through storage and marketing.

SOURCE: Stephan L. Komarik, 4810 Ronda, Coral Gables, Florida.

KNOBLAUCH SAUSAGE USING NONFAT DRY MILK

Make up this cure:

	Lb	Oz
Sodium nitrate	3	7
Sodium nitrite		5
Dextrose (corn sugar)	10	

Place ingredients in a 5-gal. glass container. Fill with water and dissolve. Use 1 qt ($2^3/4$ lb) of solution for each 100 lb of meat.

Ingredients	Lb	Oz
Bullmeat	45	
Beef trimmings	15	
Regular pork trimmings	40	
Nonfat dry milk	$4^3/4$	
Fresh onions	3	
Salt	3	
Ground white pepper		6
Ground coriander		2
Ground mace		2
Fresh garlic		5
Cure	$2^3/4$	
Chopped ice		

Procedure

Grind onions, bullmeat, and beef trimmings through $3/8$-in. plate. Grind pork trimmings through $1/4$-in. plate. Chop garlic fine and mix with cure. Place bullmeat, beef trimmings, chopped ice, salt, and cure in silent cutter. Run a few revolutions and add nonfat dry milk and chopped ice alternately a little at a time until all nonfat dry milk is used. Then add pork and seasoning, and chop fine. Stuff into beef middles or corresponding size of cellulose or fibrous casings.

Place in smokehouse at 120°F gradually raising heat to 170°F. When desired color appears take out and cook at 160°–165°F. Internal temperature should be at least 145°F. During hot weather it should be 155°F. Place under cold shower. Enough heat should remain in product to dry it.

SOURCE: American Dry Milk Institute, 130 N. Franklin, Chicago, Ill.

ACME SAUSAGE USING NONFAT DRY MILK

Make up this cure:

	Lb	Oz
Sodium nitrate	3	7
Sodium nitrite		5
Dextrose (corn sugar)	10	

Place ingredients in a 5-gal. glass container. Fill with water and dissolve. Use 1 qt (2¾ lb) of solution with each 100 lb of meat.

Ingredients	Lb	Oz
Boneless chuck	30	
Lean pork trimmings	50	
Pork cheek meat	20	
Nonfat dry milk	5	
Salt	3	
Fresh onions	4	
Fresh garlic		2
Ground white pepper		7
Ground coriander		2
Ground mustard		2
Cold water	30	
Cure		2¾

Procedure

Grind onions with chuck through ⅛-in. plate. Grind pork through ⅜-in. plate. Chop garlic fine and mix with cure.

Place all meats in mixer; while mixing, add water, salt, cure, nonfat dry milk, and seasoning; mix well. Run all through ⅜-in. plate. Stuff into wide hog casings or corresponding size cellulose casings. Link into 6-in. lengths. Hang in cooler at 38°–40°F overnight. Keep sausages at room temperature for 2 hr, then place in smokehouse. Start with 120°F and gradually increase heat to 165°–170°F until desired color appears. Cook for 15 min at 160°F. Place under cold shower. When dry, place in cooler.

SOURCE: American Dry Milk Institute, 130 N. Franklin, Chicago, Ill.

MISCELLANEOUS SAUSAGES

BROWN-AND-SERVE ALL PORK SAUSAGE

Ingredients	Lb	Oz
Lean pork trimmings 80/20	125	
Regular pork trimmings 50/50	250	
Pork shank meat	75	
Salt	10	
Corn syrup solids	5	
Sodium erythorbate		4⅓
Monosodium glutamate		7½
Ice, chopped	40	
Select type of seasoning formula given in Table 2.1		

Processing Procedure

Grind chilled pork shank meat through the ⅛-in. plate of the grinder. Transfer to a meat chopper and with the ice and 2 lb of the salt and 1 lb of the corn syrup solids chop into a fine emulsion.

Grind other pork items through the 1-in. plate of the grinder. Transfer chopped emulsion and ground pork to mechanical mixer along with the remaining salt and corn syrup solids which have previously been mixed with seasonings, sodium erythorbate, and monosodium glutamate; mix for 3 min. It is advisable to add 3% of pulverized Dry Ice in order to keep the mixture very cold. Remove mixed meat from the mixer and grind through the ³⁄₁₆-in. plate of the grinder. Stuff into 22-32 mm Cellophane casings. Link into 3½–4-in. lengths, hang on properly spaced smoke trees; keep at room temperature 2-3 hr before transferring to the smokehouse. This product is not smoked.

Preheat house to 130°F, hold sausages at this temperature for 30 min; then raise temperature to 140°F and hold for 30 min; then raise temperature to 150°F and hold at this temperature for 30 min more.

During the whole operation in the smokehouse the damper should be kept ¼ open. Sausages should reach an internal temperature of 142°F. Before removing sausages from the house, introduce live steam for 3-4 min. Remove sausages from the house, cool with a cold shower until internal meat temperature drops to 110°F. Keep sausages at room temperature until the casings are dry, then transfer to a cooler at 45°F to thoroughly chill them. Peel casing and package.

Product should be held under refrigerated temperatures during storage and marketing.

SOURCE: Stephan L. Komarik, 4810 Ronda, Coral Gables, Florida.

HEAT-AND-SERVE PORK SAUSAGE

Ingredients	Lb	Oz
Boneless, skinless picnics	500	
Salt	10	

Ice, chopped	15	
Corn sugar	1	4
Sodium erythorbate		$4^{1}/_{3}$
Select type of seasoning formula given in Table 2.1		

Processing Procedure

For best results, use fresh picnics that average 10–12 lb. Skin, bone, and remove gristle and heavy connective tissues. Cut meat into 1 lb chunks and chill to 32°–34°F before chopping. Transfer meat to a prechilled meat cutter, start machine, add chopped ice and salt which has been previously mixed with seasonings and sodium erythorbate; let machine run until meat sizes are reduced to approximately $1/4$-in. cubes. Stuff chopped meat into 22–32 mm Cellophane casings. Hang on smoke trees. Preheat smokehouse to 165°F. After sausages are placed in the house start steam and cook sausages for approximately 10 min to an internal temperature of 150°F. Cool sausages with a cold shower to an internal temperature of 100°F before putting them into a chill room at 34°F. Internal meat temperature should be reduced to 34°F before peeling. Do not use any steam in the peeling machine during the peeling operation.

Package peeled sausage. Hold under refrigeration.

SOURCE: Stephan L. Komarik, 4810 Ronda, Coral Gables, Florida.

BEST QUALITY CANNED PORK SAUSAGE

Ingredients	Lb	Oz
Boneless, skinless picnics with surface fat left on	500	
Salt	7	8
Cane sugar	7	8
Decorticated black pepper		10
Rubbed Dalmatian sage		10
Ground Jamaica ginger		2

Processing Procedure

Chill picnics to 32°–34°F. Grind through the $1/4$-in. plate of the grinder. Transfer to a vacuum mixer; add salt premixed with sugar and seasonings, and start machine. Then stop mixer, close top and pull 28 in. vacuum. Mix product for 5 min.

Meat mixture may be stuffed immediately or it can be held overnight at a temperature not higher than 35°F. If held overnight, meat mixture should be premixed under 27 in. vacuum for 2 min to make it pliable for stuffing.

Stuff in artificial casings having a minimum diameter of $1/2$ in. or a maximum diameter of $7/8$ in. and link every $4^1/2$ in. Hang links on smoke sticks

properly spaced on smoke trees, but do not smoke during the cooking schedule given below:

Preheat smokehouse to 140°F
Cook 30 min at db temp of 140°F, wb temp of 110°F
Cook 30 min at db temp of 150°F, wb temp of 120°F
Cook 5 min at db temp of 180°F, wb temp of 165°F
Internal meat temperature should reach 152°F

Chilling and Peeling.—Remove sausages from the house and chill under cold shower for 5 min then transfer to cooler at 45°F for final chilling or fast chill in a blast type chill unit; then peel them.

Packaging.—Wrap 24 oz of sausages in parchment paper. The size of the parchment should be $4^1/2$ in. high and long enough to overlap when 24 oz of sausages are encased in the paper. Place in 401 × 411 cans, fill with hot water and close cans under 27 in. vacuum.

Suggested Process

401 × 411 cans (24 oz net) 2 hr 30 min at 225°F

Check process time and temperature with can supplier or National Canners Association.

SOURCE: Stephan L. Komarik, 4810 Ronda, Coral Gables, Florida.

CANNED BULK BREAKFAST SAUSAGE WITH $3^1/2$% CEREAL ADDED

Ingredients	Lb	Oz
Hog stomachs, precooked	200	
Fresh pork hearts	200	
Pork tongues, precooked	100	
Pork snouts, precooked	100	
Wheat flour	21	
Salt	12	
Cane sugar	2	
Crushed red pepper		12
Ground red pepper		6
Ground Dalmatian sage		12
Ground nutmeg		3
Water or broth from cooked snouts	40	
Sodium nitrite		$1^1/2$

Procedure

Cook hog stomachs 2 hr, tongues 1 hr, and snouts 2 hr at water temperature of 200°–205°F. Do not chill cooked meats. Grind both the cooked meats and the raw hearts through the $1/8$-in. plate of the grinder. Transfer ground meats to a mechanical mixer. Add flour evenly while the machine is running, then add hot broth in which the sodium nitrate and sodium nitrite are dissolved, followed by the remainder of the ingredients and mix for 3 min. Pack in 307 × 409 cans (20 oz net). Close under 20 in. vacuum.

Suggested Process

2 hr 20 min at 240°F

Check process time and temperature with can supplier or the National Canners Association.

SOURCE: Stephan L. Komarik, 4810 Ronda, Coral Gables, Florida.

SAUSAGE CANNED IN VEGETABLE OIL (GOOD QUALITY)

Ingredients	Lb	Oz	Cc
Lean beef trimmings	20		
Beef cheeks, trimmed	25		
Beef hearts, trimmed	20		
Pork hearts, trimmed	30		
Ice, chopped	5		
Salt	3		
Cane sugar		8	
Sodium nitrite		1/4	
Sodium nitrate		1	
Sodium erythorbate		7/8	
Red pepper, ground		2	
Red pepper, cracked		1	
Oil of cloves[1]			0.15
Oil of nutmeg[1]			0.25
Oil of coriander[1]			0.25

[1] The equivalent of ground spices may replace the essential oils.

Procedure

Have all meats well chilled (32°-34°F) at the start of the operation.

Grind, Chop, and Mix.—Grind beef cheeks separately through the 1/8-in. plate of the grinder. Grind beef hearts and pork hearts through the 1/4-in. plate. Grind beef trimmings through the 1/8-in. plate and transfer beef trimmings to a chopper; add the chopped ice and only 1 lb of the salt and chop long enough to produce a good emulsion.

Transfer beef emulsion to a mechanical mixer. Premix remaining salt with sugar, cures, and seasonings and flavorings and add to beef emulsion. Then add remaining ground meats and mix for 3 min. If a vacuum mixer is used, mix for 3 min under 25 in. vacuum.

Stuff and Smoke.—Stuff meat mixture in medium size hog casings and link in 21 1/2-in. lengths. This length will eliminate too many round ends and pieces in the finished sausage size for the cans. Hang links on smoke trees and transfer to a preheated smokehouse at 140°F. With vents wide open, hold this temperature until casings are dry. Then close dampers to 1/4 open, apply heavy smudge, and gradually raise temperature to 160°F. Hold at this temperature until an internal meat temperature of 140°F is reached. Then remove sausages from the smokehouse and shower them with hot water for a few minutes to wash casings. Dry at room temperature until sausages reach room temperature, then transfer to a chill room (35°-40°F) for final chilling before canning.

Can.—When sausages are properly chilled and casings are dry, cut sausages to lengths that will measure 1/4-in. shorter than the height of the can that is to be used. Pack sausages in cans lengthwise and fill with vegetable oil (corn or cottonseed). Close cans under 27 in. vacuum.

Suggested Process

12 oz net cans 1 hr 45 min at 230°F
16 oz net cans 1 hr 45 min at 240°F
3 lb net cans 2 hr 15 min at 240°F
6 lb net cans 2 hr 45 min at 240°F

Check process time and temperature with can supplier or the National Canners Association.

Final Chill

After process has been completed, shut off steam and introduce cold water, and, under 15 lb of air pressure, chill to an internal can temperature of 120°F.

SOURCE: Stephan L. Komarik, 4810 Ronda, Coral Gables, Florida.

CANNED CHORIZOS IN LARD

Ingredients	Lb	Oz
Lean beef trimmings	125	
Pork hearts, trimmed (certified)[5]	125	
Lean pork trimmings (certified)	125	
Pork trimmings 50/50 (certified)	125	
Salt	17	
Spanish paprika	12	

[5] Certified pork are those fresh pork meats certified by the USDA Meat Inspection Division as being free of live trichinae. Only certified pork should be used in processing these canned sausages sinces the processing procedure does not conform otherwise to government regulations concerning destruction of live trichinae.

Black pepper (38-mesh)	8
Ground cardamom	2
Ground coriander	2
Ground oregano	$1/2$
Ground ginger	3
Garlic powder	$1/2$
Sodium nitrate	5
Sodium nitrite	1
Vinegar (45-grain)	8

Procedure

Be sure that all meat items are properly chilled to 35°F before grinding. Plates and knives of the grinder must be sharp.

Grind lean beef, pork hearts and lean pork through the $1/8$-in. plate of the grinder and regular pork trimmings through the $1/4$-in. plate. Transfer ground meat to a mechanical mixer. Dissolve the sodium nitrate and sodium nitrite in 3 pt of cold water and while the mixer is in operation, add the solution to ground meat along with the seasonings which have been mixed previously with the salt. Add vinegar and mix product for 3 min under 27 in. vacuum.

Stuffing.—Stuff mixed meat in narrow or medium hog casings (18–22 mm) and link according to the height of the can. For example, if chorizos are packed in small 208 × 208 cans, link sausages $21^1/2$-in. in length and after sausages are processed and dried, cut to the size of the height of the can. Hang sausages on smoke trees well spaced and allow meat to cure and dry the casings overnight at 50°-60°F with 70–80% RH.

Drying in Air-Conditioned Smokehouses.—Set the thermostatic control of dry bulb thermometer at 110°F and wet bulb thermometer at 98°F (relative humidity 65%). Transfer trees to the pre-heated house. Do not use smoke. Hold sausages 24 hr or until the sausages shrink at least 30% (weight loss).

In case no air-conditioned house is available, try to keep temperature between 110°-120°F, but no higher than 125°F. Keep sausages in house properly ventilated until at least a 30% shrink is obtained.

Canning.—After sausages are removed from the house, they should be packed immediately in cans in hot lard. Use lard which is already treated with an antioxidant. Add 8 oz of microfine Spanish paprika to each 100 lb of lard and heat lard to 240°F. Approximate ratio of sausages to hot lard is 55% sausages, 45% lard. Close cans immediately. If procedure is followed as given above no retorting of cans is necessary.

SOURCE: Stephan L. Komarik, 4810 Ronda, Coral Gables, Florida.

CANNED VIENNA SAUSAGES

For a top grade product, use these meats:

	Lb
Carcass beef (canner-cutter grade)	300
Pork trimmings 50/50	200
Ice, chopped	100

or

Carcass beef (canner-cutter grade)	400
Backfat	100
Ice, chopped	150

or

Bull meat	125
Carcass beef (canner-cutter grade)	125
Pork trimmings 50/50	250
Ice, chopped	125

or

Carcass beef (canner-cutter grade)	200
Beef hearts, trimmed	100
Pork trimmings 50/50	200
Ice, chopped	100

with these ingredients:

	Lb	Oz
Salt	12	8
Seasoning mixture (given below)	2	8
Sodium erythorbate		$4^1/3$
Sodium nitrate		5
Sodium nitrite		$1^1/4$

For a 2nd grade product with $3^1/2$% cereal added, use these ingredients:

	Lb	Oz
Carcass beef (canner-cutter grade)	100	
Beef cheeks, trimmed	100	
Beef tripe	100	
Sweet pickled pork trimmings	100	
Wheat flour	17	8
Seasoning mixture (given below)	2	
Sodium erythorbate		$3^1/2$
Sodium nitrate		4
Sodium nitrite		1
Salt	7	
Ice, chopped	90	

For a 3rd grade product with $3^1/2$% cereal added, use these ingredients:

	Lb	Oz
Beef cheeks, trimmed	100	
Beef trimmings	40	
Cooked and chilled ox lips	40	
Beef or pork hearts, trimmed	25	

Sweet pickled pork trimmings	20
Cooked and chilled hog stomachs	20
Beef tripe, treated	55
Wheat flour	13
Seasoning mixture (given below)	
Sodium erythorbate	$2^1/_2$
Sodium nitrate	3
Sodium nitrite	$^3/_4$
Salt	8
Ice, chopped	60

Use the following seasoning mixture with any of the above grades of Vienna sausage:

	Lb	Oz	Cc
Salt	100		
Oleoresin capsicum		17	
Oleoresin black pepper diluted			
50-50 with propylene glycol		1	25
Oil of nutmeg		13	8
Oil of coriander		4	20
Oil of cardamom		9	10
Oil of cloves		1	25

Use 8 oz seasoning mix per 100 lb meat.

Procedure

Grinding and Chopping.—Grind beef items through the $^1/_8$-in. plate of the grinder, pork items through the $^1/_4$-in. plate. If pork fat (backfat) is used it should not be ground, but cut into strips. First, chop the beef in the silent cutter with the addition of $^1/_4$ of the ice, and chop for approximately 3 min. Then add $^1/_4$ more ice[6] along with salt, seasonings, sodium erythorbate, sodium nitrate, and sodium nitrite, dissolved in 1 qt of water. Chop 3 more minutes. Add remaining ice[6] and ground pork or strips of backfat. Chop until meat temperature reaches $56°-58°F$. If cereal is used, add the cereal just 1–2 min before the end of the chopping period. After chopping, remove emulsion from the chopper, transfer it to a vacuum mixer and mix for 3 min under 27 in. of vacuum.

In case an emulsifier is used instead of a silent cutter, use the following procedure:

If fresh meats are used, the meat should be chilled to $35°F$ or lower after the grinding; use ice, or water and ice, to obtain a temperature of $35°F$ after the meats are mixed and put into the emulsifier. The mixing should be done in a regular meat mixer. Start the machine and put $^1/_2$ the amount of ice or water in the mixer. Add the salt, seasonings, and cures and then add all the ground meats (if backfat is used, grind through the $^1/_4$-in. plate and mix for 2 min before adding to the other meats). Then add the remaining ice or water (and

[6] Caution: If frozen meats are used do not use ice but only water.

flour, if used) and mix one more minute. Dump meat from mixer and immediately run through emulsifiers. The first machine should have holes 2–3 mm in diameter, and the second machine should be equipped with the superfine plate. The finished emulsion should have a temperature approximately $55°F$.

Stuffing.—Stuff in artificial casings using 22/32 or 20/32 size and link into $21^1/_2$-in. lengths. Using this method minimizes the number of round ends. Hang linked sausages on smokehouse trees and hold at room temperature for 30 min to dry casings.

Smoking and Cooking.—Transfer trees to a smokehouse preheated to $140°F$. Apply heavy smudge with dampers open for 30 min; then raise temperature to $160°F$ and continue smoking for another 30 min. Close dampers, raise temperature to $175°-180°F$ until internal temperature of the sausages reaches $145°F$. If air-conditioned houses are used, introduce steam and cook sausages to internal temperature of $155°F$. If steam cooker is used, remove trees from the smokehouse and place them in steam cooker at a temperature of $165°F$ for 4–5 min, until internal sausage temperature reaches $152°F$ on all parts of the trees. After cooking, spray with cold water until an internal temperature of $90°-100°F$ is obtained. After chilling, let casings dry at room temperature for 30–40 min before transferring to a cooler at $45°F$ until an internal temperature of $50°F$ is obtained. Now the sausages are ready for peeling, cutting, and canning.

Cutting and Canning.—Cut sausages to a length which will fit the height of the cans in which the sausages will be packed. For example, using 208 × 208 cans, the sausages should be cut $2^1/_2$ in. in length.

After sausages are placed in the cans, cans should be filled with hot water while moving along the conveyor or under a spray. The closing machine should be equipped with an automatic plunger which depresses the sausages down $^1/_4$ in. below the lip of the can. This will expel enough water to create headspace for proper vacuum. Close cans under vacuum.

Suggested Process

Can Size	Net Wt (Oz)		Time (Min)	Temp (°F)
208 × 208	4		45	230
		or	30	240
401 × 411 and				
404 × 411	22		165	225
		or	135	230
		or	105	235
		or	90	240

Check processing time and temperature with the can supplier or the National Canners Association.

SOURCE: Stephan L. Komarik, 4810 Ronda, Coral Gables, Florida.

CANNED IMITATION VIENNA SAUSAGE

Ingredients	Lb	Oz
Beef cheeks, trimmed	50	
Beef hearts, trimmed	25	
Pork hearts, trimmed	25	
Pork tripe	36	
Beef tripe, scalded	50	
Beef lungs	30	
Beef melts	12	
Cooked pork snouts, chilled	70	
Wheat flour	70	
Salt	10	
Vienna sausage seasoning	2	8
Sodium nitrate		4
Sodium nitrite		1
Sodium erythorbate		$3\frac{1}{2}$
Ice, chopped	120	

Procedure

Follow procedure given above for **Canned Vienna Sausage.**

SOURCE: Stephan L. Komarik, 4810 Ronda, Coral Gables, Florida.

CANNED VIENNA SAUSAGES WITH BEANS AND TOMATO SAUCE

Prepare Vienna Sausages

Use any of the several formulas given above for making **Canned Vienna Sausage.**

Prepare Beans

Soak and blanch beans in the following manner: Soak in cool water to cover for no less then 7 hr and no longer then 8 hr. Tanks used for soaking may be of wood, galvanized iron, or glass-lined. The best method is to have an overflow on the tank to circulate incoming water so the beans will not sour during the soaking period. After beans are properly soaked, place them in wire baskets and submerge them in boiling water for 12–15 min. Then drain well.

Prepare Sauce

Ingredients	Lb	Oz	Cc	Gal.
Tomato purée (sp. gr. 1.040)				50
Cane sugar	125			

Corn sugar	37	
Salt	31	
Onion powder		10
Oil of pimiento		10.80
Oil of cloves		5.00
Oil of nutmeg		4.00
Oil of cassia		0.60
Oleoresin capsicum		5.00
Oleoresin mace		5.00
Water to make		200

Procedure.—Mix together salt, onion powder, essential oils, and oleoresins for later use.

Put tomato purée in a steam-jacketed kettle, add corn and cane sugars and, with steady stirring, bring to a boil. To the boiling stock add the salt-seasoning mixture and continue stirring to uniformly mix ingredients. Bring volume of sauce up to 200 gal. with water and raise temperature to 200°F. Hold at this temperature for can filling.

Fill Cans

Either the 12 oz net or the 108 oz net can sizes are generally used for this product. Pack:

> 25% Vienna sausage pieces (1-in. lengths)
> 30% soaked and blanched beans
> 45% hot tomato sauce

Close cans under vacuum.

Suggested Process

300 × 308 cans (12 oz net) 95 min at 240°F
603 × 700 cans (108 oz net) 250 min at 240°F

Check processing times and temperature with the can supplier or the National Canners Association.

SOURCE: Stephan L. Komarik, 4810 Ronda, Coral Gables, Florida.

VIENNA SAUSAGES PACKED IN BARBECUE SAUCE

Select any one of the top grade canned **Vienna Sausage** formulas given above and follow procedure for making the sausages. Then make up the following barbecue sauce.

Ingredients	Gal.	Lb	Oz
Tomato purée (specific gravity 1.035)	25		
Soup stock or water	25		
Soy sauce	$1\frac{1}{2}$		
Worcestershire sauce	$\frac{1}{2}$		
Vinegar (100-grain)	1		
Wheat flour		7	8
Cornstarch		2	8
Salt		12	8

Cane sugar	10	
Spanish paprika	1	6
Ground red pepper		12
Ground cloves		$1^{1}/_{2}$
Ground mace		$1^{1}/_{2}$
Ground cinnamon		$2^{3}/_{4}$
Ground Jamaica ginger		$2^{3}/_{4}$
Ground black pepper		4
Onion powder		1
Garlic powder		$^{1}/_{2}$

Procedure

Put tomato purée in a steam-jacketed kettle. Add salt mixed together with sugar and the remaining dry ingredients. Bring temperature up to 180°F. Make a slurry of the flour and starch with 5 gal. of water and add it to the purée mixture while agitating mixture with a "Lightning" mixer. Then add soy and Worcestershire sauces, and vinegar and bring up volume to 50 gal. with added water. Raise temperature to 200°–205°F and cook for 15 min.

Canning Procedure

Cut sausages $^{1}/_{4}$ in. shorter than the height of the cans used. Can size of 300 × 309 is the usual size giving 12 oz net contents. For this size can, use 8 oz of sausages and 4 oz sauce. Close cans under 15–20 in. vacuum.

Suggested Process

300 × 309 (12 oz net) 2 hr 15 min at 225°F

Check time and temperature with can supplier or the National Canners Association.

SOURCE: Stephan L. Komarik, 4810 Ronda, Coral Gables, Florida.

COCKTAIL FRANKFURTERS IN GLASS JARS

Select any one of the top grade canned Vienna Sausage formulas given above for ingredients and procedure for making the meat emulsion. The emulsion for this product, though, is stuffed in narrow sheep casings and linked to the desired size which can be from $1^{1}/_{2}$ in. to the height of the glass jar in which they are to be packed. Follow procedure given for Vienna sausage in smoking and chilling the stuffed cocktail frankfurters. Then pack them in 6-oz jars and fill with 2% hot salt brine to within $^{1}/_{4}$ in. below top of jar. Salt brine should be at a temperature of 180°F. Close jars under 27 in. vacuum.

Retort

Place jars in baskets and transfer to the retort. Fill retort with water 20°F higher than the temperature of the brine used to fill the jars (200°F). Before closing retort, adjust water level to 6 in. below the top of the retort; and after retort is closed, adjust air pressure to 28 lb. Then introduce steam and bring retort water temperature up to 230°F. The sterilization time starts when water reaches this temperature.

Suggested Process

For the 6-oz net jar 1 hr 30 min. Check processing time and temperature with can supplier or the National Canners Association.

SOURCE: Stephan L. Komarik, 4810 Ronda, Coral Gables, Florida.

LUNCHEON MEATS, MEAT LOAVES, AND MEAT SPREADS

Many combinations of meat items and by-products can be used to make luncheon meats and meat loaves. The quality and price of the finished product that is desired will largely control the selection of meats used. But, no matter what kind of meat combination is used, it is important to have at least 25% of lean meat such as pork shank or carcass beef in the formula. This helps to coat and bind the ground meats in an emulsion and lock in the moisture which otherwise would render out during the cooking process.

Certain regulations have been prescribed by the USDA Meat Inspection Division that must be observed when processing canned meat products such as luncheon meats, nonspecific loaves, etc., in order to prevent development of the toxin which causes botulism, a very serious and often fatal illness in humans consuming food which contains this toxin produced by *Clostridium botulinum*. To accomplish this end, they require:

(1) That the product must contain 1 oz of sodium nitrate per 100 lb of meat in addition to the $\frac{1}{4}$ oz of sodium nitrite.

(2) That it must be processed to a minimum internal meat temperature of $150°$ F.

(3) That if there is no cereal present, it must have a minimum of 3.5% expressed as brine concentration of the product; and if cereal is present, the brine concentration must be 6.1%. The calculation of brine concentration is arrived at by dividing a total of moisture plus the salt, divided by the salt.

(4) That the product contain 0.5% sugar and mixed for 3 min.

A brief outline of other MID regulations is given below. For complete details of the latest revisions pursuant to the Wholesome Meat Act, contact the Meat Inspection Division, USDA Consumer and Marketing Service, Washington, D.C., and request a copy of *Meat Inspection Regulations*, Federal Register Vol. 35, No. 193, Part II, Oct. 3, 1970.

To further provide consumer safety, MID requires (following reprinted from MID *Regulations Governing Meat Inspection*):

Canning with heat processing and hermetically sealed containers; cleaning containers; closure; code marking; heat processing; incubation. (a) Containers shall be cleaned thoroughly immediately before filling, and precaution must be taken to avoid soiling the inner surfaces subsequently.

(b) Containers of metal, glass, or other material shall be washed in an inverted position with running water at a temperature of at least $180°$ F. The container-washing equipment shall be provided with a thermometer to register the temperature of the water used for cleaning the containers.

(c) Nothing less than perfect closure is acceptable for hermetically sealed containers. Heat processing shall follow promptly after closing.

(d) Careful inspection shall be made of the containers by competent establishment employees immediately after closing, and containers which are defectively filled, defectively closed or those showing inadequate vacuum, shall not be processed until the defect has been corrected. The containers shall again be inspected by establishment employees when they have cooled sufficiently for handling after processing by heating. The contents of defective containers shall be condemned unless correction of the defect is accomplished within six hours following the sealing of the containers or completion of the heat processing, as the case may be, except that (1) if the defective condition is discovered during an afternoon run the cans of product may be held in coolers at a temperature not exceeding $38°$ F under conditions that will promptly and effectively chill them until the following day when the defect may be corrected; (2) short vacuum or overstuffed cans of product which have not been handled in accordance with the above may be incubated under Division supervision, after which the cans shall be opened and the sound product passed for food; and (3) short vacuum or overstuffed cans of product of a class permitted to be labeled, "Perishable, Keep Under Refrigeration" and which have been kept under adequate refrigeration since processing may be opened and the sound product passed for food.

(e) Canned products shall not be passed unless after cooling to atmospheric temperature, they show the external characteristics of sound cans; that is, the cans shall not be overfilled; they shall have concave sides, excepting the seam side, and all ends shall be concave; there shall be no bulging; the sides and ends shall conform to the product; and there shall be no slack or loose tin.

(f) All canned products shall be plainly and permanently marked on the containers by code or otherwise with the identity of the contents and date of canning. The code used and its meaning shall be on record in the office of the inspector in charge.

(g) Canned product must be processed at such temperature and for such period of time as will assure keeping without refrigeration under usual conditions of storage and transportation when heating is relied on for preservation, with the exception of those canned products which are processed without steam-pressure cooking by permission of the Director of Division and labeled "Perishable, Keep Under Refrigeration."

(h) Lots of canned product shall be identified during their handling preparatory to heat processing by tagging the baskets, cages or cans with a tag which will change color on going through the heat processing or by other effective means so as to positively preclude failure to heat process after closing.

(i) Facilities shall be provided to incubate at least representative samples of the product of fully processed canned product. The incubation shall consist of holding the canned product for at least 10 days at about 98° F.

(1) The extent to which incubation tests shall be required depends on conditions such as the record of the establishment in conducting canning operations, the extent to which the establishment furnishes competent supervision and inspection in connection with the canning operations, the character of the equipment used, and the degree to which such equipment is maintained at maximum efficiency. Such factors shall be considered by the inspector in charge in determining the extent of incubation testing at a particular establishment.

(2) In the event of failure by an establishment to provide suitable facilities for incubation of test samples, the inspector in charge may require holding of the entire lot under such conditions and for such period of time as may, in his discretion, be necessary to establish the stability of the product.

(3) The inspector in charge may permit lots of canned product to be shipped from the establishment prior to completion of sample incubation when he has no reason to suspect unsoundness in the particular lots, and under circumstances which will assure the return of the product to the establishment for reinspection should such action be indicated by the incubation results.

NEW FDA BAN ON PREMIXED COMMERCIAL SEASONINGS CONTAINING SODIUM NITRITE

Premixed spice and flavorings ingredients from commercial suppliers are widely used in the manufacture of products such as luncheon meats and weiners. In the past, some of these premixed products also contained the recommended amount of allowable sodium nitrite. Because test data from USDA showed that an undesirable chemical (nitrosamine, a causative of cancer in test animals) may form when the nitrite preservative combined with the amines in the seasonings, the Food and Drug Administration on July 19, 1973 ordered manufacturers of meat curing premixes which combine nitrite curing agents with seasonings to package the nitrite and seasonings separately. The FDA action does not affect manufacturers of premixed seasoning ingredients who use a chemical "buffer" to separate the nitrite and the seasoning in a premix.

GENERAL INSTRUCTIONS FOR PROCESSING CANNED ITEMS UNDER STEAM OR UNDER THE COMBINATION OF STEAM AND WATER PRESSURE

High temperature sterilization process presents many problems due to the fact that physical changes are taking place in the contents of the cans.

First of all, it is necessary to know what is the best temperature to sterilize a product and how long the product must be subjected to that temperature to obtain sterilization.

All ordinary vegetative bacteria are killed at a temperature of 176°F in 30 min, but it takes 30 min to destroy spore-forming bacteria at a temperature of 230°F. At higher temperatures (over 230°F) the time of the process is reduced. At a temperature of 250°F it requires only 3 min to destroy spore-forming bacteria.

The total time to sterilize a can of food depends on (1) the size of the can; (2) the rate of heat penetration to the center of the can; (3) the processing temperature used; (4) the pH of the food; (5) the kind and number of the microorganisms present.

Heat penetration is affected by the consistency of the product and whether or not the cans are shaken or rotated during the process to obtain faster heat penetration.

Most of the canners are not equipped to work out their own problems to determine the temperature and time required to sterilize a product. The suppliers of cans maintain elaborate laboratories to furnish this information and also to indicate the type of cans best suited to the products. *It is of great importance to follow rigidly the times and temperatures of the process recommended by the can manufacturers or the National Canners Association.*

General instructions to be observed during the canning operation:

(1) Checking the seams of a few closed water-filled cans to see if the closing machine is in perfect operational condition. The whole canning operation depends on perfect can closures.

(2) Reject those cans if the lip of the cans are damaged or the lid of the can does not have proper amount of sealing compound.

(3) Rusty cans should not be used.

(4) Cans should be washed and sterilized inside and outside under hot water shower at a temperature of 180°F prior to use.

(5) Cans should not be filled up to the lip of the cans. A can should have a head space of approximately 1/4 in. to obtain proper vacuum in the cans.

(6) Cans should be inspected for proper seams and vacuum after discharge from the closing machine.

The cans should be placed in baskets for processing or in trucks for horizontal retorts, in such manner to ensure proper circulation of steam during retorting.

PROCESSING STEPS

(1) Open vents, turn on steam to allow the air to escape.

(2) Keep vents open at least until inside temperature of the retort reaches 220°F.

(3) During this period leave the drain valve partially open to allow condensed water resulting from condensed steam to escape from the bottom of the retort.

(4) Close drain valve.

(5) Sterilization time starts when temperature inside of retort reaches the designated temperature for the product to be processed.

(6) After sterilization, turn on air pressure at least 5 lb over steam pressure.

(7) As soon as the sterilization time is over, chill cans as quickly as possible. Open water supply valve and allow water to fill retort.

(8) Open overflow slightly to let the heated water escape from the retort and keep up circulation of cold water during the chilling operation.

(9) Chill cans in the retort until the internal temperature of the can reaches 120°F or lower.

(10) Close water line. Close air supply valve. Open retort and drain water. Never open retort as long as the pressure gage shows any pressure inside the retort.

(11) Give a final inspection of the cans after removal from the retort for proper vacuum and seam.

(12) The same general rules should be followed in processing food products packed in glass jars with the exception that in this case the retort will be filled with water after baskets are deposited in the retort. Air pressure is introduced in the retort after it is closed, vents are closed. The air pressure should be 10 lb over the pressure recommended to sterilize the product and the same pressure should be maintained during the chilling process also. The overflow valve should be slightly open for escaping hot water.

Exceptions to the Above Rules.—Certain products such as spreads or solid materials such as hash, or products with heavy gravies packed in small cans which do not generate instant steam in the cans when high pressure steam is introduced in the retort do not need air pressure over the steam pressure during the sterilization process, but as a safety measure, chilling under air pressure is always a good practice.

BOILING TEMPERATURE OF WATER UNDER PRESSURE

Pressure of Steam Gage Lb	Thermometer Readings °F	Pressure of Steam Gage Lb	Thermometer Readings °F
1	215.2	9	236.6
2	218.3	10	238.8
3	221.3	11	241.0
4	224.2	12	243.1
5	226.9	13	245.3
6	229.5	14	247.3
7	231.9	15	249.1
8	234.3	15.3	250.0

CANNED LUNCHEON MEATS

FINEST QUALITY SPICED PORK LUNCHEON MEAT

Spiced pork luncheon meat is canned in 12-oz oblong cans which are commercially sterile and need no refrigeration. It is also canned in 3- and 6-lb oblong cans which should be kept refrigerated throughout storage and the marketing channels.

Formula and treatment of the product ingredients as given below are the same for the 12-oz, the 3-lb, and the 6-lb packs. Canning and process time and temperature, however, differ as described.

Ingredients	Lb	Oz
Boneless, skinless picnics (fat is not removed)	500	
Salt	17	8
Cane sugar	5	
Sodium nitrate		5
Sodium nitrite		$1\frac{1}{4}$
Sodium erythorbate		$4\frac{1}{3}$
Ground white pepper		10
Ground Jamaica ginger		1
Ground nutmeg or mace		1

Procedure for All Can Sizes

Have meat well chilled (34°–36°F) at the start of grinding. Also, in order to keep the meat at a low temperature during grinding and mixing, it is very important that these operations are conducted in the chill room at 34°–36°F.

Separate about $\frac{1}{4}$ of the chilled shank portions of the picnics and put through the $\frac{1}{8}$-in. plate of the grinder. Put the remainder of the picnics through the $\frac{3}{8}$-in. plate. Transfer ground meat to a mechanical vacuum mixer. Mix together the remaining ingredients and add to the ground meat. Then mix under 27 in. vacuum for 5 min. Dump meat mixture into truck and transfer to chill room (34°–36°F) for overnight cure.

Remove cured meat and again put it in the vacuum mixer. Mix under 27 in. vacuum for 8–10 min.

Procedure for 12-Oz Oblong Cans

Can Filling and Closing.—Can filling is conducted at ambient temperature, but meat trucks supplying the stuffing machine should be kept under refrigeration prior to use. Spray cans with edible oil on the conveyor before meat is stuffed into cans. Temperature of the meat for can filling should not exceed 40°F. Pack in 12-oz net oblong cans and close under 27 in. vacuum.

Suggested Process.—$3\frac{7}{8} \times 2\frac{1}{8} \times 3\frac{1}{4}$ in. (12 oz net) oblong cans require 1 hr 10 min at 230°F.

Check processing time and temperature with can supplier or the National Canners Association.

This product is commercially sterile and needs no refrigeration through storage and marketing channels.

Procedure for 3- and 6-Lb Oblong Cans

Can Filling and Closing.—Cans are not sprayed with edible oil as with the 12-oz size. A stuffing horn is used instead and the can is lined with parchment paper. Wrap the stuffing horn with parchment before the can is placed on the horn. The parchment should be large enough to overlap the horn and long enough to be folded on the bottom and top of the can.

Close 3- or 6-lb net weight cans under 27 in. vacuum. Cans should show paneling on 3 sides of the can.

Suggested Process.—Transfer closed cans to cooking vats. Place them in such manner so as to allow proper circulation of water around each can for uniform cooking. Cooking vats should have perforated pipes on the bottom connected to an air line and a regulating valve to keep water in circulation during the cooking process.

Place cans in cooking vats with water temperature at 160°F; maintain this temperature for a cook of 3½ hr. Internal temperature of the meat should be 150°-155°F when cooking is completed. Then drain hot water from cooking vats and refill with cold water, keeping air line in operation for proper circulation of the cold water to chill cans. Open overflow valve and let warm water escape from the top of the tank. Chill cans for 2 hr. Then transfer cans to a chill room (34°-36°F) for final chilling.

This product is perishable and should always be kept under refrigeration until it reaches the consumer.

SOURCE: Stephan L. Komarik, 4810 Ronda, Coral Gables, Florida.

COMMERCIAL QUALITY SPICED PORK LUNCHEON MEAT IN 3- AND 6-LB CANS

Ingredients	Lb	Oz
Pork shank meat	125	
Pork cheeks	75	
Pork tongues	100	
Pork hearts	100	
Regular pork trimmings 50/50	100	
Ice, chopped	15	
Salt	17	8
Cane sugar	10	
Sodium erythorbate		4⅓
Sodium nitrite		1¼
Sodium nitrate		5
Ground white pepper		10
Ground Jamaica ginger		1
Ground mace or nutmeg		1

Procedure

Have all meats well chilled at start of procedure (34°-36°F). Grind chilled pork shank meat through the ⅛-in. plate of the grinder and transfer to a chopper. Add the ice, and only 3 lb of the salt mixed with only ¼ oz of the sodium nitrite; chop for 3 min.

Grind all other chilled meats through the ⅜-in. plate of the grinder. Mix together the remainder of the dry ingredients. Put all ground meats in a vacuum mixer, add the mixture of dry ingredients and, under 27 in. vacuum, mix for 3 min.

Dump mixed meat into truck and transfer to chill room at 34°-36°F for overnight cure. Next day, remix meat under 27 in. vacuum just long enough (approximately 1 min) to make meat more pliable for stuffing.

Can Filling and Closing.—A stuffing horn is used and the can is lined with parchment paper. Wrap the stuffing horn with parchment before the can is placed on the horn. The parchment should be large enough to overlap the horn and long enough to be folded on the bottom and top of the can.

Close either the 3- or the 6-lb cans under 27 in. vacuum. Cans should show paneling on 3 sides of the can.

Suggested Process.—Transfer closed cans to cooking vats. Place them in such manner so as to allow proper circulation of water around each can for uniform cooking. Cooking vats should have perforated pipes on the bottom connected to an air line and a regulating valve to keep water in circulation during the cooking process.

Place cans in cooking vats with water temperature at 160°F; maintain this temperature for a cook of 3½ hr. Internal temperature of the meat should be 150°-155°F when cooking is completed. Then drain hot water from cooking vats and refill with cold water, keeping air line in operation for proper circulation of the cold water to chill cans. Open overflow valve and let warm water escape from the top of the tank. Chill cans for 2 hr. Then transfer cans to a chill room (34°-36°F) for final chilling.

This product is perishable and should always be kept under refrigeration until it reaches the consumer.

SOURCE: Stephan L. Komarik, 4810 Ronda, Coral Gables, Florida.

CHOPPED HAM IN 12-OZ OBLONG CANS

Ingredients	Lb	Oz
Boneless, skinless fresh hams	500	
Salt	17	8
Cane sugar	5	
Sodium nitrate		5
Sodium nitrite		1¼
Sodium erythorbate		4⅓

If spiced ham is desired, use 2 lb 8 oz of the following spice mixture:

	Lb	Cc
Cane sugar	10	
Oleoresin capsicum		10.00
Oil of allspice		5.00
Oil of cloves		6.00
Oil of cassia		0.50
Oil of bay		0.50

Procedure

Have meat well chilled (34°-36°F) at the start of grinding. Also, in order to keep the meat at a low temperature during grinding and mixing, it is very important that these operations are conducted in the chill room at 34°–36°F.

Separate about ¼ of the chilled shank portions of the hams and put through the ⅛-in. plate of the grinder. Put the remainder of the ham through the ⅜-in. plate. Transfer ground meat to a mechanical vacuum mixer. Mix together the remaining ingredients and add to the ground meat. Then mix under 27 in. vacuum for 5 min. Dump meat mixture into truck and transfer to chill room (34°–36°F) for overnight cure.

Remove cured meat the next day and again put it in the vacuum mixer. Mix under 27 in. vacuum for 8–10 min.

Can Filling and Closing.—Can filling is conducted at ambient temperature, but meat trucks supplying the stuffing machine should be kept under refrigeration prior to use. Spray cans with edible oil on the conveyor before meat is stuffed into cans. Temperature of the meat for can filling should not exceed 40°F. Pack in 12-oz net oblong cans and close under 27 in. vacuum.

Suggested Process.—3⅞ × 2⅛ × 3¼ in. (12 oz net) oblong cans require 1 hr 10 min at 230°F.

Check processing time and temperature with can supplier or the National Canners Association.

This product is commercially sterile and needs no refrigeration through storage and marketing channels.

SOURCE: Stephan L. Komarik, 4810 Ronda, Coral Gables, Florida.

FINEST QUALITY PORK OR PORK-BEEF LUNCHEON MEAT

This formula is for canning in 4 × 4 × 24 in. or 6-lb capacity 2 DS molds.

Use either of these meat combinations:

	No. 1 (Lb)	No. 2 (Lb)
Fresh skinless, boneless picnics	500	
Fresh lean carcass beef		200
Fresh regular pork trimmings 50/50		250

with these ingredients:

	Lb	Oz
Salt	16	4
Cane sugar	5	
Sodium nitrite		1¼
Sodium nitrate		5
Sodium erythorbate		4⅓
Ground white pepper or dry soluble pepper	1	
Ground Jamaica ginger		1
Ground nutmeg or mace		1

Procedure for All-Pork Product

Grinding Method No. 1.—Have meat well chilled (32°–34°F) at start of operation. Remove sinews and blood clots. Separate about ¼ of the shank portions of the picnics and grind these through the ⅛-in. plate of the grinder. Grind remainder of the picnics through the 3/16-in. plate. Transfer both to a vacuum mixer. Mix together the dry ingredients and add to the ground meat; mix under 27 in. vacuum for 8 min. Pack meat mixture tightly in truck and transfer to chill room (34°–36°F) for overnight cure.

Grinding-Chopping Method No. 2.—Have meat well chilled (32°–34°F) at start of operation. Grind shank portion of the picnics through the 3/16-in. plate of the grinder and cut remainder of the picnics into 1-lb chunks. Mix together the dry ingredients. Transfer ground shank meat to a prechilled chopper, add mixture of dry ingredients, and run chopper for 1 min. Then add the meat chunks and chop until meat particles are reduced to desired size. If a rapid chopper is used, fill chopper bowl to ½ of its capacity and use only 3 knives.

Pack chopped meat tightly in meat truck and transfer to chill room (34°–36°F) for overnight cure.

Remix and Stuff.—For either method of grinding and mixing given above, after overnight cure remove meat from chill room and transfer to vacuum mixer; mix under 27 in. vacuum for 3 min to make meat more pliable for stuffing. Temperature of meat before stuffing should not be over 40°F and it is recommended that grinding and/or chopping, mixing, and possibly stuffing, be carried out in a chill room so that a low meat temperature can be maintained throughout the balance of the procedure.

Use a stuffing horn to stuff meat into molds. Wrap horns with parchment paper or plastic material before stuffing; this should be large enough to overlap the horn and long enough to be folded over the bottom and top of the mold. Fill molds and close spring attachments tightly.

Cook and Chill.—Transfer molds to a cooking vat, placed so as to permit proper circulation of water around each and every mold for uniform cooking. Vats should have perforated pipes on the bottom which are connected to an air line with a regulating valve to keep water in circulation during the cooking process. Introduce hot water (160°F) and cook for 3½ hr. Internal temperature of the meat should reach 155°F at the end of the cook. Then drain hot water from the vat and refill with cold water, keeping air line in operation for proper circulation. Open overflow valve to let warm water overflow from vat. Chill product for 2 hr or until an internal meat temperature of 100°-110°F is obtained. Transfer product immediately to cooler at 34°-36°F and chill overnight. Next day remove meat from molds. The 6-lb loaves are usually encased in pliofilm casings for sale to the trade. The long loaves (4 × 4 × 24 in.) are usually sliced and vacuum packaged in small packages for retail trade. Both loaves and sliced packages should be kept constantly refrigerated throughout storage and marketing until product reaches the consumer.

Procedure for Pork-Beef Product

Grind beef through the $3/16$-in. plate of the grinder. Use pork without grinding. Follow Grinding-Chopping Method No. 2 given above. All other steps in the procedure are identical.

SOURCE: Stephan L. Komarik, 4810 Ronda, Coral Gables, Florida.

SPICED BEEF LUNCHEON MEAT IN 12-OZ OBLONG CANS (COMMERCIALLY STERILE)

Ingredients	Lb	Oz
Fresh carcass beef (canner-cutter)	400	
Fresh beef flanks (canner-cutter)	100	
Salt	17	5
Cane sugar	5	
Sodium nitrite		$1^1/_4$
Sodium nitrate		5
Sodium erythorbate		$4^1/_3$
Decorticated black pepper (80 mesh)		1
Ground celery seed		$1/_2$
Onion powder		2
Garlic powder		$1/_4$
Ice, chopped		15

Procedure

Use only fresh beef, not older than 48 hr after slaughter. Meat should be chilled to 32°F before processing. Grind beef and flanks through the 1-in. plate of the grinder and transfer to a meat chopper. Add ice and salt (previously mix salt with sugar, sodium erythorbate, cure, and seasonings) and chop for 3 min. Transfer chopped meat to a vacuum mixer and mix for 3 min under 27 in. of vacuum.

Dump mixed meat in a truck and transfer to cooler at 30°-32°F for overnight cure. Next day, put meat in a vacuum mixer again and mix approximately 1 min to make meat pliable for filling into cans. Cans should be sprayed with edible oil on the conveyor before meat is stuffed in cans. Temperature of meat should not exceed 40°F entering cans. Close cans under 27 in. vacuum.

Suggested Process.—$3^7/_8$ × $2^1/_8$ × $3^1/_4$ size (12 oz net) oblong cans require 1 hr 10 min at 230°F.

Check processing time and temperature with can supplier or the National Canners Association.

Chilling.—Chill cans under 15 lb air pressure at least 20 min before releasing pressure. Further chilling can be at atmospheric pressure.

This product is commercially sterile and needs no refrigeration through storage and marketing.

SOURCE: Stephan L. Komarik, 4810 Ronda, Coral Gables, Florida.

NEW ENGLAND PRESSED HAM IN 3- OR 6-LB OBLONG CANS (PERISHABLE)

Ingredients	Lb	Oz
Large fresh hams, skinned, boned, and defatted to lean	500	
Salt	17	8
Cane sugar	5	
Sodium nitrate		5
Sodium nitrite		$1^1/_4$
Sodium erythorbate		$4^1/_3$
Ice, chopped		15

For flavoring, use 8 oz of the following mixture per 100 lb of meat. Dissolve oleoresin and oils in 1 oz of propylene glycol and mix thoroughly with the sugar.

Flavoring Ingredients	Lb	Cc
Cane sugar	10	
Oleoresin capsicum		10.00
Oil of allspice		5.00
Oil of cloves		6.00
Oil of cassia		0.50
Oil of bay		0.50

Procedure

Have meat well chilled (32°-34°F) before start of operation. Separate about $1/_4$ shank portion of the hams and grind through the $1/_8$-in. plate of the grinder. Transfer to a chopper; add the ice, and only 3 lb of the salt and only $1/_4$ oz of the sodium nitrite; chop for 3 min. Transfer to cooler (34°-36°F) for overnight cure.

Mix together remaining salt and sodium nitrite with the remainder of the dry ingredients and the flavoring mixture.

Put remainder of the hams through the 1- or $1^1/_2$-in. plate of the grinder. Transfer to a vacuum mixer; add salt-flavoring mixture and mix for 3 min under 27 in. vacuum. Dump mixture into truck and transfer to cooler (34°-36°F) for overnight cure.

Next day, put both the emulsion and the ground meat again in a vacuum mixer and mix for 3 min under 27 in. vacuum.

Can Filling and Closing.—A stuffing horn is used and the can is lined with parchment paper. Wrap the stuffing horn before the can is placed on the horn. The parchment should be large enough to overlap the horn and long enough to be folded on the bottom and top of the can.

Close cans under 27 in. vacuum. Cans should show paneling on 3 sides of the can.

Suggested Process.—Transfer closed cans to cooking vats. Place them in such manner so as to allow proper circulation of water around each can for uniform cooking. Cooking vats should have perforated pipes on the bottom connected to an air line and a regulating valve to keep water in circulation during the cooking process.

Place cans in cooking vats with water temperature at 160°F; maintain this temperature for a cook of 3½ hr. Internal temperature of the meat should be 150°-155°F when cooking is completed. Then drain hot water from cooking vats and refill with cold water, keeping air line in operation for proper circulation of the cold water to chill cans. Open overflow valve and let warm water escape from the top of the tank. Chill cans for 2 hr. Then transfer cans to a chill room (34°-36°F) for final chilling.

This product is perishable and should always be kept under refrigeration until it reaches the consumer.

SOURCE: Stephan L. Komarik, 4810 Ronda, Coral Gables, Florida.

NEW ENGLAND PRESSED HAM

This formula is for canning in 4 × 4 × 24 in. or 6-lb capacity 2 DS molds.

Ingredients	Lb	Oz
Large hams defatted to lean	500	
Salt	12	8
Tripolyphosphate	1	4
Cane sugar	5	
Sodium nitrate		5
Sodium nitrite		1¼
Sodium erythorbate		4⅓
Ice, chopped	40	

If spiced pressed ham is to be made, use the following flavorings in the proportion of 2 lb 8 oz of the mixture to 500 lb of meat. Dissolve oleoresin and oils in 1 oz of propylene glycol and mix with the 10 lb of cane or corn sugar.

Flavoring Ingredients	Lb	Cc
Cane or corn sugar	10	
Oleoresin capsicum		10.00
Oil of allspice		5.00
Oil of cloves		6.00
Oil of cassia		0.50
Oil of bay		0.50

Procedure

Have meat well chilled (32°-34°F) at start of operation. Remove sinews and blood clots. Sep-

arate shank portion of the hams (approximately ¼) and put through the ⅛-in. plate of the grinder. Transfer ground shank meat to a chopper; add only 2½ lb of the salt mixed with the following ingredients: only ¼ oz sodium nitrite, only 1 oz sodium nitrate, only 1 lb sugar, only ⅞ oz sodium erythorbate, only 4 oz tripolyphosphate, and only 8 oz of the flavorings (if the product is to be spiced); then add only 15 lb of the chopped ice. Let chopper run for 3 min. Dump meat emulsion into a meat tub and transfer to cooler (34°-36°F) for overnight cure.

Grind remainder of the hams through the 1- or 1½-in. plate of the grinder and transfer to a vacuum mixer. Add remaining dry ingredients and remainder of chopped ice (25 lb). Mix under 25 in. vacuum for 3 min. Dump mixture into a meat truck or tubs and transfer to a cooler (34°-36°F) for overnight cure.

Remix and Stuff.—Next day, transfer both the emulsion and the coarse ground meat to the vacuum mixer and mix under 25 in. vacuum for 3 min. Temperature of meat before stuffing should not be over 40°F.

Use a stuffing horn to stuff meat into molds. Wrap horns with parchment paper or plastic material; this should be large enough to overlap the horn and long enough to be folded over the bottom and top of the mold. Fill molds and close spring attachments tightly.

Cook and Chill.—Transfer molds to a cooking vat, placed so as to permit proper circulation of water around each and every mold for uniform cooking. Vats should have perforated pipes on the bottom which are connected to an air line with a regulating valve to keep water in circulation during the cooking process. Introduce hot water (160°F) and cook for 3½ hr. Internal temperature of the meat should reach 155°F at the end of the cook. Then drain hot water from the vat and refill with cold water, keeping air line in operation for proper circulation. Open overflow valve to let warm water overflow from vat. Chill product for 2 hr or until an internal meat temperature of 100°-110°F is obtained. Transfer product immediately to cooler at 34°-36°F and chill overnight.

Next day remove meat from molds. The 6-lb loaves are usually encased in pliofilm casings for sale to the trade. The long loaves (4 × 4 × 24 in.) are usually sliced and vacuum packaged in small packages for retail trade. Both loaves and sliced packages should be kept constantly refrigerated throughout storage and marketing until product reaches the consumer.

SOURCE: Stephan L. Komarik, 4810 Ronda, Coral Gables, Florida.

NEW ENGLAND PRESSED HAM USING NONFAT DRY MILK

Make up this cure:

	Lb	Oz
Sodium nitrate	3	7
Sodium nitrite		5
Dextrose (corn sugar)	10	

Place ingredients in a 5-gal. glass container. Fill with water and dissolve. Use 1 qt ($2^3/_4$ lb) of solution for each 100 lb of meat.

Ingredients	Lb	Oz
Cured pork blade meat[1]	80	
Bullmeat	20	
Nonfat dry milk	$4^1/_4$	
Salt		8
Ground white pepper		3
Ground cinnamon		2
Fresh garlic		$1/_2$
Cure		11
Chopped ice		

[1] Cure blade meat at the rate of $2^3/_4$ lb salt and $2^3/_4$ lb cure to 100 lb meat for 4–5 days.

Procedure

Grind cured pork blade meat through 1-in. plate. Chop garlic fine and mix with cure.

Grind fresh bullmeat through $3/_8$-in. plate. Place in silent cutter, add salt, cure, and nonfat dry milk alternately with chopped ice until all nonfat dry milk is used. Then add pepper and cinnamon; chop very fine. In all, use about 20–22 lb chopped ice. Place blade meat in mixer, add bullmeat emulsion, mix well.

Stuff in beef bungs or corresponding size cellulose casings. Place in smokehouse, starting with 120°F, gradually raising temperature to 170°F until desired color appears. Cook at 160°-165°F until internal temperature reaches 155°F (approximately $2^1/_2$ -3 hr).

This sausage can be finished in smokehouse in 8–9 hr.

SOURCE: American Dry Milk Institute, 130 N. Franklin, Chicago, Ill.

COMMERCIAL GRADE MINCED HAM IN 3- OR 6-LB OBLONG CANS (PERISHABLE)

Ingredients	Lb	Oz
Lean, boneless beef	125	
Regular pork trimmings 50/50	100	
Pork hearts	100	
Pork cheek meat	100	
Pork tongues	75	
Ice, chopped	25	
Salt	17	8
Cane sugar	5	
Sodium erythorbate		$4^1/_3$
Sodium nitrate		5
Sodium nitrite		$1^1/_4$
Ground black pepper	1	
Ground nutmeg		5
Ground allspice		$2^1/_2$
Ground Jamaica ginger		$2^1/_2$
Ground caraway seed		1

Procedure

Have all meats well chilled (32°-34°F) at start of operation. Grind beef through the $1/_8$-in. plate of the grinder and transfer to a chopper; add the chopped ice and only the following portion of the curing ingredients: 3 lb salt, $1/_4$ oz sodium nitrite, and $7/_8$ oz sodium erythorbate; chop for 5 min.

Mix together remaining dry ingredients.

Grind regular pork trimmings and pork cheeks through the $1/_8$-in. plate of the grinder; the pork hearts and tongues through the $1/_8$-in. plate of the grinder. Transfer these to a vacuum mixer along with the remaining dry ingredients; mix under 27 in. vacuum for 3 min.

Dump mixed meats into truck and transfer to chill room (34°-36°F) for overnight cure.

Remix and Stuff.—Next day remix meat in vacuum mixer for 1 min under 27 in. vacuum to make meat more pliable for stuffing.

A stuffing horn is used and the can is lined with parchment paper. Wrap the stuffing horn with parchment before the can is placed on the horn. Parchment should be large enough to overlap the horn and long enough to be folded on the bottom and top of the can. Close cans under 27 in. vacuum. Cans should show paneling on 3 sides of the can.

Suggested Process.—Transfer closed cans to cooking vats. Place them in such manner so as to allow proper circulation of water around each can for uniform cooking. Cooking vats should have perforated pipes on the bottom connected to an air line and a regulating valve to keep water in circulation during the cooking process.

Place cans in vats with water temperature at 160°F; maintain this temperature for a cook of $3^1/_2$ hr. Internal temperature of the meat should be 150°-155°F when cooking is completed. Then drain hot water from cooking vats and refill with cold water, keeping air line in operation for proper circulation of the cold water to chill cans. Open overflow valve and let warm water escape from the top of the tank. Chill cans for 2 hr. Then transfer cans to a chill room (34°-36°F) for final chilling.

This product is perishable and should always be kept under refrigeration until it reaches the consumer.

SOURCE: Stephan L. Komarik, 4810 Ronda, Coral Gables, Florida.

MINCED HAM USING NONFAT DRY MILK

Make up this cure:

	Lb	Oz
Sodium nitrate	3	7
Sodium nitrite		5
Dextrose (corn sugar)	10	

Place ingredients in a 5-gal. glass container. Fill with water and dissolve. Use 1 qt (2¾ lb) of solution for each 100 lb of meat.

Ingredients	Lb	Oz
Boneless chuck	40	
Lean pork trimmings	20	
Regular pork trimmings	40	
Nonfat dry milk	4¾	
Salt	2¾	
Ground white pepper		6
Ground coriander		2
Fresh onions	1	
Fresh garlic		1
Mapleine		2
Cold water	6	
Cure	2¾	

Procedure

Grind onions and chuck through ⅛-in. plate. Grind pork trimmings through ⅜-in. plate. Chop garlic fine and mix it and Mapleine with cure. Place all meats in mixer. Add water, salt, and cure. Then sprinkle with nonfat dry milk and seasonings. Mix well.

Stuff into beef bungs, or corresponding size cellulose or fibrous casings. Hang overnight in 38°–40°F cooler. Let stand in sausage room for about 2 hr before putting in smokehouse. If stuffed in cellulose casing, shower with hot water immediately before placing in smokehouse.

Start with 120°F. Gradually increase heat to 170°F. When 155°F internal temperature is obtained, take out. Rinse with cold water until cold. Sausage must be dry outside before placing in cooler.

SOURCE: American Dry Milk Institute, 130 N. Franklin, Chicago, Ill.

CURED BEEF TONGUES IN GLASS JARS

Preparation of Beef Tongues

Beef tongues should be carefully cleaned before curing. Tongues which are damaged or deformed should be rejected.

Use full strength 100° salinometer brine to remove slime from tongues. Use brush or scraper to clean tongues, especially at the gullet where the tongues are slimy.

Cure

Artery pump tongues with the following curing pickle, injecting 10% of the weight of the fresh tongue:

	Gal.	Lb
Water	50	
Salt		50
Cane sugar		15
Sodium nitrite		1

After tongues are pumped, transfer them in meat trucks to a chill room (35°–40°F) and cure overnight.

Cook

Use 5 gal. of cooking water for each 100 lb of tongues. Bring water to boiling, then add tongues, and cook in the boiling water until they are done (tender).

Skin and Trim

Skin and trim tongues immediately after they are removed from the cooking tank. Trimmings can be utilized in other meat spreads.

Fill Jars

Prepare Agar-agar or Gelatin Solution.—If agar-agar is used, add 5 lb of agar-agar to 95 lb of water and heat mixture to 200°F; hold at this temperature during the filling operation.

If gelatin is used, use 250 bloom, or higher gelatin. Soak overnight 1 lb of gelatin in 8 lb of water, then heat to 160°F or higher to dissolve gelatin. Hold temperature at 160°F during filling operation.

Pack tongues into jars while hot. Pour some agar-agar or gelatin solution into the bottom of the jar, then place the proper weight of tongue in the jar and close under 27 in. vacuum.

Process

Glass jars should be processed in vertical retorts filled with water under 25 lb air pressure. Heat water in retort to 240°F. Sterilization time starts when the retort temperature reaches the temperatures given below:

Suggested Process

6 oz net jars 1 hr 30 min at 230°F
12 oz net jars 1 hr 30 min at 240°F
16 oz net jars 2 hr at 240°F
22 oz net jars 2 hr at 240°F
48 oz net jars 2 hr 30 min at 230°F

Check process times and temperatures with can supplier or the National Canners Association.

SOURCE: Stephan L. Komarik, 4810 Ronda, Coral Gables, Florida.

PICKLED PIG'S FEET OR PORK HOCKS IN VINEGAR

Use 5–6 gal. of the following curing pickle per each 100 lb of pig's feet or hocks:

	Gal.	Lb
Water	50	
Salt		50
Sodium nitrite		1

Make certain that during the entire process the meat will not come in contact with any iron or copper utensils; otherwise, discoloration or greening will result in the finished product.

Select pig's feet and hocks of approximately the same size for uniform processing.

Place pig's feet or hocks in a stainless steel steam-jacketed kettle and cover with curing pickle. Raise temperature to 200°–205°F. Shut off steam, close lid on kettle, and let meat cure overnight in the heated pickle. Next morning, turn on steam again, raise temperature to 180°F and cook product until tender. Do not handle or move the feet or hocks while they are cooking. When tender, remove from the kettle and rinse under hot shower to remove all rendered fat from the surfaces. Then transfer to chill tanks equipped with a cold water inlet at the bottom of the tank and an overflow at the top.

Chill the product until it can be handled for boning, slicing, and further process. After feet or hocks are chilled it is advisable to place them in a 35-grain vinegar solution overnight.

Filling

In 1-gal. jars pack 100 oz
In 1-qt jars pack 28 oz
In 1-pt jars pack 14 oz
In 8-oz jars pack 9 oz
In 4-oz jars pack 3½ oz

Vinegar Solution to Fill Jars.—Pig's feet and hocks are packed in 45-grain vinegar (3.6% acetic acid) which is necessary to prevent bacterial spoilage. Use 100-grain vinegar in the ratio of 4¼ parts to 5½ parts water. To each 100 gal. of 45-grain vinegar add 10 lb of salt previously mixed with 5 oz ascorbic acid and, for flavor, 5 cc of oil of tarragon, if desired.

Fill Jars to Capacity.—Be sure there are no air pockets left between the pieces of meat when the jars are filled with the vinegar solution. Also, any lengthy exposure of the meat to air before packing will cause discoloration in the jars.

SOURCE: Stephan L. Komarik, 4810 Ronda, Coral Gables, Florida.

MEAT LOAVES

Meat loaves are a very important ready-to-eat item. Their preparation and manufacturing procedures are closely related to that of sausages. They fall into the following classifications: (a) prepared entirely from a meat emulsion; (b) a combination of meat emulsion and ground meat; (c) prepared entirely from ground or chopped meat; (d) a combination of precooked meats molded in a gelatin solution; and (e) those which are completely cooked in water or steam or which are baked.

Meat loaves are molded into a shape and size so that when they are sliced they are just the right shape and size for sandwiches. They are usually sliced and packaged for the consumer in transparent packaging so that the housewife can see what she is buying.

The varieties of meat loaves are so numerous that it is impossible to cover all of them in this Formulary, so only typical formulas representing each type of loaf are given. The add-to-ingredients for color and flavor are many: chopped olives, cooked macaroni, pistachio nuts, diced cheese, etc. However, if cheese is used in a meat loaf, only cheese with low-fat content should be used (sausage-makers cheese).

USE OF GELATIN AND NONFAT DRY MILK IN MEAT LOAVES

Only high grade gelatin will harden properly when mixed with water. Being an animal product, it will not keep without refrigeration, and in any case it is not advisable to hold it over. Therefore only enough jelly for daily use should be made up.

It is possible to dissolve 1 part gelatin to 6 parts water and obtain a properly hardened product. A ratio of 1-to-4 makes a very heavy, thick jelly.

To make a jelly, measure or weigh cold water. Pour the gelatin into the center of the water and let it stand until gelatin absorbs water. Do not move vessel or stir. When all water is absorbed, place vessel in a tub of hot water. Heat the water in the tub until gelatin solution reaches 160°F. Caution: If solution is heated to 170°F it will lose its binding power.

Although any amount of nonfat dry milk may be used in meat loaves, it is not advisable to use more than 12%. If more is used, the meat flavor will gradually diminish. When nonfat dry milk is used in a formula, it must be listed as an ingredient and all ingredients listed in the order of the relative amount of their content.

The use of nonfat dry milk in a formula does not affect the time or degree of temperature or smoking, cooking, or baking.

SOURCE: American Dry Milk Institute, 130 N. Franklin, Chicago, Ill.

PICKLE AND PIMIENTO LOAF

Ingredients	Lb	Oz
Bull meat or other lean beef	65	
Regular pork trimmings 50/50	35	
Ice, chopped (approximately)	45–50	
Salt	3	
Corn syrup solids	2	
Semolina flour	5	
Nonfat dry milk	5	
Soy protein concentrate	2	
Canned sweet pickles, chopped	8	
Canned pimientos, chopped	8	
Monosodium glutamate		3
Sodium nitrite		1/4
Sodium nitrate		1
Sodium erythorbate		7/8
Spanish paprika		4
Ground red pepper		1
Ground mace		1
Ground Jamaica ginger		1
Onion powder		2
Garlic powder		1/16

Procedure

Precaution.—Be sure all meats are well chilled down to 32°–34°F at start of operation.

Grind, Chop, and Mix.—Grind beef through the 1/8-in. plate of the grinder; pork trimmings through the 1/4-in. plate. Keep ground meats separated.

Mix together only the sugar, cure, and flavorings.

Put ground beef in a chopper, add 1/3 of the ice followed by the sugar-cure-flavoring mixture. Chop until ingredients are well-emulsified, adding more ice gradually so as to keep temperature at 40°F or lower. Then add remaining ice and the ground pork and chop at a temperature of 50°F. Add over the top of the emulsion the flour, nonfat milk, and protein concentrate. Let machine run just long enough to mix thoroughly and absorb the added ingredients. Then transfer mixture to a vacuum mixer, add chopped pickles and pimientos evenly over the top of the emulsion, close machine and mix for 3 min under 25 in. vacuum.

If an Emulsifier Is Used.—Grind meats as above; transfer them to a mechanical mixer; add ice and all the other ingredients except pickles and pimientos; mix thoroughly. Then put mixture first through the fine plate and then through the superfine plate of an emulsifier. Transfer emulsion to a vacuum mixer; add pickles and pimientos; if emulsion is too stiff, some ice water may be added. Close mixer and mix for 3 min under 25 in. vacuum.

Stuff and Cook.—Stuff emulsion into parchment paper-lined molds. Close molds and place them in the cooking vat so that water can circulate freely between each. Fill vat with hot water at 160°F and maintain this temperature during the cooking period. Agitate the cooking water with compressed air but do not "churn" water during cooking. Cook product for 3 hr or until an internal meat temperature of 152°F is obtained.

Chill.—Drain hot water from cooking vat and refill with cold water. Open overflow valve at the top of the tank to let hot water flow from top. Chill cooked molds approximately 2 hr or to an internal meat temperature of 80°–90°F. Remove molds from tank and immediately transfer them to chill room (34°–36°F) for overnight chilling.

After proper chilling, product may be sliced and vacuum packaged. Or, loaves cooked in 6-lb molds may be stuffed in Cellophane casings and sold in bulk to the trade.

Before slicing or encasing 6-lb loaves in Cellophane, some processors prefer to "bake" the surface of loaves by dipping the loaf in hot oil or lard (350°F) for a short time to give the loaf a brown "crust" appearance.

This is not a commercially sterile product and must be kept refrigerated throughout storage and the marketing channels.

SOURCE: Stephan L. Komarik, 4810 Ronda, Coral Gables, Florida.

PICKLE AND PIMIENTO LOAF
USING NONFAT DRY MILK

Make up this cure:

	Lb	Oz
Sodium nitrate	3	7
Sodium nitrite		5
Dextrose (corn sugar)	10	

Place ingredients in a 5-gal. glass container. Fill with water and dissolve. Use 1 qt (2³/₄ lb) of solution for each 100 lb of meat.

Ingredients	Lb	Oz
Beef trimmings	35	
Veal trimmings	25	
Pork trimmings	25	
Bullmeat	15	
Nonfat dry milk	12	
Sweet pickles	5	
Pimientos	6	
Fresh onions	5	
Salt	3¹/₂	
Ground white pepper		8
Ground marjoram		1
Fresh garlic		1
Chopped ice	45	
Cure		2³/₄

Procedure

Chop bullmeat, beef, and onions together, veal and pork separately, through ¹/₈-in. plate. Cut pickles in ¹/₄-in. pieces, pimientos in ¹/₂-in. pieces. Chop garlic fine and mix with cure.

Place ground beef-onion mixture, salt, and cure in silent cutter. After a few revolutions add chopped ice and nonfat dry milk alternately a little at a time until all nonfat dry milk is used. Then add veal, pork, and seasoning, and chop so that the emulsion is of the same consistency as for bologna. Put mixture into mixer. Add pickles and pimientos. Mix well.

For cooking, stuff into cooking molds and cook at 160°–165°F until internal temperature reaches 155°F. For baking, place in greased pans and bake at 225°–250°F until internal meat center reaches 155°F. Chill until the loaves are firmly set. Then stuff into artificial casing.

SOURCE: American Dry Milk Institute, 130 N. Franklin, Chicago, Ill.

BAKED VEAL LOAF

Ingredients	Lb	Oz	Cc
Veal trimmings	60		
Regular pork trimmings 50/50	40		
Semolina flour	10		
Nonfat dry milk	5		
Salt	3		
Corn sugar	1		
Canned pimiento, chopped	4		
Ice, chopped (approximately)	45–50		
Sodium nitrite		¹/₄	
Sodium nitrate	1		
Sodium erythorbate		⁷/₈	
Monosodium glutamate	2		
Onion powder	3		
Dry soluble pepper	4		
Oil of nutmeg			2.00
Oil of sage			4.00
Oil of thyme			0.50

Mix together dry soluble pepper and oils with the corn sugar.

Procedure

Precaution.—Be sure all meats are well chilled (32°–34°F) at start of operation.

Grind, Chop, and Mix.—Grind veal through the ¹/₈-in. plate of the grinder; pork trimmings through the ¹/₄-in. plate. Place veal in a chopper, add 10–15 lb of the ice, and, after a few revolutions, add salt previously mixed with the cures, flavorings, and seasonings. During the chopping, add enough ice to keep meat temperature at 40°F. Add pork trimmings, the remaining ice, and chop to a fine emulsion. Then add flour and nonfat dry milk and mix just long enough to thoroughly mix in these ingredients (4–5 revolutions of the chopper). Finally, add the chopped pimientos and let bowl make 2–3 more revolutions. Then transfer emulsion to a vacuum mixer and mix for 3 min under 25 in. vacuum.

Pan and Bake.—Pack finished emulsion in greased, oblong baking pans, rounding off top in loaf fashion. Pans may be sprayed with oil or heated lard.

Transfer loaves to a preheated smokehouse at 165°F and bake at this temperature for 1 hr. Then gradually raise temperature to 180°–190°F and bake until an internal meat temperature of 155°F is obtained. (A bakery oven may also be used to bake loaves: preheat oven to 175°F, bake loaves for 2 hr, then raise temperature to 200°F and bake until internal meat temperature reaches 155°F.)

Remove loaves from smokehouse (or oven) and let cool at room temperature for 2 hr. Remove loaves from pans; place on screen shelves of trucks; transfer to a chill room (40°–45°F) for overnight. Next day, slice and package in vacuum packaging or encase whole loaves in Cellophane casings.

Before slicing or encasing whole loaves, some processors prefer to brown the surface of loaves by dipping the loaves in hot oil or lard (350°F) for a short time to give the loaf a "crusty" appearance.

Product should be held under refrigeration.

SOURCE: Stephan L. Komarik, 4810 Ronda, Coral Gables, Florida.

VEAL, PORK, AND LIVER LOAF USING NONFAT DRY MILK

Make up this cure:

	Lb	Oz
Sodium nitrate	3	7
Sodium nitrite		5
Dextrose (corn sugar)	10	

Place ingredients in a 5-gal. glass container. Fill with water and dissolve. Use 1 qt (2¾ lb) of solution for each 100 lb of meat.

Ingredients	Lb	Oz
Veal trimmings	50	
Regular pork trimmings	40	
Fresh or frozen pork livers	10	
Nonfat dry milk	12	
Fresh whole eggs (approx 4 dozen)	6	
Salt	3¾	
Ground white pepper		8
Ground celery seed		2
Ground mustard		2
Ground cardamom		2
Fresh garlic		2
Chopped ice	45	
Cure	2¾	

Procedure

Grind livers and veal separately through ⅛-in. plate. Grind pork trimmings through ⅜-in. plate. Chop garlic fine and mix with cure.

Place livers in silent cutter, add salt and cure. Chop until bubbles appear on surface, then add veal, chopped ice, and nonfat dry milk alternately until nonfat dry milk is used. Then add pork, eggs, and seasoning. Chop fine. During chopping, add chopped ice so the consistency of emulsion is about the same as for bologna.

Stuff into cooking molds. Cook at 160°–165°F until internal temperature is 155°F. When chilled and firmly set, stuff into artificial casings.

The product should be held under refrigeration until used.

SOURCE: American Dry Milk Institute, 130 N. Franklin, Chicago, Ill.

CANNED VEAL LOAF IN 12-OZ OBLONG CANS (COMMERCIALLY STERILE)

Ingredients	Lb	Oz
Veal chuck, fresh	250	
Beef tripe, treated, white	175	
Pork trimmings	75	
Cream of Wheat cereal	35	
Whole eggs, frozen	12	
Salt	12	
Onion powder		10
Dry soluble pepper	1	4
Ground sage		5
Ground thyme		2.5
Garlic powder		1

Procedure

Grind chilled meat items and frozen eggs through the ⅟₁₆-in. plate of the grinder. Transfer the ground products to a vacuum mixer. Mix together the salt and other seasonings. Start mixer and add seasoning mixture until well blended; then add the Cream of Wheat. Close mixer and draw 27 in. vacuum. Run mixer for 5 min.

Pack and Process

Pack meat loaf mixture in 12-oz oblong cans which have been sprayed with an edible oil; close cans under 27 in. vacuum. Process for 90 min at 237°F. Chill cans for 30 min under 15 lb pressure, with final chilling to 110°F without pressure. Time and temperature of processing should be checked with can supplier or the National Canners Association.

Product is commercially sterile and does not need refrigeration during storage and marketing.

SOURCE: Stephan L. Komarik, 4810 Ronda, Coral Gables, Florida.

LUXURY LOAF USING NONFAT DRY MILK

Make up this cure:

	Lb	Oz
Sodium nitrate	3	7
Sodium nitrite		5
Dextrose (corn sugar)	10	

Place ingredients in a 5-gal. glass container. Fill with water and dissolve. Use 1 qt (2¾ lb) of solution for each 100 lb of meat.

Ingredients	Lb	Oz
Beef trimmings	45	
Pork blade meat	35	
Regular pork trimmings	10	
Backfat, cubed	10	
Nonfat dry milk	12	
Pimientos	5	
Cure	2¾	
Salt	3	
Pistachio	2	
Sage		1

Ground white pepper	6
Paprika	1
Mace	3

Procedure

First chop beef almost fine, then blade meat, then pork. Add backfat and chop just enough to get cubed effect. After beef is put in chopper, add nonfat dry milk, cure, and spices, adding ice during the chopping operation to make it of the right consistency. Add pimientos and run 1–2 revolutions.

When chopped fine enough, put it in pans that have been greased, then let them stand in sausage room temperature for 2 hr to complete cure. Then put in oven, bake at 225°–250°F for about 3 hr. Take center meat temperature; it should be 152°–155°F.

When this is reached, the loaves are done; take out and cool.

If it is desired to stuff loaf in artificial casing, cool about 3–4 hr to let it set. Then dip loaf in hot gelatin before stuffing.

If loaf is to be cooked, put meat in a container that has a lid that can be pressed down. Cook for 2–3 hr, according to the size loaf made. Center meat temperature should reach 152°–155°F. When done, initial cooling is in cold water in cooking tank. Then cool to room temperature. Loaves may be stuffed in artificial casings.

The product should be held under refrigeration until used.

SOURCE: American Dry Milk Institute, 130 N. Franklin, Chicago, Ill.

UTILITY LOAF
USING NONFAT DRY MILK

This loaf is intended to make practical and profitable use of bruised or other disfigured hams or shoulders. Meat should not be more than 20–25% fat and must be cured.

Ingredients	Lb	Oz
Cured pork meat	100	
Ground white pepper		6
Ground sage		1/2
Ground cloves		1/2
Mapleine (dissolved in 1 pt water)		1
Nonfat dry milk	8	
Cold water	12	

Procedure

Run cured pork through 1/2-in. plate. Add water, nonfat dry milk, and seasoning; mix well.

Place meat in molds for cooking (Frank, Hoy, or similar molds.) Cook for 3 1/2 hr at 165°F. Inside temperature should be at least 152°–155°F. After cooking, chill, and remove from containers. They can then be wrapped in pliofilm or stuffed in cellulose casing.

Loaf can be baked as follows:

Place meat in pans, smooth top with sugar syrup and bake at 200°–225°F. Bring center meat temperature to 154°F, then chill, wrap or stuff as above specified.

This product should be held under refrigeration until used.

SOURCE: American Dry Milk Institute, 130 N. Franklin, Chicago, Ill.

MEAT AND CHEESE LOAF
USING NONFAT DRY MILK

Make up this cure:

	Lb	Oz
Sodium nitrate	3	7
Sodium nitrite		5
Dextrose (corn sugar)	10	

Place ingredients in a 5-gal. glass container. Fill with water and dissolve. Use 1 qt (2 3/4 lb) of solution for each 100 lb of meat.

Ingredients	Lb	Oz
Cured beef trimmings	35	
Cured pork trimmings	15	
American process cheese	10	
Veal trimmings	15	
Pork trimmings	20	
Pork livers	15	
Nonfat dry milk	10	
Salt	2	
Fresh garlic		2
Fresh onions	2	
Ground white pepper		7
Ground marjoram		2
Ground cardamom		1
Cure	1	6
Chopped ice		

Procedure

Grind onions, veal trimmings, and pork livers through 3/8-in. plate. Grind cured pork trimmings and American process cheese, separately, through 1/4-in. plate. Grind beef trimmings through 1/8-in. plate, and pork trimmings through 3/8-in. plate. Chop garlic fine and mix with cure.

Place pork livers and veal trimmings in silent cutter, add salt, cure, and nonfat dry milk alternately with chopped ice a little at a time until all nonfat dry milk is used. Then add pork and seasoning. Make emulsion of the same consistency as for bologna.

Place all ingredients in mixer and mix thoroughly. Stuff into cooking molds. Cook at 160°–165°F until internal temperature reaches 155°F. Remove from cooking vat and chill. When cold and firmly set remove from molds and wrap or stuff into suitable containers.

The product should be held under refrigeration until used.

SOURCE: American Dry Milk Institute, 130 N. Franklin, Chicago, Ill.

MACARONI, MEAT, AND CHEESE LOAF USING NONFAT DRY MILK

Make up this cure:

	Lb	Oz
Sodium nitrate	3	7
Sodium nitrite		5
Dextrose (corn sugar)	10	

Place ingredients in a 5-gal. glass container. Fill with water and dissolve. Use 1 qt (2³⁄₄ lb) of solution for each 100 lb of meat.

Ingredients	Lb	Oz
Veal trimmings	40	
Beef trimmings	40	
Regular pork trimmings	20	
Nonfat dry milk	12	
Macaroni (cooked)	10	
Cheese	15	
Salt	3¹⁄₂	
Fresh onions	3	
Ground white pepper		8
Fresh garlic		2
Tomato purée	4	
Chopped ice	40	
Cure	2³⁄₄	

Procedure

Grind onions and beef together, and veal separately, through ¹⁄₈-in. plate. Grind pork through ³⁄₈-in. plate. Cut cheese into ¹⁄₂-in. cubes. Chop garlic fine and mix with cure.

Place beef, a little shaved ice, salt, and cure into silent cutter. After a few revolutions, add chopped ice and nonfat dry milk alternately a little at a time until all nonfat dry milk is used. Add veal trimmings. During chopping, add enough chopped ice to keep emulsion about the same consistency as for bologna. Then add pork and seasoning, chopping fine.

Place chopped material in mixer, add macaroni and cheese, mix until all is evenly distributed.

This loaf can be cooked or baked.

To Bake.—Scale into lightly-greased loaf pans and allow to stand in sausage room temperature for 2 hr to complete cure. Then transfer to oven. Bake at 225°–250°F for about 3 hr, or until internal meat temperature reaches 152°–155°F. Remove from oven and allow to cool. Stuff loaves in artificial casings, if desired, after cooling loaves 3–4 hr to let them set. Dip in hot gelatin before stuffing.

To Cook.—Put mixture in containers that have lids that can be clamped down for the cooking operation. Cook for 2–3 hr, according to size. Center meat temperature should reach 152°–155°F when done. Initial cooling is in cold water in cooking tank. Then cool to room temperature. Loaves may be stuffed in artificial casings.

The product should be held under refrigeration until used.

SOURCE: American Dry Milk Institute, 130 N. Franklin, Chicago, Ill.

BAKED PEPPER LOAF

Ingredients	Lb	Oz
Boneless, skinless, defatted picnics or extra lean pork trimmings	80	
Bull meat or lean beef	20	
Salt	3	
Corn syrup solids	2	
Ice, chopped	20	
Wheat flour	2	8
Soy protein concentrate	2	8
Monosodium glutamate	2	
Sodium nitrite		¹⁄₄
Sodium nitrate	1	
Sodium erythorbate		⁷⁄₈
Dry soluble or ground pepper	6	

Procedure

Be sure all meats are well chilled (32°–34°F) at start of operation.

Grind, Chop, and Mix.—Grind bull meat or lean beef through the ¹⁄₈-in. plate of the grinder; pork through the ¹⁄₂-in. plate.

Transfer ground beef to a chopper, add ¹⁄₃ of the ice and the salt previously mixed with the cures, corn syrup solids, and seasonings. Chop for 2 min; then gradually add remainder of the ice and chop for 2 min more. When all of the ice is incorporated in the emulsion, gradually add flour and protein concentrate; let machine run until temperature of mixture reaches 50°F.

Transfer emulsion to the mixer, add ground pork, and mix until the ground meat is fully coated with the emulsion. This takes approximately 2-3 min.

Cure and Remix.—Dump mixture into a meat truck; transfer to a cooler (36°-38°F) for overnight cure. The following day, remix in a vacuum mixer under 25 in. vacuum just long enough to make meat pliable for panning.

Pan and Bake.—Pack finished meat mixture in greased, oblong baking pans, rounding off top in loaf fashion. Pans may be sprayed with oil or heated lard. Before baking, sift cracked pepper evenly over top of each loaf, using a coarse mesh sifter.

Transfer loaves to a preheated smokehouse at 165°F and bake at this temperature for 1 hr. Then gradually raise temperature to 180°-190°F and bake until an internal meat temperature of 155°F is obtained. (A bakery oven may also be used to bake loaves: preheat oven to 175°F, bake loaves for 2 hr, then raise temperature to 200°F and bake until internal meat temperature reaches 155°F.)

Remove loaves from smokehouse (or oven) and let cool at room temperature for 3 hr. Remove loaves from pans; place on screen shelves of trucks; transfer to a chill room (40°-45°F) for overnight. Next day, slice and package in vacuum packaging or encase whole loaves in Cellophane casings.

Product is perishable and should be held in refrigeration through storage and marketing.

SOURCE: Stephan L. Komarik, 4810 Ronda, Coral Gables, Florida.

BAKED DUTCH LOAF

Ingredients	Lb	Oz
Regular pork trimmings 50/50	40	
Pork cheeks, trimmed	40	
Boneless beef or veal	20	
Salt	3	
Wheat flour	5	
Corn syrup solids	2	
Soy protein concentrate	2½	
Nonfat dry milk	2½	
Sodium nitrite		¼
Sodium nitrate	1	
Sodium erythorbate		⅞
Monosodium glutamate	2	
Onion chips		8
Dry soluble pepper or ground black pepper		4
Ground nutmeg		1
Ground sage		1
Mustard flour		2
Ice, chopped	20	

Procedure

Be sure that all the meats are chilled to 32°-34°F before processing.

Grind, Chop, and Mix.—Grind regular pork trimmings through the ⅜-in. plate of the grinder, pork cheeks through the ³/₁₆-in. plate, and veal or beef through the ⅛-in. plate.

Put ground beef or veal in a chopper, add ⅓ of the ice, then the salt (previously mixed with the cures and seasonings except the onion chips), chop for 2 min, then gradually add remaining ice and chop 2 min more. When all the ice is added to the emulsion, gradually add wheat flour, soy protein concentrate, and nonfat dry milk. Let machine run until emulsion temperature reaches 50°F.

Transfer meat emulsion and ground meats to a vacuum mixer, spread onion chips evenly over the top and mix for 3 min under 25 in. vacuum.

Pan and Bake.—Remove meat from the mixer. Form balls approximately 6-8 lb by hand; fit and shape them into round baking pans. To add gloss to the finished product brush top of loaves with sugar syrup, if desired.

Transfer loaves to a preheated smokehouse or bakery oven at 160°-165°F and bake at this temperature for 1 hr. Then gradually raise temperature to 180°-190°F and bake until an internal meat temperature of 155°F is obtained.

Chill.—Let baked loaves cool at room temperature for approximately 4 hr. Then remove loaves from pans, place them on screen shelf trucks, and move into the chill room at 45°F for final overnight chill before packaging. Product may be packaged as a whole loaf, or sliced and packaged in consumer-sized packages.

Product is perishable and should be kept under refrigeration through storage and marketing.

SOURCE: Stephan L. Komarik, 4810 Ronda, Coral Gables, Florida.

DUTCH LOAF
USING NONFAT DRY MILK

Make up this cure:

	Lb	Oz
Sodium nitrate	3	7
Sodium nitrite		5
Dextrose (corn sugar)	10	

Place ingredients in a 5-gal. glass container. Fill with water and dissolve. Use 1 qt (2¾ lb) of solution for each 100 lb of meat.

Ingredients	Lb	Oz
Lean pork trimmings	55	
Skinned bacon ends	15	

Veal trimmings	25	
Pork livers	5	
Nonfat dry milk	12	
Salt	$4\frac{1}{4}$	
Fresh onions	4	
Worcestershire sauce		8
Ground white pepper		8
Ground marjoram		2
Ground sage		2
Fresh garlic		2
Cure	$2\frac{3}{4}$	
Chopped ice		

Procedure

Grind veal trimmings, pork livers, and onions through $\frac{1}{8}$-in. plate. Grind pork trimmings through $\frac{1}{4}$-in. plate and bacon ends through $\frac{3}{8}$-in. plate. Chop garlic fine and add together with Worcestershire sauce to cure.

Place pork livers, veal trimmings, salt, and cure in silent cutter. Then add chopped ice and nonfat dry milk alternately, a little at a time, until all nonfat dry milk is used. Then add bacon ends and seasoning. Chop to about the consistency of bologna emulsion, preferably a little less stiff. Then place in mixer, add lean pork trimmings and mix well. The original Dutch loaf is placed in round pans and baked at 250°–275°F until internal heat reaches 155°F. It can also be stuffed in cooking molds. After baking, chill and wrap.

SOURCE: American Dry Milk Institute, 130 N. Franklin, Chicago, Ill.

LIVER LOAF (PERISHABLE)

Ingredients	Lb	Oz
Pork livers, fresh	250	
Pork jowls, fresh	110	
Salt pork trimmings	60	
Lean pork trimmings	80	
Salt	15	
Cane sugar	5	
Onion powder	1	8
Dry soluble pepper		1
Ground marjoram		2
Ground sage		5
Ground cloves		2
Ground allspice		1
Sodium nitrite		$1\frac{1}{4}$
Sodium nitrate		5

Preparation of Product

Use well-chilled (34°–35°F) fresh products. Trim pork livers to remove all visible tubes and surface fat, then slice into 1–1½-in. slices. Soak slices in 1% salt solution overnight. Drain.

Grind and Chop.—Grind pork jowls, salt pork, and pork trimmings through the $\frac{1}{4}$-in. plate of the grinder; and the lean pork and liver through the $\frac{1}{8}$-in. plate (keep each separate). Put ground liver in a chopper; chop approximately 10 min. Add salt previously mixed with sugar, flavoring materials, spices, and cures. Then add remaining ground pork items and chop to a fine emulsion.

Packing and Processing

Pack emulsion in parchment-lined 3- or 6-lb oblong cans and close under 27 in. vacuum.

Suggested Process.—Have water preheated to 180°F. Immerse baskets filled with cans—properly spaced so water can circulate around each individual can. Let temperature drop to 160°F and maintain this temperature for 2¾–3 hr. Internal meat temperature should reach 155°F at completion of cooking. After cooking, drain hot water and chill cans with overflowing cold water for 2 hr. Remove cans, transfer to chill room (34°–36°F) at least 8 hr before removing to holding cooler.

This product is perishable and should be kept refrigerated throughout storage and through marketing channels.

SOURCE: Stephan L. Komarik, 4810 Ronda, Coral Gables, Florida.

LIVER LOAF

Use either of these meat combinations:

Ingredients	No. 1 (Lb)	No. 2 (Lb)
Pork livers	55	50
Pork jowls	45	
Regular pork trimmings 50/50		50
Sliced backfat (for lining molds)		

with these ingredients:

	Lb	Oz
Semolina flour or cracker meal	4	
Salt	2	8
Onion powder		5
Corn syrup solids	1	
Sodium nitrite		$\frac{1}{8}$
Sodium nitrate		1
Sodium erythorbate		$\frac{7}{8}$

and with either of these seasoning combinations:

	Oz
Dry soluble pepper	4
Ground allspice	$\frac{1}{2}$
Ground cloves	$\frac{1}{2}$

Ground sage	$1/2$	
Ground marjoram	$1/2$	
Ground nutmeg	$1/2$	
Ground Jamaica ginger	$1/2$	

or

	Oz	Cc
Dry soluble pepper	4	
Oil of allspice		0.60
Oil of cloves		1.00
Oil of sage		0.60
Oil of marjoram		0.50
Oil of nutmeg		1.00
Oleoresin ginger		0.50

Thoroughly mix these seasonings with the dry soluble pepper and corn syrup solids.

Procedure

Have all the meats well chilled (32°–34°F) at start of operation.

Grind and Chop.—Grind jowls and pork trimmings through the $1/4$-in. plate of the grinder. Do not grind liver. Put liver in a chopper and chop until bubbles appear on the surface of the emulsion (approximately 10 min). Then add ground jowls or pork trimmings along with the salt previously mixed with cures, flavorings and seasonings—except for the flour or cracker meal—and chop until fat specks are no longer visible in the emulsion. Add flour or cracker meal and run machine 2–3 revolutions to disperse addition throughout mixture.

If an Emulsifier Is Used.—Grind liver through the $1/8$-in. plate of the grinder; the jowls or pork trimmings through the $1/4$-in. plate. Transfer to a mechanical mixer, premix remainder of ingredients, add to ground meats, and mix thoroughly. Without delay, put product through the fine plate of the emulsifier.

Stuff.—Use oblong molds with spring-attached cover for the top such as are used for cooking boiled hams (see Section 1). The mold is first lined with parchment paper cut to the right size to fit the inner dimension of the mold; then use one piece of parchment to cover meat crosswise and another piece lengthwise, both long enough to cover the sides and top of the loaf. After the mold is lined with parchment it should be lined crosswise with sliced backfat so that both ends of the backfat will be covered with parchment. Use only the solid skin side of the sliced backfat, otherwise it will not bind the emulsion. Fill molds, put on cover, close mold gently; do not apply springs tightly.

Cook.—Transfer filled molds to a cooking tank in which water is preheated to 180°F. Let temperature drop to 160°F and maintain this temperature until internal meat temperature reaches 152°–155°F. This takes approximately 3 hr.

Chill.—Drain hot water and refill tank with cold water. Let water overflow during chilling. Chill loaves for 2 hr, then transfer molds to the chill room at 34°–36°F and allow air circulation between molds. Chill loaves overnight.

Packaging.—Remove chilled loaves carefully from molds and stuff them in Cellophane casings. Keep loaves at cooler temperature (45°F) until shipment.

Product may also be sliced and packaged in consumer-sized retail packages. Product should be held under refrigeration during storage and marketing.

SOURCE: Stephan L. Komarik, 4810 Ronda, Coral Gables, Florida.

LIVER LOAF USING NONFAT DRY MILK

Make up this cure:

	Lb	Oz
Sodium nitrate	3	7
Sodium nitrite		5
Dextrose (corn sugar)	10	

Place ingredients in a 5-gal. glass container. Fill with water and dissolve. Use 1 qt ($2^3/4$ lb) of solution for each 100 lb of meat.

Ingredients	Lb	Oz
Pork livers, fresh or frozen	50	
Veal trimmings	10	
Regular pork trimmings	40	
Nonfat dry milk	12	
Salt	$3^1/2$	
Fresh onions	4	
Ground white pepper		8
Ground mace		2
Ground marjoram		3
Ground ginger		2
Fresh garlic		$1/2$
Chopped ice	10	
Cure	$2^3/4$	

Procedure

Grind onions with pork livers, and grind veal separately, through $1/8$-in. plate. Grind pork trimmings through $3/8$-in. plate. Chop garlic fine and mix with cure.

Place livers, salt, and cure in silent cutter. After a few revolutions, add nonfat dry milk and chopped ice alternately a little at a time until all nonfat dry milk is used. Then add veal. When chopped nearly fine enough, add pork and seasoning. Chop fine.

Place into molds suitable to trade. Put on lid

and cook at 160°-165°F until internal temperature reaches 155°F. Chill overnight. Loaves also can be stuffed into artificial casings for additional protection before removing from molds. Then give loaves a gelatin coating as described below. Loaves can also be stuffed in artificial casings for additional protection.

Coating for Meat Loaves

Ingredients	Lb
Gelatin	15
Lard	30
Nonfat dry milk	20
Salt	3
Hot water (200°F)	60

Place hot water in silent cutter. Immediately add gelatin and chop until dissolved. Then add lard and chop until well mixed. Add nonfat dry milk and salt, and chop the entire mixture until temperature is reduced to about 100°F.

Place this mixture in a container similar to a double boiler or steam-jacketed kettle. For dipping loaves, the temperature of mixture must be maintained between 95° and 100°F.

Suitable tongs can be secured from butcher supply firms that will be found helpful in dipping loaves.

SOURCE: American Dry Milk Institute, 130 N. Franklin, Chicago, Ill.

DELUXE LIVER LOAF USING NONFAT DRY MILK

Make up this cure:

	Lb	Oz
Sodium nitrate	3	7
Sodium nitrite		5
Dextrose (corn sugar)	10	

Place ingredients in a 5-gal. glass container. Fill with water and dissolve. Use 1 qt ($2^3/4$ lb) of solution for each 100 lb of meat.

Ingredients	Lb	Oz
Fresh pork livers	35	
Lean veal trimmings	10	
Regular pork trimmings	20	
Cooked pork livers	10	
Cooked backfat	10	
Skinned pork jowls	15	
Pistachio nutmeats	4	
Ripe olives	2	
Nonfat dry milk	12	
Fresh onions	4	
Salt	$3^1/2$	
Ground white pepper		6
Ground marjoram		2

Ground ginger	1
Ground sage	1
Chopped ice	12
Cure	$2^3/4$

Procedure

Grind fresh livers and onions through $1/16$-in. plate. Grind veal and pork trimmings and pork jowls through $1/8$-in. plate. Cut cooked pork livers and backfat into $1/2$-in. cubes. Pit ripe olives and cut into small pieces.

Place fresh livers, salt, and cure in silent cutter. After a few revolutions add nonfat dry milk and chopped ice. Then add veal, regular pork trimmings, and pork jowls; chop until fine.

Place all chopped meats in mixer. Add seasoning, nuts, olives, and cooked pork livers. Mix until all ingredients are evenly distributed. Stuff into cooking molds, cook at 160°-165°F until internal temperature reaches 155°F. When thoroughly chilled and set, wrap or stuff in suitable casings.

SOURCE: American Dry Milk Institute, 130 N. Franklin, Chicago, Ill.

HEADCHEESE (BRAWN)

Use any of these meat combinations:

	No. 1 Lb	No. 2 Lb	No. 3 Lb
Pork tongues, cured and cooked	100	50	75
Pork hearts, cured and cooked	50	100	75
Pork cheeks, trimmed cured and cooked	100	100	100
Pork snouts, cured and cooked	200	200	200

Cut up hearts so arteries and blood clots can be removed. Clean all mucous material from other pork products. These meats are precured before processing by immersing them in the following pickle for 7-10 days at 34°-36°F, using 5 gal. of the following pickle per 100 lb of meat:

	Gal.	Lb
Water	50	
Salt		70
Sodium nitrite		1
Sodium nitrate		1
Corn sugar (optional)		10

Pork skins are used as the binding agent in meat formulations No. 1 and No. 2. Gelatin is the binding agent in formulation No. 3.

If Pork Skins Are Used.—Use 50 lb of fresh, defatted pork skins for either No. 1 or No. 2 meat combination. Pork skins should be entirely free of fat. Cook them separately by immersing in simmering water, using just enough water to cover. Cook until tender but not mushy; do not overcook; skins lose their binding property if overcooked. Reserve pork skin cooking stock.

If Gelatin Is Used.—Granular 250 bloom gelatin is used as the binding agent in meat combination No. 3. Use 10 lb of gelatin with 40 lb of cold water. Put cold water in a container and slowly add the gelatin without stirring. Let gelatin absorb the water; then heat in steam-jacketed kettle with steady stirring until material is in a clear solution. Temperature of the finished gelatin solution should not be over 160°F.

Since all meats are precured, no additional salt or curing materials are needed. Seasoning ingredients for the meat combinations given above are the following:

	Lb	Oz
Dry soluble pepper	1	
Ground Jamaica ginger		4
Ground mace		2
Ground allspice		2
Ground caraway seed		4
Onion powder		10

Procedure

Cooking.—Transfer all cured meat to a steam-jacketed kettle, add sufficient water to cover meat, bring to boiling, then let it cool to simmering temperature (205°F) and cook for approximately 2½ hr.

Cubing and Grinding.—Grind pork skins through the ¼-in. plate of the grinder. The rest of the cooked meat should be run through a headcheese cutter or through the 1–1½-in. plate of the grinder. Bring up yield of cooked meats to 100–110% with added stock from the pork skins (if used).

Mixing.—Put all the diced or ground material in a meat truck; premix seasoning and add evenly to the meats; and mix thoroughly with a meat paddle. The material is then ready for stuffing.

If gelatin is used (formulation No. 3), thoroughly mix liquid gelatin into the meat items along with the seasonings.

Stuffing.—Stuff (with hand scoops) into artificial casings, beef bungs, hog stomachs, or 4 × 4 × 24 in. polyethylene-lined molds for pressing and cooking.

Cooking.—Transfer sausages to the cooking vat with a water temperature of 200°–205°F. Let temperature drop gradually to 180°F and cook until an internal meat temperature of 170°F is obtained. Cooking time depends on the size (diameter) of the casings. Large sizes will take

approximately 3½ hr, the product in molds requires about 3 hr.

Chilling.—Remove cooked sausages from the cooking vat and chill in cold water for 2 hr. Be sure to maintain proper circulation of the cold water. The product in 4 × 4 × 24 in. molds is transferred to the chill room at a temperature of 36°–38°F for final chilling. Sausages stuffed in natural or artificial casings are placed in spring operated oval or oblong molds such as are used to shape flat hams, and transferred to a cooler at 34°–36°F for final chill.

Smoking.—Sausages encased in beef bungs or hog stomachs are usually smoked for better appearance and keeping quality. Place chilled and formed sausages on wire screens and give them a cold smoke at house temperature not over 80°F with dampers wide open, until the desired color is obtained. Sausages which are not smoked may become moldy and slimy, especially in the summer months. To avoid this condition, sausages should be thoroughly washed with a 45-grain vinegar before shipment to the customer.

This **product** should be held under refrigeration until consumed.

SOURCE: Stephan L. Komarik, 4810 Ronda, Coral Gables, Florida.

HEADCHEESE USING NONFAT DRY MILK

The following cured pork meats will be needed:

	Lb
Snouts	20
Lips	20
Hearts	20
Cheek meat	15
Skins	15
Ears	10

with these ingredients:

	Lb	Oz
Nonfat dry milk	12	
Ground white pepper		7
Ground mustard		5
Ground sage		2
Salt		12
Fresh onions	2	
Cooking broth	45	

Procedure

Place all meat in separate nets and put in steam-jacketed kettle. Cover with water and cook at 170°–180°F until all meat is tender (time varies). Pork hearts will take longest. Reserve cooking broth. When tender, grind onions with skins through $1/16$-in. plate. Cut snouts, lips, hearts and cheeks into $3/4$-in. pieces and ears into $1/4$-in. pieces. Put all prepared meats in mixer. Sprinkle with nonfat dry milk and seasoning. Also add cooking broth, mixing well. Stuff into beef cap ends, or pork stomachs or artificial casings.

Cook for 1 hr at 165°F. Then chill in iced water. This product can be smoked. Smoke at cool temperature (120°F) for 2–3 hr.

Keep the product under refrigeration.

SOURCE: American Dry Milk Institute, 130 N. Franklin, Chicago, Ill.

HEADCHEESE SPICES

Mix together the following seasonings and use this quantity of mixture (3 lb 12 oz) per each 100 lb of headcheese mixture:

	Lb	Oz
Salt	2	
(or quantity to required taste)		
Powdered or granulated onion	1	
Powdered white pepper		6
Powdered caraway seed		3
Powdered allspice		1
Powdered marjoram		1
Powdered cloves		1

SOURCE: *Food Flavorings, 2nd Edition* by J. Merory, published by Avi Publishing Co., Westport, Conn.

SOUSE OR ASPIC LOAF

This product is identical with **Headcheese Formula No. 3** (given above) using gelatin. Curing and cooking of the meats are the same. The meat items are washed after cooking—never ground—then diced or cut in the headcheese cutter. After dicing, rinse diced meat again with hot water in order to eliminate any meat particles adhering to the surface, otherwise the gelatin becomes cloudy in the finished product.

How to Prepare Gelatin.—Put $7\frac{1}{2}$ pt of 45-grain vinegar into a stainless steel-jacketed kettle. Add 40 lb of cold water. Slowly pour in gelatin. Do not stir. Let gelatin absorb the moisture; then bring temperature up to 160°F and, with steady stirring, cook until the solution is clear and without any lumps. Temperature of the gelatin solution should not rise above 160°F. Use the following soluble formula for seasonings so as not to discolor the gelatin with ground spices:

	Cc
Oleoresin capsicum	10.00
Oil of caraway	7.50
Oil of allspice	1.25

Mix thoroughly the oleoresin and oils in 4 lb of cane sugar and 1 lb of free-flowing onion powder and add to the liquid gelatin, stirring continuously.

Stuffing.—Use the same casings as for Headcheese. Stuffing is done with a hand scoop. Cooking, chilling, and forming are identical as for Headcheese. This product is not smoked and should be kept under refrigeration.

SOURCE: Stephan L. Komarik, 4810 Ronda, Coral Gables, Florida.

HEADCHEESE (BRAWN) IN 12-OZ CANS (COMMERCIALLY STERILE)

Ingredients	Lb	Oz
Pork snouts	200	
Pork tongues	125	
Pork hearts	100	
Pork cheeks and head meat	75	
Water	50	
Salt	9	
Cane sugar	5	
Sodium nitrite		$1\frac{1}{4}$
Decorticated black pepper (38-mesh)		10
Ground coriander		5
Ground caraway seed		5

Procedure

Grind separately pork snouts, tongues, cheeks and head meat through the $1/2$-in. plate of the grinder, pork hearts through the $1/8$-in. plate. Put ground pork snouts in a steam-jacketed kettle, add 50 lb of water, and cook for 15 min at 200°–205°F. Then add ground pork tongues, pork cheeks and head meat and cook an additional 10 min, keeping the same temperature. Finally, add the ground pork hearts along with the rest of the ingredients and cook an additional 10 min at 200°–205°F. Agitate product during the cooking process; when done, turn off steam and allow the rendered fat to rise to the surface; skim off fat. After cooking, yield will be not greater than 75%.

Fill product while hot into 12-oz net cans. Temperature should not drop below 160°F before cans are closed. In case temperature drops below 160°F the cans should be closed under vacuum.

Suggested Process

12 oz net weight oblong cans 2 hr at 240°F

Check process time and temperature with can supplied or the National Canners Association.

This product is commercially sterile and needs no refrigeration through storage and marketing channels.

SOURCE: Stephan L. Komarik, 4810 Ronda, Coral Gables, Florida.

IMITATION CHICKEN LOAF IN 12-OZ, OR 3- OR 6-LB OBLONG CANS

Ingredients	Lb	Oz	Pt
Cooked hog stomachs	150		
Cooked beef tripe, treated	125		
Cooked pork trimmings	100		
Cooked veal trimmings	75		
Durum seminola flour	55		
Salt	15		
Ground celery seed		$2^{1}/_{4}$	
Ground white pepper		1	
Monosodium glutamate		10	
Vinegar (100-grain)			$4^{1}/_{2}$

Procedure

Cook hog stomachs for $2^{1}/_{2}$ hr in boiling water and remove black lining from inside stomachs. Cook treated beef tripe for 30 min. Cook veal and pork trimmings for 30 min.

Grind and Mix.—Immediately after cooking grind all meats through the $1/_{2}$-in. plate of the grinder. Transfer ground meats to a vacuum mixer. Start mixer and add salt, previously mixed with seasonings and monosodium glutamate, and flour. Then add vinegar and mix for $1/_{2}$ min. Close mixer and under 27 in. vacuum mix for $2^{1}/_{2}$ min.

Fill into 12-oz, 3- or 6-lb oblong cans immediately, while product is hot.

If product temperature in cans is kept at 160°F or higher, close cans without vacuum. If the temperature is lower than 160°F, close cans under 10–15 in. vacuum.

Suggested Process

3- and 6-lb cans	3 hr 40 min at 230°F
or	1 hr 35 min at 240°F
12-oz oblong cans	90 min at 240°F

Check processing time and temperature with can supplier or the National Canners Association.

Chilling 12-Oz Cans

After sterilization of 12-oz oblong cans, shut off steam, open cold water inlet, and chill cans under 15 lb pressure for at least 20 min. Further chilling can be at atmospheric pressure.

This product is commercially sterile and needs no further refrigeration through storage and marketing.

Chilling 3- and 6-Lb Cans

Chill 3- and 6-lb oblong cans for 2 hr under 15 lb pressure. Further chilling at atmospheric pressure in a chill room (34°–36°F).

This product is perishable and must always be kept under refrigeration through storage and marketing channels.

SOURCE: Stephan L. Komarik, 4810 Ronda, Coral Gables, Florida.

IMITATION CHICKEN LOAF IN HOY MOLDS OR 4 × 4 × 24 INCH OBLONG MOLDS

Ingredients	Lb	Oz	Pt
Precooked pork stomachs	30		
Precooked beef tripe, treated	25		
Precooked extra lean pork trimmings	20		
Precooked veal trimmings	15		
Semolina flour	10		
Salt	2	8	
Monosodium glutamate		2	
Ground celery seed		$1/_{2}$	
Vinegar (100-grain)			1

Procedure

Cook hog stomachs for $2^{1}/_{2}$ hr in boiling water and remove black linings from inside the stomachs while still hot. Cook treated beef tripe and veal and pork trimmings for 30 min.

Grind and Mix.—Grind all meat items as soon as they are removed from the cooking kettle. Grind through the $1/_{2}$-in. plate of the grinder. Transfer to a vacuum mixer. Start mixer; add vinegar; add salt which has been previously mixed with the seasonings and monosodium glutamate; add flour. After 2–3 bowl revolutions, stop mixer, close top and mix under 25 in. vacuum for $2^{1}/_{2}$ min.

Stuff and Cook.—Stuff mixture into parchment-lined Hoy molds or into 4 × 4 × 24 in. oblong molds. Transfer molds to a cooking tank and place so as to allow proper circulation of water between each mold. Fill tank with 165°F water and maintain this temperature during the cooking process. Agitate water with compressed air during cooking. Cook product approximately $3^{1}/_{2}$ hr or until an internal meat temperature of 155°F is obtained.

Chill and Package.—Drain hot water from cooking tank, refill with cold water and let warm water overflow from tank top. Chill approximately 1–$1^{1}/_{2}$ hr. Transfer molds to chill room (34°–36°F) for overnight chill.

Next day, remove loaves from molds. Those in the hoy molds are encased in Cellophane casings for bulk sale. Product in 4 × 4 × 24 in. oblong molds may be sliced and vacuum packaged in weights desired for retail trade.

This product is perishable and must always be kept under refrigeration through storage and marketing channels.

SOURCE: Stephan L. Komarik, 4810 Ronda, Coral Gables, Florida.

IMITATION CHICKEN IN ASPIC IN 3- OR 6-LB OBLONG CANS

Ingredients	Lb	Oz	Gal.	Pt
Gelatin (250 bloom)	30			
Salt	15			
Dry soluble pepper	1			
Celery seed			2¼	
Monosodium glutamate		10		
Precooked hog stomachs	300			
Precooked pork cheeks	125			
Precooked veal chucks	75			
Broth from cooked veal			15	
Vinegar (100-grain)				4

Procedure

Mix together the gelatin, salt, seasonings, and glutamate for later use.

Cook hog stomachs for 2½ hr in boiling water. Remove from water and, while stomachs are still hot, remove the black linings. Cook pork cheeks in boiling water for 45 min. Cook veal chucks in boiling water for 45 min and reserve the broth in which the veal was cooked. While the pork and veal are still hot, trim fat and remove cords from veal chucks. Then put all cooked meats through the ½-in. plate of a grinder as soon after cooking as possible before the meats have cooled. Strain the veal broth through cheesecloth to remove sediments. Transfer ground meats to the mechanical mixer and start machine. Add the gelatin mixture evenly over the meats, then the vinegar and broth. Close top of mixer and mix for 2 min under 27 in. vacuum.

Pack and Process.—Fill into 3- or 6-lb oblong cans immediately while product is still hot. If product temperature is kept at 160°F or higher, close cans without applying vacuum. If product temperature falls below 160°F, close cans under 10–15 in. vacuum.

Suggested Process

3- and 6-lb cans 4 hr at 222°F

Check processing time and temperature with can supplier or the National Canners Association.

After processing, chill cans under 15 lb pressure for 2 hr in the retort followed by final chilling under atmospheric pressure in a chill room (34°–36°F).

This product is commercially sterile and need not be held under refrigeration.

SOURCE: Stephan L. Komarik, 4810 Ronda, Coral Gables, Florida.

JELLIED IMITATION CHICKEN LOAF

Ingredients	Lb	Oz	Pt
Pork stomachs, precooked	45		
Pork cheeks, trimmed, precooked	25		
Veal chucks, trimmed, precooked	15		
Broth from cooked veal	15		
Granular gelatin (250-bloom)	4		
Salt	2	8	
Monosodium glutamate		2	
Dry soluble celery		1	
Dry soluble pepper		½	
Vinegar (100-grain)			1

Procedure

Cook hog stomachs for 2½ hr in boiling water and remove the black linings. Cook pork cheeks for 45 min. Cook veal separately for 45 min and reserve broth for later use.

Premix salt with seasonings and granular gelatin.

Grind and Mix.—While meats are still hot, first trim off fat and remove cords from veal chucks and grind all meats through the ½-in. plate of the grinder.

Strain veal broth through cheesecloth to remove sediment.

Transfer ground meats—while still hot—to a vacuum mixer. Start mixer, add salt-seasoning-gelatin mixture evenly over top of meats; then add hot broth and vinegar. Close mixer and mix for 2 min under 25 in. vacuum.

Stuff and Cook.—Loosely stuff material in Cellophane casings and place in suitable spring-cover molds. Do not apply too much pressure in closing molds.

Transfer molds to a cooking tank and place them so there is proper circulation of water between each mold. Fill tank with 160°F water and maintain this temperature during the cooking process. Agitate water with compressed air during the cooking. Cook product for 2 hr, during which time the gelatin will melt and become distributed throughout the meat mixture.

Chill and Package.—Drain hot water from cooking tank and refill with cold water, letting warm water overflow from top of tank. Chill molds approximately 1–1½ hr. Transfer to a chill room (34°–36°F) for overnight chill.

Next day, remove loaves from molds. Product may be sold in the bulk (Cellophane-encased loaf) or sliced and vacuum packaged for sale at retail.

Product is perishable and should always be kept

under refrigeration during storage and marketing channels.

SOURCE: Stephan L. Komarik, 4810 Ronda, Coral Gables, Florida.

ROAST BEEF LOAF USING NONFAT DRY MILK

Ingredients	Lb	Oz
Boneless chuck	75	
Beef plate meat	25	
Nonfat dry milk	12	
Salt	3$\frac{1}{2}$	
Ground white pepper		8
Bay leaves, crushed		2
Grated onions	2	
Tomato catsup	10	
Worcestershire sauce		3

Procedure

Grind meat through large lard plate. Put into steam-jacketed kettle with enough water to cover meat. Bring to boil, then add remaining ingredients except nonfat dry milk. Cook slowly until tender. Reserve cooking broth. Then place all in mixer. While mixing, sprinkle with nonfat dry milk and add 40–45 lb cooking broth. Mix well. Put in 5–6 lb pans and chill thoroughly. When firmly set, stuff into artificial casings.

This product should be kept under refrigeration until consumed.

SOURCE: American Dry Milk Institute, 130 N. Franklin, Chicago, Ill.

JELLIED ROAST BEEF LOAF

Ingredients	Lb	Oz	Pt
Lean beef	145		
(yield after cooking approx 87 lb)			
Beef stock from cooked beef	30		
Salt	2		
Sugar	1		
Granular gelatin (250-bloom)	4		
Dry soluble pepper		4	
Sodium erythorbate		$\frac{7}{8}$	
Onion powder		1	
Garlic powder		$\frac{1}{16}$	
Ground celery seed		$\frac{1}{8}$	
Worcestershire sauce		2	
Vinegar			$\frac{1}{2}$
Catsup (optional)			1

Procedure

Trim fat, sinews, and connective tissues from beef and cut into $\frac{1}{4}$-lb. chunks. Transfer to a steam-jacketed kettle and add just enough water to cover meat. Slowly bring up temperature to 212°F and cook at this temperature until meat is very tender. Remove meat from kettle and grind through the 1–1$\frac{1}{2}$-in. plate of the grinder directly into a meat truck. Skim foam and fat off of beef stock and cook (concentrate) to 30 lb and allow to cool to 160°F.

Mix together the salt, dry seasonings, sugar, and granular gelatin. When stock has cooled to 160°F, slowly sift in the salt-seasonings-gelatin mixture with steady agitation. Then add Worcestershire sauce, vinegar, and catsup (if used) and mix until added ingredients are thoroughly incorporated with beef stock. If this step is done carefully, the gelatin will not lump.

Pour gelatin-stock mixture evenly over the ground meat in the meat truck and mix thoroughly with a meat shovel or wooden paddle. Let product cool just enough to make stuffing easy.

Stuff material into Cellophane casings which loosely fit the molds. Before placing stuffed casings into molds, wash with a vinegar solution to remove any gelatin on outside of casings so that the loaves can be removed from molds easily. Place stuffed casings in molds, cover, press down lid and fasten springs.

Transfer molds to chill room (40°–45°F) for overnight. Next day, remove loaves from molds.

Product may be sold in the casings in bulk or sliced and vacuum packaged for retail sale.

Product is perishable and should always be kept under refrigeration throughout storage and marketing channels.

SOURCE: Stephan L. Komarik, 4810 Ronda, Coral Gables, Florida.

JELLIED CORNED BEEF LOAF

The beef for this product has to be cured. Otherwise, processing method is identical to that given above for Jellied Roast Beef Loaf.

To Cook and Cure the Beef.—Grind fresh beef through the 1$\frac{1}{2}$-in. plate of the grinder. Transfer to a steam-jacketed kettle; add just enough water to cover meat; dissolve $\frac{1}{4}$ oz sodium nitrite in 1 pt of water and stir into the kettle contents. Slowly bring temperature up to 160°F and cook until there is a "cured" color inside the center of the largest pieces of meat.

This product is perishable and should always be kept under refrigeration through storage and marketing channels.

SOURCE: Stephan L. Komarik, 4810 Ronda, Coral Gables, Florida.

CORNED BEEF LOAF USING NONFAT DRY MILK

Make up this cure:

	Lb	Oz
Sodium nitrate	3	7
Sodium nitrite		5
Dextrose (corn sugar)	10	

Place ingredients in a 5-gal. glass container. Fill with water and dissolve. Use 1 qt (2¾ lb) of solution for each 100 lb of meat.

Ingredients	Lb	Oz
Boned beef (briskets, plates, etc.)	100	
Nonfat dry milk	15	
Salt	5	
Ground black pepper		8
Ground allspice		2
Ground cloves		2
Crushed bay leaves		3
Onion powder		1
Garlic powder		½
Cure	2¾	

Procedure

Run beef through large lard cutting plate and mix well with salt and cure. Cure for 5 days at 38°–40°F. Place meat in nets for easier handling. Place in steam-jacketed kettle, cover with water, and cook for about 3½ hr at 165°–170°F. Place spices in a muslin bag and add to meat while cooking. After cooking, remove bag of spice. Place meat in mixer and sprinkle with nonfat dry milk, adding cooking water to give it proper consistency.

Put in pans or molds of desired size and cool overnight. It can be stuffed into artificial casings.

This product should be kept under refrigeration until consumed.

SOURCE: American Dry Milk Institute, 130 N. Franklin, Chicago, Ill.

JELLIED BARBECUED BEEF LOAF

Ingredients	Lb	Oz	Gm
Lean beef	145		
(yield after cooking approx 87 lb)			
Beef stock from cooked beef	30		
Salt	2		
Cane sugar	2		
Sodium ascorbate			⅞
Granular gelatin (250-bloom)	4		
Tomato paste	5		
Cider vinegar (45-grain)		8	
Worcestershire sauce		2	
Ground red pepper		1	

	Lb	Oz
Onion powder	1	
Garlic powder		¹⁄₁₆
Ground cloves		4
Ground mace		2
Ground cinnamon		4
Ground Jamaica ginger		4
Ground celery seed		3½

Procedure

Trim fat, sinews, and connective tissues from beef and cut into ¼-lb chunks. Transfer to a steam-jacketed kettle and add just enough water to cover meat. Slowly bring up temperature to 212°F and cook at this temperature until meat is very tender. Remove meat from kettle and grind through the 1–1½-in. plate of the grinder directly into a meat truck. Skim foam and fat off of beef stock and cook (concentrate) to 30 lb and allow to cool to 160°F.

Mix together the salt, dry seasonings, sugar, sodium erythorbate, and granular gelatin. When stock has cooled to 160°F, slowly sift in the salt-seasonings-gelatin mixture with steady agitation. Then add tomato paste, vinegar, and Worcestershire sauce and mix until added ingredients are thoroughly incorporated with beef stock. If this step is done carefully, the gelatin will not lump.

Pour gelatin-stock mixture evenly over the ground meat in the meat truck and mix thoroughly with a meat shovel or wooden paddle. Let product cool just enough to make stuffing easy.

Stuff, Chill, and Package.—These steps are identical to those given for **Jellied Roast Beef Loaf.**

Product is perishable and should always be kept under refrigeration throughout storage and marketing channels.

SOURCE: Stephan L. Komarik, 4810 Ronda, Coral Gables, Florida.

BARBECUE-STYLE PORK LOAF USING NONFAT DRY MILK

Ingredients	Lb	Oz
Pork cheeks	60	
Pork giblets	15	
Nonfat dry milk	12	
Salt	2½	
Ground white pepper		3
Chili powder		3
Dry gelatin	3½	
Tomato catsup	3 No. 10 cans	

Procedure

Grind meats through 1-in. plate. Mix catsup with dry gelatin.

Put pork cheeks and pork giblets in a steam-jacketed kettle. Barely cover meat with water and cook until tender. Sprinkle nonfat dry milk and seasoning over meat. Add water, stirring constantly. Do not cook. When thoroughly mixed, add catsup-gelatin mixture and mix well. Then put mixture into molds and chill. Can be wrapped or stuffed into artificial casings.

SOURCE: American Dry Milk Institute, 130 N. Franklin, Chicago, Ill.

CANNED SPREADS

DEVILED HAM SPREAD (FINEST QUALITY)

Ingredients	Lb	Oz
Cured and precooked hams	250	
Ham fat from hams	125	
Ham broth from cooking hams	125	
Mustard flour, yellow	1	12¾
White pepper (62-mesh)		8¾
Ground turmeric		1½
Ground red pepper		1½
Ground Spanish paprika, microfine		½

Selection and Curing of Hams

Select hams 25 lb and over in weight. Prepare the following pumping pickle:

	Gal.	Lb
Water	50	
Salt		70
Sodium nitrite		1
Sodium nitrate		4
Cane sugar		16

Pump 10% of the raw weight of the ham through arterial system, or stitch pump pickle into hams, using the above formula. Then reduce salinometer reading to 50° by adding water and cover hams with the reduced-strength pickle. Cure for 10 days.

Cook Hams

Remove hams from pickle; scrub and wash them with hot water; then skin, defat (reserve fat for later use in formula), and remove bones. Cut boneless hams into uniform 1-lb chunks, transfer them to a steam-jacketed kettle, cover with water, and cook at simmering water temperature (200°–205°F for 1 hr). Reserve cooking broth. Cooking shrink will be approximately 41–42%. Ham fat is not precooked.

Grind and Mix

Grind hams hot from the cooking kettle along with ham fat through the ½-in. plate of the grinder. Transfer to a meat truck. Dissolve sea-sonings in hot ham broth and add to the ground meat. Stir mixture occasionally until ground meat absorbs broth. Regrind mixture through the ¹/₁₆-in. plate of the grinder.

If an emulsifier is used: After grinding through the ½-in. plate, transfer ground meat to a mechanical mixer, add seasoned broth and mix until meat absorbs the added broth, then put material through the 2 mm plate of the emulsifier.

Reheat and Fill Cans

Use a steam-jacketed mixer or a Patterson pre-heater to keep emulsion hot before it enters cans. The emulsion should not drop below 160°F before cans are closed.

Suggested Process

208 × 108 cans (3 oz net) 1 hr 30 min at 230°F

Check process time and temperature with can supplier or the National Canners Association.

SOURCE: Stephan L. Komarik, 4810 Ronda, Coral Gables, Florida.

DEVILED HAM SPREAD (COMMERCIAL GRADE)

Ingredients	Lb	Oz
Precooked lean hams	220	
Raw ham fat	112	
Ham broth from cooking hams	168	
Salt	10	
Sodium nitrite		1¼
Sodium nitrate		13¾
Mustard flour		2
Worcestershire sauce		2
Red pepper		½
Dry soluble pepper or ground white pepper		10

Preparation of Meat

Large hams 25 lb and over should be used. Skin, defat, and bone hams; then cut boneless hams into uniform 1-lb chunks; transfer to a steam-jacketed kettle, cover with water, and cook at simmering temperature (200°–205°F) for 1 hr. Reserve broth. Cooking shrink is approximately 41–42%. Ham fat is not precooked.

Grind and Mix

Grind cooked hams, hot from the cooking kettle along with the ham fat through the $1/2$-in. plate of the grinder and put into a meat truck. Dissolve seasonings, salt, sodium nitrite, and sodium nitrate in the hot broth and add to the ground meat. Stir the mixture occasionally until ground meat absorbs broth. Regrind mixture through the $1/16$-in. plate of the grinder.

If an emulsifier is used: After grinding, transfer meat to a mechanical mixer; add seasonings, salt, sodium nitrite, and sodium nitrate to the hot broth and mix until meat absorbs the broth; then put material through the 2 mm plate of the emulsifier.

Some processors prefer to use a meat chopper to produce a finer emulsion. In this case, grind the precooked hams and the raw ham fat together through the $1/8$-in. plate of the grinder. Transfer to chopper and chop meat for 5 min. Then gradually add the hot broth in which salt, cures, and flavorings are dissolved and chop an additional 5 min.

Reheat and Fill Cans

A steam-jacketed mixer or a Patterson preheater should be used to keep the emulsion hot before it enters the cans. The emulsion should not cool below 160°F before cans are closed.

Suggested Process

208 × 108 cans (3 oz net) 1 hr 30 min at 230°F

Check process time and temperature with can supplier or the National Canners Association.

SOURCE: Stephan L. Komarik, 4810 Ronda, Coral Gables, Florida.

HAM AND TONGUE SPREAD

Ingredients	Lb	Oz
Smoked hams	260	
Pork tongues (cured, cooked weight 65 lb)	100	
Fat trimmings from smoked hams	45	
Butter	5	
Meat stock or water (hot)	125	
Salt	3	
Mustard flour	2	
Red pepper		2
Dry soluble pepper		10

Cure and Cook Tongues

Prepare the following curing solution: 50 gal. water, 80 lb salt, and 1 lb sodium nitrite. Use 5 gal. of pickle per 100 lb of tongues. Heat curing solution to 195°–200°F; cook and cure tongues in the curing solution until they are well done and gullet bones can be removed easily. Remove gullet bones. (Dispose of curing solution after tongues are removed.)

Grind and Chop

Grind smoked hams, tongues, and fat trimmings from the hams through the $1/8$-in. plate of the grinder. Transfer meats to the chopper; add salt, seasonings, and butter and chop for 5 min. Gradually add hot meat stock, if available, or hot water to the chopper and chop 5 min.

If an emulsifier is used: After grinding, transfer meat to a mechanical mixer, add remainder of the ingredients and mix thoroughly, then put through the finest plate of the emulsifier.

Reheat and Fill Cans

Use a steam-jacketed mixer or a Patterson preheater to keep emulsion hot before filling the cans. The emulsion should not drop below 160°F before the cans are closed.

Suggested Process

208 × 108 cans (3 oz net) 1 hr 30 min at 230°F

Check process time and temperature with can supplier or the National Canners Association.

SOURCE: Stephan L. Komarik, 4810 Ronda, Coral Gables, Florida.

CANNED POTTED MEAT (BUFFET SPREAD)

Ingredients	Lb	Oz
Beef tripe (cooked weight)	75	
Hog stomachs (cooked weight)	75	
Beef lungs (cooked weight)	80	
Lean pork trimmings (cooked weight)	50	
Bacon skins (cooked weight)	45	
Broth from pork trimmings	25	
Salt	7	
Cane sugar	2	
Mustard flour	3	
Black pepper, ground		14
Red pepper, ground		1
Coriander, ground		8
Nutmeg, ground		2
Onion powder		3
Sodium nitrite		$1/2$

Prepare Meats and By-products

Cook hog stomachs and beef lungs after the windpipes are removed in the following curing solution: 50 gal. of water, 1 oz sodium nitrite. Cook hog stomachs until tender, beef lungs 30 min. The purpose of cooking hog stomachs in curing solution is to prevent the inside lining of the stomachs from turning black as they do when cooked in plain water. Sodium nitrite gives the lining a "cured" color, therefore it is not necessary to remove the lining of the stomachs. Cook beef tripe until tender and bacon skins until they are very soft. Cook pork trimmings separately and reserve broth for use in meat mixture.

Grind and Chop

Keep all meats hot; grind meats right from the cooking tanks through the $1/8$-in. plate of the grinder; and while they are still hot transfer them to the chopper and chop for 5 min. Add premixed salt, sugar, seasonings, and sodium nitrite, then gradually add the hot broth from the pork trimmings and chop an additional 5 min.

If an emulsifier is used: After grinding, transfer meat to a mechanical mixer, add all the ingredients including hot broth, and make a uniform mixture; then run material through the finest plate of the emulsifier.

Reheat and Fill Cans

Use a steam-jacketed mixer or a Patterson preheater to keep emulsion hot before it enters cans. The emulsion should not drop below 160°F before the cans are closed.

Suggested Process

208 × 108 cans (3 oz net) 1 hr 30 min at 230°F

Check process time and temperature with can supplier or the National Canners Association.

SOURCE: Stephan L. Komarik, 4810 Ronda, Coral Gables, Florida.

CANNED LIVER SPREAD

Ingredients	Lb	Oz
Cooked pork liver	100	
Cooked beef tripe	100	
Cooked pork snouts	40	
Cooked smoked pork jowls	50	
Cooked pork trimmings, lean	90	
Broth (from cooked pork trimmings and jowls)	100	
Salt	10	
Onion powder	2	
Dry soluble pepper	1	
Ground nutmeg		1
Ground marjoram		2
Ground sage		5
Ground cloves		2
Ground allspice		1
Sodium nitrite		1

Prepare Meat and By-products

Pretreat Tripe.—Use an ordinary wooden or glass-lined tank to soak tripe for pretreatment before use in this formula. Prepare a vinegar solution in the proportion of 96 gal. of water to 12 gal. of 90-grain vinegar. Immerse tripe in solution for 20 min, stirring twice during this period. Then transfer tripe to a vat filled with cold water and hold it immersed for 10 min with occasional stirring. Rinse thoroughly and cook for 30 min. Note: Half the tripe may be replaced with hog stomachs. If used, cook stomachs until tender and remove the black linings.

Soak and Leach Livers.—Trim livers to remove all visable tubes and surface fat. Then slice 1-in. thick and leach slices in a well-iced 1% salt solution overnight. Next day, cook them in fresh water at 160°F for 30 min.

Snouts, Jowls, and Pork Trimmings.—Select snouts as uniform in size as possible and cook 1 hr 30 min.

Skin pork jowls and cook together with pork trimmings for 30 min, reserving the broth of these two cooked items for use later.

Grind and Chop

Grind all items through the $1/8$-in. plate of the grinder immediately after removal from the cooking tanks. Transfer immediately to the chopper and chop for 5 min. Add salt, previously mixed with the flavoring ingredients and sodium nitrite then gradually add the hot broth. Chop an additional 5 min. If an emulsifier is used: After grinding, transfer meats to a mechanical mixer, add all the other ingredients and make a uniform mixture, then put the material through the finest plate of the emulsifier.

Reheat and Fill Cans

Use a steam-jacketed kettle to keep the emulsion hot before it is put in the cans. The emulsion should not cool below 160°F before cans are closed.

Suggested Process

208 × 108 cans (3 oz net) 1 hr 30 min at 230°F

Check process time and temperature with can supplier or the National Canners Association.

SOURCE: Stephan L. Komarik, 4810 Ronda, Coral Gables, Florida.

CANNED MOCK CHICKEN SPREAD

Ingredients	Lb	Oz
Treated, cooked beef tripe	200	
Cooked pork snouts	40	
Lean pork (75-25%)	140	
Broth from cooked pork	100	
Salt	10	
Dry soluble pepper		8
Celery salt		7
Monosodium glutamate		8
Vinegar (100-grain)	2	

Prepare Meat and By-products

Pretreat Tripe.—Use an ordinary wooden or glass-lined tank to soak tripe for pretreatment before use in this formula. Prepare a vinegar solution in the proportion of 96 gal. of water to 12 gal. of 90-grain vinegar. Immerse tripe in solution for 20 min, stirring twice during this period. Then transfer tripe to a vat filled with cold water and hold it immersed for 10 min with occasional stirring. Rinse thoroughly and cook for 30 min.

Note: Half the tripe may be replaced with hog stomachs. If, used, cook stomachs until tender and remove the black linings.

Snouts and Pork.—Select snouts as uniformly in size as possible and cook 1 hr 30 min.

Cook pork 30 min and reserve this broth for later use.

Grind and Chop

Grind all items through the $1/8$-in. plate of the grinder right after removal from the cooking tanks. Transfer immediately to the chopper and chop for 5 min. Add salt, previously mixed with flavorings and vinegar, then gradually add hot broth from the pork trimmings. Chop an additional 5 min. In case an emulsifier is used: after grinding, transfer meats to a mechanical mixer and add all the ingredients; make a uniform mixture; then put material through the finest plate of the emulsifier.

Reheat and Fill Cans

Keep emulsion hot before it enters the cans in a steam-jacketed mixer or a Patterson preheater. The emulsion should not drop below 160°F before the cans are closed.

Suggested Process

208 × 108 cans (3 oz net) 1 hr 30 min at 230°F

Check process time and temperature with can supplier or the National Canners Association.

SOURCE: Stephan L. Komarik, 4810 Ronda, Coral Gables, Florida.

METTWURST SAUSAGE SPREAD

This sausage is soft in texture so it can be spread but also firm enough so it can be sliced, if desired. Texture is somewhat similar to Braunschweiger.

Use any of these meat combinations:

	No. 1 Lb	No. 2 Lb	No. 3 Lb	No. 4 Lb
Certified[1] pork trimmings, 60/65% lean	500	375	250	250
Lean beef		125	175	200
Backfat			75	50

with these ingredients:

	Lb	Oz
Salt	12	8
Corn syrup solids	5	
Sodium nitrite		$1/4$
Sodium nitrate		$12 1/2$
Sodium erythorbate		$4 1/3$

and one of these three seasoning formulas using purified and sterilized spices:

	Lb	Oz
No. 1		
Ground black or white pepper	1	8
No. 2		
Ground black or white pepper	1	8
Whole mustard seeds		8
No. 3		
Ground black or white pepper	1	8
Ground caraway seed		2
Ground coriander		3
Garlic powder		$1/4$

Procedure

Select beef light in color and pork trimmings from hams, shoulders, and bellies with a minimum of 60% lean. Remove all sinews, connective tissues, and skins from meats. It is most important to chill all meat products down to 32°F before use.

Grind.—Grind pork trimmings and backfat, if used, through the $1/2$-in. plate of the grinder; grind beef through the $1/8$-in. plate. Transfer ground meats to the mechanical mixer, add the rest of the ingredients and mix to a uniform mixture.

---

[1] Certified pork are those fresh pork meats certified by the USDA Meat Inspection Division as being free of live trichinae. Only certified pork should be used in processing this sausage since the processing procedure does not conform otherwise to government regulations concerning destruction of live trichinae.

Cure.—Pack ground meat tightly (avoid air pockets) in pans not over 6 in. deep; transfer to cooler at 34°–36°F and cure for 24 hr.

Regrind.—After curing regrind meat through the 1/8-in. plate of the grinder.

Stuff.—Pack stuffer tightly (avoid air pockets). Use beef rounds or wide hog casings precut to 16–18 in. and tied on one end with twine; then fill casings. Tie open end in such manner that enough twine is left over to close the open end of the next sausage and leave a distance about 4 in. between. Perforate with a needle paddle to let any air under the casings escape. Hang on smoke trees properly spread so that sausages will not touch each other. Shower with cold water.

Ripen (Green Room).—Transfer to green room at 70°–75°F with 75–80% RH and cure for 3 days.

Smoke.—Temperature of the house should not be over 70°–80°F with 80–85% RH otherwise sausages may sour. Transfer smoke trees into the house with dampers wide open to dry casings fully, (approximately 30 min). Adjust dampers 1/4 open, then introduce heavy smudge. Smoke sausages for 24–48 hr. After removing the sausages from the house, dip momentarily in simmering water to shrink casings and remove any fat particles.

Chill.—From the smokehouse sausages are transferred to a cooler at 45°F until an internal meat temperature of 50°F is obtained.

Fast Curing Method

Ingredients and procedure for grinding, curing, and stuffing are the same as for the regular Mettwurst, but this method does not give the same ripe flavor that results from the long ripening given regular Mettwurst.

In the fast cure method, increase sodium nitrite to 1 1/4 oz and decrease sodium nitrate to 5 oz per 500 lb of raw meat.

As soon as sausages are stuffed, transfer to the smokehouse and smoke under the same conditions as regular Mettwurst. However, smoking time can be reduced to 8 hr.

TEEWURST SAUSAGE SPREAD

Use any of these meat combinations:

	No. 1 Lb	No. 2 Lb	No. 3 Lb
Lean beef		100	300
Certified[2] lean pork trimmings 80/85%	300	250	
Backfat	200	150	200

with these ingredients:

	Lb	Oz	Pt
Salt	12	8	
Corn syrup solids	5		
Sodium nitrite		1/4	
Sodium nitrate		12 1/2	
Sodium erythorbate		4 1/3	
Ground white pepper	1	2	
Ground allspice		4	
Spanish paprika		5	
Ground cardamom		2	
Jamaican rum			2

Procedure

Follow procedure given above for Mettwurst Sausage Spread.

SOURCE: Stephan L. Komarik, 4810 Ronda, Coral Gables, Florida.

TEEWURST SAUSAGE SPREAD (FAST METHOD)

Ingredients and procedure are identical with those just given for regular Teewurst Sausage Spread. But, of course, this product will not have the same ripe flavor as that produced by the longer curing method.

For the fast curing method, use the full amount of sodium nitrite (1 1/4 oz per 500 lb of raw meat) and only 5 oz of sodium nitrate.

After sausages are stuffed, transfer them immediately to the smokehouse and smoke under the same conditions given for the regular Teewurst Sausage Spread, but smoking time with the fast method can be reduced to 8 hr.

SOURCE: Stephan L. Komarik, 4810 Ronda, Coral Gables, Florida.

---

[2] Certified pork are those fresh pork meats certified by the USDA Meat Inspection Division as being free of live trichinae. Only certified pork should be used in processing this sausage since the processing procedure does not conform otherwise to government regulations concerning destruction of live trichinae.

CANNED CORNED BEEF PRODUCTS

CANNED CORNED BEEF

The beef used is ordinary carcass meat, canner or cutter grade. After beef is boned, and skins, tendons, and connective tissues are removed, put the meat through the meat slicer and slice into 1–1½ in. strips. Carry sliced meat in wire baskets to cooking tanks and cook in simmering water (195°–200°F) while stirring continuously until a 35% shrink from the raw weight has been obtained. Use cooking water only four times. Remove cooking water to the extract room. Reinspect meat for sinews and cords on a conveyor system. Then transfer to grinders and grind through either the ¾-, 1-, or 1½-in. plate, depending upon the size of cans to be packed. Transfer ground meats to mixers. To each 100 lb of meat, add a mixture of 3 lb salt and ¼ oz sodium nitrite and thoroughly mix (approximately 3 min are required).

In case spiced corned beef is desired the following seasonings are added to the above mixture: 2 oz ground pepper (80 mesh), 2 oz onion powder, and ½ oz celery seed.

Immediately pack meat mixture into cans while still hot. Cold meat will not pack tightly in the cans; it will lose its elasticity.

Close cans under 27 in. vacuum.

Suggested Process

12-Oz round cans 2 hr at 240°F
24-Oz round cans 2 hr 30 min at 240°F

Check process times and temperature with can supplier or the National Canners Association.

After processing, chill under 15 lb water pressure.

SOURCE: Stephan L. Komarik, 4810 Ronda, Coral Gables, Florida.

CANNED CORNED BEEF HASH

Ingredients	Lb	Oz
Carcass beef, canner or cutter grade	54	
Diced dehydrated potatoes	12	
Water	34	
Salt	1	8
Black pepper, 48 mesh		1
Mustard flour		2
Onion powder		5
Sodium nitrite		⅛

Procedure

Grind meat through the ⅜-in. plate of a grinder. Transfer meat to the mechanical mixer; add remaining ingredients and mix just long enough to have a uniform mixture.

Fill cans through filling machine and close under 27 in. vacuum.

Suggested Process

303 × 400 cans (16 oz net) for 95 min at 240°F
603 × 700 cans (108 oz net) for 250 min at 240°F

Time and temperature of processing should be checked with can supplier or the National Canners Association.

SOURCE: Stephan L. Komarik, 4810 Ronda, Coral Gables, Florida.

CORNED BEEF HASH USING BRAISED MEAT

Ingredients	Lb	Oz
Carcass beef (canner or cutter grade)	50	
Dehydrated potatoes (weight after reconstituted, 48 lb)	11	
Salt	1	8
Onion powder		5
Black pepper (80-mesh)		3
Mustard flour		1
Sodium nitrite		⅛

Procedure

Grind beef through the ⅜-in. plate of the grinder. Mix dry ingredients listed above. Transfer ground meat to a steam-jacketed kettle, add seasonings and curing mixture along with 2 qt of water and braise meat by steady stirring until it is free-flowing. Remove meat from the jacketed kettle, add enough water to bring weight to 50 lb. Soak dehydrated diced potatoes in hot water at a temperature of 180°F until drained weight of the reconstituted potatoes reaches 48 lb.

Transfer braised meat and dehydrated potatoes to a mechanical mixer; mix approximately 3 min or until the ingredients are uniformly distributed. Fill cans through a filling machine. Close cans under vacuum.

Suggested Process

303 × 400 size cans (16 oz net) 95 min at 240°F
603 × 700 size cans (108 oz net) 255 min at 240°F

Check processing time and temperature with can supplier or the National Canners Association.

SOURCE: Stephan L. Komarik, 4810 Ronda, Coral Gables, Florida.

CORNED BEEF HASH
USING SOUTH AMERICAN CANNED CORNED BEEF

Ingredients	Lb	Oz
Canned corned beef	35	
Dehydrated diced pota-		
toes	12	
Water	36	
Fresh ground onions	3	
(or 5 oz onion powder)		
Salt	1	
Black pepper (48-mesh)		1
Mustard flour		2

Procedure

Remove corned beef from the cans and grind through the $1/4$-in. plate of the grinder.

Put 12 lb of dehydrated diced potatoes in 36 lb boiling water and allow them to remain until the potatoes absorb all the water. Place reconstituted potatoes, ground corned beef, and the remainder of the ingredients in a mechanical mixer; mix just long enough to have a uniform mixture. Fill cans through the filling machine and close under 27 in. vacuum.

Suggested Process

303 × 400 cans (16 oz net) 95 min at 240°F

Check process time and temperature with can supplier or the National Canners Association.

SOURCE: Stephan L. Komarik, 4810 Ronda, Coral Gables, Florida.

DEVILED CORNED BEEF (HOT PACK)

Ingredients	Lb	Oz
Cured, precooked beef carcass		
(canner-cutter grade)	150	
Cured, precooked beef flanks		
or plates	50	
Beef stock (from uncured meat)	50	
Ground pepper (60-mesh)		4
Onion powder		5
Celery seeds (ground)		$1^1/_2$

Procedure

Put beef through the meat slicer, cutting into 1-in. strips. Transfer sliced meat to cooking tanks and cook in simmering water at 195°–200°F, stirring continuously until a 35% shrink from the raw weight has been obtained. Use the same cooking water for four batches to condense broth (if more batches are made during the day). Always use 5 gal. of water per 100 lb of meat. After meat

is cooked, transfer it to another vat containing the following pickle: 50 gal. water; 60 lb salt; 9.6 oz sodium nitrite.

First, heat pickle to 180°F before adding meat. Let meat stand in pickle until thoroughly cured (approx 1–1$^1/_2$ hr). During this operation maintain the temperature of the pickle at 180°F. Use 5 gal. of pickle per 100 lb meat.

Deviling Procedure.—After meat is properly cured, transfer to the grinder and grind through the $1/8$-in. plate. Transfer ground meat to the silent cutter, and with the addition of 25 lb hot beef broth, chop for 5 min. Add seasonings along with another 25 lb hot beef broth and chop an additional 5 min.

In case a meat emulsifier is used: after meat is ground through the $1/8$-in. plate, transfer it to a steam-jacketed mixer, add the hot broth along with the seasonings, and mix thoroughly; then put it through the finest plate of the emulsifier.

Keep meat hot during all these operations. After emulsification, the meat emulsion also has to be kept hot (not lower than 160°F) before filling into the cans. This can be accomplished by using steam-jacketed mixers or a jacketed hopper right on the filling machine or by means of a Patterson heating unit.

Suggested Process

208 × 108 cans (3 oz net) 1 hr 20 min at 230°F

Check process time and temperature with can supplier or the National Canners Association.

SOURCE: Stephan L. Komarik, 4810 Ronda, Coral Gables, Florida.

CREAMED CORNED BEEF (HOT PACK)

Ingredients	Lb	Oz
Beef chucks, rounds, or clods	50	
Nonfat dry milk	18	
Shortening or vegetable oil	12	
Wheat flour	19	
Dry soluble pepper		6
Monosodium glutamate		5
Ground celery seeds		$1/_2$
Salt		4
Sodium nitrite		$1/_8$
Water to make 40 gal.		

Procedure

Grind beef through $1/2$-in. plate of the grinder. Heat shortening or oil in the kettle, add ground beef, and 2 qts of water containing the sodium nitrite. Braise meat until it is free-flowing, stirring constantly. Add approximately half of the water to the kettle, then add salt, and seasonings and hold temperature at 180°F. In a bakery mixer, make a smooth slurry with the remaining water by adding slowly the flour and nonfat dry milk; run machine until the slurry is free of lumps. By continuous stirring add slurry to the heated stock. Bring volume to 40 gal. with additional water.

Hold temperature at 180°–200°F for 15 min or until the product is thick enough to hold the meat in suspension. Fill cans while product is hot. Internal temperature of the product in the cans should be 160°F or higher when they are closed. In case temperature drops under 150°F close cans under 10–15 in. vacuum.

Suggested Process

300 × 409 Cans (1 lb net) 90 min at 240°F

Check process time and temperature with can supplier or the National Canners Association.

SOURCE: Stephan L. Komarik, 4810 Ronda, Coral Gables, Florida.

MEAT DISHES, MEAT LOAVES, AND MEAT PATTIES USING PLANT PROTEIN EXTENDERS

Plant proteins, better known as vegetable proteins, are isolated, high purity protein products removed from vegetables such as soy beans. These products—which are textured, spun, concentrated, etc.—are available commercially and sold under various trade names. They are excellent extenders for use in comminuted meat formulas to provide more nourishment per serving with little or no increase in cost of ingredients. They are being recommended and used widely for school lunches and mass feeding programs where nutritional intake may be substandard.

ADVANTAGES OF PLANT PROTEINS AS EXTENDERS IN MEAT PRODUCTS

Real innovations in the food industry have come from expanding our imagination into concepts which will utilize raw materials in new ways and apply them effectively for the millions of people who demand variety and convenience in their daily diet. Today, the spotlight is being focused on a product which has supplied energy for many generations, but it has been objectively and effectively modified to give the meat industry a new commodity whereby they can improve and tailor their food products.

Plant proteins deserve this spotlight, not because they are new but because they have been modified to fill a need in our modern processing plants.

The real innovation in plant proteins came only about 16 yr ago when we learned how to force a solution of isolated soy protein along with selected blends of other proteins through tiny holes in a spinnerette and come out with high purity protein fibers.

As yet, plant protein products have not gained the stature as a complete food in their own right with the general public, only in selected groups. Plant protein has always been combined with other supplementary proteins to improve texture, functional characteristics, and nutritional properties.

All plant protein products today which are used in other foods are not in the form of fibers. Extruded plant protein products are available which are made from soy flours and soy concentrates. These relatively high protein ingredients are mixed with water, flavor, and color and then cooked under pressure. As they are extruded into the atmosphere, they expand in the same manner as cereal-based snack foods are extruded and expanded.

Size and shape of the products are controlled by the configuration of the dies used and the speed of the cutting knife. These extruded products when dried can be used also in small amounts as an extender for conventional foods. Many extruded vegetable proteins are used today as extenders and in place of comminuted meat in items such as chili, sloppy joes, spaghetti sauce, patties, meat loaves, etc.

Spun protein fibers today are opening a new horizon to the meat processor who is interested in expanding the quality of his food as well as expanding the volume. As the protein fibers have the same texture as meat fibers, a ground meat product can be mixed with the fibered extenders to complement the texture of the meat.

Meat extenders made with spun vegetable protein fiber have a shelf-life longer than the product which they are extending. They contain no enzymes to accelerate deterioration; they are stable under refrigeration much longer than the natural product; they do not become mushy upon storage; and because of their fibered texture they're very similar to the ground meat to which they are added.

Fibered extenders have a stabilizing effect on comminuted meat products. They will hold the fat and other ingredients in a matrix of protein particles and eliminate weeping and loss of flavor. They will inhibit shrinkage when these extended products are cooked; and the final cooked product is tender and moist.

The price of fibered extenders is lower than the cost of the natural product and therefore the final convenient extended meat item is more economical to the consumer. As the fibered extender contains more protein than natural meat, the nutritional value from the protein standpoint is higher in an extended product than a natural product. Fibered extenders (such as Temptein™) contain no fat. If no additional fat is added to the mixture, the final meat product has a lower calorie value than the natural product by itself. If it is desirable to reduce the cost of the product even more, a small amount of fat can be added which will bring the terminal fat content equal to that of the normal product. This extended product will have an identity which is very similar to the natural product.

Plant proteins have given the meat processor a modern and significantly advantageous way to provide variety and improved product function to the consumer. While the cost of food increases universally, cost of fibered plant protein extenders has been gradually going down. It is rare in the annals of product development where one can reduce the price of his commodity and still improve acceptance. . . .Extentions of food products have long been practiced. . . .meat loaf with bread and other cereals. . . .hamburgers with cracker crumbs and onions. . . .crab cakes with potatoes. . . .Now that meat can be extended without loss of texture, the entire horizon of new product development is open for the alert food processor.

SOURCE: Excerpted from Plant Proteins: Their Advantages as Extenders in Meat Products by R. F. Robinson, Marschall Div., Miles Laboratories, Inc., published in *Meat Processing*, February 1971.

USING TEXTURED VEGETABLE PROTEIN WITH GROUND MEATS

Any ground or chopped meat product either bulk or pattied should be considered satisfactory to combine with textured vegetable protein. The following formulas are suggested formulas and mixing procedures. Formula No. 3 has been found most acceptable and Formula No. 2 should be considered the maximum usage.

| | Formulas | | |
| | No. 1 | No. 2 | No. 3 |
Ingredients	Lb	Lb	Lb
Beef, 22–25% fat	84	100	100
Textured vegetable protein	4	5	4
Water	12	15	12

Procedure

Allow textured vegetable protein to rehydrate in 40°F water (amount as indicated above) for 10–15 min (cold tap water may suffice with some textured vegetable proteins).

Place normal blend of cuts (chucks, flanks, plates, trimmings, etc.) into grinder hopper and distribute the rehydrated textured vegetable protein throughout. Then grind through a ½- or ⅜-in. plate mixer. Mix for 60–90 sec (if mixer is not available, tumble 3–4 times by hand).

Advantages

When ground beef, veal, or pork is conditioned with textured vegetable protein, the end product should:
1. Be more machinable in automatic equipment.
2. Shrink 10–15% less.
3. Have improved tenderness and juiciness.
4. Be lower in total formulation cost by 5–7% per cwt.

Advantages in using a product with a percentage replacement of textured vegetable protein:
1. Less shrinkage in frying or grilling than an all-meat patty.
2. Patty is "juicy" rather than dry or tough.
3. Will not "weep" upon thawing after being frozen.
4. Will give a quality patty with more bun coverage.

Note: The lower the temperature of the processed meat, the longer shelf-life of the patty or loaf.

SOURCE: Swift Edible Oil Company, Vegetable Protein Products Div., 115 W. Jackson Blvd., Chicago, Ill.

MEAT DISHES

SALISBURY STEAK WITH TEXTURED VEGETABLE PROTEIN

The following meat mixtures are given with varied percentages of hydrated textured vegetable protein replacement:

	Hydrated Textured Vegetable Protein Replacement		
	30%	21%	12%
	Lb	Lb	Lb
Economy beef chuck	41	46	51
Premium beef flank	27	30	33
Textured vegetable protein (Texgran No. 10100 or 10900)	10	7	4
Water	20	14	8

Other Ingredients		
	Lb	Oz
Salt		14.4
Dehydrated onion		12.8
Nonfat dry milk	2	1.6
Beef flavor—any of the following:		6–8
McCormick Flavor Cap No. 20, 601		
Florasynth Beef Flavor No. 870		
I.F.F. Imitation Beef No. 29, 759		
Pfizer Beef "Corral"		

Procedure

Mix textured vegetable protein (Texgran), water, salt, nonfat dry milk, flavor, and dehydrated onion together and allow to fully hydrate (15–20 min). Place hydrated mixture over rough cuts of meat and grind or flake to particle size of $1/2$ in. Mix and grind through $1/2$-in. plate and form into patties through a $3/8$-in. Hollymatic plate.

SOURCE: Swift Edible Oil Co., Vegetable Protein Products Div., 115 W. Jackson Blvd., Chicago, Ill.

SALISBURY STEAK PREPARED WITH PEANUT GRITS TEXTURIZED PROTEIN

Quality as well as economy are the essence of a good Salisbury steak. Peanut Grits texturized protein are designed to provide these features for comminuted meat dishes such as Salisbury steak which can be portion-controlled.

Ingredients	Lb
Beef trimmings (28% fat)	100
Nonfat dry milk	3.5
Peanut Grits	5
Precooked wheat fines	2
Ice water	20
Tomato purée	5
Salt	1.4
Seasonings to taste	

Procedure

1. Cut beef in silent cutter or cube and pass through $1/2$-in. plate of the grinder.
2. Presoak the remaining ingredients (Peanut Grits, precooked wheat fines, tomato purée, nonfat dry milk, salt, and seasonings) in ice water for 15 min.
3. Blend meat and presoaked mixture in silent cutter or similar equipment.
4. Grind through desired plate, i.e., $3/8$-in. or $1/8$-in.
5. Form into patties on automatic pattie maker.
6. Bake at 350°F until done.

SOURCE: Gold Kist, Inc., P.O. Box 2210, Atlanta, Ga.

SALISBURY STEAK WITH TEXTURED VEGETABLE PROTEIN

Meat portion:

Ingredients	%
Beef	70
Textured vegetable protein (Edi-Pro® 200)	30

The following ingredient percentages are based on the meat portion:

Ingredients	%
Salt	1.30
Beef-type flavor powder D-93455 (available from Haarmann & Reimer, Springfield, N.J.)	0.50
Lemon flavor	0.05
Black pepper	0.04
Bell pepper	0.04
Worcestershire powder (available from R. T. French Co., Rochester, N.Y.)	0.03
Garlic powder	0.02

Procedure

1. The beef and textured vegetable protein (Edi-Pro® 200) are mixed for 5 min in a Hobart mixer.
2. Spices and flavoring are then added and thoroughly mixed.

3. The resulting mixture is ground twice through a $^3/_{16}$-in. plate.

4. Form into patties and freeze.

5. Thawed patties are cooked at 400°F until done.

SOURCE: Ralston Purina Company, Checkerboard Square, St. Louis, Mo.

SWEDISH MEAT BALLS WITH TEXTURED VEGETABLE PROTEIN

Ingredients	%	By Weight Lb	By Weight Oz	By Measure
Ground beef	48.12	15.0		
Ground pork	24.06	7.5		
Powdered onion	1.50		7.5	
Textured vegetable protein (Mira-Tex 230-1)	9.62	3.0		
Water (hot)	9.37			6 cups
Minced parsley	0.11			$^3/_4$ cup
Salt	0.81			$^1/_2$ cup
Pepper	0.02			$1^1/_2$ tsp
Worcestershire sauce	0.57			$^1/_3$ cup
Eggs (medium)	5.82			15

Procedure

Hydrate textured vegetable protein (Mira-Tex 230-1) in hot water until water is absorbed. Thoroughly blend in all ingredients. Shape into meat balls. Fry or bake until done. Cook meat balls in mushroom soup (or gravy) 15–20 min.

SOURCE: A. E. Staley Mfg. Co., Decatur, Ill.

GROUND BEEF AND SPAGHETTI WITH TEXTURED SOY PROTEIN

Ingredients	By Weight Lb	By Weight Oz	or By Measure
Spaghetti	4		1 gal. $1^3/_4$ qt
Boiling water			4 gal.
Salt		1	$1^1/_2$ tbsp
Ground beef	10	2	
Hydration water	2	12	$5^1/_2$ cups
Textured soy protein (Maxten)	1	12	$9^1/_2$ cups
Onions, chopped	3		2 qt
Cheese, shredded	2		2 qt
Tomato paste	4	12	2 qt
Tomato purée	3	6	$1^1/_2$ qt
Salt		$5^1/_4$	$^1/_2$ cup
Sugar			2 tbsp

YIELD: 100 portions of about $^2/_3$ cup each providing the equivalent of a 2-oz serving of cooked lean meat.

Procedure

1. Cook spaghetti in boiling salted water until done (about 10–12 min); drain.

2. Add hydration water to textured soy protein (Maxten) and allow to stand for 5 min. Then mix with ground beef.

3. Brown the beef mixture lightly; add onions and cook until onions are clear but not browned. Drain.

4. Blend cheese with meat mixture. Add remaining ingredients. Stir in spaghetti. Reheat and serve.

SOURCE: Miles Laboratories, Inc., Marschall Division, Elkhart, Ind.

ITALIAN-STYLE MEAT SAUCE WITH TEXTURED VEGETABLE PROTEIN

The following meat mixtures are given with varied percentages of textured vegetable protein replacement in the formula:

Ingredients	12% Lb	12% Oz	21% Lb	21% Oz	30% Lb
Boneless cow chuck	52	13	47	6	42
Choice trimmed flank	35	3	31	10	28
Water	8		14		20
Textured vegetable protein (Texgran 52300-T.A.)	4		7		10

Procedure.—Hydrate textured vegetable protein (Texgran) in designated amount of tap water and allow to hydrate 30 min with occasional agitation. Pass chucks and beef flanks through $^7/_{32}$-in. grinder plate. Combine hydrated Texgran with ground beef and mix thoroughly. Pass the meat mixture once again through a $^7/_{32}$-in. grinder plate. Sauté meat until cooked, stirring frequently to brown.

Sauce Formulation

Ingredients	Lb	Oz
Water	100	
Tomato purée	60	
Tomato paste	40	
Grated Parmesan cheese	2	8
Salt	2	
Sugar	1	
Oregano leaf		5
Basil leaf		$2^1/_2$
Garlic juice		$2^1/_2$
Fennel seed, ground		$1^1/_4$
Black pepper		$1^1/_4$

Procedure.—Add all sauce ingredients to cooked meat mixture. Stir in and simmer to the finished cooked weight designated below according to meat replacement:

	12%	21%	30%
Pounds of cooked meat and sauce	225–230	240–245	255–260

SOURCE: Swift Edible Oil Co., Vegetable Protein Products Div., 115 W. Jackson Blvd., Chicago, Ill.

SPAGHETTI WITH MEAT SAUCE WITH TEXTURED VEGETABLE PROTEIN

Ingredients	By Weight Lb Oz	or	By Measure
Spaghetti	4		1 gal. 1¾ qt
Boiling water			2 gal.
Salt	1		2 tbsp
Meat Mixture			
Beef trimmings	10 2		
Textured vegetable protein (Mira-Tex 210-1)	1 8		
Water (hot)	3		1½ qt
Oil	8		
Onions, chopped	3		2 qt
Sauce			
Cheese, shredded	2		2 qt
Tomato paste	4 12		2 qt
Tomato purée	3 6		1½ qt
Salt	6		¾ cup
Sugar			2 tbsp
Water			2 qt

YIELD: 100 portions; about ⅔ cup provides the equivalent of 2 oz protein-rich food and ¼ cup of vegetable.

Procedure

1. Cook spaghetti in the salted boiling water about 15 min; drain.
2. Combine textured vegetable protein (Mira-Tex 210-1) with hot water and let stand 10–15 min until hydrated; then combine with beef and grind twice, first through a ⅜-in. plate, then through a ³⁄₁₆-in. plate.
3. Brown beef mixture; add onions and cook until onions are clear but not brown. Drain excess fat.
4. Blend cheese with meat mixture and add remaining ingredients. Stir in spaghetti. Reheat and serve.

SOURCE: A. E. Staley Mfg. Co., Decatur, Ill.

MEAT BALLS WITH TEXTURED VEGETABLE PROTEIN

The following meat mixtures are given with varied percentages of hydrated textured vegetable protein replacement:

	Hydrated Textured Vegetable Protein Replacement					
	30%		21%		12%	
Ingredients	Lb	Oz	Lb	Oz	Lb	Oz
Economy beef Chuck	41	5	46	10	51	14
Premium beef flank	27	8	31	1	34	10
Textured vegetable protein (Texgran 10,000-DTA)	9	13	6	14	3	15
Water	19	10	13	12	7	14

Other ingredients	Oz
Dehydrated minced onion	10
Salt	8
Nonfat dry milk	5
Black pepper	¾
Dehydrated parsley flake	¾
Beef flavor—any of the following:	2½
McCormick Flavor Cap No. 20,601	
Florasynth Beef Flavor No. 870	
I.F.F. Imitation Beef No. 29,759	
Pfizer Beef "Corral"	

Procedure

Mix nonfat dry milk and beef flavor in designated amount of tap water. Add dehydrated minced onion and hydrate 10 min. Add textured vegetable protein (Texgran) and remaining dry ingredients. Hydrate 30 min. Pass chucks and flanks through ½-in. grinder plate. Combine hydrated textured vegetable protein mixture with ground beef and mix in thoroughly. Then pass meat mixture through a ⁵⁄₃₂-in. grinder plate. Form into desired weight patties.

SOURCE: Swift Edible Oil Company, Vegetable Protein Products Div., 115 W. Jackson Blvd., Chicago, Ill.

ITALIAN-STYLE MEAT BALLS WITH TEXTURED VEGETABLE PROTEIN

The following meat mixtures are given with varied percentages of textured vegetable protein replacement in the formula:

	30% Lb	21% Lb	12% Lb
Economy beef chuck	42	47	52
Premium beef flank	27	31	35

	Oz	Oz	Oz
Textured vegetable protein (Texgran)	10	7	4
Water	20	14	8

The following spice mix ingredients are suggested; they may be substituted with your own formula:

	Oz	Gm
Salt	13.1	
Garlic juice	2.5	
Sweet basil	1.2	
Parsley flakes	1.2	
Black pepper	0.8	
Oregano leaf	0.8	
Rosemary, ground		5
Beef flavor—any of the following:	4–8	
Florasynth Beef Flavor No. 870		
I.F.F. Imitation Beef No. 29,759		
Pfizer Beef "Corral"		
McCormick Flavor Cap		
No. 20,601		

Procedure

Combine textured vegetable protein (Texgran), seasonings, and water; mix and let stand for 10 min, then add to rough cuts of meat and grind through a $1/2$-in. die; mix and grind through a $1/8$-in. die. Form into meatballs.

SOURCE: Swift Edible Oil Company, Vegetable Protein Products Div., 115 W. Jackson Blvd., Chicago, Ill.

BARBECUED BEEF WITH SPUN TEXTURED VEGETABLE PROTEIN OR TEXTURED SOY PROTEIN

	By Weight		or	By Measure
Ingredients	Lb	Oz		
Oil or melted fat		4		$1/2$ cup
Vinegar		10		$1^1/_4$ cups
Water	3			$1^1/_2$ qt
Catsup	5	10		$2^1/_4$ qt
Brown sugar		7		1 cup, packed
Onions, chopped		12		2 cups
Celery, chopped	2			1 qt $3^1/_2$ cups
Dry mustard		1		$1/4$ cup
Salt		2		3 tbsp
Hydration water	2	4		$4^1/_2$ cups
Spun textured vegetable protein (Temptein) or textured soy protein (Maxten)	1	8		9 cups
Cooked beef, coarsely chopped	8	12		
Hamburger rolls				100

YIELD: 100 portions with one sandwich providing the equivalent of 2 oz cooked lean meat and a serving of bread.

Procedure

1. Combine fat, liquids, catsup, sugar, vegetables, and seasonings. Heat thoroughly but do not cook enough to soften the vegetables.

2. Add hydration water to spun textured vegetable protein (Temptein) or textured soy protein (Maxten) and allow to stand for about 5 min. Then mix with beef and add mixture to sauce. Reheat to serving temperature.

3. Cut rolls in half and toast, if desired. Use No. 12 scoop for portioning ($1/3$ cup), putting barbecued beef mixture on bottom half or roll and topping with other half. Serve hot.

SOURCE: Miles Laboratories, Inc., Marschall Division, Elkhart, Ind.

PIZZA WITH TEXTURED VEGETABLE PROTEIN

	By Weight		or	By Measure
Ingredients	Lb	Oz		
Dough				
Active dry yeast		$1^1/_2$		$4^1/_2$ tbsp
Lukewarm water				$1^1/_4$ qt
Oil or melted fat		7		1 cup less 2 tbsp
Nonfat dry milk		$3^1/_4$		$2/3$ cup
Sugar				2 tbsp
Salt				$3^1/_2$ tbsp
All-purpose flour	4	4		$4^1/_2$ qt (approx)
Meat Mixture				
Beef trimmings	6	2		
Textured vegetable protein (Mira-Tex 210-1)	1			
Water (hot)	1	12		$3^1/_2$ cup
Sauce				
Tomato paste	4	12		2 qt
Oregano				1 tbsp
Garlic powder				$3/4$ tsp
Sugar		$2^1/_4$		$1/3$ cup
Water				$1^1/_4$ qt
Cheddar cheese, shredded	6	4		1 gal $2^1/_4$ qt

YIELD: 100 portions; 1 piece ($3^1/_4 \times 5$ in.) provides equivalent of 2 oz protein-rich food and a serving of bread.

Procedure

For Yeast Dough.—Add yeast to lukewarm water in a 10–15 qt bowl. Stir about 10 min. Add fat, milk, sugar, and salt. Slowly add flour using dough hook until dough leaves sides of bowl. Dough should mix about 15 min and be soft but not sticky. Cut into 4 equal balls. Roll each ball of dough thin and line 4 sheet pans (18 × 26 in.) with dough.

For Meat Sauce.—Combine the textured vegetable protein (Mira-Tex 210-1) with hot water and let stand 15–20 min until all water has been absorbed. Mix with meat. Then grind twice, first through a $^3/_8$-in. plate, then through a $^3/_{16}$-in. plate. Brown meat mixture for 25 min in a hot oven at 400°F. Drain. Mix tomato paste, seasonings, sugar, and water; add to cooked meat and mix well. Spread warm filling (about 3 lb 3 oz or $1^1/_2$ qt) over each pan of dough to within $^1/_2$ in. of edges.

Bake about 10 min at 425°F. Remove from oven and top with shredded cheese (1 lb 9 oz or $1^1/_2$ qt per pan). Return to oven and bake 5 min longer.

SOURCE: A. E. Staley Mfg. Co., Decatur, Ill.

CHILI WITH TEXTURED VEGETABLE PROTEIN

Ingredients	%
Kidney beans in water (available from Bush Brothers & Co., Dandridge, Tenn.)	36.24
Meat portion (beef, 70%; textured vegetable protein Edi-Pro® 200, 30%)	33.54
Canned tomatoes, drained	20.74
Tomato sauce	6.92
Chili seasoning	1.71
Salt	0.67
Ground cumin seed	0.18

Procedure

1. Make up meat portion by mixing textured vegetable protein (Edi-Pro® 200) and beef 5 min in a Hobart mixer.
2. Double grind through a $^3/_{16}$-in. plate.
3. Sear the meat mixture until brown.
4. Add the tomatoes, kidney beans, and seasoning; mix thoroughly.
5. Heat to a boil and simmer 15 min before serving.

SOURCE: Ralston Purina Company, Checkerboard Square, St. Louis, Mo.

CHILI WITH BEANS EXTENDED WITH TEXTURED VEGETABLE PROTEIN

Ingredients	%
Soaked kidney beans	28.93
Water	24.22

Textured vegetable protein (Supro 50™, dry)	10.00
Ground beef, 30% fat	30.00
Shortening	2.00
Tomato paste, 30% solids	4.00
Starch (Staley Tenderfil 8)	0.844
Sorbitol	0.004
Bratarome flavor (available from Haarmann & Reimer, Springfield, N.J.)	0.002
	100.000

Chili spice mix: use quantity sufficient to provide flavor level required

Procedure

Place 80% of the water in a steam kettle, add the Bratarome flavor, then add the textured vegetable protein (Supro 50™), shortening, and sorbitol. Heat to 210°F, hold for 3 min. Then add the ground beef and continue to braise until the meat is cooked. Add the tomato paste, balance of water, spice mix, starch, and kidney beans. Cook until the spices are fully blended.

SOURCE: Ralston Purina Company, Checkerboard Square, St. Louis, Mo.

CHILI CON CARNE WITH BEANS AND TEXTURED SOY PROTEIN OR SPUN TEXTURED VEGETABLE PROTEIN

	By Weight	or	By Measure
Ingredients	Lb Oz		
Ground beef	6 8		
Hydration water	1 8		3 cups
Textured soy protein (Maxten) or spun textured vegetable protein (Temptein)	1		6 cups
Onions, chopped	1		$2^2/_3$ cups
Tomato purée	9		1 gal.
Bean liquid and water	4		2 qt
All-purpose flour	4		1 cup
Water	8		1 cup
Cooked kidney or pinto beans, drained	10 6		1 gal. $2^1/_4$ qt
Salt	2		$^1/_4$ cup
Chili powder	1		$^1/_3$ cup

YIELD: 100 portions with about $^1/_2$ cup providing the equivalent of a 2-oz serving of cooked lean meat.

Procedure

1. Add hydration water to textured soy protein (Maxten) or spun textured vegetable protein

(Temptein) and allow to stand for 5 min. Then mix with ground beef.

2. Brown the beef mixture lightly; add onions and cook until onions are clear but not browned. Drain.

3. Add tomato purée and liquid; simmer until beef is tender.

4. Make a paste of flour and water; add to beef mixture, stirring constantly. Then add beans and seasonings.

5. Cover and cook 1–1½ hr or until flavors are well blended and mixture is thickened. Stir occasionally to prevent sticking.

SOURCE: Miles Laboratories, Inc., Marschall Division, Elkhart, Ind.

CHILI CON CARNE WITH TEXTURED VEGETABLE PROTEIN

Ingredients	By Weight Lb	By Weight Oz	or	By Measure
Textured vegetable Protein (Mira-Tex 210-1)	1			
Water (hot)	1	12		3½ cup
Beef trimmings	6	4		
Oil	8			1 cup
Onions, chopped	1			2⅔ cup
Tomato purée	9			1 gal.
Bean liquid and water				2 qt
Corn starch		2		
Water				1 cup
Cooked kidney or pinto beans	10	6		1 gal. 2¼ qt
Salt		2		¼ cup
Chili powder				⅓ cup

YIELD: 100 portions; ½ cup provides equivalent of 2 oz protein-rich food.

Procedure

1. Combine textured vegetable protein (Mira-Tex 210-1) and hot water and allow to stand about 15 min until all water has been absorbed; then combine with beef trimmings. Grind mixture twice; first through a ⅜-in. plate, then through a ⅛-in. plate.

2. Brown meat mixture. Add onions and cook until onions are clear but not brown. Drain excess fat. Add purée and liquid and simmer until beef is tender.

3. Mix corn starch and water; add to beef mixture stirring constantly. Then add beans and seasonings.

4. Cover and cook 1–1½ hr or until flavors are well blended and mixture is thickened, stirring occasionally to prevent sticking.

SOURCE: A. E. Staley Mfg. Co., Decatur, Ill.

CHILI WITHOUT BEANS WITH TEXTURED VEGETABLE PROTEIN

The following meat mixtures are given with varied percentages of textured vegetable protein replacement in the formula:

Ingredients	12% Lb	12% Oz	21% Lb	21% Oz	30% Lb
Boneless cow chuck	52	13	47	6	42
Choice trimmed beef flank	35	3	31	10	28
Water	8		14		20
Textured vegetable protein (Texgran 52300-T.A.)	4		7		10

Procedure.—Hydrate textured vegetable protein (Texgran) in designated amount of tap water and allow to hydrate 30 min with occasional agitation. Pass chucks and flanks through ⁷⁄₃₂-in. grinder plate. Combine hydrated Texgran with ground beef and mix in thoroughly. Pass the meat mixture once again through a ⁷⁄₃₂-in. grinder plate. Sauté meat until cooked, stirring frequently to brown.

Sauce Formulation

Ingredients	Lb	Oz
Water	100	
Tomato purée	90	
Dehydrated minced onion	2	8
All-purpose flour	1	10
Salt	1	14
Chili powder		10
Cumin		10
Black pepper		3
Oregano, ground		1½
Garlic juice		1½

Procedure.—Add all sauce ingredients (except flour) to cooked meat. Stir to blend thoroughly. Mix flour with 1 gal. cold water to form a slurry. Stir into *simmering* chili until well blended. Simmer meat and sauce mixture to the finished cooked weight designated below according to meat replacement:

	12%	21%	30%
Pounds of cooked meat and sauce	225–230	240–245	255–260

SOURCE: Swift Edible Oil Company, Vegetable Protein Products Div., 115 W. Jackson Blvd., Chicago, Ill.

SLOPPY JOE WITH TEXTURED VEGETABLE PROTEIN

Ingredient	%
Meat portion (beef 50%, textured vegetable protein Edi-Pro® 200 50%)	39.77
Tomato purée (sp. gr. 1.06)	32.55
Water	24.07
Sloppy Joe seasoning mix No. 61008 (available from Stange Co., Chicago)	2.42
Salt	0.60
Chili powder	0.23
Beef-type flavor powder D-93455 (available from Haarmann & Reimer, Springfield, N.J.)	0.23
Worcestershire powder (available from R. T. French Co., Rochester, N.Y.)	0.08
Garlic powder	0.03
Red pepper	0.02

Procedure

1. Mix the textured vegetable protein (Edi-Pro® 200) and beef in a Hobart mixer for 5 min.
2. Grind the resulting mixture through a $3/16$-in. plate, twice.
3. Sear the meat mixture until brown.
4. Add the seasoning mix, tomato purée, and other ingredients.
5. Mix all ingredients, while heating mixture to a boil.
6. Simmer for 20 min before serving.

SOURCE: Ralston Purina Company, Checkerboard Square, St. Louis, Mo.

CANNED SLOPPY JOE (BARBECUE SAUCE WITH BEEF) WITH HYDROLYZED PLANT PROTEIN

Ingredients	%
Hydrolyzed plant protein (Maggi HPP Type Super 3H Powder)	0.400
Beef trimmings, $3/8$-in. grind, precooked	35.000
Water	17.750
Beef broth	15.000
Tomato paste (30% solids)	12.500
Sugar	4.500
Flour	4.500
Sweet pickle relish	3.100
Vinegar (50-grain)	2.500
Worcestershire sauce	1.500
Salt	1.500
Onion, dehydrated granulated	0.750
Waxy maize starch	0.500
Spice blend (see below)	0.250
Garlic powder	0.125
Red pepper-salt, soluble	0.125
	100.000

Spice Blend Ingredients	%
Celery salt	32.50
Garlic powder	12.50
Clove, soluble	7.50
Bay, soluble	7.50
Pimiento, soluble	8.75
Turmeric (Alleppey)	31.25

Procedure

Mix ingredients and heat to 180°F. Fill into cans and process.

Suggested Process

301 × 411 (16 oz net) 20 min at 212°F

Check process time and temperature with can supplier or the National Canners Association.

SOURCE: Nestlé Company, Food Ingredients Division, 100 Bloomingdale Road, White Plains, N.Y.

SLOPPY JOE WITH TEXTURED VEGETABLE PROTEIN

The following meat mixtures are given with varied percentages of textured vegetable protein replacement in the formula:

Ingredients	12% Lb	Oz	21% Lb	Oz	30% Lb
Boneless cow chuck	52	13	47	6	42
Choice trimmed beef flank	35	3	31	10	28
Water	8		14		20
Textured vegetable protein (Texgran 52300-T.A.)	4		7		10

Procedure.—Hydrate textured vegetable protein (Texgran) in designated amount of tap water and allow to hydrate 30 min with occasional agitation. Pass chucks, flanks, and hydrated textured vegetable protein through $7/32$-in. grinder plate. Mix thoroughly. Pass meat mixture once more through $7/32$-in. grinder plate. Sauté meat until cooked, stirring frequently to brown.

Sauce Formulation

Ingredients	By Weight Lb	Oz	or By Measure
Oil	2	8	$2^1/4$ qt.
Chopped celery	10		
Chopped onion	7		
Cider vinegar	9		$4^1/2$ qt
Brown sugar	4	8	
Catsup	54		$6^3/4$ gal.
Mustard powder		6	
Salt	1	8	

Water	10	
Canned diced green pepper (optional)	2	1 qt
Worcestershire sauce (optional)	1	1 pt
All-purpose flour	12	
Water	2	

Procedure.—In a large steam kettle, sauté celery and onions in oil. Add vinegar and brown sugar. Simmer 5 min. Add cooked meat mixture and all remaining ingredients, except flour and last 2 lb of water. Combine flour and water to make a slurry. Add to mixture slowly while stirring. Simmer meat and sauce mixture to the finished cooked weight designated below according to meat replacement:

	12%	21%	30%
Pounds of cooked meat and sauce	150–155	160–165	170–175

SOURCE: Swift Edible Oil Company, Vegetable Protein Products Div., 115 W. Jackson Blvd., Chicago, Ill.

SLOPPY JOE WITH TEXTURED VEGETABLE PROTEIN

Ingredients	%
Meat portion (beef, 70%; textured vegetable protein Edi-Pro® 200, 30%)	55.99
Tomato sauce	21.33
Water	19.20
Sloppy Joe seasoning No. 61008 (available from Stange Co., Chicago)	2.95
Salt	0.53

Procedure

1. Mix the beef and textured vegetable protein (Edi-Pro® 200) for 5 min in a Hobart mixer.
2. A double grind of the resulting mixture is accomplished on a $3/16$-in. plate.
3. Sear the beef mixture until brown.
4. Add the other ingredients and stir until uniformly distributed.
5. Heat the mixture to a boil, then simmer 20 min before serving.

SOURCE: Ralston Purina Company, Checkerboard Square, St. Louis, Mo.

NOT-SO-SLOPPY JOE WITH TEXTURED VEGETABLE PROTEIN

	By Weight		By or Measure
Ingredients	Lb	Oz	
Meat Mixture			
Textured vegetable protein (Mira-Tex 210-1)	1	12	

Water (hot)	3	4	1½ qt
Beef trimmings	12		
Sauce			
Brown sugar			⅓ cup
Paprika			3 tbsp
Salt			3 tsp
Dry mustard			3 tsp
Chili powder			¾ tsp
Cayenne pepper			¼ tsp
Worcestershire sauce			⅓ cup
Vinegar			½ cup
Tomato juice			3 cups
Catsup			1½ qt
Water			3 qt

YIELD: 100 portions

Procedure

Combine textured vegetable protein (Mira-Tex 210-1) and hot water and let stand about 10 min until all water is absorbed. Mix meat chunks and moist textured vegetable protein and grind mixture twice: first through a $3/8$-in. plate, then through a $1/8$-in. plate. Brown meat mixture 25 min at 400°F (hot oven). Drain.

Combine sauce ingredients and mix well. Combine meat mixture and sauce. Heat in pan or steam tray until recipe is hot and meat becomes tender.

SOURCE: A. E. Staley Mfg. Co., Decatur, Ill.

SLOPPY JOE EXTENDED WITH TEXTURED VEGETABLE PROTEIN

	A	B
Ingredients	%	%
Beef, 30% fat, $3/16$-in. grind	36.79	26.27
Textured vegetable protein (Supro 50$_{TM}$, regular)	5.25	8.76
Water	39.27	46.195
Sloppy Joe seasoning No. 61008 (available from Stange Co., Chicago)	2.63	2.63
Tomato paste, 32% solids	15.62	15.62
Sugar	0.44	0.44
Salt		0.075
Chili peppers, ground		0.01
	100.00	100.000

Formula A replaces 30% of the beef with Supro 50$_{TM}$
Formula B replaces 50% of the beef with Supro 50$_{TM}$

Procedure

1. Place the textured vegetable protein (Supro 50$_{TM}$) in a steam kettle with water to hydrate, using a 2:1 water to Supro 50$_{TM}$ ratio.
2. Heat to 210°F, add the ground beef, and continue to cook until the mixture is uniformly braised.

3. Add the remainder of the ingredients in any order and stir until homogeneous.

4. Simmer 15 min, stir occasionally.

SOURCE: Ralston Purina Company, Checkerboard Square, St. Louis, Mo.

MEAT LOAVES

MEAT LOAF OR MEAT LOAF PATTIES WITH TEXTURED VEGETABLE PROTEIN

The following meat mixtures are given with varied percentages of hydrated textured vegetable protein replacement in the formula:

	Hydrated Textured Vegetable Protein Replacement		
	30%	21%	12%
Ingredients	Lb	Lb	Lb
Economy beef chuck	42	47	53
Premium beef flank	28	32	35
Textured vegetable protein (Texgran No. 10100 or No. 10900)	10	7	4
Water	20	14	8

The following flavoring mix ingredients are suggested; they may be substituted with your own:

	Lb	Oz
Bread crumbs	3	
Nonfat dry milk (high heat)		11
Dehydrated onions		13
Frozen whole egg	3	12
Salt		11.5
Black pepper		1.6
Dehydrated parsley flake		1.25
Beef flavor—any of the following:		6–10
Pfizer Beef "Corral"		
McCormick Flavor Cap No. 20,601		
Florasynth Beef Flavor No. 870		
I.F.F. Imitation Beef No. 29,759		

Procedure

Blend textured vegetable protein (Texgran), spices, and all other ingredients except meat with water. Mix and let hydrate for 10–15 min. Add hydrated mixture to rough cuts of meat and grind through a $1/2$-in. die; mix and grind again through a $1/8$- or $5/16$-in. die. Form into loaves or into patties of desired weight.

SOURCE: Swift Edible Oil Company, Vegetable Protein Products Div., 115 W. Jackson Blvd., Chicago, Ill.

MEAT LOAF PREPARED WITH PEANUT GRITS TEXTURIZED PROTEIN

Meat loaf can be extended with Peanut Grits texturized protein resulting in a tasty and economical finished product.

Ingredients	Lb	Oz
Lean Beef (80/20)	70	
Pork trimmings or beef plates (50/50)	30	
Nonfat dry milk	4	
Tomato purée	1	
Dehydrated sweet red peppers		1
Dehydrated sweet green peppers		1
Salt	1	
Water	20	
Peanut Grits	6	
Seasonings to taste		

Procedure

1. Cut beef in silent cutter or cube and pass through the $1/2$-in. plate of the grinder.

2. Presoak remaining ingredients (Peanut Grits, seasonings, salt, tomato purée, and nonfat dry milk) in ice water for 15–20 min.

3. Blend meat and presoaked mixture in silent cutter or similar equipment.

4. Grind through the $1/8$-in. plate of the grinder.

5. Form into meat loaves of desired size.

6. Loaves may be frozen as made up (fresh); or they may be baked at 325°F to an internal temperature of 150°F and then frozen.

SOURCE: Gold Kist, Inc., P.O. Box 2210, Atlanta, Ga.

EMULSION-TYPE MEAT LOAF WITH SOY PROTEIN CONCENTRATE

Ingredients	Lb
Lean beef (90% lean)	50.0
Beef cheek	15.0
Lean pork (75% lean)	15.0
Pork jowls	20.0
Soy protein concentrate (Promosoy-100)	10.0
Nonfat dry milk	10.0
Cereal	5.0
Water	70.0
Spice, salt, cure, seasonings to suit	

Procedure

1. Chop lean meats with moisture, salt, cure, and spices for about 2 min.
2. Add soy protein concentrate (Promosoy-100) and chop for an additional 3 min.
3. Add fat meats and complete chop.
4. Stuff and cook, using usual cooking procedure.

SOURCE: Central Soya Co., Chemurgy Division, 1825 N. Laramie St., Chicago, Ill.

PICKLE-PIMIENTO LOAF WITH TEXTURED SOY PROTEIN

Ingredients	Lb	Oz
Beef trimmings	30	
Regular pork trimmings	50	
Beef plates	10	
Partially defatted pork fatty tissue	10	
Sweet pickles	10	
Pimientos or red peppers	10	
Salt	$3^1/_2$	
Swift's food protein (S.F.P.)	12	
Fresh onions	5	
Ground white pepper		8
Ground marjoram		1
Fresh garlic		1
Chopped ice	50	
Sodium ascorbate		$^7/_8$
Sodium nitrite		$^1/_4$
Sodium nitrate		$^3/_4$

Procedure

Chop beef and onions together, and pork separately, through $^1/_8$-in. plate. Cut pickles in $^1/_4$-in. pieces, pimientos in $^1/_2$-in. pieces. Chop garlic fine and mix with cure. Place beef, salt, and cure in silent cutter. Cut for $^1/_2$ min, add chopped ice and food protein (S.F.P.) a little at a time until all the S.F.P. has been used. Then add pork and seasonings, and chop so that the emulsion is of the same consistency as for bologna. Put mixture into mixer. Add pickles and pimientos. Mix well.

Cook, stuff and mold under your individual conditions.

SOURCE: Swift Edible Oil Co., Vegetable Protein Products Div., 115 W. Jackson Blvd., Chicago, Ill.

SPICED LUNCHEON LOAF WITH SOY PROTEIN CONCENTRATE

Ingredients	Lb
Lean beef (90% lean)	30.0
Beef plates	20.0
Beef hearts	25.0
Pork jowls	10.0
Regular pork trimmings (50% lean)	15.0
Soy protein concentrate (Promosoy-100)	5.0
Nonfat dry milk	5.0
Corn syrup	5.0
Water	25.0
Spice, salt, cure, seasonings to suit	

Procedure

1. Chop lean meats with moisture, salt, cure, and spices for about 2 min.
2. Add soy protein concentrate (Promosoy-100) and chop for an additional 3 min.
3. Add fat meats and complete chop.
4. Stuff and cook using usual cooking procedure.

SOURCE: Central Soya Co., Chemurgy Division, 1825 N. Laramie St., Chicago, Ill.

SAUSAGE-FLAVORED PORK LOAF PREPARED WITH PEANUT GRITS TEXTURIZED PROTEIN

Ingredients	Lb
Pork trimmings (55% fat)	80
Pork hearts	20
Peanut Grits	10
Ice water	28
Bread crumbs	1.4
Nonfat dry milk	4.1
Sausage seasoning	3.1

Procedure

1. Presoak Peanut Grits, bread crumbs, nonfat dry milk, and sausage seasoning in ice water for 15 min.
2. Cube meat ($1^1/_2$–1 in. cubes) and blend meat and presoaked mixture in silent cutter.
3. Grind through desired plate of the grinder.
4. Form into loaves of desired size.
5. Loaves may be frozen as made up (fresh); or they may be baked at 325°F to an internal temperature of 185°F and then frozen.

SOURCE: Gold Kist, Inc., P.O. Box 2210, Atlanta, Ga.

MEAT LOAF WITH TEXTURED VEGETABLE PROTEIN

This formula has excellent juice and volume retention.

Ingredients	Oz
Textured vegetable protein (Texgran No. 10,900)	11
Bread crumbs	8
Water	33
Milk	15
Minced onions	18

Salt	2
Black pepper	$\frac{1}{4}$
Chopped parsley	$\frac{1}{4}$
Eggs, slightly beaten	12
Ground beef	160

Procedure

Blend textured vegetable protein (Texgran), bread crumbs, water, milk, and spices. Allow 15 min for textured vegetable protein to absorb water. Add eggs and mix in ground beef. Pack into greased loaf pans and bake for $1\frac{1}{4}$ hr at 375°F.

SOURCE: Swift Edible Oil Company, Vegetable Protein Products Div., 115 W. Jackson Blvd., Chicago, Ill.

MEAT LOAF WITH TEXTURED VEGETABLE PROTEIN

	By Weight		By
Ingredients	Lb	Oz	or Measure
Textured vegetable protein (S.F.P.— Swift's Food Protein)		11	$3\frac{1}{2}$ cups
Water	2	1	
Milk		15	$1\frac{7}{8}$ cups
Bread crumbs		8	8 cups
Onions, minced	1	2	3 cups
Ground beef	10		
Salt		2	$\frac{1}{4}$ cup
Black pepper		$\frac{1}{4}$	$\frac{1}{2}$ tbsp
Parsley, chopped			$\frac{1}{2}$ cup
Eggs, slightly beaten			6
Oil		14	$1\frac{3}{4}$ cups

Procedure

Rehydrate textured vegetable protein (S.F.P.) in designated amount of water; let stand 15 min to allow for complete absorption of water. An alternate method is to cover food protein with tap water; allow 15 min for rehydration; pour off unabsorbed water. The latter method is preferred because it can be done in a large mixing pot (Hobart, etc.).

Beat bread and milk in a mixer 2 min on low speed. Combine bread mixture and S.F.P. (Swift's Food Protein) with all other ingredients. Mix in mixer 3 min at low speed.

Pack in greased loaf pan (4 × 10 × 4 in.). Bake at 375°F for 1 hr 10 min.

SOURCE: Swift Edible Oil Co., Vegetable Protein Products Div., 115 W. Jackson Blvd., Chicago, Ill.

MEAT LOAF WITH TEXTURED VEGETABLE PROTEIN

Ingredients	%
Beef	63.31
Textured vegetable protein (Edi-Pro® 200)	26.20
Bread crumbs	6.11
Salt	1.83
Minced onion	1.40
Beef-type flavor powder D-93455 (available from Haarmann & Reimer, Springfield, N.J.)	0.87
Black pepper	0.18
Ground bell pepper	0.10

Procedure

1. Mix the textured vegetable protein (Edi-Pro® 200) and beef for 5 min in a Hobart mixer.
2. Add all other ingredients and continue mixing for 3 min.
3. After uniform distribution has been accomplished, the mixture is ground twice through a $\frac{3}{16}$-in. plate.
4. The ground material is then molded into loaf pans and baked at 350°F for 50 min.

SOURCE: Ralston Purina Company, Checkerboard Square, St. Louis, Mo.

MEAT LOAF WITH TEXTURED VEGETABLE PROTEIN

	By Weight		By
Ingredients	Lb	Oz	or Measure
Textured vegetable protein (Mira-Tex 210-1)	1	6	
Water (hot)	2	10	$1\frac{1}{3}$ qt
Beef trimmings (28–30% fat)	9	2	
Bread slices	1		
Milk			$1\frac{1}{2}$ qt
Onions, chopped		12	2 cups
Celery, chopped		12	$2\frac{3}{4}$ cups
Salt		2	$\frac{1}{4}$ cup
Worcestershire sauce		$2\frac{1}{4}$	$\frac{1}{4}$ cup
Eggs	2	13	25 large

YIELD: 100 portions; 1 slice about $\frac{3}{4}$-in. thick provides the equivalent of 2 oz of protein-rich food.

Procedure

1. Combine textured vegetable protein (Mira-Tex 210-1) and hot water; hydrate for 10–15 min.

Combine with beef trimmings and grind first through a $3/8$-in. plate, then through a $1/8$-in. plate.

2. Beat bread and milk 2 min in mixer on low speed, or soak bread in milk. Combine bread and meat mixture with other ingredients. Mix well 3 min on low speed.

3. Place meat mixture in 2 greased pans (about $12 \times 20 \times 2$ in.), about 10 lb 8 oz (or $1 1/4$ gal.) per pan. Shape mixture into 2 equal lengthwise loaves in each pan.

4. Bake 1 hr 10 min at $375°F$ (moderate oven). Pour off liquid and fat that accumulate during cooking.

SOURCE: A. E. Staley Mfg. Co., Decatur, Ill.

MEAT LOAF WITH TEXTURED SOY PROTEIN OR SPUN TEXTURED VEGETABLE PROTEIN

	By Weight		or	By Measure
Ingredients	Lb	Oz		
Bread slices	2			
Milk	3			$1 1/2$ qt
Onions, chopped		12		2 cups
Celery, chopped		12		$2 3/4$ cups
Ground beef	10	8		
Hydration water	2	13		$5 1/2$ cups

MEAT PATTIES

BEEF PATTIES WITH SPUN TEXTURED VEGETABLE PROTEIN OR TEXTURED SOY PROTEIN

	By Weight	or	By Measure
Ingredients	Lb	Oz	
Ground beef	12	4	
Hydration water	3	2	$6 1/4$ cups
Spun textured vegetable protein (Temptein) or textured soy protein (Maxten)	2	2	12 cups
Salt		2	3 tbsp

YIELD: 100 portions with one patty the equivalent of a 2-oz serving of cooked lean meat.

Procedure

1. Add hydration water to spun textured vegetable protein (Temptein) or textured soy protein (Maxten) and allow to stand for 5 min. Then combine all ingredients and mix thoroughly.

Textured soy protein (Maxten) or spun textured vegetable protein (Temptein)	1	11	$9 1/2$ cups
Salt		2	3 tbsp
Worcestershire sauce		$2 1/4$	$1/4$ cup
Parsley, chopped (if desired)		$1/2$	$1/2$ cup
Eggs	1	9	14 large

YIELD: 100 portions with a $3/4$-in. thick slice providing the equivalent of a 2-oz serving of cooked lean meat.

Procedure

1. Beat bread and milk for 2 min in mixer on low speed, or soak bread in milk.

2. Add hydration water to textured soy protein (Maxten) or spun textured vegetable protein (Temptein) and allow to stand for 5 min.

3. Combine bread mixture with hydrated Maxten or Temptein, ground beef, and remaining ingredients. Mix well for 3 min on low speed.

4. Place meat mixture in 2 greased oblong pans (approx $12 \times 20 \times 2$ in.) with about 11 lb 12 oz (or 1 gal. $1 3/4$ qt by measure) in each pan. Shape into two equal loaves lengthwise in each pan.

5. Bake 1 hr 10 min at $375°F$ (moderate oven). Drain excess fat, slice and serve.

SOURCE: Miles Laboratories, Inc., Marschall Division, Elkhart, Ind.

2. Portion mixture with No. 12 scoop ($1/3$ cup) onto sheet pans (approx 18×26 in.). Flatten each portion gently into patties about $3/4$ in. wider than desired size when cooked.

3. Bake at $400°F$ (hot oven) for 10 min.

4. Serve as a meat accompaniment on luncheon plate or between sliced, heated hamburger roll.

SOURCE: Miles Laboratories, Inc., Marschall Division, Elkhart, Ind.

BEEF PATTIES WITH TEXTURED VEGETABLE PROTEIN

Ingredients	%
Ground beef	68.84
Textured vegetable protein (Edi-Pro® 200)	29.50
Spicing mix (see below)	1.36
Beef-type flavor powder D-93455 (available from Haarmann & Reimer, Springfield, N.J.)	0.30

Spices are used with percentages based on beef plus textured vegetable protein:

Spice Ingredients	%
Salt	1.200
Chili powder	0.300
Onion powder	0.050
Black pepper	0.030
Ground mustard seed	0.020
Garlic powder	0.005

Procedure

1. Mix textured vegetable protein (Edi-Pro® 200) in Hobart mixer for 5 min.
2. Add ground beef to mixing bowl and blend for 1 min.
3. Add remaining ingredients and mix for 3 min.
4. Form patties from the resulting mixture and freeze.
5. Cook thawed patties at 400°F until done.

SOURCE: Ralston Purina Company, Checkerboard Square, St. Louis, Mo.

BREAKFAST PATTIES WITH TEXTURED VEGETABLE PROTEIN

Ingredients	Lb
Textured vegetable protein (Texgran No. 10,000 or 10,300)	13
Regular pork trimmings	85
Lean pork trimmings	85
Pork sausage seasoning	4
Water (chilled 35°–40°F)	31

Procedure

Combine the textured vegetable protein (Texgran), seasoning, and water. Mix and let stand for 10–15 min. Add these ingredients (uniformly) to the meat and grind through $^3/_8$-in. or $^1/_2$-in. die plate. Add 10 lb shaved ice as grinding process continues. Mix for 2–3 min; then grind through $^1/_8$-in. plate. May be pattied through a Hollymatic 8S plate.

SOURCE: Swift Edible Oil Company, Vegetable Protein Products Div., 115 W. Jackson Blvd., Chicago, Ill.

BEEF PATTIES WITH TEXTURED VEGETABLE PROTEIN

These patties have a moist, chewy and palatable texture with little cook-out shrinkage.

Ingredients	Lb
Meat (85–90% lean)	50
50/50 meat (50% lean)	50

Water	13$^1/_2$
Textured vegetable protein (Texgran)	4
Hydrolyzed vegetable protein	$^1/_2$

Procedure

Generally, textured vegetable protein (Texgran) should be hydrated and ground with rough cuts of meat. Recommended starting level when using Texgran (No. 10,000, 10,100, or 10,900) in beef patties is 4% (dry weight). Texgran is hydrated with 337% cold water ($3.37 \times 4 = 13^1/_2$ lb water) for 15–20 min with periodic mixing. Hydrated Texgran and any excess water are added to rough meat cuts, then ground through a $^1/_2$-in. plate and "pattied out."

Depending upon product, Texgran-rehydrating water can be varied from 200 to 337%. Level of Texgran can be increased to an 8% maximum, provided meat flavor is added to compensate for natural meat flavor's dilution.

SOURCE: Swift Edible Oil Company, Vegetable Protein Products Div., 115 W. Jackson Blvd., Chicago, Ill.

FROZEN BEEF PATTY GRILL WITH TEXTURED VEGETABLE PROTEIN

Ingredients	Lb
90/10 lean beef (frozen)	65
50/50 beef plates	285
Textured vegetable protein (Bontrae® rehydrated crumbles)	145
Salt	2$^1/_2$
Beef patty seasoning	2$^1/_2$

Procedure

Hydrate textured vegetable protein in meat tub using 48 lb Bontrae® and 97 lb water. Weigh out meat and coarse grind through a $^1/_2$-in. plate. Add hydrated textured vegetable protein. Blend with meat in Reitz or Hobart mixer; then fine-grind mixture putting it through a $^1/_8$-in. plate. Form into patties with Hollymatic or Acupac. Freeze patties and package in desired size freezing cartons.

SOURCE: General Mills, Inc., 9200 Wayzata Blvd., Minneapolis, Minn.

BEEF PATTIES WITH TEXTURED VEGETABLE PROTEIN

	By Weight		or	By Measure
Ingredients	Lb	Oz		
Textured vegetable protein (Mira-Tex 210-1)	1	14		
Water (hot)	3	6		1$^2/_3$ qt

Beef trimmings	12	4
Salt	2	¼ cup

YIELD: 100 portions; 1 patty provides 2 oz cooked meat.

Procedure

1. Combine textured vegetable protein (Mira-Tex 210-1) with hot water and allow to stand about 15 min until all water has been absorbed; then mix with beef and salt. Grind mixture twice, first through a ³/₈-in. plate, then through a ¹/₈-in. plate.

2. Portion with a No. 12 scoop (¹/₃ cup) onto greased sheet pans; flatten with a spatula.

3. Bake single layers at 400°F (hot oven): 15 min for medium, 20 min for well done.

SOURCE: A. E. Staley Mfg. Co., Decatur, Ill.

ECONOMY HIGH-FAT BEEF PATTIES WITH PEANUT GRITS TEXTURIZED PROTEIN

The use of Peanut Grits texturized protein in ground meat combinations allows a wide latitude in formulation variations. The following formulas are designed for precooked or frozen patties with 24–25% finished fat.

Ingredients	No. 1 Lb	No. 2 Lb
Beef (40% fat)	60	60
Peanut Grits	10	6
Precooked wheat fines		4
Ice water	27	27
Salt	1	1
Seasonings to taste		

Procedure

1. Cut beef in silent cutter or cube and pass through the ¹/₂-in. plate of the grinder.

2. Combine Peanut Grits, ice water, salt, and seasonings and allow to stand for 15–20 min.

3. Blend meat and presoaked mixture.

4. Grind combined ingredients through ¹/₈-in. plate.

5. Form into patties on automatic pattie maker.

SOURCE: Gold Kist, Inc., P.O. Box 2210, Atlanta, Ga.

HAMBURGERS EXTENDED WITH TEXTURED VEGETABLE PROTEIN

Ingredients	% A	% B
Lean cow meat (11% fat)	38.8	38.8
Choice flank meat (68% fat)	31.2	31.2
Textured vegetable protein (Supro 50™, minced)	10.0	15.0

Water	19.5	14.5
Salt	0.5	0.5
	100.0	100.0

Formula B can be used when it is desired to have a slightly drier product with a higher protein level.

Procedure

1. Grind cow meat and flank meat separately through a ¹/₂-in. plate.

2. Hydrate the textured vegetable protein (Supro 50™) with the water (2–3 min).

3. Mix the hydrated textured vegetable protein (Supro 50™), ground lean, and ground flank in a Hobart mixer, low speed 2–3 min.

4. Sprinkle in the salt and mix for an additional 5 min.

5. Grind the entire mixture through a ¹/₈-in. plate and make into patties.

Note: Final product: 25% fat. Proportions of lean and flank meat will vary to obtain consistent fat levels.

SOURCE: Ralston Purina Company, Checkerboard Square, St. Louis, Mo.

MEAT PATTIES WITH TEXTURED VEGETABLE PROTEIN

Ingredients	Formula 1 %	Formula 2 %
Ground meat (20–30% fat)	90.00	86.46
Textured vegetable protein (Mira-Tex 210)	3.50	5.00
Hot water (140°F)	6.47	8.50
Meat pattie seasoning (or season to suit)	0.03	0.04

Procedure

Add seasoning to hot water and mix well. Hydrate textured vegetable protein (Mira-Tex 210) in hot water-seasoning mixture until water is absorbed. Combine with meat and grind to desired particle size. Form into patties and package.

SOURCE: A. E. Staley Mfg. Co., Decatur, Ill.

BEEF PATTIES WITH TEXTURED VEGETABLE PROTEIN

The following meat mixtures are given with varied percentages of hydrated textured vegetable protein replacement in the formula:

Ingredients	Hydrated Textured Vegetable Protein Replacement		
	30% Lb	21% Lb	12% Lb
Economy beef chuck	27	31	34
Premium beef flank	40	45	50
Textured vegetable protein (Texgran No. 10100 or No. 10900)	9.5	6.5	3.9
Water	19	13	7.8

The following spice mix ingredients are suggested; they may be substituted with your own:

	Lb	Oz
Cheddar whey	1	7.8
Salt		15.9
Dehydrated onions		4.8
Water	1	7.8
Monosodium glutamate		6.4
Black pepper		0.8
Beef flavor—any of the following:		4–8
I.F.F. Imitation Beef No. 29,759		
Pfizer Beef "Corral"		
McCormick Flavor Cap No. 20,601		
Florasynth Beef Flavor No. 870		

Procedure

Combine textured vegetable protein (Texgran), spices, and water. Mix and let stand to hydrate for 10–15 min. Hydrated mixture should then be added to rough cuts of meat and ground through a $1/2$-in. die. Mix for 1–3 min, then grind through a $1/8$-in. die. Patty out.

SOURCE: Swift Edible Oil Company, Vegetable Protein Products Div., 115 W. Jackson Blvd., Chicago, Ill.

MEAT PATTIES WITH TEXTURED VEGETABLE PROTEIN

Ingredients	%
Beef flank (approx 45% fat)	50
Boneless lean beef (approx 15% fat)	20
Textured soy protein (Maxten)	30
Seasoning	Optional

Procedure

Hydrate textured soy protein (Maxten) in the proper amount of water. Warm water is best; if not available or desirable, cold water may be used. Add hydrated vegetable protein to the combined meats in the chopper and chop for approximately 30 sec. Grind the meat mixture through a conventional plate die. (Additional grinding and mixing steps can be added if desired.) Form the ground meat mixture on an automatic patty former.

SOURCE: Miles Laboratories, Inc., Marschall Division, Elkhart, Ind.

MISCELLANEOUS CANNED MEAT PRODUCTS

GENERAL INSTRUCTIONS TO BE OBSERVED FOR PROCESSING CANNED ITEMS UNDER STEAM OR UNDER THE COMBINATION OF STEAM AND WATER PRESSURE

High temperature sterilization process presents many problems due to the fact that physical changes take place in the contents of the cans.

First of all, it is necessary to know what is the best temperature to make the product sterile and how long the product must be subjected to that temperature to obtain sterilization.

All ordinary vegetative bacteria are killed off at a temperature of 176°F in 30 min; but it takes 30 min to destroy spore-forming bacteria at a temperature of 230°F. At higher temperatures (over 230°F) the time of the process is reduced. At a temperature of 250°F it requires only 3 min to destroy spore-forming bacteria.

The total time to sterilize a can of food depends on (1) the size of the can, (2) the rate of heat penetration to the center of the can, and (3) the processing temperature which is used to obtain a wholesome product.

Heat penetration is affected by the consistency of the product and whether or not the containers can be shaken or rotated during the process to obtain faster heat penetration.

Most of the canners are not equipped to work out their own problems to determine the temperature and time required to sterilize a product. The suppliers of cans maintain elaborate laboratories to furnish this information, and also to indicate the type of containers best suited to the product. It is of great importance to follow rigidly the times and temperatures of the process recommended by the can manufacturer.

General Instructions

(1) Check the seams of a few closed, water-filled cans to see if the closing machine is in perfect operating condition. The whole canning operation depends upon perfect can closures.

(2) Reject those cans where the lip of the can is damaged or the lid of the can does not have proper amount of sealing compound.

(3) Rusty cans should never be used.

(4) Cans should be washed and sterilized inside and outside under hot water shower at a temperature of 180°F.

(5) Cans should not be filled up to the lip of the can. There should be a headspace of approximately 1/4 in. to obtain proper vacuum in the can.

(6) Cans should be inspected for proper seams and evacuation after discharge from the closing machine.

Retort Procedure During Cooking and Chilling Operations

Place cans in baskets for processing (or in trucks for horizontal retorts) in such a manner to ensure proper circulation of steam during retorting.

(1) Open vents, turn on steam to allow the air to escape.

(2) Keep vents open at least until inside temperature of the retort reaches 220°F.

(3) During this period leave the drain valve partially open to allow condensed water resulting from condensed steam to escape from the bottom of the retort.

(4) Close drain valve.

(5) Sterilization time starts when temperature inside of retort reaches the designated temperature for the product to be processed.

(6) As soon as the sterilization time is over, chill cans as quickly as possible. Open air pressure valve as soon as steam pressure is turned off. Maintain air pressure at the same level as steam pressure was applied to sterilize the product, to avoid buckling the cans; i.e., replace 10 lb steam pressure with 10 lb air pressure.

(7) Open overflow slightly to let the heated water escape from the retort and keep up circulation of cold water during the chilling operation.

(8) Chill cans in the retort until the internal product temperature in the can reaches at least 120°F.

(9) Close water line. Close air supply valve. Open retort and drain water. Never open retort as long as the pressure gage shows any pressure inside the retort.

(10) After removal from the retort give a final inspection to the cans for proper vacuum and seal.

The same general rules should be followed in processing food products packed in glass jars with the exception that in this case the retort is filled with water after baskets are deposited in the retort. Air pressure is introduced in the retort after it is closed, i.e., vents are closed. The air pressure should be 10 lb over the pressure recommended to sterilize the product and the same pressure also should be maintained during the chilling process. Overflow should be slightly open for escaping hot water.

Exceptions to the Above Rules.—Certain products such as spreads, hash, Vienna sausages packed in small cans do not need air pressure during the chilling process. But as a safety measure chilling under air pressure is always a good practice.

AMOUNT OF MONOSODIUM GLUTAMATE TO USE IN VARIOUS PRODUCTS

Product	Oz/100 Lb	%
Fish fillets (fresh or frozen)	2–3	0.13–0.19
Meat and sausage products	2–5$^{1}/_{4}$	0.13–0.34
Poultry, dressed (fresh or frozen)	2–3	0.13–0.19
Poultry, canned	3–5	0.19–0.31
Soups and gravies, canned	3–5$^{1}/_{2}$ [1]	
Stews, hash, gravy	2–4	0.13–0.25
Vegetables (canned or frozen)	2$^{1}/_{2}$–4	0.16–0.25
Potato chips and snack items	1 lb MSG per 10 lb salt	

[1] Ounces per 12 gal. soup or gravy.

SOURCE: *Food Flavorings, 2nd Edition* by J. Merory, published by Avi Publishing Co., Westport, Conn.

BROWN GRAVY (RETORT TYPE)

Ingredients	(%)
Water	90.26
Starch (Sta-O-Paque)	4.82
Whole milk solids (28% butterfat)	0.76
Sweet whey solids	0.36
Sugar	0.35
Hydrogenated vegetable oil	0.09
Salt	0.05
Caramel color	0.08
Beef flavor base (Asmus 97P-95-2)	3.23

Procedure

Blend dry ingredients thoroughly. Add to water and make a smooth slurry. Cook until mixture thickens. This gravy will not cook clear.

SOURCE: A. E. Staley Mfg. Co., Decatur, Ill.

BROWN GRAVY

Ingredients	Lb	Oz
Cornstarch	6	
Wheat flour	10	
Cracker flour	8	
Rendered beef fat (oleo stock)	12	
Salt	4	
Beef extract	5	
Plant protein hydrolyzate	5	
Monosodium glutamate	2	
Garlic powder		$^{1}/_{4}$
Onion powder	3	
Spanish paprika (fine mesh)	2	
Ground celery seed		1
Caramel color (powder)	1	4
Dry soluble pepper		2
Tomato paste (28% solids)	10	
Water to make 50 gal.		

Procedure

Put 25 gal. water in a steam-jacketed kettle. Add all ingredients except wheat and cracker flours and cornstarch and bring temperature up to 160°F. Put 15 gal. water in a bakery mixer and make a slurry free of lumps by slowly adding the flours and cornstarch. Add slurry to ingredients in the steam kettle with steady agitation. Then bring volume up to 50 gal. Allow gravy to simmer at 200°-205°F for 15 min.

Pack while hot at a temperature not lower than 160°F.

Suggested Process

603 × 700 cans (6 lb 12 oz net) 240 min at 240°F
300 × 409 cans (16 oz net) 75 min at 240°F

Check processing times and temperature with can supplier or the National Canners Association.

Suggested Uses

This brown gravy can be used in making beef stew, served over roast beef, provide the gravy for Swiss and Salisbury steaks, etc.

Sliced canned mushroom pieces may be added when using the gravy; or the pieces may be added to the gravy when processing it for canning. If used in the canned product, cans should be labeled accordingly.

SOURCE: Stephan L. Komarik, 4810 Ronda, Coral Gables, Florida.

BROWN GRAVY WITH SLICED BEEF (SEMICOLD PACK)

Prepare Beef Slices

Use commercial grade of beef rounds or clods and remove sinews, connective tissues, gristle, and fat. Cut meat into strips approximately 2 X 3 in. Place each strip on the shelf of an open truck in single layers in such a manner that they do not touch each other. Move truck to freezer and keep strips at freezer temperature just long enough to solidify (but not thoroughly freeze) them so they can be sliced on a slicing machine. Slice beef 1/4-in. thick.

Prepare Gravy

Ingredients	Lb	Oz	Pt
Salt	14		
Pepper (dry soluble, sugar base)	1		
Cane sugar	4		
Oleoresin celery (water-soluble)		1	
Garlic powder		2	
Hydrolyzed plant protein liquid			1
Tomato paste (28% solids)			15
Caramel color			1
Oleoresin paprika (HCV, water-soluble)		2	
Wheat flour	47		
Onion powder	4		

Place 55 gal. of water in a steam-jacketed kettle, apply steam and bring temperature to 180°F. Add all ingredients except the flour and onion powder. Put 15 gal. of water in a bakery mixer and while the machine is running, slowly add the flour and onion powder; mix until the slurry is free from lumps. Add slurry to other ingredients in kettle while mixer is running and bring volume of the gravy up to 70 gal. Temperature in the kettle will drop with the addition of the slurry, so bring temperature up to 200°F and keep gravy cooking for 10–15 min.

Pack 60% hot gravy with 40% sliced beef. Close under 15 in. vacuum.

Suggested Process

300 X 409 cans (16 oz net) 90 min at 240°F
404 X 200 cans (12 oz net) 60 min at 240°F

Check process times and temperature with can supplier or the National Canners Association.

SOURCE: Stephan L. Komarik, 4810 Ronda, Coral Gables, Florida.

BEEF AND GRAVY (COLD PACK) (70% BEEF, 30% GRAVY)

Ingredients	Lb	Oz
Carcass beef (canner-cutter grade)	350	
Wheat flour	17	14
Pregelatinized wheat flour	5	12
Salt	7	8
Onion powder		9
Plant protein hydrolyzate		7 1/2
Black pepper (34-mesh)		4 1/2
Powdered caramel color		4 1/2
Monosodium glutamate		1 1/2
Water	95	
Tomato paste (26–28% solids)	23	

Procedure

Dice raw beef into 2-in. cubes or grind it through the 1 1/2-in. plate of the grinder.

Make a uniform mixture of flours, caramel color, and flavorings. Put water in a mixer and slowly add the flour-flavoring mixture; run the mixer until gravy is smooth and free from lumps. Then add tomato paste.

Place cubed or ground beef in a mechanical mixer and add the gravy mix (150 lb). Mix until meat is evenly coated with gravy.

Hand pack in cans. After cans have been filled and before they go through the vacuum closing machine, run a spatula or similar instrument down the side of each can so that any entrapped air on the bottom can be eliminated. Close cans under 27 in. vacuum.

Suggested Process

404 X 404 cans (30 oz net) 2 hr 30 min at 240°F
401 X 411 cans (30 oz net) 2 hr 30 min at 240°F
300 X 409 cans (16 oz net) 95 min at 240°F

Check process times and temperature with can supplier or the National Canners Association.

After the sterilization process, use only cold water in the can washer; hot water will cause the gravy paste to congeal on the outside of the cans.

SOURCE: Stephan L. Komarik, 4810 Ronda, Coral Gables, Florida.

BEEF AND GRAVY (COLD PACK)

Ingredients	Lb	Oz
Carcass beef (canner-cutter grade)	500	
Wheat flour	18	13
Salt	7	4
Black pepper (34-mesh)		5
Onion powder		8
Powdered caramel color		4
Water	18	
Tomato purée (sp. gr. 1.035)	11	

Procedure

Dice raw beef into 2-in. cubes. Make a uniform mixture of flour, salt, seasonings, and caramel color. Put water in a mixer; slowly add flour-seasoning mixture and run mixer until gravy is smooth without any lumps. Then add tomato purée.

Place cubed beef in a mechanical mixer and add 55 lb of gravy mixture. Mix until meat is evenly coated with gravy.

Hand pack in cans. After cans have been filled and before they go through the vacuum closing machine, run a spatula or similar instrument down the side of each can so any entrapped air on the bottom may be eliminated. Close cans under 27 in. vacuum.

Suggested Process

404 X 404 cans (30 oz net) 2 hr 30 min at 240°F
401 X 411 cans (30 oz net) 2 hr 30 min at 240°F
300 X 409 cans (16 oz net) 95 min at 240°F

Check process times and temperature with can supplier or the National Canners Association.

After the sterilization process, use only cold water in the can washer; hot water will cause the gravy paste to congeal on the outside of the cans.

SOURCE: Stephan L. Komarik, 4810 Ronda, Coral Gables, Florida.

SLICED BEEF IN GRAVY (FOR 100-GALLON BATCH)

Ingredients	Lb
Derivatized cross-bonded waxy maize cornstarch	35.55
Beef gravy seasoning	44.33
Water sufficient to make 100 gal.	

Procedure

Mix seasoning and cornstarch with a portion of the water to make a smooth paste. Add remaining water to required gage, heat slowly with continuous stirring to 190°F. Pour over sliced beef prepared as directed.

Use commercial outside rounds and handle in the following manner: Cut rounds in sections to give a reasonable slice of meat but not too small for a No. 300 container. Then immerse meat in a 30% dextrose solution, slice approximately $1/2$-in. thick, deep fry in vegetable shortening or vegetable corn oil for no more than 35 sec at 350°-375°F, drain and weigh into can.

Use 6 oz meat per No. 300 can, top with hot gravy, fill, seam and sterilize. Retort at 240°F for 60 min. Type of can should be determined by can supplier.

Check process time and temperature with can supplier or the National Canners Association.

SOURCE: CPC International Inc., Industrial Division, Englewood Cliffs, N.J.

SWISS STEAK IN GRAVY

Ingredients	Lb	Oz	Pt
Beef steaks	465		
Tomato purée (sp. gr. 1.035)	30		
Water	100		
Salt	10		
Wheat flour	10		
Onion powder		9	
Plant protein hydrolyzate		8	
Black pepper (34-mesh)		4	
Powdered caramel color		4	
Monosodium glutamate		4	
Worcestershire sauce			2

Prepare Meat

Strip loins, sirloin butts, or rounds are the most suitable materials of commercial grade beef for making this product.

Cut meat into approximately $4 1/2$-X-$4 1/2$-in. oblong strips. Lay each strip on the shelf of an open truck in single layers. The cuts should not touch each other. Place trucks in the freezer and keep them there just long enough to solidify the meat but not completely freeze it; it can then be easily sliced into steaks approximately $7/8$–1 in. thick. Roll steaks in wheat flour and fry in deep fat for approximately 3–4 min at 350°F. The steaks will shrink approximately 15–20% from the raw weight. The best method to fry steaks is in an oblong tank through which a conveyor equipped with baskets carries the meat a predetermined time through the heated fat in the tank.

Prepare Gravy

Put 80 lb of water in a steam-jacketed kettle, add tomato purée, and the remainder of the ingredients except the flour. Make a slurry free of lumps with the flour and 20 lb of water in a bakery mixer. Add slurry to the batch and make a mark on a measuring stick at the gravy level. Bring temperature up to 200°F and cook gravy for 20 min with steady stirring. Bring volume back up to its original mark with added water.

Fill and Close

Pack 75% steaks and 25% hot gravy.

Place sauce on the bottom of the can, then add steaks placing a circular cut parchment in between. Close cans under 15 in. vacuum.

Suggested Process

401 X 411 cans (30 oz net) 2 hr at 240°F

Check process time and temperature with can supplier or the National Canners Association.

SOURCE: Stephan L. Komarik, 4810 Ronda, Coral Gables, Florida.

BEEF STEW
CANNED WITH PRECOOKED GRAVY
OR COLD GRAVY

This product is made up of 25% diced, lean beef, 35% mixed vegetables, and 40% precooked or cold gravy.

Dice fresh lean beef into 1-in. cubes.

Mix together the following vegetables:

	%
Rehydrated diced potatoes	53
Sliced frozen carrots (defrosted)	28
Frozen peas (defrosted)	15
Dehydrated minced onion	4

Reconstitute 50 lb dehydrated potatoes in hot water (200°F) until they pick up 120–130 lb of water (rehydrated weight of potatoes should be 220–230 lb).

Dehydrated minced onions need not be reconstituted prior to use. If fresh onions are used, increase the weight of the fresh eight times that of the dehydrated product.

Precooked Gravy Procedure

Ingredients	Lb	Oz
Salt	20	
Cane sugar	5	8
Oleoresin celery		1.6
Black pepper (38-mesh)		12
Monosodium glutamate	1	8
Garlic powder		3
Corn sugar	1	8
Wheat flour 4X	27	8
Potato starch	4	8
Tomato paste (28% solids)	21	
Hydrolyzed plant protein (liquid)		3
Caramel color (liquid)		8
Oleoresin paprika (HCV; water-soluble)		2
Water to make 90 gal.		

Heat 75 gal. water in a steam-jacketed kettle to 200°F. Add all ingredients except flour and starch. Mix with a "Lightning" mixer. Put 15 gal. of water in a bakery mixer and, while mixer is running, slowly add the flour and starch and mix until the slurry is free of lumps. Add slurry to the contents of the steam kettle while the mixer is running. Bring volume up to 90 gal. if necessary. Temperature will drop with the addition of ingredients and slurry, therefore bring temperature of the gravy up to 200°F and maintain this temperature for 10–15 min more.

Pack and Process.—Fill cans first with 25% diced, cooked beef; then add 35% mixed vegetables, followed by 40% hot gravy. Close cans under vacuum.

Cold Gravy Procedure

Preparation of the cubed beef and the mixed vegetables is the same as that given above.

Ingredients for the cold gravy are identical to those given above for the precooked gravy *except* pregelatinized wheat flour and pregelatinized potato starch are used in place of the regular wheat flour 4X and potato starch.

By using pregelatinized flours and starches, the precooking of gravy is eliminated. The addition of the proper amount of cold water to the treated flours and starches to make the cold gravy produces a consistency in which the added solid ingredients, such as diced meat and vegetables, are kept in perfect suspension and ready to fill into cans through proper adjustment of the filling machines.

To Make Cold Gravy.—Put water in a mechanical mixer. Start mixer and add tomato paste, the oleoresins (celery and paprika), plant protein, and caramel color. Mix together thoroughly the remaining dry ingredients and slowly add them to the contents of the mixer. Continue mixing until the gravy is uniformly mixed and free from any lumps. Bring up volume with added water to make 90 gal. and let mixer run until the added water is uniformly dispersed through the contents.

Mix and Process.—In a mechanical meat mixer, put 40% cold gravy and start machine. Then add 25% diced beef and 35% mixed vegetables. Let machine run until all ingredients are uniformly distributed. Fill cans. Close under 27 in. vacuum.

Suggested Process for Either Type of Gravy

603 X 700 cans (6 lb 12 oz) 250 min at 240°F
404 X 309 cans (1 lb 8 oz) 150 min at 240°F
300 X 409 cans (16 oz) 95 min at 240°F

Check processing times and temperature with the can supplier or the National Canners Association.

After sterilization, shut off steam and introduce cold water in the retort under 15 lb pressure and chill cans to an internal temperature of 120°–130°F.

SOURCE: Stephan L. Komarik, 4810 Ronda, Coral Gables, Florida.

BEEF STEW WITH DEHYDRATED POTATOES

Ingredients	%
Trimmed carcass beef	27.4
Beef suet	1.0
Dehydrated potato dice	18.8
Onion flakes	1.0
Carrots, diced	8.4
Peas	6.9
Tomato paste (25% solids)	1.5
Water	23.0
Amioca starch (Clearjel)	1.7
Flour	1.7
Salt	0.8
Black pepper	0.1
Additional water	7.6
Caramel coloring	0.1

Procedure

1. Fill trimmed beef and suet into cans manually.

2. Bring to a boil the following ingredients: the large quantity of water designated in the ingredients (23%), dehydrated potatoes, onion flakes, carrots, peas, and tomato paste.

3. Mix the following ingredients thoroughly in a Hobart Mixer: amioca starch (Clearjel), flour, salt, pepper, water (7.6%), and caramel coloring. Add to vegetable mixture and bring back to a boil.

4. Fill over meat in cans, seal, and retort: No. 303's for 90 min at 240°F; No. 404's for 110 min at 240°F. Check processing times and temperature with can supplier or with National Canners Association.

SOURCE: National Starch and Chemical Corp., 1700 W. Front St., Plainfield, N.J.

SOUTHERN-STYLE BRUNSWICK STEW (HOT PACK)

Ingredients	Lb	Oz	Pt	Gal.
Carcass beef (canner-cutter grade)	125			
Canned sweet corn	100			
Crushed dehydrated potatoes	30			
Tomato paste (28% solids)	22			
Smoked bacon ends	30			
Water				10
Stale bread	30			
Salt	5			
Dehydrated onion powder	1			
Paprika (microfine)	1			
Black pepper (80-mesh)		6		
Monosodium glutamate		8		
Plant protein hydrolyzate (liquid)		8		
Caramel color (liquid)		4		
Worcestershire sauce			4	

Procedure

Grind beef through the 1-in. plate of the grinder; grind the bacon ends through the $1/4$-in. plate. Transfer to a steam-jacketed kettle and braise meats until done. Regrind meats through the $1/2$-in. plate of the grinder.

Make a paste out of the stale bread with 10 gal. of water in a bakery dough mixer. Transfer meat, bread paste, tomato paste, sweet corn, and the rest of the ingredients to a steam-jacketed kettle and bring volume up to 70 gal. Raise temperature to 180°F, and, with steady stirring, cook product until sauce thickens. Then pack hot into cans. Temperature should not drop under 160°F while filling and closing cans. Close without any vacuum.

Suggested Process

404 X 309 cans (16 oz net) 90 min at 240°F

Check process time and temperature with can supplier or the National Canners Association.

SOURCE: Stephan L. Komarik, 4810 Ronda, Coral Gables, Florida.

BEEF STROGANOFF (HOT PACK)

Ingredients	Lb	Oz	Pt
Braised diced beef, canner-cutter grade (400 lb raw weight minus 35% shrink)	260		
Tomato purée (sp. gr. 1.035)	6		
Sour cream	30		
Wheat flour	15		
Salt	6		
Sliced canned mushrooms	12		
Spanish paprika (microfine)	2		
Onion powder	1		
Monosodium glutamate		12	
Plant protein hydrolyzate		12	
Garlic powder			2

Dry soluble pepper (salt base)	1	
Worcestershire sauce		8
Sherry cooking wine		4
Beef broth and water	190	

Prepare Meat

Dice meat into 1-in. cubes. Transfer to jacketed kettle. Add 1 gal. of water and braise meat approximately 10 min or until 35% shrink is obtained. If shrink is over 35% adjust it with added beef stock which meat will absorb. Remove meat but hold beef stock in the kettle.

Prepare Gravy

Add 20 gal. of water to beef stock in jacketed kettle. Add purée, sour cream, mushrooms, sherry wine, and all dry ingredients except flour. Raise temperature to 180°–185°F.

Make a slurry of 5 gal. of water and flour in a bakery mixer. Run machine until the slurry is free from lumps. Add slurry to sauce mixture and bring volume up to 33 gal. Cook gravy for an additional 10–15 min at 180°F.

Pack

Pack equal weights of braised beef and gravy in 16-oz cans. Close cans under 15–20 in. vacuum.

Suggested Process

300 × 409 cans (16 oz net) 90 min at 240°F

Check process time and temperature with can supplier or the National Canners Association.

SOURCE: Stephan L. Komarik, 4810 Ronda, Coral Gables, Florida.

GEORGIA HASH (HOT PACK)

Ingredients	Lb	Oz
Carcass beef (canner-cutter grade)	100	
Boneless, skinless hog picnics	100	
Tomato paste (28% solids)	12	
Crushed dehydrated potatoes	20	
White vinegar (100-grain)	5	
Worcestershire sauce	4	
Salt	5	
Cracker meal	5	
Black pepper (80-mesh)		12
Paprika		12
Hydrolyzed plant protein		8
Monosodium glutamate		4
Sodium nitrite		1/2
Water to make 50 gal.		

Procedure

Grind both beef and picnics through the 3/8-in. plate of the grinder and transfer to a steam-jacketed kettle. Turn on steam, and add 4 qt of water in which the sodium nitrite is dissolved. Braise the meat with steady stirring until it is free flowing. Add 10 gal. of water to the batch, then, with steady stirring, add the rest of the ingredients. Bring volume up to 50 gal. and raise temperature to 180°F. Maintain 180°F for an additional 15 min and fill cans at this temperature.

Suggested Process

603 × 700 cans (108 oz net) 250 min at 240°F
303 × 400 cans (16 oz net) 90 min at 240°F

Check process times and temperature with can supplier or the National Canners Association.

SOURCE: Stephan L. Komarik, 4810 Ronda, Coral Gables, Florida.

GEORGIA HASH (COLD PACK)

Use the same ingredients given above for Georgia Hash (Hot Pack).

Procedure

Add the ground meats and sodium nitrite to 25 gal. of water and mix thoroughly. Slowly add the rest of the ingredients except dehydrated potatoes and cracker meal. Bring volume up to 40 gal. Then add potatoes and cracker meal and mix for several minutes so these ingredients can absorb some of the moisture. Bring volume up to 50 gal. and mix an additional 3 min.

Fill cans and close cans under vacuum.

Process

Because the product is cold, the sterilization period should be longer than that given the hot-packed product.

Consult your can company or National Canners Association for proper sterilization time and temperature giving them the can size and the internal temperature of the product prior to closing the cans.

SOURCE: Stephan L. Komarik, 4810 Ronda, Coral Gables, Florida.

HUNGARIAN-STYLE BEEF AND VEGETABLE DINNER (COLD PACK)

Ingredients	Lb	Oz	Gal.
Carcass beef, canner-cutter grade	150		
Fresh onions	50		
Diced dehydrated potatoes	22		
Diced fresh carrots	20		
Diced fresh green peppers	16		
Green peas frozen	16		

Tomato purée (sp. gr. 1.045)	16		
Pregelatinized wheat flour	15		
Salt	4	8	
Hungarian paprika (or Spanish)	2		
Ground white pepper		3	
Garlic powder		1/4	
Ground caraway seeds		1/2	
Water			18

Procedure

Grind beef through the 1/2-in. plate of the grinder, and the fresh onions through the 1/4-in. plate. Dice carrots and green pepper into 1/4-in. pieces. Defrost green peas.

Put the tomato purée and 18 gal. of water into a mechanical mixer; add salt, seasonings, and precooked wheat flour; run mixer until a slurry free of lumps is obtained. Add meat and vegetables and mix until all the ingredients are uniformly distributed. Fill cans and close under 27 in. vacuum.

Suggested process

300 × 409 cans (16 oz net) 90 min at 240°F

Check process time and temperature with can supplier or the National Canners Association.

For Pork and Vegetable Dinner

Use same method and ingredients described above and replace beef with lean pork.

SOURCE: Stephan L. Komarik, 4810 Ronda, Coral Gables, Florida.

HUNGARIAN-STYLE GOULASH (HOT PACK)

Ingredients	Lb	Oz	Gal.
Beef chucks (canner-cutter grade)	500		
Lard	20		
Tomato purée (sp. gr. 1.035)			4
Salt	12		
Diced fresh green peppers	10		
Hungarian paprika	10		
Wheat flour	10		
Ground white pepper		10	
Garlic powder		4	
Ground caraway seed		2	
Ground red pepper		2	
Onion powder	20		
Water to make 60 gal. of gravy			

Prepare Meat

Trim beef chucks closely. Remove back cords, sinews, and connective tissues. Dice meat into 1-in. cubes. Dice green peppers into 1-in. squares.

Place diced meat in a steam-jacketed kettle; add lard and green pepper and braise meat until it is free flowing (approximate shrinkage, 40%). Remove meat and green peppers.

Prepare Gravy

To the rendered meat juices in the steam kettle, add tomato purée, 20 gal. of water, and the seasonings. Make a slurry of the flour and 2 gal. of water in a bakery mixer. With steady agitation of the gravy (using a "Lightning" mixer), add slurry to the batch. Bring volume up to 60 gal. with water. Raise temperature to 200°–205°F and simmer for 20 min.

Fill and Close

Pack 40% meat and 60% hot gravy. Temperature of the product should not be below 160°F when cans are closed. Close cans under 10–15 in. vacuum.

Suggested Process

300 × 409 cans (16 oz net) 90 min at 240°F

Check processing time and temperature with the can supplier or the National Canners Association.

SOURCE: Stephan L. Komarik, 4810 Ronda, Coral Gables, Florida.

HUNGARIAN BEEF GOULASH (COLD PACK)

Ingredients	Lb	Oz	Gal.
Carcass beef (canner-cutter grade)	500		
Tomato purée (sp. gr. 1.045)			4
Water			3
Wheat flour	16		
Salt	9		
Black pepper (80-mesh)		10	
Hungarian sweet paprika	6		
Onion powder	4		
Garlic powder		2	
Ground caraway seed		1	

Procedure

Make a uniform mixture of flour, salt, paprika and flavorings. Dice raw beef into 1 1/2-in. cubes. Put 3 gal. of water in a mixer and add the previously prepared mixture; run the machine until the gravy is smooth and free from lumps, then add the tomato purée.

Place 500 lb of cubed beef in a mechanical mixer, add 91 lb of gravy mix. Mix until the meat is evenly coated with gravy. Hand pack into cans. After cans have been filled and before they go to the vacuum closing machine, put spatula or similar instrument down the side of the can so that any air trapped on the bottom of the can may be eliminated. Close cans under 27 in. vacuum.

Suggested Process

404 × 404 cans (30 oz net) 2 hr 30 min at 240°F
401 × 411 cans (30 oz net) 2 hr 30 min at 240°F
300 × 409 cans (16 oz net) 95 min at 240°F

Check times and temperature with can supplier or the National Canners Association.

After processing, wash cans in cold water in can washer.

SOURCE: Stephan L. Komarik, 4810 Ronda, Coral Gables, Florida.

PORK AND RICE CREOLE DINNER

Ingredients	Lb	Oz
Lean pork trimmings	125	
Cooked Patna rice	75	
Tomato purée (sp. gr. 1.045)	125	
Fresh onions	50	
Canned diced green peppers	10	
Canned diced pimiento	10	
Salt	7	
Cane sugar	7	
Spanish paprika	1	
Hydrolyzed plant protein		8
Dry soluble pepper		8
Water including brine from diced green peppers and pimiento	125	

Procedure

Use 1 gal. of cooking water for each 1 lb of rice. Bring water to boil, add rice and cook for 10 min. Drain water and wash rice. Grind meat through the ½-in. plate of the grinder. Drain brine from both diced red and green peppers and add enough water to make a weight of 125 lb. Transfer all products to a mechanical mixer and mix for 3 min.

Use a mechanical filling machine and fill 16 oz to the can. Close cans under 27 in. vacuum.

Suggested Process

300 × 409 cans (16 oz net) 90 min at 240°F

Check process time and temperature with can supplier or the National Canners Association.

SOURCE: Stephan L. Komarik, 4810 Ronda, Coral Gables, Florida.

LIMA BEANS WITH HAM (HOT PACK)

Ingredients	Lb	Oz
Smoked hams	63	
Wheat flour	15	
Cornstarch	3	
Ham fat from smoked hams	18	
Salt	6	
Dry soluble pepper		3
Celery salt (or 12% ground celery)		2
Monosodium glutamate		6
Plant protein hydrolyzate		2
Cooked lima beans	300	
Water to make 40 gal. of sauce		

Prepare Hams

Skin and bone smoked hams, and separate fat from lean. Grind fat through the ⅛-in. plate of the grinder. Cube lean into ½-in. dice.

Prepare Lima Beans

Soak lima beans in slowly overflowing fresh water overnight. Drain, then cook in boiling water for 30 min.

Make Gravy

Put ground ham fat in the steam-jacketed kettle, apply steam and braise fat until it is rendered. Add 30 gal. of water and raise temperature to approximately 160°F; add all ingredients except ham, beans, flour, and starch. Make a lump-free slurry of flour and starch with 5 gal. of water in a bakery mixer. Add slurry to the hot batch while the gravy is agitated with a "Lightning" mixer. Bring volume up to 40 gal. Raise temperature to 200°–205°F and cook gravy for 20 min.

Fill and Close

In each 11 oz net can put 5½ oz lima beans, 1 oz cubed ham, and 4½ oz hot gravy.

Suggested Process

208 × 410 cans (11 oz net) 1 hr at 240°F

Check process time and temperature with can supplier or the National Canners Association.

SOURCE: Stephan L. Komarik, 4810 Ronda, Coral Gables, Florida.

CREAMED CHIPPED BEEF

Step 1

Ingredients	%
Microcrystalline cellulose (Avicel RC-591)	1.00

Water	36.95
Xanthan gum (such as Keltrol available from Kelco Co., San Diego)	0.10
Vegetable oil	1.14
Butter	0.70
Whole milk powder	0.50

Disperse Avicel RC-591 in the water with maximum agitation. Mix for 5 min until smooth and a visible thickening occurs. Add xanthan gum to the vortex. Slowly add vegetable oil, butter, and milk powder to the vortex. Continue mixing for an additional 5 min. Homogenize at 2000 psi first stage; 500 psi second stage. (Homogenization is not necessary but it will produce a thicker, whiter emulsion.)

Step 2

Ingredients	%
Modified waxy maize starch (available from National Starch & Chemical Corp., New York)	2.50
Wheat flour	0.90
Sucrose	0.46
Monosodium glutamate (MSG)	0.25

Under maximum agitation add the above ingredients to the above emulsion and mix until smooth—about 5 min mixing time.

Step 3

Ingredients	%
Water	30.00
Chipped beef	25.50

Preheat beef in water. Blend white sauce prepared from Steps 1 and 2 into preheated beef. Heat under agitation to cook starch.

Process

Hot fill and retort. Check process time and temperature with can supplier or the National Canners Association.

SOURCE: FMC Corp., Avicel Division of American Viscose Co., Marcus Hook, Pa.

CREAMED CHIPPED BEEF (HOT PACK)

Ingredients	Lb	Oz
Chipped beef[1]	50	
Nonfat dry milk	8	
Shortening or vegetable oil	12	
Wheat flour	19	
Salt	2	8
Dry soluble pepper		6

Monosodium glutamate	5	
Ground celery seeds		1/4
Water to make 40 gal.		

[1] To cure dried beef for chipping, see Section 1, Dried Beef for Slicing (Fast Method).

Procedure

Grind beef through the 1/2-in. plate of the grinder. Heat shortening or oil in a steam kettle and add chipped beef. With a wooden paddle, stir meat until the chips are covered with the heated oil. Add half of the water to the kettle; then add salt and seasonings and bring up temperature to 180°F.

In a bakery mixer make a smooth slurry with the remaining water slowly adding the flour and nonfat dry milk. Run machine until slurry is free of lumps. Add slurry to the heated stock with continuous stirring.

Bring volume up to 40 gal. Keep temperature at 180°-200°F for 15 min, or until the product is thick enough to carry the chipped beef in suspension. Can while product is hot. Internal temperature should not drop below 160°F in the cans before they are closed.

Suggested Process

300 × 409 cans (16 oz net) 90 min at 240°F

Check process time and temperature with can supplier or the National Canners Association.

SOURCE: Stephan L. Komarik, 4810 Ronda, Coral Gables, Florida.

STUFFED GREEN PEPPERS IN TOMATO SAUCE

Select fresh green peppers of uniform size. Wash peppers and cut out stem ends; remove pulpy sections and seeds from inside of each pepper.

Prepare Filling

Ingredients	Lb	Oz
Carcass beef (canner-cutter grade)	100	
Regular pork trimmings 50/50	100	
Patna rice	80	
Frozen whole eggs	40	
Onion powder	1	4
Salt	6	
Dry soluble pepper	8	
Mustard flour	4	
Spanish paprika	8	
Garlic powder		1/2

For each 1 lb of rice, use 1 gal. of cooking water. Bring water to boil, add rice, and cook for 10 min. Then drain, and wash. (Cooked rice will weigh approximately 200 lb.)

Grind meats through the $3/8$-in. plate of the grinder along with the frozen eggs. Transfer rice to a mechanical mixer. Premix salt with seasonings and add to rice in mixer; then add ground meat-egg mixture and mix for 3 min.

Prepare Sauce

Ingredients	Lb	Oz	Gal.
Wheat flour	30		
Onion powder	1	8	
Garlic powder		2	
Cane sugar	25		
Salt	10		
Dry soluble pepper	1		
Ground sweet basil		1	
Tomato purée (sp. gr. 1.045)			50
Water to make			100

Put tomato purée in steam-jacketed kettle and bring temperature up to 180°F. Make a slurry of flour and the rest of the dry ingredients in 10 gal. of water; then add slurry to the heated tomato purée. Bring volume of sauce up to 100 gal. and raise temperature to 200°F. Cook 10 min.

Assemble, Fill Cans, and Close

Fill peppers with meat-rice mixture and stuff 2 peppers in each 24-oz can. Place them in the can adjoining each other at the stem-end, stuffed side. Fill void in the can with hot sauce. Close under vacuum.

Suggested Process

307 × 508 cans (24 oz net) 90 min at 240°F

Check process time and temperature with can supplier or the National Canners Association.

SOURCE: Stephan L. Komarik, 4810 Ronda, Coral Gables, Florida.

CHOP SUEY WITH VEGETABLES AND BEEF OR PORK

Ingredients	Lb	Oz
Bean sprouts	50	
Celery (chopped in 1-in. lengths)	50	
Bamboo shoots	5	
Water chestnuts (sliced)	5	
Cooked lean beef or pork	30	
Onions (fresh, sliced $1/8$-in. thick)	7	
Diced red pepper (canned)	3	
Vegetable oil	2	
Meat stock (from cooked beef or pork)	30	
Cornstarch	3	8
Salt	1	8
Cane sugar		8
Monosodium glutamate		4
Protein hydrolyzate	1	
Ground celery seed		1
Dry soluble pepper		3
Caramel color to obtain desired shade		

Procedure

If fresh bean sprouts are used, blanch 15 min in boiling water. Wash in cold water; then drain. Mix blanched bean sprouts with celery, bamboo shoots, water chestnuts, onions, and red pepper with a meat fork to obtain a uniform mixture.

Cut meat into 1-in. thick slices and add 5 gal. of water to each 100 lb meat; cook at a temperature of 190°–200°F until meat loses 35% of the raw weight. Chill meat then dice.

Put meat stock and vegetable oil in a steam-jacketed kettle. Mix salt, cornstarch, and the remainder of the dry ingredients and add to meat stock which has been preheated to 180°F. Then add caramel color to obtain the shade desired. Shut off steam. Stir until stock thickens. Prolonged cooking makes it too thick to handle.

Pack 2 oz diced cooked beef or pork on the bottom of the can, add 11 oz mixed vegetables, and 3 oz sauce in each 16 oz can. Close cans under vacuum.

Suggested Process

300 × 409 cans (16 oz net) 90 min at 240°F

Check process time and temperature with can supplier or the National Canners Association.

SOURCE: Stephan L. Komarik, 4810 Ronda, Coral Gables, Florida.

SMOKED HAM WITH RAISIN SAUCE

Ingredients	Lb	Oz
Smoked ham meat (boneless, skinless, defatted)	82	
White raisins	7	
Cane sugar	7	
Pregelatinized starch	3	
Seasoning mixture (given below)		4
White vinegar (45-grain)		12

Seasoning Mixture	Cc	Lb
Oleoresin capsicum	10.00	
Oil of cloves	10.00	
Oil of pimiento	10.00	
Oil of bay	2.50	
Oil of cassia	0.50	
Cane sugar		10

Procedure

Premix sugar, starch and seasoning mixture. Remove skins, bones, and fat from hams and dice meat into 2–2½-in. pieces. Transfer dice to a mechanical mixer. Start mixer and add sugar-seasoning mixture, raisins, and vinegar evenly over the meat. Run mixer until meat is evenly coated with the added materials. Total mixing time should not be over 2 min and the temperature of the product when filled into cans should not be warmer than 50°F. Close cans under 27-in. vacuum.

Suggested Process

404 × 414 cans (36 oz net) 3 hr 30 min at 235°F

Check process time and temperature with can supplier or the National Canners Association.

SOURCE: Stephan L. Komarik, 4810 Ronda, Coral Gables, Florida.

CANNED HAM SALAD SPREAD

This retortable salad dressing system, stabilized with Keltrol®, has been successfully adapted to a canned ham salad spread, using equal portions of ground smoked ham and salad dressing.

To Prepare Meat

The appearance of the final product depends mainly on the quality of the ham used. Economical ham cuts containing large portions of fat will produce a sandwich spread where the reddish meat color will be less evident then in a product prepared with high quality lean ham. Tenox 6 is used in the formulation to aid in the prevention of oxidative discoloration and rancidity.

Grind the smoked ham through the ¼-in. plate of the grinder. Then place the ground ham with an equal weight of water in a kettle and simmer for 30 min. Reserve the resulting ham broth for use in making the salad dressing.

To Prepare Dressing

Ingredients	%
Xanthan gum (Keltrol®)	0.40
Black pepper	0.01
Garlic powder	0.02
Citric acid	0.05
Tenox 6 (available from Eastman Chemical Products)	0.10
Sodium nitrate	0.10
Ascorbic acid	0.10
Onion powder	0.15
Celery salt	0.20
Monosodium glutamate	0.20
Dispersible titanium dioxide (available from Kohnstamn & Co.)	0.30
Mustard powder	0.30
Lemon juice	0.50
Salt	1.00
Dehydrated egg yolk	1.00
Starch (Purity NCS available from National Starch & Chemical Co.)	1.00
Avicel RC-501 (available from American Viscose Div., FMC Corp.)	2.50
Vinegar (100-grain)	7.00
70% sorbitol solution	10.00
Vegetable oil	25.00
Ham broth	50.07
	100.00%

Vigorously agitate the ham broth and add Avicel RC-501. Mix for 10 min. Blend together the balance of the dry ingredients and add to the broth mixture. Mix for 15 min. Then add the vegetable oil in a slow and continuous stream. Mix for 5 min.

Combine Tenox 6, lemon juice, and the sorbitol solution with the vinegar and add to the emulsion. Mix for 10 min.

Homogenize the emulsion at 2500 psi single stage and record salad dressing viscosity. It should be between 4500 and 5500 cps measured with a Brookfield Viscometer LVT, spindle No. 4.

Combine, Fill, and Process

Mix ground ham with the salad dressing in equal portions. Fill cans, seal and retort at 240°F to sterility.

Check with can supplier or the National Canners Association for correct times and temperature for can sizes used.

SOURCE: Kelco Company, 20 N. Wacker Drive, Chicago, Ill.

MEAT BALLS IN TOMATO SAUCE (INSTITUTIONAL PACK IN NO. 10 TINS)

Prepare Meat Balls

Ingredients	Lb	Oz
Beef (canner-cutter grade)	150	
Beef flanks, trimmed	150	
Frozen whole eggs (or fresh)	15	
Reconstituted minced onion (approx 4 lb dehydrated)	30	
Cracker meal	40	
Salt	10	
Black pepper (62-mesh)		10

At least 1 hr before preparation of the meat mixture, reconstitute the dehydrated minced onions in the ratio of 1 part to 7 parts of hot water. If frozen, the whole eggs should be defrosted in tap water until they can be removed from container and then chopped up with a cleaver and ground through the 1-in. plate of the grinder. Grind well-chilled meat (at 34°F) through the 1-in. plate of the grinder.

Place ground meat and eggs in a mechanical mixer and while the machine is running, add reconstituted minced onions, cracker meal, and salt previously mixed with the black pepper. Mix 3 min. Regrind meat mixture immediately through the $^3/_{16}$-in. plate of the grinder. Dump meat mixture into a meat truck, chill at least 2 hr in the cooler before forming balls. Form balls through the forming machine. Recommended size is $1^1/_4$ oz per ball. As balls come down the conveyor dust with flour so they will not stick together while being placed in the cans.

Prepare Sauce

Ingredients	Lb	Oz
Tomato paste (26–28% solids)	189	
Fresh celery	5	
Fresh carrots (cooked)	5	
Aged cheddar cheese	5	
Vegetable oil	8	
Bread crumbs (finest mesh)	20	
Salt	10	
Cane sugar	3	
Toasted onion powder	6	
Monosodium glutamate	3	
Spanish paprika (microfine)	2	
Ground rosemary		7
Garlic powder		5
Ground pickling spice		4
Dry soluble pepper		3
Water to make 100 gal.		

Grind fresh celery, cooked carrots and cheddar cheese through the $^1/_8$-in. plate of the grinder. Blend bread crumbs, salt, sugar, and seasonings together. Measure out 75 gal. of water in a steam-jacketed kettle. Add tomato paste and ground celery, carrots, and cheese. Apply steam and with steady stirring, using a "Lightning" mixer, add the bread crumbs-seasoning mixture. Bring volume up to 100 gal. by adding water. Raise temperature to 205°–210°F and cook sauce 10–15 min with steady stirring.

Fill, Close, and Process

Measure 29 oz of very hot sauce into No. 10 cans and immediately add 60 meat balls to each can. It is important to have the sauce very hot if the balls are not prefried. The hot sauce immedi-ately cooks the surface of the balls and will keep them apart without matting together.

Close cans under 10 in. vacuum.

Suggested Process

Process time depends upon the internal temperature of the contents of the cans immediately prior to closing cans:

Can Closing Temp (°F)	Process Time (Min)	Process Temp (°F)
160	250	240
140	265	240
120	280	240

Check process time and temperature with can supplier or the National Canners Association.

Chill

After sterilizing, cans should be chilled in water at least 30 min under 15 lb air pressure before releasing pressure.

SOURCE: Stephan L. Komarik, 4810 Ronda, Coral Gables, Florida.

MEAT BALLS IN BROWN GRAVY (INSTITUTIONAL PACK IN NO. 10 TINS)

Prepare Meat Balls

The ingredients for meat balls and their preparation are identical with the formula given above for Meat Balls in Tomato Sauce.

Prepare Gravy

Ingredients	Lb	Oz
Tomato paste (26–28% solids)	42	
Wheat flour	17	
Bread crumbs (finesh mesh)	13	
Salt	7	
Toasted onion powder	3	
Monosodium glutamate	3	
Garlic powder		8
Ground Jamaica ginger		$^1/_4$
Dry soluble pepper		4
Dry soluble thyme		$^1/_8$
Dry soluble celery		1
Dry soluble mace		$^1/_4$
Beef extract	3	
Plant protein hydrolyzate (liquid)	3	
Worcestershire sauce	2	
Cane sugar	2	
Dehydrated caramel color	3	
Water to make 100 gal.		

Blend flour, bread crumbs, salt, sugar, and seasonings together. Measure 75 gal. of water in a steam-jacketed kettle, add tomato paste, plant protein hydrolyzate, beef extract, Worcestershire sauce, and caramel color. Apply steam and, with steady stirring using a "Lightning" mixer, add the bread crumbs-seasoning mixture. Bring volume up to 100 gal. with added water. Raise temperature to 205°–210°F and cook gravy 10–15 minutes with steady stirring.

Fill, Close, Process, and Chill

Procedure for these steps is the same as that given above for **Meat Balls in Tomato Sauce.**

SOURCE: Stephan L. Komarik, 4810 Ronda, Coral Gables, Florida.

MEAT BALLS IN SPAGHETTI SAUCE

Prepare Meat Balls

Ingredients	Lb	Oz
Beef chucks, canner-cutter grade	150	
Beef flanks, trimmed	150	
Fresh onions	30	
Frozen whole eggs	15	
Cracker meal	40	
Salt	7	
Black pepper (62-mesh)		4

Grind chucks, flanks, onions, and frozen eggs through the 1/8-in. plate of the grinder. Transfer mixture to a mixer. Start machine and add cracker meal evenly over mixture. Mix salt with pepper and add to mixture. Mix for 3 min.

Put mixture through forming machine and make into balls 1/2 oz in size. Dust balls with flour as they come down the conveyor to prevent their sticking together.

Prepare Sauce

Ingredients	Lb	Oz
Tomato paste	340	
Cane sugar	45	
Wheat flour	20	
Cornstarch	10	
Bread crumbs	30	
Salt	23	
Cheddar cheese, aged	15	
Garlic powder		6
Onion powder	1	
Plant protein hydrolyzate	9	
Black pepper		10
Ground red pepper		4
Ground sweet basil		2
Bicarbonate of soda		8

	Lb	Oz
Imitation cheese flavor		1 1/2
Dry soluble seasoning mixture (see below)	1	11
Cottonseed or corn oil	12	
Water to make 200 gal.		

Dry Soluble Seasoning Mix	Lb	Cc
Oleoresin capsicum		4.00
Oleoresin ginger		1.40
Oleoresin mace		0.16
Oil of dill seed		0.20
Oil of cloves		3.60
Oil of cardamom		0.80
Oil of cassia		2.40
Oil of pimiento		26.40
Oil of bay		0.80
Salt to mix	2	

Use 4 gm mixture per 1 gal. sauce

Grind cheese through the 1/4-in. plate of the grinder. Blend together sugar, salt, flour, cornstarch, bread crumbs, and seasonings. In a bakery mixer, put 2 gal. of warm water (140°F) and add ground cheese; make a slurry free of lumps. Put 150 gal. of water in a steam-jacketed kettle, add tomato paste and bicarbonate of soda. Use a "Lightning" mixer and agitate sauce as sugar-seasoning mixture is slowly added; then add cheese slurry and oil with continued agitation. Raise temperature to 180°F, continuing agitation, and add water to bring sauce volume up to 200 gal. When temperature reaches 180°F, cook an additional 15 min.

Fill Cans and Process

For 16-oz cans, pack 8 oz meat balls and 8 oz sauce. Close under vacuum and process.

Suggested Process

300 X 409 cans (16 oz net) 90 min at 240°F

Check process time and temperature with can supplier or the National Canners Association.

SOURCE: Stephan L. Komarik, 4810 Ronda, Coral Gables, Florida.

SPAGHETTI AND MEAT BALLS IN TOMATO SAUCE WITH CHEESE

Prepare Meat Balls

Ingredients	Lb	Oz
Beef chucks, canner-cutter grade	150	
Beef flanks, trimmed	150	
Fresh onions	30	
Frozen whole eggs	15	
Cracker meal	40	
Salt	7	
Black pepper (62-mesh)		10

Grind chucks, flanks, onions, and frozen eggs through the $\frac{1}{8}$-in. plate of the grinder. Transfer mixture to a mixer. Start machine and add cracker meal evenly over mixture. Mix salt with pepper and add to mixture. Mix for 3 min.

Put mixture through forming machine and make into balls $\frac{1}{2}$ oz in size. Dust balls with flour as they come down the conveyor to prevent their sticking together.

Prepare Sauce

Ingredients

Tomato paste, 26–28% solids	38 No. 10 cans	
	Lb	**Oz**
Wheat flour	36	
Salt	36	
Cane sugar	26	
Cheddar cheese, aged	35	
Bicarbonate of soda		8
Corn or cottonseed oil	12	
Spanish paprika (microfine)	4	8
Dry soluble pepper (sugar base)		8
Ground basil		4
Onion powder	3	
Garlic powder	1	
Dry soluble seasoning mixture (see below)		8
Water to make 200 gal.		

Dry Soluble Seasoning Mix	**Lb**	**Cc**
Oleoresin capsicum		4.00
Oleoresin ginger		1.40
Oleoresin mace		0.16
Oil of dill seed		0.20
Oil of cloves		3.60
Oil of cardamom		0.80
Oil of cassia		2.40
Oil of pimiento		26.40
Oil of bay		0.80
Salt to mix	2	

Use 4 gm mixture per 1 gal. sauce

Grind cheese through the $\frac{1}{4}$-in. plate of the grinder. Put cheese together with 5 gal. of warm water (140°F) in a bakery mixer and make a slurry, free of lumps. Blend sugar, salt, flour and seasonings together. In a steam-jacketed kettle, put 150 gal. of water and add tomato paste and bicarbonate of soda. Agitate tomato paste mixture with "Lightning" mixer and slowly add the blend of salt-sugar-seasonings. Then add the cheese slurry and the oil. With steady agitation, bring temperature up to 180°F. Add water to bring volume up to 200 gal. After sauce temperature reaches 180°F, cook an additional 15 min.

Prepare Spaghetti

For each pound spaghetti, use approximately 1 gal. of water with 2% salt added. Bring water to boil and add spaghetti broken into thirds. Boil for 12 min; drain; wash and rinse in cold water; then drain before packing into cans.

Assemble and Pack

For 16-oz cans, allow 4 meat balls (2 oz), 4.25 oz cooked spaghetti, and 9.75 oz hot sauce.

Close cans under vacuum.

Suggested Process

300 × 409 cans (net 16 oz) 60 min at 240°F

Check process time and temperature with can supplier or the National Canners Association.

SOURCE: Stephan L. Komarik, 4810 Ronda, Coral Gables, Florida.

SPAGHETTI MEAT SAUCE (HOT PACK)

Ingredients	**Lb**	**Oz**
Tomato paste (26–28% solids)	340	
Lean beef chuck	50	
Trimmed steer flanks	50	
Cane sugar	45	
Wheat flour	20	
Cornstarch	10	
Bread crumbs (80-mesh)	30	
Salt	23	
Garlic powder		6
Onion powder	3	
Plant protein hydrolyzate	2	
Dry soluble seasoning mix (see below)		8
Black pepper (62-mesh)		10
Ground red pepper		4
Ground sweet basil		2
Bicarbonate of soda	1	8
Imitation cheese flavor		1$\frac{1}{2}$
Aged American cheddar cheese	15	
Water to make 200 gal.		

Dry Soluble Seasoning Mix	**Lb**	**Cc**
Oleoresin capsicum		4
Oleoresin ginger		1.4
Oleoresin mace		0.16
Oil of dill seed		0.2
Oil of cloves		3.6
Oil of cardamom		0.8
Oil of cassia		2.4
Oil of pimiento		26.4
Oil of bay		0.8
Salt to mix	2	

Use 4 gm per 1 gal. sauce.

Procedure

Grind beef chucks, steer flanks and cheese separately through the $1/4$-in. plate of the grinder. Blend together sugar, salt, wheat flour, cornstarch, bread crumbs, and seasonings.

Place the ground steer flanks in a small steam-jacketed kettle and braise until the fat is rendered; add ground beef chuck and braise with steady stirring until meat is free flowing. In a large jacketed kettle, put 150 gal. of water. Add tomato paste, braised meat, and ground cheese. Then agitate sauce with a "Lightning" mixer and add slowly the previously blended sugar-seasoning mixture. Raise temperature to 180°F and bring volume up to 200 gal. Cook an additional 15 min.

Fill cans while hot. Internal temperature before closing cans should not drop under 160°F.

Suggested Process

300 × 409 cans (16 oz net) 1 hr 15 min at 240°F

Check process time and temperature with can supplier or the National Canners Association.

SOURCE: Stephan L. Komarik, 4810 Ronda, Coral Gables, Florida.

COCKTAIL MEAT BALLS (DRY PACK)

Ingredients	Lb	Oz
Boneless, skinless picnics	340	
Stale white bread	70	
Ice water	35	
Frozen whole eggs	35	
Wheat flour	10	
Salt	7	
Monosodium glutamate		10
Plant protein hydrolyzate		2
Onion powder		10
Black pepper (38-mesh)		10
Garlic powder		1

Prepare Mixture

Use fresh pork shoulders averaging 6–8 lb. Bone and skin but leave fat on. Grind meat through the $3/8$-in. plate of the grinder.

Break up frozen eggs and transfer them to a mixer. Add water, stale bread, and flour and mix thoroughly until bread absorbs moisture. Then grind through the $3/8$-in. plate of the grinder. Transfer egg-bread mixture to a mixer along with the ground meat. Start mixer and slowly add salt, previously mixed with the rest of the flavoring ingredients; mix just long enough to obtain a uniform mixture. Transfer meat to the ball-forming machine and form $3/4$-oz balls.

Fry or Broil

To Fry.—Heat hydrogenated vegetable oil to 320°F and maintain that temperature during the frying process. Allow frying time of 3 min from entering the frying medium to discharge. This should result in a shrink of 30%.

To Broil.—If the balls are broiled on a conveyor or under infrared rods, the timing has to be adjusted so that a 30% shrink of the balls will be obtained.

Drain, Pack, and Fill

Drain balls of excess fat and pack immediately in parchment-lined cans. Pack 7 oz of meat balls in 300 × 310 cans and close under 6–8 in. vacuum.

Suggested Process

300 × 310 cans 90 min at 240°F

Check process time and temperature with can supplier or the National Canners Association.

Chill

This product should not be chilled in the retort. Remove baskets after process then chill cans under shower of cold water.

SOURCE: Stephan L. Komarik, 4810 Ronda, Coral Gables, Florida.

BEEF AND MACARONI IN CHEESE SAUCE (HOT PACK)

Ingredients	Lb	Oz
Macaroni (raw)	100	
Beef chucks (canner-cutter)	180	
Cheddar cheese (2 yr old)	25	
Wheat flour	25	
Vegetable oil	6	
Carrots	6	
Whey powder	6	
Butter	5	
Salt	6	
Cane sugar	5	
Onion powder		8
Sodium citrate	1	
Monosodium glutamate		8
Dry soluble pepper (sugar base)		8
Water to make 50 gal.		

Prepare Meat

Grind meat through the $1/4$-in. plate of the grinder. Transfer ground meat to a steam-jacketed kettle; add 3 qt of water and by steady stirring braise meat to effect an approximate 25–30% shrink. Remove meat from kettle.

Prepare Cheese Sauce

In another vessel, precook carrots until tender, then grind through the smallest plate of the grinder. Grind cheese through the $1/8$-in. plate.

Put 10 gal. of water in the jacketed kettle; add sodium citrate, ground carrots and cheese, vegetable oil, butter, and salt which is previously mixed with the seasonings and flavorings. Cook at low temperature (not over 160°F) until cheese is melted and the sauce is smooth. Then add 10 gal. more of water and bring temperature up to 180°F. Add braised meat.

Put 10 gal. of water in a bakery mixer and slowly add whey powder and flour and let mixer run until slurry is free of lumps.

With steady agitation of the sauce, add slurry and bring volume of the sauce up to 50 gal. Then raise temperature to 200°F.

Prepare Macaroni

Use 1 gal. of water per 1 lb of macaroni or 100 gal. for this prescribed batch. Add 2% salt to the cooking water and bring to a boil. Break macaroni sticks into thirds and add to the boiling water. Cook for 12 min. Wash and rinse in cold water immediately after cooking; then drain. Never let the macaroni stand in cold water longer than 30 min. Yield 300%.

Pack

5 oz cooked macaroni and 11 oz hot sauce in each 16-oz can. Internal temperature should not drop under 160°F during closing. If this happens close cans under vacuum.

Suggested Process

300 × 409 cans (16 oz net) 90 min at 240°F

Check process time and temperature with can supplier or the National Canners Association.

SOURCE: Stephan L. Komarik, 4810 Ronda, Coral Gables, Florida.

BEEF AND NOODLE DINNER

Prepare Meat

Ingredients	Lb	Gal.
Beef canner-cutter grade	200	
Precooked egg noodles	175	
Gravy		50

Grind beef through the 1-in. plate of the grinder. Transfer to a steam-jacketed kettle and add 2 gal. of water; braise meat until it is free flowing. The shrink will be approximately 30%. Remove meat and save meat juices.

Prepare Egg Noodles

Use best quality egg noodles specially manufactured for canning purposes ($1/2$-in. width, 10% eggs). Cook in boiling water containing 2% salt for 10 min; then drain and wash. Use 1 gal. of cooking water to each pound of noodles.

Prepare Gravy

Ingredients	Lb	Oz
Wheat flour	19	
Cornstarch	8	
Rendered beef fat (oleo stock)	12	
Salt	7	
Plant protein hydrolyzate	3	
Monosodium glutamate	1	
Onion powder	5	
Garlic powder		$1/4$
Ground celery seed		1
Dry soluble pepper		4
Spanish paprika		2
Caramel color (powder)		12
Water to make 50 gal.		

Add 25 gal. of water to the beef stock in the same kettle in which the meat was braised. Add remainder of the ingredients except flour and cornstarch. Raise temperature to 160°F. Make a slurry with the flour and cornstarch in 10 gal. of water in a bakery mixer. Add slurry to the hot batch, stirring the gravy with a "Lightning" mixer. Bring volume up to 50 gal. with added water. Raise temperature to 200°–205°F and cook gravy for 20 min.

Pack

Fill each 16 oz net can with 3 oz braised beef, 4 oz cooked noodles, and 9 oz hot gravy. Close cans. If the internal temperature of the filled cans is 160°F or higher, close cans without drawing any vacuum. If the temperature is lower, close cans under 10–15 in. vacuum.

Suggested Process

300 × 409 cans (16 oz net) 90 min at 240°F

Check process time and temperature with the can supplier or the National Canners Association.

SOURCE: Stephan L. Komarik, 4810 Ronda, Coral Gables, Florida.

PORK AND BEANS IN TOMATO SAUCE (HOT PACK)

Prepare Pork and Beans

Soak beans no longer than 8 hr and no less than 7 hr. Tanks used for soaking may be wood, galvanized iron, or glass-lined. The best method for soaking is to have an overflow on the tank to circulate incoming water so the beans will not sour during the soaking period. After beans are properly soaked, place them in wire baskets and submerge in boiling water for 12–15 min. Drain.

Dice salt pork into cubes approximately $1/2$– $5/8$-in. weighing about $1/2$ oz.

Prepare Sauce

Ingredients	Gal.	Lb	Oz	Cc
Tomato purée (sp. gr. 1.040)	50			
Cane sugar		125		
Corn sugar		37		
Salt		31		
Onion powder			10	
Oil of pimiento				10.80
Oil of cloves				5.00
Oil of nutmeg				4.00
Oil of cassia				0.60
Oleoresin capsicum				5.00
Oleoresin mace				5.00
Water to make	200			

Mix together salt, onion powder, essential oils, and oleoresins for later use.

Put tomato purée in a steam-jacketed kettle, add corn and cane sugars and, with steady stirring, bring to a boil. To the boiling stock add the salt-seasoning mixture and continue stirring to uniformly mix ingredients. Bring volume of sauce up to 200 gal. and raise temperature to 200°F.

Fill Cans

Using 300 X 409 cans (16 oz net), fill each can with 8.5 oz blanched beans, 7.0 oz hot tomato sauce, and top with $1/2$-oz piece of salt pork. Hold product at 160°F or higher for filling. Close cans under vacuum.

Suggested Process

300 X 409 cans (16 oz net) 2 hr at 240°F

Check process time and temperature with can supplier or the National Canners Association.

SOURCE: Stephan L. Komarik, 4810 Ronda, Coral Gables, Florida.

RANCH-STYLE BEANS WITH MEAT BALLS

Prepare Beans

Soak pinto beans overnight in cooler temperature. Next morning cook beans for 12 min in boiling water.

Prepare Meat Balls

Ingredients	Lb	Oz
Beef chucks (canner-cutter grade)	100	
Beef flanks (canner-cutter grade)	300	
Fresh onions	30	
Frozen whole eggs	15	
Cracker meal	30	
Salt	10	
Pepper (62-mesh)		10

Grind beef chucks and trimmed flanks, onions, and frozen eggs through the $1/8$-in. plate of the grinder. Transfer to mixer. Mix together salt and pepper. Start mixer and add cracker meal and salt-pepper mixture evenly over meat mixture and mix for 3 min. Put meat mixture through a forming machine and form into $1/2$-oz balls. Dust meat balls with flour as they come down the conveyor so they will not stick together.

Prepare Sauce

Ingredients	Gal.	Lb	Oz
Tomato purée (sp. gr. 1.045)	35		
Cane sugar		12	8
Salt		32	
Cornstarch		45	
Rendered beef fat		35	
Chili pepper (34 mesh)		12	
Paprika (domestic)		13	
Onion powder		9	
Garlic powder		2	
Ground cumin		8	
Ground oregano		4	
Water to make 200 gal.			

Mix together all ingredients. Put tomato purée in a steam-jacketed kettle and stir in dry ingredients. Heat beef fat and, with steady stirring, add to tomato purée mixture. Bring volume of sauce up to 200 gal., heat to 212°F, and cook for 20 min.

Pack and Process

Hold beans and sauce at 160°F or above. Pack 2 oz (4) meat balls, 6 oz beans, and 8 oz sauce in 16-oz cans.

Suggested Process

300 X 409 cans (16 oz net) 2 hr at 240°F

Check process time and temperature with can supplier or the National Canners Association.

SOURCE: Stephan L. Komarik, 4810 Ronda, Coral Gables, Florida.

CHILI WITH BEANS WITH TEXTURED SOY FLOUR

This is a generalized formula and procedure for producing a canned chili with beans containing Texgran Brand textured soy flour.

Ingredients	%
Water	39.00
Red chili beans, cooked	28.00
Beef, raw	25.00
Seasonings and flavorings, salt and sugar	3.25
Starch	2.00
Textured soy flour (Texgran[1])	1.50
Flour, wheat or potato	1.25

[1] Texgran Code No. 52000 is most often used which is listed in the ingredient statement as "Textured Soy Flour—Caramel Color Added." Alternates, such as Code No. 10000 or No. 70000, are listed as "Textured Soy Flour."

Procedure

Blanch beans to yield of 200%. Blend textured soy flour and salt with meat and grind to desired size. Preblend starch and flour as a cold water slurry. Preheat water in mixer; add seasonings and blend before adding meat mixture and slurry to mixer ingredients. Heat to set starch and pump to filling equipment. Retort process canned product according to National Canners Association recommendations.

SOURCE: Swift Edible Oil Company, Division of Swift & Company, 115 W. Jackson Blvd., Chicago, Ill.

CHILI CON CARNE WITH OR WITHOUT BEANS

Ingredients	Lb	Oz	Gal.
Beef kidney suet (ground through $^3/_8$-in. plate)	20		
Fresh beef (ground through $^3/_8$-in. plate)	80		
Salt (to taste)	1	6 (approx)	
Powdered onion (optional)	4		
Water[1]			6 (approx)
Chili powder (Gentry)	5	5	
Garlic powder (Gentry "CO") (optional)		4½	
Mexican or red kidney beans (optional)	20		

[1] Tomato juice or the equivalent amount of tomato purée may be substituted in part for the water.

YIELD: Approximately 20 gal. without beans; approximately 27.5 gal. with beans.

Procedure

Render suet either in a steam-jacketed or gas-fired kettle. Remove cracklings. Add meat and salt and cook until the meat is tender and the water in the meat has evaporated. The mixture should be stirred at all times to keep it from adhering to the sides of the kettle. Add water gradually together with powdered onion and cook for at least 20 min. Add chili powder and garlic powder and finish cooking (approx 10 min).

Simmer beans separately until nearly soft. Beans may either be mixed with the other ingredients or weighed into cans which are then filled with the hot mixture. If the latter procedure is used, beans should be hot when added to the cans.

Processing and Cooling.—The following processes are suggested for chili con carne, chili con carne with beans, and meatless chili:

		Initial	Processing Time in Min at	
Can Size		Temp °F	240°F	250°F
No. 1	211 X 400	180	75	55
No. 300	300 X 407	180	90	65
No. 2	307 X 409	180	105	80
No. 2½	401 X 411	180	125	95
No. 10	603 X 700	180	240	200

Processes longer than those listed above are sometimes used in order to produce a softer bean. A process which is at all questionable in sterilizing value should never be used for a product of this kind, inasmuch as the quality is in no way impaired by an adequate cook. In order to attain the desired sterilizing value it is essential that the initial temperature (can center at the start of the process) be at least as high as indicated above. If lower temperatures are used the process must be increased. Check process times and temperatures with the can supplier or the National Canners Association.

This type of product is subject to thermophilic spoilage if not properly cooled. In order to reduce the danger from this type of spoilage, cans should be promptly and thoroughly cooled in water after the process. All cans larger than No. 2½ size should be pressure cooled in order to prevent buckle formation and strained ends.

SOURCE: Gentry International, Inc., P.O. Box 37, Gilroy, Calif.

PLAIN CHILI CON CARNE (HOT PACK)

Ingredients	Lb
Carcass beef (canner-cutter grade)	175
Oleo stock or kidney suet	18
Freshly ground onions (or onion powder, $2^1/_2$ lb)	24
Tomato purée (sp. gr. 1.035)	18
Salt	6
Wheat flour	18
Chili seasoning mix	12

Chili Seasoning Mix	Lb	Oz
Ground chili pepper (best quality)	59	
Finely ground Spanish paprika	20	8
Finely ground cumin seeds	12	
Garlic powder	2	4
Black pepper (62-mesh)	1	12
Ground oregano	3	
Red pepper		8

Procedure

Grind beef through the $^3/_8$-in. plate of the grinder and if fresh onions are used grind them through the $^1/_4$-in. plate. Put oleo stock or rendered kidney suet in a steam-jacketed kettle; add onions and fry until they turn golden yellow. Then add ground meat and, with continuous stirring, braise meat until free flowing (this takes approximately 15 min). If onion powder is used braise meat without the fresh, ground onion. Add salt and chili seasoning mixture. Make a slurry of the flour, tomato purée (and onion powder, if used) in 5 gal. of water and, with continuous stirring, add it to the cooking batch. Add enough water to bring volume up to 425 lb. It is important that the product be agitated continuously until flour thickens to the proper consistency. Fill cans while maintaining the product temperature at 160°F. There is no need to vacuum pack this product.

Suggested Process

300 × 409 cans (16 oz net) 95 min at 240°F

Check process time and temperature with can supplier or the National Canners Association.

SOURCE: Stephan L. Komarik, 4810 Ronda, Coral Gables, Florida.

CHILI CON CARNE WITH BEANS (HOT PACK)

Ingredients	Lb	Oz
Carcass beef (canner-cutter grade)	140	
Beef suet	60	
Tomato purée (sp. gr. 1.035)	20	
Wheat flour	10	
Salt	6	4
Soaked and precooked beans (Michigan Red or California Pink)	100	
Onion powder	2	
Garlic powder		8
Paprika emulsion (HCV water-soluble)		14
Chili seasoning mix[1]	10	
Water to make 520 Lb		

[1] Use the same seasoning mix ingredients given above for Plain Chili Con Carne (Hot Pack).

Procedure

Soak beans overnight in cold water. Soaking tank should be fed by water entering the bottom of the tank so water can slowly overflow at the top of the tank keeping water in motion to prevent beans from souring. Then blanch beans for 15 min in boiling water.

Grind beef through the $^1/_2$-in. plate of the grinder and beef suet through the $^1/_4$-in. plate. Put beef suet in a steam-jacketed kettle and braise meat until it is free flowing. Add the chili seasoning mix and stir continuously. Make a slurry (free of lumps) of the flour, onion and garlic powders, and tomato purée in 5 gal. of water and by continuous stirring add to the braised meat along with the paprika emulsion. Add blanched beans. Bring volume up to 520 lb and cook product until the flour thickens the product.

Fill cans while maintaining product temperature at 160°F.

Suggested Process

603 × 700 cans (6 lb 12 oz net) 4 hr at 240°F
300 × 409 cans (16 oz net) 2 hr at 240°F

Check process times and temperatures with the can supplier or the National Canners Association.

SOURCE: Stephan L. Komarik, 4810 Ronda, Coral Gables, Florida.

CHILI CON CARNE WITH BEANS (COLD PACK)

Ingredients	Lb	Oz
Carcass beef (canner-cutter grade)	150	
Beef suet	60	
Soaked blanched beans	160	
Tomato purée (sp. gr. 1.035)	50	
Pregelatinized yellow corn flour	10	
Onion powder	2	
Chili seasoning mix[1]	10	8
Salt	6	4
Water	150	

[1] Use the same chili seasoning mix ingredients given above for Plain Chili Con Carne (Hot Pack).

Procedure

Soak beans overnight in cold water. Soaking tank should be fed by water entering the bottom of the tank so water slowly overflows at the top of the tank, keeping water in motion. Otherwise beans may sour overnight. Then blanch for 15 min. in boiling water.

Grind beef through the 1/2 -in. plate of the grinder, beef suet through 1/4 -in. plate. Put approximately 80 lb of water (10 gal.) in a mechanical mixer, add flour, salt, seasonings, and tomato purée and run machine until the paste is free of lumps. Add blanched beans along with the salt; then add ground meat and remaining water (70 lb). Mix until all ingredients are uniformly distributed.

Fill cans; close under 27 in. vacuum.

Suggested Process

603 × 700 cans (6 lb 12 oz net) 5 hr 20 min at 240°F
300 × 409 cans (16 oz net) 2 hr 30 min at 240°F

Check process times and temperatures with can supplier or the National Canners Association.

SOURCE: Stephan L. Komarik, 4810 Ronda, Coral Gables, Florida.

CHILI MAK (COLD PACK)

Ingredients	Lb	Oz
Carcass beef (canner-cutter grade)	150	
Beef suet	60	
Cooked spaghetti (or macaroni)	160	
Tomato purée (sp. gr. 1.035)	50	
Pregelatinized yellow corn flour	10	
Onion powder	2	
Chili seasoning mix[1]	10	8
Salt	6	4
Brown sugar	2	
Water	150	

Plus water to bring weight to 600 lb

[1] Use the same chili seasoning mix ingredients given above for **Plain Chili Con Carne (Hot Pack)**.

Procedure

For each pound of spaghetti, use approximately 1 gal. of water containing 2% salt. Bring water to boil and add spaghetti (broken into thirds) or macaroni. Boil for 12 min. After cooking, wash and rinse in cold water, then drain; washing and rinsing should not exceed one-half hour. Yield: 300% of original weight.

Grind beef through the 1/2 -in. plate of the grinder, beef suet through the 1/4 -in. plate.

Put approximately 80 lb of water in a mechanical mixer, add flour, salt, seasoning, and tomato purée to the mixer, and let machine run until the paste is free of lumps. Add suet, meat, and the remaining water (70 lb). After all ingredients are properly distributed add cooked spaghetti or macaroni. Mix just long enough for even distribution.

Fill and close cans under vacuum.

Suggested Process

300 × 409 cans (16 oz net) 95 min at 240°F

Check process time and temperature with can supplier or the National Canners Association.

SOURCE: Stephan L. Komarik, 4810 Ronda, Coral Gables, Florida.

HOT DOG CHILI SAUCE WITH MEAT (HOT PACK)

Ingredients	Lb	Oz
Carcass beef (canner-cutter grade)	90	
Beef suet	90	
Tomato purée (sp. gr. 1.045)	180	
Dry chili beans soaked and cooked	116	
Yellow corn flour	10	
Salt	11	8
Onion powder	6	
Cane sugar	10	
Plant protein hydrolyzate		6
Sodium nitrite		1/4
Water	360	
Chili seasoning mix[1]	10	8

[1] Use the same chili seasoning mix ingredients given above for **Plain Chili Con Carne (Hot Pack)**.

Procedure

Soak beans overnight in cold water. Soaking tank should be fed by water entering the bottom of the tank so water will slowly overflow from the top keeping water in motion. Otherwise beans may sour overnight. Then blanch beans 30 min in boiling water.

Grind beef and suet through the 1-in. plate of the grinder. Braise meat and suet in a steam-jacketed kettle until it is free flowing. Remove braised meat-suet mixture and reserve rendered juices. Grind beans and meat through the 1/4 - in. plate of the grinder. To the rendered juices in the steam kettle add tomato purée, and the ground beef-beans mixture. Using a "Lightning" mixer, add enough water to bring volume to 50 gal. Then add the remainder of the ingredients except the flour. Make a slurry of flour and 5 gal. of water and mix until slurry is free of lumps. Add slurry to batch, bring volume up to 100 gal. and, with steady stirring, raise temperature to 200°F; cook an additional 30 min.

Fill cans while sauce is hot. Temperature of the sauce should not drop below 160°F. If temperature drops below 160°F, close cans under vacuum.

Suggested Process

208 × 408 cans (10½ oz net) 90 min at 240°F

Check process time and temperature with can supplier or the National Canners Association.

SOURCE: Stephan L. Komarik, 4810 Ronda, Coral Gables, Florida.

PIZZA FILLER WITH BEEF (HOT PACK)

Ingredients	Lb	Oz
Mozzarella cheese	25	
Tomato paste (28% solids)	144	
Corn oil	8	
Cracker meal	24	
Beef (chuck)	35	
Cane sugar	16	
Salt	12	
Monosodium glutamate	1	
Plant protein hydrolyzate		8
Ground oregano	1	4
Ground fennel	1	4
Onion powder		10
Ground anise		10
Garlic powder		10
Water to make 65 gal.		

Procedure

Grind beef chuck and the cheese through the ⅛-in. plate of the grinder. Place corn oil in a steam-jacketed kettle, add ground meat, turn on heat and braise until meat is free flowing. Add tomato paste and seasonings and about half the volume of water. With continuous agitation raise temperature to 180°F. Put approximately 15 gal. of water in a bakery mixer and while the machine is in operation add cracker meal and ground mozzarella cheese; mix until slurry is free of lumps. Add slurry to meat mixture, stirring continuously. Increase volume to 65 gal. Raise temperature to 180°F and hold this temperature for 10–15 min.

Fill cans while product is hot; temperature should not drop below 160°F.

Suggested Process

300 × 400 cans (16 oz net) 90 min at 240°F
211 × 400 cans (11 oz net) 60 min at 240°F

Check process times and temperatures with can supplier or the National Canners Association.

SOURCE: Stephan L. Komarik, 4810 Ronda, Coral Gables, Florida.

SLOPPY JOE WITH TEXTURED SOY FLOUR

This is a generalized formula and procedure for producing a canned or frozen Sloppy Joe containing Texgran Brand textured soy flour.

Ingredients	%
Beef, raw	40.00
Water	37.00
Onion, chopped	8.45
Salt, sugar, seasoning	5.50
Starch	3.00
Tomato powder	2.50
Textured soy flour (Texgran Code No. 52000)	2.50
Nonfat dry milk solids	1.00
Coloring	0.05

Procedure

Blend textured soy flour (Texgran) and salt with beef and grind to desired size. Preblend starch and nonfat dry milk as a cold water slurry. Preheat water in mixer; add seasoning and blend before adding meat mixture and slurry to mixer contents. Heat to set starch and pump to filling equipment.

Retort canned product according to National Canners Association recommendations; or, package for freezing.

SOURCE: Swift Edible Oil Co. Div., Swift & Company, 115 W. Jackson Blvd., Chicago, Ill.

SLOPPY JOE (COLD PACK)

Ingredients	Lb	Oz
Carcass beef (canner-cutter grade)	200	
Trimmed beef flanks	100	
Tomato purée (sp. gr. 1.045)	147	
Sweet pickle relish	48	
Cider vinegar (45-grain)	36	
Pregelatinized starch	12	
Light brown sugar	12	
Cane sugar	12	
Salt	9	
Plant protein hydrolyzate		10
Monosodium glutamate	1	
Ground chili pepper	7	
Ground cumin seeds	1	
Garlic powder		4
Onion powder		12
Black pepper		4
Red pepper		1
Ground oregano		7
Ground cloves		1½
Ground cinnamon		1½
Smoke flavor, if desired could be used sparingly		

Procedure

Grind meats through $1/2$-in. plate of the grinder. Mix salt with the seasonings, plant protein hydrolyzate, and monosodium glutamate. Put ground meat in a mechanical mixer. Start machine; add tomato purée; then add slowly and evenly the precooked starch and mix until the starch is uniformly distributed and there are no lumps. Add vinegar, sugars, sweet relish, and mixed seasonings and let machine run until all the ingredients are uniformly distributed.

Fill and close cans under 27 in. vacuum.

Suggested Process

300 × 409 cans (16 oz net) 95 min at 240°F

Check process time and temperature with can supplier or the National Canners Association.

SOURCE: Stephan L. Komarik, 4810 Ronda, Coral Gables, Florida.

GROUND BEEF IN BARBECUE SAUCE (HOT PACK)

This product is made up of 50% braised beef and 50% barbecue sauce.

Cook Meat

Grind meat through the 1-in. plate of the grinder and transfer it to a steam-jacketed kettle. Add 2 qt of water per 100 lb of meat and braise meat just long enough to make meat free flowing in the kettle. Drain meat juices (stock) and reserve it for use in making the sauce.

Make Sauce

Ingredients	Lb	Oz	Gal.
Tomato purée (sp. gr. 1.035)			25
Braised meat juices and water			25
Soy sauce			$1^1/_2$
Worcestershire sauce			$^1/_2$
Vinegar (100-grain)			1
Wheat flour	7	8	
Cornstarch	2	8	
Salt	12	8	
Ground red pepper		4	
Black pepper (62-mesh)		4	
Onion powder		1	
Garlic powder		$^1/_2$	
Barbecue seasoning mix:	2	13	

	%
Spanish paprika (HCV)	50
Ground red pepper	28
Ground cloves	6.5
Ground mace	3.0
Ground Batavia cinnamon	6.0
Ground African ginger	6.5

Put the tomato purée in a steam-jacketed kettle and heat to 180°F. Add salt blended with seasonings, barbecue seasoning mix, garlic, and onion powder. Make a paste of flour and cornstarch in 5 gal. of water and add to the tomato purée mixture. Bring volume up to 50 gal. with the addition of meat juices and water. Add soy sauce, Worcestershire sauce, and vinegar and cook for 15 min. During the entire sauce-making procedure agitate sauce with a mixer.

Fill

Use 50% braised meat and 50% sauce to fill cans. Close under 27 in. vacuum.

Suggested Process

603 × 700 cans (6 lb 12 oz net) 300 min at 240°F
300 × 409 cans (16 oz net) 90 min at 240°F
300 × 308 cans (12 oz net) 60 min at 240°F

Check process times and temperature with the can supplier or the National Canners Association.

SOURCE: Stephan L. Komarik, 4810 Ronda, Coral Gables, Florida.

GROUND BEEF IN BARBECUE SAUCE (SEMICOLD PACK)

Ingredients	Lb	Oz
Lean beef (utility grade)	533	
Tomato paste (26% solids)	40	
Water	16	
Wheat flour	25	
Cornstarch	5	
Brown sugar	17	8
Soy sauce	12	8
Worcestershire sauce	4	8
Vinegar (100-grain)	8	
Salt	9	
Onion powder	3	
Garlic powder		8
Spanish paprika		$10^1/_2$
Red pepper (cayenne)		$2^1/_2$
Mace		1
Batavia cinnamon		$1^1/_2$
Jamaica ginger		$1^1/_2$
Cloves		$1^1/_2$

Procedure

Cut meat into slices 2 in. thick. Transfer it to a steam-jacketed kettle; add enough water to cover meat and cook for 10 min at 200°F to obtain approximately 10% shrink. Reserve stock. Remove meat from the kettle and grind it through the $1^1/_2$-

in. plate of the grinder. Reweigh meat and add enough stock to bring product up to the original raw weight of 533 lb. Transfer to a mechanical mixer; add tomato paste, 16 lb of the stock, brown sugar, and salt previously mixed with the seasonings and flavorings. Then add vinegar and Worcestershire sauce. Make a slurry of the flour and starch (free of lumps) with the remaining meat stock and water to make exactly 50 lb; add slurry to the mixer. Mix product approximately 3 min to obtain a uniform mixture; then fill cans. Close cans under 27 in. vacuum.

Suggested Process

603 × 700 cans (6 lb 12 oz net) 300 min at 240°F
300 × 409 cans (16 oz net) 95 min at 240°F
300 × 308 cans (12 oz net) 65 min at 240°F

Check process times and temperature with can supplier or the National Canners Association.

SOURCE: Stephan L. Komarik, 4810 Ronda, Coral Gables, Florida.

SLICED BEEF IN BARBECUE SAUCE (HOT PACK)

Prepare Meat

Use commercial grade of beef rounds or clods. Remove sinews and connective tissues, gristle, and fat. Cut meat into approximately 2-×-3-in. oblong strips. Lay each strip on the shelf of an open truck in single layers. Cuts should not touch each other. Put truck into the freezer and keep it there just long enough to solidify the meat (but not completely freeze it) so it can be sliced on a slicing machine. Slice meat 1/4-in. thick.

Put 15 gal. water in a steam-jacketed kettle equipped with a perforated basket. Bring temperature to 180°F; then add 200 lb of sliced beef. Cook meat while it is being slowly agitated with a wooden paddle until there is a 40% shrink from its original weight. The water temperature should be maintained at 180°F during cooking. Lift basket out of the kettle by means of a hoist and move it to the canning line. To obtain the beef stock concentration needed for preparing the sauce, repeat this operation three times with fresh sliced meat.

It is important to keep the sliced, cooked meat hot during the canning operation. If it gets cold, it will lose its pliability and will be hard to pack into cans without breaking.

Prepare Sauce

Ingredients and procedure are identical with the barbecue sauce given above for Ground Beef in Barbecue Sauce (Hot Pack).

Fill Cans

Fill 8 oz of sliced beef and 8 oz of hot barbecue sauce in 300 × 409 cans. Use spatula or some other instrument around the side of the can before closing to eliminate air pockets which may be trapped on the bottom of the can. Internal temperature of product should be maintained at least at 160°F when cans are closed. If closing temperature drops below 160°F, close cans under 15 in. vacuum.

Suggested Process

300 × 409 cans (16 oz net) 90 min at 240°F

Check processing time and temperature with the can supplier or the National Canners Association.

SOURCE: Stephan L. Komarik, 4810 Ronda, Coral Gables, Florida.

SLICED PORK IN BARBECUE SAUCE

To Prepare Meat

Use only fresh defatted hams (24 lb or over) or large defatted picnics, and follow preparation procedure given above for beef cooked and sliced for Sliced Beef in Barbecue Sauce. (If cured hams are used, product should be labeled Ham in Barbecue Sauce.)

To Prepare Sauce

Use ingredients and preparation procedure given above for barbecue sauce in Ground Beef in Barbecue Sauce (Hot Pack).

To Process

Check processing times and temperature with the can supplier or the National Canners Association.

SOURCE: Stephan L. Komarik, 4810 Ronda, Coral Gables, Florida.

BARBECUED BEEF IN SAUCE (HOT PACK)

This product is made by barbecuing meat over wood or charcoal fire and should not be confused with the product called Beef in Barbecue Sauce.

Barbecue the Beef

Beef round, clods or chucks are best for this canned item. Trim meat free of fat, connective tissues, and sinews and cut into uniform chunks of approximately 2 lb each. Place chunks on large trays equipped with drain pipes to permit collection of the rendered juices into a container.

Transfer beef to a specially-built barbecue house equipped with steal rod shelves and a fire pit. Heat the house by burning hard wood. Place trays of meat on the shelves, connect the drain pipes, and barbecue the meat at 300°–350°F until the meat reaches an internal temperature of 130°F. After barbecuing the meat it is ground through the 1-in. plate of the grinder.

Prepare Sauce

Ingredients	Lb	Gal.	Qt
Tomato purée (sp. gr. 1.035)		55	
Beef broth		48	
Soy sauce		3	1
Worcestershire sauce		2	1
White vinegar (100-grain)		3	2
Salt	43		
Cane sugar	17		
Seasoning mix:	10		

	Lb	Oz
Spanish paprika	5	
Ground red pepper	2	12
Ground cloves		10
Ground mace		5
Ground cinnamon		10
Ground Jamaica ginger		11

Put all sauce ingredients in a steam-jacketed kettle and bring temperature to 180°F and it is ready for canning.

Fill Cans and Close

Pack 65% barbecued beef and 35% sauce. Temperature of product for filling should not be lower than 160°F.

Suggested Process

300 × 400 cans (16 oz net) 90 min at 240°F
211 × 400 cans (11 oz net) 60 min at 240°F

Check processing times and temperature with the can supplier or the National Canners Association.

SOURCE: Stephan L. Komarik, 4810 Ronda, Coral Gables, Florida.

BARBECUE PARTY DIP

Ingredients	Lb	Oz	Pt
Pinto beans, soaked and cooked	315		
Water	70		
Smoked bacon ends	35		
Fresh green peppers	40		
Onion powder	10		
Diced, canned red pepper	10		
Vinegar (100-grain)			2
Salt	12	8	
Ground chili pepper	4	4	
Ground Spanish paprika	1	8	

Ground black pepper (62-mesh)	2
Ground red pepper (60-mesh)	1/2
Ground cumin	14
Ground oregano	2 1/2
Garlic powder	2 1/2

Procedure

Soak beans overnight (8 hr). The best method is to have an overflow on the container in which the beans are soaking so that water will circulate and beans will not sour during the soaking period. After soaking, drain; then cook beans until tender. A pressure vessel can be used for fast cooking of beans. Grind bacon through the 1/8-in. plate of a grinder. Clean green peppers, removing stems, seeds, and veins; then coarsely dice. Transfer cooked beans to a meat chopper; add ground bacon and chop mixture to a fine consistency. Mix together salt and the dry seasoning ingredients. Add seasoning ingredients together with water and vinegar to bean-bacon mixture. Chop and mix until all ingredients are uniformly distributed (approx 3 min). Then add green and red peppers and let chopping machine make a few revolutions to reduce these ingredients to approximately 1/4-in. pieces and distribute them throughout mixture.

Use automatic filling machine to fill cans. Close under 27 in. vacuum.

Suggested Process

208 × 410 cans (11 oz net) 2 hr at 240°F

Check process time and temperature with can supplier or the National Canners Association.

SOURCE: Stephan L. Komarik, 4810 Ronda, Coral Gables, Florida.

CORN MEAL MUSH WITH BACON

Ingredients	Lb	Oz	Gal.
Yellow corn meal	80		
White corn meal	80		
Bacon ends and pieces	40		
Salt	8		
Butter or vegetable oil	8		
Cane sugar	3		
Monosodium glutamate		12	
Dry soluble pepper	1		
Water			70

Procedure

Grind bacon ends and pieces through the quarter inch plate of the grinder. Bring water to boiling in a steam-jacketed kettle. Shut off steam and with continuous stirring add the remainder of the ingredients. The product should be smooth, free from any lumps.

Use a mechanical filling machine and fill 16 oz into each can while product is hot.

Suggested Process

300 × 409 cans (16 oz net) 2 hr at 240°F

Check process time and temperature with can supplier or the National Canners Association.

SOURCE: Stephan L. Komarik, 4810 Ronda, Coral Gables, Florida.

PHILADELPHIA SCRAPPLE

Ingredients	Lb	Oz
Pork head meat	100	
Beef cheeks, hearts, or shank meat	20	
Treated beef tripe, or hog stomachs	40	
Meat stock from cooked meats	148	
White corn meal	92	
Toasted onion chips	1	
Salt	6	
Dry soluble pepper		8
Ground celery seed		1
Monosodium glutamate		6
Ground Dalmatian sage		1½
Ground marjoram		1
Sodium nitrite		¼

Procedure

Except treated beef tripe, all meat weights given above are precooked weights. Put 5 gal. of water in a steam-jacketed kettle; add salt, sodium nitrite, pork head meat, and beef cheeks (or hearts or shank meat); cook slowly until meats are tender. Remove meats; bring stock volume up to 18 gal. with water; hold stock at 180°F.

If fresh hog stomachs are used, cook them separately. To each 100 lb of hog stomachs, use 5 gal. of water and ¼ oz of sodium nitrite. Cook until stomachs are tender. (Sodium nitrite turns stomach linings a pink color so linings do not have to be removed. Without sodium nitrite, linings turn black during cooking and have to be removed.) Discard cooking liquid from the stomachs.

Grind all the cooked meats and treated beef tripe through the ³⁄₈-in. plate of the grinder.

Bring temperature of meat stock up to boiling. Shut off steam and with steady agitation using a scraping-type agitator, add first the salt, seasonings, monosodium glutamate, and onion chips. Then slowly add corn meal while continuing with agitation to avoid lumps. Finally add ground meats. When all items are properly distributed in the mix-

ture, fill into cans through a filling machine. Do not let temperature of the mixture drop below 160°F. Close cans under vacuum.

Suggested Process

300 × 409 cans (16 oz net) 2 hr at 240°F

Check process time and temperature with can supplier or the National Canners Association.

SOURCE: Stephan L. Komarik, 4810 Ronda, Coral Gables, Florida.

MINCE MEAT PIE FILLING

Ingredients	Pt	Gal.	Lb	Oz
Water		8		
Dehydrated apple slices			50	
Brown sugar			40	
Corn syrup			100	
Beef suet			15	
Beef			60	
Seedless raisins			100	
Spices			1½	
Sodium benzoate				9
Salt				1½
Wine		2		
Alcohol	2			

Procedure

Soak apples and raisins overnight in the water. Drain liquid and reserve for use in formula.

Cook beef until tender, then put through a meat grinder.

Put soaked apples and raisins through the grinder.

Put liquid from apples and raisins in a steam jacketed kettle and add sugar, corn syrup, salt, and sodium benzoate. Bring mixture to a boil. Then add ground beef and cook to proper consistency. Shut off steam and add spices, wine, and alcohol; mix with an agitator.

Put beef suet through the grinder and add to the product as it is cooling down in the kettle or cooling pan, continuing with the agitation. (The ground suet may also be added with the meat to the hot batch and thoroughly mixed in.)

Fill and Process

Follow recommendations of jar supplier or the National Canners Association for filling procedure and process time and temperature.

SOURCE: *Handbook of Food Manufacture* by Feine and Blumenthal, published by Chemical Publishing Co., New York, N.Y.

RUM FLAVORING FOR MINCE MEAT

Mix together the following:

	Fl Oz
Jamaica rum flavor	42.0
Raisin concentrated extract	44.0
Wine bitter aperitif flavor	42.0
Total fl oz	128.0

Recommended use: 16–32 fl oz per 1000 lb.

SOURCE: *Food Flavorings, 2nd Edition* by J. Merory published by Avi Publishing Co., Westport, Conn.

BRANDY FLAVORING FOR MINCE MEAT

Mix together the following:

	Fl Oz
Imitation brandy flavor	20.0
Alcohol, 95%	20.0
Sherry wine flavor	26.0
Raisin true fruit concentrated extract	12.0
Wine bitter aperitif flavor	50.0
Total fl oz	128.0

Recommended use: 16–32 fl oz per 100 lb.

SOURCE: *Food Flavorings, 2nd Edition*, by J. Merory published by Avi Publishing Co., Westport, Conn.

ENGLISH-STYLE PORK KIDNEYS IN LEMON SAUCE

Ingredients	Lb	Oz
Pork kidneys, precooked	400	
Lard or hydrogenated vegetable oil	20	
Fresh onions	40	
Wheat flour	20	
Salt	10	
Hydrolyzed plant protein	2	
Monosodium glutamate	1	
Ground black pepper		4
Ground bay leaves		1
Spanish paprika		8
Juice of 5 dozen lemons		
Rinds of 3 dozen lemons		
Caramel color		5
Water to make 40 gal.		

Procedure

Trim kidneys and soak them in 2% salt water overnight. Next day blanch kidneys 15 min in boiling water; then drain water and cover kidneys with fresh water. Bring temperature to 200°–205°F and simmer 15 min. Drain; rinse in cold water and slice as trade desires.

Grind onions through the ¼-in. plate of the grinder. Put lemon peels through the ⅛-in. plate of the grinder. Premix lemon peels with salt and other dry ingredients.

Put lard or vegetable oil in steam-jacketed kettle and add onions; cook onions lightly to a golden color, then add flour and, with steady stirring, brown flour. Add lemon peel-seasoning mixture and, with steady stirring, add enough boiling water to make 40 gal. Stir lemon juice and caramel color into sauce and bring temperature up to 200°–205°F; simmer for 10 min.

Fill into cans using 50% cooked, sliced kidneys and 50% hot sauce.

Suggested Process

208 × 408 cans (12 oz net) 1 hr at 240°F
300 × 409 cans (16 oz net) 1 hr 30 min at 240°F

These process times and temperature should be checked with the can supplier or the National Canners Association.

SOURCE: Stephan L. Komarik, 4810 Ronda, Coral Gables, Florida.

CANNED RABBIT MEAT

Rabbit may be canned in two general ways: pick the meat from the bones and can the meat only; or, cut the rabbit into suitably sized pieces and can without boning.

To Can the Meat

Skin, clean, and thoroughly wash rabbit carcasses in cold water; take care that all blood is removed. Place carcasses in a steam-jacketed kettle and cover with water. Bring kettle contents to a boil and simmer gently until meat is tender. Reserve liquid in which the meat was cooked. Carefully remove bones from meat.

Pack the desired weight of meat into cans and fill with either the hot concentrated broth in which the meat was cooked (as described below) or a gelatin mixture of the broth.

Boil down the liquid in which the rabbit meat was cooked to approximately ½ its volume; add salt in the ratio of ½ lb salt per 1 gal. of broth. If a jelly is desired in the finished canned product, add 1 lb of best grade gelatin per 6 gal. concentrated broth. First soak gelatin in cold water for 1 hr before adding it to the broth.

Meat products of this kind may be packed in flat cans holding from ¼ to 1 lb. A can 3⁷⁄₁₆ in. in diameter and 2 in. high will hold about ½ lb, and a can 4¹⁄₁₆ in. in diameter and 2¹¹⁄₁₆ in. high holds about 1 lb.

Pass the filled cans through a steam exhaust to remove entrapped air and to heat up the contents to at least 140°F at the center; close cans immediately and process.

To Can Pieces

Pack cleaned, cut-up pieces firmly into cans and add $\frac{1}{3}$ tsp of salt per pound of meat. Cover can contents with either the hot concentrated broth or a broth-gelatin mixture as described above for canning meat only. Pass filled cans through a steam exhaust to remove entrapped air and to heat up the contents to at least 140°F at the center; close cans immediately and process.

A larger size of can than that used for the meat only will be preferable for pieces. Approximately $1\frac{1}{2}$ lb of pieces can be packed into cans $5\frac{7}{16}$ in. in diameter and $2\frac{25}{32}$ in. high (net contents with added broth, about 2 lb). Approximately 1 lb of pieces can be packed into cans $4\frac{30}{32}$ in. in diameter and $2\frac{19}{32}$ in. high (net contents with added broth, about $1\frac{1}{2}$ lb).

Process

Check processing times and temperatures for meat only or rabbit pieces with can supplier or the National Canners Association.

SOURCE: *A Complete Course in Canning* by Lopez, published by Canning Trade, Baltimore, Md.

CANNED FROG LEGS

Small quantities of frog legs are canned commercially in the Gulf of Mexico and Mississippi River areas. As a rule, the hind legs only are canned, the meat from the fore legs and body being utilized in the preparation of specialty dishes similar to chicken a la king. Information is not available in the canning of "frog a la king," although a limited amount is canned commercially. Both common or "giant" bull frog (*Rana catesbciana*) and the smaller green frogs (*R. clamitans*) are used. The frogs are taken in the coastal bayous and river marshes by "torching" at night. A bright light is placed in the bow of a canoe or skiff. Frogs are attracted or dazed by the light so that they may be approached near enough to be taken by spearing, or in a dip net. Some are brought in alive. Frogs are said to be best from August through October.

The hind legs are separated from the rest of the body; the edge of the skin at the top of the legs is loosened, turned downward and pulled off over the toes, which are then cut off. The legs are soaked 15 min in a brine testing about 50° salinometer, after which they are washed thoroughly in cold water.

The legs are next drained and placed in a kettle with sufficient meat stock to cover. They are parboiled for 8 min, the stock is drawn off and the legs are packed in cans, usually No. 1 picnic (211 × 400), and squat (307 × 208) cans. The legs should be filled in carefully so that a good fill is obtained, with no large spaces. The fill-in weight of frog legs should be approximately 8 oz for both sizes of container.

The cans are filled with the hot meat stock, leaving a headspace of $\frac{3}{16}$ in., and are sealed immediately by closing machine without exhaust or mechanical vacuum seal. The process for both sizes is 45 min at 240°F (10 lb pressure). The product is water-cooled in tanks after processing.

Processing time and temperature should be checked with the can supplier or the National Canners Association.

SOURCE: Fish and Wildlife Services, U.S. Dept. of Interior, Washington, D.C.

CANNED HAM AND EGGS

Ingredients	Lb	Oz
Skinless, boneless, smoked hams	250	
Frozen whole eggs	250	
Ground white pepper (80-mesh)		$1\frac{1}{4}$

Procedure

Defrost frozen eggs at room temperature or in warm water just long enough so they can be removed from the containers; then chop up the mass and grind through the $\frac{1}{4}$-in. plate of the grinder.

Bone and skin hams and grind meat through the $\frac{1}{4}$-in. plate of the grinder.

Transfer both ham and eggs to a steam-jacketed mixer. Sprinkle pepper evenly over the top of the mixture; and while the mixer is running warm the product to 150°F, just under the coagulation point of the egg albumin.

Use a filling machine to fill cans. Before filling the cans, spray cans on the conveyor line with heated lard or some edible oil (corn, cottonseed); this will prevent material from sticking to the cans Temperature of the meat-egg mixture should remain at 150°F when filling cans. If temperature drops below 150°F, close under 10 in. vacuum.

Suggested Process

404 × 414 cans (34 oz net) 2 hr 30 min at 240°F
300 × 106 cans ($3\frac{3}{4}$ oz net) 1 hr 30 min at 230°F

Check process times and temperatures with can supplier or the National Canners Association.

SOURCE: Stephan L. Komarik, 4810 Ronda, Coral Gables, Florida.

CANNED BRAINS WITH GRAVY

Ingredients	Lb	Oz
Hog brains	450	
Salt	7	
Monosodium glutamate		5
Sodium nitrite		1/2
Water	50	

Procedure

Wash brains in overflowing cold water then carefully remove thin skin covering. This is a very important procedure because if it is not done the product will turn black in the cans after the process. Dissolve salt, monosodium glutamate and sodium nitrite in the water. After the brains have been washed and the thin films have been removed, place brains in a stainless steel truck, add brine, and mix thoroughly with a wooden paddle.

Filling the cans should be done through a filling machine and the cans closed under 27 in. vacuum.

Suggested Process

208 × 408 cans (10½ oz net) 90 min at 240°F

Check process time and temperature with can supplier or the National Canners Association.

SOURCE: Stephan L. Komarik, 4810 Ronda, Coral Gables, Florida.

CANNED BEEF TRIPE

Selection of Tripe

All excessively dark or yellow tripe, or tripe that is extremely thin or soft, should be rejected. Frozen tripe should not be used for canning purposes. Beef tripe should be delivered to the canning plant in the scalded, finished, and chilled form. It must be treated in the canning room as soon as possible after it is received.

Treatment Prior to Canning

Immerse 750 lb of beef tripe in vinegar solution (96 gal. of water and 12 gal. of 90-grain vinegar) in an ordinary 250-gal. wooden or glass-lined tank. Keep the tripe submerged in the vinegar solution for 20 min, stirring twice during this period.

At the end of this treatment, transfer tripe to a vat filled with cold water and hold it submerged for 10 min with occasional stirring; then rinse thoroughly. It is then ready for canning.

The vinegar solution in the vat may be used for an entire day's operation but should not be held overnight.

Fill Cans

After tripe has been prepared as described above, cut it into strips gaging the width of the strips to the height of the cans. Roll strips and fill into cans.

Then fill cans with milk to which enough salt is added to give 1% in the canned product.

Close cans under vacuum.

Suggested Process

300 × 409 (16 oz net) 2 hr 30 min at 235°F

Check process time and temperature with can supplier or the National Canners Association.

SOURCE: Stephan L. Komarik, 4810 Ronda, Coral Gables, Florida.

FROZEN MEAT, MEAT DISHES, SAUCES AND GRAVIES

HOW MULTIPLATE FREEZERS OPERATE

The Birdseye multiplate freezer developed by Birdseye and Hall and used commercially by the General Foods Corporation, consists of a number of superimposed hollow metal plates actuated by means of hydraulic pressure in such a manner that they may be opened to receive products between them and then closed on the product with any desired pressure. The entire freezing apparatus is enclosed in an insulated cabinet. The smaller machines, six stations and less, are self-contained and have compressor, compressor motor, condenser, hydraulic lift cylinder, hydraulic oil tank, and pressure pump located beneath the insulated freezing chamber. The larger machines require separate refrigerating systems.

The plates are made of rolled aluminum alloy and although they may be considered hollow, actually they are provided with sinuous passages. The ammonia, Freon, or brine is circulated through these passages. From one end of each plate a rubber hose connects to a header which feeds the plates with the refrigerant. The other end of the plate is also connected by a rubber hose to another header which carries the gas (in an ammonia type) to a surge drum located on top of the machine. Both headers are connected to the surge drum as it also acts as an accumulator for the liquid refrigerant.

In the older, as well as the smaller types of machines, the plates are actuated by means of pantagraphs or lazy tongs, the hydraulically operated cylinder, located under the bottom plate, being the means for imparting motion to and pressure on, the plates. The ten-station machines are so constructed that as pressure is applied on the under side of the first plate, it lifts its load until it meets the second plate, which in turn is raised with its load, and so on up.

Before the product to be frozen (usually in packages) is placed in the machine, the plates are cooled to the desired low temperature. After loading, the hydraulic cylinder is raised to squeeze the product between the plates, the cabinet doors are closed and the product left therein until its temperature reaches about $0°F$. The freezing time varies with the thickness of the package as well as the nature of the product to be frozen. In general, 2-in. packages of fish and meats can be completely frozen in less than 90 min. Fruits and vegetables require about 2 hr.

Usually sticks of wood, as long as the depth of the plate, and slightly less in height than the height of the packages that are to be frozen, are placed on each side of the machine between each plate, to prevent any excess pressure on the packages. In this way, sufficient pressure to obtain the desired results is exerted, yet excess pressure which might break the cartons is eliminated.

SOURCE: *The Freezing Preservation of Foods, 3rd Edition, Vol. 1* by Tressler and Evers published by Avi Publishing Co., Westport, Conn.

HOW PRECOOKED STEAKS ARE FREEZE DRIED

Freeze drying may be defined as removal of water from material by sublimation from the frozen state. Initial freezing may be accomplished by conventional methods such as air blast freezing or plate freezers, or by evaporative cooling effected by the vacuum established in the freeze drying chamber. The latter method always carries with it the hazard of causing a surface layer to dry from the unfrozen state, thus producing some undesirable case hardening. In order to have true freeze drying, with minimum changes in quality, it is imperative that the material be completely frozen and remain frozen throughout the freeze-drying cycle. If thawing takes place at any time during drying, a shrinkage of tissue and the formation of a hard core difficult to rehydrate, will result. In freezing meat, supercooling without freezing is apparently possible down to $-40°F$, which sets the lowest necessary temperature for any meat product. Once frozen, the product may be warmed to any point short of the eutectic melting point without incurring drying damage in the subsequent dehydration process. The higher the product ice temperature the faster the drying rate. Maximum permissible product ice temperature for animal tissues has been stated to range from 23° to 14°F.

Precooking of the steaks should be carried out in deep fat at 325°-350°F for 25 sec. Steaks should be tempered at 26°-30°F, and run through a modified cube steak machine prior to freeze drying, in order to increase drying surface and reduce drying time. Freeze drying should be conducted either by contact plate heating above and below the loaded tray, or by radiant heating with plates 3 or 4 in. above and below the product. Drying times for the contact plate method for plate temperatures of 110°, 165°, and 210°F, should be 12-14, 10-11, and 5-7 hr, respectively. For radiant heating with plate temperatures at 210°F, drying times are 7-9 hr for a 3 in. plate separation and 8-10 hr for a 4 in. separation. In the radiant heating applications, plates should be anodically blackened, since the resulting increased heat input reduces drying times by as much as 6 hr. Product temperature should be held below 110°F, by controlling thermocouples inserted in four pieces of product located at widely separated points on the drier shelves.

SOURCE: *Food Dehydration, 2nd Edition, Vol. 2* by Van Arsdel *et al.* published by Avi Publishing Co., Westport, Conn.

STEAKS, STEWS, POT PIES, AND MISCELLANEOUS MEATS

FROZEN SWISS STEAK

Ingredients	Lb	Oz
Beef, bottom round, trimmed	8	
Salt		1
White pepper		$1/7$
Peanut oil		7
Carrots, diced		7
Onions, diced		7
Celery, outside stalks, diced		7
Water		80
Spice bag to hold 3 cloves, 1 bay leaf, $1/10$ oz rosemary, $1/10$ oz thyme		
Red wine, domestic		12
Modified starch		3
Dehydrated onion powder		$1/2$
Dehydrated garlic powder		$1/2$

Procedure

Cut trimmed meat into $9^1/2$-oz steaks and sprinkle with salt and pepper. Pound steaks on both sides to tenderize. Brown in hot oil. Add diced carrots, onions, and celery and lightly brown also. Add water and the spice bag; cover and bring to a boil. Reduce heat and simmer 2 hr or until steaks are tender. Remove steaks and strain gravy. Add wine to starch and stir until smooth; add to gravy and heat to 180°F stirring constantly. Add onion and garlic powders.

Package each steak in 12 in. × 8 in. vacuum boil-in-bag pouch and add 7 oz gravy evenly distributed over meat. Close pouch and blast freeze for 30 min.

SOURCE: *The Freezing Preservation of Foods, 4th Edition, Vol. 4* by Tressler *et al.* published by Avi Publishing Co., Westport, Conn.

FROZEN AMERICAN POT ROAST

Ingredients	By Weight		or	By Measure
	Lb	Oz		
Beef, bottom round	7	8		
Peanut oil		7		
Carrots, diced		7		
Onions, diced		7		
Celery, outside stalks, diced		7		
Salt		1		(2 tbsp)
Pepper				1 tbsp
Water				3 qt
Sachet bag:				
Cloves				3
Bay leaf				1
Rosemary				1 tbsp
Thyme				2 tsp
Dry white wine, domestic				1 cup
Modified starch		$4^1/2$		
Instant onion powder				1 tbsp + 1 tsp
Instant garlic powder				2 tsp
Prepared gravy color				1 tbsp

YIELD: 10 portions using 9 oz beef and 7 oz gravy

Procedure

Brown meat carefully in hot oil then place meat in deep stew pan. Add carrots, diced onions, and celery and brown. Add water, salt, pepper, sachet bag; cover and bring to a boil. Then reduce heat and simmer for $2^1/2$ hr or until meat is tender. Remove meat from gravy and when meat is cool slice thinly and divide into 9-oz portions. Strain gravy through a fine sieve (there should be about $1\frac{1}{2}$ qt) and bring to a boil while stirring. Slowly add wine to modified starch, stirring until smooth; add to gravy and heat to 180°F, stirring constantly. Add instant onion, instant garlic, and prepared gravy color; blend gravy ingredients.

Package a 9-oz portion in 12 × 8-in. vacuum boil-in-bag pouch and add 7 oz gravy evenly distributed over meat slices. Blast freeze for 30 min.

SOURCE: Cornell Hotel & Restaurent Administration Quarterly, Statler Hall, Ithaca, N.Y.

FROZEN SLICED BEEF IN BROWN GRAVY

Prepare Beef

Use beef clods, Spencer rolls, outside or knuckles of rounds from a good grade of beef. Cut 600 lb of fresh beef in strips 3–4 in. wide and the full length of meat pieces. Put strips on a shelf truck and place in the freezer just long enough to partially freeze strips so they can be sliced easily on a slicing machine. Slice $\frac{1}{4}$ in. thick.

In a steam-jacketed kettle equipped with a wire basket, put 40 gal. of water and heat to 180°F. Add meat slices and, with gentle agitation with a wooden paddle, cook 20–25 min or until slices are tender.

It is important to keep meat warm and moist until it is packaged. Dry meat will lose its pliability and will break up during handling.

Prepare Gravy

Ingredients	Gal.	Lb	Oz
Beef stock	60		
Chilled beef stock or water	10		
Wheat flour		10	
Cornstarch		6	
Cracker flour (fine)		6	
Plant protein hydrolyzate		4	
Salt		5	
Monosodium glutamate		2	
Onion powder		4	
Tomato paste (28% solids)		10	
Dry caramel color		1	10
Ground black pepper			5
Garlic powder			$\frac{1}{4}$

Measure out 70 gal. of water in a steam-jacketed kettle and make a mark at water level on a measuring stick so finished gallonage can be gaged. Drain water.

Place 60 gal. of the beef broth in the kettle and heat to 180°F. In a bakery mixer, make a slurry free of lumps with 10 gal. of chilled beef stock or water and the flours and starch. Mix salt with

the remaining dry ingredients and add to the hot stock. While agitating hot stock with a "Lightning" mixer, add slurry along with the tomato paste. Bring volume up to 70 gal. and cook 15–20 min at 200°F.

Package and Freeze

Using 1-lb-net boil-in-bag Mylar bags put 6.4 oz of meat in bag and top with 9.6 oz gravy evenly distributed over meat. Vacuumize and seal bags. Prechill product in cooler at 34°–36°F before moving to a sharp freezer at −20°F.

SOURCE: Stephan L. Komarik, 4810 Ronda, Coral Gables, Florida.

FROZEN CHIP STEAK

Chip steak is made by cutting frozen beef into thin slices and then combining several of these wafers of meat to form a tender beef steak. The product is usually marketed in frozen form for institutional trade.

SOURCE: The Freezing Preservation of Foods, 3rd Edition, Vol. 1 by Tressler and Evers published by Avi Publishing Co., Westport, Conn.

FROZEN BREADED VEAL CUTLETS

Carefully cut and trim veal into 4-oz pieces and feed through a fully automatic batter dipping and breading machine. The pieces are conveyed through the batter mix for uniform coating on all sides. Following this, the pieces go directly to the breader, moving through a turning drum so as to be gently tumbled for a complete coating of breading mix. As cutlets are discharged from the breader, pack 40–42 portions in each foil-lined telescopic freezing carton and transfer product to the freezers. Either air-blast or multiplate freezers may be used.

SOURCE: The Freezing Preservation of Foods, 3rd Edition, Vol. 1 by Tressler and Evers published by Avi Publishing Co., Westport, Conn.

FROZEN BEEF POT PIES

Ingredients	Gal.	Lb	Oz
Beef broth	90		
Water	10		
Frozen peas		100	
Tomato paste (28% solids)		20	
Rendered beef fat		30	
Wheat flour		45	
Cornstarch		12	
Fresh carrots		126	
Onion powder		3	
Caramel color		4	

Dry soluble pepper	1	
Salt	14	8
Monosodium glutamate	2	8
Plant protein hydrolyzate	1	8
Garlic powder		$1/4$
Oleoresin celery	1	

Salt	0.40
Paprika	0.25
Dehydrated onion chips	0.25
Worcestershire sauce	0.25
Caramel (brown shade)	0.01
Burnt sugar	0.01

Procedure

Prepare Meat and Vegetables.—Cook a sufficient amount of well-trimmed beef chucks or clods in 90 gal. of water to produce enough diced meat to fill $1^{1}/_{4}$ oz in each 8-oz net aluminum foil pie shell. Shrinkage can be estimated at 45% from the raw weight.

Dice carrots to desired size, then blanch in boiling water for 15 min. Defrost peas.

Prepare Gravy.—In a bakery mixer make a slurry free of lumps with the water and the flour. Mix together salt, flavorings, and seasonings.

Heat broth in a steam-jacketed kettle to 200°F; add fat and tomato paste. Using a "Lightning" mixer add salt-seasoning mixture, then caramel coloring and slurry. Lastly add carrots and peas. Heat gravy to 200°F and cook 20 min with slow agitation.

In each individual aluminum foil pie shell (8 oz net) put $1^{1}/_{4}$ oz beef, over which put $6^{3}/_{4}$ oz gravy (keep well mixed so carrots and peas will be evenly distributed). Top with unbaked pastry circle, encase individual pies in cartons suitable for freezing. Prechill product at 34°–36°F before placing in a sharp freezer to freeze at -20°F.

SOURCE: Stephan L. Komarik, 4810 Ronda, Coral Gables, Florida.

FROZEN BEEF POT PIES

The contents of each 8-oz beef pie is as follows:

Ingredients	Oz
Diced cooked beef	$1^{1}/_{2}$
Crust	$2^{1}/_{2}$
Peas and carrots	1
Gravy	$3^{1}/_{4}$
Total	$8^{1}/_{4}$

Prepare the Gravy

The recommended gravy formula in percentage by weight is as follows:

Ingredients	%
Broth (from cooking beef)	62.00
Water	23.00
Vegetable shortening	6.00
Flour	5.83
Commercial seasonings	2.00

Mix together dry ingredients. Melt shortening in kettle and slowly add dry ingredients, stirring constantly, and cook 2 min.

Blanch commercially frozen peas and carrots in small amount of boiling water for $1^{1}/_{2}$ min. Use this blanching water as part of the water designated. Also, dissolve coloring in some of the water.

Combine all remaining gravy ingredients and add to hot shortening mixture in kettle, stirring constantly for 3 min, or until thickened. Cool gravy to 40°F or below, before using.

Cook the Beef

Beef used in making frozen pot pies should be of good commercial chuck or better, should be lean and easily diced. Cook the beef slowly. Fast cooking has a tendency to toughen the beef fibers. Always skim fat from broth before using. Strain broth through a fine screen or muslin.

A shrinkage of from 25 to 40% will result in cooking the beef depending on the quality of beef and method of cooking. Beef that is too fat will produce a greasy gravy and waste meat as all fat will have to be discarded in the dicing of the cooked beef.

Usual Commercial Procedure in Makeup

Most frozen meat pies are made on a pie machine. Empty rigid aluminum foil pie plates are stacked at the start of this operation. One plate is placed in each of four pockets that form a cluster. Next, the dough for the bottom crust is rolled and placed over the four plates. A docker forms the dough to the pie plates. The pies then pass under a gravy filler and then on to a section where weighed portions of beef and other ingredients are added. After this, the pies pass on to a section where a sheet of dough is rolled and placed by hand over the four pie plates to form the top crust. Top crust is crimped in place and trimmings cut away.

The completed pies usually pass on to an automatic cartoning line where each pie is placed in a package and overwrapped. It is then ready for the freezer.

SOURCE: *Freezing Preservation of Foods, 4th Edition, Vol. 4* by Tressler *et al.* published by Avi Publishing Co., Westport, Conn.

FROZEN BEEF STEW

Prepare Beef and Vegetables

Use trimmed beef chucks or rounds of good quality. Dice into 1-in. cubes. For each 100 lb of beef, use 5 gal. of water. Put water in a steam-jacketed kettle and heat to 180°F. Add meat and cook approximately 20–25 min gently agitating contents with a wooden paddle. Remove meat and reserve broth for use in gravy.

Soak large size dehydrated potato cubes in hot water (180°F) for 1¾ hr or until potatoes increase 480% in weight.

Dice fresh carrots into ½-in. dice. Cook in boiling water until tender, but not too soft.

Defrost peas.

Prepare Gravy

Ingredients	Lb	Oz
Salt	20	
Cane sugar	5	8
Tomato paste (28% solids)	21	
Wheat flour	27	8
Potato starch	4	8
Monosodium glutamate	1	8
Plant protein hydrolyzate (liquid)	3	
Corn sugar	1	8
Onion powder	1	8
Garlic powder		3
Black pepper (38-mesh)		12
Oleoresin paprika (HCV)		2
Oleoresin celery		1½
Caramel color (dry)		8
Water to make 90 gal. using beef broth		

Put 90 gal. of water in a steam-jacketed kettle and make a mark on a measuring stick so gallonage of finished gravy can be gaged. Drain water. Fill kettle ¾ full of water and heat to 200°F. Add all ingredients except flour and starch. Use a "Lightning" mixer to agitate gravy. Put 15 gal. of water in a bakery mixer and while mixer is running, add slowly the flour and starch; run mixer until the slurry is free of lumps. Add slurry to the hot, agitated gravy. Bring volume up to 90 gal. with the stock in which the beef was cooked. Bring temperature up to 200°F and cook 20 min longer.

Package and Freeze

In 1-lb-net polyethylene Mylar bags, first put 4 oz beef, 3 oz potatoes, 1½ oz carrots, and 1 oz peas. Evenly distribute over these ingredients 6½ oz of gravy. Vacuumize and seal bags.

Transfer to a cooler at 34°–36°F to prechill before transferring product to a sharp freezer at -20°F.

SOURCE: Stephan L. Komarik, 4810 Ronda, Coral Gables, Florida.

FROZEN BEEF STEW

Ingredients	%
Beef (1–1½-in. cubes)	30.50
Potatoes, diced[1]	25.00
Carrots, diced	5.44
Flour	1.88
Shortening	1.88
Onions, diced	0.88
Salt	0.52
Pepper	0.08
Worcestershire sauce	0.12
Water	33.70

[1] As an alternate, ¼ of the diced potatoes may be replaced with cooked peas in the proportion of 6.25% peas and 18.75% potatoes.

Procedure

Brown beef cubes with the shortening in a kettle. Then add approximately half the water (preheated). Simmer until beef is tender. Cook vegetables separately in the remainder of the water until they are tender. Then add vegetables to the cooked beef. Make a paste of the flour with cold water and add to stew mixture. Heat stew with agitation until it thickens. Season with salt and pepper and simmer stew for about 30 min. Cool to 120°–130°F; add Worcestershire sauce and cooked peas. Fill into suitable containers for freezing and freeze as rapidly as possible.

SOURCE: *Freezing Preservation of Foods, 4th Edition, Vol. 4* by Tressler *et al.* published by Avi Publishing Co., Westport, Conn.

FROZEN VEGETABLE AND BEEF STEW

Ingredients	Lb	Oz
Ground beef	140	
Carrots	106	
Potatoes	110	
Tomato juice	111	
Celery stalks	35	10
Waxy rice flour	22	
Rice	10	
Dehydrated onion powder	1	
Salt	3	
Monosodium glutamate	1	6
YIELD: 100 gal.		

For Strained Vegetables with Beef

Cook ground beef in a steam-jacketed kettle in 35 gal. of water for 30 min; then comminute in a Fitzpatrick mill or equivalent. Return comminuted beef to steam kettle; add rice and salt and continue cooking for 15 min. Wash potatoes, peel in an abrasive peeler or by some other method. Wash, trim, and peel carrots. Wash and trim celery. Then chop vegetables and add to meat ingredients in steam kettle; continue cooking for about 25 min. Make an aqueous slurry of waxy rice flour; add to meat mixture together with tomato juice, salt, onion powder, and monosodium glutamate. Make contents of steam kettle up to 100 gal. with addition of water.

Put the stew through a rotary cylindrical finisher fitted with a screen having 0.033-in. openings. Pump the resultant purée through a tubular flash-heater or sterilizer to raise the temperature to about 270°F. Immediately cool to filling temperature by passing mixture through a heat exchanger.

Fill product into cartons for freezing; or, fill into cans or glass jars and process, following directions of container representative or National Canners Association.

For Chopped Vegetables with Beef

Use ingredients indicated above. The partially cooked meat is chopped in a Buffalo cutter. The vegetables are cut into 1/2-in. dice and cooked in a steam-jacketed kettle in 35 gal. of water for 30 min. Otherwise, follow procedure given for strained vegetables with beef up to the point where the finished stew is run through the finisher. Instead, product is either immediately filled into cans or glass containers and processed, or packaged in cartons for freezing.

SOURCE: *Freezing Preservation of Foods, 4th Edition, Vol. 4* by Tressler *et al.* published by Avi Publishing Co., Westport, Conn.

FROZEN LAMB STEW

Ingredients	%
Lamb (cut in 1-in. cubes)	31.87
Potatoes, diced	29.75
Hot water	17.00
Turnips, diced	8.50
Peas (cooked)	4.25
Onions, sliced	4.25
Tomato purée	1.70
Shortening	1.25
Flour	0.85
Salt	0.50
Ground pepper	0.08

Procedure

Lightly brown lamb cubes in shortening in kettle; then add sliced onions and salt and cook until onion slices are golden. Add pepper and flour and brown slightly before adding the hot water and tomato purée. Simmer mixture until lamb is tender; this requires a little over 1 hr.

Cook potatoes, carrots, and turnips in a separate kettle until tender; add to stew along with the cooked peas.

Cool stew and let excess fat rise to surface so it can be skimmed off. Fill stew into containers for freezing and freeze as rapidly as possible.

SOURCE: *Freezing Preservation of Foods, 4th Edition, Vol. 4* by Tressler *et al.* published by Avi Publishing Co., Westport, Conn.

FROZEN BARBECUED RIBS

Prepare Sauce

Ingredients	Gal.	Lb	Oz
Tomato paste	10		
Water	10		
White vinegar (100-grain)	6		
Brown sugar		40	
Cane sugar		15	
Salt		7	
Precooked cornstarch		5	
Onion powder			10
Garlic powder			3 1/2
Ground cinnamon			1/2
Ground yellow mustard flour			7
Ground celery seeds			1/2
Ground red pepper			2

Add flavorings and seasonings to 1 gal. of the water and steep for 1 hr. In a kettle equipped with an agitator, add the remaining water (9 gal.) and add the steeped seasonings. Then add salt and sugars and agitate until ingredients are dissolved. With the agitator still operating, add vinegar and slowly add starch. When sauce is smooth, add tomato paste and let agitator run until a uniform mixture is obtained.

Barbecue Ribs

Make up the following curing pickle: 50 gal. water, 60 lb salt, and 1 lb sodium nitrite. Use 10 gal. of pickle per 100 lb ribs; pickle can be reused for one day's operation only.

Heat pickle to 160°F and cook ribs in pickle until almost tender (approximately 30 min for small ribs). Remove ribs from hot pickle and dip in sauce. Hang ribs on sausage trees using bacon combs. Have smokehouse preheated to 140°F; transfer trees to smokehouse and with all drafts wide open, give ribs a light smoke. Hold ribs in smokehouse until sauce has dried on surface of the ribs; then transfer to a chill room (34°–36°F). When ribs are properly chilled, pack in Cryovac bags, vacuumize and close. Pack in cartons suitable for freezing and freeze at –20°F.

Note: Ribs need not be defrosted before heating to serving temperature, but remove from vacuum package and place directly in the oven at 350°F for 10–15 min.

SOURCE: Stephan L. Komarik, 4810 Ronda, Coral Gables, Florida.

FROZEN SLICED BEEF IN BARBECUE SAUCE

Prepare Meat

Select approximately 600 lb of beef clods, Spencer rolls, or outside or knuckles of rounds from good grade of beef. Cut meat in strips 3–4 in. wide and the full length of pieces. Put strips of meat on a shelf truck and place in a freezer just long enough to partially freeze meat so it can be sliced on a slicing machine. Slice pieces 1/4 -in. thick.

Put 20 gal. of water in a steam-jacketed kettle equipped with a wire basket and heat to 180°F. Add a basketful of meat slices and, with gentle agitation with a wooden paddle, cook 20–25 min or until meat is tender. Remove meat and keep warm and moist until it is packaged. Dry meat loses its pliability and breaks up in the packaging operation.

Note: The meat juices plus the water in which the meat is cooked will yield more broth than is used in preparing the sauce; so make a more concentrated broth by reusing the broth at least 3 times for cooking the sliced meat, maintaining the volume of broth for each cooking at 20 gal.

Prepare Sauce

Ingredients	Gal.	Lb	Oz
Tomato purée (sp. gr. 1.035)	25		
Beef broth	25		
Soy sauce	1 1/2		
Worcestershire sauce	1/2		
Vinegar (100-grain)	1		
Cane sugar		30	
Wheat flour		5	
Cornstarch		2	
Cracker flour (fine)		3	
Onion powder		1	
Salt		12	8
Seasoning mix (see below)		2	13
Black pepper			4
Garlic powder			1/2

Seasoning Mix	Cc
Spanish paprika	50.0
Ground red pepper	28.0
Ground cloves	6.5
Ground mace (Bonda)	3.0
Ground cinnamon (Batavia)	6.0
Ground ginger (Jamaica)	6.5

In order to gage gallonage in a steam-jacketed kettle, measure out 50 gal. of water in kettle and make a mark on a measuring stick at the water level; then drain kettle. Put tomato purée in kettle and heat to 180°F. Mix salt with dry seasonings and flavorings; add to purée. In a bakery mixer, make a slurry free of lumps with 5 gal. of water and the flour, starch, and cracker flour. Add slurry to purée stirring continuously with a "Lightning" mixer. Add soy and Worcestershire sauces and vinegar to purée mixture and bring sauce volume up to 50 gal. with added broth. Cook sauce 15 min longer.

Package

Using 1-lb-net boil-in-bag Mylar bags, fill with 6.4 oz of sliced beef and evenly distribute over meat 9.6 oz hot sauce. Vacuumize and seal bags. Transfer to chill room at 34°–36°F to prechill product before freezing at –20°F.

SOURCE: Stephan L. Komarik, 4810 Ronda, Coral Gables, Florida.

FROZEN CREAMED CHIPPED BEEF

Ingredients	Lb	Oz
Chipped beef	50	
Nonfat dry milk	8	
Wheat flour	16	
Cornstarch	4	
Shortening	12	
Salt	2	8
Dry soluble pepper		4
Monosodium glutamate		6
Ground celery seeds		1/4
Water to make 40 gal.		

Procedure

Put 40 gal. of water in a steam-jacketed kettle; make a mark at water level on a measuring stick so finished gallonage can be gaged.

Grind chipped beef through the 1/2-in. plate of the grinder. Heat shortening in the steam-jacketed kettle; add chipped beef and stir with a wooden paddle until the chips are evenly coated with the heated oil. Add half the water (20 gal.) to the kettle; then add seasonings and salt, and bring temperature up to 180°F. In a bakery mixer, make a smooth slurry free of lumps of flour, starch, nonfat dry milk, and the remaining water (20 gal.). Add slurry to the batch and bring volume up to 40 gal. Raise temperature to 200°F and cook for 20 min.

Fill into 16-oz boil-in-bag Mylar packages. Close under vacuum and transfer to chill room at 34°-36°F to chill before freezing in a sharp freezer at -20°F.

SOURCE: Stephan L. Komarik, 4810 Ronda, Coral Gables, Florida.

FROZEN SMOKED SAUSAGES WITH BEANS IN TOMATO SAUCE

Prepare Beans

Soak white navy beans in wood, galvanized iron, or glass-lined containers for 8-10 hr. The best method is to have an overflow on the top of the containers to circulate incoming water during the soaking period, otherwise beans may sour, especially during warm weather.

Put soaked beans in a wire basket in a steam-jacketed kettle and precook for 30 min. Remove beans and drain.

Prepare Sausages

Select any kind of the best grade of smoked sausages such as Polish or breakfast pork sausages. Cut into 1-1½ in. lengths.

Prepare Sauce

Ingredients	Gal.	Lb	Oz	Cc
Tomato purée (sp. gr. 1.045)	25			
Cane sugar		63		
Corn sugar		18		
Salt		15		
Onion powder			5	
Oil of pimiento				5.40
Oil of cloves				2.50
Oil of nutmeg				2.00
Oil of cassia				0.30
Oleoresin capsicum				2.50
Oleoresin mace				2.50
Water to make	100			

Put 100 gal. of water in a steam-jacketed kettle and mark water level on a measuring stick so finished gallonage can be gaged; then drain water from kettle and put in tomato purée. Make a mixture of salt, onion powder, essential oils, and oleoresins and add to the purée; with steady stirring, bring temperature up to 180°F. Then add water to bring volume up to 100 gal., add 840 lb of precooked beans and, with occasional stirring, bring temperature up to 200°F. Simmer sauce with beans until beans are soft but not mushy.

Package and Freeze

In 1-lb-net polyethylene Mylar bags, pack 4 oz sausage pieces and 12 oz bean-tomato sauce mixture, distributing sauce evenly over sausage. Close packages under vacuum. Transfer to chill room at 34°-36°F to prechill before transferring product to a sharp freezer at -20°F.

SOURCE: Stephan L. Komarik, 4810 Ronda, Coral Gables, Florida.

FREEZING RABBIT MEAT

Southern California is the center for this industry. Most of the rabbit meat that reaches the country's consumers is processed there.

Domestic rabbits are generally milk fed, with a supplement of high protein feeds in order to produce quick growth and a finish of finely grained, all white meat at 7-10 weeks. Packed under U.S. government inspection, the cutting and packaging methods are closely aligned with disjointed poultry.

Live animals are collected each day, held overnight, and are taken to the killing room in the morning where they are rendered unconscious by a sharp blow on the head before being killed. Each rabbit is decapitated and three of the feet are severed from the body. The carcass is then hung by the fourth foot on poultry type hooks moving on an overhead monorail. The hides are removed before the rabbits are conveyed into the eviscerating room. The viscera are removed and placed in pans similar to the "on the table" system used in poultry plants. The carcasses and viscera are both inspected carefully.

After the rabbits are inspected they pass through spray washers and then are taken down from the hooks. The remaining foot is removed and the dressed carcass is dropped into a circulating cool water bath. Now the carcasses are placed on a rack and are moved into a chill room which holds a temperature range of 30°-40°F. The chilled rabbits are moved into the cutting room where a power saw is used to separate the carcasses into six pieces. These six pieces, plus the liver, are then packaged, overwrapped, and heat-sealed. The average weight per package is between 2 and 3 lb. The cartons are placed in an airblast freezer at -25°F.

Rabbit carcasses, unlike most other skinned edible animals, have little or no natural protective fatty tissues. For this reason, it is more susceptible to severe freezer-burn during storage than almost any other form of carcass meat. Highly impervious moisture-vapor wrapping materials are necessary and careful attention should be paid to folds and end seals. Aluminum foil, moisture-proof Cellophane and Pliofilm are satisfactory.

SOURCE: *The Freezing Preservation of Food, 3rd Edition, Vol. 1* by Tressler and Evers published by Avi Publishing Co., Westport, Conn.

FREEZING FROG LEGS

Legs of large bullfrogs are the kind usually frozen, although the smaller spotted leopard or meadow frog legs and the small pickerel frog legs are equally delicious.

Trucks from freezing plants pick up the frogger's catch each morning. When the load reaches the freezing plant, the frog legs are placed in a re-frigerated holding room until they can be inspected for color and imperfections.

In preparing legs for freezing, the hind legs are usually cut off in pairs (called saddles).

After inspection for color and imperfections, the saddles are graded for size: small, medium, and jumbo or large. They are then skinned, washed in cold water, and drained. Each saddle is wrapped individually in moisture-proof Cellophane or some other equally moisture-proof sheeting and packed in 1-lb cartons or in 10-lb institutional size packages.

Freezing is usually accomplished at temperatures well below zero and the packaged, frozen product is stored at $-10°F$ until shipped.

SOURCE: *The Freezing Preservation of Foods, 3rd Edition, Vol. 1* by Tressler and Evers published by Avi Publishing Co., Westport, Conn.

LOAVES, FABRICATED STEAKS, PATTIES, MEAT BALLS

FROZEN ALL-PURPOSE MEAT LOAF

Ingredients	Lb	Oz
Carcass beef (canner-cutter grade)	100	
Regular pork trimmings	250	
Trimmed pork cheeks	150	
Semolina flour	30	
Nonfat dry milk	10	
Soy protein concentrate	10	
Salt	10	
Mustard flour	5	
Monosodium glutamate	1	
Plant protein hydrolyzate	1	
Onion powder	1	4
Ground black pepper (62-mesh)		10
Ground nutmeg		5
Garlic powder		1
Rubbed sage		5
Sodium nitrite		$1^{1}/_{4}$
Sodium erythorbate (optional)		$4^{3}/_{8}$
Ice, chopped	100	

Procedure

Have meats well chilled at start of operation. Grind beef through the $1/8$-in. plate of the grinder; pork trimmings and cheeks through the $1/4$-in. plate. Transfer beef to a meat chopper, add $1/3$ of the ice, and start machine. Add salt previously mixed with sodium nitrite, sodium erythorbate, seasonings, and flavorings. Chop for 5 min. Add remaining ice. Then add flour, nonfat dry milk, and soy protein concentrate evenly over top of the mixer ingredients and run machine just long enough so that the binding ingredients are uniformly chopped into the emulsion.

In case an emulsifier is used: Put ground beef in a mechanical mixer; add all the ice followed by the salt mixture, and add, lastly, the binding ingredients. Run mixer until all ingredients are properly distributed then put mixture through the fine plate of an emulsifier. Transfer emulsion to a vacuum mixer, add ground pork meats, and, under 27 in. vacuum, run mixer for 3 min.

Pack finished meat mixture in 2-lb oblong aluminum freezing containers. For a nice gloss to the finished baked product, brush top of loaves with a 90% sugar solution. Close containers and freeze at $-20°F$.

Baking Optional.—Meat loaves may be baked before they are frozen. Bake in a rotating bakery oven with a starting temperature of 150°F. Gradually raise temperature to 185°F and bake until an internal meat temperature of 150°F is obtained. Close containers, prechill, and freeze at $-20°F$.

SOURCE: Stephan L. Komarik, 4810 Ronda, Coral Gables, Florida.

HAM LOAF

The formula given below is for the fresh-baked product for institutional food service. However, this is a product that can be frozen unbaked in aluminum foil loaf pans and marketed for retail as well as institutional trade.

Ingredients	Weight Lb	Oz	Approx Measure
Water or tomato juice			2½ qt
Fine, dry bread crumbs	2		
Salt		1	
Pepper			2 tsp
Dry mustard			2 tsp
Nonfat dry milk	1	8	(2¼ qt instant)
Whole eggs, beaten	2		(20)
Cured ham, ground	16		
Veal, ground	8		

YIELD: 10 3-lb loaves with 10 portions per loaf (100 servings)

Procedure

In the bowl of a mixer, let crumbs stand in liquid (water or tomato juice) until softened. Then, using paddle attachment on 1st speed, blend in salt, pepper, mustard, and dry milk. Then add beaten eggs and blend into mixture. Lastly, add ground ham and veal.

Pack in lightly greased loaf pans, scaling 3 lb per pan. Bake at 350°F for 1½ hr.

Note: Broiled peach halves are a nice accompaniment.

SOURCE: American Dry Milk Institute, 130 N. Franklin St., Chicago, Ill.

HOT PORK LOAF

The formula given below is for the fresh-baked product for institutional food service. However, this is a product that can be frozen unbaked in aluminum foil loaf pans and marketed for retail as well as institutional trade.

Ingredients	Weight Lb	Oz	Approx Measure
Dry bread crumbs	1		
Nonfat dry milk	1	8	(2¼ qt instant)
Salt		2½	
Pepper			1 tsp
Water			2 qt
Ground pork	18		
Finely chopped celery	2		
Finely chopped onions	8		
Chopped parsley			1¼ cups

YIELD: 10 3-lb loaves with 10 portions per loaf (100 servings)

Procedure

At low speed in a mixer with paddle attachment, blend together the bread crumbs, dry milk, salt, pepper, and water. Then add pork, celery, onions, and parsley and mix at low speed until ingredients are well blended. Pack in lightly greased loaf pans,

scaling 3 lb per pan. Bake at 350°F for 1½ hr. Let stand 15 min before slicing.

SOURCE: American Dry Milk Institute, 130 N. Franklin St., Chicago, Ill.

LIVER LOAF

The formula given below is for the fresh-baked product for institutional food service. However, this is a product that can be frozen unbaked in aluminum foil loaf pans and marketed for retail as well as institutional trade.

Ingredients	Weight Lb	Oz	Approx Measure
Sliced liver	20		
Onions			6 medium
Pork sausage	6		
Whole eggs, beaten	2		(30)
Soft diced bread cubes	3		(6 qt)
Nonfat dry milk	2		(3 qt instant)
Salt		2	
Pepper			1½ tsp
Water			3 qt

YIELD: 10 3-lb loaves with 10 portions per loaf (100 servings)

Procedure

Cook liver in lard or drippings until lightly browned. Cool and grind liver with onions. Then in a mixer at 1st speed and using a paddle attachment, blend liver and onions with the pork sausage, beaten eggs, and bread cubes.

Sprinkle dry milk, salt, and pepper on water and blend until smooth. Add to liver-sausage mixture and mix at 1st speed until all ingredients are uniformly disbursed.

Pack into greased loaf pans, scaling 3 lb per pan. Bake at 325°F for 1½ hr. Let stand a few minutes before slicing.

Note: Serve hot with tomato sauce. Serve sliced cold on salad plates.

SOURCE: American Dry Milk Institute, 130 N. Franklin St., Chicago, Ill.

FROZEN SALISBURY STEAK (BEST QUALITY)

Ingredients	Lb	Oz
Trimmed beef chucks or clods	250	
Trimmed steer flanks	250	
Salt	7	
Onion powder	1	4
Monosodium glutamate		10
Plant protein hydrolyzate		6
Dry soluble pepper		3

Procedure

Have meats well chilled to 34°–36°F at start of operation. Grind them through the 1-in. plate of the grinder and transfer to a mechanical mixer. Mix salt with seasonings and flavorings and add evenly over top of meat while mixer is running; mix for 3 min. Transfer to a meat truck and hold in a cooler (34°F) overnight. Then regrind through the $\frac{1}{8}$-in. plate of the grinder. Put meat through a patty-making machine to produce portions of desired weight and size. Pack in cartons suitable for freezing, separating portions with parchment. Transfer to a sharp freezer at –20°F.

SOURCE: Stephan L. Komarik, 4810 Ronda, Coral Gables, Florida.

FROZEN SALISBURY STEAK (COMMERCIAL GRADE)

Ingredients and procedure are the same as that given above for Frozen Salisbury Steak (Best Quality) except: In the first mixing operation, add 25 lb bread crumbs or soy grits, 50 lb water, and 1 lb salt. In case debittered soy grits are used, first soak grits in water until saturated.

SOURCE: Stephan L. Komarik, 4810 Ronda, Coral Gables, Florida.

FROZEN COMMINUTED PEPPER "STEAKS"

Ingredients	Lb	Oz
Beef chucks or clods, trimmed	250	
Steer flanks, trimmed	250	
Diced fresh green peppers	5	
Canned diced red peppers	5	
Salt	8	
Onion powder	1	4
Monosodium glutamate		10
Plant protein hydrolyzate		6
Garlic powder		1
Ground black pepper (34-mesh)		6
Ground celery seeds		1

Procedure

Have meats well chilled at start of operation. Grind meats through the 1-in. plate of the grinder. Transfer to a mixer; add salt previously mixed with flavorings and seasonings; then add diced red and green peppers; mix for 3 min. Dump mixture into meat truck and chill overnight in a cooler at 34°F. Next day, regrind mixture through the $\frac{1}{8}$-in. plate of the grinder. Transfer product to a molding machine and form "steaks" to desired shape and weight.

Pack in cartons suitable for freezing, placing parchment discs between pieces. Transfer to a sharp freezer at –20°F.

If "steaks" are to be breaded, then prefreeze before coating with batter and breading mix.

SOURCE: Stephan L. Komarik, 4810 Ronda, Coral Gables, Florida.

FROZEN COMMINUTED MUSHROOM "STEAKS"

Ingredients	Lb	Oz
Beef chucks or clods, trimmed	250	
Steer flanks, trimmed	250	
Salt	8	
Monosodium glutamate	1	
Onion powder		10
Plant protein hydrolyzate		8
Garlic powder		$\frac{1}{4}$
Powdered mushrooms (Sokol)		10
Canned mushroom stems and pieces with liquid	5 No. 10 tins	

Procedure

Have meats well chilled at start of operation. Grind meats through the 1-in. plate of the grinder. Transfer to a mixer; add salt previously mixed with flavorings and seasonings; then add mushrooms and liquid; mix for 3 min. Dump mixture into meat truck and chill overnight in a cooler at 34°F. Next day, regrind mixture through the $\frac{1}{8}$-in. plate of the grinder. Transfer product to a molding machine and form "steaks" to desired shape and weight.

Pack in cartons suitable for freezing, placing parchment discs between pieces. Transfer to a sharp freezer at –20°F.

If "steaks" are to be breaded, then prefreeze before coating with batter and breading mix.

SOURCE: Stephan L. Komarik, 4810 Ronda, Coral Gables, Florida.

FROZEN COMMINUTED ONION "STEAKS"

Ingredients	Lb	Oz
Beef chucks or clods, trimmed	250	
Steer flanks, trimmed	250	
Fresh onions	40	
(or, 1 lb of dehydrated minced onions reconstituted in 7 lb of water may be substituted)		
Salt	8	
Monosodium glutamate		10
Plant protein hydrolyzate		6
Black pepper (62-mesh)		6
Garlic powder		$\frac{1}{4}$

Procedure

Have meats well chilled at start of operation. Grind meats through the 1-in. plate of the grinder; onions through the 1/4-in. plate. Transfer meat and onions to a mechanical mixer; add salt previously mixed with the flavorings and seasonings; mix to distribute ingredients. Dump mixture in meat truck and transfer to a cooler at 34°F for overnight. Next day, regrind mixture through the 1/8-in. plate of the grinder. Transfer to a molding machine and form "steaks" in the desired shape and weight. Pack in cartons suitable for freezing, placing a parchment disc between each "steak" and transfer product to a sharp freezer at −20°F.

If "steaks" are to be breaded, then prefreeze before coating with batter and breading mix.

SOURCE: Stephan L. Komarik, 4810 Ronda, Coral Gables, Florida.

FROZEN CHEESEBURGERS

Ingredients	Lb	Oz
Trimmed steer flanks	250	
Beef chucks or clods	200	
Cheddar cheese	50	
Salt	6	8
Onion powder	1	
Monosodium glutamate		5
Plant protein hydrolyzate		3
Dry soluble pepper		5
Garlic powder		1/8

Procedure

Have meats well chilled at start of operation. Grind meats through the 1-in. plate of the grinder. Dice cheese into 1/2-in. cubes. Mix salt with seasonings and flavorings.

Transfer meat to a mechanical mixer and add cheese; start mixer and add salt mixture evenly over meat-cheese mixture. Mix approximately 3 min. Dump product in a meat truck and transfer it to a chill room at 34°–36°F for overnight. Next day regrind mixture through the 1/8-in. plate of the grinder. Form into patties in patty-making machine.

Pack patties, separated with parchment, into containers suitable for freezing in sizes for consumer and/or institutional use. Freeze at −20°F.

Patties also may be fried before freezing. The most efficient method is to run them through a tunnel heated by infrared rods or lamps, turning patties in midsection of the tunnel to fry evenly on both sides. Prechill before packaging for freezing.

SOURCE: Stephan L. Komarik, 4810 Ronda, Coral Gables, Florida.

FROZEN ROAST BEEF HASH PATTIES

Ingredients	Lb	Oz
Carcass beef (canner-cutter grade)	260	
Dehydrated potato dice (reconstituted weight: 240 lb)	50	
Ground black pepper (38-mesh)	1	
Salt	10	8
Onion powder	1	4
Mustard flour		4

Procedure

Grind beef through the 1/2-in. plate of the grinder. Soak potato dice in water at 180°F for 1 3/4 hr or until they increase in weight 480%; then drain. Transfer meat and potato dice to a mechanical mixer, add salt previously mixed with the remainder of the ingredients, and mix until ingredients are uniformly distributed. Remove from mixer and regrind product through the 1/4-in. plate of the grinder.

Stuff in "Easy Peel" fibrous casings and cook in water bath at 180°F for 3 hr. Chill in running cold water for 1 hr; then transfer in sausage trucks to a cooler at 34°F for overnight. Slice the product next day to the desired thickness and remove casing.

Package and Freeze

Pack slices in cartons by putting parchment discs between slices. Overwrap cartons with moisture-vaporproof paper and transfer to a sharp freezer at −20°F.

SOURCE: Stephan L. Komarik, 4810 Ronda, Coral Gables, Florida.

FROZEN CORNED BEEF HASH PATTIES

Follow the formula given above for **Frozen Roast Beef Hash Patties** except: dissolve 5/8 oz of sodium nitrite in 1 pt of water and add it to the meat in the mechanical mixer.

SOURCE: Stephan L. Komarik, 4810 Ronda, Coral Gables, Florida.

FROZEN VEAL PATTIES

Ingredients	Lb	Oz
Veal trimmings	400	
Beef suet	100	
Bread crumbs	25	
Salt	8	
Crushed ice	35	
Monosodium glutamate		10
Plant protein hydrolyzate		6
White pepper (60-mesh)		2 1/2

Procedure

Grind well-chilled veal together with suet through the 1-in. plate of the grinder and transfer to a mechanical mixer. Add ice, bread crumbs, and salt which has been previously mixed with the flavorings and pepper; mix to uniformly distribute all ingredients. To keep temperature at a low level (32°–34°F) use chipped Dry Ice (approximately 4–5 lb per 100 lb meat) and regrind through the $1/8$-in. plate of the grinder. Transfer meat to a molding machine and form patties or portions to the desired size and weight.

Pack in cartons suitable for freezing with parchment separating portions. Transfer to a sharp freezer at – 20°F.

If product is to be breaded, freeze first, then coat with batter and breading mix before packaging.

SOURCE: Stephan L. Komarik, 4810 Ronda, Coral Gables, Florida.

FROZEN HAM PATTIES

Ingredients	Lb	Oz
Fresh boneless hams	500	
Iced water	30	
Salt	10	
Cane sugar	2	8
Tetrasodium pyrophosphate	1	4
Sodium nitrite		$1^{1}/_4$
Sodium erythorbate		$4^{3}/_8$

Procedure

Skin, defat surface, and bone hams. Surface layer of fat should not be over $1/4$-in. thick; fat content of the boned hams should not be higher than 20%. Cut hams into 1-lb chunks and spread evenly on smoke screens; move into a cold smokehouse and smoke with heavy smudge for 15–20 min. House temperature should not be over 75°F.

Note: Smoking operation can be eliminated by using a true smoke flavor, diluting it in the ice water and adding it in the iced water at the first mixing operation (below).

Grind meat through the 1-in. plate of the grinder, then transfer to a mechanical mixer. Add salt previously mixed with dry ingredients; then add iced water and mix for 3 min. Dump mixture in a meat truck and transfer to a cooler at 34°F for overnight cure. Next day regrind mixture through the $1/4$-in. plate of the grinder and remix under 27 in. vacuum for 2 min. Form patties to desired shape and weight through a forming machine.

Pack in cartons suitable for freezing, placing parchment discs between patties; transfer to a sharp freezer at – 20°F.

If ham patties are breaded, prefreeze before coating with batter and breading mix.

SOURCE: Stephan L. Komarik, 4810 Ronda, Coral Gables, Florida.

FROZEN BREADED HAM STICKS

Ingredients	Lb	Oz
Fresh boneless hams	400	
Fresh ham shanks	100	
Iced water	30	
Salt	10	
Cane sugar	2	8
Tetrasodium pyrophosphate	1	4
Sodium nitrite		$1^{1}/_4$
Sodium erythorbate		$4^{3}/_8$

Procedure

Use heavy hams, 25 lb and over. Skin, defat and bone. Surface layer of fat should not be over $1/4$-in. thick. Have meat well chilled at start of operation (34°F). Grind the shank meat through the $1/8$-in. plate of the grinder, hams through the $3/8$-in. plate. Transfer ground meats to a vacuum mixer and with the addition of salt, previously mixed with the dry ingredients, and iced water, mix for 3 min under 27 in. vacuum. Dump meat in a meat truck and transfer to cooler at 36°F for overnight cure. Next day, remix cured meat in a vacuum mixer under 27 in. vacuum for 8–10 min. Stuff mixture in 4 × 4 × 24 in. oblong paper-lined molds and cook in preheated water at 160°F for $3^{1}/_2$ hr. Then chill immediately in cold water until internal meat temperature is reduced to 100°F. Transfer to a chill room at 32°–34°F for thorough chilling.

After thorough chilling, remove product from molds and, in a cutting device, cut loaves into $2^{1}/_2$ × $3/4$ × $3/4$-in. sticks. Prefreeze sticks before breading. Then coat with batter and breading mix. Pack in cartons suitable for freezing, separating layers with parchment sheets. Freeze at – 20°F.

SOURCE: Stephan L. Komarik, 4810 Ronda, Coral Gables, Florida.

FROZEN BREADED MOCK CHICKEN LEGS

Ingredients	Lb	Oz
Lean pork trimmings	150	
Veal trimmings	350	
Cracker flour (fine)	10	
Iced water	10	
Salt	6	4
Monosodium glutamate		10
Ground celery seeds		$1^{1}/_2$

Procedure

Have meat well chilled (34°–36°F) at start of operation. Grind meats through the 1-in. plate of the grinder; transfer to a mixer; start machine and add iced water; then add salt previously mixed with the flavorings, adding mixture evenly over the meat. Add cracker flour and let machine run until the product is thoroughly mixed (about 3 min). Then regrind mixture through the $^1/_{16}$-in. plate of the grinder. Transfer to a cooler (34°F) and chill overnight. Next day, remix mixture in a vacuum mixer under 27 in. vacuum just long enough to make mixture pliable for the molding machine. Mold into "drumsticks" of shape, size, and weight desired. Coat with batter and breading mix and insert a skewer in small end of each and package in cartons suitable for freezing. Freeze at –20°F.

Produce may be fried before freezing: After molding and breading operation, fry in oil at 350°F until internal temperature reaches 160°F. Prechill, insert skewers, package, and freeze.

SOURCE: Stephan L. Komarik, 4810 Ronda, Coral Gables, Florida.

FROZEN ITALIAN SPAGHETTI AND MEAT BALLS WITH SOY PROTEIN CONCENTRATE

Prepare Meat Balls

Ingredients	%
Beef trimmings and plates	71.13
Soy protein concentrate (Ultra-Soy 200, cc)	4.18
Water	8.37
Grated Parmesan cheese	2.93
Dehydrated parsley flakes	0.05
Garlic powder	0.10
Oregano, crushed	0.16
Bread crumbs	0.63
Milk	11.30
Salt	0.84
Black pepper	0.10
Dehydrated minced onions	0.21
	100.00

1. Presoak soy protein concentrate (Ultra-Soy), bread crumbs, Parmesan cheese, and seasonings in milk and water.
2. Blend the meat and presoaked mixture in the silent cutter. Then grind through the $^3/_{16}$-in. plate of the grinder.
3. Form into meat balls on Hollymatic 200.
4. Brown the meat balls and cook until done. Drain.

Prepare Spaghetti and Sauce

Ingredients	%
Chopped onions	3.34
Garlic cloves, minced	0.02
Olive oil	2.68
Canned tomatoes	33.45
Tomato paste	25.09
Water	16.72
Sugar	0.84
Salt	0.88
Black pepper	0.08
Bay leaf	0.01
Crushed oregano	0.17
Uncooked spaghetti	16.72
Grated Parmesan cheese as garnish	
	100.00

Spaghetti.—Cook spaghetti in boiling salted water until tender; drain; then rinse in cold water.

Sauce.—Cook onions and garlic in hot oil until tender but not brown. Add remaining ingredients and simmer uncovered for 30 min. Remove bay leaf.

Package for Freezing

Put measured amounts of spaghetti and meat balls in bottom of cartons or containers suitable for freezing; using sizes for retail or institutional trade. Cover with measured amount of sauce. Close cartons or containers and freeze at –20°F.

SOURCE: Far-Mar-Co, Research Division, 960 N. Halstead, Hutchinson, Kansas.

FROZEN COCKTAIL MEAT BALLS

Ingredients	Lb	Oz
Boneless, skinless picnics	340	
Stale white bread, sliced	70	
Whole fresh milk	35	
Frozen whole eggs, partially defrosted	35	
Wheat flour	10	
Salt	7	
Monosodium glutamate	1	
Plant protein hydrolyzate		8
Onion powder		10
Garlic powder		$^1/_2$
Black pepper (34-mesh)		5

Procedure

Use fresh picnics averaging 6–8 lb. Bone and skin, but leave fat on. Have meat well chilled to 34°F at start of operation. Grind picnics through the $^3/_8$-in. plate of the grinder. Break up partially defrosted eggs; transfer to a mechanical mixer, add milk, bread, and flour and run mixer until bread absorbs the moisture; then grind through the $3/8$-in. plate of the grinder. Transfer egg-bread mixture back to the mixer and add the ground meat. Start mixer; slowly add salt previously mixed with the rest of the seasonings, and flavoring ingredients; mix just long enough to distribute materials uniformly. Chill overnight at 34°F.

Transfer product to a ball forming machine and form into $3/4$-oz balls. Then deep fry or broil.

If balls are deep fried, fry at 350°F for 3 min. Or, if infrared rod broiling equipment is available, broil balls to a 30% shrinkage. Drain balls of excess fat and prechill before packaging.

Pack in Cellophane-lined freezing cartons and sharp freeze at −20°F.

SOURCE: Stephan L. Komarik, 4810 Ronda, Coral Gables, Florida.

FROZEN ALL-PURPOSE MEAT BALLS

Ingredients	Lb	Oz
Beef chucks, trimmed	150	
Steer flanks, trimmed	150	
Fresh onions	30	
(or, 8 lb of onion powder and 22 lb of water may be substituted)		
Fresh whole eggs	15	
Cracker meal or bread crumbs	40	
Salt	7	
Ground black pepper (38-mesh)		4

Procedure

Grind chucks, flanks, onions, and frozen eggs through the $1/8$-in. plate of the grinder. Transfer to a mechanical mixer; add salt previously mixed with pepper; while mixer is in operation add cracker meal or bread crumbs evenly to the meat mixture; mix for 3 min. Form balls into desired size through a forming machine and dust with fine cracker meal as the balls come down the conveyor so they will not stick together. Freeze balls through a tunnel freezer before packaging. Then pack in cartons suitable for freezing with separating sheets of parchment. Transfer to freezer.

To Serve

Product needs no defrosting prior to cooking. Fry in deep fat at 350°F to internal temperature of 160°F. May be served with spaghetti sauce, with brown gravy and noodles, etc., as a main dinner dish.

SOURCE: Stephan L. Komarik, 4810 Ronda, Coral Gables, Florida.

BARBECUED MEAT BALLS

The formula given below is for the fresh-made product for institutional food service. However, this is a product that can be frozen in appropriate packages for freezing and marketed for retail as well as institutional trade.

Prepare Meat Balls

Ingredients	Weight Lb	Oz	Approx Measure
Ground beef	16		
Ground pork	6		
Soft bread cubes	2½		(5 qt)
Nonfat dry milk	2		(3 qt instant)
Whole eggs	1½		(12)
Salt	1½		
Pepper			1½ tsp
Monosodium glutamate			1½ tbsp
Water			2 qt

YIELD: 200 2-oz balls

Using mixer at 1st speed and paddle attachment, mix together all ingredients; do not overmix (overmixing will cause meats to "smear"). Form into balls using No. 16 scoop (or put through a forming machine to make 2-oz balls). Place balls in counter pan, close together, in one layer only. Cover with sauce (below).

Prepare Barbecue Sauce

Ingredients	Lb	Oz	Approx Measure
Lemons, thinly sliced			3
Chopped onions	1		
Chili powder			¼ cup
Celery seed			¾ cup
Brown sugar		¾	(2 cups)
Vinegar			3 cups
Worcestershire sauce			¾ cup
Catsup			3 qt
Water			1 gal.

Reserve lemon slices to lay over top of meat balls. Mix remaining ingredients and heat to boiling. Cover meat balls with sauce and add lemon slices. Bake at 325°F for 1 hr.

SOURCE: American Dry Milk Institute, 130 N. Franklin St., Chicago, Ill.

SWEDISH MEAT BALLS IN WHITE SAUCE WITH SOY PROTEIN CONCENTRATE

The formula given below is for the fresh-made product for institutional food service. However, this is a product that can be frozen in appropriate packages for freezing and marketed for retail as well as institutional trade.

Prepare Meat Balls

Ingredients	%
Beef trimmings and plates 70/30	56.76
Pork trimmings 80/20	17.47
Soy protein concentrate (Ultra-Soy 100's, caramel)	4.37
Water	8.73
Bread crumbs	0.87
Light cream	8.73
Dehydrated minced onions	1.75
Salt	1.09
White pepper	0.06
Nutmeg	0.11
Allspice	0.03
Dried parsley flakes	0.03
	100.00

1. Presoak soy protein concentrate (Ultra-Soy), bread crumbs, and all seasonings for the meat balls in water and light cream.
2. Blend the meat and soaked mixture in the silent cutter. Then grind through the 3/16-in. plate of the grinder.
3. Form into meatballs on the Hollymatic 200.

Prepare Sauce

Ingredients	%
Margarine or butter	10.07
Flour	5.04
Milk	83.96
Salt	0.63
White pepper	0.10
Nutmeg	0.05
Dried parsley flakes	0.05
Allspice	0.10
	100.00

1. Melt margarine or butter, add flour, salt, pepper, nutmeg, and allspice.
2. Stir mixture into milk.
3. Cook and stir constantly until sauce is thickened. Add parsley flakes.

Combine Meat Balls and Sauce

Brown the meat balls and cook until done. Drain well. Then combine meat balls and sauce.

SOURCE: Far-Mar-Co, Research Division, 960 N. Halstead, Hutchinson, Kansas.

SWEDISH MEAT BALLS

The formula given below is for the fresh-made product for institutional food service. However, this is a product that can be frozen in appropriate packages for freezing and marketed for retail as well as institutional trade.

Prepare Meat Balls

Ingredients	Weight Lb	Oz	Approx Measure
Fresh bread cubes	1		(2 qt)
Nonfat dry milk	1		(1½ qt instant)
Water			2 qt
Whole eggs, beaten	1	4	(10–12)
Chopped onions		12	
Salt		3	
Pepper			2 tbsp
Ground beef	8		
Ground pork	6		
Ground veal	4		

YIELD: 400 1-oz balls

In bowl of mixer, let bread cubes, dry milk, and water stand until bread is quite soft. Then add beaten eggs, onions, salt and pepper and blend at low speed with paddle attachment until ingredients are well mixed. Meats should be ground very fine. Add meats to bread-milk mixture and blend to a uniform mixture (do not overmix). Using a No. 40 scoop, form into small balls (or use a forming machine and make 1-oz balls). Brown balls in hot fat. Remove; drain; and place in layers in baking pans. Cover with the following gravy.

Prepare Gravy and Bake

Ingredients	Weight Lb	Oz	Approx Measure
Drippings from frying meat balls	1		(2 cups)
Flour		12	
Nonfat dry milk		12	(4½ cups instant)
Salt			1½ tbsp
Pepper			1½ tsp
Warm water			1½ gal.

Blend flour, dry milk, and seasonings with small amount of water until mixture is smooth. Add to remaining water and drippings. Cook, while stirring, until mixture is hot and beginning to thicken. Pour over meat balls in baking pans. Bake for 1 hr at 325°F.

SOURCE: American Dry Milk Institute, 130 N. Franklin St., Chicago, Ill.

SAUCES AND GRAVIES

FROZEN SPAGHETTI MEAT SAUCE

Prepare Meat

Ingredients	Lb
Trimmed beef flanks	50
Lean beef chucks	50

Grind flanks and chucks separately through the ¼-in. plate of the grinder. Put ground flanks in a steam-jacketed kettle and braise until fat is rendered out. Then add ground chucks and braise with steady stirring until meat is free flowing.

Prepare Sauce

Ingredients	Lb	Oz
Tomato paste (26–28% solids)	340	
Cane sugar	45	
Cheddar cheese (aged)	25	
Wheat flour	20	
Cornstarch	10	
Bread crumbs	30	
Salt	23	
Onion powder	3	
Plant protein hydrolyzate	9	
Dry soluble seasoning mix (see below)	1	8
Bicarbonate of soda	1	8
Garlic powder		6
Ground red pepper		4
Ground sweet basil		2
Imitation cheese flavor		1½
Water to make 200 gal.		

Dry Soluble Seasoning Mix	Cc	Lb
Oleoresin capsicum	4.00	
Oleoresin ginger	1.40	
Oleoresin mace	0.16	
Oil of dill	0.20	
Oil of cloves	3.60	
Oil of cardamom	0.80	
Oil of cassia	2.40	
Oil of pimiento	26.40	
Oil of bay	0.80	
Salt		2

Mix all ingredients thoroughly with the salt. Use 4 gm per 1 gal. sauce.

Put 200 gal. of water in a steam-jacketed kettle; make a mark at water level on a measuring stick so finished gallonage can be gaged. Drain water. Grind cheese through the ¼-in. plate of the grinder. Mix together sugar, salt, flour, cornstarch, bread crumbs, and seasonings.

Put 150 gal. of water in a large steam-jacketed kettle. Add tomato paste, bicarbonate of soda, cheese, and the braised meat together with its juices. Agitate sauce with a "Lightning" mixer, then slowly add salt-seasoning mixture. Bring sauce volume up to 200 gal. and raise temperature to 200°F. Cook 20 min.

Package and Freeze

Package product for consumer use in boil-in-bag vacuumized bags (1 lb net) and/or institutional packs of 5-lb net. Prechill product after packaging at 34°–36°F before freezing at −20°F.

SOURCE: Stephan L. Komarik, 4810 Ronda, Coral Gables, Florida.

FROZEN SLOPPY JOE

Ingredients	Lb	Oz
Carcass beef (canner-cutter grade)	200	
Beef flanks, trimmed	100	
Tomato paste	147	
Sweet pickle relish	48	
Cider vinegar (45-grain)	36	
Wheat flour	12	
Light brown sugar	12	
Cane sugar	12	
Monosodium glutamate	1	
Ground chili pepper	7	
Ground camino seeds	1	
Plant protein hydrolyzate		10
Onion powder		12
Garlic powder		4
Black pepper		4
Red pepper		1
Ground oregano		7
Ground cloves		1½
Ground cinnamon		1½
Smoke flavor (optional; use sparingly to taste)		

Procedure

Grind beef through the ¼-in. plate of the grinder and transfer to a steam-jacketed kettle. Add 30 lb of water and braise meat with steady stirring.

Make a thorough mixture of all dry ingredients including flour. To the braised meat add tomato paste, relish, and vinegar. Then, with steady stirring, add dry mixture to the batch. Bring temperature up to 200°F and cook for 15 min.

For consumer use: pack in boil-in-bag Mylar bags and close under vacuum. For institutional use: pack in 5-lb freezing containers. Prechill product at 34°–36°F before transferring to a sharp freezer at −20°F.

SOURCE: Stephan L. Komarik, 4810 Ronda, Coral Gables, Florida.

FROZEN ALL-PURPOSE BROWN GRAVY

Ingredients	Gal.	Lb	Oz
Water	70		
Tomato paste (28% solids)		10	
Wheat flour		10	
Cornstarch		6	
Cracker flour (fine)		6	
Rendered beef fat		12	
Salt		4	
Beef extract		5	
Plant protein hydrolyzate		5	
Monosodium glutamate		2	
Onion powder		3	
Garlic powder			1/4
Spanish paprika		2	
Dry soluble pepper		2	
Ground celery seed		1	
Caramel color		2	4

Procedure

Measure 70 gal. of water in a steam-jacketed kettle and make a mark at water level on a measuring stick so finished gallonage can be gaged. Drain water.

Put 60 gal. of water in the kettle and heat to 180°F. Add tomato paste, beef fat, beef extract, plant protein hydrolyzate, and caramel color. Add salt previously mixed with the remainder of ingredients except flours and starch. In a bakery mixer, make a slurry free of lumps with the remaining water (10 gal.) and the flours and starch. Add slurry to the batch while agitating with a "Lightning" mixer. Bring volume up to 70 gal. and cook for 15–20 min at 200°F.

For consumer use: pack in boil-in-bag Mylar bags, vacuumize and seal. For institutional use: pack in 5-lb containers suitable for freezing. Transfer product to chill room at 34°–36°F and prechill before transferring to a sharp freezer at -20°F.

SOURCE: Stephan L. Komarik, 4810 Ronda, Coral Gables, Florida.

FROZEN NATURAL PAN GRAVY EXTENDER

This product is used as an extender of natural meat juices rendered during roasting. Also, by adding thickening to the thawed product, it can be used as the gravy on hot roast beef or pork sandwiches.

Ingredients	Gal.	Lb	Oz
Water	50		
Beef extract (S.A.)		3	
Rendered kidney suet		6	
Salt		4	
Monosodium glutamate		1	8

Plant protein hydrolyzate	12
Onion powder	2
Ground turmeric (Alleppey)	1/2
Ground celery seeds	1/4
Spanish paprika	1/4
Ground white pepper	1/2
Garlic powder	1/16
Caramel color, if desired	

Procedure

Put water in a steam-jacketed kettle and heat to 200°F. Add beef extract dissolved in 1 gal. of hot water, the fat from the rendered suet, and the remaining ingredients. Cook 15 min. If a darker shade is desired in the finished product, add a small amount of caramel coloring.

Pack for institutional use in 5-lb water-tight containers suitable for freezing. Prechill product before freezing at -20°F.

SOURCE: Stephan L. Komarik, 4810 Ronda, Coral Gables, Florida.

FROZEN GRAVY CONCENTRATE

Ingredients	(%)
Starch (Sta-O-Paque)	12.0
Nonfat dry milk	3.0
Sweet whey solids	3.0
Corn syrup solids (Star-Dri 24R)	3.75
Rendered beef fat	2.20
Salt	3.58
Monosodium glutamate	0.60
Spice blend (Asmus 9632)	5.13
Water	66.74

Procedure

Disperse all the ingredients in cold water. Heat to 130°F and hold until fat is completely melted. Heat to 190°F and hold for 5 min. Cool, package, and freeze.

To Use Product

Add 3 parts water to 1 part concentrate; heat and serve.

SOURCE: A. E. Staley Mfg. Co., Decatur, Ill.

BEEF GRAVY FOR FROZEN MEAT PIES

Ingredients	Lb	Gal.
Beef broth	375–390	
Derivatized cross-bonded waxy corn starch	16	
Wheat flour	9 1/2	
Tomato purée	(as desired)	

Fat (part beef, part margarine)	15	
Water		1-2
Meat pie seasonings	4	

Procedure

(1) Slurry starch and flour in water.
(2) Heat broth to 190°F.
(3) Add starch suspension and cook 5-10 min.
(4) Add purée and fat.
(5) Add pie seasonings.
(6) Fill into pie shells in desired proportion with meat and vegetables.

SOURCE: CPC International, Inc., Industrial Division, Englewood Cliffs, N.J.

SAUCE FOR FROZEN CREAMED CHIPPED BEEF

This product makes a sauce for creamed chipped beef that has a smooth, creamy consistency; does not become grainy upon thawing; retards syneresis; and maintains sufficient viscosity when heated.

Ingredients	%
Whole milk (3.5% fat)	25.00
Nonfat dry milk	3.50
Vegetable oil	2.00
Starch (Col Flo 67)	2.00
Stabilizer (Germantown No. 242)	0.75
Water and seasonings	66.75

Procedure

1. Dry mix the stabilizer with other dry ingredients and disperse mixture in the water and oil with good agitation.
2. Heat mixture to 180°F and hold for 5 min.
3. Fill into containers with chipped beef, using 1 part beef to 4 parts sauce. Freeze or refrigerate.

SOURCE: Germantown Manufacturing Company, 505 Parkway, Broomall, Pa.

AMERICAN-STYLE FOREIGN DISHES

FROZEN CONCENTRATED BRICK CHILI CON CARNE

Ingredients	Lb	Oz
Beef (canner-cutter grade)	170	
Beef kidney suet	130	
Fresh ground onions	20	
Water	28	
Tomato purée (sp. gr. 1.045)	40	
Domestic paprika (HCV)	5	
Salt	15	
Wheat flour	53	
Ground chili pepper	14	8
Ground camino seeds	1	12
Ground black pepper		4
Ground oregano	8	8
Onion powder	2	4
Garlic powder		4

Procedure

Grind beef through the 3/8-in. plate of the grinder; suet through the 1/4-in. plate. Render suet in a steam-jacketed kettle; then add beef and onions and braise meat until done. Make a thorough mixture of wheat flour, salt, and seasonings; with steady stirring, add mixture gradually to the braised meat and stir until the product is smooth. Add water, tomato purée; with slow agitation, cook product 15-20 min at 200°F.

Fat for Topping Bricks.—Heat 40 lb of beef fat and 2 lb of lard flakes in a steam-jacketed kettle to 240°F. Add 2 lb Spanish paprika and cook for 15 min. Strain fat through a cloth.

Pack and Freeze.—For institutional use, pack in 5-lb bricks in oblong freezing cartons or in molds and allow to remain at room temperature until surfaces harden, then pour enough of the hot fat on top of each brick to cover the surface (about 1/8-in. thick).

For consumer use, pack in 1-lb bricks in freezing cartons or aluminum foil containers of suitable size, topping each brick with the melted fat after surface hardens, as described above.

Freeze product at -20°F.

To Use Product

This is a concentrated product. To use, add 2 qt of water to each 5-lb brick and heat to serving temperature. Add 4/5 pt of water to the consumer-sized brick weighing 1 lb and heat to serving.

SOURCE: Stephan L. Komarik, 4810 Ronda, Coral Gables, Florida.

FROZEN CONCENTRATED BRICK CHILI CON CARNE WITH BEANS

Except for the addition of beans, ingredients and procedure are identical with that given above for **Frozen Concentrated Brick Chili Con Carne.**

Use Michigan Red or California Pink dried beans. For the ingredients given above, 210 lb of cooked beans will be needed.

Soak beans overnight in running cold water so beans do not sour during soaking period. Cook beans in fresh water in a steam-jacketed kettle until beans are tender. Drain cooking water and let beans dry in the kettle before adding them to the batch. Add beans at the end of the cooking operation and thoroughly incorporate beans into the batch ingredients.

SOURCE: Stephan L. Komarik, 4810 Ronda, Coral Gables, Florida.

BEEF ENCHILADAS WITH SOY PROTEIN CONCENTRATE

Prepare Sauce

Ingredients	%
Minced onions	3.2
Fat	3.6
Flour	1.3
Tomato purée	50.9
Garlic powder	0.1
Chili pepper	1.0
Cumin	0.5
Salt	0.8
Tobasco sauce	0.4
Water	38.2
	100.0

1. Cook onions in fat until golden.
2. Add flour, water, tomato purée, and seasonings.
3. Simmer 10–15 min until slightly thickened.

Prepare Enchiladas and Filling

Ingredients	%
Ground beef trimmings	57.2
Soy protein concentrate (Ultra-Soy minced caramel)	5.0
Rehydration water	10.1
Onions, chopped	5.0
Salt	1.3
Cheddar cheese, shredded	20.1
Chili pepper	1.3
	100.0

1. Rehydrate soy protein concentrate (Ultra-Soy) in water.
2. Brown beef and onions; add rehydrated soy protein and seasonings.
3. Stir in shredded cheese.
4. Dip corn tortillas in warm sauce to soften and coat them.

5. Put a rounded tablespoon of filling on each tortilla and roll.

Package and Freeze

Using oblong aluminum foil freezing containers, place rolled tortillas in each. Add measured amount of sauce. Sprinkle shredded cheese over top. Close containers and freeze at −20°F.

SOURCE: Far-Mar-Co, Research Division, 960 N. Halstead, Hutchinson, Kansas.

LASAGNA WITH SOY PROTEIN CONCENTRATE

The formula given below is for the fresh-made product for institutional food service. However, this is a product that can be frozen in appropriate packages for freezing and marketed for retail as well as institutional trade.

Ingredients	%
Beef trimmings (30% fat) ground through $^3/_{16}$ -in. plate	16.76
Soy protein concentrate (Ultra-Soy Minced, caramel)	1.00
Rehydration water (iced)	2.51
Tomato paste	16.34
Water	16.76
Dehydrated minced onions	0.67
Bay leaves, crumbled	0.01
Dehydrated parsley flakes	0.04
Basil	0.05
Oregano	0.05
Salt	0.34
Black pepper	0.10
Garlic powder	0.10
Lasagna noodles	10.89
Small curd cottage cheese	16.34
Mozarella cheese, shredded	16.34
Parmesan cheese, grated	1.70
	100.00

Procedure

1. Rehydrate the soy protein concentrate (Ultra-Soy), salt, pepper, garlic powder, onions, bay leaves parsley, basil, and oregano in ice water.
2. Add rehydrated soy protein concentrate and seasoning to the ground meat and combine in the mixer 2–3 min.
3. Brown meat stirring constantly.
4. Add tomato paste and water. Mix well. Cover and simmer 1 hr over low heat.
5. Cook noodles.
6. Place 1/3 of meat sauce in bottom of greased pans.

7. Lay half of the noodle strips on top of sauce. Add half the cottage cheese. Top with half the mozarella cheese.

8. Repeat layers topping with the remaining $1/3$ of the meat sauce.

9. Sprinkle Parmesan cheese on top.

10. Bake at 375°F. for 30 min.

SOURCE: Far-Mar-Co, Research Division, 960 N. Halstead, Hutchinson, Kansas.

FROZEN BEEF STROGANOFF

Ingredients	Lb	Oz
Beef, top round (cut into strips $1^1/4$ in. long, $1/2$ in. thick)	6	
Peanut oil		7
Onions, chopped fine	2	
Butter		$3^1/2$
Hungarian paprika		$1/7$
Water		32
Dry red wine		$3^1/12$
Salt		1
Pepper		$1/12$
Dry sherry		5
Modified starch		$3^1/2$
Modified cream		5
Evaporated milk		15
Instant onion powder		$1/2$
Instant garlic powder		$1/4$
Mushrooms (sliced lengthwise and sautéed)		$1^1/2$

Procedure

Sauté beef strips in hot oil. Place in stew pan. Sauté onions in butter until transparent and add to meat. Add paprika, water, and wine. Cover and simmer for $1^1/4$ hr or until tender. Add salt and pepper. Remove meat from sauce. There should be 2 qt plus 1 cup of sauce. Bring sauce to a boil. Slowly add sherry to the modified starch and stir until smooth and add modified cream. Add starch-cream mixture to sauce; heat to 180°F stirring constantly. Add evaporated milk, powdered onion, and garlic and blend well.

Packaging.—In 12 × 8 in. vacuum pouches, put $6^1/2$ oz of beef strips and 1 oz sautéed mushroom slices; over these ingredients evenly distribute 7 oz sauce. Blast freeze (30 min).

YIELD: 10 pouches with above ingredients

Cooked noodles (5 oz) may be packaged and frozen separately in 8 × $6^1/2$ in. vacuum pouches and assembled with the packaged Stroganoff for retail distribution or institutional use.

SOURCE: *Freezing Preservation of Foods, 4th Edition, Vol. 4* by Tressler *et al.* published by Avi Publishing Co., Westport, Conn.

FROZEN BEEF STROGANOFF

Ingredients	Lb	Oz	Pt
Carcass beef (good grade)	580		
Sour cream	30		
Wheat flour	16		
Canned sliced mushrooms	12		
Tomato purée (sp. gr. 1.035)	6		
Spanish paprika	2		
Onion powder	1		
Salt	6		
Monosodium glutamate		12	
Plant protein hydrolyzate		12	
Garlic powder		2	
Dry soluble pepper (salt base)		8	
Worcestershire sauce		8	
Cooking sherry			4
Water to make final gravy volume of 38 gal.			

Procedure

Put 38 gal. of water in a steam-jacketed kettle; make a mark at water level on a measuring stick so finished gallonage can be gaged. Drain water.

Dice beef into 1-in. cubes. Transfer to the kettle and add 5 gal. of water. Heat to 180°F and cook until beef is tender. Shrinkage in the cooked beef will be approximately 45% resulting in 300 lb cooked beef. Remove meat and strain stock through a fine mesh wire sieve.

Return stock to the jacketed kettle; heat to 180°F. Make a slurry free of lumps with 3 gal. of water and the flour. Add slurry to the stock with steady agitation. Thoroughly mix together salt and the dry ingredients and add to sauce; mix to uniformly distribute seasonings. Then add sour cream, Worcestershire sauce, tomato purée, mushrooms, and lastly the sherry. Bring volume of gravy up to 38 gal.; raise temperature to 200°F and cook 15 min.

Pack in boil-in-bag 1-lb-net Mylar bags: put 8 oz beef in bag and distribute 8 oz gravy evenly over the meat; vacuumize and seal bags. Product may also be packaged in 5-lb containers suitable for freezing for institutional use. In either case, prechill product at 34°–36°F before transferring packages to a sharp freezer at −20°F.

SOURCE: Stephan L. Komarik, 4810 Ronda, Coral Gables, Florida.

FROZEN HUNGARIAN BEEF GULYAS

Ingredients	Lb	Oz	Qt
Beef (shank meat, trimmed and cut in $1^1/4$-in. cubes)	10		
Oil		7	
Butter		$1/2$	
Onions, chopped	2		

Hungarian paprika	$^1/_3$
Salt	1
Sachet bag:	
3 cloves	
1 bay leaf	
$^1/_{10}$ oz rosemary	
$^1/_{10}$ oz thyme	
Tomato sauce	$10^1/_2$
Water	2
Red wine	8
Modified starch	1
Instant onion powder	$^1/_2$
Instant garlic powder	$^1/_4$

YIELD: 10 portions of 10 oz meat, 7 oz sauce

Procedure

Heat oil and butter in deep pan; add onions and sauté until transparent. Then add meat cubes, paprika, salt, and sachet bag and blend well. Cover and simmer $^1/_2$ hr, occasionally stirring mixture from bottom. Add tomato sauce and water; cover and simmer $1^1/_2$ hr or until meat is tender. Remove meat from sauce. Bring sauce to a boil and remove sachet bag. Slowly add wine to modified starch and stir until smooth. Add starch-wine mixture to sauce and heat to 180°F stirring constantly. Add onion and garlic powders and blend well.

Package in 12 × 8 in. vacuum pouches with 10 oz of meat and add 7 oz sauce distributed evenly over meat. Blast freeze (30 min).

Cooked spaetzles (Hungarian style noodles) may be packaged (5 oz) and frozen separately in 8 × 6$^1/_2$ in. vacuum pouches and assembled with the Beef Gulyas for retail distribution or institutional use.

SOURCE: *Freezing Preservation of Foods, 4th Edition, Vol. 4* by Tressler *et al.* published by Avi Publishing Co., Westport, Conn.

FROZEN HUNGARIAN-STYLE GOULASH

Ingredients	Lb	Oz
Beef chucks, clods, or rounds (good grade)	250	
Fresh onions	100	
Vegetable shortening	10	
Tomato purée (sp. gr. 1.045)	16	
Salt	5	
Wheat flour or cracker meal	6	
Fresh green peppers	5	
Spanish paprika	5	
Ground black pepper		5
Ground caraway seeds		1
Ground red pepper		1
Garlic powder		$^1/_4$
Monosodium glutamate		8

Procedure

If chucks are used, trim cords, skin, and connective tissue. Dice beef into 1-in. cubes. Dice fresh onions through the dicing machine into $^1/_4$-in. cubes. Core green peppers and dice into $^1/_2$-in. squares.

Put shortening in a steam-jacketed kettle; add onions and, with steady stirring, fry until golden yellow; add meat and cook until meat is done, stirring gently with a wooden paddle. Mix salt with flour or meal, monosodium glutamate, and seasonings; add mixture to meat and mix well. Then add tomato purée and green pepper. Cook an additional 15 min, stirring gently.

Drain and weigh sauce. Remove meat from kettle and weigh. Estimate ratio of sauce to meat and pack accordingly, putting meat in containers first and then evenly distributing sauce over meat. For consumer use: pack in boil-in-bag Mylar bags (1 lb net) and close bags under vacuum. For institutional use: pack in 5-lb Cellophane-lined freezer cartons. Prechill product before freezing at -20°F.

SOURCE: Stephan L. Komarik, 4810 Ronda, Coral Gables, Florida.

BEEF STROGANOFF (FORMULA NO. 1) WITH SOY PROTEIN CONCENTRATE

The formula given below is for the fresh-made product for institutional food service. However, this is a product that can be frozen in appropriate packages for freezing and marketed for retail as well as institutional trade.

Ingredients	%
Round steak, cut in $^1/_2$-in. cubes	35
Soy protein concentrate (Ultra-Soy 100's, caramel)	2
Water to rehydrate the protein concentrate	4
Flour	2
Salt	0.7
Paprika	0.15
Shortening	4
Chopped onions	5
Beef consommé	23
Water	9
Mushrooms, sliced	6
Sour cream	9
Garlic salt	0.15
	100.00

Procedure

1. Mix flour, salt, paprika, and garlic salt. Add meat to coat. Reserve the remaining mixture of flour.

2. Rehydrate the soy protein concentrate (Ultra-Soy) in water 15-20 min.

3. Heat shortening. Add meat and brown well. Add onions and rehydrated soy protein concentrate (Ultra-Soy) and cook until onions are transparent.

4. Add remaining flour mixture, water, and consommé. Mix well. Cover and cook slowly for 1-1½ hr. Stir occasionally.

5. Remove cover, add mushrooms, and continue cooking (uncovered) until the mixture is slightly thickened.

6. Add sour cream just before serving.

7. Serve over hot buttered rice or noodles.

SOURCE: Far-Mar-Co, Research Division, 960 N. Halstead, Hutchinson, Kansas.

BEEF STROGANOFF (FORMULA NO. 2) WITH MINCED SOY PROTEIN CONCENTRATE

The formula given below is for the fresh-made product for institutional food service. However, this is a product that can be frozen in appropriate packages for freezing and marketed for retail as well as institutional trade.

Ingredients	%
Ground beef trimmings, 25-30% fat	35
Soy protein concentrate (Ultra-Soy Minced, caramel)	3.5
Rehydration water	6.5
Flour	2
Salt	0.7
Paprika	0.15
Garlic salt	0.15
Chopped onions	5
Beef consommé	23
Water	9
Canned sliced mushrooms with liquid	6
Sour cream	9
	100.00

Procedure

1. Rehydrate the soy protein concentrate (Ultra-Soy) with seasonings in water.

2. Brown ground beef, add rehydrated soy protein concentrate and onions and cook until onions are transparent.

3. Add flour, water and consommé; mix well. Simmer 20-30 min, stirring occasionally until thickened.

4. Add mushrooms and simmer 5 min more.

5. Add sour cream just before serving.

6. Serve over buttered noodles or rice.

SOURCE: Far-Mar-Co, Research Division, 960 N. Halstead, Hutchinson, Kansas.

CABBAGE ROLLS WITH SOY PROTEIN CONCENTRATE

The formula given below is for the fresh-made product for institutional food service. However, this is a product that can be frozen unbaked in oblong aluminum foil freezing containers and marketed for retail as well as institutional trade.

Ingredients	%
Ground beef trimmings (28%)	25.17
Soy protein concentrate (Ultra-Soy Minced, caramel)	1.48
Water	2.96
Salt	0.67
Black pepper	0.07
Garlic powder	0.04
Sweet basil	0.01
Fresh onions, finely diced	1.48
Cooked rice or bulgur (5.9 lb raw)	17.77
Canned tomatoes	29.62
Tomato juice[1]	20.73
	100.00

Cabbage leaves: 444 leaves per 100 lb of filling

[1] Tomato soup or tomato purée and water may be substituted for juice

Procedure

1. Presoak soy protein concentrate (Ultra-Soy) and dry seasonings in water.

2. Combine the presoaked mixture, cooked rice, and ground beef and mix well.

3. Core the cabbage heads. Place cabbage heads in boiling salted water 7-10 min, pulling off leaves as they become limp and soft. Drain leaves.

4. Place about 2 rounded tablespoons of the meat mixture on each cabbage leaf and wrap.

5. Place rolls in casserole pouring tomatoes and tomato juice over the top.

6. Cover and place in 325°F oven for 1½-2 hr.

SOURCE: Far-Mar-Co, Research Division, 960 N. Halstead, Hutchinson, Kansas.

FROZEN SAUERBRATEN

Ingredients	By Weight Lb	Oz	or	By Measure
Beef, eye of bottom round	7			
Cider vinegar				1 pt
Brown sugar		8		
Sachet bag:				
Bay leaves				2
Cloves				3
Rosemary				1 tbsp
Thyme				1 tsp

Peanut oil		1 cup
Carrots, diced	7	
Onions, diced	7	
Celery, diced	7	
Salt		2 tbsp
White pepper		2 tsp
Water		2½ qt
Dry white wine, domestic		½ cup
Modified starch		1 cup
Modified cream	7	
Instant onion powder		1 tbsp + 1 tsp
Instant garlic powder		2 tsp

YIELD: 10 portions consisting of 7 oz meat and 7 oz gravy

Procedure

Place beef in deep pot which can be covered. Combine vinegar and sugar; pour over beef, add sachet bag; cover and refrigerate 3 days before cooking. Remove beef and save marinade. Slowly brown meat on all sides in oil. Add carrots, onion, and celery and brown lightly. Transfer meat to deep stew pan; add 1 pt of marinade, salt, pepper, and water. Cover and simmer for 2½ hr or until tender. Remove meat from gravy and hold in a covered container. Slowly add wine to starch and modified cream stirring until smooth; add to gravy with onion and garlic powders. Bring to 180°F stirring constantly. Strain through a fine sieve.

In a 12 × 8-in. vacuum boil-in-bag pouch, package 7 oz sliced meat and 7 oz gravy, evenly distributing gravy over meat slices. Blast freeze 30 min.

SOURCE: Cornell Hotel & Restaurant Administration Quarterly, Statler Hall, Ithaca, N.Y.

FROZEN STEAK AND KIDNEY PIE

	By Weight		By
			Measure
Ingredients	Lb	Oz	
Beef, cut in 1-in. cubes	10		
Veal kidney, cut in 1-in. cubes	2	8	
Onions, finely chopped	4		
Shallots, finely chopped	1	8	
Butter	1		
Beef stock			1 gal.
Oysters, shucked, drained			3½ qt
Eggs			3
Parsley, chopped			½ cup
Flour		4	
Purity 69 starch (available from National Starch & Chemical Co.)		4	
Water, cold			¾ qt

| Salt | | to taste |
| Pepper | | to taste |

YIELD: 50 portions of 5 oz each in individual aluminum pie shells

Procedure

1. Sauté beef cubes, kidney, onions, and shallots in butter.

2. Prepare stock and add it to pan, cover and simmer beef and kidney until tender.

3. Add oysters, eggs, and parsley. Cook for 10 min.

4. Prepare a wash of flour, starch, and water. Thicken stock with wash, stirring constantly until thick and hold temperature at 180°F. Adjust seasoning.

5. Bag and freeze: Cut unbaked pie crust to size of individual aluminum pie shells. Ladle 5 oz of meat and sauce into pan and cover with crust. Package in suitable cartons for freezing and freeze.

SOURCE: Cornell Hotel & Restaurant Administration Quarterly, Ithaca, N.Y.

FROZEN KIDNEY STEW

Ingredients	%
Beef kidneys (cut in 1-in. dice)	27.50
Water	27.50
Potatoes, diced	13.70
Canned tomatoes (drained)	13.70
Onions, diced	5.43
Carrots, sliced	3.40
Butter or margarine	3.40
Celery tops, chopped	3.30
Barley (medium)	1.65
Salt	0.28
Ground pepper	0.14
Bay leaves, crushed	To taste

Procedure

First step in preparing kidney stew is to soak washed barley in water for about 2 hr. Kidneys should be "skinned," trimmed free of fat and tough membranes, and diced (1-in. cubes). Brown in butter or margarine, add onions and continue cooking for about 5 min. Add water, soaked barley, salt, tomatoes, pepper, and bay leaves. Cover kettle and simmer stew until both the barley and kidneys are tender (about 1 hr). Then add potatoes, carrots, and celery tops; simmer mixture for ½ hr longer or until vegetables are tender. Add more water if necessary. Cool the stew, fill into appropriate freezing containers, and freeze as rapidly as possible.

SOURCE: *Freezing Preservation of Foods, 4th Edition, Vol. 4* by Tressler *et al.* published by Avi Publishing Co., Westport, Conn.

AMERICAN-STYLE ORIENTAL DISHES

FROZEN VEGETABLE CHOP SUEY OR CHOW MEIN BASE

Excluding any meat that may be packed with Chinese food, there appears to be no basic difference between the standard chop suey and chow mein. Chow mein is commonly served with fried noodles, while chop suey is served with cooked rice.

The basic ingredients in either chop suey or chow mein are celery, onions, bean sprouts, monosodium glutamate, sugar, salt, soy sauce, chicken broth or beef stock or bouillon, and spices.

One of several types of meat, or shellfish, or chicken may be added to a vegetable chop suey (or chow mein) base thereby converting it to Chicken Chop Suey, Pork Chop Suey, Shrimp Chop Suey, etc. (or Chow Mein). Water chestnuts, a more costly ingredient, may be included in the best quality products (as they are included in the higher-priced dishes in a Chinese restaurant). Mushrooms are often added to enhance the flavor mixture. Almonds (lightly sautéed) are added to both chop suey and chow mein dishes which are then called "Subgum," e.g., Subgum Chicken Chop Suey or Subgum Chicken Chow Mein.

Following is a formula for preparing vegetable chop suey or chow mein base.

Ingredients	Gal.	Lb	Pt
Sliced fresh onions		37^1/$_2$	
Lard or shortening		6	
Celery, ^{1}/$_4$-in. dice		24	
Water	4^1/$_2$	(plus)	1^1/$_2$
Meat concentrate (such as Armour's Vitalox or Wilson's B-V)		4^1/$_2$	
Sliced mushrooms		6	
Sliced green peppers		6	
Bean sprouts		18	
Cornstarch		2	

Procedure

In a kettle, lightly brown onions in lard or shortening. Add celery and 4^1/$_2$ gal. of water and simmer ^{1}/$_2$ hr. Then add the meat concentrate dissolved in a small amount of water, sliced mushrooms, sliced green peppers, and bean sprouts. Bring contents of kettle to boil and thicken with paste made of the cornstarch and the 1^1/$_2$ pt of water.

Fill into containers suitable for freezing. Pre-chill product in cooler at 34°–36°F prior to transfer to a sharp freezer at -20°F.

SOURCE: *The Freezing Preservation of Foods, 3rd Edition, Vol. 2* by Tressler and Evers published by Avi Publishing Co., Westport, Conn.

FROZEN BEEF OR PORK CHOP SUEY

Prepare Meat and Vegetables

Ingredients	Lb
Carcass beef or pork, lean	350
Vegetable oil	10
Vegetable mix	1220
(made up of the following: 50% blanched celery, 43% bean sprouts, 5% sliced onions, and 2% diced canned pimiento)	

Cut meat into 1-in. oblong strips and place on a shelf truck so that 4 or 6 strips are placed together to form a block, with each block separated from others. Transfer to freezer and hold meat until it is partially frozen so it can be sliced easily. Slice blocks into ^{1}/$_4$-in.-thick slices. Put vegetable oil in a steam-jacketed kettle and add beef slices; while agitating gently with a wooden paddle, braise until slices are separated. Drain rendered meat juices and reserve for sauce.

If fresh bean sprouts are used, blanch in boiling water for 15 min; then drain thoroughly so as not to thin the sauce. Cut celery stalks into 1-in. pieces (green top portion of stalks may be used for this) and blanch in boiling water for 3 min. Slice fresh onions and dice drained pimientos into ^{1}/$_4$-in. dice.

Prepare Sauce

Ingredients	Gal.	Lb	Oz
Meat stock	50		
Soy sauce	5		
Cornstarch		32	
Monosodium glutamate		1	
Plant protein hydrolyzate		2	
Salt		8	12
Cane sugar		2	8
Dry soluble pepper			12
Caramel color to obtain desired brown color			

Put 55 gal. of water in a steam-jacketed kettle; make a mark at water level on a measuring stick so finished gallonage can be gaged. Drain only half the water and heat to 160°F. Mix salt with sugar and flavorings. Make a slurry free of lumps of the cornstarch in 10 gal. of water. With a "Lightning" mixer, add salt mixture, then the slurry, followed by the hot stock, soy sauce, and juices from the braised meat. Add caramel color and bring temperature of sauce up to 180°F; cook until sauce thickens. Bring volume of sauce up to 55 gal.

Package and Freeze

In 1-lb-net boil-in-bag Mylar bags, first put 10 oz of vegetable mix and 2 oz meat slices; then evenly distribute 4 oz sauce over meat and vegetables. Vacuumize and close bags. Prechill before transferring product to a sharp freezer at -20°F.

SOURCE: Stephan L. Komarik, 4810 Ronda, Coral Gables, Florida.

FROZEN EGG ROLLS

This product is packed and sold as is, or added to the tray and sold as part of a frozen Chinese dinner. Egg rolls are most often made with the following ingredients: celery, shrimp, pork, flour, vegetable shortening, eggs, onions, water scallions, salt, sugar, monosodium glutamate, and spices.

The procedure and packaging for egg rolls in one plant may be described as follows:

Shrimp, celery, pork, and onions are diced, then mixed along with spices in approximately 40-lb batches. An Urschel slicer cuts celery into 1/8-in. dice. About 2 oz of this mix is placed on a sheet of egg-noodle dough (purchased according to specifications from a local macaroni manufacturer), and then hand formed into a roll (1 1/4 × 5 in.). An egg paste is used to seal the dough.

Rolls are packed 72 to a wire-basket tray, and 20 trays are loaded onto a portable rack that's pushed to the kitchen. Here, a trayload of egg rolls is submerged 2 1/2 min in 1 of the 3 batch-type, deep-fat fryers. Temperature of the cooking fat is 350°F.

The trayload of rolls is then removed from the fryer and placed on an inclined table attached to the fryer. Draining of excess fat takes about 2 min.

Trays are then loaded onto racks for room-temperature cooling. Then the rolls are packed three to each carton. Cartons are Cellophane-wrapped by a Hayssen machine.

The egg rolls are also packed 2 to a plastic bag as well as 25, 50, or 100 to a carton for institutions and restaurants.

Freeze egg rolls in an airblast freezer at -20°F or below.

SOURCE: *The Freezing Preservation of Foods, 4th Edition, Vol. 4* by Tressler *et al.* published by Avi Publishing Co., Westport, Conn.

FROZEN SWEET AND SOUR PORK

Ingredients	Gm
Soy sauce	100
Fresh ginger root	20
Scallions, cut in 4-in. lengths	20
Garlic cloves, slightly crushed	10
Salt	8
Passion fruit nectar	17
Pork, cut in 3/4-in. cubes	450
Water	385
Vegetable oil	28
Garlic cloves, slightly crushed	5
Chili sauce	40
Sweet mixed pickle juice	60
Pineapple syrup (canned)	380
Pineapple tidbits (canned)	190
Water chestnuts (canned 1/4-in. slices)	78
Mixed sweet pickles (1/2- to 1-in. pieces)	80
Pimientos, coarsely diced (1/2-in. pieces)	64
Fresh green pepper, coarsely diced (1/2 to 3/4 in.)	57
Cornstarch	24
Water	35

Procedure

Combine 75 gm soy sauce, ginger root, scallions, 4 cloves garlic (10 gm), salt, passion fruit nectar, and pork, mix well. Let stand for 2 hr. Add 350 gm water and place in pressure cooker. Cook under 15 lb pressure for 12 min. Cool immediately. Let meat cool in stock. Drain and pick out pieces of ginger, garlic, and scallion.

Heat oil and add 2 cloves garlic (5 gm); let sizzle for 5 sec. Remove garlic and add remainder of soy sauce (25 gm), chili sauce, pickle juice, and pineapple syrup. Heat to boiling point. Combine cornstarch and water; mix until blended and stir into hot liquid. Cook stirring constantly, until mixture thickens. Add pork and remaining ingredients.

Cool, package, and freeze.

SOURCE: *The Freezing Preservation of Foods, 4th Edition, Vol. 4* by Tressler *et al.* published by Avi Publishing Co., Westport, Conn.

CHINESE SWEET AND SOUR PORK WITH SOY PROTEIN CONCENTRATE

The formula given below is for the fresh-made product for institutional food service. However, this is a product that can be frozen in appropriate packages for freezing and marketed for retail as well as institutional trade.

Ingredients	%
Pork shoulder, cut in 1/2-in. cubes	30.3
Soy protein concentrate (Ultra-Soy 100's, caramel)	3.0
Rehydration water	6.1
Flour	2.2
Ginger	0.2
Salad oil	2.9
Canned pineapple chunks, drained	10.9
Drained pineapple syrup plus water	11.6
Vinegar	3.2
Soy sauce	3.6
Worcestershire sauce	0.4
Sugar	4.0
Salt	0.5
Black pepper	0.1
Green pepper, cut in strips	3.4
Canned bean sprouts, drained	6.9
Canned water chestnuts, drained and thinly sliced	8.5
Chili sauce	2.2
	100.0

Procedure

1. Trim any excess fat from the pork and cut in 1/2-in. cubes. Rehydrate soy protein concentrate (Ultra-Soy) in water.
2. Combine half of the flour and ginger and coat the pork, a few pieces at a time.
3. Heat oil and brown the pork on all sides, removing pieces as they brown.
4. Add water to pineapple syrup to make total liquid; gradually stir remaining flour and ginger into the pineapple liquid.
5. Add flour mixture, vinegar, and soy and Worcestershire sauces to pork drippings. Heat to boiling, stirring constantly. Boil for 1 min.
6. Stir in sugar, salt, pepper, rehydrated soy protein concentrate (Ultra-Soy), and meat. Simmer for 1 hr or until the meat is tender, stirring occasionally.
7. Add pineapple chunks and green pepper strips. Cook uncovered 10 min.
8. Stir in bean sprouts, water chestnuts, and chili sauce. Cook 5 min longer.

SOURCE: Far-Mar-Co, Research Division, 960 N. Halstead, Hutchinson, Kansas.

FROZEN SWEET AND SOUR SPARERIBS

Cook Spareribs

Ingredients	Gm
Soy sauce	65
Fresh ginger root, slices	2
Scallions, cut in 4-in. lengths	2
Garlic cloves, slightly crushed	4
Salt	8
Passion fruit nectar	17
Spareribs, cut in 1-in. lengths	900
Water	340

Combine soy sauce, ginger, scallions, garlic, salt, and nectar. Add spareribs and marinate for 2 hr, turning over once at the end of 1 hr. Place spareribs, marinating sauce, and water in a pressure cooker. Cook under 15 lb pressure for 15 min. Let ribs cool before removing from liquid.

Prepare Sauce

Ingredients	Gm
Garlic, crushed	5
Vegetable oil	24
Soy sauce	25
Chili sauce	22
Mixed sweet pickle juice	57
Pineapple syrup (canned)	380
Pineapple tidbits (canned)	190
Water chestnuts (canned 1/4-in. slices)	78
Sweet pickles, sliced	80
Diced pimiento	57
Diced green pepper	57
Cornstarch	16
Water	24

Let garlic sizzle in oil a few seconds, then discard garlic cloves. Combine soy sauce, chili sauce, pickle juice, and pineapple juice drained from the canned tidbits; add mixture to the hot oil and mix well. Then add pineapple, chestnuts, pickles, pimiento, and green pepper. Bring to a boil. Blend cornstarch and water and stir into sauce mixture; stirring constantly, cook until mixture comes to a boil.

Combine, Package, Freeze

Reheat cooked spareribs in preheated oven at 250°F for 10 min. Add 900 gm hot sauce to spareribs and let product cool.
Package and freeze.

SOURCE: *The Freezing Preservation of Foods*, 4th Edition, *Vol. 4* by Tressler *et al.* published by Avi Publishing Co., Westport, Conn.

JAPANESE SUKIYAKI WITH TEXTURED SOY PROTEIN CONCENTRATE

The formula given below is for the fresh-made product for institutional food service. However, this is a product that can be frozen in appropriate packages for freezing and marketed for retail as well as institutional trade.

Ingredients	%
Fat or vegetable oil	0.93
Round steak	15.83
Textured soy protein concentrate (Ultra-Soy Chiplets 100 Caramel)	0.93
Hot water	8.38
Beef bouillon, dissolved in above hot water	0.37
Soy sauce	3.72
Canned, sliced mushrooms, drained	4.66
Celery, angle-sliced	4.66
Onions, thinly sliced	7.45
Fresh green onions, cut in 1½-in. lengths	1.86
Bamboo shoots	6.52
Raw spinach leaves	6.52
Water chestnuts, sliced	5.59
Bean sprouts, drained	13.97
Cooked rice (approx 6 lb raw cooked with 13 lb salted water)	18.61
	100.00

Procedure

1. Cut round steak in bit-size pieces and brown in fat.

2. Add soy protein concentrate (Ultra-Soy) and beef bouillon to hot water and soy sauce. Simmer 2-3 min.

3. Add all other ingredients (except rice and spinach) and simmer 10 min or until vegetables are tender.

4. Add spinach leaves and simmer 5 min longer.

5. Serve on or with rice.

SOURCE: Far-Mar-Co, Research Division, 960 N. Halstead, Hutchinson, Kansas.

SOUPS, GRAVIES, AND SAUCES (INCLUDING MIXES)

MAKING STOCKS, EXTRACT, AND MIXES

BEEF SOUP STOCK

Use the bony parts of canner grade beef. Trim off all the fat and strip the meat from the bones. Crack the bones. Place separated meat and bones in wire baskets to prevent small bone particles getting into the broth or mixed into the meat. To 1000 lb of beef and bones add 200 gal. of water. Turn on steam bring temperature to 190°-200°F, and simmer stock for 8-10 hr. During this time, skim off fat and co agulated albumin occasionally. After cooking, remove baskets containing meat and bones. Increase vol ume of stock to 200 gal. by adding water. Cooked meat should be properly chilled, then diced and use in soups such as Beef with Vegetables.

If stronger stock is required, add 1 lb of beef extract or plant protein hydrolyzate to each 50 gal. o stock. Chill stock to solidify the fat. Do not remove fat until stock is used. Before removing fat, drain of clear stock from the precipitated sediment.

Beef Stock with Vegetables Added

The flavor of beef stock can be improved by addition of vegetables such as celery or carrots; they should be diced, sliced or chopped, placed in wire baskets and added to the cooking stock to be blanche a short time just before the end of the cooking time. Many soup formulas contain carrots, celery an other kinds of vegetables in an emulsified form. In this case these vegetables should be added to the cooking stock at an earlier stage so they will be thoroughly cooked and then emulsified through pulping machine.

SOURCE: Stephan L. Komarik, 4810 Ronda, Coral Gables, Florida.

CHICKEN SOUP STOCK

Put 600 lb eviscerated and thoroughly washed chicken in 200 gal. water in a steam-jacketed kettle. Bring temperature up to 190°-200°F and simmer until meat can easily be removed from the bones. Remove meat from bones and return bones to the stock; cook an additional 2 hr. Remove bones and add water to bring volume of the stock to 200 gal. Skim off coagulated albumin as it rises to the top during the cooking process. Remove chicken fat from the top of the stock at end of the process. Drain off clear stock over the precipitated sediment.

SOURCE: Stephan L. Komarik, 4810 Ronda, Coral Gables, Florida.

BEEF EXTRACT

Collect beef trimmings in a storage tank at a temperature of 170°-180°F, until sufficient quantities are obtained for continuous evaporation. Prior to evaporation, boil the meat in water for 1 hr, then hold at the approximate boiling temperature for at least another hour prior to filtering. Then pass the extract through a filter press and transfer to condensing pans. Take care to prevent grease and scum from the surface from entering the evaporators.

Evaporate in a single, double, or triple effect evaporator of the type used for condensing milk. Operate the single-stage evaporator at approximately 25 in. vacuum and 130°F. Continue the operation until a product of 40% solids is obtained. In the second stage, concentrate the product at 25-29 in. vacuum and 130°F to 60% solids. Finally, concentrate to 80% solids in open, shallow steam-jacketed finishing pans equipped with agitators at 140°-150°F. During entire procedure, steam coils must be covered by the concentrate to prevent scorching.

SOURCE: *Food Flavorings, 2nd Edition* by J. Merory published by Avi Publishing Co., Westport, Conn.

MANUFACTURE OF DRY SOUPS AND GRAVY MIXES

General Tips

Where all ingredients in a formula are dry powders, it is preferable to have each as uniform in screen size as is possible in order to prevent segregation of coarse and fine particles during the subsequent handling and filling operations.

In the event that noodles, flours, or starches are redried prior to use in a given formula, convey the redried materials by belt from drying equipment to a storage bin.

When pastes are to be manufactured, it is not necessary to melt the fat. It needs only to be softened enough so that it will mix thoroughly with the dry ingredients. In formulations in which small quantities of fat are used, it is preferably melted beforehand and then sprayed into the dried ingredients during the mixing operation.

Components such as dehydrated vegetables need to be handled with a minimum of grinding or rubbing to prevent powdering of the brittle vegetable pieces. Blended mixtures of vegetables are best conveyed to a hopper at the filling machine by means of a belt.

The first step of weighing or measuring formula ingredients for a standard batch is done by hand in small-scale operations. In large volume plants, it may be completely automated.

Small-Scale Production

Bring ingredients to a scale and weigh out successively each ingredient required for the batch. Transfer the scaled-off components to mixing equipment and blend for a sufficient time to bring about uniformity of ingredients.

A tumbling-type mixer, if properly designed, may prove more advantageous in obtaining uniformity than would a ribbon-type mixer. For mixtures high in fat or viscous in consistency, like noodle soup mix in paste form or soup and gravy base for U.S. Army onion soup, a dough-type mixer is required.

Experience will dictate the order of adding ingredients and the length of time given to their blending.

Large-Scale Production

For larger installations, a series of hoppers is usually installed side by side for the separate storage of each ingredient. These hoppers are filled from the floor above as required. Each hopper is fitted with a valve mechanism which can be actuated automatically to deliver ingredients sequentially into a tote bin positioned in turn under each successive hopper. This tote bin serves as a weighing bin also, being suspended from a suitable weighing mechanism and preferably transported on an overhead rail from hopper to hopper.

In completely automated systems, an electronic computer is installed in which each formula is entered on a punch card. These cards are fed into the computer as desired and any given number of batches automatically scaled off. With such a system, the tote bin containing the weighed ingredients is conveyed on an overhead trolley to mixing equipment. The blended mix is then dumped into another tote bin and conveyed to a hopper which feeds filling machines.

SOURCE: *Food Dehydration, 2nd Edition, Vol. 2* by Van Arsdel *et al.* published by Avi Publishing Co., Westport, Conn.

SOUPS

CANNED BEEF CONSOMMÉ

Ingredients	Gal.	Lb	Oz
Beef stock (clarified)	100		
Salt		16	
Mixed pulped vegetables			
(onions, 95%; parsnips, 5%)	9		
Rendered beef fat		2	
Monosodium glutamate		2	8
Plant protein hydrolyzate		1	8
Beef extract		5	
Wheat flour, browned		10	
Onion powder			4
Garlic powder			1/2
Ground celery seeds			1
Ground turmeric			1
Dry soluble pepper			4
Caramel color			4

Procedure

To brown wheat flour: Put flour and rendered fat in a steam-jacketed kettle, apply steam and, with steady stirring, brown flour until it is deep brown. Add 8 gal. of stock to the browned flour, and, with steady stirring make a slurry, free of lumps.

Put 92 gal. of stock in a steam-jacketed kettle with the remainder of the ingredients. Raise temperature to 200°F then, with steady stirring, add slurry and cook an additional 10–15 min. Before canning run hot consommé through a filter.

Fill

Pack hot consommé in 211 × 400 size cans. Filling temperature should not drop below 180°F.

Suggested Process

211 × 400 cans (10½ oz net) 30 min at 250°F

Check process time and temperature with can supplier or the National Canners Association.

SOURCE: Stephan L. Komarik, 4810 Ronda, Coral Gables, Florida.

CANNED JELLIED BEEF CONSOMMÉ

Follow formula given above for **Canned Beef Consommé** except add gelatin.

Use 16 lb of 200-bloom gelatin (presoaked in cold water) per 100 gal. of filtered consommé. Heat until all of the gelatin is dissolved; add, while stirring, to the filtered consommé.

Pack while product is 180°F or hotter, using 211 × 400 cans.

Suggested Process

211 × 400 cans (10½ oz net) 30 min at 250°F

Check process time and temperature with can supplier or the National Canners Association.

SOURCE: Stephan L. Komarik, 4810 Ronda, Coral Gables, Florida.

SPANISH BEAN SOUP (SINGLE STRENGTH)

Ingredients	Gal.	Lb	Oz
Water	120		
Diced onions		250	
Bacon ends and pieces		15	
Garbanzo beans		75	
(soaked weight 150 lb)			
Sliced chorizos		16	
Olive oil		4	
Salt		16	
Cane sugar		5	
Monosodium glutamate		2	8
Plant protein hydrolyzate		1	4
Spanish paprika		2	

Ground celery seeds	1
Garlic powder	½
Dry soluble pepper	4
Ground bay leaves	½
Ground turmeric	1
Potato starch	15

Procedure

Soak garbanzos overnight in 2% salt water. Dice potatoes into 1½-in. cubes and blanch in boiling water for 3 min. Chill and keep in fresh water to avoid discoloration. Dice onions in ¼-in. cubes. Grind bacon through the ⅛-in. plate of the grinder. Use the best grade dried chorizos and slice into 3/16-in. slices. Put water in a steam-jacketed kettle, add bacon, olive oil, salt, and sugar mixed with seasonings and flavorings. Bring temperature to 200°F and simmer soup stock for 1 hr. Make slurry of potato starch in 2 gal. of water and with steady stirring add the slurry to the heated stock.

If clear soup stock is desired, without onion or bacon particles, then filter stock through a fine-mesh screen.

Fill 300 × 409 size can with 2 chorizo slices, 2 oz beans, 1 oz potatoes, and 11 oz hot soup stock at 180°F or higher.

Suggested Process

300 × 409 cans (16 oz net) 1 hr at 250°F

Check process time and temperature with can supplier or the National Canners Association.

SOURCE: Stephan L. Komarik, 4810 Ronda, Coral Gables, Florida.

FROZEN GAZPACHO

Ingredients	%
Maggi Granulated Beef Bouillon	1.00
Maggi Granulated Chicken Bouillon	1.20
Cucumbers, peeled and without seeds	27.25
Tomato purée, heavy concentrated	11.70
Fresh onions, coarsely chopped	4.70
Cider vinegar	0.95
Corn oil	0.95
Granulated dehydrated garlic	0.01
Ground cumin	0.01
Granulated sugar	0.25
Green pepper, diced fine	1.60
Water	50.38
	100.00

Procedure

Mash cucumbers and onions. Combine with remainder of ingredients and heat to 190°F. Fill into containers suitable for freezing. Cool to 120°F and freeze.

SOURCE: Nestlé Company, Food Ingredients Division, 100 Bloomingdale Road, White Plains, N.Y.

CANNED CHICKEN BROTH

Procedure

Chicken broth is prepared from the stock obtained in precooking chickens for canning as boned chicken or chicken a la king. This stock or broth may be fortified by boiling chicken skins and bones in a small amount of water in a pressure cooker for 3–4 hr at 220°F. This extract is added to the broth in the tanks where the chickens have been precooked.

Chicken broth should be strained through sterilized muslin or some other suitable filter to remove small bone fragments and bone marrow, which, if included, would detract from the clarity of the product. The broth is then seasoned as desired before canning.

Some packers add a teaspoonful of barley or rice (regular or converted) to each small can and a proportionate amount to larger cans before filling with the broth. The broth is then filled into the cans mechanically at a temperature of 180°–190°F, after which the cans are closed and processed.

Suggested Process

307 × 409 cans (No. 2) or smaller 30 min at 240°F
603 × 700 cans (No. 10) 45 min at 240°F

Check process times and temperature with can supplier or the National Canners Association.

The cans should be thoroughly water-cooled after processing.

SOURCE: *Poultry Products Technology* by Mountney published by Avi Publishing Co., Westport, Conn.

CHICKEN-FLAVORED SOUP WITH TEXTURED VEGETABLE PROTEIN

Ingredients	%
Textured vegetable protein (Mira-Tex 210)	1.35
Chicken-flavored soup base (Vico-Asmus)	3.36
Fine egg noodles	3.36
Water	91.91

Procedure

Add textured vegetable protein (Mira-Tex 210), chicken-flavored soup base (Vico-Asmus), and

noodles to water. Bring to boil with agitation. Hold at boiling 5–7 min.

SOURCE: A. E. Staley Mfg. Company, Decatur, Ill.

CANNED CHICKEN GUMBO SOUP

Ingredients	Lb	Oz	Gal.
Chicken soup stock			20
Ham, fresh	10		
Cooked chicken	12		
Onions, diced	2		
Butter	3		
White pepper		1	
Salt	1		
Wheat flour	2		
Louisiana gumbo filé		10	

Procedure

Cut ham into cubes; mince the chicken; chop onions very fine. Cook ham in the soup stock about 1 hr. Make a thin paste of the flour; add flour paste along with salt, pepper, butter, minced chicken, and onions to the soup stock. Bring mixture to a boil and add gumbo filé (or powdered okra may be used) mixed with 2 qt of water. Fill into No. 1 cans; exhaust 3 min.

NOTE: A richer product can be made by lightly browning the flour in butter and adding this to the product instead of making a paste of flour and water.

Suggested Process

No. 1 cans process 40 min at 250°F

Check process time and temperature with can supplier or the National Canners Association.

SOURCE: *Poultry Products Technology* by George J. Mountney published by Avi Publishing Co., Westport, Conn.

CONDENSED BEEF BOUILLON OR BROTH

Ingredients	Gal.	Lb	Oz
Beef stock (clarified)	100		
Salt		16	
Cane sugar		1	14
Monosodium glutamate		3	
Plant protein hydrolyzate		1	8
Onion powder			4
Garlic powder			1/8
Ground celery seeds			1
Ground turmeric (Alleppey)			1
Ground white pepper			1
Caramel color (liquid or dry)			4

Procedure

Heat stock to 200°F. Make a mixture of salt and flavorings and add with the caramel color to the heated stock. Then refilter.

Pack in 211 × 400 cans at a temperature of 180°F or higher.

Suggested Process

211 × 400 cans (10½ oz net) 30 min at 250°F

Check process time and temperature with can supplier or the National Canners Association.

SOURCE: Stephan L. Komarik, 4810 Ronda, Coral Gables, Florida.

CONDENSED BEEF BOUILLON OR BROTH WITH RICE

Use the same ingredients given above for Condensed Beef Bouillon or Broth.

Use Patna or Malechized rice only. Blanch in boiling water for 30 min using fine mesh wire baskets.

Fill into 211 × 400 cans using 2 oz rice and 8½ oz hot broth. Temperature of broth during filling should be 180°F or higher.

Suggested Process

211 × 400 cans (10½ oz net) 30 min at 250°F

Check process time and temperature with can supplier or the National Canners Association.

SOURCE: Stephan L. Komarik, 4810 Ronda, Coral Gables, Florida.

CANNED CONDENSED CHICKEN BROTH

Ingredients	Gal.	Lb	Oz
Chicken stock (clarified)	100		
Mixed pulped vegetables (carrots, onions, celery)		9	
Salt		16	
Monosodium glutamate		3	
Plant protein hydrolyzate		1	8
Chicken fat		6	
Dry soluble pepper			4
Ground celery seeds			½
Onion powder			4
Garlic powder			⅛

Procedure

Put all ingredients in a steam-jacketed kettle. Raise temperature to 200°F then filter before canning.

In case no pulped vegetables are available, the following may be added to the stock: 1 oz ground turmeric, 1 oz onion powder. In this case, no filtering is necessary.

Fill cans while product is 180°F or hotter.

Suggested Process

211 × 400 cans (10½ oz net) 30 min at 250°F

Check process time and temperature with can supplier or the National Canners Association.

SOURCE: Stephan L. Komarik, 4810 Ronda, Coral Gables, Florida.

CANNED CONDENSED CHICKEN AND NOODLE SOUP

Use the formula as given above for Condensed Chicken Broth but make a heavier stock by adding 4 lb of cornstarch to the ingredients and pack with cooked noodles and diced, cooked chicken meat.

Use egg noodles with 10% egg solids. Cook noodles in boiling water containing 2% salt for 10 min. Use 1 gal. of water to each pound of noodles. After cooking, drain, wash in cold water, and drain again.

Pack in 211 × 400 cans using 2 oz noodles, 1 oz chicken dice, and 7½ oz hot chicken broth. Fill cans while broth is 180°F or hotter.

Suggested Process

211 × 400 cans (10½ oz net) 30 min at 250°F

Check process time and temperature with can supplier or the National Canners Association.

SOURCE: Stephan L. Komarik, 4810 Ronda, Coral Gables, Florida.

CANNED CONDENSED CHICKEN BROTH WITH RICE

Use the formula given above for Condensed Chicken Broth and add cooked rice.

Use either Patna or Melachized rice. Cook in a fine wire basket in boiling water for 30 min.

Fill into 211 × 400 size cans using 2 oz rice and 9½ oz hot chicken broth at 180°F or hotter.

Suggested Process

211 × 400 cans (10½ oz net) 30 min at 250°F

Check process time and temperature with can supplier or the National Canners Association.

SOURCE: Stephan L. Komarik, 4810 Ronda, Coral Gables, Florida.

CONDENSED BEEF AND NOODLE SOUP

Prepare Beef and Noodles

Cook beef and cut into $1/4$-in. dice. Boil egg noodles for 2 min in water containing 2% salt, using 1 gal. water per 1 lb noodles. Wash in cold water; drain.

Prepare Base

Ingredients	Gal.	Lb	Oz
Water	100		
Salt		16	
Cane sugar		2	
Monosodium glutamate		2	8
Plant protein hydrolyzate		1	4
Rendered beef fat		4	
Beef extract		10	
Carrot emulsion		2	
Potato starch		2	
Onion powder			8
Garlic powder			$1/8$
Turmeric (Alleppey)			1
Ground celery seeds			$1/2$
Dry soluble pepper			2
Caramel color (dry or liquid)			4

Heat water to 200°F to make stock using beef extract, carrot emulsion, rendered beef fat, and the remainder of the ingredients. Cook an additional 10 min.

Fill

In 211 × 400 cans pack 2 oz noodles, 1 oz beef dice, and $7 1/2$ oz hot stock. Temperature for filling should not fall below 180°F.

Suggested Process

211 × 400 cans ($10 1/2$ oz net) 30 min at 250°F

Check process time and temperature with can supplier or the National Canners Association.

SOURCE: Stephan L. Komarik, 4810 Ronda, Coral Gables, Florida.

CANNED CONDENSED BEEF SOUP WITH VEGETABLES AND BARLEY

Ingredients	Gal.	Lb	Oz
Beef stock	50		
Water	45		
Salt		16	
Beef fat		6	
Cornstarch		8	
Potato starch		6	
Wheat flour		2	
Tomato paste (28% solids)		20	
Monosodium glutamate		3	
Plant protein hydrolyzate		1	8
Onion powder			4
Garlic powder			$1/8$
Dry soluble pepper			4
Ground celery seeds			1
Caramel color			4

Prepare Base

Put beef stock and water in a steam-jacketed kettle and add remainder of the ingredients except flour and starches. Bring temperature up to 200°F. Make a slurry of flour and starches with 5 gal. of water in a bakery mixer; add to the heated stock. Agitate stock during cooking. Cook an additional 10 min at 200°F.

Prepare Vegetables and Meat

Ingredients	%
Cooked beef, diced	34.50
Diced carrots, blanched	14.50
Diced potatoes, blanched	14.50
Diced celery, blanched	2.50
Frozen peas, defrosted	1.00
Chopped parsley	0.50
Precooked pearl barley	32.50

Cut carrots, potatoes, and celery into $1/2$-in. dice. Defrost frozen peas. Chop parsley into small pieces. Put all vegetables and barley in kettle and cook until softened and vegetables have gained about 100% in weight.

Use beef from beef stock; chill, then cut into $1/4$-in. cubes.

Fill

Make a thorough mixture of the vegetables and beef.

In 211 × 400 cans pack $4 1/2$ oz meat-vegetable mixture and $6 1/2$ oz hot soup. Temperature should be 180°F or higher before closing cans.

Suggested Process

211 × 400 cans ($10 1/2$ oz net) 45 min at 240°F

Check process time and temperature with can supplier or the National Canners Association.

SOURCE: Stephan L. Komarik, 4810 Ronda, Coral Gables, Florida.

CONDENSED CREAM OF CHICKEN SOUP

Ingredients	Gal.	Oz
Chicken broth	7	
Chicken meat, diced		7
Chicken fat		3

Corn oil	1
Cream (32%)	8
Nonfat dry milk	1
Wheat flour	5.50
Derivatized cross-bonded waxy cornstarch	4.75
Salt	3
Sugar	0.25
Monosodium glutamate	0.50
Cream of chicken soup seasoning	0.60
Water (total quantity needed)	$7/8$

Procedure

Blend flour, starch, nonfat dry milk, and cream in mixer with $1/2$ pt water. Add sugar, salt, monosodium glutamate, and seasoning and blend thoroughly. Then add $1 1/2$ pt water and blend to smooth consistency.

Put remaining water ($5/8$ gal.) in kettle, add broth, meat, fat, and oil (gage: $3/4$ gal.). Heat to boiling and add the above blend. Reheat to 190°–195°F and fill.

Suggested Process

Using No. 1 can, plain bodies, C enamel ends and lids, process at 240°F for 65 min.

Check process time and temperature with can supplier or the National Canners Association.

SOURCE: CPC International, Inc., Industrial Division, Englewood Cliffs, N.J.

CANNED CONDENSED CREAM OF CHICKEN SOUP

Ingredients	Gal.	Lb	Oz
Chicken stock (clarified)	100		
Cooked chicken meat		40	
Carrot emulsion		30	
Wheat flour		35	
Cornstarch		6	
Cream (30% butterfat)		20	
Salt		16	
Nonfat dry milk		6	
Monosodium glutamate		3	
Plant protein hydrolyzate		1	8
Onion powder			4
Garlic powder			$1/8$
Ground turmeric			1
Dry soluble pepper			4
Ground celery seeds			$1/2$

Procedure

Grind the cooked chicken meat through the $1/4$-in. plate of the grinder.

Put 80 gal. of stock, carrot emulsion, cream, and the remainder of the ingredients except flour,

starch, and nonfat dry milk, in a steam-jacketed kettle; bring temperature to 200°F. Put flour, starch, and nonfat dry milk in a bakery mixer; add 20 gal. of well-chilled stock and make a slurry free of lumps. Add slurry, with steady stirring, to the heated stock. Add chicken meat and bring temperature back to 200°F; let simmer an additional 10 min.

Fill into $10 1/2$ oz cans while product is 180°F or hotter.

Suggested Process

211×400 cans ($10 1/2$ oz net) 30 min at 250°F

Check process time and temperature with can supplier or the National Canners Association.

SOURCE: Stephan L. Komarik, 4810 Ronda, Coral Gables, Florida.

CANNED CONDENSED CHICKEN VEGETABLE SOUP

Prepare Meat and Vegetables

Cook chicken meat and dice into $1/4$-in. cubes ($1/2$ oz as needed per can).

Cut fresh carrots and celery into strips $1 \times 1/4 \times 1/4$ in. Blanch both products in boiling water for 3 min and drain. Needed for pack: $1/4$ oz per can of each, cooked weight.

Defrost frozen peas; use $1/4$ oz per can of the pack.

Egg noodles in the amount of 1 oz cooked weight are added per can. Use $1/4$-in. wide, 1 in. long egg noodles and cook in boiling water to which 1% salt has been added; use 1 gal. of water per pound of egg noodles. Cook for 10 min; then drain, wash, and drain again.

Prepare Soup

Ingredients	Gal.	Lb	Oz
Chicken soup stock (clarified)	100		
Tomato purée (sp. gr. 1.035)	1		
Salt		16	
Chicken fat		5	
Potato starch		4	
Monosodium glutamate		2	8
Plant protein hydrolyzate		1	8
Dry soluble pepper			4
Ground celery seeds			1
Onion powder			4
Garlic powder			$1/8$
Turmeric			1

Heat stock to 200°F. Make a mixture of all dry ingredients and add the mixture to the hot stock, with continuous stirring, along with tomato purée, and chicken fat. Stir. Cook an additional 10 min at 200°F.

Fill

Pack into each 211 × 400 size cans: ¹/₂ oz chicken; 1 oz noodles; ¹/₄ oz carrots; ¹/₄ oz celery; ¹/₄ oz peas, and 8¹/₂ oz hot soup.

Filling temperature should not drop below 180°F.

Suggested Process

211 × 400 cans (10¹/₂ oz net) 30 min at 250°F

Check process time and temperature with can supplier or the National Canners Association.

SOURCE: Stephan L. Komarik, 4810 Ronda, Coral Gables, Florida.

CONDENSED OLD-FASHIONED VEGETABLE SOUP

Prepare Vegetable-Macaroni Mixture

Ingredients	%
Carrot strips (¹/₂ × ¹/₄ × ¹/₄ in.), blanched	27
Potato strips (¹/₂ × ¹/₄ × ¹/₄ in.), blanched	15
Small dried lima beans (soaked overnight)	13
Canned or frozen peas	15
Green beans, sliced ¹/₄ in.	6
Celery, sliced ¹/₂ in.	8
Cabbage, chopped	4
Rutabagas, diced ¹/₄-oz pieces	2
Macaroni O's, dry, ¹/₈-in. diam	10

Prepare Soup Base

Ingredients	Gal.	Lb	Oz
Beef stock (clarified)	100		
Salt		16	
Carrot emulsion		8	
Potato starch		15	
Monosodium glutamate		2	8
Hydrolyzed plant protein		1	4
Cane sugar		1	
Vegetable oil		2	
Rendered beef fat		2	
Cooked beef, finely ground		2	
Toasted onion chips			12
Garlic powder			¹/₂
Ground turmeric			1
Dry soluble celery			1
Dry soluble pepper			3
Caramel color			4

Heat stock to 200°F. Make a mixture of salt and flavoring materials and add to stock along with fat, oil, beef and carrot emulsion. Make a

slurry of the potato starch and 10 gal. of chilled stock or water and, with steady stirring, add to the hot stock. Cook an additional 10 min.

Fill

Fill cans half full with the vegetable-macaroni mixture. Then fill cans with hot soup base at a temperature not lower than 180°F.

Some manufacturers prefer to add the vegetable-macaroni mixture directly to the soup base before filling cans. In this case, soup has to be thick enough to keep the vegetables in proper suspension and soup should be agitated during the filling procedure.

Suggested Process

211 × 400 cans (10¹/₂ oz net) 45 min at 240°F

Check process time and temperature with can supplier or the National Canners Association.

SOURCE: Stephan L. Komarik, 4810 Ronda, Coral Gables, Florida.

CANNED CONDENSED PEA SOUP

Ingredients	Gal.	Lb	Oz
Beef stock	100		
Split peas or Scotch peas		150	
Smoked ham		15	
Bacon ends and pieces		30	
Salt		16	
Cane sugar		8	
Wheat flour		10	
Cornstarch		2	
Monosodium glutamate		2	8
Plant protein hydrolyzate		1	8
Dry soluble pepper			10
Ground celery seeds			¹/₂
Ground nutmeg			¹/₂
Onion powder		1	8
Garlic powder			¹/₂

Procedure

Soak peas overnight, then steam cook for 35 min in a retort at 230°F.

Grind smoked ham through the ¹/₄ in. plate of the grinder; bacon through the ¹/₈-in. plate.

Make a slurry in a bakery mixer of the flour and starch in 5 gal. of water or chilled beef stock.

Add 50 gal. of the beef stock to half of the steamed peas and grind through a pulping machine. Add remaining beef stock and peas to the pulped peas and raise temperature to 200°F. Mix together flavorings and seasonings and add to hot soup mixture along with ham, bacon, and slurry with

steady stirring. Keep soup agitated, and cook an additional 10 min.
Pack at a temperature of 180°F or hotter.

Suggested Process

211 × 400 cans (10½ oz net) 35 min at 250°F

Check process time and temperature with can supplier or the National Canners Association.

SOURCE: Stephan L. Komarik, 4810 Ronda, Coral Gables, Florida.

CANNED CONDENSED LENTIL SOUP

Use the formula given above for **Condensed Pea Soup** and substitute lentils instead of peas.
Pack at a temperature of 180°F or hotter.

Suggested Process

211 × 400 cans (10½ oz net) 35 min at 250°F

Check process time and temperature with can supplier or the National Canners Association.

SOURCE: Stephan L. Komarik, 4810 Ronda, Coral Gables, Florida.

CANNED CONDENSED CREAM OF CELERY SOUP

Ingredients	Gal.	Lb	Oz
Beef stock	33		
Cooked and pulped celery	33		
Fresh milk	33		
Wheat flour		8	
Cornstarch		2	
Salt		16	
Butter		8	
Monosodium glutamate		2	8
Plant protein hydrolyzate		1	4
Dry soluble pepper			8

Procedure

Put all the ingredients except the cornstarch and wheat flour in a steam-jacketed kettle and bring to boil. Agitate slowly. Make a slurry in a bakery mixer of flour and starch with 5 gal. of water or soup stock. Add slurry to the boiling soup with steady stirring and let it simmer for 10 min more.

In case chopped (not pulped) celery is desired in the soup, then reduce the pulped celery 25% and replace it with precooked chopped celery. Agitate soup during filling cans so as to obtain even distribution of chopped celery in the cans.

Fill into cans while the product is 180°F or hotter.

Suggested Process

211 × 400 cans (10½ oz net) 30 min at 250°F

Check process time and temperature with can supplier or the National Canners Association.

SOURCE: Stephan L. Komarik, 4810 Ronda, Coral Gables, Florida.

CANNED CONDENSED CREAM OF ASPARAGUS SOUP

Use the formula given above for **Cream of Celery Soup** and substitute cooked, pulped asparagus instead of the celery.
Pack while product is 180°F or hotter.

Suggested Process

211 × 400 cans (10½ oz net) 30 min at 250°F

Check process time and temperature with can supplier or the National Canners Association.

SOURCE: Stephan L. Komarik, 4810 Ronda, Coral Gables, Florida.

CANNED CONDENSED CREAM OF SPINACH SOUP

Ingredients	Gal.	Lb	Oz
Chicken stock	35		
Cooked, pulped spinach	30		
Fresh milk	35		
Wheat flour		15	
Cornstarch		2	
Butter		20	
Salt		16	
Monosodium glutamate		2	8
Plant protein hydrolyzate		1	8
Dry soluble pepper			4
Onion powder			4
Garlic powder			⅛

Procedure

Put all the ingredients except the wheat flour and cornstarch in a steam-jacketed kettle. Agitate slowly and bring to a boil. In a bakery mixer, make a slurry free of lumps of flour and starch with 5 gal. of water or chilled soup stock. Add slurry to the boiling soup, with steady stirring, and let it simmer for 10 min.
Pack while product is 180°F or hotter.

Suggested Process

211 × 400 cans (10½ oz net) 35 min at 250°F

Check process time and temperature with can supplier or the National Canners Association.

SOURCE: Stephan L. Komarik, 4810 Ronda, Coral Gables, Florida.

CANNED CONDENSED ONION SOUP

Ingredients	Gal.	Lb	Oz
Beef stock (clarified)	100		
Salt		16	
Butter		8	
Sliced and chopped onions		80	
Monosodium glutamate	2		12
Plant protein hydrolyzate	1		8
Cane sugar	1		14
Onion powder			6
Caramel color			4
Oleoresin celery			$\frac{1}{2}$

Procedure

Fry the onions in a steam-jacketed kettle in the butter until the onions are golden yellow. Heat beef stock to 200°F and then add remainder of the premixed ingredients.

Using 211 × 400 can size, pack 1 oz fried onions and $9\frac{1}{2}$ oz hot broth, while temperature is 180°F or higher.

Suggested Process

211 × 400 cans ($10\frac{1}{2}$ oz net) 30 min at 250°F

Check process time and temperature with can supplier or the National Canners Association.

SOURCE: Stephan L. Komarik, 4810 Ronda, Coral Gables, Florida.

CANNED CONDENSED MULLIGATAWNY SOUP

Ingredients	Gal.	Lb	Oz
Beef stock (clarified)	80		
Tomato purée (sp. gr. 1.035)	3		
Chutney	3		
Apple sauce	3		
Blanched carrots, $\frac{1}{4}$-in. dice		45	
Dehydrated minced onion		5	
Salt		16	
Cane sugar		6	
Cornstarch		40	
Curry powder		8	
Monosodium glutamate	2		8
Plant protein hydrolyzate	1		8
Ground allspice			4
Ground cloves			2
Ground bay leaves			2
Ground thyme			2
Ground marjoram			2
Garlic powder			$\frac{1}{4}$

Procedure

Put stock in a steam-jacketed kettle, add tomato purée, chutney, apple sauce, carrot dice, onions,
and salt premixed with the remainder of the ingredients except cornstarch; stir. Bring temperature to 200°F. Make a slurry of cornstarch in 10 gal. of chilled beef stock (or water) in a bakery mixer. Add slurry while agitating the hot soup. Cook an additional 15 min at 200°F.

Fill into 211 × 400 cans at 180°F or higher.

NOTE: Cooked, diced chicken or beef is often added to Mulligatawny. If this ingredient is used, put $\frac{1}{4}$-$\frac{1}{2}$ oz of the diced meat in each can before filling with the hot soup.

Suggested Process

211 × 400 cans ($10\frac{1}{2}$ oz net) 30 min at 250°F

Check process time and temperature with can supplier or the National Canners Association.

SOURCE: Stephan L. Komarik, 4810 Ronda, Coral Gables, Florida.

CANNED CONDENSED OXTAIL SOUP

Ingredients	Gal.	Lb	Oz
Oxtails		500	
Stock from cooked oxtails	100		
Tomato purée (sp. gr. 1.035)	8		
Blanched carrots ($\frac{1}{4}$-in. dice)		45	
Salt		16	
Cane sugar		6	
Wheat flour		10	
Cornstarch		2	
Dehydrated toasted onion chips		5	
Monosodium glutamate	2		8
Plant protein hydrolyzate	1		4
Ground allspice			4
Ground cloves			1
Ground bay leaves			1
Ground celery seeds			2
Ground white pepper			4
Garlic powder			$\frac{1}{2}$
Caramel color			14

Procedure

Cut oxtails into small pieces; add 100 gal. water and simmer slowly for 1 hr. Remove oxtails and skim fat from stock. Put 90 gal. of soup stock, tomato purée, salt, and the remainder of the ingredients except flour and starch into a steam-jacketed kettle. Heat to a temperature of 200°F. Make a slurry of flour and starch with 10 gal. of chilled soup stock (or water) in a bakery mixer. Add the slurry to the heated stock. Bring temperature up to 200°F and cook for 10 min.

Fill 211 × 400 cans with 1 oz oxtail pieces, $\frac{1}{4}$ oz carrots, and 9 oz hot soup. Filling temperature of hot soup should be 180°F or higher.

Suggested Process

211 × 400 cans (10½ oz net) 30 min at 250°F

Check process time and temperature with can supplier or the National Canners Association.

SOURCE: Stephan L. Komarik, 4810 Ronda, Coral Gables, Florida.

CANNED CONDENSED MOCK TURTLE SOUP

Ingredients	Gal.	Lb	Oz
Calf heads		500	
(yield will be approx 100 lb of cooked, diced meat)			
Stock from cooked heads	100		
Fresh lemons (in ¼-in. dice)		10	
Chopped fresh onions		10	
Chopped parsley		2	
Butter		36	
Wheat flour		45	
Salt		16	
Monosodium glutamate		2	8
Plant protein hydrolyzate		1	8
Ground white pepper			4
Ground thyme			4
Ground coriander			6
Caramel color			4
Sherry wine	4		

Procedure

Cover calf heads with 100 gal. of water. Bring temperature up to 200°F and cook until meat can be removed. Chill and dice in ¼-in dice.

Melt butter in a steam-jacketed kettle and, with steady stirring, add flour; raise temperature to 240°F and brown flour.

Heat soup stock to 200°F in another steam-jacketed kettle. Add chopped onions, parsley, and salt mixed with the remainder of the seasonings and flavorings. While agitating the stock slowly, add the browned flour, then the meat and lemon dice. Bring temperature up to 200°F and cook soup 10 min longer. Add sherry wine just before filling cans.

Fill into 211 × 400 size cans at a temperature of 180°F or higher.

Suggested Process

211 × 400 cans (10½ oz net) 30 min at 250°F

Check process time and temperature with can supplier or the National Canners Association.

SOURCE: Stephan L. Komarik, 4810 Ronda, Coral Gables, Florida.

GREEN TURTLE SOUP

Green turtle soup is canned in New York and one or two other localities on the Atlantic seaboard, utilizing green turtles (*Chelonia mydes*) imported from Central America, especially from Yucatan, British Honduras, Nicaragua and the West Indies. Some of these turtles are taken by hand when they come up on land, but most are caught in tangle nets, a type of gill net.

The turtles which weigh from 100–300 lb are held in tanks or pens and shipped live to Fulton Market in New York City. Several published formulas are available but are useful only as guides and must be modified as experience indicates. The formula given below is of that type.

Ingredients	Lb	Oz
Turtle meat	20	
Beef bones (or parts of the turtle; see below)	20	
Water (10 gal.)		
Onions, diced	2	
Sherry wine (2 qt)		
Olive oil (1½ pt)		
Flour	1	
Salt		4–8
Worcestershire sauce		8
Minced parsley		3
Cayenne pepper		2
Celery, diced	½	
Marjoram		1
Thyme		1
Bay leaves		½

Procedure

Instead of beef bones to make the stock, the turtle head, liver, lungs, heart, flippers and shell may be used. Boil beef bones (or turtle parts) in the water together with the celery, marjoram, thyme, bay leaves, and parsley to prepare the soup stock.

While stock is cooking, dice turtle meat into small cubes and cook slightly over low heat for 15–20 min in ¾ pt of the olive oil. With the remainder of the olive oil (¾ pt), cook the diced onions until brown; then strain onions out of oil and slowly add the flour to the oil, while stirring; cook and stir until a smooth brown roux is obtained.

Filter stock until clear and gradually add the roux, mixing continuously so the soup will not be lumpy. Then add the cooked meat together with salt and cayenne pepper. When soup approaches boiling temperature, add the Worcestershire sauce and sherry. Stir the soup vigorously while filling containers (so ingredients are well distributed).

Containers should be filled and sealed immediately while soup is hot.

Suggested Process

Turtle soup is packed in containers varying from No. 1 picnic (211 × 400) to No. 2½ (401 × 411) cans. Representative processes are: for No. 1 cans 45 min and for No. 2½ containers 65 min at 240°F (10 lb pressure). Water cool the pack in tanks immediately after processing. The process time and temperature should be checked with the can supplier or the National Canners Association.

Some published formulas include lemon juice and chopped hard boiled egg yolks. It is understood that better results are obtained when these ingredients are added to taste by the consumer. Cooking sherry may be used; imported sherry is favored for a fancy product. Some chefs prefer turtle soup without sherry, adding it to taste when serving the soup.

SOURCE: Fish and Wildlife Service. U.S. Department of the Interior, Washington, D.C.

SNAPPING TURTLE SOUP

Two species of snapping turtle are canned to some extent, the common snapping turtle (*Chelydra serpentina*) and the hardshell, or alligator turtle (*Macrochelys lacertina*). The common snapping turtle may reach a maximum weight of 40 lb, but is usually much smaller. The common snapping turtle is taken commercially in the states around the Great Lakes, along the Mississippi River, and in New Jersey, Delaware, and Virginia. Snapping turtles are taken commercially by fyke nets, fish pots, haul seines, gaffs, hand lines, trot lines, and by hand, that is, simply picked up by the fishermen. Snapping turtles should be alive when marketed. It is believed that the females are best for canning.

"Snapper soup" may be made using the formula given above for **Green Turtle Soup**, or the following ingredients and procedure may be used.

Ingredients	Gal.	Lb	Oz
Snapper meat		30	
Water	10		
Tomatoes (10 No. 1 cans)			
Minced onions			2
Lard			1
Flour			1
Minced garlic			2
Minced parsley			2
White pepper			2
Whole cloves			2
Mace			½
Bay leaves			½
Salt, to taste			

Procedure

Behead turtles and hang head down until blood ceases to drip. Then clean turtles, taking care not to break the gall bladder. Separate meat from bones and cut meat into small dice. Add the turtle dice, parsley, cloves, mace and bay leaves to the water and simmer about 15 min. Then remove the meat and strain the liquid to obtain the soup stock. Drain the meat and fry lightly in ham fat or bacon drippings until meat surface is a light brown.

Fry onions in the lard until they are brown; then strain onions out of fat and slowly add the flour, while stirring; cook and stir until a smooth brown roux is obtained. While stirring the stock, gradually add the roux, followed by the tomatoes and meat; and when soup boils, add the pepper and salt to taste.

Fill into 211 × 400 cans and seal immediately while soup is hot.

Suggested Process

For 211 × 400 cans process 40–45 min at 240°F with 10 lb pressure. Check process time and temperature with can supplier or the National Canners Association.

The pack is usually water-cooled in tanks to about 100°F.

SOURCE: Fish and Wildlife Service, U.S. Department of the Interior, Washington, D.C.

BEEF-FLAVOR SOUP AND GRAVY BASE MIX

Ingredients	%
Maggi's Hydrolyzed Plant Protein 4BE Powder	44.20
Monosodium glutamate	10.00
Onion powder	6.50
Maggi low sodium yeast	4.00
Sugar	12.00
Celery salt	1.20
Caramel powder	1.00
Beef fat	2.75
Salt	18.30
Cayenne pepper	0.05
	100.00

Procedure

Mix ingredients until a uniform mixture is obtained.

To Use.—Dissolve 7 gm in 8 oz of hot water.

SOURCE: Nestlé Company, Food Ingredients Division, 100 Bloomingdale Road, White Plains, N.Y.

BEEF-TYPE BROTH MIX (LOW SODIUM)

Ingredients	%
Maggi HPP Type Super BE powder	48.00
Monopotassium glutamate	10.00
Maggi autolyzed yeast extract, low sodium powder	5.00
Caramel color powder	1.75
Beef extract, dried	1.50
Spice blend (see below)	5.00
Instant Clearjel	5.00
Oleoresin celery	0.015
Sugar	13.735
Nonfat dry milk, spray dried	10.00
	100.00

Spice Blend Ingredients	%
Garlic powder	1.74
White pepper	1.33
Ground rosemary	0.40
Ground cloves	0.13
Cayenne pepper	0.20
Onion powder	96.20
	100.00

Procedure

Mix ingredients until a uniform mixture is obtained.

To Use.—Dissolve 3.5 gm in 6 oz of boiling water.

Sodium Content: 3.5 gm per 6-oz serving—245 mg Na

Caloric Content: 3.5 gm per 6-oz serving—10.23 cal

SOURCE: Nestlé Company, Food Ingredients Division, 100 Bloomingdale Road, White Plains, N.Y.

BEEF BROTH BASE MIX (PASTE FORM)

Ingredients	Lb	Oz
Cheese salt	32	
Corn sugar	16	
Monosodium glutamate	10	
Plant protein hydrolyzate	5	
S.A. beef extract	10	
Rendered beef fat	16	
Cornstarch	4	
Onion powder	2	
Dry soluble pepper	1	
Dry caramel color	1	
Oleoresin celery		2
Garlic powder		2

Procedure

Put sugar, salt, monosodium glutamate, plant protein hydrolyzate, starch, caramel color and flavorings in a mechanical mixer and mix thoroughly. Heat beef extract with fat to 180°F then add to mixer contents and mix until smooth texture is obtained.

Pack product in any size drum, jar, or moisture-vaporproof envelope.

Recommended Use.—Use 4 oz per 1 gal. of water and simmer 10 min before serving.

SOURCE: Stephan L. Komarik, 4810 Ronda, Coral Gables, Florida.

BEEF SOUP MIX

Ingredients	%
Beef powder*	23.10
Wheat flour*	23.10
Carrot powder*	23.08
Onion powder*	17.30
Salt*	8.78
Beef fat	1.88
Monosodium glutamate	1.66
Hydrolyzed vegetable protein*	0.88
Ground white pepper	0.15
Caramelline powder H6168	0.07

Procedure

Mix all ingredients thoroughly. If desired, the ingredients marked * may be predried together to lower the final moisture content.

Use 4-ply laminated soup pockets and fill 56 gm of mix into each and heat-seal.

To Reconstitute

Mix the contents of a packet with 1 pt of water. Bring to a boil and simmer for 5 min.

SOURCE: Henningsen Foods, Inc., 60 East 42 St., New York, N.Y.

JELLIED BEEF CONSOMMÉ BASE MIX

Ingredients	Lb	Oz
Cheese salt	32	
Corn sugar	26	
Monosodium glutamate	10	
Plant protein hydrolyzate	6	
Beef extract	10	
Onion powder	4	
Dry soluble pepper	1	
Dry caramel color	1	
Oleoresin celery		4
Garlic powder		2
Gelatin (200-bloom fine granulation)	60	

Procedure

Put cheese salt and gelatin in a mechanical mixer and mix thoroughly. Heat beef extract to 180°F, and add to mixture. Run mixer until salt and gelatin are coated with the extract without any lumps, then add remainder of the ingredients and mix thoroughly.

Pack in any size drum, can, jar, or moisture-vaporproof envelope.

Recommended Use.—Use 6 oz to 1 gal. of water and simmer 10 min before chilling and serving.

SOURCE: Stephan L. Komarik, 4810 Ronda, Coral Gables, Florida.

BEEF NOODLE SOUP BASE MIX

Ingredients	%
Maggi HPP Type 4BE Powder	12.00
Maggi Super BE Powder	11.00
Beef fat	8.00
Cornstarch, dried	12.00
Monosodium glutamate	10.00
Salt	24.00
Spice blend (see below)	2.00
Turmeric	0.10
Caramel color powder	0.50
Sugar	10.40
Maltodextrin	10.00
	100.00

Spice Blend Ingredients	%
Celery salt	16.20
Garlic powder	1.45
White pepper	1.21
Rosemary	0.32
Cloves	0.08
Cayenne pepper	0.16
Granulated onion	80.58
	100.00

Procedure

Mix ingredients until a uniform mixture is obtained.

To Use.—Add 28 gm of base and 30 gm of noodles to 1 qt of water. Bring to a boil while stirring. Simmer partly covered for 4 min.

For a beef noodle soup with diced beef meat, add 3 gm of freeze-dried beef dice.

SOURCE: Nestlé Company, Food Ingredients Division, 100 Bloomingdale Road, White Plains, N.Y.

BEEF NOODLE SOUP MIX

Ingredients	%
Freeze-dehydrated beef dice	23.22
Salt	21.12
Corn syrup solids	9.85
Cornstarch	9.29
Monosodium glutamate	7.66
Rendered beef fat	7.47
Beef extract	5.57
Hydrolyzed plant protein	4.64
Dehydrated onion slices	4.64
Freeze-dehydrated carrot slices	4.64
Celery on salt	1.16
Garlic powder	0.28
Caramel	0.23
C.O.S. black pepper (Cream of Spice)	0.23

Procedure

All of the dry ingredients should be warmed to room temperature and thoroughly mixed together in a Hobart mixer or a tumbling-type mixer. Melt beef fat and add it last, taking care to add it slowly while the mixer is operating.

Package 21.53 gm of mix with 21 gm noodles in a buried-foil pouch.

To Use

Stir contents of 1 envelope into 1½ pt of boiling water and simmer for 7 min with saucepan partially covered.

SOURCE: *Food Dehydration, 2nd Edition, Vol. 2* by Van Arsdel *et al.* published by Avi Publishing Co., Westport, Conn.

CHICKEN-TYPE BROTH MIX (LOW SODIUM)

	Formula	
	No. 1	No. 2
Ingredients	%	%
Maggi HPP Type Super 3H Powder	46.00	46.00
Dehydrated chicken broth	2.00	2.00
Monopotassium glutamate	12.50	12.50
Nonfat dry milk, spray dried	5.00	10.50
Onion powder, fresh flavor	2.00	2.00
White pepper	0.20	0.20
Parsley granules	0.10	0.10
Oleoresin celery	0.015	0.015
Sugar	15.485	15.485
Instant Clearjel	15.50	10.00
Turmeric, soluble	0.20	0.20
Salt substitute (see below)	1.00	1.00
	100.000	100.000

Salt Substitute Ingredients	%
Potassium chloride	82.0
Monopotassium glutamate	15.0
Ammonium chloride	3.0
	100.0

Procedure

Mix ingredients until a uniform mixture is obtained.

To Use.—Dissolve 3.5 gm in 6 oz of boiling water. Either of the above formulas provide the following:

Sodium Content: 3.5 gm per 6-oz serving—
244 mg Na

Caloric Content: 3.5 gm per 6-oz serving—
9.88 cal

SOURCE: Nestlé Company, Food Ingredients Division, 100 Bloomingdale Road, White Plains, N.Y.

CLEAR CHICKEN SOUP BASE MIX

Ingredients	Lb	Oz
Salt	32	
Monosodium glutamate	12	
Plant protein hydrolyzate	6	
Mixed soluble seasonings	2	4

Soluble Seasoning Ingredients	Gm	Cc
Oleoresin pepper	42.50	
Oleoresin celery	7.00	
Oleoresin turmeric	10.00	
True oil of onions		4.12
True oil of garlic		0.12
Propylene glycol		60.00

Dissolve oleoresins and oils in the propylene glycol then mix in 2 lb of sugar.

Procedure

Mix all ingredients thoroughly in a mechanical mixer. Pack in any size of drum, tin, or moisture-proof envelope.

Recommended Use

Use 2½ oz to 1 gal. of water. Heat 10 min at simmering temperature. If desired, 1 tsp of butter added to the broth will make a richer soup.

SOURCE: Stephan L. Komarik, 4810 Ronda, Coral Gables, Florida.

JELLIED CHICKEN SOUP BASE MIX

Use the formula given above for Clear Chicken Soup Base Mix, and to each 52 lb 4 oz add a mix-

ture of 50 lb 200-bloom gelatin and 2 oz dry caramel color.

Pack in any size drum, can, jar or moisture-vaporproof envelope.

Recommended Use

Use 5 oz to 1 gal. of water. Cook 10 min at simmering temperature, then chill before serving.

SOURCE: Stephan L. Komarik, 4810 Ronda, Coral Gables, Florida.

SOUP, DEHYDRATED, CHICKEN (TYPE II WITH NOODLES)

Ingredients	Parts by Weight
Egg noodles	70.0
Chicken fat	3.5
Dehydrated chicken meat solids	0.5
Hydrogenated vegetable fat	3.5
Hydrolyzed protein	1.0
Monosodium glutamate	4.0
Onion powder	1.0
(Not more than the following:)	
Salt	11.0
Sugar	1.5
Starch or dextrin (or both)	4.0
Spices and flavorings	1.0

The above specification includes a method for preaward testing by a consumer preference panel of not less than 30 persons, using a 9-point hedonic scale. A standard reference sample is used for comparison purposes.

SOURCE: U.S. Military Specification No. S-1049C, Nov. 20, 1962.

CHICKEN NOODLE SOUP MIX

Ingredients	%
Salt	37.86
Monosodium glutamate	21.70
Chicken fat	16.30
Dehydrated chicken	14.08
Wheaten base	3.26
Onion powder	2.72
Sugar	1.74
Hydrolyzed vegetable protein	1.36
Dried parsley	0.54
Ground white pepper	0.22
Ground turmeric	0.22

Procedure

Mix all ingredients thoroughly.
Use 4-ply laminated soup pockets. Fill 17 gm of

the above soup mix and 40 gm of fine noodles into each pocket and heat-seal.

To Rehydrate

Add contents of a packet to 1 pt of boiling water. Simmer until noodles are tender (approx 5–7 min).

SOURCE: Henningsen Foods, Inc., 60 East 42 St., New York, N.Y.

CREAM OF CHICKEN SOUP BASE MIX

Ingredients	Lb	Oz
Precooked wheat flour	140	
Cornstarch	24	
Butter	24	
Rendered chicken fat	16	
Dehydrated chicken meat	16	
Nonfat dry milk	24	
Cheese salt	32	
Monosodium glutamate	10	
Plant protein hydrolyzate	6	
Free flowing onion powder	1	
Dehydrated carrot dice (1/4-in.)	4	
Dehydrated pimientos	4	
Dry soluble pepper		4
Garlic powder		1
Turmeric (Alleppey)		4
Ground celery seeds		2

Procedure

Heat chicken fat and butter to 160°F. Add ground turmeric and celery to the heated fats and mix thoroughly. Put salt, monosodium glutamate, plant protein hydrolyzate, garlic, and onion powder in a mechanical mixer. Start machine; then add heated fats and mix thoroughly; then add remaining ingredients and let machine run until all ingredients are uniformly distributed.

Pack in any size drum, tin, or moisture-vapor-proof envelopes.

To Use

Use 12 oz of base mix per 1 gal. of water. Make a slurry of the base mix with 1 qt of water, then add 3 qt of hot water. Stir and cook for 15 min before serving.

SOURCE: Stephan L. Komarik, 4810 Ronda, Coral Gables, Florida.

CREAM OF CHICKEN SOUP MIX

Ingredients	%
Dehydrated chicken meat	28.25
Wheat flour*	24.60
Nonfat dry milk*	22.70
Chicken fat*	18.20
Salt	3.55
Monosodium glutamate	1.13
Onion powder*	0.57
Hydrolyzed vegetable protein*	0.55
Sugar	0.38
White pepper (on salt)	0.04
Celery (on salt)	0.03

Procedure

Mix all ingredients thoroughly. If desired, the ingredients marked * may be predried together to lower the final moisture content.

Use 4-ply laminated soup pockets. Fill 91 gm of mix into each and heat-seal.

To Rehydrate

Mix the contents of a packet with 1 pt of cold water. Bring to a boil and simmer for 10–15 min.

SOURCE: Henningsen Foods, Inc., 60 East 42 St., New York, N.Y.

CHICKEN NOODLE SOUP MIX (DRY STYLE)

Ingredients	%
Corn syrup solids	32.10
Salt	32.00
Monosodium glutamate	12.65
Cornstarch	8.00
Chicken fat	7.16
Chicken stock, dehydrated	2.44
Powdered chicken meat	2.30
Dehydrated onion powder	2.25
Dehydrated parsley leaves	0.24
Hydrolyzed vegetable protein	0.20
C.O.S. black pepper (Cream of Spice)	0.20
C.O.S. celery (Cream of Spice)	0.45
C.O.S. thyme (Cream of Spice)	0.01

Procedure

Mix ingredients in dough type mixer until a uniform mixture is obtained.

Package 22.1 gm dry mix with 41.7 noodles in laminated buried-foil pouch.

To Rehydrate

Stir contents of 1 package into 4 cups boiling water; keep pan partially covered and soup simmering for 7 min with occasional stirring.

SOURCE: Food Dehydration, 2nd Edition, Vol. 2 by Van Arsdel et al. published by Avi Publishing Company, Westport, Conn.

CHICKEN NOODLE SOUP MIX (PASTE STYLE)

Ingredients	%
Salt	34.0
Hydrogenated vegetable oil	15.04
Monosodium glutamate	12.75
Corn syrup solids	11.55
Hydrolyzed plant and milk protein	6.00
Powdered chicken meat	5.74
Chicken fat	4.63
Dextrose, anhydrous	4.23
Wheat starch	2.54
Dehydrated white onion powder	2.20
C.O.S. celery (Cream of Spice)	0.45
Dehydrated parsley leaves	0.23
Vegetable gum (C.M.C.)	0.22
C.O.S. black pepper (Cream of Spice)	0.214
Turmeric	0.20
C.O.S. clove (Cream of Spice)	0.004
Rosemary powder	0.002

Procedure

Mix ingredients in dough type mixer until a uniform mixture is obtained.

Package 21.7 gm paste with 35 gm noodles in a laminated buried-foil pouch.

To Rehydrate

Stir contents of 1 package into 1 qt boiling water and cook for 5–7 min.

SOURCE: *Food Dehydration, 2nd Edition, Vol. 2 by Van Arsdel et al.* published by Avi Publishing Company, Westport, Conn.

CHICKEN-FLAVORED SOUP BASE MIX

Ingredients	%
Hydrogenated vegetable oil	16.42
Rendered chicken fat	6.00
Starch (Mira-Cleer® 340)	9.55
Corn syrup solids (Star-Dri® 24R)	14.40
Powdered chicken	2.25
Dextrose (Staleydex® 333)	0.70
Chicken seasoning blend (Vico-Asmus 91N-74)	50.68

Procedure

Blend fats with starch (Mira-Cleer®), corn syrup solids (Star-Dri®), and dextrose (Staleydex®). Add and blend in powdered chicken and seasoning blend.

SOURCE: A. E. Staley Mfg. Company, Decatur, Ill.

CREAM OF MUSHROOM SOUP MIX

Ingredients	%
Maggi HPP Type 3H3-4 Powder	6.80
Nonfat dry milk	23.00
Hydrogenated vegetable oil	5.22
Wheat flour, dried	15.70
Cornstarch, dried	10.45
Sugar	4.70
Salt	6.26
Onion powder	1.05
Mushroom powder	2.10
Turmeric	0.02
Freeze-dried mushroom dice	2.10
Monosodium glutamate	6.80
C.O.S. pepper (Cream of Spice)	0.10
Dry sweet whey	15.70
	100.00

Procedure

Mix ingredients until a uniform mixture is obtained.

To Use.—Put 84 gm in a saucepan. Gradually stir in 2¼ cups of water. Bring to a boil, stirring constantly. Reduce heat and simmer for 3 min. Add ¾ cup of milk and heat gently. Do not boil.

SOURCE: Nestlé Company, Food Ingredients Division, 100 Bloomingdale Road, White Plains, N.Y.

INSTANT ONION SOUP MIX

Ingredients	%
Maggi HPP Type 4BE-2	3.75
Maggi HPP Type 3H3 Powder	3.00
Hydrogenated vegetable oil	5.00
Salt	20.75
Sugar	18.00
Monosodium glutamate	6.00
Dehydrated ground onion, toasted	6.00
Onion powder	11.50
Caramel color	0.60
Pregelatinized starch	6.00
Lactose	18.40
Paprika	1.00
	100.00

Procedure

Mix ingredients until a uniform mixture is obtained.

To Use.—Combine 12 gm of mix with 6 oz hot water (195°F). Stir until uniform.

SOURCE: Nestlé Company, Food Ingredients Division, 100 Bloomingdale Road, White Plains, N.Y.

OXTAIL SOUP MIX

Ingredients	%
Wheat flour*	45.20
Salt*	18.10
Beef extract*	8.52
Brown bean powder*	4.52
Beef powder*	4.52
Beef fat	4.52
Hydrolyzed yeast protein	4.52
Onion powder	4.52
Monosodium glutamate	2.26
Hydrolyzed vegetable protein*	2.26
Ground thyme	0.23
Caramel	0.23
Ground white pepper	0.12
Ground paprika	0.12
Ground coriander	0.12
Ground bay	0.12
ICI Edicol Supra Orange AG	0.12

Procedure

Mix all ingredients thoroughly. If desired, the ingredients marked * may be predried together to lower the final moisture content.

Use 4-ply laminated soup pockets. Fill 44 gm of mix into each and heat-seal.

To Reconstitute

Mix the contents of a packet with 1 pt of cold water, bring to a boil and simmer for 3–5 min before serving.

SOURCE: Henningsen Foods, Inc., 60 East 42 St., New York, N.Y.

MULLIGATAWNY SOUP MIX

Ingredients	%
Wheat flour*	33.70
Beef powder*	27.00
Salt*	11.09
Tomato powder	8.41
Sugar	6.74
Curry powder	5.04
Onion powder	3.57
Beef fat	1.95
Monosodium glutamate	0.88
Ground paprika	0.67
Ground turmeric	0.44
Hydrolyzed vegetable protein*	0.34
Caramelline H6168	0.20
Ground marjoram	0.07
Ground clove	0.05
Ground thyme	0.05

Procedure

Mix all ingredients thoroughly. If desired, the ingredients marked * may be predried together to lower the final moisture content.

Use 4-ply laminated soup pockets. Fill 56 gm of mix into each pocket and heat-seal.

To Reconstitute

Mix contents of a packet with 1 pt of cold water. Bring to a boil and simmer for a few minutes before serving.

SOURCE: Henningsen Foods, Inc., 60 East 42 St., New York, N.Y.

MOCK TURTLE SOUP MIX

Ingredients	%
Wheat flour*	27.30
Beef powder*	17.02
Onion powder*	13.65
Carrot powder*	11.40
Tomato powder	10.80
Salt*	9.10
Monosodium glutamate	2.85
Beef fat	2.85
Hydrolyzed vegetable protein*	2.27
Hydrolyzed yeast protein*	2.27
Ground thyme	0.15
ICI Edicol Supra Orange AG	0.11
Ground bay	0.07
Ground coriander	0.06
Ground paprika	0.05
Ground white pepper	0.05
	100.00

Procedure

Mix all the ingredients thoroughly. If desired, the ingredients marked * may be predried together to lower the final moisture content.

Fill 56 gm of mix into each 4-ply laminated soup pocket and heat-seal.

To Reconstitute

Mix the contents of a packet with 1 pt of cold water, bring to a boil and simmer for a few minutes before serving.

SOURCE: Henningsen Foods, Inc., 60 East 42 St., New York, N.Y.

BEET SOUP MIX (BORSCHT)

Ingredients	Lb	Oz
Beet powder	45	
Salt	36	

Ingredients		
Monosodium glutamate	12	
Plant protein hydrolyzate	6	
Cane sugar	110	
Cornstarch	73	
Vegetable oil	12	
Onion powder	3	12
Citric acid	2	4
Ground celery seed	2	
Garlic powder		$1/2$
Dry soluble pepper	4	

Procedure

Put salt in a mechanical mixer and while the machine is running, add ground celery seed, dry soluble pepper, garlic powder, and citric acid. Add vegetable oil. After a few minutes add the remainder of the ingredients and mix thoroughly.

Pack in any size drum, tin, or moisture-vapor-proof envelope.

Recommended Use.—Use 12 oz per 1 gal. of water. Make a slurry of 12 oz of soup base to 1 qt of water (free of lumps) then add slurry to the remaining 3 qt of hot water. Stir and cook an additional 15 min.

SOURCE: Stephan L. Komarik, 4810 Ronda, Coral Gables, Florida.

GRAVY FOR FROZEN POT PIES

For Chicken Pies

Ingredients	Lb
Chicken broth	300
Wheat flour	$9^{1}/2$
Derivatized cross-bonded waxy cornstarch	$15^{1}/2$
Chicken fat	25
Chicken pie seasoning	$3^{1}/4$

(1) Slurry flour and starch in 2–3 gal. of the cold broth. Heat remaining broth in kettle to 190°F.

(2) Stir in starch-flour slurry and continue to heat until broth thickens.

(3) Add fat and seasoning.

(4) Fill into aluminum pans over meat and vegetable pieces. Bottom crust is optional.

For Turkey Pies

Follow formula given above but use turkey pie seasoning instead.

For Tuna Pies

Use formula given above except: replace chicken broth with water; replace chicken fat with shortening; and use tuna pie seasoning.

SOURCE: CPC International. Inc., Industrial Division, Englewood Cliffs, N.J.

FROZEN EXTENDER FOR ROAST CHICKEN OR TURKEY GRAVY

Use this gravy extender with the natural roast chicken or turkey juices rendered during roasting of these products.

Ingredients	Gal.	Lb	Oz
Water	50		
Salt		4	
Gelatin (200-bloom)		6	
Monosodium glutamate	1	8	
Plant protein hydrolyzate		12	
Onion powder		2	
Ground turmeric (Alleppey)			$1/2$
Ground celery seeds			$1/4$
Spanish paprika			$1/4$
White pepper			$1/2$
Garlic powder			$1/16$
Caramel color		1	

Procedure

Put water in a steam-jacketed kettle and heat to 200°F. Mix salt, gelatin, and remainder of ingredients together and stir into the hot water. Stir and cook 15 min.

Pack for institutional use. Prechill before freezing.

To Use.—Defrost product in refrigerator overnight; or, if product is packaged in water-tight cans, accelerated defrosting can be done in warm water. Heat product to serving temperature and thoroughly mix in the natural juices rendered during roasting of chickens or turkeys.

SOURCE: Stephan L. Komarik, 4810 Ronda, Coral Gables, Florida.

FROZEN GIBLET GRAVY

Prepare Giblets

Ingredients	Gal.	Lb
Water	5	
Chicken or turkey gizzards or hearts		80
Carrot emulsion		22
Chopped cooked carrots		5

Remove stomach linings of gizzards and all surface fat from both gizzards and hearts and wash well in cold water. Cook in water until giblets are tender; then chop or grind to $1/4$ in. in size.

Cook carrots for the emulsion until very soft in a pressure cooker; then put product through a finisher to make a smooth emulsion.

For the chopped cooked carrots, cook product until tender but not mushy; then dice into $1/4$-in. cubes.

Prepare Gravy

Ingredients	Gal.	Lb	Oz
Water	45		
Rendered chicken fat		25	
Wheat flour		20	
Cornstarch		5	
Salt		5	
Monosodium glutamate		1	8
Plant protein hydrolyzate			12
Onion powder			2
Garlic powder			1/8
Ground turmeric (Alleppey)			1/2
Ground celery seeds			1/4
Ground white pepper			1
Spanish paprika			1/4
Caramel color			1-2

In a bakery mixer, make a slurry of the flour and starch with 5 gal. of the water. Premix salt with flavorings and seasonings.

Put remainder of the water in a steam-jacketed kettle and heat to 200°F. Add salt mixture and, with continuous stirring, add slurry. Then add chicken fat, carrot emulsion, and the diced carrots and giblets. Bring temperature back up to 200°F and cook 15–20 min.

Pack for institutional use in 5-lb containers suitable for freezing. Prechill product before freezing.

To Use

If product is warmed over low heat to serving temperature, it need not be fully defrosted before warming. Otherwise, defrost overnight in refrigerator; or, if product is packaged in water-tight containers, defrosting can be accelerated by placing it in warm water.

SOURCE: Stephan L. Komarik, 4810 Ronda, Coral Gables, Florida.

DRY MIX SOUP AND GRAVY BASE, BEEF

Ingredients	Not Less Than	Not More Than
	Parts by Weight (as-is basis)	
Hydrolyzed protein	18.0	
Beef extract	11.5	
Monosodium glutamate	10.0	
Onion powder	6.5	
Autolyzed yeast (salt-free solids)	3.0	
Rendered beef fat		3.0
Sugar		12.0
Soluble celery flavoring		12.0

Caramel color	1.5
Salt, spice, or spice flavorings, and other seasonings to make up 100 parts	

The finished soup product can contain no more than 22% salt as NaCl, 3.0% moisture, and 2.5% fat.

SOURCE: U.S. Military Specification No. 3271C

AU JUS GRAVY MIX

Ingredients	%
Maggi HPP Type 245 Powder	12.50
Maggi HPP Type 4BE-2 Powder	6.25
Caramel color	2.50
Beef fat	5.00
Monosodium glutamate	8.00
Cornstarch, dried	23.00
Granulated salt	9.00
Granulated sugar	10.00
Dehydrated onion powder, toasted	1.00
Ground paprika	1.00
Corn syrup solids	21.75
	100.00

Procedure

Mix ingredients until a uniform mixture is obtained.

To Use.—In a saucepan, combine 20 gm of mix with 8 oz of water. Bring to a boil while stirring. Simmer for 2 min.

SOURCE: Nestlé Company, Food Ingredients Division, 100 Bloomingdale Road, White Plains, N.Y.

GRAVY MIX FOR BEEF POT ROAST

Ingredients	%
Waxy maize starch (pregelatinized)	40.5
Caramel color (powder)	2.0
Onion powder (white)	2.5
Onion chips (golden brown, dehydrated)	5.0
Salt	20.5
Monosodium glutamate	1.5
Black pepper, ground	0.5
Worcestershire sauce	3.5
Hydrolyzed vegetable protein	1.5
Oleo stock	17.5
Lard flakes	4.0
Citric acid	1.0
	100.0

Procedure

First thoroughly mix the dry ingredients in a mechanical mixer (e.g., Hobart). Melt and combine lard flakes and oleo stock and slowly add the warm shortening to the dry ingredients while the mixer is slowly running; then slowly add the Worcestershire sauce, continuing to slowly run the mixer until all ingredients are thoroughly incorporated.

To Use.—While rapidly agitating product, slowly add mix in the desired concentration to hot water.

SOURCE: *Food Dehydration, 2nd Edition, Vol. 2* by Van Arsdel *et al.* published by Avi Publishing Co., Westport, Conn.

BROWN GRAVY MIX

Ingredients	%
Maggi HPP Super BE Powder	7.50
Maggi HPP 4BE Powder	7.50
Cornstarch	16.00
Tapioca starch	12.00
Wheat flour	14.00
Monosodium glutamate	10.00
Soluble pepper	0.10
Dehydrated onion powder, toasted	4.00
Caramel color powder	0.90
Sugar	2.50
Hydrogenated vegetable oil	3.00
Sour cream solids	1.50
Emulsifier, mono- and diglycerides	1.00
Tetrasodium pyrophosphate	2.00
Sodium caseinate	2.00
Oleoresin paprika	0.10
Salt	5.50
Maltodextrine	10.40
	100.00

Procedure

Mix ingredients until a uniform mixture is obtained.

To Use.—Add 22.7 gm of mix to 8 oz of water and bring to a boil while stirring. Simmer for 2 min.

SOURCE: Nestlé Company, Food Ingredients Division, 100 Bloomingdale Road, White Plains, N.Y.

BROWN GRAVY MIX (DRY)

This product exhibits excellent freeze-thaw and heat stability. Finished products using this gravy are versatile as viscosity remains constant over a wide temperature range. Gravy made from this mix also gives clean mouth-feel and good flavor release.

Ingredients	%
Xanthan gum (Keltrol® F)	3.47
Garlic powder	0.098
Celery salt	0.196
White pepper	0.196
"Corral" beef extract (a Pfizer product)	1.43
Monosodium glutamate	2.45
Caramel color	2.45
Onion flakes	4.21
Fat (oleomargarine)	4.55
Nonfat dry milk	9.40
Brown sugar	9.40
Salt	9.40
Maggi HVP4BE (a Nestlé product)	11.75
Wheat flour	41.00
	100.000

Procedure

Mix ingredients until a uniform mixture is obtained.

To Use.—Disperse 24.40 gm (⅞ oz) of dry mix per cup of cold water. While stirring, slowly heat to boil.

SOURCE: Kelco Company, 20 N. Wacker Drive, Chicago, Ill.

CHICKEN GRAVY MIX (DRY)

This product exhibits excellent freeze-thaw and heat stability. Finished products using this gravy are versatile as viscosity remains constant over a wide temperature range. Gravy made from this mix also gives clean mouth-feel and good flavor release.

Ingredients	%
Xanthan gum (Keltrol® F)	3.47
Turmeric powder	0.014
Garlic powder	0.039
White pepper	0.050
Celery salt	0.056
Onion powder	0.16
Monosodium glutamate	3.78
Chicken fat	4.54
Nonfat dry milk	8.16
Dry sweet whey	8.43
Salt	9.151
Sugar	9.40
Maggi HVP3H3-4 (a Nestlé product)	11.75
Wheat flour	41.00
	100.000

Procedure

Mix ingredients until a uniform mixture is obtained.

To Use.—Disperse 24.40 gm (⅞ oz) of dry mix per cup of cold water. While stirring, slowly heat to boil.

SOURCE: Kelco Company, 20 N. Wacker Drive, Chicago, Ill.

CHICKEN-FLAVORED GRAVY MIX (COOK-UP TYPE)

Ingredients	%
Cornstarch (Mira-Cleer 300)	26.60
Pure food powdered starch (Staley's)	18.40
Salt	10.00
Dextrose (Staleydex 333)	5.80
Sweet whey solids	6.50
Nonfat dry milk solids	4.68
Rendered chicken fat	5.07
Corn syrup solids (Star-Dri 24R)	5.02
Chicken seasoning (Asmus 97P-107B)	17.93

Procedure

Blend all ingredients together until a uniform mixture is obtained.

To Prepare Gravy.—Mix 20–24 gm per cup of water until smooth. Cook until mixture thickens.

SOURCE: A. E. Staley Mfg. Company, Decatur, Ill.

CHICKEN-FLAVORED GRAVY MIX

Ingredients	%
Maggi HPP Type 3H3-4 Powder	10.00
Granulated salt	6.00
Soluble onion	0.30
Wheat flour, dried	20.00
Cornstarch, dried	21.70
Hydrogenated vegetable oil	6.00
Spice blend (see below)	0.20
Dehydrated minced green onion	0.20
Monosodium glutamate	8.00
Nonfat dry milk	27.58
Turmeric (Alleppey)	0.02
	100.00

Spice Blend Ingredients	%
Turmeric (Alleppey)	26.139
Celery salt	37.341
Granulated garlic	23.824
White pepper	7.469
Mustard powder	0.563
Coriander	4.664
	100.000

Procedure

Mix ingredients until a uniform mixture is obtained.

To Use.—Combine 1 oz with 8 oz of cold water. Bring to a boil while stirring. Simmer for 2 min.

SOURCE: Nestlé Company, Food Ingredients Division, 100 Bloomingdale Road, White Plains, N.Y.

TURKEY-FLAVORED INSTANT GRAVY MIX

Ingredients	%
Maggi HPP Type 3H3-4 Powder	5.00
Maggi HPP Type 245 Powder	4.00
Salt	8.00
Onion powder, fresh flavor	1.00
Chicken fat	6.00
Spice blend (see below)	0.30
Parsley granules	0.20
Nonfat dry milk	35.00
Monosodium glutamate	10.00
Precooked starch	8.00
Guar gum	6.00
Vegetable gum	5.00
Dry sweet whey	11.50
	100.00

Spice Blend Ingredients	%
Turmeric (Alleppey)	26.139
Celery salt	37.341
Granulated garlic	23.824
White pepper	7.469
Mustard powder	0.563
Coriander	4.664
	100.000

Procedure

Mix ingredients until a uniform mixture is obtained.

To Use.—To 22 gm of mix add 8 oz of hot water. Stir until smooth. For a frozen food sauce, cold water may be used.

SOURCE: Nestlé Company, Food Ingredients Division, 100 Bloomingdale Road, White Plains, N.Y.

MUSHROOM GRAVY MIX

Ingredients	%
Maggi HPP Type 4BE-2 Powder	7.00
Maggi HPP Type 3H3 Powder	6.00
Caramel powder	2.00
Hydrogenated vegetable oil	5.00
Chicken fat	3.00
Wheat flour	25.00
Cornstarch, dried	14.00
Monosodium glutamate	6.00
Onion powder, fresh flavor	1.00
White pepper	0.15
Oleoresin paprika	0.10
Salt	5.00
Sugar	6.00
Celery seed, microground	0.20
Dry sweet whey	11.55
Freeze-dried mushroom powder	2.00
Freeze-dried mushroom dice	6.00
	100.00

Procedure

Mix ingredients until a uniform mixture is obtained.

To Use.—Combine 24 gm of mix with 8 oz cold water. Bring to a boil and simmer for 1 min.

SOURCE: Nestlé Company, Food Ingredients Division, 100 Bloomingdale Road, White Plains, N.Y.

HAM-STYLE GRAVY MIX

Ingredients	%
Maggi HPP Type 3-FS Powder	4.50
Maggi HPP Type 3H3-4 Powder	4.50
Maggi 4BE Powder	3.75
Salt	7.35
Wheat flour, dried	27.25
Cornstarch, dried	13.65
Sugar	4.90
Monosodium glutamate	7.00
Granulated onion	1.47
C.O.S. celery (Cream of Spice)	0.40
C.O.S. pepper (Cream of Spice)	0.12
Mustard powder	7.75
Tomato powder	9.00
Imitation pineapple flavor	0.02
Ground cloves	0.04
Allspice	0.05
Caramel color	1.50
Hydrogenated vegetable oil	6.75
	100.00

Procedure

Mix ingredients until a uniform mixture is obtained.

To Use.—Combine 22 gm of mix with 8 oz of water. Bring to a boil while stirring. Simmer for 2 min.

SOURCE: Nestlé Company, Food Ingredients Division, 100 Bloomingdale Road, White Plains, N.Y.

SAUCES

BORDELAISE SAUCE FOR FREEZING

	Ingredients	%
(A)	Water	42.5
	Beef broth	36.6
	Tomato paste	6.2
(B)	Starch (Col-Flo 67)	3.2
	Salt	1.2
	Onion flakes	0.5
	Monosodium glutamate	0.2
	Pepper	0.1
(C)	Red wine	9.5

Procedure

1. Blend all ingredients in (A) together.
2. Blend all ingredients in (B) together.
3. Slowly add (B) to (A) while stirring.
4. Heat to 185°F and hold 3 min.
5. Remove from heat and slowly add (C), stirring constantly.
6. Add solids, place in desired containers and freeze.

SOURCE: National Starch and Chemical Corp., 1700 W. Front St., Plainfield, N.J.

BOTTLED MEAT SAUCE

Ingredients	Lb	Oz
Fat	12	
Modified thick boiling waxy maize starch		3
Ground carrots	5	
Ground onions	5	
Tomato pureé	5	
Garlic		4
Ground bay leaves	1	
Ground whole cloves		10
Ground thyme		5
Ground pepper		8
Tobasco sauce		½
Brown sugar	3	
Beef stock	100	

YIELD: 130 lb

Procedure

Melt fat in kettle over low heat. Add ground onions and carrots and simmer at low heat for 5 min. Add garlic.

While stirring gently add tomato pureé, ground spices, and tobasco. Add the brown sugar. Add 80 lb of the beef stock and bring to 195°F.

While stirring slowly add 20 lb of beef stock in which has been slurried the modified waxy maize starch. Continue heat at 180°F until thick.

Strain and pack in bottles, then process.

Check process time and temperature with bottle supplier or the National Canners Association.

SOURCE: CPC International, Inc., Industrial Division, Englewood Cliffs, N.J.

FROZEN SAUCE A LA BARBARA WITH HAM-LIKE TEXTURED VEGETABLE PROTEIN DICE

Ingredients	%
Vegetable oil	7.90
Onions, diced	4.50
Mushrooms	6.75
Flour	4.50
Chicken stock	27.04
Milk	18.00
Textured vegetable protein (Bontrae® Ham)	26.00
Romano cheese	4.50
Nutmeg, ground	0.30
Salt	0.45
White pepper	0.02
Parsley	0.04

Procedure

Weigh oil into steam kettle; add onion and heat until tender. Add flour and spices to form a paste. Add milk while stirring. Add Bontrae® and remaining ingredients and bring to a boil.
Package in boil-in-bag pouches and freeze.

SOURCE: General Mills, Inc., 9200 Wayzata Blvd., Minneapolis, Minn.

MARINARA SAUCE BASE MIX

Ingredients	%
Garlic powder	24.55
Salt	16.45
Maggi Type 4BE-2 Powder	12.40
Sugar	11.80
Oregano	0.82
Basil	0.41
Thyme	0.41
Maltodextrine 2% (Yellow No. 5)	9.85
Monosodium glutamate	4.93
Red pepper	0.61
Marjoram	0.21
Torulla yeast	4.10
Rosemary	0.24
Spray-dried Romano cheese (available from Rogers Products)	0.82
Dextrose	12.40
	100.00

Procedure

Mix ingredients until a uniform mixture is obtained.

To Use.—To 14 gm of base mix, add the following: 8-oz can plum tomatoes, 8-oz can tomato sauce, and 2-3 tbsp of olive oil. Bring contents to a boil while stirring. Reduce heat, cover, and cook gently for another 5-10 min.

SOURCE: Nestlé Company, Food Ingredients Division, 100 Bloomingdale Road, White Plains, N.Y.

BARBECUE SAUCE

Ingredients	%
Tomato paste (28% solids)	37.95
Water	30.82
White distilled vinegar (50-grain)	12.66
Lemon juice, single strength	8.07
Brown sugar	5.65
Salt	2.42
Modified waxy maize starch (Polar Gel 10, available from American Maize-Products Co.)	1.00
Onion	0.80
Microcrystalline cellulose (Avicel RC-581 or RC-591)	0.33
Paprika	0.30
	100.00

Procedure

(1) Add dry blend of Avicel RC-581 or RC-591 and starch to the total water requirements and mix for 3 min.
(2) Add tomato paste, sugar, salt, onion, and paprika.
(3) Slowly blend in vinegar and lemon juice.
(4) Allow temperature to reach 190°-195°F (stirring constantly) over a period of 3-4 min to fully develop the thickener.
(5) Hot fill into containers.
Check process time and temperature with can supplier or the National Canners Association.

SOURCE: FMC Corp., American Viscose Division, Marcus Hook, Pa.

BARBECUE SAUCE MIX

Ingredients	%
Lard flakes	1.8
Oleo stock	25.1
Dehydrated apple sauce	12.8
Worcestershire sauce	11.6
Onion powder (white)	10.7
Tomato flakes (salt-free)	10.7
Salt	7.3
Brown sugar	6.0
Dehydrated grapefruit juice	4.65
Beef extract	2.7
Dry vinegar	1.75
Hydrolyzed vegetable protein	1.5
Paprika (50A)	1.16
Yeast extract	0.15

Garlic powder	0.5
Soluble celery seasoning	0.28
Black pepper, ground	0.31

Procedure

Mix together all dry ingredients in a Hobart mixer or a tumbling type mixer, after which thoroughly incorporate lard flakes and oleo stock.

Percentage of sauce ingredients given above (100%) for 100-lb of barbecued meat ingredients.

SOURCE: *Food Dehydration, 2nd Edition, Vol. 2* by Van Arsdel *et al.* published by Avi Publishing Co., Westport, Conn.

BARBECUE SAUCE MIX

Ingredients	%
Xanthan gum (Keltrol® F)	1.32
Onion powder	2.64
Spaghetti sauce seasonings	6.60
Salt	9.24
Barbecue spice[1]	19.80
Sugar	20.80
Tomato solids	39.60
Total	100.00

[1] See **Oil Spice for Barbecue Sauce** formula following.

Procedure

Mix together all ingredients until a uniform mixture is obtained.

To Use.—Place 1 cup of water in mixing bowl. Add 75.75 gm of sauce mix and mix at low speed. Mixing time for electric mixers is approximately 3 min; for hand mixers 1½–2 min. Just before end of mixing period, add 1 tbsp of vinegar.

SOURCE: Kelco Company, 20 N. Wacker Drive, Chicago, Ill.

OIL SPICE FOR BARBECUE SAUCE

Mix together the following and use as much as suffices:

	Gm
Oil of sweet marjoram	13.2
Oil of bay leaves 55/60% phenol content	24.2
Oil of thyme, white	24.2
Oil of coriander	35.2
Oil of black pepper	88.0
Oil of pimenta leaf	59.4

SOURCE: *Food Flavorings, 2nd Edition* by J. Merory, published by Avi Publishing Co., Westport, Conn.

GROUND BEEF IN BARBECUE SAUCE (HOT PACK)

This product is made up of 50% braised beef and 50% barbecue sauce.

Cook Meat

Grind meat through the 1-in. plate of the grinder and transfer it to a steam-jacketed kettle. Add 2 qt of water per 100 lb of meat and braise meat just long enough to make meat free flowing in the kettle. Drain meat juices (stock) and reserve it for making the sauce.

Make Sauce

Ingredients	Lb	Oz	Gal.
Tomato pureé (sp. gr. 1.035)			25
Braised meat juices and water			25
Soy sauce			1½
Worcestershire sauce			½
Vinegar (100-grain)			1
Wheat flour	7	8	
Cornstarch	2	8	
Salt	12	8	
Ground red pepper		4	
Black pepper (62-mesh)		4	
Onion powder		1	
Garlic powder		½	
Barbecue seasoning mix:	2	13	

	%
Spanish paprika (HCV)	50
Ground red pepper	28
Ground cloves	6.5
Ground mace	3.0
Ground Batavia cinnamon	6.0
Ground African ginger	6.5

In a steam-jacketed kettle, put the tomato pureé and heat to 180°F. Add salt blended with seasonings, barbecue seasoning mix, garlic, and onion powder. Make a paste of flour and corn-starch in 5 gal. of water and add to the tomato pureé mixture. Bring volume up to 50 gal. with the addition of meat juices and water. Add soy sauce, Worcestershire sauce, and vinegar and cook for 15 min. During the entire sauce-mixture procedure agitate sauce with a mixer.

Fill

Use 50% braised meat and 50% sauce to fill cans. Close under 27 in. vacuum.

Suggested Process

603 × 700 cans (6 lb 12 oz net) 300 min at 240°F
300 × 409 cans (16 oz net) 90 min at 240°F
300 × 308 cans (12 oz net) 60 min at 240°F

Check process times and temperature with the can supplier or the National Canners Association.

SOURCE: Stephan L. Komarik, 4810 Ronda, Coral Gables, Florida.

GROUND BEEF IN BARBECUE SAUCE (SEMICOLD PACK)

Ingredients	Lb	Oz
Lean beef (utility grade)	533	
Tomato paste (26% solids)	40	
Water	16	
Wheat flour	25	
Cornstarch	5	
Brown sugar	17	8
Soy sauce	12	8
Worcestershire sauce	4	8
Vinegar (100-grain)	8	
Salt	9	
Onion powder	3	
Garlic powder		8
Spanish paprika		$10\frac{1}{2}$
Red pepper (cayenne)		$2\frac{1}{2}$
Mace		1
Batavia cinnamon		$1\frac{1}{2}$
Jamaica ginger		$1\frac{1}{2}$
Cloves		$1\frac{1}{2}$

Procedure

Cut meat into slices 2 in. thick. Transfer it to a steam-jacketed kettle; add enough water to cover meat and cook for 10 min. at 200°F to obtain approximately 10% shrink. Reserve stock. Remove meat from the kettle and grind it through the $1\frac{1}{2}$-in. plate of the grinder. Reweigh meat and add enough stock to bring product up to the original raw weight of 533 lb. Transfer to a mechanical mixer; add tomato paste, 16 lb of the stock, brown sugar, and salt previously mixed with the seasonings and flavorings. Then add vinegar and Worcestershire sauce. Make a slurry of the flour and starch (free of lumps) with the remaining meat stock and water to make exactly 50 lb; add slurry to the mixer. Mix product approximately 3 min to obtain a uniform mixture; then fill cans. Close cans under 27 in. vacuum.

Suggested Process

603 × 700 cans (6 lb 12 oz) 300 min at 240°F
300 × 409 cans (16 oz net) 95 min at 240°F
300 × 308 cans (12 oz net) 65 min at 240°F

Check times and temperature of processing with can supplier or the National Canners Association.

SOURCE: Stephan L. Komarik, 4810 Ronda, Coral Gables, Florida.

BARBECUE SAUCE PREPARED WITH PEANUT FLOUR

Ingredients	Lb	Oz
Tomato paste	33	
Worcestershire sauce		10
Hot sauce		6.5
Lemon juice	10	
Dark brown sugar	5	
Vinegar	2	10
Peanut oil	7	
Water	59	
Peanut flour	7	
Sugar	1	8
Salt	1	5
Spice blend	2	8

Procedure

1. Mix peanut flour with part of the water (approx $2\frac{1}{2}$ times the weight of the flour).
2. Mix peanut flour-water mixture with tomato paste. Add remaining water.
3. Add remaining ingredients, mixing well.
4. Heat until sauce thickens.
5. May be used in canning procedure of products such as sliced beef or pork. Or, may be canned as a sauce only. If the latter, follow recommendations of the can supplier or the National Canners Association.

SOURCE: Gold Kist, Inc., P.O. Box 2210, Atlanta, Ga.

BARBECUE SAUCE

Ingredients	%
Tomato paste (32% solids)	20.00
Liquid smoke	1.43
Brown sugar	8.30
White distilled vinegar (50-grain)	13.70
Spice mix	6.10
Water	49.72
Stabilizer (Multi-Sta Special)	0.75

Processing Pointers

In tomato paste, pureé, or sauces, which have a large percentage of water, the stabilizer (Multi-Sta Special) could readily be incorporated by one of the following methods:

1. Add water of formula first to processing tank. Under good agitation add stabilizer directly into the water. Multi-Sta Special hydrates slowly at first so that good dispersion can be obtained.
2. If necessary mix stabilizer with 5 times its weight of sugar. Add this mixture to the batch whenever the best agitation is available.

Generally speaking, the best time to add Multi-Sta Special is early in batch assembly when the vat is about ¼ to ⅓ full and also before heat has been applied.

SOURCE: Germantown Manufacturing Company, 505 Parkway, Broomall, Pa.

CANNED SWEET BARBECUE SAUCE (CAN BE USED WITH RELISH AND/OR CHUTNEY)

Ingredients	%
Amioca starch (Clearjel)	3.0
Lime juice	1.9
Sugar	15.0
Salt	0.3
Paprika	0.2
Cinnamon	0.4
Ground cloves	0.2
Raisins	3.0
Tomato pureé	32.4
Minced onions	5.3
Worcestershire sauce	6.6
Water	25.7
Vinegar	6.0

10% relish and/or chutney can be added

Procedure

Cook all ingredients together with agitation until desired consistency is obtained (at about 180°–185°F). Can, seal, and retort. Follow recommendations of can company representative or National Canners Association for proper retorting time and temperature.

SOURCE: National Starch and Chemical Corp., 1700 W. Front St., Plainfield, N.J.

CANNED BARBECUE SAUCE

Ingredients	%
Tomato paste (28% solids)	37.95
Water	30.82
White distilled vinegar (50-grain)	12.66
Lemon juice (single strength)	8.07
Brown sugar	5.65
Salt	2.42
Modified waxy maize starch (Polar Gel)[1]	1.00
Onion, chopped	0.80
Microcrystalline cellulose (Avicel RC-581 or RC-591)	0.33
Paprika	0.30

[1] Product of American Maize-Products Co.

Procedure

Add dry blend of Avicel and starch to the total water requirements and mix for 3 min. Add tomato paste, sugar, salt, onion, and paprika. Slowly blend in vinegar and lemon juice. Allow temperature to reach 190°–195°F (while stirring constantly) over a period of 3–4 min to fully develop the thickener.

Hot fill into containers and process. Check processing time and temperature with can supplier or National Canners Association.

SOURCE: FMC Corp., American Viscose Division, Marcus Hook, Pa.

POULTRY PRODUCTS

FREEZING WHOLE, PARTS, ROLLS, AND MEAT OF POULTRY

FREEZING ROASTING CHICKENS AND TURKEYS

Chickens

Whole, ready-to-cook birds are trussed and formed into a compact attractive shape, often by inserting the legs under a specially cut strip of skin below the body cavity or by inserting a formed wire retainer to hold legs close to body of the bird. Giblets are wrapped separately in parchment paper and may be inserted in the crop cavity at the neck or in the visceral cavity.

Birds are then packaged in form-fitting plastic bags that are translucent, fairly tough, and reasonably impermeable to moisture and air. Form fitting is achieved in most cases by the ability of the plastic film to shrink when the sealed bag containing the bird is immersed for a few seconds in water somewhat below the boiling point.

Turkeys

Turkeys are similarly trussed and prepared for packaging and packaged in form-fitting plastic bags which are shrunk by immersion of the packaged turkey in hot water.

Turkeys should be packed in fiberboard cartons or similar containers for handling in frozen storage and shipment. These cartons should be rectangular and of a shape to facilitate palletizing and strong enough to withstand stacking loads 16 ft high in refrigerated warehouses. If birds are to be frozen after placing them in the cartons, it is often desirable to cut out sections of the sides or ends of the carton to permit rapid air flow across the carcass surfaces in the air-blast freezer and thus accomplish rapid freezing.

SOURCE: *The Freezing Preservation of Foods, 4th Edition, Vol. 3* by Tressler *et al.* published by Avi Publishing Co., Westport, Conn.

FREEZING POULTRY ROLLS (RAW, COOKED, CURED AND SMOKED)

Poultry rolls are made up as a raw product, as a cooked product, and also as a cured, smoked product. They can be made in a number of shapes: in cylindrical form, in tied rolls where the skin is used as the casing, in formed rolls in a plastic casing, in rectangular molded shapes, and oblong tied shapes. Generally, they are seasoned with salt, pepper, and sometimes monosodium glutamate is added. When the meat is precooked for rolled poultry, gelatin or another binder, such as wheat gluten, is added and the rolls are molded under pressure.

The following percentages of white and dark meat and ratio of large pieces to small pieces in a roll can be followed as a guide to making a quality product:

	%
Large pieces of white meat (e.g., $\frac{1}{2}$ turkey breast)	35–38
Large pieces of dark meat (e.g., 1 turkey leg and thigh section)	32–35
Skin (e.g., from one side of bird backbone to breast-bone)	10–12
Small meat pieces	18–20

Raw Poultry Rolls

Poultry rolls sold as raw meat are tightly packed in casings (such as Cryovac) suitable for freezing and are frozen at $-20°F$ and held in frozen storage ($0°F$ or below) until cooked. Low storage temperatures for all poultry rolls will extend shelf-life of these products.

Cooked Poultry Rolls

Rolls sold as a cooked product are tightly packed in a fibrous casing and sealed. (If precooked meat is used, a binder is added as casings are filled.) Rolls are placed in cooking vats with water temperature at 165°–175°F and cooked until an internal meat temperature of 150°F is reached. Chill rolls, first in cold water, then in a cooler (34°–36°F) before freezing at –20°F. Product should be held in frozen storage (see above).

Cured, Smoked Poultry Rolls

First step is to cure and smoke the birds, after which they are boned. (At this stage the birds bone very easily.) Separate skin and fat. Chop $^2/_3$ of the meat pieces into $^1/_2$-in. cubes. Grind the remaining meat including the skin and fat, using a very fine blade or a blender. Mix together thoroughly the cubed meat and the ground meat; sprinkle gelatin on mixture (1% of meat by weight) and blend thoroughly. Method of cooking determines the type of casing into which the mixture is stuffed. Stuff in permeable casings if cooked in a smokehouse; hang at smokehouse temperature of 180°F until internal meat temperature reaches 150°F. Or, stuff in fibrous casings and process in water bath at 165°–175°F until internal meat temperature reaches 150°F. Prechill rolls before freezing. Those cooked in permeable casings in the smokehouse should be adequately protected with moisture-vaporproof packaging for frozen storage. Those cooked in fibrous casings should also be overwrapped for frozen storage.

Freeze product at –20°F and hold in frozen storage at 0°F or below. Low storage temperature will extend shelf-life of this product considerably.

SOURCE: *Poultry Products Technology* by George J. Mountney published by Avi Publishing Co., Westport, Conn.

FREEZING CUT-UP POULTRY

A completely cut-up bird consists of breast (may be cut into two or more pieces), two wings, two legs, (thighs and drumsticks may or may not be separated), back (whole or cut into pieces) and neck, plus gizzard, heart, and liver. The dismembered birds are also packed as all-legs, all-breasts, or all-wings. Regardless of how packed and sold, to-day's modern plant uses the "on-the-line" method of cutting up poultry.

Birds to be cut up are removed from the chilling tanks and hung on a shackle. Usually this shackle is of a type different from those used on the dressing and eviscerating lines, in order to hold the bird more firmly making it easier to perform the various cutting operations. The birds are hung by the hocks with the breast of all birds facing in the one direction. The wings are cut off first, then the entire breast is removed. One leg is removed from the shackle and cut away from the backbone. Then the backbone is cut from the other leg and the second leg is removed from the shackle. If the backs are cut in two and the breasts split, these operations are done off the conveyor on a saw.

The individual pieces of each bird are placed in a Cellophane-lined or laminated board carton in accordance with a standard predetermined pattern. Usually the less meaty pieces, such as the front and rear half of the back and the wrapped giblets, are placed in the bottom of the carton. The better-appearing, more meaty pieces, such as the breast, wings, legs, and thighs, are then packed as a second or top layer.

The cartons are closed and the product is frozen, usually in a multiplate freezer.

SOURCE: *The Freezing Preservation of Foods*, 3rd Edition, Vol. 1 by Tressler and Evers published by Avi Publishing Co., Westport, Conn.

FROZEN DEBONED CHICKEN MEAT

Precook young chickens (steaming is recommended) sufficiently so that meat may be removed easily from bones. Remove bones and separate meat from wing ends, backs, etc., and skins. Cool, pack in cartons or other containers suitable for freezing. Freeze as rapidly as possible.

When thawed, this frozen product has a wide variety of uses: Cut into chunks and use in pot pies, salads, creamed chicken, chicken a la king, cold plates, chicken chow mein or chop suey, and many other specialties. Grind (using a large proportion of meat from wings, backs, and necks) and use in chicken croquettes, Brunswick stew, sandwich and canapé spreads, in soups, and with other meat combinations. Make a congealed loaf of chicken pieces and slice for cold plates, salads, sandwiches. Use in combination with other ingredients for chicken and dumplings, chicken gumbo (with okra), chicken and gravy. Chicken meat may be diced and dehydrated. It may be ground and made into chicken sausage. Other by-products might include rendered chicken fat, bouillon cubes, extracted gelatin, or chicken seasoning paste.

SOURCE: *The Freezing Preservation of Foods*, 3rd Edition, Vol. 2 by Tressler and Evers published by Avi Publishing Co., Westport, Conn.

FREEZE DRYING CHICKEN

Freeze-dried chicken meat is used extensively in dry chicken soup mixes and in combination with other ingredients to make soups, stews, and other prepared dishes.

Poultry meat is diced and first quick frozen in preparation for freeze drying. After freezing, the meat is placed in a vacuum chamber where removal of water is accomplished in three steps. Heat is added to accelerate sublimation, water is removed from the subliming ice within the product, and finally the water vapor which reaches the surface must be removed.

To accelerate the drying process during freeze drying, heat can be furnished by conduction, radiation, or dielectric heating. Heat by conduction is most commonly used. In the final drying stages, the temperature is raised to just below the point where heat damage to the product would occur.

To prevent growth of microorganisms, the moisture content must be below 10%, but to prevent deterioration from other causes during storage the moisture content should not be over 1%.

SOURCE: *Poultry Products Technology* by George J. Mountney published by Avi Publishing Co., Westport, Conn.

FREEZING STUFFED TURKEYS

All sanitation aspects of any plant freezing stuffed turkeys is under the supervision of the Poultry Inspection Service of USDA and each turkey so processed is "Government Inspected and Approved for Wholesomeness."

Following is a general outline of the procedure:

1. Each bird is washed three times and individually inspected to insure complete cleanliness. Then the birds are chilled to 35°F and washed and inspected again.

2. Stuffing is mechanically mixed in a closed system which is sealed off from contamination. Both the birds and stuffing are kept at temperatures below 35°F at all times.

3. The turkeys are mechanically stuffed in a matter of seconds.

4. The stuffed turkeys are packaged and placed in the freezer in a very few minutes. The birds are frozen at an average temperature of 40°F below zero. This results in extremely low bacterial counts.

5. Stuffed turkeys are under constant laboratory control. Samples are taken regularly to check bacteria counts, thus assuring that rigid quality standards are met.

SOURCE: *The Freezing Preservation of Foods, 3rd Edition, Vol. 2* by Tressler and Evers, published by Avi Publishing Co., Westport, Conn.

BONING WHOLE TURKEYS

There are several different ways of boning whole turkeys. One method consists of releasing the legs by cutting the skin flap or removing the wire tie with pliers to release the legs and stretch them out from the body. Then cut the skin between the leg and the body as close to the leg as possible to leave the maximum amount of skin on the breast. Continue with the point of the knife to cut along the breast to the point where the thigh is joined to the body. Next, score the leading edge of the oyster and then pull the leg from the body releasing the oyster. Cut through the remaining skin freeing the drumstick and thigh. Generally, drumsticks are not boned so cut into the joint between the thigh and drumsticks, then cut along the length of the thigh to the bones and with the tip of the knife remove the bones. Cut off the wing tips at the second joint and cut along the length of the bone on the underside of the remaining wing portions so the bone and artery can be removed after the breast meat is freed. Turn the turkey on its breast then score the meat behind the shoulder blades and cut along the top of the shoulder blades freeing scapula meat followed by a cut along the rib cage releasing breast meat from the ribs on each side of the skeleton and follow on down on each side of the keel bone. Release the meat from the bone on the wing sections and lift the skeleton from the flesh. Remove the heavy arteries from the thigh and wing meat and any visible blood clots. The meat is now ready to be rolled or tied into the desired shape.

SOURCE: George J. Mountney, Research Management Specialist, Food Service Programs, USDA, Washington, D.C.

FREEZING WHOLE BONED TURKEY ROLLS

The following is excerpted from military specifications for whole boned turkey rolls:

Turkeys shall be boned and skinned in such a manner as to yield a minimum number of pieces of skin, and dark and white meat. The skin to be used in preparation of the finished product shall be removed in not more than two pieces. (Skin to be excluded may be removed in any number of pieces as long as the skin to be used does not exceed two pieces.) The dark meat shall be removed in as nearly two pieces as possible and the white meat shall be removed in as nearly two pieces as possible. Small pieces of dark and white meat shall not exceed a total of 5% of the total dark and white meat used in manufacture of the finished product. Meat from the wing tips (that meat covering the carpus, metacarpus, and phalanges), neck (that meat covering the cervical vertebrae), tail (that meat covering the coccygel vertebrae), interior of the body cavity (including fat, giblets, and other organs or glands), shall be excluded from the finished product. All tendons shall be removed from the legs and excluded with all bones, cartilages, and ligaments. The skin to be used shall be scraped clean of protruding pin-feathers, feathers, loose pieces of fat, and extraneous material, and shall be practically free from nonprotruding pin-feathers. Blood clots shall be removed wherever possible. The boning operation shall be performed as expeditiously as possible. The boning operation shall be accomplished in a room with a temperature not exceeding 60°F and the time interval from removal of the dressed birds from refrigeration for boning and processing to entry of the finished product into the freezer shall not exceed 1 hr, unless the boning room temperature is 50°F or lower in which case 2 hr will be the maximum.

The specifications give three ways in which the whole boned turkey may be formed: cylindrical (molded), rectangular (molded), and roll tied. Specifications for roll tieing are as follows:

The roll (tied) turkey, shall be approximately elliptical or oblong to cylindrical in shape, 5 to 7 in. at the greatest diameter, and 9 to 14 in. in length. White and dark meat shall be in the proportion of not less than 55% white and not more than 45% dark meat, but including all the white and dark meat from the turkeys with the exception of the meat from the excluded components. The final product shall consist of one layer of dark meat and one layer of light meat, seasoned as specified (see below), and completely encased in skin and tied (with cotton twine) at intervals of not more than 3 in. nor less then 2 in. around the circumference from one end to the other. Holes larger than 1/4 of an inch in the skin encasing the finished product must be sewn; however, reasonable care shall be taken to avoid the occurrence of holes, by careful boning. The weight of the skin shall not exceed 16% of the total weight of the dark and white meat in any case.

The seasoning mentioned above may be of two types: No. 1 shall consist of 1 lb 12 oz salt, 4 oz of monosodium glutamate, and 8 oz of sugar per 100 lb of total meat. No other ingredients shall be added. No. 2 shall consist of 1 lb of salt, 1/2 oz of pepper, and 4 oz of monosodium glutamate per 100 lb of total meat and skin. No other ingredients shall be added.

When rolled and tied, Cryovac packaging for freezing is well suited to this product.

SOURCE: *The Freezing Preservation of Foods, 3rd Edition, Vol. 1* by Tressler and Evers published by Avi Publishing Co., Westport, Conn.

TURKEY FILLETS

One type of cut-up turkey being merchandised is turkey fillets. The white meat as a chunk is removed from each side of the breast of raw turkey, trimmed, wrapped, and packaged in the same manner as a fish fillet. These packaged turkey fillets are frozen and sold principally to the institutional trade. The remainder of the carcass is cooked by boiling and the meat stripped for turkey meat to be used in many types of canned and frozen products.

SOURCE: *The Freezing Preservation of Foods, 3rd Edition, Vol. 1* by Tressler and Evers published by Avi Publishing Co., Westport, Conn.

HOW TO UTILIZE POULTRY SKIN AND MEAT BITS IN POT PIES

Turkey as well as chicken may be used for pot pies. The cooked carcasses are deboned with the skin and meat bits and meat pieces sorted into separate batches. Both are then chilled to approximately 36°F for 3–4 hr after which the meat pieces are run through a dicer and the skins and meat bits are run through a meat grinder followed by passing them through a comminuter. The comminuted skin and meat bits are added to the gravy ingredients adding more liquid if necessary to obtain the proper consistency.

SOURCE: *Poultry Products Technology* by George J. Mountney published by Avi Publishing Co., Westport, Conn.

FREEZING CORNISH GAME HENS

After killing and bleeding, the birds are wet plucked following a semiscald at 126°F for 45 sec. Plucking is done primarily by hand; leg and wing finishers cannot be used because the birds would be pulled apart, and the skin would be barked and lose its bloom. (No bird with skin damage or loss of bloom is accepted as a "first.")

After plucking, birds are chilled and packed in ice to take the animal heat out of the carcass immediately. This assures more flavor and finer textured meat. This again is special handling, since larger birds are eviscerated hot which makes for an easier job and a higher percentage of yield (by 3%). Eviscerating equipment is usually semiautomatic standard equipment. After eviscerating, birds are drained in racks to eliminate all excess moisture. They are then stuffed in Cryovac bags, vacuum-sealed, and dipped in boiling water so that the bag will shrink tight around the bird. They are then placed in wire baskets, 18 to a basket, and frozen at −40°F. They remain in the freezer for about 3 hr after which they are taken out and packed, 12 in a box for the retail trade and 25 to a master carton for the institutional trade. The holding room maintains a temperature of 0°F.

These birds are packed in squab size for individual serving and in a larger size to serve two people. The squab size weighs on an average 14 oz and is packed in a polyethylene bag.

SOURCE: *The Freezing Preservation of Foods, 3rd Edition, Vol. 2* by Tressler and Evers published by Avi Publishing Co., Westport, Conn.

FREEZING DUCKS

After delivery at the packing plant, ducks are first weighed; then they are held for 1–2 hr to settle down before slaughter. Carcasses are scalded twice in rocker scalders, first at 140°F for 2½ min and then at 142°–145°F. Next they are picked on batch type pickers which hold 20 birds per lot. After drying, the carcasses are dipped in wax at 195°F for 15 sec and then dipped a second time at 160°F. They are then cooled in water at 55°F. Wax is removed by a wax stripping machine and the remainder by pinners. Next the ducks are eviscerated and chilled in a continuous chiller and then packaged in Cryovac and frozen at −28°F for 24 hr.

SOURCE: *Poultry Products Technology* by George J. Mountney published by Avi Publishing Co., Westport, Conn.

FREEZING GEESE

Geese are generally slaughtered at 17 weeks of age at which time they usually average 6–7 lb live weight. Dressing yields generally are about 70% with a pick-up of about 4.5% during chilling.

For processing, birds are delivered to a holding corral. Then they are forced to swim through a canal to clean their feathers. After hanging on the conveyor line they are stunned and bled with an electric knife and then scalded at 150°–154°F in a homemade rocking scalder.

Flight and shoulder feathers are removed as soon as the carcasses leave the scalder. Then carcasses are released automatically from shackles and dropped into a hopper. At preset intervals the hopper drops groups of carcasses into a centrifuge-type picker to remove the remaining feathers. Any remaining pinfeathers left by the picker are removed with an on-the-line picker after which the carcasses are dried with a jet of compressed air and hung in a triangular suspension with the breast down. Then the carcasses are dipped in molten wax at 220°F for 3–5 sec, cooled, redipped at 160°F for 3–5 sec and dipped in cold water to harden the wax. The head is removed from the shackle which breaks the wax so it can be stripped from the carcass in several large pieces. The remaining wax is removed by a drum picker and then the carcasses are dipped in water at 180°F to tighten the skin. Tightening the skin makes it easy for pinners to remove the remaining pinfeathers. Carcasses are then eviscerated and inspected. The carcasses are chilled, packaged in Cryovac or other plastic sheeting which can be heat-shrunk and frozen in an air-blast freezer at a temperature of −20°F.

SOURCE: *Poultry Products Technology* by George J. Mountney published by Avi Publishing Co., Westport, Conn.

CANNED CHICKEN PRODUCTS

CANNED WHOLE CHICKEN

Whole chickens should weigh 2 lb 4 oz after cleaning and eviscerating.

Two types of broth are used for canning whole chickens.

Ingredients for Plain Broth

	Gal.	Lb	Oz
Water	100		
Salt		14	
Plant protein hydrolyzate		2	
Monosodium glutamate		5	
Dry soluble pepper			2
Ground celery			1
Ground turmeric			1¼
Garlic powder			⅓
Paprika			1
Onion powder			5

Ingredients for Broth with Gelatin Added

	Gal.	Lb	Oz
Water	100		
Gelatin (200-bloom)		80	
Seasonings same as above			

Procedure

For Plain Broth.—Put 100 gal. of water in a steam-jacketed kettle, bring to boil, add salt and seasonings and boil for 10 min.

For Broth with Gelatin Added.—Put 80 gal. of water in a steam-jacketed kettle, bring to boil, then add salt and seasonings. Shut off steam. Put 20 gal. of cold water in a large container; slowly pour gelatin into water, and let soak for 1 hr. Stir soaked gelatin into heated stock and raise temperature to 180°F.

Fill Cans

Use 404 × 700 size cans. Place chicken in the can neck down. Be sure the skin is not covering the opening of the breast cavity. (Proper packing in the cans will allow good circulation of the broth during the processing period.) Add 1 lb of either broth to the cans. Temperature of the broth should be at least 160°F. Close cans under 18 in. vacuum.

Suggested Process

404 × 700 cans (3 lb 4 oz net) 75 min at 240°F

Check process time and temperature with can supplier or the National Canners Association.

Chill

After process, shut off steam and introduce cold water under 10 lb air pressure at least 10 min, keep overflow valve open for proper circulation of the cold water. Final chilling should be at atmospheric pressure.

SOURCE: Stephan L. Komarik, 4810 Ronda, Coral Gables, Florida.

CANNED CHICKEN OR TURKEY MEAT

Thoroughly eviscerate and wash whole birds. Transfer to cooking tanks and add enough water to cover; cook at 195°-200°F until meat can be removed from bones easily. Use the same broth to cook at least four batches of birds so that broth becomes concentrated.

Skim fat from broth and to each 10 gal. of concentrated broth add 3 oz monosodium glutamate and 2 oz plant protein hydrolyzate.

Remove bones from birds and separate skin from meat. Grind skins through the ⅛-in. plate of the grinder and slice meat (size of slices depends upon size of can to be used). To 75 lb of sliced meat, add and mix 8 lb of ground skin and 5 lb of rendered fat (skimmed from broth).

Pack 78% meat mixture tightly in cans and add 22% seasoned broth. Close cans under 27 in. vacuum.

Suggested Process

300 × 409 cans (16 oz net) 2 hr 30 min at 240°F

Check process time and temperature with can supplier or the National Canners Association.

SOURCE: Stephan L. Komarik, 4810 Ronda, Coral Gables, Florida.

CANNED CHICKEN FRICASSE

Prepare Chicken

Thoroughly clean, eviscerate, and wash chickens. Disjoint into legs, thighs, and breasts (cut into 2–4 pieces); and separate wings, necks, and backs to make emulsion. Parboil chicken pieces in water at 180°F for 20 min using 5 gal. of water for each 100 lb of chicken pieces. Reserve broth for gravy.

Cook wings, necks, and backs separately in simmering water (200°F) until skins and meat can be removed easily from bones. While still hot, grind skins and meat through the ⅛-in. plate of the grinder and mix with the same weight of stock in which these were cooked. Chop into a fine emulsion or run through the finest plate of a meat emulsifier.

Prepare Gravy

Ingredients	Gal.	Lb	Oz
Chicken broth	100		
Wheat flour		30	
Cornstarch		10	
Rendered chicken fat		10	
Butter		3	
Salt		16	
Monosodium glutamate		2	8
Plant protein hydrolyzate		1	
Dry soluble pepper			8
Ground celery seeds			1
Ground turmeric			1½
Spanish paprika			3
Garlic powder			½
Onion powder			6

Put 60 gal. of broth in a steam-jacketed kettle along with the chicken emulsion. Add chicken fat, butter, salt, and the remainder of the ingredients except flour and starch. Use a "Lightning" mixer to agitate gravy. Make a slurry of flour and starch in 20 gal. of water (or well-chilled broth) and, with continuous agitation, add slurry to gravy. Bring volume of gravy up to 100 gal. by adding hot water. Cook at 200°F for 30 min.

Fill Cans and Close

A quality product should have at least 50% chicken pieces in 50% hot gravy.

If internal can temperature of the product is not lower than 160°F, close cans without drawing any vacuum; otherwise close under 15 in. vacuum.

Suggested Process

300 × 409 cans (16 oz net) 90 min at 240°F

Check process time and temperature with can supplier or the National Canners Association.

SOURCE: Stephan L. Komarik, 4810 Ronda, Coral Gables, Florida.

CANNED CHICKEN STEW

Ingredients needed to assemble:

	%
Cooked chicken, diced 1-in. cubes	18
Mixed vegetables	32
Gravy	50

Prepare Vegetables

Ingredients	%
Reconstituted dehydrated potato dice (³/₄-in.)	40
Reconstituted dehydrated carrot dice (¹/₄-in.)	22
Dehydrated minced onion	11
Fresh celery, ½-in. dice	9
Frozen peas, defrosted	9
Canned, diced sweet red pepper	9

Reconstitute potato dice in hot water (200°F) until 100 lb pick up 120–130 lb moisture. Reconstitute carrots similarly. Minced onions need no rehydration. Drain sweet peppers well before using. Defrost peas.

Prepare 90 Gal. of Gravy

Ingredients	Lb	Oz
Salt	17	
Wheat flour	40	
Cornstarch	10	
Monosodium glutamate	1	
Plant protein hydrolyzate	1	
Dry soluble pepper		8
Ground turmeric		2
Oleoresin paprika (HCV)		2
Garlic powder		1
Cane sugar	5	
Chicken broth to make 90 gal.		

Make a slurry free of lumps with flour, starch and 20 gal. of water. Heat 70 gal. of broth to 200°F and add all the other ingredients except slurry. Using a "Lightning" mixer stir slurry slowly into gravy mixture. Bring volume up to 90 gal. and raise temperature to 200°F. Cook 15 min.

Fill and Close Cans

Fill cans with 18% chicken dice, 32% mixed vegetables, and 50% hot gravy. Close cans under vacuum.

Suggested Process

300 × 409 cans (16 oz net) 95 min at 240°F
404 × 309 cans (1 lb 8 oz) 150 min at 240°F
603 × 700 cans (6 lb 12 oz) 250 min at 240°F

Check process times and temperature with can supplier or the National Canners Association.

After sterilization process, shut off steam, introduce cold water under 15 lb air pressure, and chill cans to an internal temperature of about 120°F.

SOURCE: Stephan L. Komarik, 4810 Ronda, Coral Gables, Florida.

CANNED CHICKEN AND DUMPLINGS

Prepare Chicken

Approximately 67 lb of cooked, diced chicken meat will be needed for the ingredients given in this formula.

Clean chickens and cook in simmering water until bones can be removed easily. Remove bones and skin and chill meat well before dicing. Dice to desired size. Reserve broth for gravy.

Prepare Dumplings

Approximately 67 lb of precooked dumplings will be needed. When cooked, dumplings will gain from 250 to 300% in weight.

Noodle manufacturers offer dumplings for canned products. Recommended size is 2 × 1 × ⅛ in.

Cook dumplings in 2% salt water for 15 min, using 1 gal. of water per pound of dumplings. Drain dumplings, wash in cold water, then drain again.

Prepare Gravy

Ingredients	Gal.	Lb	Oz
Chicken broth	40		
Rendered chicken fat		10	
Cornstarch		30	
Salt		8	8
Monosodium glutamate		4	8
Hydrolyzed plant protein		1	8
Dry soluble pepper			8
Ground celery seeds			1
Ground Spanish paprika			2
Ground turmeric			1½
Onion powder			4
Garlic powder			¼
Water (or chicken broth)	10		

In a bakery mixer, make a slurry of the water (or chilled chicken broth), cornstarch, and other dry seasonings and flavorings. Put 40 gal. of chicken broth in a steam-jacketed kettle, add chicken fat, and raise temperature to 150°F. Add slurry to hot broth and bring volume of broth up to 50 gal. Raise temperature to 200°–205°F and cook gravy for 20 min.

Pack 12.5% diced meat, 12.5% dumplings, and 75% hot gravy in 16 oz cans. If internal temperature of can contents does not drop below 160°F, close cans without drawing any vacuum.

Suggested Process

300 × 409 cans (16 oz net) 95 min at 240°F

Check process time and temperature with can supplier or the National Canners Association.

SOURCE: Stephan L. Komarik, 4810 Ronda, Coral Gables, Florida.

CANNED TURKEY AND DUMPLINGS

Use the above formula for **Canned Chicken and Dumplings** replacing chicken with cooked turkey dice.

SOURCE: Stephan L. Komarik, 4810 Ronda, Coral Gables, Florida.

CANNED HAM AND DUMPLINGS

Use the above formula for **Canned Chicken and Dumplings** replacing chicken with smoked ready-to-eat ham dice.

SOURCE: Stephan L. Komarik, 4810 Ronda, Coral Gables, Florida.

CANNED CHICKEN AND NOODLE DINNER

Broth is made by first concentrating the water used in precooking the chickens. To each 10 gal. of broth add about 8 oz of salt, 1–2 oz of white pepper, and monosodium glutamate for seasoning.

The broth is generally strained through a flannel drip cloth. Fat is added after the stock is concentrated.

Use noodles containing at least 5½% egg solids; blanch at least 5–20 min to remove air. Mix blanched noodles with cut-up chicken meat and weigh mixture directly into washed glass containers.

Hot broth (135°F) is measured into the containers (usually automatically) to provide a 90–94% fill. Jars are then sealed and tumbled.

Suggested Process

Generally, a 16-oz container requires a processing time of 75–90 min at 240°F, depending upon the contents. Check process time and temperature with can supplier or the National Canners Association.

After partial cooling in the retort, cool the jars to below 110°F, then rinse with a hot water detergent solution before labeling and packing.

SOURCE: *Poultry Products Technology* by George J. Mountney published by Avi Publishing Co., Westport, Conn.

CANNED CHICKEN NOODLE DINNER

Ingredients	Gal.	Lb	Oz
Cooked chicken meat, sliced		180	
Broth in which chicken is cooked	60		
Cooked egg noodles		640	
Rendered chicken fat		6	

Salt	6
Monosodium glutamate	6
Dry soluble pepper	6
Dry soluble celery	2

Procedure

Use noodles manufactured for canning with 10% egg content. Cook in boiling water containing 2% salt for 15 min, using 1 gal. of water per pound of noodles. Drain; wash with cold water to avoid matting of cooked noodles; then drain again.

Slice the cooked chicken meat thin, reserving larger sizes of breast meat slices to decorate side of glass jar. Mix rendered fat with sliced meat.

Filter broth in which chickens were cooked. It should be crystal clear for this product. Add salt and flavorings to the clear stock and raise temperature to 100°F.

Pack 50% noodles, 12½% sliced meat, and 37½% broth in 16 oz glass jars. Close jars under 27 in. vacuum.

Suggested Process

Glass jars 16 oz net process 1 hr at 240°F

Check process time and temperature with jar supplier or the National Canners Association.
Chill jars under water pressure.

SOURCE: Stephan L. Komarik, 4810 Ronda, Coral Gables, Florida.

CANNED CHICKEN, MUSHROOMS AND NOODLES

Ingredients	Lb
Canned sliced mushrooms	150
Cooked chicken meat, diced	150
Cooked egg noodles	150
Cream (20%)	150
Butter	45
Water	1035
Chicken broth	75
Flour	90
Salt	22
Canned pimientos, diced	60
Frozen peas, defrosted	60
Monosodium glutamate	2
Plant protein hydrolyzate	1

Procedure

Make a smooth paste of flour and approximately 300 lb of water. Put remaining water, cream, butter, salt, and broth in a steam-jacketed kettle and bring to a boil. Stir in flour paste and cook 20 min.

Boil noodles in 1% salt water for 5 min. Then drain, wash, and drain again and promptly add to the sauce to avoid matting.

Add remaining ingredients; mix thoroughly and pack in 16-oz cans and close under 25 in. vacuum.

Suggested Process

300 × 409 cans (16 oz net) 90 min at 240°F

Check process time and temperature with can supplier or the National Canners Association.

SOURCE: Stephan L. Komarik, 4810 Ronda, Coral Gables, Florida.

CANNED CHICKEN, MUSHROOMS AND MACARONI

Ingredients	Lb	Oz	Gal.
Canned sliced mushrooms	38		
Cooked chicken meat, diced	38		
Cooked elbow macaroni	38		
Cream (20%)	38		
Butter	10		
Chicken broth	20		
Wheat flour	22		
Salt	5		
Canned diced pimiento	15		
Frozen peas (defrosted)	15		
Water			32
Monosodium glutamate		4	
Dry soluble pepper		3	
Dry soluble celery salt		3	
(to make: mix together 12 cc oil of celery with 10 lb of salt)			

Procedure

Drain canned mushrooms and save brine which will be added to the stock.

Make a slurry free of lumps of wheat flour and 5 gal. of water.

Cook elbow macaroni for 12 min in boiling water (with 2% salt added), using 1 gal. of water to each 1 lb of macaroni. Drain, rinse in cold water, and drain again.

Put remainder of water (27 gal.) in a steam-jacketed kettle. Add cream, butter, salt, brine from mushrooms, broth, and seasonings. Bring temperature up to 160°F and, while stirring steadily with a "Lightning" mixer, add slurry to hot batch and cook for 20 min at 200°–205°F. Add remaining ingredients, mix thoroughly and pack.

Fill cans while product is hot. Internal product temperature should not drop below 160°F when cans are filled. If temperature drops below 160°F, close cans under 10–15 in. vacuum.

Suggested Process

300 × 409 cans (16 oz net) 90 min at 240°F

Check process time and temperature with can supplier or the National Canners Association.

SOURCE: Stephan L. Komarik, 4810 Ronda, Coral Gables, Florida.

CANNED GIBLET AND NOODLE DINNER

Prepare Giblets

Remove linings of gizzards and wash gizzards and hearts clean, removing all fat from giblets. Cook giblets using 5 gal. of water and $\frac{1}{4}$ oz of sodium nitrite for each 100 lb giblets. Cook until giblets are a nice pink color, then slice about $\frac{1}{8}$-in. thick. Cooking water should be discarded.

Prepare Noodles

For this product, select noodles with 10% eggs which are manufactured for processed foods. Use 1 gal. of water for each 1 lb of noodles and cook 15 min in boiling water. Wash noodles thoroughly in cold water after cooking so they will not stick together.

Prepare Stock

Ingredients	Gal.	Lb	Oz
Chicken broth	60		
Salt		3	
Rendered chicken fat		5	10
Monosodium glutamate			6
Plant protein hydrolyzate			4

Put all ingredients in a steam-jacketed kettle and bring temperature up to 200°F.

Fill Jars and Close

Using 16 oz jars, pack 2 oz sliced giblets, 8 oz noodles, and 6 oz stock. Close jars under 27 in. vacuum.

Suggested Process

Process 16 oz net jars under 28 lb water pressure for 1 hr and 30 min at 240°F. Check process time and temperature with can supplier or the National Canners Association.

SOURCE: Stephan L. Komarik, 4810 Ronda, Coral Gables, Florida.

CANNED CHICKEN A LA KING (FINEST QUALITY)

Prepare a la King Ingredients

	Lb
Cooked chicken meat	280
Canned pimientos, diced	50
Frozen peas	50
Canned mushrooms, sliced	100

Thoroughly clean, eviscerate and wash chickens. Cook in boiling water until bones can be removed easily. Reserve broth for use in sauce. Remove skin and bones from meat and cut meat into large cubes ($\frac{1}{2}$ to $\frac{3}{4}$ in.).

If canned whole pimientos are used, drain and dice into $\frac{1}{4}$-in. cubes.

Defrost peas before use.

Prepare Sauce

Ingredients	Gal.	Lb	Oz	Pt
Whole milk	75			
Chicken broth (chilled)	25			
Wheat flour		40		
Cornstarch		10		
Salt		14		
Butter		50		
Monosodium glutamate		1		
Dry soluble pepper			2	
Ground celery seed			$\frac{1}{2}$	
Ground turmeric			$\frac{3}{4}$	
Sherry wine (optional)				1

Put milk in a steam-jacketed kettle and raise temperature to almost boiling, *but do not boil.* Add salt, butter, seasonings, and monosodium glutamate and simmer for 10 min at 180°–190°F. Make a slurry free of lumps of chicken broth, starch, and flour. Add slurry with steady stirring to milk mixture and continue to simmer for 10 min at 180°–190°F.

Assemble Ingredients and Pack

Add cubed chicken and all other a la King ingredients to hot sauce, adding sherry wine last (if used). Bring product temperature back up to 190°F before filling cans.

Fill 16 oz net cans while product temperature is maintained at least at 160°F. If product temperature drops below 160°F, close cans under 15–18 in. vacuum.

Suggested Process

300 × 409 cans (16 oz net) 95 min at 240°F

Check process time and temperature with can supplier or the National Canners Association.

Variations

Diced, cooked turkey or flaked, canned tuna may be used in the above formula instead of chicken.

Method of preparation and assembly of ingredients are the same.

This formula also may be used for Ham a la King, substituting smoked ham for the chicken. Select 16–18 lb smoked hams. Bone, skin, and trim fat. Then put the meat through a dicing machine, making $1/4$–$3/8$-in. dice.

SOURCE: Stephan L. Komarik, 4810 Ronda, Coral Gables, Florida.

CANNED CHICKEN A LA KING (GOOD QUALITY)

Prepare a la King Ingredients

	Lb
Cooked chicken meat, diced	200
Canned pimientos, diced	42
Frozen peas	50
Canned mushrooms, sliced	31

Follow procedure for preparing these components given above for **Chicken a la King (Finest Quality).**

Prepare Sauce

	Lb	Oz	Gal.	Pt
Whole milk			40	
Water			40	
Chicken broth			20	
Nonfat dry milk	37			
Wheat flour	40			
Cornstarch	10			
Salt	14			
Butter	25			
Cream (20%)	25			
Monosodium glutamate	1			
Dry soluble pepper		2		
Ground celery			$1/2$	
Ground turmeric			$3/4$	
Sherry wine (optional)				1

Put milk, broth, and half the water (20 gal.) in a steam-jacketed kettle. Bring to a boil and add salt, butter, cream, and monosodium glutamate. Let mixture simmer at 180°–190°F for 10 min. Make a slurry free of lumps using the remaining water (20 gal.) with seasonings, flour, starch, and nonfat dry milk. With steady stirring, add slurry to hot sauce mixture and cook an additional 10 min at 180°–190°F.

Assemble Ingredients and Pack

Add cubed chicken and all other a la King ingredients to hot sauce, adding sherry wine last (if used). Bring product temperature back up to 190°F, stirring gently to uniformly mix ingredients.

Fill 16 oz net cans while product is hot. Maintain filling temperature not lower than 160°F. Close cans under 27 in. vacuum.

Suggested Process

300 X 409 cans (16 oz net) 95 min at 240°F

Check process time and temperature with can supplier or the National Canners Association.

SOURCE: Stephan L. Komarik, 4810 Ronda, Coral Gables, Florida.

CANNED CHICKEN CHOW MEIN

Prepare Chicken Dice

Eviscerate and clean 100 lb of whole chickens. Cook in 5 gal. of water at 190°–200°F until meat is tender enough to easily remove the bones. Remove bones and chill meat before dicing. Dice in $1/2$-in. cubes.

Prepare Vegetables

Ingredients	Lb
Bean sprouts	50
Bamboo shoots	5
Water chestnuts (sliced)	5
Celery, cut in 1-in. lengths	50
Onions, fresh sliced $1/8$-in.	7
Canned diced red pepper	3

If fresh bean sprouts, bamboo shoots, and water chestnuts are used, blanch separately in boiling water for 15 min. If these products are canned, no blanching is necessary.

Mix together all vegetables with a meat fork to obtain a uniform mixture.

Prepare Sauce

Ingredients	Lb	Oz
Broth from cooked chickens	30	
Rendered chicken fat	2	
Cornstarch	3	8
Salt	1	12
Cane sugar		8
Monosodium glutamate		4
Plant protein hydrolyzate		8

Ground celery seed	1
Dry soluble pepper	3

Put chicken broth and rendered chicken fat in a steam-jacketed kettle and heat to 180°F. Premix salt, cornstarch, and remaining dry ingredients and stir mixture into hot stock. Shut off steam. Prolonged cooking makes the sauce too thick to handle.

Fill into Cans

Using 16 oz net cans, fill with 2 oz chicken on the bottom of the can, add 11 oz mixed vegetables, and top with 3 oz sauce. Close cans under vacuum.

Suggested Process

300 × 409 cans (16 oz net) 90 min at 240°F

Check process time and temperature with can supplier or the National Canners Association.

SOURCE: Stephan L. Komarik, 4810 Ronda, Coral Gables, Florida.

CANNED CURRIED CHICKEN

Prepare Chicken Meat

Clean chickens and cook in simmering water until bones can be removed easily. Separate skin from meat.

Grind skin while still hot through the $1/8$-in. plate of the grinder; add hot chicken broth and chop to a fine emulsion.

Chill meat well before dicing; then dice to desired size.

Prepare Gravy

Ingredients	Gal.	Lb	Oz
Chicken broth	4		
Water		2	
Tomato pureé (sp. gr. 1.035)		2	
Skin emulsion		4	4
Wheat flour		2	4
Rendered bacon fat		3	
Salt		1	8
Curry powder		1	8
Monosodium glutamate			2
Plant protein hydrolyzate			1

Make a thin paste of 1 gal. of water and flour. In a steam-jacketed kettle, heat broth to 200°F and add tomato pureé, remaining 1 gal. water, and bacon fat. Then stir in the flour paste and skin emulsion, salt, and flavorings. Cook, with steady stirring, for 10 min.

In 16 oz net cans, pack 8 oz chicken meat and 8 oz gravy. Close cans under 27 in. vacuum.

Suggested Process

300 × 409 cans (16 oz net) 90 min at 240°F

Check process time and temperature with can supplier or the National Canners Association.

SOURCE: Stephan L. Komarik, 4810 Ronda, Coral Gables, Florida.

CANNED CHICKEN IN BARBECUE SAUCE

Approximately 130 lb of cooked, diced chicken will be needed for the amount of sauce ingredients given:

	Gal.	Lb	Oz
Tomato pureé	25		
Chicken broth	25		
Soy sauce	$1 1/2$		
Worcestershire sauce	$1/2$		
Vinegar (100-grain)	3		
Onion juice			$3 3/4$
Garlic juice			5
Sugar		45	
Salt		12	
Wheat flour		10	
Cornstarch		$2 1/2$	
Ground cloves			$3 3/4$
Ground cumin			$3 3/4$
Ground ginger			$3 1/2$
Ground mace			2
Ground red pepper		2	

Procedure

Put pureé in steam-jacketed kettle. Mix salt, sugar, flour and seasonings together and add to pureé, stirring constantly. Add broth and cook 20 min. Add soy and Worcestershire sauces, onion and garlic juices, and vinegar and cook an additional 3 min.

Using 12 oz net cans, fill with 4 oz chicken dice and 8 oz hot barbecue sauce.

Suggested Process

12 oz net cans 60 min at 240°F

Check process time and temperature with can supplier or the National Canners Association.

SOURCE: Stephan L. Komarik, 4810 Ronda, Coral Gables, Florida.

CANNED HUNGARIAN-STYLE CHICKEN PAPRIKA

Prepare Chicken

Thoroughly clean, eviscerate, and wash chickens. Disjoint into legs, thighs, and breasts (cut into 2-4 pieces); and separate wings, necks, and backs to make emulsion. Parboil chicken pieces in water at 180°F for 20 min using 5 gal. of water for each 100 lb of chicken pieces. Reserve broth for gravy.

Cook wings, necks, and backs separately in simmering water (200°F) until skins and meat can be removed easily from bones. While still hot, grind skins and meat through the 1/8-in. plate of the grinder and mix with the same weight of stock in which these were cooked. Chop into a fine emulsion or run through the finest plate of a meat emulsifier.

Prepare Gravy

Ingredients	Gal.	Lb	Oz
Chicken broth	75		
Tomato pureé (sp. gr. 1.035)	20		
Sour cream	5		
Wheat flour		20	
Cornstarch		10	
Salt		16	
Monosodium glutamate		3	
Plant protein hydrolyzate		1	
Diced fresh green pepper		10	
Hungarian or Spanish paprika		20	
Onion powder		10	
Garlic powder			2
Dry soluble pepper		1	
Ground celery seeds			1
Ground caraway seeds			2

Put 55 gal. hot broth in a steam-jacketed kettle along with the emulsified chicken skins and meat. Add tomato pureé and remainder of the premixed dry ingredients except flour, starch, and sour cream. Use a "Lightning" mixer to agitate gravy. Make a slurry of flour, starch, and sour cream in 20 gal. of water (or well-chilled chicken broth). With continuous agitation, add slurry to gravy. Bring gravy volume up to 100 gal. and cook at 200°F for 30 min.

Fill and Close Cans

A quality product should have at least 50% chicken and 50% hot gravy. If internal product temperature in cans is not lower than 160°F, close cans without drawing vacuum. Otherwise, close cans under 18 in. vacuum.

Suggested Process

300 × 409 cans (16 oz net) 90 min at 240°F

Check process time and temperature with can supplier or the National Canners Association.

SOURCE: Stephan L. Komarik, 4810 Ronda, Coral Gables, Florida.

CANNED CHICKEN LIVER PATÉ

This product is heat-stabilized with the use of Keltrol® and offers interesting possibilities since a number of similar products are feasible by simply mixing the basic emulsion blend with fowl, beef, pork or ham.

Basic Emulsion Blend	%
Xanthan gum (Keltrol®)	0.40
Locust bean gum (available from Hathaway Allied Products, Harbor City, Calif.)	0.40
Avicel-RC-501 (available from FMC Corp., American Viscose Div., Marcus Hook, Pa.)	3.00
Dehydrated egg yolk	2.50
Purity NCS starch (available from National Starch & Chemical Corp., New York, N.Y.)	1.00
Titanium dioxide	0.20
Vinegar (50-grain)	10.00
Sugar	5.00
Vegetable oil	30.00
Salt	1.00
Mustard powder	0.50
Onion powder	1.00
Garlic powder	0.01
Water	44.99
	100.00

Can Fill	%
Cooked chicken liver paste	60.00
Basic emulsion blend	40.00

Procedure

1. Simmer fresh liver in water for 10 min. Discard the resulting broth and grind the cooked liver through a sufficiently fine plate to make a paste.

2. Disperse the Avicel in the water with a high shear mixer or in a planetary blender, such as a Hobart.

3. Dry blend the xanthan gum (Keltrol®), starch, egg yolk, onion powder, garlic powder, sugar, and mustard powder.

4. Add Step No. 3 to Step No. 2 and mix for 10 min to dissolve the xanthan gum.

5. Add the oil in a slow and continuous stream.

6. Mix for 15 min to allow the formation of the emulsion.

7. Mix salt with the vinegar; add and mix for 5 min.

8. Homogenize at 2500 psi, single stage.

9. Take viscosity reading. It should be between 7000 and 8000 cps measured with Brookfield Viscometer Model LVF, spindle No. 4 at 60 rpm.

10. Mix basic emulsion blend (40%) with the

liver paste (60%). Fill into cans, seal, and process to sterility. Check process time and temperature with can supplier or the National Canners Association.

SOURCE: Kelco Co., 20 N. Wacker Drive, Chicago, Ill.

CANNED POTTED CHICKEN (SANDWICH SPREAD)

Ingredients	Lb	Oz
Chicken	90	
Salt pork	10	
Onions, sliced	5	
Salt	4	
Parsley	1	
Ground white pepper	$1/2$	
Ground whole cloves	$1/4$	
Mace		2
Bay leaves		1

Procedure

Cook and skin the salt pork; draw and clean the chickens and cut into pieces. Place pork and chicken pieces in kettle with 2 lb of the salt, onions, parsley, cloves, mace, and bay leaves; cover with cold water, bring to a boil and simmer until chicken is tender.

Remove chicken pieces from kettle; remove skin and bone. Grind to a fine paste and mix in the remainder of the salt (2 lb) and the pepper. Fill into cans, seal and process. Check processing time and temperature with can supplier or with National Canners Association.

Uses for Broth

The liquor—strained—in which the chickens were cooked may be used for chicken soup. Or, if concentrated to $1/2$ its bulk, it may be used or marketed as concentrated chicken broth.

Fill into 1-gal. cans, seal, and process 70 min at 250°F. Check time and temperature of processing with can supplier or with the National Canners Association.

SOURCE: *Poultry Products Technology* by George J. Mountney published by Avi Publishing Co., Westport, Conn.

CANNED SAVORY CHICKEN OR TURKEY SPREAD

Ingredients	Lb	Oz
Cooked chicken or turkey meat	175	
Cooked chicken or turkey skin	140	
Chicken or turkey fat, either raw or rendered		35
Salt		8

Vinegar (100-grain)	2	
Chicken or turkey broth	90	
Dry soluble pepper		8
Celery salt		7
Monosodium glutamate		8

Procedure

Cooked meat and skins should be ground immediately after cooking. Grind meat, skins, and raw fat (if used) through the $1/8$-in. plate of the grinder. Transfer immediately to chopper and chop for 5 min. Add salt premixed with flavorings, vinegar, and, if rendered fat is used, add it also at this time. Then gradually add hot broth. Chop an additional 5 min.

In case an emulsifier is used: after grinding, transfer meats to a mechanical mixer; add all the ingredients and make a uniform mixture; then run material through the finest plate of an emulsifier.

Use a steam-jacketed mixer or a Patterson preheater to keep emulsion hot while filling cans. The emulsion should not cool below 160°F before the cans are closed.

Suggested Process

208 × 108 cans (3 oz net) 1 hr 30 min at 230°F

Check process time and temperature with can supplier or the National Canners Association.

SOURCE: Stephan L. Komarik, 4810 Ronda, Coral Gables, Florida.

CANNED GIBLET SPREAD

Ingredients	Lb	Oz
Cooked chicken or turkey skins	165	
Cooked chicken or turkey gizzards	98	
Cooked chicken or turkey hearts	44	
Raw chicken or turkey fat	35	
Blanched chicken or turkey livers	60	
Broth from cooked skins	90	
Salt	10	
Toasted onion powder		12
Dry soluble pepper		8
Ground nutmeg		1
Ground marjoram		2
Ground sage		2
Ground cloves		2
Ground allspice		1
Sodium nitrite		1

Procedure

Thoroughly wash hearts and gizzards and cook until tender.

Soak livers in cold water at least 2 hr; change water several times or allow it to overflow to carry away blood and cleanse of any bitterness caused by improper handling in removing gall bladders. Then blanch livers at 160°F for 10 min.

Cook skins until tender, reserving the broth for use in the formula. If frozen precooked chicken or turkey skins are used, defrost them in a steam-jacketed kettle, using sufficient water to cover; apply steam and cook just long enough to bring temperature to 200°F.

Meats should be kept hot at all times. Grind all meat items and raw fat through the $1/8$-in. plate of the grinder. Transfer to a chopper and chop for 5 min. Then add salt premixed with flavorings, seasonings, and sodium nitrite. Then gradually add hot broth and chop an additional 5 min.

In case an emulsifier is used: after grinding, transfer meat to a mechanical mixer and add all ingredients including hot broth; mix to a uniform mixture; then put through the finest plate of an emulsifier.

Use a steam-jacketed mixer or a Patterson preheater to keep emulsion hot while filling cans. The emulsion should not cool below 160°F for filling.

Suggested Process

208 × 108 cans (3 oz net) 1 hr 30 min at 230°F

Check process time and temperature with can supplier or the National Canners Association.

SOURCE: Stephan L. Komarik, 4810 Ronda, Coral Gables, Florida.

FROZEN CHICKEN PRODUCTS

FROZEN BAKED DRESSING

This product merely needs to be removed from its outer wrapping and heated in a moderate oven to serving temperature and it is ready to be sliced and served with either roast meats or roast poultry.

Ingredients	Lb	Oz
Regular pork trimmings (50/50)	20	
Sliced, stale bread	100	
Water	70	
Carrot emulsion	5	
Fresh or frozen whole eggs	15	
Nonfat dry milk	5	
Salt	3	
Fresh parsley	1	
Monosodium glutamate		8
Plant protein hydrolyzate		4
Onion powder		4
Garlic powder		$1/8$
Black pepper (38-mesh)		2
Rubbed sage		2
Ground marjoram		$1/4$
Ground rosemary		$1/4$

Procedure

Grind pork trimmings through the $1/4$-in. plate of the grinder. Cook carrots in boiling water until soft and, with 5 lb of hot water, convert into an emulsion in a bakery mixer. Chop parsley into small pieces. Mix salt with flavorings, seasonings, and nonfat dry milk. If frozen eggs are used, defrost before use.

Place bread in a mechanical mixer and add eggs, carrot emulsion, pork, water, and chopped parsley. Start mixer and add salt mixture. Let mixer run until all ingredients are thoroughly mixed (approximately 1-2 min). Then regrind mixture through the $1/2$-in. plate of the grinder.

Pack mixture in oblong aluminum foil baking pans and bake at 375°F to an internal temperature of 165°-170°F. Cool at room temperature, then insert lids and carton for the freezer. Prechill in a cooler at 34°-36°F before transferring to a sharp freezer at -20°F.

SOURCE: Stephan L. Komarik, 4810 Ronda, Coral Gables, Florida.

FROZEN GIBLET DRESSING

Ingredients and procedure are identical with that given above for **Frozen Baked Dressing** except: Instead of pork trimmings, substitute 10 lb of chicken or turkey hearts and gizzards and 10 lb of raw chicken or turkey fat. Grind these items through the $1/4$-in. plate of the grinder.

SOURCE: Stephan L. Komarik, 4810 Ronda, Coral Gables, Florida.

FROZEN CHICKEN POT PIE FILLING

	By Weight		By Measure
Ingredients for 10 Portions	Lb	Oz	
Chicken, cooked white and dark meat	8		
Chicken base		14	

Chicken broth		$1^1/_2$ qt
Nonfat dry milk	3	
Evaporated milk	14	
Modified starch (Puritan 69)		$1^1/_4$ cup
Dry sherry	2	
Lemon juice		2 tbsp
Yellow food color		20 drops
Carrots	$1^3/_4$	
Celery	$1^3/_4$	
Mushrooms	$1^3/_4$	
Peas, frozen	2	
Pearl onions, frozen		30–40

Procedure

Select chickens weighing $3^1/_4$–$3^1/_2$ lb; eviscerate and clean well. Cook until tender; skin and debone; use white and dark meat from breasts, thighs, and legs (utilizing other portions and skin for other products). Cut meat in chunks 1 × $^1/_2$ × $^1/_4$ in. in size. Wash and trim carrots and celery stalks; cut carrots in strips approximately 1 in. long and $^1/_4$ in. wide; slice celery stalks $^1/_4$-in. thick crosswise; cook each separately until just tender. Quarter mushrooms and sauté lightly.

To make sauce, add chicken base to broth in kettle. Slowly add evaporated milk to the modified starch and nonfat dry milk; stir until smooth and add to broth. Heat to 180°F stirring constantly. Add sherry, lemon juice, and color. Blend well.

In each 12 × 8 in. vacuum pouch, put $2^3/_4$ oz chicken pieces, $1^1/_2$ tbsp carrots, 1 tbsp each of celery, mushrooms, and peas and add 3–4 pearl onions. Evenly distribute over these ingredients 8 oz sauce. Seal and blast freeze (30 min).

To Use Frozen Product

Contents of pouches can be heated in boiling water to cover for 6 min, then emptied into pot pie dishes and topped with a round of unbaked pastry. Bake in 400°F oven for 8 min.

SOURCE: *The Freezing Preservation of Foods, 4th Edition, Vol. 4* by Tressler *et al.* published by Avi Publishing Co., Westport, Conn.

Carrot emulsion	30	
Nonfat dry milk	17	
Monosodium glutamate	3	
Salt	12	8
Plant protein hydrolyzate	1	8
Onion powder		6
Dry soluble pepper		4

Procedure

Cook sufficient amount of chicken or turkey to produce enough boneless, diced meat to fill pies or pouches with $1^1/_4$ oz each.

Blanch carrots in boiling water for 15 min and dice in $^1/_4$-in. cubes. Defrost frozen peas.

Make Emulsions.—To make carrot emulsion: cook 15 lb of carrots in 15 lb of water in pressure cooker until carrots are very soft. Put cooked product through a vegetable finisher and make an emulsion of the carrots and water.

To make skin emulsion: Cook chicken or turkey skins until tender and, while still hot, put through the $^1/_8$-in. plate of the grinder. Add some hot broth and chop to a fine emulsion in a meat chopper or put through finest plate of an emulsifier.

Make Gravy and Assemble.—Put 6 gal. of water in a bakery mixer and make a slurry with the flour, cornstarch, and dry milk.

Heat broth to 200°F in a steam-jacketed kettle. Add carrot and skin emulsions, fat, and salt previously mixed with seasonings and flavorings. With continuous stirring, add slurry. Then add carrot dice and defrosted peas. Cook an additional 20 min at 200°F with gentle agitation.

Individual pies may be made up, packaged, and frozen using $1^1/_4$ oz diced meat in bottom of aluminum foil pans, topped with $6^3/_4$ oz gravy-vegetable mixture, and sealed with a top crust. Or, for institutional use, filling only may be frozen separately in boil-in-bag pouches. In this case, put $1^1/_4$ oz diced meat in bottom of pouch and evenly distribute $6^3/_4$ oz gravy-vegetable mixture over meat; vacuum seal pouches and freeze.

SOURCE: Stephan L. Komarik, 4810 Ronda, Coral Gables, Florida.

FROZEN CHICKEN OR TURKEY POT PIES

Ingredients	Gal.	Lb	Oz
Chicken or turkey broth	80		
Water	6		
Wheat flour		35	
Cornstarch		15	
Cooked chicken or turkey skins		66	
Carrots, diced $^1/_4$ in.		50	
Frozen peas, defrosted		50	
Chicken or turkey fat		50	

FROZEN CHICKEN OR TURKEY CROQUETTES

Ingredients	Lb	Oz
Cooked chicken or turkey meat	230	
Cooked chicken or turkey skins	30	
Chicken or turkey broth	190	
Rendered chicken or turkey fat	2	
Precooked wheat flour (Aquatex)	35	
Salt		7

Monosodium glutamate	2	
Plant protein hydrolyzate	1	
Onion powder		12
Garlic powder		$1/16$
Dry soluble pepper		2
Ground turmeric (Alleppey)		$1/2$
Ground celery seeds		$1/2$

Procedure

Grind well-chilled meat through the $1/4$-in. plate of the grinder; put skins through the $1/16$-in. plate.

Mix together salt and dry flavors and seasonings.

Put well-chilled broth in a mixer; add salt-seasoning mixture. While machine is in operation, slowly add flour; then add fat and run machine until mixture is smooth. Reduce mixer speed to slow and add ground meat and skins. Run machine until ingredients are uniformly distributed. Transfer product to cooler and chill to $34°-40°F$. In a forming machine, form product to desired shape and size. Coat with bread crumbs.

The breaded croquettes may be packaged and frozen as they come off the breading line or they may be deep fried and frozen as a ready-to-heat-and-eat product.

In the latter case, fry croquettes in deep fat at $350°F$ until an internal temperature of $180°F$ is obtained. Drain a few minutes before packaging for freezing.

Sharp freezing at $-20°F$ is recommended.

SOURCE: Stephan L. Komarik, 4810 Ronda, Coral Gables, Florida.

FROZEN CHICKEN OR TURKEY PATTIES

Ingredients	Lb	Oz
Raw chicken or turkey meat	450	
Cooked chicken or turkey skins	50	
Salt	7	
Monosodium glutamate	2	
Plant protein hydrolyzate	1	
Ice, chopped	15	
Dry soluble pepper		2
Ground celery seeds		$1/2$
Onion powder		3
Garlic powder		$1/16$

Procedure

Have meat and cooked skins well chilled ($34°-36°F$).

Grind skins first through the $1/4$-in. plate of the grinder; then regrind through the $1/8$-in. plate. If frozen cooked chicken or turkey skins are used, slice the frozen block with a frozen meat cutter into slices approximately $1/2$ in. thick before grinding and grind without defrosting.

Grind 50 lb of raw dark meat through the $1/8$-in. plate of the grinder and the remaining raw meat through the $1/4$-in. plate. Transfer ground skins and dark meat to meat chopper; add only 2 lb of salt and ice; chop mixture to a fine emulsion (or put the mixture through an emulsifier).

In a mechanical mixer, thoroughly mix skin mixture, dark meat emulsion, the remaining salt which has been previously mixed with the seasonings and flavorings, and the ground raw meat. Let mixer run 3–4 min. Dump into truck and transfer to a cooler for overnight chilling at $36°-38°F$.

Next day, transfer to patty-making machine connected with a conveyor to carry patties through the batter coating and breading operation. Pack between parchment paper dividers in cartons suitable for freezing and freeze at $-20°F$.

SOURCE: Stephan L. Komarik, 4810 Ronda, Coral Gables, Florida.

FROZEN BREADED CHICKEN STICKS

Prepare Chicken Sticks

Ingredients	Lb	Oz
Boned, raw chicken meat	90	
Golden cereal binder (a mixture of corn, wheat, oats, rye, and barley)	1.8	
Nonfat dry milk	4.5	
Seasoning (a commercial blend of seasoning for chicken loaves is recommended)		10.5
Salt		21
Water	4	
Vinegar (4–5% acidity)		28

Grind chicken meat through the $1/2$-in. plate of the grinder and then regrind through the $1/8$-in. plate. Blend together all dry ingredients. Put all ingredients in a mechanical mixer and mix well.

One of two methods may be used to form the mixture into sticks $3/4 \times 3/4 \times 3$ to $3 1/2$ in.:

(1) Thoroughly chill mixture down to $32°-34°F$ and feed it through a forming machine. Then freeze sticks prior to coating with batter and breading mix.

(2) Pack mixture in pans $3/4$-in. deep and freeze. Then cut into sticks of desired thickness and length. Since product is already frozen, sticks are ready to be coated with batter and breading mix.

For Batter Coating

A commercially-prepared batter mix may be used to coat the sticks, or the following batter may be made:

	Lb	Oz
Flour	4	
Fresh or frozen whole eggs (or 3/4 lb dehydrated whole eggs may be used)	3	
Seasoning (as desired)		4
Water to make 2 gal. of batter		

Defrost frozen eggs, if used. Mix together thoroughly all ingredients.

For Breading

A commercially-prepared breading mix may be used. An alternative is to bread the sticks in corn-flake crumbs. This type of crumb coating gives the product an attractive appearance both before and after cooking. About 13 lb of cornflake crumbs will be needed for the amount of ingredients given in the formula.

Package and Freeze

Package finished sticks in cartons suitable for freezing, separating layers with parchment paper. Refreeze product after coating sticks and store at $-10°$F.

SOURCE: *Poultry Products Technology* by George J. Mountney published by Avi Publishing Co., Westport, Conn.

FROZEN CHICKEN A LA KING

Prepare the following a la King ingredients:

	Lb
Cooked, diced chicken meat	200
Canned, diced pimientos	42
Canned, sliced mushrooms	31
Frozen peas, defrosted	50

Prepare Sauce

Ingredients	Gal.	Pt	Lb	Oz
Whole milk	40			
Water	40			
Chicken broth	20			
Nonfat dry milk			37	
Wheat flour			25	
Cracker flour			25	
Salt			14	
Butter			25	
Cream			25	
Monosodium glutamate			2	
Plant protein hydrolyzate			1	
Dry soluble pepper				2
Ground celery seeds				1/2
Ground turmeric (Alleppey)				3/4
Sherry wine		1		

Put milk, chicken broth, and half (20 gal.) of the water in a steam-jacketed kettle. Bring to boil. Add salt mixed with the seasonings, monosodium glutamate, and plant protein hydrolyzate along with the butter and cream. Let simmer for 10 min. In a bakery mixer, make a slurry (free of lumps) of dry milk, wheat flour, and cracker flour in 20 gal. of water. Add slurry to the milk-broth mixture with steady stirring. Cook an additional 20 min at 200°F. Add all the a la King ingredients and the sherry wine; mix thoroughly. Pack in polyethylene Mylar bags. Transfer to chill room at 34°–36°F to prechill before transferring to sharp freezer.

SOURCE: Stephan L. Komarik, 4810 Ronda, Coral Gables, Florida.

FROZEN CHICKEN A LA KING

Ingredients for 10 portions	By Weight Lb	Oz	By Measure
Chicken, cooked white and dark meat	10		
Chicken base		2	
Nonfat dry milk		3 1/2	
Chicken stock			2 1/2 qt
Evaporated milk		4 1/2	
Modified starch (Purity 69)		4 1/2	
Dry sherry		3 3/4	
Yellow food color			20 drops
Lemon juice			1 Lemon
Green pepper, diced and cooked			1/2 tsp
Pimiento, diced			1/2 tsp
Mushrooms, sautéed, sliced lengthwise		1	

Estimated Quantities for 1000 Portions

	Lb	Gal.
Chicken, raw	1030	
Sauce		60
Green pepper and pimiento	11	
Mushrooms	50	

Procedure

Select chickens weighing 3 1/4–3 1/2 lb; eviscerate and clean well. Cook until tender; skin and debone; use white and dark meat from breasts, thighs and legs (utilizing other portions and skin for other products). Cut into pieces approximately 1 in. long, 1/2 in. wide, and 1/4 in. thick. To the designated amount of chicken broth in which the chickens were cooked, add chicken base and nonfat milk. Slowly add evaporated milk to modified starch; stir until smooth and add to broth mixture. Heat to 180°F, stirring constantly. Add sherry, color, and lemon juice. Blend thoroughly.

In 12 X 8 in. vacuum boil-in-bag pouches, put 4½ oz chicken, 1 tsp each of peppers and pimientos, and 1 tsp of mushroom slices in each pouch. Add 8½ oz sauce, distributing sauce evenly over ingredients. Seal pouches and blast freeze (30 min).

SOURCE: *The Freezing Preservation of Foods, 4th Edition, Vol. 4* by Tressler *et al.* published by Avi Publishing Co., Westport, Conn.

FROZEN CREAMED CHICKEN PATTY FILLING

Ingredients	By Weight Lb	By Weight Oz	By Measure
Chicken, cooked and cubed (1 X ½ X ¼ in.)	8		
Chicken base		1¾	
Chicken broth			2 qt
Nonfat dry milk		2¾	
Evaporated milk		3½	
Modified starch		3½	
Dry sherry		2¾	
Yellow food coloring			20 drops
Lemon juice			2 tbsp

YIELD: 10 portions consisting of 3½ oz chicken and 7 oz sauce

Procedure

Chickens of 3¼-3½ lb weight are most economical. Boil gently in water until tender; skin and debone; cube both light and dark meat. Bring chicken broth to boiling; add chicken base and nonfat dry milk to broth. Slowly add evaporated milk to starch, stirring until smooth; add to broth mixture; heat to 180°F stirring constantly; then add sherry, lemon juice, and coloring.

In 12 X 8 in. vacuum boil-in-bag pouch put 3½ oz cubed chicken; add 7 oz sauce distributing sauce evenly over chicken. Heat-seal and blast freeze 30 min.

SOURCE: Cornell Hotel & Restaurant Administration Quarterly, Statler Hall, Ithaca, N.Y.

FROZEN CHICKEN IN PORT WINE

Ingredients	By Weight Lb	By Weight Oz	By Measure
Chicken legs			6
Chicken breasts with wings			3
Butter	¼		
Salt			1 tsp
Pepper			¼ tsp
Dry port wine, domestic			¾ cup
Chicken broth			2 qt
Nonfat dry milk		2¾	
Evaporated milk		15	
Modified starch		2¾	
Instant onions		15	
Espagnole extract			¼ cup + 1 tbsp
Mushrooms, cooked and sliced lengthwise		7	

YIELD: 6 portions using 1 leg and ½ breast each

Procedure

Wash chicken pieces in cold water. Remove breast bones and cut breasts in half; sever wings to the second joint leaving wing bone in. Sauté chicken pieces in butter until golden brown. Add salt and pepper and place in a deep pot. Add chicken broth and only half the wine; cover and simmer 25-30 min or until chicken is tender. Remove chicken. Add nonfat dry milk to broth. Slowly add evaporated milk to modified starch stirring until smooth; add mixture to broth. Heat to 180°F stirring constantly. Add instant onions, Espagnole extract, and remaining wine and blend ingredients.

Package 1 leg and ½ breast in 12 X 8-in. vacuum boil-in-bag pouch; add 7 oz sauce and evenly distribute sauce over meat pieces. Blast freeze for 30 min.

SOURCE: Cornell Hotel & Restaurant Administration Quarterly, Statler Hall, Ithaca, N.Y.

FROZEN CHICKEN CURRY

Ingredients	By Weight Oz	By Measure
Chicken legs		6
Chicken breasts with wings		3
Butter	2	
Salt		1 tsp
Curry powder		1 tbsp + 1 tsp
Chicken broth		1 qt + 1 cup
Apples, peeled and diced	4	
Celery, ¼-in. cubes	2½	
Mango chutney, ⅜-in. cubes	3	
Dry white wine, domestic		½ cup
Modified starch	½	

Modified cream   1
Evaporated milk $10^1/_2$

> YIELD: 6 portions using 1 leg and $^1/_2$ breast each

Procedure

Wash chicken pieces in cold water. Remove breast bones and cut breasts in half; sever wings to the second joint leaving wing bone in. Sauté chicken pieces in butter until golden brown. Add salt, curry powder, broth; cover and simmer 15 min. Remove chicken pieces. Add apples, celery, and chutney and simmer 5 min. Slowly add wine to modified starch stirring until smooth; add to sauce and heat to 180°F stirring constantly. Add modified cream and evaporated milk and blend well.

Package 1 leg and $^1/_2$ breast in 12 × 8-in. vacuum boil-in-bag pouch. Add 7 oz sauce and evenly distribute sauce over meat pieces. Blast freeze 30 min.

SOURCE: Cornell Hotel & Restaurant Administration Quarterly, Statler Hall, Ithaca, N.Y.

FROZEN CHICKEN TAHITI

Ingredients	Gm
Butter or margarine	200
Flour	90
Chicken stock, heated	910
Cream, heavy	115
Celery strips	320
Chinese cabbage stems, sliced	320
Chicken, cooked and diced	675
Bamboo shoots, canned	40
Water chestnuts, canned, sliced	80
Pimiento, canned, diced	40
Almonds, slivered and toasted	80
Coconut, fresh, diced	150

Procedure

Melt butter; add flour and stir over low heat for 2–3 min. Add heated chicken stock and cook, stirring constantly until mixture comes to a boil. Stir in cream, celery, and cabbage. Heat again to a boil. Stir in remaining ingredients and season to taste with salt and pepper.

Package in cartons or pouches suitable for freezing and freeze in airblast or multiplate freezer.

SOURCE: *The Freezing Preservation of Foods, 4th Edition, Vol. 4* by Tressler *et al.* published by Avi Publishing Co., Westport, Conn.

FROZEN CHICKEN PAPRIKA

Ingredients	By Weight Oz	By Measure
Chickens legs		6
Chicken breasts with wings		3
Butter	$3^1/_2$	
Salt		1 tsp
Hungarian paprika	$^3/_4$	(1 tbsp + 1 tsp)
Chicken broth		$^3/_4$ qt
Dry white wine, domestic		$^1/_2$ cup
Modified starch	$^1/_2$	
Modified cream	$1^1/_2$	($^1/_2$ cup + 1 tsp)
Evaporated milk	9	
Dehydrated instant onions	$^3/_4$	
Pimientos, diced	4	
Fresh mushrooms, cooked and sliced lengthwise	8	

> YIELD: 6 portions using 1 leg and $^1/_2$ breast each

Procedure

Wash chicken pieces in cold water. Remove breast bones and cut breasts in half; sever wings to the second joint leaving wing bone in. Sauté chicken pieces in butter until golden brown. Add salt, paprika and broth; cover and simmer for 20 min. Remove chicken pieces. Slowly add wine to modified starch; stir until smooth and add to broth; heat to 180°F stirring constantly. Add modified cream and evaporated milk; add instant onions and pimientos and blend well.

Package 1 leg and $^1/_2$ breast in 12 × 8 in. vacuum boil-in-bag pouch; add approximately 1 oz sliced mushrooms and 7 oz sauce; distribute sauce evenly over meat pieces. Blast freeze for 30 min.

SOURCE: Cornell Hotel & Restaurant Administration Quarterly, Statler Hall, Ithaca, N.Y.

FROZEN CHICKEN CACCIATORE

Ingredients	By Weight Oz	By Measure
Chicken legs		6
Chicken breasts with wings		3
Butter	$3^1/_2$	
Salt		1 tsp
White pepper		$^1/_4$ tsp
Instant garlic		1 tsp
Instant onion		1 tbsp + 1 tsp

Espagnole extract	$1\frac{1}{2}$	
Chicken broth		$\frac{3}{4}$ qt
Tomato sauce	7	
Canned Italian tomatoes, diced and seeds removed	12	
Fresh mushrooms, sliced lengthwise	4	
Green peppers, $\frac{1}{2}$-in. squares, cooked	$2\frac{1}{2}$	
Dry white wine, domestic		$\frac{1}{2}$ cup
Modified starch	$\frac{1}{2}$	(2 tbsp)

YIELD: 6 portions using 1 leg and $\frac{1}{2}$ breast each

Procedure

Wash chicken pieces in cold water. Remove breast bones and cut breasts in half; sever wings to the second joint leaving wing bone in. Sauté chicken pieces in butter until golden brown. Add salt, pepper, garlic, onion, Espagnole extract, and broth; cover and simmer 15 min. Add tomato sauce, tomatoes, mushrooms, peppers, and simmer 5 min. Remove chicken pieces. Slowly add wine to modified starch; stir until smooth; add to sauce and heat to 180°F stirring constantly.

Package 1 leg and $\frac{1}{2}$ breast plus 7 oz sauce in vacuum boil-in-bag pouch 12 × 8 in., evenly distributing sauce over meat pieces. Blast freeze for 30 min.

SOURCE: Cornell Hotel & Restaurant Administration Quarterly, Statler Hall, Ithaca, N.Y.

FROZEN CORNISH GAME HEN WITH PEACHES

	By Weight		By Measure
Ingredients	Lb	Oz	
Cornish Game Hens split lengthwise			24 halves
Salt		1	
Pepper			$\frac{1}{2}$ tsp
Butter, melted		4	
Chicken base		6	
Espagnole base		2	
Water, hot (a)			1 qt
Peach juice, drained from canned sections			1 No. 5 can
Lemon juice			$\frac{1}{2}$ cup
Sugar	1		
Margarine		4	
Peach brandy			1 cup
Ground cinnamon			$\frac{1}{3}$ tsp
Ground cloves			$\frac{1}{2}$ tsp

Purity 69 starch (available from National Starch & Chemical Co.)	4	
Flour	4	
Water, cold (b)		1 qt
Peach sections, drained		1 qt

YIELD: 24 portions of $\frac{1}{2}$ Cornish game hen and 6 oz sauce

Procedure

1. Season split hens with salt and pepper. Place the split halves in baking pan, skin side up, brush with butter and bake uncovered at 375°F for 30 min, or until tender.

2. Dissolve chicken base and Espagnole base in 1 qt hot water (a). Add peach and lemon juices. Bring to a boil. Reduce temperature and simmer.

3. Caramelize sugar in large heavy saucepan. Add margarine and simmer until foaming stops. Stir caramel mixture and brandy into juice-stock mixture. Add cinnamon and cloves.

4. Prepare a wash of Purity 69 starch (waxy maize starch), flour, and 1 qt cold water (b). Whip into stock and heat to 180°F, stirring constantly. Reduce heat. Add peach sections. Adjust seasonings.

5. Place each half of game hen in freezer bag and distribute 6 oz of sauce evenly over meat. Seal bag and freeze.

SOURCE: Cornell Hotel & Restaurant Administration Quarterly, Statler Hall, Ithaca, N.Y.

FROZEN FRENCH-FRIED CHICKEN

Chicken breasts and thighs are used for French frying chicken for freezing. Season the cleaned chicken pieces with a mixture of salt, monosodium glutamate, and pepper. Prepare a breading using a mixture of wheat flour, milk, eggs, monosodium glutamate, salt, and pepper. (Additional seasonings may be used in the breading mixture if desired.) Bread chicken pieces and fry in deep fat (2 in. deep or more) for such time as is necessary to obtain a golden brown exterior color and an internal temperature of 190°F. Drain excess fat from fried chicken pieces immediately after cooking.

It is essential that only a high quality frying fat be used. Stainless steel equipment is recommended above copper, copper alloy, or aluminum, and it should be designed to hold the minimum amount of fat required to do a good frying job. Frequent heating and cooling periods of the fat should be avoided. Continuous use of the frying fat at any one time will ensure better turnover and eliminate the bad effects of holdover of used fats.

Cool the product to room temperature or below. Then package in moisture-vaporproof packages and quick freeze at -20°F. Store frozen product at 0°F or below.

SOURCE: *The Freezing Preservation of Foods, 3rd Edition, Vol. 2* by Tressler and Evers published by Avi Publishing Co., Westport, Conn.

BOIL-IN-BAG FROZEN SMOKED CHICKEN IN BARBECUE SAUCE

Prepare Chicken and Smoke

Cook eviscerated, cleaned chickens in water to cover just until meat is tender. Separate meat from bones. Spread meat on screens and transfer to smokehouse. Smoke meat without heat for 10–15 min. Chill meat thoroughly; then dice into 3/4–1-in. cubes. Hold meat in cooler for freezer until ready to use.

Prepare Sauce

Ingredients	Gal.	Lb	Oz
Tomato purée (sp. gr. 1.035)	17		
Chicken broth	17		
Vinegar (45-grain)	4		
Worcestershire sauce	1/2		
Soy sauce	1/2		
Chicken skin emulsion		50	
Cane sugar		30	
Wheat flour		5	
Cracker flour (fine)		3	
Cornstarch		2	
Salt		12	
Onion powder		1	
Spanish paprika		1	6
Garlic powder			1/2
Ground red pepper			1
Ground cloves			2 1/2
Ground mace			1
Ground cinnamon			2
Ground Jamaica ginger			3
Dry soluble pepper			8
Chicken broth to make 50 gal.			

Put 50 gal. of water in a steam-jacketed kettle and make a mark at water level on a measuring stick. Drain water. Put purée and 17 gal. of broth into kettle and heat to 160°F.

Grind 25 lb of chicken skins through the fine plate of the grinder and add an equal amount (25 lb) of hot chicken broth; mix thoroughly. Chop to a fine emulsion in a meat chopper or put product through the finest plate of an emulsifier. Add emulsion to heated tomato-broth mixture.

Make a slurry free of lumps with the flours, cornstarch, and 5 gal. of water or chilled chicken broth; add to batch with steady agitation using a "Lightning" mixer. Mix together sugar, salt, and other flavorings and seasonings and add to sauce. Finally add vinegar, Worcestershire and soy sauces and bring volume up to 50 gal. with chicken broth. Cook sauce 20 min.

Pack and Freeze

Using 1-lb net Mylar boil-in-bags, pack 7.2 oz diced meat and 8.8 oz barbecue sauce. Vacuumize and seal bags. Move into chill room (34°–36°F) for prechilling before transferring product to sharp freezer at -20°F.

SOURCE: Stephan L. Komarik, 4810 Ronda, Coral Gables, Florida.

BAG-IN-BOX FROZEN SMOKED CHICKEN IN BARBECUE SAUCE

Prepare Chicken and Smoke

Cook approximately 1000 lb of eviscerated, cleaned chickens in simmering water (200°F) until just tender. Bone out and place meat on screens in smokehouse. Cold smoke meat without heat for 10–15 min. Chill meat thoroughly; then dice into 3/4–1-in. cubes. Hold meat in cooler or freezer until ready to use.

Prepare Sauce

Ingredients	Gal.	Lb	Oz
Chicken stock		150	
Tomato purée (sp. gr. 1.045)		106	
Cane sugar		30	
Vinegar (45-grain)	4		
Worcestershire sauce		5	
Ground chicken skins		50	
Wheat flour		50	
Salt		10	
Seasoning mix (see below)		1	1
Water to make 376 lb			

Seasoning Mix Ingredients	Oz
Garlic powder	1 1/4
Onion powder	1 3/4
Ground red pepper	1 1/2
Ground cloves	2 1/2
Ground mace	1 1/4
Ground cinnamon	2 1/2
Ground ginger	2 1/2
Ground Spanish paprika	1 3/4
Ground black pepper	2

In a bakery mixer, make a slurry of 25 lb of water and the flour. Put stock, tomato purée, vinegar, seasoning, sugar, Worcestershire sauce, and chicken skins in a steam-jacketed kettle. Heat to 180°F and, while stirring slowly, add slurry and bring temperature up to 212°F. Cook for 15–20 min. Bring weight of sauce up to 376 lb with added water and bring sauce temperature back up to 212°F. Allow sauce to cool before packaging for freezing.

Package and Freeze

Using bag-in-box cartons, put 45% chicken dice in bottom of carton and distribute 55% sauce evenly over meat. Heat-seal cartons and transfer to sharp freezer at –20°F.

SOURCE: Stephan L. Komarik, 4810 Ronda, Coral Gables, Florida.

FROZEN CHICKENBURGERS

Large chickens are more economical to use since ratio of meat to bones is greater. Thoroughly clean and wash whole chickens; sever wing tips at the second joint and reserve for use in making emulsion. Remove all skin from birds, which also is used in making an emulsion (below). Remove raw meat from legs, thighs, base of wings, and breasts.

Cook necks, wing tips, skeletons, and bones in water to cover in a steam-jacketed kettle. Cook until meat can be removed easily from bones. Then grind through the 1/4-in. plate of the grinder.

Put skins in a steam-jacketed kettle, add enough water to cover, and cook until tender. Then grind through the 1/8-in. plate of the grinder. Combine ground skins and ground meat from the necks, wing tips, etc., and transfer to a silent cutter. Add an equal amount of broth and chop to a fine emulsion. Pack in trays and chill thoroughly in a cooler at 34°F.

Grind the raw chicken meat through the 1/4-in. plate of the grinder. Transfer to a mechanical mixer and add the chilled skin emulsion along with 2 lb salt, 3 oz monosodium glutamate, and 1 1/2 oz plant protein hydrolyzate per each 100 lb of meat mixture. Mix for 3 min until all ingredients are thoroughly distributed. Hollymatic into patties of desired size and shape.

Package in cartons suitable for freezing. Sharp freezing is recommended. Patties may also be frozen and then coated with batter and breading prior to packaging for the freezer.

SOURCE: Stephan L. Komarik, 4810 Ronda, Coral Gables, Florida.

FROZEN TURKEYBURGERS

Formula is identical with that given above for **Frozen Chickenburgers.** Substitute turkey meat for chicken meat.

To facilitate boning turkeys, leg tendons should be pulled when the birds are killed.

SOURCE: Stephan L. Komarik, 4810 Ronda, Coral Gables, Florida.

FROZEN CHICKEN GIBLET CON CARNE WITH BEANS

Ingredients	Lb	Oz
Chicken gizzards	65	
Chicken hearts	10	
Kidney suet or raw chicken fat	25	
Cooked Michigan red beans	86	
Tomato paste	10	
Wheat flour	6	8
Onion powder	1	6
Seasoning mix (see below)	5	
Salt	3	2
Water	93	

Seasoning Mix Ingredients	Oz
Chili pepper	57
Paprika (high color value)	22
Ground cumin	13
Garlic powder	2
Ground black pepper	2
Ground red pepper	6
Oregano	3

Prepare Meats

Thoroughly clean gizzards and hearts, removing all surface fat. Place giblets in steam-jacketed kettle with enough water to fully cover and cook until tender. Then grind giblets through the 1/4-in. plate of the grinder.

Prepare Beans

Soak beans in cold water overnight in vats with an overflow device; let cold water slowly overrun during soaking to prevent beans from souring. Cook in fresh water until tender.

Assemble Ingredients

Put suet (or fat, if used) through the 1/4-in. plate of the grinder. Transfer to a steam-jacketed kettle and render. Add ground giblets and, with continuous stirring, braise approximately 15 min. Then, while stirring, add flour, seasoning mix, and salt mixed with the onion powder; stir until sauce is smooth. Add tomato paste and, finally, the water. Cook for approximately 1/2 hr at 212°F. Add cooked beans and mix ingredients well. Bring volume up to 300 lb with added water. Cool product and pack in polyethylene Mylar bags. Freeze.

SOURCE: Stephan L. Komarik, 4810 Ronda, Coral Gables, Florida.

TURKEY PRODUCTS

FROZEN TURKEY ROLLS (EMULSION TYPE)

The use of large birds with an eviscerated weight of 24 lb or more is generally recommended for this product as being the most economical. Line-bone turkeys and remove entire skin which is used to make the following skin emulsion.

Ingredients	Lb	Oz
Skin	100	
Ice, chopped	18	
Salt	1	2
Monosodium glutamate		4
Sodium erythorbate		2

Grind skin through the $1/8$-in. plate of the grinder. Transfer to chopper and add salt, monosodium glutamate, and sodium erythorbate along with the gradual addition of chopped ice. Chop to a fine emulsion.

The meat is portioned into white and dark meat and made up separately into rolls using the following ingredients:

	White Rolls		Dark Rolls	
	Lb	Oz	Lb	Oz
Coarse-cut meat	100		125	
Meat in pieces	50		25	
Skin emulsion	22		12	
Salt	2	8	2	8
Monosodium glutamate		7		7

Procedure for Making Rolls

Procedure is the same for making either the white turkey meat rolls or the dark turkey meat rolls.

Put coarse-cut meat and pieces in a meat type mixer and mix for 2 min. Add salt and monosodium glutamate and continue mixing for 2 min. Then add skin emulsion; and mix for 4 min. Dump meat mixture and divide into 7 lb 6 oz portions. Place each portion in a Semco Pneumatic Stuffer and stuff into presoaked fibrous casings. Recheck and adjust weight. Pressure pack casing with 50 lb air pressure in a Tipper Tie machine and seal casing. Place sealed rolls in tanks for cooking; fill tanks with water and raise temperature to 150°F by direct steam. Hold at this temperature and cook for $2^{1/2}$ hr. Then raise temperature to 175°F and cook another $1^{1/2}$ hr or until an internal meat temperature of 164°–167°F is reached. Shut off steam and introduce cold running water until rolls and water are approximately the same temperature. Then add slush ice to the tank water and allow product to chill overnight in a cooler at 42°F.

The next morning, remove rolls, allow them to dry, then weigh each and freeze.

SOURCE: Stephan L. Komarik, 4810 Ronda, Coral Gables, Florida.

CANNED TURKEY NOODLE DINNER IN JARS

Ingredients	Gal.	Lb	Oz
Turkey stock (broth)	60		
Salt		3	
Monosodium glutamate			6
Plant protein hydrolyzate			3
Turkey fat		5	10

Procedure

After the turkeys are killed, cleaned and drawn, they are chilled in cold water. They are then transferred to the steam-jacketed kettle or cooking vat, covered with water, and cooked (simmered) at 190°–200°F until the meat can be easily removed from the bones. Remove the fat from the top of the broth. Mix this fat with the meat before it is packed in the glass jars, using 5 lb 10 oz of fat to 60 gal. of turkey broth.

Put the broth through a sieve, or filter it so that foam and particles developed during cooking are removed. After the broth is cleaned in this way, add the salt and seasoning, bring to a boil; the broth is then ready to can.

Noodles made with 10% eggs should be used. Cook noodles 15 min in boiling water, using 1 lb of noodles to 1 gal. of water. Wash noodles thoroughly in cold water after cooking, so they will not stick together.

Pack 1-lb jars as follows: 2 oz sliced cooked turkey meat, 8 oz cooked noodles, 6 oz turkey broth.

Close jars under 27 in. vacuum and process under 25 lb water pressure 1 hr 30 min at 240°F. Check processing time and temperature with jar supplier or with the National Canners Association.

SOURCE: Stephan Komarik, 4810 Ronda, Coral Gables, Florida.

CANNED TURKEY A LA KING

Prepare a la King Ingredients

	Gal.	Lb
Cooked turkey meat		14
Fresh green peppers		3
Fresh mushrooms		5

Fresh pimientos		2½
Sherry wine		⅛

Thoroughly clean and wash turkeys and soak in cold water for at least 2 hr. Then put whole turkeys in a steam-jacketed kettle, cover with water, and simmer until meat is tender and can be removed easily from bones. Remove skin and bones and cut meat into uniform size pieces.

Stem and clean green peppers and pimientos. Dice in ¾-in. squares. Blanch in boiling water for 3 min.

Wash and clean mushrooms and slice ⅛-in. thick.

Prepare Sauce

Ingredients	Gal.	Lb	Oz
Whole milk	5		
Butter		2½	
Wheat flour		2½	
Salt			13
Monosodium glutamate			1
Wheat protein hydrolyzate			½

In a steam-jacketed kettle, melt butter and stir in flour; with steady sitrring, cook for 10 min to obtain a roux.

In the meantime, heat milk to boiling and hold at this temperature for 10 min. Add salt mixed with monosodium glutamate, and plant protein hydrolyzate; stir into milk thoroughly. Then add hot milk slowly to the roux, stirring continuously with a "Lightning" mixer so as to avoid a lumpy sauce. Cook sauce for 10 min. Add the a la king ingredients, adding sherry wine last (wine should be clear and free of sediment). Mix all ingredients thoroughly.

Close cans with product temperature not lower than 160°F.

Suggested Process

300 × 409 cans (16 oz net) 90 min at 240°F

Check process time and temperature with can supplier or the National Canners Association.

Label Requirement

Pure food regulations require the following to appear on the label of this product: "Flavored with a wheat protein derivative and monosodium glutamate."

SOURCE: Stephan L. Komarik, 4810 Ronda, Coral Gables, Florida.

FROZEN COMMINUTED TURKEY "STEAKS"

Ingredients	Lb	Oz
Boneless fresh turkey meat	250	
Cooked turkey meat	30	
Cooked turkey skins	45	
Semolina flour	50	
Turkey broth	70	
Ice, chopped	50	
Salt	10	
Monosodium glutamate	3	
Plant protein hydrolyzate	1	8
Ground white pepper		1
Ground celery seeds		¾
Onion powder		4
Garlic powder		⅛

Procedure

Tendons of turkey legs should be pulled when the birds are killed and dressed.

Premix salt with the flavorings and seasonings.

Skin large whole birds, except the wing tips (which are severed at the second joint and cooked as described below). Reserve skins for skin emulsion (below). Bone legs, thighs, breasts, and base of wings.

Grind 35% of the leg and thigh meat through the ⅛-in. plate of the grinder; transfer to a meat chopper and add ½ the salt-seasoning mixture; with the chopped ice, chop into a fine emulsion. Grind remaining boneless meat through the ¼-in. plate. Put the emulsion and the ground meat separately in meat trays not deeper than 4 in. and chill overnight at 34°F.

Cook necks, wing tips, skeletons, and bones from legs and thighs in a steam-jacketed kettle. Separate skin and meat taken from the bones. Add skins to the cooked skins (below) to make emulsion. Grind meat through the ¼-in. plate of the grinder. Cooking stock is used also in the skin emulsion.

To Make Skin Emulsion.—Put skins in a steam-jacketed kettle, add enough water to cover, and simmer until tender. Add cooked skins from necks, wing tips, etc. While skins are still hot, grind through the ⅛-in. plate of the grinder. Transfer to chopper with the broth and flour and chop to a fine emulsion. Transfer to cooler at 42°F for overnight chill.

Assemble Ingredients.—In a mechanical mixer, put the chilled, ground raw meat and the cooked ground meat together with the chilled meat emulsion. Start mixer and add remaining ½ of the salt-seasoning mixture; run mixer for 1 min. Then add the freshly-made skin emulsion and run mixer for 2 min more under 27 in. vacuum.

Stuff, Cook, and Chill.—Stuff product tightly into the desired size of "Easy Peel" fibrous casings.

Transfer to preheated cooking tank at 160°F and cook to an internal meat temperature of 150°F. Chill in cold water to an internal meat temperature of 100°F. Then to form product—still in casings—put into wire molds of the same type used to shape flat boneless hams. Transfer molds to chill room at 34°F for overnight.

Slice, Coat, and Freeze.—Place molds in freezer room and semifreeze product just enough to be able to slice in the slicing machine to the desired thickness. First remove molds and casings; slice to desired thickness; then coat with batter and breading mix. Package in cartons suitable for freezing and freeze.

SOURCE: Stephan L. Komarik, 4810 Ronda, Coral Gables, Florida.

SMOKED TURKEY

Prepare the following curing solution:

Ingredients	Gal.	Lb	Oz
Water	50		
Sugar		15	
Salt		53	
Sodium nitrite			13½

The sodium nitrite in the curing solution will give a pink cast to the smoked meat. If this color is objectionable, omit this ingredient in the curing solution.

Procedure

Turkeys should be eviscerated, washed, and dressed promptly after slaughter. Then pump turkeys with curing solution using 10% of the weight of the turkey. Place pumped turkeys in ice water to chill for 3–4 hr. Remove from chill water and place in cover pickle of the same strength as the pumping pickle. Temperature of cover pickle should be 38°–40°F. Transfer to cooler (38°–40°F) and allow to cure for 48 hr.

NOTE: If it is not possible to pump turkeys as outlined above, submerge them in the pickle made with the above brine and cure them at cooler temperature (38°–40°F) for a period of 4–5 days depending on the size of the birds.

Remove turkeys from cure, hang on smoke sticks, and transfer to the smokehouse for the following smoking schedule: Preheat house to 130°F. Smoke at this temperature for 6 hr. Raise temperature to 140°F; hold for 4 hr. Raise temperature to 165°F; hold at this temperature until internal meat temperature of the fleshy parts reaches 155°F.

Remove smoked turkeys from smokehouse and let them hang at room temperature until bird temperature drops to at least 100°F, then transfer to chill room (42°F) for finish chilling.

This is a perishable product and should be held under refrigeration.

SOURCE: Stephan L. Komarik, 4810 Ronda, Coral Gables, Florida.

TURKEY LOAF

The formula given below is for the fresh-baked product for institutional food service. However, this is a product that can be frozen unbaked in aluminum foil loaf pans and marketed for retail as well as institutional trade.

Ingredients	Weight Lb	Oz	Approx Measure
Fresh bread cubes	1	4	(2½ qt)
Cooked rice (1 cup uncooked rice yields 1 qt cooked)	3	8	(2⅓ qt)
Salt		1½	
Chopped pimientos		11½	
Chopped onions		1½	
Egg yolks	1		(24)
Turkey broth and water			1 gal.
Nonfat dry milk	1	8	(2¼ qt instant)
Diced turkey	10		
Butter, melted	1		
Egg whites	1	8	(24)

YIELD: 96 servings approximately 3 × 3⅓ in.

Procedure

Combine bread cubes, rice, salt, pimientos, and onions.

Beat egg yolks and add to broth-water liquid; then sprinkle dry milk on top and beat until ingredients are well blended. Add to bread-rice mixture. Then add turkey and melted butter and mix to blend ingredients.

Beat egg whites until stiff but not dry (about 8 min). Fold into turkey mixture. Divide into 4 counter pans (12 × 20 × 2½ in.) and bake at 375°F for 1 hr.

SOURCE: American Dry Milk Institute, 130 N. Franklin St., Chicago, Ill.

TURKEY LOAF

Ingredients	Lb	Oz
Boneless, cooked turkey meat	60	
Gelatin solution (1 part gelatin, 8 parts chicken stock)	40	
Salt	2	
Monosodium glutamate		2
Plant protein hydrolyzate		1

Procedure

Turkey may be boned before or after cooking. Cover meat with water and cook until tender (do not overcook so that meat falls apart). Meat normally has a shrinkage during cooking of approximately 40%. Use stock to make the gelatin solution. Heat gelatin solution to 160°F; then add salt and chicken flavor.

This product is usually stuffed in Cellophane casings and pressed in oblong molds. Use Cellophane casings that fit ham molds equipped with spring attachments which presses the stuffed casing into shape.

First put some gelatin solution in the casing; then pack casing with meat putting attractive slices to the outside and filling center with chunks and pieces. As casings are being filled, add enough gelatin solution to keep out air pockets. Proper meat : gelatin ratio should be maintained in each casing: 6 parts meat to 4 parts gelatin solution.

Chill stuffed product in the molds overnight at 42°F. Then remove molds, package, and ship. This is a very perishable product and should be held under refrigeration until sold.

SOURCE: Stephan L. Komarik, 4810 Ronda, Coral Gables, Florida.

TURKEY LOAF IN CHUBS

These loaves are made from a combination of fresh boneless and cooked turkey meat. The formula is so constructed that the finished yield of the completely processed loaf is virtually 100% of the eviscerated, boned, raw turkey, not including giblets.

Ingredients	Lb	Oz
Boneless raw turkey meat	48.36	
Ice, chopped	10	
Cooked turkey meat	6	
Cooked skins	9	
Cereal binder (fine)[1]	9	
Turkey broth	14.64	
Salt	3	
Monosodium glutamate		3
Plant protein hydrolyzate		1

[1] A mixture of corn and wheat flours.

Procedure

Tendons of turkey legs should be pulled when the birds are killed and dressed. Skin large whole birds, except the wing tips (which are severed at the second joint and cooked as described below). Reserve skins for skin emulsion (below). Bone legs, thighs, base of wings, and breasts.

Grind 35% of the raw meat (legs, thighs) through the ⅛-in. plate of the grinder. Transfer to a chopper and with the chopped ice (10% of the whole batch) and half of the salt (1½ lb) chop to produce a fine emulsion. Grind remaining raw meat through the ¼-in. plate. Put meat emulsion and ground raw meat in trays and chill thoroughly overnight at 34°F.

Cook necks, wing tips, skeletons, and bones in a steam-jacketed kettle. Separate skin and meat taken from bones. Add skins to the cooked skins (below) to make the skin emulsion. Grind meat through the ¼-in. plate of the grinder. Reserve cooking stock to use in skin emulsion.

To Make Skin Emulsion.—Put skins in a steam-jacketed kettle, add enough water to cover, and simmer until tender. Add cooked skins from necks, wing tips, etc. While skins are still hot, grind through the ⅛-in. plate of the grinder. Transfer 9 lb of the ground skins to a chopper and with the hot stock, cereal binder, seasonings, and remaining salt (1½ lb) chop to a fine emulsion. Pack in trays and chill overnight at 34°F.

Assemble Ingredients.—In a mechanical mixer, put the chilled, ground raw meat and the cooked ground meat together with the chilled meat emulsion. Start mixer and run 1 min. Then add skin emulsion and let machine run an additional 2 min, or until all ingredients are evenly distributed.

Stuff, Cook, and Chill.—Stuff product in Saran chubs, using a chub machine, if available. Cook in 160°F water until an internal meat temperature of 152°–155°F is reached. Chill in cold water to 105°F before transferring product to chill room.

This product is perishable and should be kept under refrigeration in storage and through marketing channels. Storage life will be prolonged if product is held in a freezer until marketed.

SOURCE: Stephan L. Komarik, 4810 Ronda, Coral Gables, Florida.

TURKEY LOAVES IN 6-LB OBLONG CANS

Except for substituting semolina flour for the cereal binder, ingredients and procedure for making the meat mixture are identical with that given above for **Turkey Loaf in Chubs.**

Stuffing, Cooking, Chilling for Oblong Cans

Transfer made-up meat mixture to stuffer and stuff into parchment-lined oblong cans. Close cans under 27 in. vacuum.

Preheat water in cooking tank to 160°F before immersing cans and cook product until an internal meat temperature of 150°F is obtained (approximately 3½ hr). Chill for 2 hr in cold water then transfer to chill room at 34°F for thorough chilling.

This product is perishable and should be kept under refrigeration in storage and through marketing channels.

Storage life will be prolonged if product is held in a freezer until marketed.

SOURCE: Stephan L. Komarik, 4810 Ronda, Coral Gables, Florida.

TURKEY PATTIES WITH TEXTURED VEGETABLE PROTEIN

Ingredients	%
Ground turkey thigh meat	60.46
Textured vegetable protein (Edi-Pro® 200)	24.78
Ground turkey skin	13.88
Salt	0.74
Imitation Roast Turkey Flavor 104 (available from Knickerbocker Mills Co., Totowa, N.J.)	0.14

Procedure

1. The deboned thigh meat is ground through a $1/2$-in. plate.
2. Grinding of the skin is accomplished through a $1/8$-in. plate.
3. Textured vegetable protein (Edi-Pro® 200) is chopped in a silent cutter for 3 min.
4. Mix all ingredients in a Hobart mixer for 3 min.
5. Grind the resulting mixture once through a $3/16$-in. plate.
6. Patties may then be formed for freezing until used.
7. Thawed patties are cooked at 350°F until done.

SOURCE: Ralston Purnia Company, Checkerboard Square, St. Louis, Mo.

FROZEN TURKEY STICKS

Except for substituting semolina flour for the cereal binder, ingredients and procedure for making the meat mixture are identical with that given above for **Turkey Loaf in Chubs.**

Stuffing, Cooking, Preparing Sticks

Transfer made-up meat mixture to stuffer and stuff into $4 \times 4 \times 24$ in. oblong molds. Close molds.

Preheat water in cooking tank to 160°F; immerse molds and cook loaves to an internal meat temperature of 150°F (approximately $3 1/2$ hr). Chill for 2 hr in cold water then transfer to chill room at 34°F for thorough chilling. Remove molds and cut loaves to desired dimension of sticks, using

a mitre box or cubing machine. Batter dip and bread sticks before encasing for the freezer. Package in cartons suitable for freezing and transfer to sharp freezer room.

SOURCE: Stephan L. Komarik, 4810 Ronda, Coral Gables, Florida.

TURKEY LIVERWURST (PATÉ) IN CHUBS

Ingredients	Lb	Oz
Blanched turkey livers	30	
Cooked turkey skins	30	
Cooked turkey gizzards	26	
Cooked turkey hearts	14	
Turkey fat, raw	10	
Salt	2	
Black pepper (fine mesh)		4
Ground nutmeg		$1/4$
Ground marjoram		$1/2$
Ground sage		$1/2$
Ground mustard		1
Ground cloves		$1/4$
Ground allspice		$1/4$
Onion powder		3
Stock (hot) from cooked skins	25	

Procedure

Soak livers in cold water for 2 hr with overflow of water to wash out blood and any bitterness caused by improper handling of gall bladders. Then blanch livers in water at 160°F for 10 min. Cook hearts and gizzards until done. Grind all meat items through the $1/8$-in. plate of the grinder. Transfer to a mixer and add the remaining ingredients including hot stock; mix thoroughly. Pass product through the fine plate of an emulsifier. Stuff in Saran chubs and cook at 160°F for 30 min. Prechill product in cold water before transferring it to a chill room at 40°–42°F for thorough chilling.

Product is perishable and should be kept under refrigeration through storage and marketing channels. Storage life will be prolonged if product is held in a freezer until marketed.

SOURCE: Stephan L. Komarik, 4810 Ronda, Coral Gables, Florida.

TURKEY SPREAD IN CHUBS

Ingredients	Lb	Oz	Gm
Cooked turkey meat from necks and carcasses	50		
Cooked turkey skins	40		
Turkey fat	10		
Salt	2		
Monosodium glutamate			3

Plant protein hydrolyzate	1$\frac{1}{2}$
Vinegar (100-grain)	8
Chicken stock (hot)	25

Procedure

Cook turkey skins until tender. Then with the rest of the cooked turkey meat grind through the $\frac{1}{8}$-in. plate of the grinder. Transfer meat to a mixer and add the rest of the ingredients including the hot stock. Mix thoroughly and then put product through the fine plate of an emulsifier. Stuff in Saran chubs and cook at 160°F for 30 min. Prechill in cold water; then transfer product to a chill room at 40°-42°F.

Product is perishable and should be kept under refrigeration through storage and marketing channels. Storage life will be prolonged if product is held in a freezer until marketed.

SOURCE: Stephan L. Komarik, 4810 Ronda, Coral Gables, Florida.

TURKEY BOLOGNA

Use either of these meat mixtures

	No. 1	No. 2
Ingredients	Lb	Lb
Boneless raw turkey meat	50	50
Cooked turkey skins	9	9
Raw turkey fat	10	
Pork jowls		10

with these ingredients

	Lb	Oz
Semolina flour	10	
Ice, chopped	10	
Turkey broth	9	
Salt	3	
Sodium nitrite (use only if a pink color is desired in finished product)		$\frac{1}{4}$
Monosodium glutamate		3
Plant protein hydrolyzate		1

Procedure

Have turkey meat and turkey fat (or pork jowls) well chilled. Grind meat through the $\frac{1}{8}$-in. plate of the grinder. Grind fat or jowls through the $\frac{1}{4}$-in. plate. Cook turkey skins until tender; then grind through the $\frac{1}{4}$-in. plate. After grinding, chill all the meat products and the broth down to 30°-32°F.

Next day, regrind skins through the $\frac{1}{8}$-in. plate of the grinder. Put reground skins and meat in a silent cutter. Start chopping while adding chopped ice, salt, and seasonings. Chop 5 min; then add

broth (temperature 32°F) and ground fat; chop 3 min more. Add flour and chop 2 min more to a smooth emulsion. Total chopping time: 10 min.

If an emulsifier is used: mix all ingredients in a mechanical mixer and put product through the superfine plate of an emulsifier.

Stuff and Smoke.—Stuff in Cellophane casings of desired size. Hang on smokehouse trees properly spaced and rinse with cold water. Transfer sausages to the smokehouse and smoke as follows: Preheat smokehouse to 130°-135°F and hold sausages at this temperature for $\frac{1}{2}$ hr with dampers wide open to dry casings. Then introduce smoke (heavy smudge) and smoke for 2$\frac{1}{2}$-3 hr. Raise temperature gradually to 175°F until internal meat temperature of 155°F is obtained.

Remove sausages from smokehouse and shower with cold water until internal meat temperature has dropped to 110°F. Then allow to cool and dry at room temperature for 30-60 min before transferring product to holding cooler at 45°F.

Product is perishable and should be kept under refrigeration through storage and marketing channels. Storage life of product will be prolonged if product is held at frozen temperatures until marketed.

SOURCE: Stephan L. Komarik, 4810 Ronda, Coral Gables, Florida.

CANNED TURKEY CHILI CON CARNE

Ingredients	Lb	Oz
Raw turkey meat	125	
Raw turkey fat	30	
Tomato purée (sp. gr. 1.035)	15	
Processed semolina wheat flour	10	
Salt	5	
Ground chili pepper	5	
Ground Spanish paprika	1	10
Ground cumin	1	
Onion powder	1	
Garlic powder		2$\frac{1}{2}$
Ground black pepper		2$\frac{1}{4}$
Ground red pepper		$\frac{1}{2}$
Ground oregano		4
Water	114	

Procedure

Have turkey meat and turkey fat well chilled. Grind turkey meat through the $\frac{1}{2}$-in. plate of the grinder; the fat through the $\frac{1}{4}$-in. plate. Mix together flour, salt, and the seasonings. Measure out water in a mechanical mixer; start mixer and slowly add the flour-seasoning mixture; then add tomato purée, and finally the ground meat and fat.

Let machine run a few minutes until all ingredients are thoroughly distributed.

Fill into 16 oz net cans and close under 27 in. vacuum.

Suggested Process

300 × 409 cans (16 oz net) 95 min at 240°F

Check process time and temperature with can supplier or the National Canners Association.

After approximately 15 min chilling in the retort, cans should be removed and thoroughly shaken before storing.

SOURCE: Stephan L. Komarik, 4810 Ronda, Coral Gables, Florida.

CANNED TURKEY CHILI CON CARNE WITH BEANS

Ingredients	Lb	Oz
Raw turkey meat	75	
Raw turkey fat	30	
Presoaked pinto beans	80	
Tomato purée (sp. gr. 1.035)	25	
Processed wheat flour	4	
Salt	3	2
Ground chili pepper	3	
Ground Spanish paprika	1	
Onion powder	1	
Garlic powder		1½
Ground cumin		10
Ground black pepper		1¼
Ground red pepper		¼
Ground oregano		2¼
Water	76	

Procedure

Soak pinto beans overnight in water, allowing water to overflow so beans will not sour during soaking.

Grind well-chilled turkey meat through the ½-in. plate of the grinder; turkey fat (also well-chilled) through the ¼-in. plate.

Mix flour, salt, and seasonings. Measure out water in a mechanical mixer and, while machine is running, slowly add the flour-salt-seasonings mixture; then add tomato purée; finally, add the soaked beans and ground meat and fat. Run machine a few minutes until all ingredients are thoroughly distributed.

Fill 1-lb cans and close under 27 in. vacuum.

Suggested Process

300 × 409 cans (16 oz net) 2 hr 30 min at 240°F

Check process time and temperature with can supplier or the National Canners Association.

Chill.—After approximately 15 min of chilling in the retort, cans should be removed and thoroughly shaken before storage.

SOURCE: Stephan L. Komarik, 4810 Ronda, Coral Gables, Florida.

MISCELLANEOUS POULTRY PRODUCTS

COOKED BONELESS POULTRY ROLLS AND ROASTS

Ingredients	Lb	Oz
Boneless, skinless poultry meat	85	
Emulsified skins and meat fines	10	
Water	2	
Salt	1½	
Spice mix	1½	
Sodium polyphosphate (Kena®)		8
Sodium erythorbate (Neo-Cebitate®)		⅞

Procedure

Place deboned, skinless poultry meat into mixer. Make a slurry of sodium polyphosphate (Kena®) and sodium erythorbate (Neo-Cebitate®) and add it to the poultry meat. Mix until evenly distributed. Add salt and spice mix and mix for approximately 2 min. Add emulsified skin and meat fines and mix thoroughly into batch. Stuff into appropriate casings.

Oven roast at 250°F to internal temperature of 160°F. Or, water cook at 180°–190°F to internal temperature of 160°F.

Chill immediately.

Products such as these are perishable and should be kept refrigerated at all times. Shelf-life will be extended if product is stored in a freezer until marketed.

SOURCE: Merck Chemical Division, Merck and Company, Rahway, N.J.

BREADED POULTRY PATTIES WITH 15% MEAT REPLACEMENT

Ingredients	Lb	%
Poultry meat (cooked)	100.00	83.06
Bread crumbs	2.00	1.66
Soy protein concentrate (S.F.P. Regular TA)	5.85	4.86
Water (cold)	11.70	9.72
Maggi Poultry Base 102-F	0.75	0.62

Onion powder	0.04	0.03
Ground celery seed	0.03	0.02
Ground white pepper	0.02	0.02

Procedure

1. Mix poultry base and spices with designated amount of water. Add protein concentrate (S.F.P.) and hydrate 10–15 min.

2. Coarse grind or flake poultry meat. Add S.F.P.-spice mixture. Mix in bread crumbs.

3. Pass entire blended ingredients through medium grind plate.

4. Form into patties of desired weight.

5. Batter and bread with commercial breading material designed for poultry patties to be fried.

SOURCE: Swift Edible Oil Co., Vegetable Protein Products Division, 115 W. Jackson Blvd., Chicago, Ill.

CHICKEN LOAF WITH TEXTURED VEGETABLE PROTEIN

Ingredients	%
Minced deboned chicken	53.76
Textured vegetable protein (Edi-Pro® 200)	37.63
Calcium protolac (available from Borden Co., Columbus, Ohio)	3.22
Imitation chicken flavor 5839-DB (available from Monsanto Flavor/Essence, St. Louis)	1.58
Maggi RF-C (available from Nestlé Co., White Plains, N.Y.)	1.58
Salt	1.08
Egg Albumin (available from Seymour Foods Co., Topeka, Kansas)	0.89
Flavor Potentiator (available from Monsanto Flavor/Essence, St. Louis)	0.26

Procedure

1. Mix textured vegetable protein (Edi-Pro® 200) in Hobart mixer for 3 min.

2. Add thawed, minced deboned chicken and mix for an additional 2 min.

3. Mix in other ingredients one at a time until uniformly distributed.

4. Place the mixed ingredients in a spring loaded pan.

5. Suggested cooking is in 190°F water bath until an internal temperature of 175°F is reached.

SOURCE: Ralston Purina Company, Checkerboard Square, St. Louis, Mo.

JELLIED CHICKEN LOAF

Ingredients for 200 lb of loaves	Lb	Oz
Dressed stewing hens	300	
Carrots	20	
Celery	17	
Salt	9	
Pimiento	5	
Pepper		7
Onion powder		7
Monosodium glutamate		3.5
Gelatin (per 100 lb chicken broth)	8	

Procedure

Dismember chickens. Place in pot with necks. Cover with water. Add salt, pepper, onion powder, and monosodium glutamate. Place carrots and celery in stockinettes and add to the pot. Cook at boiling temperature for 3½–4 hr. Remove chicken and strain broth through clean cheese cloth. Cool both chicken and broth in cooler and remove surface layer of fat that forms on the broth. Heat chicken broth to 160°F in steam kettle. Dissolve gelatin; add to broth and allow to cool to a temperature suitable for handling.

Remove meat from chicken bones, discarding bones, skin, and necks. A 30% yield can be anticipated including cooking losses. Dice the chicken meat and mix with diced pimiento. Add mixture to cooled gelatin-broth mixture (1:1 ratio). Pour mixture through a wide-mouth funnel into suitably prepared 80 MP fibrous casings. Tie casings, wash with hot water or vinegar solution. Transfer to cooler immediately.

Product is perishable and should be kept under refrigeration through storage and marketing channels. Shelf-life of product will be extended if product is held in a freezer.

SOURCE: *Poultry Products Technology* by George J. Mountney published by Avi Publishing Co., Westport, Conn.

CHICKEN SANDWICH SPREAD

Ingredients	Lb	Oz	Gal.
Cooked chicken meat and skins	80		
Onions, chopped	2		
Salt	2		
Ground white pepper		1	
Ground cloves		1	
Ground mace		1	
Chicken broth			1
Flour (if desired)	4		

Procedure

Put the cooked chicken meat and skins through a fine grinder and mix together with remaining ingredients.

Mixture may be packed in cartons and frozen or may be processed for canning.

SOURCE: *Poultry Products Technology* by George J. Mountney, published by Avi Publishing Co., Westport, Conn.

CHICKEN-FLAVORED SANDWICH SPREAD WITH TEXTURED VEGETABLE PROTEIN DICE

Ingredients	By Weight Lb	By Measure
Chicken-flavored textured vegetable protein (Bontrae® Dice)	5	(1 carton)
Celery, diced	1	(1 qt)
Sweet pickle relish		1 cup
Mayonnaise or salad dressing		1 qt
Salt		2 tbsp
White pepper		1 tsp
Salad mustard		1 tbsp
Eggs, hard cooked and diced		6

YIELD: Allowing for 2-oz portions, this formula will make 60 sandwiches

Procedure

Using a food chopper or coarse meat grinder, grind the frozen textured vegetable protein dice (Bontrae®) .... do not thaw before grinding. Combine with diced celery and pickle relish. Blend salt, pepper, salad mustard, and diced eggs with dressing; add to textured vegetable protein mixture and blend well.

SOURCE: General Mills, Inc., Food Service & Protein Products Division, Minneapolis, Minn.

CHICKEN SALAD WITH TEXTURED VEGETABLE PROTEIN

Ingredients	By Weight Lb	Oz	or	By Measure
Chicken, cooked, diced	6	4		
Textured vegetable protein (Mira-Tex 200)	1			
Water (hot)	1	12		(3½ cup)
Mayonnaise	10			
Celery, chopped	3	3		
Sweet pickle relish	2	9		
Pitted olives, chopped	1	4		

Hard cooked eggs, chopped		24
Salt		2

YIELD: 100 portions of ⅔ cup provides equivalent of 2 oz protein-rich food

Procedure

1. Combine textured vegetable protein (Mira-Tex 200) and hot water and allow to stand 15–20 min or until the water has been absorbed.

2. Grind the softened textured vegetable protein once, using a ³/₁₆-in. plate.

3. Mix all ingredients together; blend well. Chill.

Variations.—*Tuna Salad.*—Use 6 lb, 4 oz flaked, canned tuna in place of chicken. One ⅔-cup portion provides equivalent of 2 oz protein-rich food.

Turkey Salad.—Use 6 lb, 4 oz diced cooked turkey in place of chicken. One ⅔-cup portion provides equivalent of 2 oz protein-rich food.

SOURCE: A. E. Staley Mfg. Co., Decatur, Ill.

CHICKEN PIE WITH TEXTURED VEGETABLE PROTEIN

Ingredients	By Weight Lb	Oz	or	By Measure
Textured vegetable protein (Mira-Tex 200)	1	5		
Water (hot)	2	7		(1¼ qt)
Carrots, diced	3			(2 qt 1½ cup)
Celery, diced	3			(2 qt 3½ cup)
Water				2 qt 1½ cup
Salt				1¾ tsp
All-purpose flour	2	4		(2¼ qt)
Salt		2¾		(⅓ cup)
Chicken fat, butter, or melted margarine	2	4		(1 qt ½ cup)
Broth (skimmed) plus hot vegetable cooking liquid				2½ gal.
Cooked green peas, drained	2	8		(1 qt 2¾ cup)
Onions, chopped	1			(2⅔ cup)
Cooked chicken, diced	8	12		
Unbaked biscuits				100

YIELD: 100 portions; ¾ cup plus 1 biscuit provides 2 oz cooked meat, ¼ cup vegetable, 1 serving of bread

Procedure

1. Combine textured vegetable protein (Mira-Tex 200) with hot water and allow to stand 15–20 min or until all water has been absorbed; then grind through $1/8$-in. plate and mix lightly with the diced chicken.

2. Cook carrots and celery together in boiling salted water 15 min; drain and reserve liquid for gravy.

3. Blend flour, salt, and fat; stir into hot liquid; cook and stir constantly until thickened. Combine gravy, vegetables, and chicken mixture.

4. Place in 4 greased baking pans ($12 \times 20 \times 2$ in.) allowing about 10 lb, 4 oz ($4^3/4$ qt) per pan. Bake 30 min in hot $425°F$ oven.

5. Remove from oven and top with unbaked biscuits. Return to oven and bake 12–15 min at $450°F$ (very hot oven).

SOURCE: A. E. Staley Mfg. Co., Decatur, Ill.

A LA KING USING TEXTURED VEGETABLE PROTEIN DICE WITH CHICKEN-LIKE FLAVOR

Ingredients	By Weight (Lb)	By Measure
Water		9 qt
a la King sauce mix (General Mills)	3	(2 cans)
Textured vegetable protein dice with chicken-like flavor (Bontrae®)	10	(2 cartons)
Frozen peas	2	(2 qt)

YIELD: 75 portions of 6 oz each

Procedure

Bring 6 qt of water to a boil. Combine a la King sauce mix with remaining 3 qt of water. Add sauce mix to boiling water while stirring with a wire whip. Cook until thickened. Add vegetable protein dice (Bontrae®) and peas. Simmer until thoroughly heated. Serve over biscuit or puff pastry shell.

SOURCE: General Mills, Inc., Food Service & Protein Products Division, Minneapolis, Minn.

CHICKEN A LA KING WITH TEXTURED SOY PROTEIN CHIPLETS

Ingredients	%
Chicken fat or margarine	6.31
Flour	4.21
Salt	0.53
Paprika	0.11
White pepper	0.11
Chicken broth	21.03
Light cream	21.03
Cooked chicken, diced	29.43
Textured soy protein chiplets (Ultra-Soy Chiplets 100, uncolored)	1.26
Chicken broth to rehydrate soy protein chiplets	2.94
Sliced mushrooms	4.21
Canned pimiento, chopped	2.10
Frozen peas, cooked	4.21
Green peppers, chopped	2.52

Procedure

1. Melt chicken fat and blend in flour, salt, paprika and white pepper.

2. Add chicken broth and light cream. Cook stirring constantly until the sauce is thick and bubbly.

3. Rehydrate the soy protein chiplets (Ultra-Soy) in chicken broth.

4. Add the rehydrated chiplets, diced chicken, peas, green pepper, mushrooms, and pimiento to the sauce and simmer 20 min.

5. Product may be prechilled and then packed in cartons suitable for freezing and frozen at $-20°F$.

SOURCE: Far-Mar-Co., Inc., Research Division, 960 N. Halstead, Hutchinson, Kansas.

CHICKEN LIVER PATÉ IN CHUBS

Ingredients	Lb	Oz
Blanched chicken livers	40	
Cooked chicken gizzards	30	
Cooked chicken hearts	10	
Cooked chicken skins	10	
Chicken fat (raw)	10	
Bread crumbs	5	
Seasoning mixture (see below)	4	12
Salt	3	
Stock from cooking chickens	25	

Seasoning Mix Ingredients	Oz
Black pepper	4
Ground nutmeg	$1/2$
Ground marjoram	$1/2$
Rubbed sage	$1/2$
Ground cloves	$1/2$
Ground allspice	$1/2$

Procedure

Soak livers in cold water for 2 hr with overflow of water to wash out blood and any bitterness caused by improper handling of gall bladders.

Blanch livers in water at 160°F for 10 min. Cook hearts and gizzards for 45 min at 212°F. If raw skins are used, cook along with gizzards and hearts; otherwise do not recook.

Grind all meats and fat through the 1/8-in. plate of the grinder. Transfer to a silent cutter and chop for 3 min. Then add the remainder of the ingredients, gradually adding the stock last. Chop for an additional 7 min.

To avoid air pockets in the stuffed product, it is advisable to transfer product to a vacuum mixer and mix for 3 min under 27 in. vacuum before stuffing.

Stuff in Saran chubs and cook at 160°F for 30 min. Prechill product in cold water before transferring it to the cooler at 34°F for thorough chilling.

Product is perishable and should be kept under refrigeration through storage and marketing channels. Storage life will be prolonged if product is held at frozen temperatures until marketed.

SOURCE: Stephan L. Komarik, 4810 Ronda, Coral Gables, Florida.

BASE MIX FOR CHICKEN CROQUETTES

Ingredients	%
Maggi HPP Type 3H3 powder with partially hydrogenated vegetable oil added	1.60
Maggi HPP Type 245 powder with partially hydrogenated vegetable oil added	2.00
Waxy maize cornstarch	19.50
Nonfat dry milk	19.50
Monosodium glutamate	2.70
Minced green onions	0.30
Salt	3.90
Ground rosemary	0.20
Ground sage	0.10
Ground tarragon	0.15
Ground celery seed	0.10
Turmeric	0.02
Cracker meal, fine	49.93
	100.00

Procedure

Mix ingredients until a uniform mixture is obtained.

Directions for Sample Evaluation.—In double boiler, combine 90 gm of base mix with 270 cc of water and 140 gm of cooked, finely diced chicken meat. Stir until smooth and lump free. Heat until mixture thickens (at approx 150°F). Cool and shape into croquettes.

SOURCE: Nestlé Company, Food Ingredients Division, 100 Bloomingdale Rd., White Plains, N.Y.

DRY MIX CHICKEN STEW WITH VEGETABLES

Ingredients	Oz
Freeze-dried chicken pieces	26.5
Freeze-dried white potato dice	14.5
Freeze-dried green peas	7.25
Freeze-dried carrot dice	4.00
Dehydrated minced onions	0.50
Dehydrated red pepper, diced	0.50
Gravy mix for chicken stew	20.75

Procedure

For a batch, successively weigh out ingredients as given above and mix together thoroughly. Since this stew mix is made up of pieces of chicken and vegetables, use a tumbling-type mixer in order to prevent segregation of coarse and fine pieces.

For retail distribution the product is usually packed in a buried-foil type of pouch.

SOURCE: *Food Dehydration*, *2nd Edition*, *Vol. 2* by Van Arsdel *et al.* published by Avi Publishing Co., Westport, Conn.

CHICKEN CHOP SUEY WITH TEXTURED SOY PROTEIN

Ingredients	%
Cooked chicken cut into medium-to-large pieces	18.85
Textured soy protein (Ultra-Soy, minced, uncolored)	1.11
Chicken broth and bean sprout liquid	39.90
Celery cut into 1-in. pieces	11.09
Fresh onions, sliced	5.54
Salt	0.33
Black pepper	0.06
Monosodium glutamate	0.06
Sugar	0.67
Mushrooms broiled in butter, sliced, undrained	1.77
Water chestnuts, sliced	1.77
Cornstarch	2.66
Cold water	2.66
Canned bean sprouts, drained	9.98
Soy sauce	3.55
	100.00

Procedure

1. Simmer chicken, textured soy protein (Ultra-Soy), chicken broth, and bean sprout liquid in water for 20–30 min.

2. Add celery, onions, salt, pepper, sugar, monosodium glutamate, mushrooms, and water chestnuts. Simmer 5–10 min.

3. Blend cornstarch with cold water and stir

into the mixture. Simmer 15 min, stirring frequently.

4. Add bean sprouts and soy sauce and simmer 5 min more. Additional soy sauce may be added to suit individual taste.

5. Product may be prechilled and then packed in cartons suitable for freezing and frozen at −20°F.

SOURCE: Far-Mar-Co., Inc., Research Division, 960 N. Halstead, Hutchinson, Kansas.

CHOW MEIN WITH CHICKEN-FLAVORED TEXTURED VEGETABLE PROTEIN DICE

	By Weight		or	By Measure
Ingredient	Lb	Oz		
Cooking oil		8		(1 cup)
Celery, sliced	7			(2 gal.)
Onions, diced	3			(3 qt)
Water	5			(5 qt)
Soup base, chicken-flavored				¼ cup
Bean sprouts, drained	3			
Salt				2 tbsp
White pepper				1 tbsp
Cornstarch		10		(2½ cups)
Soy sauce				2 cups
Textured vegetable protein dice (Bontrae®)	5			(1 carton)

YIELD: 50 servings of 6-oz portions

Procedure

Sauté celery and onions in oil for approximately 5 min; add water and soup base and simmer for an additional 10–15 min. Add bean sprouts and seasonings. Combine cornstarch with soy sauce and add to simmering mixture, stirring continuously. Add textured vegetable protein dice and simmer for 5 min. Serve over cooked rice or chow mein noodles.

SOURCE: General Mills, Inc., Food Service & Protein Products Division, Minneapolis, Minn.

SMOKED CHICKEN

The following brine solution ingredients should be sufficient for about 25 fryers:

	Lb	Gm
Salt	12	
Light brown sugar	6	
Sodium nitrite		80
Water	9	

Procedure

Stir together the above ingredients until dissolved. Cool to 34°–36°F. Soak cleaned, eviscerated, whole fryers in solution for 48 hr; then in cold water for 1 hr to remove excess salt.

Smoke with legs up at 180°F for 1 hr, then at 130°F for an additional 5–12 hr. Yields of 85% were reported for this method.

After smoking, cook the carcasses at either 5 lb pressure for 10 min, or in steam for about 25 min or until the internal temperature of the meat reaches 165°F.

After cooking and cooling, package the smoked chicken in suitable packaging. Product is perishable and should be held under refrigerated temperatures at all times until consumed. Shelf-life will be extended if product is held in a freezer.

SOURCE: *Poultry Products Technology* by George J. Mountney published by Avi Publishing Co., Westport, Conn.

POULTRY SAUSAGE

Sausage may be made from poultry meat, making a novel bulk or link sausage product. Here is a laboratory formula giving the basic ingredients. Additional fat should be incorporated with the ingredients shown below:

Ingredients	Lb	Tbsp
Poultry meat	6	
Salt		3
Black pepper		1½
Red pepper		¼
Nonfat dry milk	¼	

Use poultry meat free of skin, bones, and tendons. Coarsely grind and mix with seasonings, then regrind. May be packaged as bulk poultry sausage or stuffed into links.

SOURCE: *Poultry Products Technology* by George J. Mountney published by Avi Publishing Co., Westport, Conn.

CHICKEN FRANKFURTERS

Ingredients	Lb	Oz
Raw chicken meat	50	
Cooked chicken skins	9	
Raw chicken fat	20	
Semolina flour	9	
Chilled chicken broth	9	
Chopped ice	10	
Salt	2	8
Monosodium glutamate		3
Plant protein hydrolyzate		1½
Dry soluble pepper		2

Procedure

Have meat and fat well chilled. Grind meat through the $^1/_8$-in. plate of the grinder; the fat through the $^1/_4$-in. plate. Cook chicken skins until tender and grind through the $^1/_4$-in. plate. After grinding the meat items, put in separate trays and chill overnight in a cooler at $30°-32°F$.

Next day regrind skins through the $^1/_8$-in. plate of the grinder. Put skins and meat in a silent cutter. Start chopping while adding ice, chilled broth ($32°F$), salt, seasonings, and flour; chop for 5 min. Then add raw fat and chop 5 min more to a smooth emulsion (total chopping time: 10 min).

If an emulsifier is used: mix all ingredients in a mechanical mixer then put product through the superfine plate of the emulsifier.

Stuff, Smoke, and Cook.—Stuff emulsion into 28/32 mm artificial casings and link sausages to desired length.

Preheat smokehouse to $160°F$. Bring in sausages and hold at this temperature for 1 hr 15 min. Apply dense smoke for at least $^1/_2$ hr. Then raise temperature to $170°F$ and hold until internal meat temperature reaches $152°F$. Apply cold water shower for 3-4 min to bring internal meat temperature down to $90°F$. Then transfer sausages to cooler at $45°F$ for final chilling.

Product is perishable and should be kept under refrigeration through storage and marketing channels. Storage life of product will be prolonged if product is held in a freezer until marketed.

SOURCE: Stephan L. Komarik, 4810 Ronda, Coral Gables, Florida.

FEDERAL AND MILITARY SPECIFICATIONS FOR POULTRY PRODUCTS

Space in this volume of formulas does not allow for the full reproduction of the federal and military specifications which are here given. These are excerpted, boiled-down versions taken from various abbreviated specifications for poultry products as issued by the government. The authors recommend to anyone interested in processing any poultry product for the U.S. Government that he procure the full set of specifications by writing to the Quartermaster General, U.S. Army, Pentagon, Washington, D.C.

FROZEN READY-TO-COOK TURKEYS

Turkeys shall be processed subsequent to date of contract. The ready-to-cook product shall have been eviscerated warm followed by immediate chilling to $40°F$ or below. The packaging and placing of the chilled product into the freezer shall be accomplished within 36 hr from the time of slaughter. When the packaging of the product is not accomplished immediately after chilling, the turkeys shall be maintained at a temperature of $38°F$ or lower during the holding period. The time between packaging and placing in the freezer shall not exceed 6 hr. The turkeys shall be frozen in a manner so as to bring the internal temperature at the center of the package to $0°F$ or below within 72 hr from the time of entering the freezer. Grading shall be done prior to packing and tolerance for undergrade birds shall not apply.

Weight ranges for ready-to-cook turkeys (giblets and necks included) are as follows:

Class	Weight Range Per Carcass Min Lb	Max Lb
Yearling hen turkeys	None	8
	Over 8	10
	Over 10	12
	Over 12	14
	Over 14	None
Yearling tom turkeys and mature or old turkeys (hens or toms)	None	8
	Over 8	10
	Over 10	12
	Over 12	14
	Over 14	16
	Over 16	18
	Over 18	20
	Over 20	22
	Over 22	24
	Over 24	None

Processing

Eviscerating of dressed turkeys that have been previously frozen shall not be permitted. Although removal of the epidermis (or cuticle) is permissible, there shall be no excessive wearing away of the skin by machining in order to achieve feather and pinfeather removal. At no time shall the skin be permitted to become dry to the extent of darkening (in color) prior to delivery. Turkeys to be chilled in air shall be processed in such a manner as to leave the epidermis (or cuticle) substantially intact. Giblets (liver, heart, and gizzard) shall be properly trimmed, washed, chilled, and wrapped.

Style 1, Ready-To-Cook Whole.—This Style is applicable to all classes. The neck shall be cut off at its junction with the body and placed in the body cavity.

Style 2, Ready-To-Cook, Halved and Split.—This Style is confined to Class 1 (fryer-roasters), Class 2 (young hens), and Class 3 (young toms). Immediately following eviscerating or chilling, whichever is applicable, the carcass shall be prepared by making a full-length back and breast split so as to produce approximately equal right and left sides. The neck shall be cut off at its junction with the body and placed with the giblets.

Style 3, Ready-To-Cook, Quartered.—This Style is confined to Class 1 (fryers-roasters), Class 2 (young hens), and Class 3 (young toms). Immediately following evisceration or chilling, whichever is applicable, the carcass shall be split and the resulting halves shall be cut crosswise at almost right angles to the backbone, so as to produce forequarters of all white meat and hindquarters of all dark meat of approximately equal size. The neck shall be cut off at its junction with the body and placed with the giblets.

Style 4, Ready-To-Cook, Cut-Up.—This Style is confined to Class 1 (fryer-roaster turkeys). Immediately following evisceration or chilling, whichever is applicable, the carcass shall be cut in such a manner as to produce the following pieces from each turkey: 2 wings, 2 drumsticks, 2 breast halves, 2 thighs, 2 back halves, 1 neck with giblets (gizzard, heart, and liver).

Pieces shall be packed in the proportions as they appear in the carcasses. However, there need be no relation in any individual package between the turkey parts and the whole turkey(s) from which they are removed. In addition, if a turkey piece does not meet the grade quality required at time of packaging, because of a bruise or for some other defect, such piece may be removed and a similar piece of the required grade may be substituted, provided it is within the desired weight range. The part(s) so excluded shall not be packed in any grade as defined in this specification. The separation of the wings, thighs, and neck from the carcass and the separation of the drumstick from the thigh shall be accomplished in a neat manner. The breast shall be separated from the back by means of a cut starting at the shoulder joint, going backward through the junction of the sternal and vertebral ribs. Neck skin shall not be included with the breast. The separation of the carcass into the prescribed component parts shall be accomplished at the articulation (joint) without undue mutilation of adjacent muscle and bone and without producing bone splinters. All parts shall be disjointed by knife except for the back and breast, which may be cut by saw. The neck may be removed in any manner desired.

Unless otherwise specified, all Styles shall be ice-packed. Types I to IV, Styles 2 to 4, shall be prepared from chilled carcasses (with or without the necks) and the parts shall not be rechilled in ice and water or water.

Temperatures at time of shipment and receipt shall be in accordance with MIL-T-43372.

All deliveries shall conform in every respect to the provisions of the Federal Food, Drug, and Cosmetic Act and Regulations Promulgated Thereunder.

The product shall be prepared, processed, and packaged under modern sanitary conditions and by such methods as will reflect food standards of workmanship and quality in the finished product.

Packaging

Whole Turkeys.—Each turkey shall be inserted into a bag made from a copolymer of vinyl chloride-vinylidene chloride, heat-shrinkable polyethylene, or heat-shrinkable polyethylene terephthalate film in the thickness specified. The bag shall be heat-sealed, or shall be closed with a twist of wire or malleable metal clip, or with pressure-sensitive tape. The bag shall cling tightly to the turkey as a result of vacuumizing or heat shrinking. The giblets and neck of the individual turkey shall be wrapped in one of the materials specified and inserted into the neck or body cavity. Alternatively, the neck need not be wrapped prior to insertion into the neck or body cavity with the wrapped giblets.

When specified, each turkey bagged as specified shall be packaged in an individual commercial carton. Alternatively, each turkey, without bagging but with the giblets and neck wrapped as specified, shall be packaged in a carton as specified.

Halved Turkeys.—Each turkey side shall be individually wrapped in one of the materials specified. An even number of sides in proportion to a number of whole turkeys shall be packed directly into the container. The giblets and necks corresponding to the whole number of turkeys packaged shall be wrapped in one of the materials specified and placed on top of the wrapped turkey sides in the shipping container.

Quartered Turkeys.—Quartered turkey shall be packaged in accordance with specifications. Giblets and necks shall be excluded from the carton, but shall be wrapped in one of the materials specified and placed on top of the quarters in the shipping container.

Cut-Up Turkeys.—Cut-up turkey shall be packaged in accordance with specifications and giblets shall be wrapped separately and placed on top of the parts in the carton or shipping container.

Wrapping materials

The wrappers shall be made of the following materials and shall be heat-sealed, string-tied, secured with pressure-sensitive tape, or closed with a twist of wire, rubber band or metal clip. The wrapper may be prefabricated into a bag or pouch.

Waxed Paper.—The paper before waxing shall be bleached, semibleached, or unbleached deodorized kraft, or sulphite having a minimum basis weight of 26 lb per ream (24 × 36-500). The paper (or vegetable parchment) shall be wet-waxed on both sides with a total of not less than 9 lb per ream of a fully refined paraffin having a melting point of not less than 125°F. The quantity of wax on the surface shall be sufficient to show the presence of wax on the fingernail when it has been scraped lightly across the sheet. The waxed sheets shall have a bursting strength of not less then 22 psi and a tearing resistance of not less then 18 gm in either direction.

Parchment Paper.—Vegetable parchment paper shall have a minimum basis weight of 26 lb per ream (24 × 36-500). The sheet shall have an average bursting strength of 22 psi and an average tearing resistance of not less than 18 gm in either direction.

Plastic Films.—The materials shall be one of the following: (a) Polyvinyl chloride with food-grade plasticizers, not less than 0.003 in. thick. (b) A copolymer of vinylidene chloride-vinyl chloride. The film shall be not less than 0.001 in. thick. (c) A shrinkable polyethylene terephthalate film 0.00065 in. nominal thickness. (d) Polyethylene 0.002 in. thick. (e) Heat-shrinkable polyethylene 0.001 in. thick. (Note: Polyethylene shall be tested in accordance with L-P-378.) (f) A rubber-hydrochloride-base plastic film not less than 0.001 in. thick.

SOURCE: Military Specification PP-T-7915, Sept. 26, 1968.

FROZEN BONELESS TURKEY RAW OR COOKED

Component Materials Requirements

Turkeys—(a) Fresh chilled or frozen (frozen less than 90 days). (b) Young tom or hen turkeys less than 1 yr old of USDA Grade B or better, as defined in Regulations Governing the Grading and Inspection of Poultry and Edible Products Thereof and United States Classes, Standards, and Grades with Respect Thereto. (c) Shall be in sound, wholesome condition with no evidence of off-condition

such as off-odor, slightly sticky, etc. (d) The internal temperature at the center of the thigh shall not exceed 40°F at the start of the boning operation.

Salt—Salt shall be white refined sodium chloride with or without anticaking agent. Iodized salt shall not be used.

Pepper—Pepper shall be ground, white or black pepper complying with specifications.

Wheat Gluten—Wheat gluten shall be free from foreign flavor, color, and odor. The wheat gluten shall not be denatured as determined by testing in accordance with specifications.

Gelatin—Gelatin shall comply with Type I of C-D-221 specifications except that the gel strength shall be 275 ± 10 gm.

Processing Requirements

The following amounts of seasoning and binders shall be added to each 100 lb of raw, boned turkey:

Type	Salt Lb	Pepper Oz	Wheat Gluten Lb	Gelatin Lb
I and II	1	1/2	—	—
III	1 1/2	3/4	2	—
IV	1 1/2	3/4	—	2

The ingredients shall be uniformly distributed on the surfaces of the meat as the product is being formulated.

Type IV product shall have a raw uncooked weight of not less than 9 lb.

Cooking Types III and IV: The formed product shall be cooked in a water bath to an internal temperature of not more than 175°F nor less than 170°F in the thickest part of the product. The temperature of water bath shall not exceed 190°F.

Finished Product Requirements

1. All Types shall be free from pinfeather, blood clots and bruises, and bone or hard tendons whose greatest dimension is 1/4 in. or greater.

2. A unit shall have at least 50% by weight of white meat and not less than 80% of the unit shall be whole or halved breasts and thighs.

3. The thickness of skin and fat combined shall not exceed 1/4 in. at any point.

4. There shall be no loose pieces (tag ends) of skin, muscle tissue, fat, casing, or string which exceeds more than 1/2 in. from the surface of any unit.

5. The product shall be arranged so the breast meat is opposite the thigh meat or in alternate layers of dark and light meat.

6. The product shall contain no ground or comminuted meat or skin.

7. The product shall be packaged in accordance with specifications as applicable.

8. The boneless turkey, after being properly packed, shall be placed in a freezer within 4 hr after processing, and frozen to a temperature of $0°F$ in the thickest part of the product within 72 hr from the completion of processing. After being frozen and until time of delivery temperature of product should be $0°F$ or below.

Preparation for Delivery

The product shall be packaged in accordance with specifications as applicable to type of product.

Type I.—The product shall be tightly wrapped in a sheet of aluminum foil (coated side towards the product) of sufficient size to cover the block completely. The aluminum foil shall be 0.002 in. thick and shall be coated on one side with not less than 3 lb per ream (24 X 36-480) of a vinyl or vinyl copolymer base plastic coating. The coating shall be colored with a nontoxic coloring material to facilitate identification of the coated side. The aluminum foil may be embossed to ensure dead-fold characteristics. The long end of the wrapper shall be brought face to face and closed by means of a confectioner's fold. The ends of the wrapper shall be folded tightly against the product.

The vinyl coating shall: (a) Impart no odor, flavor, or color to the product. (b) Have a composition which has been approved for contact with food products by the Federal Food, Drug and Cosmetic Act and General Regulations for Its Enforcement. (c) Be satisfactory in resisting oven baking temperature of approximately $450°F$ for 30 min.

Types II and III.—The product shall be inserted into a bag constructed from one of the materials specified. The bag shall be closed with a malleable metal clip, or other equivalent method. The bag shall cling tightly to the product as the result of shrinking, vacuumizing, or mechanical means, or a combination of two or more of these methods. The bag shall be of sufficient diameter and length to result in a product complying with the applicable size requirements.

Bag Materials.—Bags shall be constructed from one of the following materials: (a) A frozen food grade film formed by copolymerizing vinylidene chloride. The film shall average not less than 0.0015 in. thick. (b) A shrinkable polyethylene terephthalate film 0.00065 in. nominal thickness. (c) Polyvinyl chloride with suitable food grade plasticizers not less than 0.0020 in. thick. (d) A shrinkable polyethylene 0.001 in. thick.

SOURCE: Military Specification MIL-T-1660D, April 1965.

FROZEN COOKED SLICED TURKEY WITH GRAVY

Turkey with gravy shall be prepared in accordance with the following formula:

	% By Weight
Turkey, sliced	31
Gravy	69
	100

Gravy Ingredients	% By Weight
Caramel food color	0.07
Celery powder	0.04
Hydrolyzed vegetable protein	0.09
Margarine	4.40
Monosodium glutamate	0.01
Onion powder	0.07
Pepper, white	0.03
Pregelatinized starch	8.70
Poultry seasoning	0.04
Salt	0.58
Soup and gravy base, chicken flavor	1.45
Water	84.52
	100.00

Preparation

Turkey shall be cooked by any suitable means to an internal temperature of not less than $170°F$. Head, feet, metacarpus-phalanges section of wings, giblets, viscera, bones, coarse connective tissue, blood clots exceeding $1/4$ in. in any dimension, skin, and bruised and discolored meat exceeding $1/4$ in. in any dimension shall be excluded. Cooked turkey meat shall be sliced into slices approximately $1/8$-in. thick.

Margarine shall be melted. All ingredients, except starch and margarine shall be mixed together in cold water. Starch shall then be added and mixed thoroughly and entire mixture shall be heated. Margarine shall be added as heating takes place and mixture shall be brought to minimum temperature of $180°F$. Turkey shall be weighed into trays and gravy poured over it. Any process which produces an equivalent product shall be acceptable.

Freezing

After the containers have been sealed, the finished packages shall be placed in a blast freezer at $-20°$ to $-40°F$ within 20 min of the time containers are filled. The product shall be solidly frozen to $0°F$ or lower before removal to the holding freezer. Temperature of holding freezer shall be $0°F$ or lower.

Time and Temperature Limitations

The materials and products shall be so handled as to comply with the following limitations:

(1) Maximum time turkey rolls may be frozen before being used in final product: 30 days.

(2) Maximum temperature for storage of frozen rolls: 0°F.

(3) Maximum temperature of turkey meat during holding or processing prior to slicing: 40°F.

(4) Maximum temperature of turkey meat subsequent to boning: 40°F.

(5) Maximum time from completion of thawing, if frozen turkey rolls are used, until sliced turkey is used in final product: 48 hr.

(6) Maximum time from completion of slicing until sliced turkey is used in final product if frozen after slicing: 10 days. (Sliced turkey prepared from turkey rolls may be frozen only if fresh turkey rolls not previously frozen are used.)

(7) Maximum temperature for holding frozen sliced turkey: 0°F.

(8) Maximum time gravy may be held before use: 8 hr.

(9) Maximum time from packing until product is frozen to 0°F: 4 hr.

SOURCE: Purchase Description LP/P DES 22-70, May 12, 1970.

CANNED BONED CHICKEN OR TURKEY

Chickens and Turkeys

Chickens and turkeys shall conform to the quality requirements for consumer Grade B or better or procurement Grade I as specified in Regulations Governing the Grading and Inspection of Poultry and Edible Products Thereof and United States Classes, Standards, and Grade with Respect Thereto.

Chickens shall be roasters (4 lb or over) or fowl, or a combination of roasters and fowl.

Turkeys shall be young tom turkeys, yearling hen turkeys, or yearling or mature turkeys.

Chicken or Turkey Fat

The chicken or turkey fat shall be in excellent condition (this shall exclude but not be restricted to fat which is moldy or discolored, or has a foreign flavor or odor).

A good quality chicken or turkey fat meeting requirements may be substituted for each other providing the finished product meets the requirements. Correctness of ingredients statement when fats are substituted is the responsibility of the supplier.

Salt

The salt (sodium chloride) shall be white, refined, with or without anticaking agents. Iodized salt shall not be used.

Processing

The product shall be formulated from raw or cooked, skinned, trimmed, boned chicken or turkey meat in natural proportions from the whole bird except that back, legs, necks, and wings may be used in less than natural proportions. Skin and giblets (gizzard, heart, and liver) shall not be used.

For Class 1 products, both Types I and II, salt, and, if necessary, broth and rendered chicken or turkey fat to produce a product complying with specifications shall be used.

Class 2 products shall contain 20% broth, chicken or turkey, as applicable. Chicken or turkey broth shall represent the first extraction when the meat is cooked in accordance with recognized good commercial practice. When precooked meat is used, the broth shall be prepared from chickens and turkeys meeting the requirements. The broth may be frozen provided it is handled in accordance with specifications.

Sodium chloride shall not be used in the preparation of dietetic pack products.

The fowl shall be cooked by any suitable means until tender.

Class 2 products shall be chilled and mechanically diced with dicer settings set at $5/8 \times 5/8$ in. ($\pm 1/8$ in.). (NOTE: The meat from the back, legs, necks, and wings shall be excluded in order to meet this requirement.) Cooked diced chicken or turkey may be frozen.

The product including broth, as applicable, shall be filled into cans which shall then be vacuumized, sealed, and heat treated in a manner which will stabilize the product for conformance.

Time and Temperature Limitations

(1) Maximum temperature of meat during holding or processing prior to initial cooking: 40°F.

(2) Maximum holding temperature of meat subsequent to boning, or broth after preparation: 40°F.

(3) Maximum time from start of cooking until diced meat is used in final product if the diced meat is not frozen or of holding broth prior to use: 24 hr.

(4) Maximum time from start of cooking until diced meat is used in final product, if frozen after dicing or after broth preparation: 20 days.

(5) Maximum temperature for holding frozen diced meat and broth before use: 0°F.

Physical Requirements of Finished Product

The finished product shall comply, on a unit container basis, with specified requirements.

SOURCE: Proposed Federal Specification PP-C-1802.

CANNED TURKEY LOAF

Turkey Preparation

The breast, upper part of the wing (humerus portion) and legs shall be raw boned to supply the raw boned turkey meat required in the formulation. Turkey carcasses (whole or after raw boning) shall be cooked in water to supply the cooked turkey meat required. The raw turkey meat shall be ground through a plate having holes approximately $1\frac{1}{2}$ in. in diameter. The turkey skin shall be ground through a plate having holes approximately $\frac{1}{8}$ in. in diameter.

Loaf Formulation

The product shall consist of the following components in the amounts indicated for approximately 110 lb of product:

	Lb	Oz
Raw boned turkey meat	70	
Turkey skin	20 (max)	
Cooked turkey meat	5-15	
Cracker meal	5	
Salt	1	8

Turkey fat: a sufficient amount so that final product shall not exceed 10%

Canning

The product shall be thoroughly mixed, filled, vacuumized, sealed, and heat treated in a manner which will stabilize the product for extended storage.

SOURCE: Military Specification MIL-T-38996, June 9, 1971.

COOKED DEHYDRATED CHICKEN AND CHICKEN PRODUCTS

Carcass Preparation

The carcass or parts shall be skinned and boned. The head, feet, metacarpus-phalanges section of wings, giblets, and viscera shall be excluded. Bones, coarse connective tissue, blood clots, skin, and bruised and discolored meat exceeding $\frac{1}{4}$ in. in any dimension shall be excluded. Ligaments, tendons, and cartilage shall be removed so that the final product shall comply with specifications.

Cooking and Dicing

The chicken meat shall be cooked by any suitable means until it is tender. A minimum internal temperature of 170°F shall be reached during the cooking process. The meat shall be drained, cooled, and diced. Dicing shall be accomplished by machine. Dice size shall be approximately $1 \times 1 \times \frac{3}{8}$ in. for Types I and II products and approximately $\frac{1}{2} \times \frac{1}{2} \times \frac{3}{8}$ in. for Type III products. Cooking and dicing shall be so conducted that the final product shall comply with specifications.

Dehydration

The chicken shall be freeze dehydrated (conversion of water directly from solid to vapor phase, omitting the liquid phase entirely) at an absolute pressure not to exceed 1.5 mm of mercury. Momentary increases of pressure for short periods of time, due to operational factors, shall be permitted provided that at no time shall the pressure be high enough to thaw the product. After dehydration is completed, the pressure shall be equilized to atmospheric level with nitrogen, and the product shall be packaged immediately as specified below. If it becomes necessary to hold the product between dehydration and packaging, the product shall be adequately protected from oxygen and moisture by either holding under a nitrogen atmosphere with 2.0% or less oxygen, or under a vacuum of at least 27 in. of mercury for the entire period. If vacuum is used, it shall be broked with nitrogen.

Gravy

Gravy for Type II product shall consist of the following ingredients in the amounts indicated for each 100 lb:

	Lb	Oz
Chicken-flavored soup and gravy base	45	8
Waxy maize starch	31	
Nonfat dry milk solids	21	
Dehydrated minced onions	1	8
Dehydrated diced celery		13
Black pepper		3

Gravy ingredients shall be uniformly and thoroughly blended in a suitable mixer.

Gravy for Type III product shall consist of the following ingredients in the amounts indicated for each 100 lb:

	Lb	Oz
Chicken-flavored soup and gravy base	21	12
Salt	5	8
Poultry seasoning		3

	Monosodium glutamate		1
	Waxy maize starch	36	4
	Nonfat dry milk solids	36	4

Gravy ingredients shall be uniformly and thoroughly blended in a suitable mixer.

Formulation of Finished Products

Finished product shall consist of the following components in the percentages indicated, packaged in accordance with specifications given below.

Type	Ingredient	% By Weight
I	Cooked, dehydrated chicken pieces	100.0
II	Cooked, dehydrated chicken pieces	77.0
	Gravy[1]	23.0
III	Cooked, dehydrated chicken pieces	35.5
	Gravy[1]	28.0
	Cooked, dehydrated white diced potatoes	20.5
	Precooked, dehydrated green peas	10.0
	Precooked, dehydrated diced carrots	5.0
	Dehydrated minced onions	0.5
	Dehydrated diced red peppers	0.5

[1] Gravy for Type II and III products shall be in a separate package enclosed in the container of formulated product in accordance with specifications given below.

Packaging

In the proportions specified above, 24 oz of Type I product, 28.5 oz of Type II product, or 32.0 oz of Type III product shall be packaged in a size 603 × 700 open-style, round metal can with soldered side seam and compound lined, double-seamed ends. The cans shall be made throughout from not less than commercial 0.25 lb per base box electrolytic tin plate and shall be coated on the outside with a coating conforming to specifications. Gravy for Type II and III products shall be packaged in 8 × 10 in. bags made from not less than 0.001-in. thick polyethylene. The bags shall be closed by wrapping the unsealed end of the bag around the portion of the bag holding the product, and holding it in place with a piece of tape which will impart no flavor or odor to the product. The product shall be gas packaged by first removing the air from the filled can and replacing it with nitrogen. The oxygen content of the gases in the sealed container shall not exceed 2.0%. The cans shall be hermetically sealed. The cans shall be clean and free from defects such as rust, dents, improper closures, or holes.

SOURCE: Military Specification MIL-C-0043135 C(GL), Nov. 7, 1960.

FREEZE-DRIED CHICKEN STEW

Chicken stew shall be prepared in accordance with the following formula.

Stew Ingredients	% By Weight
Chicken, cooked and diced	29.0
Potatoes, diced raw	21.0
Peas, slit or perforated	4.5
Carrots, diced	5.0
Vegetable oil	2.5
Water	32.0
Gravy mix	6.0
	100.0

Gravy Mix Ingredients	% By Weight
Chicken-flavored soup and gravy base	25.00
Salt	10.60
Poultry seasoning	0.21
Monosodium glutamate	0.10
Nonfat dry milk	30.00
Starch, instant	30.00
Pepper, white	0.60
Garlic powder	0.09
Onions, dehydrated	3.40
	100.00

Gravy mix ingredients and water shall be mixed thoroughly. Peas, carrots, potatoes, and oil shall be added and the mixture heated to a minimum of 185°F, with stirring, until tender. Stirring shall be gentle enough so that the cooked vegetables are not broken up. The diced chicken shall be added and the mixture heated to a minimum of 180°F. Any process which produces an equivalent product shall be acceptable. The prepared product shall be spread on dehydrator trays, frozen, and freeze dehydrated to a moisture content of 2.0%.

SOURCE: Military Specification MIL-C-431350.

DEHYDRATED COOKED CHICKEN WITH RICE

The chicken and rice shall be prepared in accordance with the following formula.

	% By Weight
Chicken, cooked and diced	38.5
Rice, instant	9.6
Chicken-flavored soup and gravy base	2.5
Salt	0.4
Water	41.5
Vegetable oil	4.8
Pimientos, diced	2.7
	100.0

Preparation

Chicken.—The chicken carcass or parts shall be skinned and boned raw. The head, feet, metacarpus-phalanges section of wings, giblets, and viscera shall be excluded. Bones, coarse connective tissue, blood clots exceeding $1/4$ in. in any dimension and skin or bruised and discolored meat exceeding $1/4$ in. in any dimension shall be excluded. The chicken meat shall be cooked in suitable casings or metal molds by any suitable means until it is tender. A minimum internal temperature of $170°F$ shall be reached during the cooking process. The cooked meat shall be chilled (not less than $25°F$) and mechanically diced with the dicer setting at approximately $1/2 \times 1/2 \times 1/4$ in. If frozen chicken is used, the diced chicken meat shall not be refrozen before being used in preparation of the product.

Cooking.—All ingredients except rice and chicken shall be heated with stirring to a minimum temperature of $180°F$. The rice shall be added and the mixture brought to a boil, then allowed to stand 5 min. The chicken shall be added with gentle stirring and the mixture brought to a minimum temperature of $180°F$. Any process which produces an equivalent product shall be acceptable. If it is found that less water than specified can be used, the quantity of water may be decreased. However, increased amounts of water shall not be used. The prepared product shall be spread on dehydrator trays and frozen.

Dehydration.—The product shall be freeze dehydrated at an absolute pressure not to exceed 1.5 mm of mercury and a product temperature as indicated by suitable instruments, not to exceed $150°F$. If the platen temperature is maintained at $155°F$ or below with radiant heating, the product temperature may be disregarded. After dehydration is completed, the pressure shall be equalized to atmospheric level with nitrogen and the product shall be packaged immediately. If it is necessary to hold the product more than 1 hr between dehydration and packaging, it shall be adequately protected from oxygen and moisture by either holding under a nitrogen atmosphere with 2.0% or less oxygen, or under a vacuum of at least 27 in. of mercury. If vacuum is used, it shall be broken with nitrogen.

SOURCE: Military Specification MIL-43289 A, Sept. 4, 1969.

FROZEN CHICKEN POT PIE (CASSEROLE)

Each casserole shall consist of the following:

	Oz
Chicken	$2^3/4$
Sauce	$4^3/4$
Carrots	$3/4$
Peas	1
Total filling	$9^1/4$
Crust	$2 \pm 1/3$ oz
Total casserole	$11^1/4$

Chicken Preparation

The ready-to-cook chicken shall be covered with water and cooked for such time as is necessary to allow for removal of the meat from the bones in as large and unbroken pieces as possible. In no case shall the birds be cooked to the extent that the meat falls from the bones. The cooked chicken shall not be cooled in water or broth. Each portion of cooked chicken (free of skin and bone) shall consist of 60% ± 20% light meat and 40% ± 20% dark meat. The large pieces of chicken shall be cut into pieces $3/4$-in. long (± $1/4$ in.). Not less than 75% of the blended cooked chicken shall be of the specified size.

Sauce and Vegetable Preparation

The sauce shall consist of chicken broth, flour, rice flour, chicken fat, salt, monosodium glutamate, celery salt, and pepper. The carrots shall be cut as specified. Chopped onions may be added for seasoning as specified. The peas and carrots shall be prepared as outlined. In order to facilitate rapid thawing and reheating, the sauce must maintain a thin-to-medium consistency after the product has been frozen, thawed, and reheated.

Crust Preparation

The crust shall consist of the following ingredients: flour, shortening, water, and salt. The quantity of shortening content shall be not less than 50% of the weight of the flour used. Milk or egg wash to aid in the browning will be permitted. The crust shall be rolled, placed on the assembled pie uncooked, and then baked for approximately 25 min at $400°F$ or until done and light brown.

Alternatively, the crust may be rolled, cut to size, baked in a hot oven (425°–450°F) for approximately 10 min or until done and placed on the assembled pie. (CAUTION: A minimum of water shall be used in the formulation. The crust shall be processed and rolled with an absolute minimum of mixing and manipulation. The crust shall be thoroughly baked prior to freezing.) The baked crust shall weigh 2 oz ± $^1/_3$ oz.

NOTE: The above calls for a crust (and finished pie) that is baked prior to freezing. The reason for this is that there is neither sufficient time nor temperature available in the warm-up oven to accomplish this baking. Most, if not all, commercially available frozen pot pies are merchandized with an unbaked crust.

SOURCE: Military Specification MIL-M-13966A, Oct. 11, 1956.

FROZEN COOKED CHICKEN A LA KING

All materials shall be in excellent condition, clean, sound, wholesome, and free from evidence of insect infestation, foreign and undesirable odors, flavors, colors, and extraneous materials. They shall be so handled and processed that the end product shall comply with the finished product requirements of the specifications.

Chicken Meat

The chicken shall meet the commodity requirements for U.S. Grade B or better. U.S. procurement Grade I chickens, complying with regulations governing the grading of poultry may be used in lieu of Grade B or better chickens. Frozen chickens shall not be used.

Cooking and Dicing.—The chickens shall be cooked by any suitable means until tender. After cooking, the chicken carcass or parts shall be skinned and boned. The head, feet, metacarpus-phalanges section of wings, giblets, viscera, bones, coarse connective tissue, blood clots, and skin, or bruised and discolored meat shall be excluded so that specification requirements shall be met. The meat shall be chilled and mechanically diced with dicer settings at approximately 1 × 1 × $^1/_2$ in. Alternatively, the chicken may be raw-boned, cooked, and diced; or partially cooked for boning, boned, recooked, and diced. Cooked diced chicken may be frozen.

Other Ingredients

Margarine: Margarine shall comply with the commodity requirements excluding soybean oil and butter as components.

Evaporated milk: Evaporated milk shall comply with the commodity requirements.

Mushrooms: Mushrooms shall be extra standard or above, any style or size in compliance with the commodity requirements. Mushrooms shall be mechanically diced with the dicer setting approximately $^1/_4$ × $^1/_4$ × $^1/_4$ in.

Onion powder: Onion powder shall comply with the commodity requirements, standard grade or better.

Pepper, white: White pepper shall comply with the commodity requirements.

Pimientos, canned: Pimientos shall be any style, and shall meet the commodity requirements for Grade C or better.

Salt, noniodized: Salt shall be white, refined, sodium chloride with or without anticaking agent.

Chicken-flavored soup and gravy base: Chicken-flavored soup and gravy base shall comply with the commodity requirements.

Pregelatinized, edible starch: Pregelatinized, edible starch shall be in compliance with the commodity requirements.

Preparation

Chicken a la King shall be prepared in accordance with the following formula:

	% By Weight
Cooked, diced chicken	30.0
Sauce	70.0
	100.0

Sauce Ingredients	% By Weight
Mushrooms, diced	6.40
Pimientos, diced	4.27
Evaporated milk	12.85
Salt, noniodized	0.30
Pepper, white	0.03
Onion powder	0.10
Soup and gravy base, chicken-flavored	1.45
Water	66.00
Starch, pregelatinized	4.30
Margarine	4.30
	100.00

Margarine shall be melted and starch added and heated for 5 min with stirring. All other ingredients, except chicken, shall be added to the margarine-starch mixture and heated to 180°F with constant stirring. The diced chicken shall be put in aluminum trays and the sauce added to bring to final weight. Any process which produces an equivalent product shall be acceptable.

Time and Temperature Limitations

The materials and products shall be handled so as to comply with the following limitations:

(1) Maximum temperature of chicken meat during holding or processing prior to initial cooking: 40°F.

(2) Maximum holding temperature of chicken meat subsequent to boning: 40°F.

(3) Maximum time from start of cooking until diced chicken is used in final product if the diced chicken is not frozen: 24 hr.

(4) Maximum time from start of cooking until diced chicken is used in final product if frozen after dicing: 20 days.

(5) Maximum temperature for holding frozen diced chicken: 0°F.

(6) Maximum time sauce may be held before use: 8 hr.

Freezing

After filling, the containers shall be placed in a blast freezer (-20° to -40°F) within 20 min from the time they are filled. The product shall be frozen to 0°F or lower and maintained at that temperature until it is shipped.

SOURCE: Military Purchase Description LP-PDES 12-70, March 1970.

FROZEN CHICKEN CACCIATORE

Chicken cacciatore shall be prepared in accordance with the following formula:

	% By Weight
Chicken, cooked	38.0
Tomatoes	20.0
Mushrooms, diced	5.0
Water	30.5
Seasoning (see below)	2.5
Tomato paste	4.0
	100.0

Seasoning Ingredients	% By Weight
Chicken-flavored soup and gravy base	36.0
Salt	15.0
Oregano	1.5
Pepper, black	2.5
Monosodium glutamate	0.5
Pregelatinized starch	37.5
Onion powder	4.0
Thyme	1.0
Capsicum pepper	0.5
Allspice	0.5
Garlic powder	1.0
	100.0

All ingredients, except chicken, shall be mixed and heated to 180°F with stirring. The boned, cooked chicken shall be placed in containers for freezing as specified and each shall contain at least 8 1/4-breast pieces in each pan. The mixture of other ingredients shall be added to bring to final weight. Any process which produces an equivalent product shall be acceptable.

After the containers have been sealed, the finished packages shall be placed in a blast freezer (-20° to -40°F) within 20 min of the time containers are filled. The product shall be solidly frozen to 0°F or lower before being removed to the holding freezer. Temperature of the holding freezer shall be 0°F or lower.

SOURCE: Limited Purchase Description LP/P DES 20-70-27, April 1970.

READY-TO-COOK DUCKS, GEESE, GUINEAS, AND SQUABS

Weight range for these poultry products is as follows:

	Weight Range per Carcass			
	Min		Max	
	Lb	Oz	Lb	Oz
Ducks (all classes)	Over 3	0	4	0
	Over 4	0	5	0
	Over 5	0	6	0
	Over 6	0	7	0
	Over 7	0	None	
Geese (all classes)	6	0	8	0
	Over 8	0	10	0
	Over 10	0	12	0
	Over 12	0	14	0
	Over 14	0	None	
Guineas (all classes)	1	0	1	4
	Over 1	4	1	8
	Over 1	8	1	12
	Over 1	12	2	0
	Over 2	0	2	4
	Over 2	4	2	8
	Over 2	8	None	
Squabs[1]	0	6	0	8
	Over 0	8	0	10
	Over 0	10	0	12
	Over 0	12	0	14
	Over 0	14	0	16
	Over 0	16	None	

[1] Dressed squabs, when specified, shall conform to the weight ranges specified for ready-to-cook, except that weights under 8 oz are not permitted.

Material Requirements

All birds, except Class 8, shall be processed and chilled or frozen under continuous government inspection in accordance with the U.S. Department of Agriculture Regulations Governing the Inspection of Poultry and Poultry Products.

Holding Temperature

All products shall be in excellent condition at time of delivery. Types II, III, and IV products, after being frozen and until time of delivery, shall be held at a uniform temperature not higher than 0°F. The supplier shall provide evidence that the internal temperature of the product at time of shipment does not exceed 0°F.

Type I, Fresh Chilled.—Birds shall be processed subsequent to date of contract. Unless otherwise specified, the ready-to-cook product shall be eviscerated warm, followed by immediate chilling of the eviscerated bird. In addition, unless otherwise specified, the bird, after packing, shall be chilled to an internal temperature not higher than 36°F and delivered to destination at an internal temperature not higher than 38°F within 4 days after slaughtering.

Type II, Frozen Not More Than 60 Days.—Birds shall be solidly frozen in accordance with U.S. Department of Agriculture Regulations Governing the Inspection of Poultry and Poultry Products. The product shall be eviscerated warm followed by immediate chilling. Plate freezers shall not be used on Style 1. Freezer storage time shall be limited to 60 days. Storage time shall include the date put into the freezer and shall be computed from the time of initial inspection.

Type III, Frozen More Than 60 Days.—Birds shall comply with Type II except for time in storage. Unless otherwise specified in the invitation for bids, freezer storage time shall be limited to 120 days when product is being procured for export purposes and 180 days when it is being procured for domestic purposes.

Type IV, Frozen (Special).—Product shall be processed subsequent to date of contract. The ready-to-cook product shall have been eviscerated warm followed by immediate chilling to 40°F or below. The packaging and placing of the chilled product into the freezer shall be accomplished within 36 hr from the time of slaughter. When the packaging of the product is not accomplished immediately after chilling, the birds shall be maintained at a temperature of 38°F or lower during the holding period. The time between packaging and placing in the freezer shall not exceed 6 hr. The birds shall be frozen in a manner so as to bring the internal temperature at the center of the package to 0°F or below within 72 hr from the time of entering

the freezer. Grading shall be done prior to packaging and tolerances for undergrade birds shall not apply.

Classes

Class descriptions for Class 1 to Class 8 shall be those set forth in the Regulations Governing the Grading and Inspection of Poultry and Edible Products Thereof and U.S. Classes, Standards, and Grades with Respect Thereto (7 CFR, Part 70).

Styles

Style 1: Ready-to-cook, whole birds.
Style 2: Ready-to-cook, halved (split) birds.
Style 3: Ready-to-cook, quartered birds.

Grades

The interpretation of requirements shall be in accordance with standards of quality set forth in Regulations Governing the Grading and Inspection of Poultry and Edible Products Thereof and U.S. Classes, Standards, and Grades with Respect Thereto (7 CFR, Part 70).

Pygostyle (tail) may be removed without affecting grade. In geese, the parts of the wing beyond the second joint may be removed without affecting the grade, if removed at the joint and both wings are so treated.

Processing

Evisceration of dressed birds that have been previously frozen shall not be permitted. Although removal of the epidermis (or cuticle) is permissible, there shall be no excessive wearing away of the skin by machining in order to achieve feather and pinfeather removal. At no time shall the skin be permitted to become dry to the extent of darkening (in color) prior to delivery. Birds to be chilled in air shall be processed in such a manner as to leave the epidermis (or cuticle) substantially intact. Giblets (liver, heart, and gizzard) shall be properly trimmed, washed, chilled, and wrapped.

Style 1, Ready-To-Cook Whole.—This Style is applicable to all classes. The neck shall be cut off at its junction with the body and placed with the giblets.

Style 2, Ready-To-Cook Halved (Split).—This Style is applicable to all classes. Immediately following evisceration or chilling, whichever is applicable, the carcass shall be prepared by making a full-length back and breast split so as to produce approximately equal right and left sides. The neck shall be cut off at its junction with the body and placed with the giblets.

Style 3, Ready-To-Cook Quartered.—This Style is applicable to all classes. Immediately following evisceration or chilling, whichever is applicable, the carcass shall be split as specified in Style 2 and the resulting halves shall be cut crosswise at almost right angles to the backbone so as to produce forequarters of all white meat and hindquarters of all dark meat of approximately equal size. The neck shall be cut off at its junction with the body and placed with the giblets.

Unless otherwise specified, Type I product, all Styles, shall be ice-packed. Types I to IV, Styles 2 and 3, shall be prepared from chilled carcasses (with or without the necks) and the parts shall not be placed in ice and water or water.

Class 8, Squab, when specified may be commercially dressed birds. Styles 1 to 3 shall be processed in a plant operating under the supervision of the Poultry Inspection Service, Consumer and Marketing Service, USDA, in accordance with Regulations Governing the Grading and Inspection of Poultry and Edible Products Thereof and U.S. Classes, Standards, and Grades with Respect Thereto or in a plant approved by the Veterinary Corps of the U.S. Army or Air Force and inspected and passed for wholesomeness by either of these organizations.

Packaging

Bags.—Each bird shall be inserted into a bag made from one of the materials specified for plastic films. The bag shall be heat-sealed, or shall be closed with a twist of wire or malleable metal clip, or with pressure-sensitive tape. The bag shall cling closely to the bird as a result of shrinking or vacuumizing. The giblets and neck of the individual bird shall be wrapped in one of the materials specified: waxed paper, parchment paper, plastic film, Cellophane, or kraft paper; and shall be inserted directly into the neck or body cavity before bagging. Alternatively, the necks need not be wrapped prior to insertion into the neck or body cavity with the wrapped giblets.

Cartons.—The carton shall contain individual birds, bagged as specified above and shall be packaged in individual commercial cartons normally used for the product. Alternatively, each bird, without bagging, but with giblets and neck wrapped or bagged and inserted into the bird as specified above, shall be packaged in a carton as specified above.

Not more than 15 lb of halved birds, corresponding to a number of whole birds, shall be packaged in a folding or set-up carton of solid bleached sulfite, solid bleached or semibleached sulfate, or solid manila boxboard or of board having inner and outer liners of these materials. All of the inside surfaces shall be completely lined or laminated with one of the materials specified for plastic films. Cartons need not be lined if the interior surface is waxed or coated with polyethylene and the cartons are overwrapped with one of the specified plastic films or Cellophane. Giblets and necks corresponding to the number of whole birds packaged, shall be wrapped or bagged in one of the specified materials and packaged with the birds.

Wrapping Materials

The wrappers shall be made of the following materials. The wrapper shall be heat-sealed, string-tied, secured with pressure-sensitive tape, or closed with a twist of wire, rubber band, or plastic or metal clip. The wrapper may be prefabricated into a bag or pouch.

Waxed Paper.—The paper, before waxing, shall be bleached, semibleached, or unbleached deodorized kraft, sulphite, or vegetable parchment having a minimum basis weight of 26 lb per ream (24 × 36-500). The paper (or vegetable parchment) shall be wet-waxed on both sides with a total of not less than 9 lb per ream of a fully refined paraffin having a melting point of not less than 125°F. The quantity of wax on the surface shall be sufficient to show the presence of wax on the fingernail when it has been scraped lightly across the sheet. The waxed sheets shall have a bursting strength of not less than 22 psi and a tearing resistance of not less than 18 gm.

Parchment Paper.—Vegetable parchment paper shall have a minimum basis weight of 26 lb per ream (24 × 36-500). The sheet shall have an average bursting strength of 22 psi and an average tearing resistance of not less than 18 gm in any direction.

Plastic Films.—The materials shall be one of the following:

(a) A copoylmer of vinylidene chloridevinyl chloride not less than 0.0006 in. thick.

(b) Polyvinyl chloride with food grade plasticizers, not less than 0.002 in. thick.

(c) Heat shrinkable polyethylene 0.001 in. thick.

(d) Polyethylene 0.0015 in. thick.

(e) A shrinkable polyethylene terphthalate film 0.0006 in. nominal thickness.

(f) A special frozen-food grade rubber hydrochloride-base plastic film not less than 0.001 in. thick.

Cellophane.—The Cellophane shall be 0.0010-in. thick gage in accordance with Type V, Class 2 specifications.

Materials for Giblets Only.—In addition to the materials specified above, either of the materials specified below may be used.

(a) A wrapper made from wet-strength bleached kraft paper which shall have a minimum average dry bursting strength of 18 psi. Bleached kraft paper shall have a minimum basis weight of 27 lb per ream (24 × 36-500).

(b) A wrapper consisting of a rippled or non-rippled parchmentized kraft paper, made from No. 1 kraft, having a minimum basis weight of 27 lb per ream (24 × 36-500) and a minimum average dry bursting strength of 18 psi and a minimum wet bursting strength of 5 psi.

For Level C Products (All Types, Classes, and Styles).—Unless otherwise specified in procurement documents, commercial packaging will be acceptable.

SOURCE: Federal Specification PP-D-745 G, Febr. 20, 1970.

FISH PRODUCTS

SEPARATING FISH FLESH FROM BONES AND SKIN MECHANICALLY

The fish flesh separator works by squeezing the flesh from the skin and bones of fish and passing the flesh through perforations on a stainless steel plate or drum. The skin and bones do not pass through the perforations and are separated by the machine. The comminuted fish flesh can then be used in many food products; e.g., fish sticks, sandwich spreads, hors d'oeuvres, etc.

The flesh separator has (1) a stainless steel drum (approx $8^1/_2$ in. in length and $6^1/_2$ in. in diameter) perforated with closely spaced holes $1/_8$-in. in diameter, and (2) a continuous rubber belt (approx 41 in. long and $8^1/_4$ in. wide) which runs over a series of moving rollers. Position of the rollers is adjustable to regulate the pressure exerted against the drum by the rubber belt.

Here is how the machine works: Headed and gutted fish are fed into the machine and pass between the belt and perforated drum. Pressure applied by the belt on the fish forces the fish flesh through the perforations of the drum while the skin and bones pass to the "waste" discharge chute. The operator can adjust the pressure exerted by the belt to remove most of the light meat during the first pass through the machine. If it is desired to remove the remaining light meat and dark flesh under the skin, the "waste" can be passed through the machine again after pressure exerted by the belt has been increased. Alternatively, pressure exerted by the belt can be adjusted to the maximum so that one pass removes all the fish flesh—both light and dark.

Following is a Table showing yield of flesh and waste for a number of common varieties of Pacific Ocean fish using the mechanical fish flesh separator.

YIELD OF FLESH AND WASTE FROM SOME PACIFIC OCEAN FISH PASSED THROUGH A LABORATORY-MODEL FLESH SEPARATOR

Common Name	Scientific Name	Weight of Fish Used Kg	Yield of Flesh: 1st Pass %	Yield of Flesh: 2d Pass %	Yield of Flesh: Total %	Yield of Waste: Head and Viscera %	Yield of Waste: Skin and Bones %	Yield of Waste: Total %
Northern anchovy	*Engraulis mordax*	4.8	41.4	20.2	61.6	33.5	4.9	38.4
Spiny dogfish	*Squalus acanthias*	14.5	20.9	16.0	36.9	52.1	11.0	63.1
English sole	*Parophrys vetulus*	15.2	40.2	20.0	60.2	28.4	11.4	39.8
Pacific hake (Puget Sound)	*Merluccius productus*	17.7	33.0	16.0	49.0	44.6	6.4	51.0
Pacific herring	*Clupea harengus pallasi*	10.3	38.2	28.4	66.6	29.5	3.9	33.4
Lingcod	*Ophiodon elongatus*	266.2	26.2	20.8	47.0	39.0	14.0	53.0
Silvergray rockfish	*Sebastodes brevispinis*	19.8	35.8	10.7	46.5	42.3	11.2	53.5
Starry flounder	*Platichthys stellatus*	67.0	27.1	15.8	42.9	46.0	11.1	57.1
Pacific cod	*Gadus macrocephalus*	17.4	32.5	5.3	37.8	45.5	16.7	62.2

Note 1: Yield is affected largely by the anatomy of the species used; those species with relatively large heads and viscera masses give relatively low yields of flesh. All yields are based on whole fish.

Note 2: The data on waste skin and bones were obtained indirectly by calculation: weight of skin and bones = weight of fish used minus the sum of the weight of recovered flesh and weight of head and viscera.

SOURCE: The *Freezing Preservation of Foods, 4th Edition, Vol. 3* by Tressler *et al.* published by Avi Publishing Co., Westport, Conn.

REDUCING DRIP LOSS IN FISH FILLETS

The loss of drip in fresh and thawed fillets is effectively controlled by the addition of small amounts of sodium tripolyphosphate (TPP) to the fillets prior to either their distribution fresh to retail or in preparation for freezing.

If fish fillets are treated with sodium tripolyphosphate, the surface layer of protein is modified so that its ability to hold water is greatly increased. This surface layer of modified protein prevents the escape of fluid from the interior of the fillet, with the result that drip formation is prevented.

Sodium tripolyphosphate can be applied to fillets by two methods: fillets may be dipped in appropriate concentration of TPP solutions, or the solution can be sprayed directly onto the fillets.

Treatment for Freezing

With fillets that are to be frozen, the most effective dip solution is 12% TPP containing 4% salt.

The drip during thawing of red snapper and sole fillets is reduced about 50% by TPP treatment before freezing.

Results of Tests on Fresh Fish

Tests show that the loss of drip in fresh (refrigerated) fillets can be effectively minimized by spraying with 7.5–10% TPP solution containing 2% salt. Treated fillets such as sole, ocean perch, cod, and halibut steaks lost no more than 0.5–1.0% drip during their effective refrigerated shelf-life. Drip lost in untreated fish ranged from 3 to 6% during the same storage period.

SOURCE: Bureau of Commercial Fisheries Technological Laboratory, Seattle, Wash.

MANUFACTURING FISH FLOUR (FISH PROTEIN CONCENTRATE)

Fish flour (fish protein concentrate) is an inexpensive source of protein of high quality and may find wide use in improving nutritional quality of many prepared dishes as well as improving the diet of people whose food is largely grains such as rice and corn.

Raw, frozen fresh fish is used such as hake or other less costly fish which is in plentiful supply. The frozen fish is ground up, then placed in an open stainless steel mixing kettle. To the ground fish is added isopropanol solvent and extraction takes place, at well below the ambient temperature. The resulting slurry is separated in a centrifuge, and the isopropanol phase goes to solvent recovery while the solids enter a second-stage extractor (a covered, jacketed mixing vessel). Here extraction takes place at about 170°F, near the boiling point of the solvent. The phases are separated again, and third-stage extraction proceeds at 170°F, using fresh (recovered) solvent. After final centrifuging, solid material goes to a vacuum tumbler dryer that removes residual solvent. Once dried, the fish solids enter a mill where they are ground to a light gray powder.

SOURCE: U. S. Bureau of Commercial Fisheries, Washington, D.C.

SALTED AND PICKLED FISH

SALTING FISH

There are two classes of commercial methods of salting fish: brine-salting and dry-salting. The term "dry-salted" refers to the method of salting and not to the procedure followed in packing or storing fish; it should not be confused with dried, salted fish.

Brine-Salting.—Brine-salting is of relatively little importance compared with dry-salting, as the chief fish that is salted by brine is the alewife or river herring. The cleaned fish are placed in large vats partially filled with concentrated salt solution. A small amount of salt is put on top of the fish floating in the brine. The fish should be stirred daily to prevent the brine from becoming too dilute at any one point in the vat.

Dry-Salting.—The exact procedure to follow depends upon the kind of fish and the custom practiced in a particular locality. But, for general consideration, the following description is sufficiently detailed.

The round, gibbed, beheaded or split fish are washed and then packed in water-tight containers with an excess of dry salt. The proportion of salt to fish varies greatly depending upon the kind of fish, the weather, and the custom of the salter, varying from 10 to 35% of the weight of the fish. Usually, the fish are rubbed in salt as they are packed and each layer of fish is then sprinkled with salt. After a few hours, sufficient pickle has formed to cover the fish which are not disturbed until they are completely salted. Then the fish should either be repacked in fresh pickle or removed and dried.

The dry-salt method has been found to obtain more rapid penetration of salt into the fish and to inhibit decomposition more quickly. Evidently, in dry-salting the brine remains more nearly saturated, probably because of the greater surplus and better distribution of the dry salt.

SOURCE: *Marine Products of Commerce* by D. K. Tressler published by Chemical Catalog Co., New York, N.Y.

SALTING OF COD, LUSK, HADDOCK, HAKE, AND POLLOCK

Cleaning

The fish are cleaned (eviscerated) at sea. The heads are broken off, the fish split open, and $2/3$ of the backbone removed (that portion from the head to the lower end of the abdominal cavity). The fish are then washed.

Salting

Butt Method.—In summer all fish must be salted in butts or other water-tight containers, but in winter they are often salted in kenches. A butt is a large barrel (formerly a molasses hogshead) and is about 3 ft in diameter and 4 ft high. The salters throw the cod face (flesh side) up into butts and sprinkle salt uniformly over each layer. When coarse salt is used, 6.5–7 bu are required for each butt of fish. If finer salt is used, a slightly larger quantity is often added; and in hot weather more salt is required. The fish are piled high above the top of the butt; and the last few layers which are exposed are placed with backs up. A pile of salt is placed on top of the fish. The salt and fish settle slowly and within a day or two sink below the top of the butt. After the fish have settled, a bushel or more of salt is placed on top. About 3 weeks' time is required for the completion of the salting process.

Kench Method.—During winter or on board schooners, these fish are often salted in kenches. A kench is a regular pile of fish made by laying them on their backs with napes and tails alternating. A considerable quantity of salt is spread over each layer. The top layer of fish is turned with backs up. As the salt extracts the water from the fish it runs to the floor and is drained off. Since the fish do not stand in brine it is much more difficult to obtain uniform penetration of salt by the kench method; therefore, there is much greater danger of spoilage (souring) by this procedure than by the butt method. About 20 lb of salt are used on each 100 lb of fish.

Drying

Water-Horsing.—When fish are to be dried, they are removed from butts or kenches and washed with sea water or brine to remove any objectionable slime. They are then hauled to a building or room having a good concrete floor. Here they are kenched on frames about 8 in. above the floor. Weights of various kinds are placed on the kenches to press surplus brine out of the fish. The fish drain and slowly dry in the kenches; the longer they remain on kenches the less time they must remain on the flakes for final drying.

Drying on Flakes.—After kenching, the partially-dried fish are placed flesh side up on flakes for further drying. A flake is a rack or lattice bed about 3 ft wide constructed of triangular strips about 1 in. wide (at the base) and nailed about 3 in. apart to a substantial framework. These are built in the open air about 30 in. above the floor. The weather is watched carefully, and when a rainstorm is imminent the fish are collected in piles and covered with small rectangular boxes with peaked roofs called "flake boxes."

The time which the fish remain on the flakes depends chiefly upon the weather and the amount of drying and bleaching desired. When there is a strong dry wind, two lots may be dried in a single day; but during bad weather, a week or more may be required.

The degree to which the fish are dried depends upon the trade. If they are to be sold in the southern states, they must be much drier than if they are to be marketed locally. Fish for export must be dried as completely as possible. For export, flake drying is usually insufficient in the moist New England climate where the bulk of the salting is done; therefore, such fish are dried further in specially-constructed, heated driers.

When sufficiently dry the fish are carted to a storehouse where they are kenched until needed for packing, or skinning and boning.

Skinning and Boning

The fish are sorted as to quality and size. The skin is pulled off and discarded. All of the bones still remaining are pulled out and the salted product is cut into strips to fit the boxes or cartons in which it is to be packed. Usually, fine salt containing 4% boric acid is sprinkled over the salt fish as it is packed.

SOURCE: *Marine Products of Commerce* by D. K. Tressler published by Chemical Catalog Co., New York, N.Y.

SALTING MACKEREL

Salting of mackerel begins at sea aboard the fishing trawler. Each mackerel is split so that it will lie open and flat after the viscera has been removed. The splitting knife is held by the fingers and guided by the thumb and slides along the upper side of the fish. After splitting, each fish goes to a tray where the gibber opens the fish with a jerk causing it to break lengthwise along the lower end of the ribs. Viscera and gills are removed and the fish is thrown into a "wash" barrel partly filled with clean salt water; the fish is thrown into the barrel "open and face down." Here the blood is soaked from the fish. They remain in the salt water until the splitting is finished, which may be 6–8 hr, or even longer. Then the deck is cleaned up and the men proceed to salting.

The mackerel are removed from the salt water by emptying the wash barrels onto the clean deck and are rinsed by throwing buckets of clean water over them. They are then dipped into fine salt, such as Liverpool No. 2, and placed in a barrel flesh side down, except that 2–3 bottom layers have the flesh side up. Coarse salts are not used as they give the fish a "ragged" appearance. The barrels of salted mackerel are then not disturbed until the vessel arrives in port. Here they are removed to a cool storehouse and remain until needed for market. From time to time, additional brine is added to the barrels to replace any loss by leakage or evaporation. This is important as any exposed fish soon "rust" and cannot be marketed.

Before marketing, the salted mackerel are carefully repacked and covered with fresh brine. Tops of the barrels are removed, the brine poured off and discarded, and the fish emptied out into a "culling crib," a box of planed boards with slat bottom, usually about 5 ft long, 3 ft wide, and 8–10 in. deep on legs about 3 ft high. Here the mackerel are sorted into recognized trade grades and put into weighing tubs with perforated bottoms. Each tub holds about 100 lb and is weighed on a beam scale. After weighing, the fish are packed in barrels, kegs, or kits with the various grades packed separately. A small amount of salt is sprinkled on the bottom of the barrel or keg; 2–3 layers of fish are placed flesh side up with the remaining layers placed flesh side down. A large handful of salt is sprinkled over each layer as it is packed with about 35 lb needed for each 200-lb barrel. When filled, the barrel is turned on its side and filled with strong brine.

SOURCE: *Marine Products of Commerce* by D. K. Tressler published by Chemical Catalog Co., New York, N.Y.

SALTING SALMON

In dressing salmon for pickling, first remove the head; then split the fish along the back ending the cut with a downward curve at the tail. Remove the viscera and $2/3$ of the backbone; scrape away the blood, gurry, and black stomach membrane. Thoroughly scrub and wash the dressed fish in cold water. Place them in pickling butts with about 15 lb of half-ground salt to every 100 lb fish. Lay fish in a tier, flesh side up, sprinkle salt evenly over each tier and repeat until tank is full. Several boards are then laid across the fish with the boards weighted down in order to keep the fish submerged in the pickle which will form. Allow the fish to stand in the pickle about 1 week, holding the brine at about 90°F. Remove the fish from the pickle, rub clean with a scrub brush, and repack in market barrels, using 1 sack of salt to every 3 barrels of 200 lb fish. About 40–52 red salmon, 25–35 coho salmon, 70–80 humpback salmon, 10–14 king salmon, and 25–30 dog salmon will be required to fill each when packing a market barrel of dressed, salted salmon.

SOURCE: *Marine Products of Commerce* by D. K. Tressler published by Chemical Catalog Co., New York, N.Y.

SALTING MULLET

Dry-Salting

The best method for curing mullet in the warm weather of the southern states is dry-salting, a combination of salting and drying. If the fish are strictly fresh and handled carefully, the product will be of good quality. A recommended procedure follows.

Procedure.—Split the fish along the back, "mackerel style," so they will lie flat in a single piece, leaving the backbone in. Heads may or may not be removed. Roe is saved and salted separately. In cleaning the fish, they should be eviscerated and washed to remove all traces of blood from under the backbone and clear away the dark belly cavity skin. If heads are left on, clean out all traces of the gills. Score each fish longitudinally along the backbone and also through the flesh on the top side of the fish. Then wash and soak in a light brine solution for about 30 min to remove all traces of blood and slime. Remove from brine and drain for about 15 min.

Use "dairy fine" mined salt and dredge each fish in the salt, rubbing some into the scored cuts on each side. A shallow pan or box about 2 ft square is convenient for this operation. Pack the salted fish, layer by layer, into barrels or tubs with flesh side up except for the top layer which is packed flesh side down. A little salt is sprinkled on the bottom of the container and over each layer of fish. Place a weight on top of the pack to keep the fish under the surface of the brine that forms. Allow the fish to cure in this brine 36–48 hr, after which they are removed and allowed to drain for 15–20 min.

The fish are now ready for the drying racks. These are frames of wood covered with wire mesh and standing on legs 3–4 ft high. Drying is done best in the shade under a roof without walls and so located that as much of a current of air as possible will pass over the fish. Oxidation or "rusting" sets in immediately if drying is done under the direct rays of the sun. The salted fish are laid on the racks skin side down, but are turned 3–4 times the first day. At night, to prevent spoilage through dampness which causes souring and molding, fish are taken to a sheltered cover (inside if possible). The time required for drying usually averages 4 days but is dependent upon weather conditions during the drying period and size of the fish. The dryer the finished product is, the less danger there will be of reddening or rusting. If the surface looks dry and hard and the thumb can be pressed into the thick part of the flesh without leaving an impression, the fish can be considered cured.

Should high humidities make air-drying impossible, the following procedure should be used: When the fish are "struck through," having absorbed enough salt for curing purposes, they should be taken out of the salt, scrubbed in brine, and piled in stacks with the flesh side down. Weight the stacks heavily in order to press moisture out of the fish. After 10–18 hr in stacks, repack the fish in dry salt, again weighted down, and put in storage in a cool, dry place.

Brine-Salting

In an effort to stimulate production and use of brine-salted mullet in the soutern states, technologists of the U.S. Fish and Wildlife Service devoted considerable time to a study of methods of curing. Their recommended procedure may be summarized as follows:

In the preparation of brine-salted mullet, the fish should be dressed as soon as possible after removal from nets or seines (within 6 hr at the most). Split fish down the back and along the backbone; the heads are cut through so that the fish can be laid out flat. The viscera can also be easily pulled out after cutting through the heads. Roe, in season, is usually separated and dried, salted or smoked as a profitable by-product. Gills are removed and the appearance of the product is improved if the black membrane of the belly cavity is also removed. Heads and foreparts of the backbone are often taken out of larger fish (those weighing more than 1½ lb). After thorough cleaning, the fish are washed in clean sea water or light brine to remove blood and slime. Soaking for ½ hr in brine will make this cleaning easier.

The fish are now ready for salting. A mined or refined salt is preferable to sea salt, as it is cleaner and contains less chemical impurities. Ocean salts are also carriers of the bacteria that cause reddening of the fish. In packing, a heavy layer of salt is placed on the bottom of the barrel and covered by a layer of fish, open side up. Sprinkle layer of fish liberally with salt. Repeat fish and salt layers until container is full. The fish are usually packed "fanwise" with heads out and tails toward the center. Take care that the fish in the layers do not overlap. Every surface should be exposed to the action of the salt. Place the top layer of fish in the barrel cut side down, cover with salt, and place a weight on top of the filled barrel to keep fish submerged in the brine that forms. The fish should be "struck through" with the salt in 4–10 days, depending upon size of the fish. If possible, they should be held in a cool room at a temperature not exceeding 50°F during the "striking through" period.

Repacking can be done any time after the fish are struck. They are graded and sorted for size and condition, and any remaining blood, salt, scales, etc., are rinsed off in the brine. Repacking is usually done in smaller kegs or barrels with a layer of salt on the bottom and on the top with a light sprinkling between fish layers. After the containers are "headed" sufficient concentrated brine is added to fill the containers. The product should be refrigerated if it is to be stored for very long.

SOURCE: *Marine Products of Commerce, 2nd Edition* by Tressler and Lemon published by Reinhold Publishing Corp., New York, N.Y.

BISMARK HERRING AND VARIATIONS

True marinated fish, according to the Germans, are those which are cured with strong salt and vinegar pickles without being cooked. Examples of the German products are Bismark herring, mustard or Kaiser-Friedrich herring, and Russian sardines.

Bismark Herring.—These are prepared from herring of uniform size. The fish are first washed in a special washing machine consisting of a large revolving drum equipped with a spray of water. The washed and scaled fish are then cleaned, beheaded, and boned. They are then rinsed with water and brushed inside to remove the black lining of the belly cavity. They are then placed in salt brine for 2–3 hr. Following this, they are put into a vinegar pickle (from 5–6% acetic acid) containing a moderate amount of salt. They remain in the pickle for 2 days after which they are packed tightly in boxes with slices of onion, and some pepper and mustard seed. A vinegar sauce (from 2.2 to 2.4% acetic acid) containing some sugar is added and the box is closed and wrapped for marketing. The herring are usually shipped immediately; but, if stored, are kept in cool, dry rooms.

Mustard or Kaiser-Friedrich Herring.—These are prepared in exactly the same manner as Bismark herring. However, a mustard sauce, instead of sweetened vinegar, is added when the fish are packed. The mustard sauce is usually prepared in special factories and is merely thinned preparatory to use in the marinating factory.

Other Variations.—Other marinated fish are prepared by the addition of Remoulade, wine, bouillon, tomato, or Cumberland sauce to the vinegar-prepared fish. Sauce prepared from the milts of herring constitute another favorite marinade. In cutting the herring the milts are collected and mixed with vinegar sauce. When desired for use as the sauce, the milts are strained through a sieve so that the membranes are removed. As the herring are packed in boxes, any of a number of combination of spices may be used, depending upon the preference of the packer. These include black pepper, pimiento, onion, clove, bay leaf. These are sprinkled over each layer of fish as they are packed. The milt sauce is added and the boxes are then closed and wrapped in the same way as plain Bismark herring.

Canned Marinated Herring.—These are prepared by washing choice herring of uniform size in a revolving cylindrical screen which also removes scales. The fish are then dressed by removing heads, tails, and bones by hand; they are then rinsed and placed in about 75° brine for 2–3 hr. From the brine tanks they are transferred to a vinegar pickle of 5–6% acidity, containing considerable salt. After about 2 days the fish are ready to pack in cans, in which they are placed in layers, with onions, peppers, and mustard seed on each layer. A small amount of 2¼% vinegar and a little sugar is added to each can. Cans are exhausted, sealed, and processed.

SOURCE: *Marine Products of Commerce, 2nd Edition* by Tressler and Lemon published by Reinhold Publishing Corp., New York, N.Y.

CUT SPICED HERRING

Formula No. 1

Ingredients	Lb	Qt	Oz
Salt herring	10		
Vinegar (6% acidity)		2	
Water		2	
Sugar			2½
Onions, sliced			4
Mustard seed			2
Bay leaves			1
Whole allspice			1
Whole black peppers			1
Whole white peppers			1
Whole red chili peppers			1
Whole cloves			½

Cut herring across the body in pieces 1–2 in. long. Pack pieces in wooden tubs holding 10–20 lb, or, if they are to be repacked in individual glass containers, in kegs holding 100 lb. Mix together the dry spices. Place a few spices, a bay leaf or two, and several slices of onion in the bottom of the tub or keg, then a layer of cut herring, over which are laid onion slices and a sprinkling of spices. Repeat until tub or keg is filled. Dissolve sugar in the water and mix with vinegar. Cover cut herring with sugar-vinegar mixture. Store at 40°F for 10 days to cure. At the end of this time, if fish are to be repacked, fill cut pieces into 8-, 16-, or 32-oz glass containers. The curing vinegar may be used to fill containers but should be strained before reuse. Some packers prefer to use fresh vinegar diluted to 3% acidity. Place a few spices, 1 or 2 bay leaves, and a little chopped onion in each jar. Vacuum seal the containers, wipe containers clean and label; pack 1 or 2 dozen to the carton.

Formula No. 2

Use vinegar-salt cured herring. The formulas given here are for 10 lb, but may be multiplied for larger packs. Cut herring across the body in pieces 1–2 in. long. Pack into 8-, 16-, or 32-oz glass containers with whole mixed spices, using the spice ingredients given in Formula No. 1. Use

1 tsp spices to 8-oz jar, 2 tsp to 16-oz jar, and 1 tbsp to 32-oz jar. Also add to each jar a slice or two of onion, 1 or 2 bay leaves, and, if desired for color, a strip of canned pimiento placed around the side of the container. Make up the following vinegar-spice mixture and fill each container: To 1 gal. vinegar (diluted to $2\frac{1}{2}\%$ acidity) add $\frac{1}{2}$ lb sugar, $\frac{1}{4}$ lb salt, and 10 drops each of oil of cloves, allspice, and oil of cardamom. The spice oils are usually added to the sugar before dissolving the sugar in the vinegar; this distributes the spice flavor more evenly. The amount and variety of spice flavors may be altered to suit the taste and preference of the packer and his market. Vacuum seal the containers, wipe containers clean, label, and pack 1 or 2 dozen jars to the carton.

The shelf-life of this product depends upon the care in manufacture and temperature of storage. If held refrigerated (40°F), the product should remain in good condition for at least 6 months. Exposure to light causes deterioration more rapidly even if held under refrigeration, as in a refrigerated showcase.

SOURCE: U.S. Bureau of Commerical Fisheries, Washington, D.C.

PICKLED HERRING FOR ROLLMOPS, CUT SPICED, OR BISMARK HERRING

A variety of methods are used of which the following is typical.

If herring are only dressed, behead and eviscerate. If herring are cut across the body in pieces, pieces should be cleaned thoroughly. Special cleaning attention should be paid to removal of the kidney which is the dark streak along the backbone in the rib cage. Rinse fish in fresh water; place in a curing tank and cover with a brine testing 80°–90° salinometer that contains 120-grain distilled vinegar with acidity of about $2\frac{1}{2}\%$. Allow fish to remain in the brine until the salt has struck through and completely penetrated the flesh. But remove the fish, however, before the skin starts to wrinkle or lose color. The length of cure depends on judgment of the curer since it depends on temperature conditions and freshness and size of fish. The average length of cure is 5 days, although various sources of information give curing times varying from 3 to 7 days. When herring are sufficiently cured, pack into barrels. As a rule, no attempt is made to pack in regular layers; the herring are simply shoveled in until the barrel will hold no more. Head the barrels and fill with a salt-vinegar brine testing 70° salinometer.

The barrels are shipped to marketing centers for final manufacture where they are then repacked in kegs which are filled with a solution of distilled vinegar diluted with water to a 3% acidity and containing sufficient salt to test 35° salinometer. Before repacking dressed herring, they may be cut into fillets or the backbone may be removed leaving the fish otherwise whole. The repacked kegs should be put into cold storage at 34°F and held until required.

The final process of manufacture is begun by soaking the herring in a tank of cold water from 8 to 10 hr. Remove the herring and drain. Place the fish in a solution of vinegar, salt and water for 72 hr. Make up the solution in the following proportion: 1 gal. of 6% white distilled vinegar to 1 gal. of water, and 1 lb of salt. Be certain the fish are well covered with the solution. Then make them up into cut spiced herring, rollmops, or Bismark herring.

SOURCE: U.S. Bureau of Commercial Fisheries, Washington, D.C.

HERRING IN WINE SAUCE

Wine sauce formulas in general are like the standard spice sauce formulas for herring, with the exception that the amount of vinegar is reduced $\frac{1}{2}$ or $\frac{3}{4}$ and wine used instead. A dry white or burgundy-type red wine must be used, as sweet wines are not suitable. Following is a sample wine sauce which may be used with 10 lb of fish.

Ingredients	Qt	Pt	Oz
White wine	1		
Vinegar, distilled white		1	
Onions, chopped			4
Sugar			$2\frac{1}{2}$
Whole cloves			$\frac{1}{4}$
Mustard seed			$\frac{1}{4}$
Chili peppers			$\frac{1}{4}$
Bay leaves			$\frac{1}{8}$
Whole black peppers			$\frac{1}{8}$
Whole white peppers			$\frac{1}{8}$
Whole allspice			$\frac{1}{4}$
Ground nutmeg			$\frac{1}{16}$
Cracked cinnamon			$\frac{1}{16}$
Cracked ginger			$\frac{1}{16}$
Crushed cardamom			$\frac{1}{16}$

Put all ingredients into a large jar with cover. Place jar in a large enough cooking pot to which water can be added to the depth of the ingredients in the jar; bring water to a boil and boil for 2 hr. Then allow jar to stand overnight. When sauce is ready to be used, strain to remove the spices.

If vinegar-salt cure herring are used, cut the fillets in pieces of suitable size, rinse in fresh water, drain, and pack in sterilized jars with a few fresh spices and a slice of lemon. Fill jars with wine sauce. Seal.

If ordinary salt herring are used, fillet and freshen in water. Drain the fillets; pack in a stoneware crock; cover with 1 qt distilled vinegar (3% acidity) and let stand 48 hr. Remove the fillets from the vinegar and cut in pieces of suitable size; pack into sterilized jars and fill with wine sauce.

SOURCE: U.S. Bureau of Commercial Fisheries, Washington, D.C.

"SCOTCH-CURED" HERRING

Do not wash herring, but "pip" them immediately after they are unloaded; i.e., the gills and gib (gall, liver, intestines, etc.) are removed by means of a small knife. After gutting, sort for size and content of roe or milt. Sort for size as follows:

	Inches	No. per 250-Lb Scotch-Style Barrel
Large fulls	11¼	600–650
Fulls	10¼	700–750
Matfulls	9¼	800–850
Matties	8½	950–1000

When sufficient "pipped" herring have been sorted they are "roused" with salt by placing them in a large tub and covering them with fine salt; mix thoroughly by hand until the entire surface of each herring is evenly covered with salt. Then pack either in tight 250-lb or 125-lb barrels. The standard Scotch barrel (250-lb) is made of staves about ¾-in. thick; is 30 in. high and has a head 17 in. in diameter; its capacity is 32 U.S. gal. Carefully pack the fish in layers with back side down, taking care to keep the rows even so the layers are uniform. Pack the second layer at right angles to the first layer. Using Liverpool No. 2 fishery salt, half-ground Spanish salt, or half-ground double washed California salt, sprinkle enough salt over each layer to almost cover them. More salt is required on fish containing milt or roe. But in any case, an excess of salt should not be used as the completely cured fish should be free from undissolved salt.

Some salters of herring allow the fish to make their own pickle; others add some saturated brine immediately after the fish are packed into barrels. Adding the brine is advisable during warm weather and when curing extra large herring for it enables the pickle to "strike the bone" immediately from the inside and outside as well.

On the first or second day after salting when the herring have settled somewhat, the barrel is filled with herring of the same day's pack. Put the head on the barrel and place it on its side for 8–10 days. At the end of this time, up-end the barrel, head up, and remove the head. Bore a bung-hole in the center of the side of the barrel and drain the pickle as far down as the bung-hole. Pour the drained pickle over the top tiers of fish in the barrel 2–3 times which will cause the herring to settle. Again fill the barrel with salted herring of the same day's pack. In repacking the barrel, sprinkle a very small quantity of salt over each additional layer except the last layer to which no salt is added. When the layers of salted fish reach the top of the staves, the head is "jumped" in. After tightening the hoops, place the barrel on its side and fill with saturated brine. Replace the bung and brand with name of packer, trademark, grade, and place of cure. Approximate weight of the contents is also usually stamped on the bottom of the barrel.

SOURCE: *Marine Products of Commerce* by D. K. Tressler published by Chemical Catalog Co., New York, N.Y.

ROLLMOPS

Ingredients	Qt	Lb	Oz
Salt herring		10	
Chopped onions			4
Sugar			2½
Whole cloves			¼
Mustard seed			¼
Chili peppers			¼
Bay leaves			⅛
Whole black peppers			⅛
Whole white peppers			⅛
Whole allspice			¼
Powdered nutmeg			1/16
Cracked cinnamon			1/16
Cracked ginger			1/16
Crushed cardamom			1/16
Distilled vinegar (5% acidity)	2		
Dill pickles	8		

Procedure

Put the bay leaves and chili peppers in a small cloth bag so they can be easily separated for later use. Place this bag together with the balance of the spices and ¾ qt of the vinegar in a covered receptacle. Bring to boil and allow to simmer for 1½–2 hr. Violent boiling causes loss of the volatile acetic acid. A very simple way is to put the spices in a common fruit jar and place in boiling water for 2 hr. Allow to stand 1–2 weeks after boiling to ensure still greater extraction of the spicing materials. Remove the chili peppers and bay leaves which are to be used for decorative purposes. Strain the pickle through a cloth bag to remove the spices. These should be well mixed, ready for adding to the jars before packing. Slightly less than $^3/_4$ qt of pickle will be obtained.

Preparation of the Fish.—Remove heads, scale, and wash. Split into two fillets and trim. Freshen $2^1/_2$ hr in running water, then drain. Ten pounds of medium size herring should give about 6 lb drained weight.

Preliminary Vinegar-Cure.—Pack the fillets skin down in a stone crock. Cover with $1^1/_4$ qt of vinegar. If necessary, put a light weight on top to keep the fillets well covered. Allow to cure in a cool place for 40–48 hr. Remove and drain. The vinegar should now test about 2% acid and show a salinometer reading of about 30°. The fish have absorbed much of the acid and have lost some salt.

Packing.—Cut each dill pickle lengthwise into 4 parts, then each of these across the center, making 8 pieces in all.

Roll the fillets around a piece of pickle and fasten with a fresh clove. A clove serves the purpose just as well as a toothpick and adds to the attractiveness of the pack.

Place 1 tsp of mixed used spices on the bottom of the jar, then pack the fish. With a medium sized herring, 3 rolls will pack nicely into a No. 306 jar (6 fluid ounces capacity) if placed on end. Decorate around the sides with a couple of chili peppers and a bay leaf. Add sufficient pickle to fill (from 25 to 35 cc) (this is about equivalent to 2 level tablespoonsful). The net weight should be $5^1/_2$ oz or over. Seal the jars immediately after packing. Vacuum sealing is preferable.

Store in a cool place. Cold storage at about 35°F is advisable to ensure longest preservation.

NOTE: If vinegar-salt-cured herring are used, the preparation and preliminary vinegar-cure steps will be unnecessary. (It is believed that a better product will be obtained if the vinegar-salt-cure herring are used.) In this case, the spice-vinegar sauce should be diluted to 3% acidity and the rollmops should be cured in the spice sauce for 10 days. They should then be repacked in jars with a few spices and the jars filled with fresh 3% vinegar to which are added 2 tbsp sugar and 1 tbsp salt per quart. Store at 34°–40°F.

SOURCE: U.S. Bureau of Commercial Fisheries, Washington, D.C.

HERRING IN SOUR CREAM SAUCE

For a 1-gal. keg of Holland-Style Herring use the following ingredients:

	Pt	Oz
Dry white wine	1	
Sour cream	1	
Sweet cream	1	
Distilled vinegar	$^1/_2$	
Mixed spices		$^1/_2$
Onions, thinly sliced		2 cups

Procedure

Use the mild-cured herring (Holland style). Fillet and save the milts. Soak fillets in cold water for 2 hr. Rub the milts through a fine sieve. Drain fillets of surplus moisture. Boil together the vinegar, wine, and mixed spices for 3–5 min; cool and remove spices. Blend together the sour cream, sweet cream, milts, and cooled vinegar. Pack fillets in a large container with sliced onions, cover with the cream-vinegar sauce, and marinate in a cool place for one week. Pack fish and onion slices in glass jars and fill jars with the sauce.

SOURCE: U.S. Bureau of Commercial Fisheries, Washington, D.C.

MATJESHERING

This is a spiced-herring product considered very choice in northern Europe. It is prepared from fresh, full herring (herring with milt or roe). The formula given is for the European unit quantity, a small keg of 75 herring.

Wash the herring and scale. Remove the gills and pull the intestines out through the gill opening so that the throat or belly walls are not cut open. Soak the cleaned fish in a 7% white wine vinegar solution for 12 to 18 hr (they must be removed from this solution before the skin becomes soft and flabby). Wipe fish dry. Roll in a curing mixture of:

	Lb	Oz
Salt	2.2	
Brown sugar	1.1	
Sodium nitrate		4

Pack herring in a small keg in straight layers with backs up. Scatter some of the curing mixture between the fish as they are packed and sprinkle some over each layer. Allow to stand 24 to 48 hr. Then repack fish, using the original brine that has collected. If not enough brine has formed, make up additional brine to cover herring by boiling together 1 part salt-sugar mixture (as above) to 4 parts water; cool and filter before using. Close kegs and store at 40°F for at least 1 month before using.

SOURCE: U.S. Bureau of Commercial Fisheries, Washington, D.C.

GAFFELBITER

Ingredients	Lb	Qt	Oz
Mild-cure herring	16		
Vinegar (6% distilled)		1	
Water		1	
Onions, chopped			8
Whole black peppers			1/4
Whole white peppers			1/4
Whole cloves			1/4
Mustard seed			1/4
Bay leaves			1/8

Procedure

Select fat, mild-cure salt herring; cut into fillets and skin. Freshen in running water 2–3 hr depending upon size of the herring, whether mild or heavy cure, and local market preferences. Cut fillets into 1-in. sections; pack into tubs or crocks and mix in the chopped onions and spices; cover with the distilled vinegar. Store in cool place (about 40°F) and allow to cure for 48 hr. Then repack herring pieces in sterilized glass containers. Fill containers with either fresh vinegar or the vinegar used for curing, but strain before using. Seal containers and pack for market distribution.

This formula differs from gaffelbiter as prepared in the Scandinavian countries. The formula was originally obtained from a Scandinavian-American fish curer and is descriptive of the method developed in the United States for the Scandinavian-American market.

SOURCE: U.S. Bureau of Commercial Fisheries, Washington, D.C.

GABELBISSEN

Ingredients	Lb	Oz
Fresh herring	220	
Salt	22–35	
Sugar	4	
Black peppers	2.2	
White peppers	2.2	
Allspice		18
Coriander		11
Cardamom		4
Ginger		2
Hops		6
Cloves		2
Cinnamon		2
Sodium nitrate		3

Procedure

Fresh fat herring are used for gabelbissen. The round herring are first cured for 30–40 hr in a brine testing 90° salinometer. In some instances,

however, this preliminary brine cure is omitted and the fresh fish are packed directly into barrels. A special curing mixture is scattered on the bottom of the barrel between the fish and over each layer. The herring are packed much as described for the packing of whole salt herring, with bellies straight up and tails overlapping. The layers of fish are packed in rather loosely. The barrels are headed up and put in cold storage at about 40°F, where they are held for several months to cure and ripen.

At the end of about three months the herring are removed from storage, drained well, headed, boned, and skinned. The fillets may be cut into sections and packed in glass containers, or whole fillets may be cut in oval or oblong flat cans. A bay leaf and a thin slice of lemon may be laid in each can. The containers may be filled up with the original curing brine diluted 1/2 with distilled vinegar or they may be packed in wine sauce, dill sauce, or curry sauce. The containers are sealed, cleaned, packed in cartons and held under refrigeration until sold to the retail consumer.

SOURCE: U.S. Bureau of Commercial Fisheries, Washington, D.C.

GERMAN DELICATESSEN ANCHOVIES

In Sweden, Finland, and Germany, many anchovies and small herring are preserved by packing in salt, sweetened and flavored with sugar, sodium nitrate, pepper, cloves, mace, cinnamon, ginger, sandalwood, Spanish hops, bay leaves, etc. In Finland, the sprats or anchovies are thoroughly washed and are packed in the round condition; but in Sweden the fish are eviscerated, beheaded, and thoroughly cleaned. Only the fatter fish are used as lean fish produce an inferior product.

The following preservation and spicing mixtures are given for 1-liter tins:

Ingredients	No. 1 Gm	No. 2 Gm	No. 3 Gm
Luneburg salt	125–150	150	
Liverpool salt			150
Sugar	50	100	100
Sodium nitrate	1.5	2	
Jamaica pepper	3.5		4
Black pepper	1	2	3
Cayenne pepper			0.04
Cloves	1.5	1.5	2
Mace	1		1
Sandalwood		1	1
Cinnamon	0.5		1
Ginger	0.5	1	2
Spanish hops		1	2
Bay leaves	1.5	2	2

Procedure

Weigh out salt, sugar, and sodium nitrate and thoroughly mix together. Then weigh out the remaining spice ingredients and mix thoroughly with the salt-sugar mixture.

Spread some of the spice mixture on the bottom of the 1-liter tins and between each layer of fish. Place the first layer of fish in rows with backs down; the second layer in rows obliquely to the rows below with backs of the fish down. Repeat until there are four layers in the tin. Place 1 bay leaf on the bottom of the tin, 1 between each layer, and 1 on top. The lid is then put on and, for local use, made air-tight with paraffin. Store the tins in a cool place, preferably under refrigeration.

SOURCE: *Marine Products of Commerce* by D. K. Tressler published by Chemical Catalog Co., New York, N.Y.

SCANDINAVIAN ANCHOVIES

The true anchovy is not used in the preparation of this product. The bristling or sprat (*Clupea sprattus*) is used. In contrast to the Spanish or Portuguese anchovies, Norwegian or Swedish anchovies are flavored with spices and the curing is not primarily a fermentation process. Various spice mixtures are used and the methods differ in detail but the following formulas are typical.

Formula No. 1

From 25 to 30 lb of bristling are cured for 12 hr in a brine made of $4^{1}/_{2}$ lb of Liverpool salt and 7 qt of water. At the end of the salting period the fish are laid on a wire screen to drain. The following spice mixture is then made up with all spices well pulverized and the ingredients thoroughly blended:

	Lb	Oz
Luneberg salt	$2^{1}/_{4}$	
Black pepper		3
Allspice		3
Sugar		3
Cloves		$^{1}/_{2}$
Nutmeg		$^{1}/_{2}$
Cayenne		$^{1}/_{2}$

Use half of the spice mixture and mix well with the sprats. Then pack them in a large container and cure for 14 days. Then repack in individual containers in layers, bellies up. Some of the remaining spice mixture is scattered between each layer with pieces of chopped bay and cherry leaves. On the bottom and top of each container, lay two whole bay leaves. The brine formed in the

original spice cure is filtered and used to fill the small containers after packing. During the first few days after the containers are closed, they must be rolled about and inverted at least every other day.

Tin containers are preferred to wooden kegs which are often leaky and the air-tight seal of a tin container permits a longer period of preservation.

Formula No. 2

For 40 lb of bristling prepare the following spice mixture well pulverized and thoroughly blended:

	Lb	Oz
Luneberg salt	$2^{1}/_{4}$	
Black pepper		7
Allspice		7
Sugar		7
Cloves		$1^{1}/_{8}$
Nutmeg		$1^{1}/_{8}$
Spanish hops		$1^{1}/_{8}$

Fresh bristling are placed in a strong salt brine from 12 to 24 hours. They are drained on a screen, and are packed in layers in small kegs after being rolled in a spice-curing mixture. Some of this mixture is scattered between the layers of fish. At the top, bottom, and in the middle of the keg, several bay leaves are laid. The kegs are packed tightly and are rolled about or inverted for 14 days. The anchovies may be repacked in tins in 14 days in summer or after 4–8 weeks in winter.

Formula No. 3

In this formula, from German sources, the bristling are brine-salted in Norway in barrels holding about 100 kg (220 lb). When the bristling are to be manufactured into anchovies, the barrels are taken out of cold storage and the fish washed thoroughly in a light brine testing 40° salinometer. After draining, the fish are packed loosely in new barrels with some of the following spice mixture scattered between each layer of fish. This quantity of spice mixture is for one barrel original weight:

	Lb	Oz
Black peppers	2	
Allspice	1	
Sugar (best raw)	$1^{1}/_{2}$	
Sodium nitrate	1	
Bay leaves	1	
Spanish hops		6
Mace		2
Cloves		2
Cinnamon		2
Ginger		2

The brine used for washing and the original brine are filtered and poured into the barrels after filling. The barrels are placed in cool storage for several months for the fish to ripen or acquire an aromatic flavor. The barrels should be rolled about daily or at the least, at intervals of 2–3 days. When the fish have completely absorbed the spice flavor they are repacked in small individual containers, small kegs holding about 7 lb, cans holding from 2–5 lb, and glass jars. The brine used in curing is filtered and filled into the containers when they have been packed with fish. In summer 0.5% benzoic acid may be added to the brine.

SOURCE: U.S. Bureau of Commercial Fisheries, Washington, D.C.

RUSSIAN SARDINES

Ingredients	Lb	Oz	Gal.
Fresh herring	120		
Vinegar			2
Allspice		1.8	
Bay leaves		1	
Cloves		8	
Ginger		8	
Sliced onions	4		
Horseradish	2		
Chili peppers		8	
Coriander seed		8	
Capers		2.5	

Procedure

Pack fresh small herring (5–7 in.) in 90°–100° salinometer brine as soon as possible after catching. They should be held in the brine about 10 days until they are thoroughly salt-cured or struck through. The exact time depends on the size of the fish and the weather. After salting, they are then headed, pulling out the viscera with the same stroke of the knife without tearing the belly open. Wash in clean water and place on wire trays for draining. Allow herring to drain for several hours. Then sort for size and pack each size separately in small kegs holding about 7 lb of fish. They are packed in this manner: Mix together all spices and flavorings. Scatter a thin layer of these ingredients in the bottom of the keg over which is placed a layer of herring with backs up. Lightly press down layer, scatter another thin layer of spice ingredients over fish, and add a little vinegar. Repeat this process until keg is filled. As much vinegar as the keg will hold is then poured in and the keg headed up. The fish require some time to season before they are ready for the market. In summer, they are ready for sale in 4–5 days; but in winter, 3–4 weeks may be required. If the

product is held in refrigeration at about 40°F, it will remain in good condition for 1 yr.

SOURCE: U.S. Bureau of Commercial Fisheries, Washington, D.C.

POTTED HERRING

This is a pickled herring greatly appreciated in the British Isles. Small mackerel are also cured by this method. Fresh herring or mackerel are always used.

The herring are first scaled, headed, split down the belly, and washed thoroughly. After draining, the inside of each fish is rubbed with a mixture of black pepper and fine salt. The herring are then laid in layers in a baking dish with a few whole cloves and bay leaves scattered over the layer of fish. When the dish is filled the fish are half-covered with vinegar and the dish is baked in a moderate oven (about 350°F). This product will keep about 2 weeks at ordinary temperatures.

SOURCE: U.S. Bureau of Commercial Fisheries, Washington, D.C.

FISH PICKLED IN WINE

This method is used for sturgeon, pike, pickerel, salmon, herring, trout, and other fish. It is a commercial formula of German origin. Wash 10 lb of fish well and cut in small individual serving-size portions, from 2 to 4 oz each. These pieces are dredged in fine salt and left standing from 1 to 3 hr. The salt is rinsed off, the pieces are dried, and brushed with good cooking oil. They are laid on a grill and broiled over a hot fire until both sides are a light brown. They should be brushed with cooking oil during the process. The fish is allowed to cool, then packed in glass containers with a slice or two of lemon, bay leaves, onion, and a scattering of rosemary, whole black peppers, and whole cloves between the layers of fish. The jars are filled with a marinade made of white wine, vinegar and water, sealed immediately, and stored in a dry, cool place.

Thyme may be substituted for rosemary, and the spice combination may be otherwise altered to suit the individual preference.

SOURCE: U.S. Bureau of Commercial Fisheries, Washington, D.C.

PICKLED HADDOCK FILLETS

Ingredients	Qt	Lb	Oz
Haddock fillets		10	
Distilled vinegar (6% acidity)	2		

Water	1
White peppers	½
Red chili peppers	½
Allspice	½
Cloves	¼
Mustard seed	¼
Bay leaves	¼
Sliced onions	¼

Procedure

The fish are covered with a solution of 2 parts vinegar and 1 part water, adding a small piece of alum about the size of a walnut. Boil slowly until the fish may be pierced easily with a fork. After cooling, the product is packed in glass containers, adding a few fresh spices, a bay leaf, and a slice of lemon around the side of the jar for decoration. A few slices of onion may also be packed with the fish. Strain the vinegar sauce, heat it, and pour over the fish until the top is well covered. Seal the containers immediately. For maximum preservation, store this product under refrigeration.

SOURCE: U.S. Bureau of Commercial Fisheries, Washington, D.C.

PICKLED SALMON

Formula No. 1

This method may also be used for shad and other large fish.

Ingredients	Qt	Cup	Tbsp
Distilled vinegar	1		
Water	1		
Olive oil		½	
Onions, thinly sliced		1	
Bay leaves			½
White peppers, whole			1
Mustard seed			1
Cloves			½
Black peppers, whole			½
Fresh salmon	(10 lb)		

Cut salmon into individual serving portions. Wash well in cold water, drain, and dredge in fine salt. Allow to stand for 30 min, drain off leakage, and slowly simmer salmon until done. Place the warm fish pieces in an earthenware crock. Cover with a vinegar-spice sauce made as follows: Saute onions in olive oil slowly until they are yellow and soft. Add remainder of ingredients and simmer gently for 45 min; cool sauce, then pour it over the fish making sure that all pieces are covered. Let fish stand in sauce for 48 hr then repack in pint jars with a slice of lemon, slice of onion, and 1 bay leaf inserted around sides of jar

for decoration. Filter the spice sauce before pouring it over the fish; fill container with sauce, then seal. This product should be held under refrigeration (40°F).

Formula No. 2

Use only strictly fresh salmon. Wash it well. Remove backbone and trim sides of the very thin belly flesh. Cut salmon in pieces of about ¼-lb each; simmer in well-salted water until they are done but not soft. Remove fish and filter cooking water. Make a sauce of the filtered cooking water and equal parts of white wine and vinegar. Pack salmon pieces in wide-mouth glass jars with 2–3 thin slices of lemon, 2 bay leaves, 4 cloves, and 4 whole black peppers to each jar. Pour warm sauce over fish, making sure that all pieces are covered in the jar, then pour in a top layer of olive oil (¾-in. thick). Seal jars and store in a dry, cool place.

Some mild-cure salmon is cut into 2-in. cubes, freshened in cold water, and packed in spiced vinegar sauce or in wine sauce.

SOURCE: U.S. Bureau of Commercial Fisheries, Washington, D.C.

PICKLED AND SPICED MACKEREL FILLETS

Ingredients	Qt	Pt	Lb	Oz
Fresh mackerel fillets			10	
Distilled vinegar	2			
Water		3		
Chopped onions	1			
Sugar				2

Seasonings: 1 clove of garlic chopped; and 1 tbsp of each of the following: allspice, cloves, black peppers, bay leaves, and crushed nutmeg

Procedure

This formula, developed for mackerel, may be used for other fish. It has been obtained from German sources. The fish are cleaned and washed thoroughly, then cut into fillets, removing the backbone. Divide the fillets into 2-inch lengths and dredge in fine salt. Pick up pieces with as much salt as will cling to the flesh and pack in a crock or tub. Let the fish stand for 1–2 hr, then rinse in fresh water. Cook the vinegar, water and other ingredients slowly and gently for 10 min after reaching boiling point. Add the fish and cook slowly for 10 min longer, counting from the time at which the solution again begins to boil after the fish has been put in. Remove the fish and allow the pieces to drain, then pack them in sterilized jars, adding some chopped onion, a bay leaf, a few spices, and a slice of lemon to each jar.

Strain the spice vinegar sauce and bring to a boil. Fill the containers with hot sauce and seal immediately. Store in a cool, dry place.

SOURCE: U.S. Bureau of Commercial Fisheries, Washington, D.C.

PICKLED EELS

This dish is a favorite in northern Europe, from the British Isles to Sweden. Clean and skin the eels and cut them into pieces about $3/4$-in. thick. Wash and drain the pieces, then dredge in fine salt and allow to stand from 30 min to 1 hr. Rinse off the salt, wipe the pieces dry, and rub them with a cut clove of garlic. Brush the eel with melted butter and broil until both sides are a light brown. As an alternative, pieces may be sauted in olive oil or other good salad oil. Place the pieces of cooked eel on absorbent paper. When the pieces are cool, pack them in layers in a crock with a scattering of sliced onion, allspice, bay leaves, mustard seed, whole cloves, peppers, and mace between the layers of fish. Weight the mixture down to keep it compressed. Cover the fish with a cold vinegar sauce made of vinegar, water, onions, and a few bay leaves cooked for 15–20 min. After standing for 48 hr in a cool place pack the eels in glass tumblers with a thin slice of lemon, a bay leaf, a slice of onion, and a few fresh whole spices for decoration. Fill the tumblers with sauce used in curing, which has been filtered. Seal the containers immediately. Store in a cool, dry place. This article remains in good condition for a considerable period of time.

SOURCE: U.S. Bureau of Commercial Fisheries, Washington, D.C.

CANNING FROZEN-AT-SEA TUNA

Tuna caught at sea are frozen in "wells" while the vessel is at sea. The freshly-caught fish are put in a well and refrigerated sea water is circulated around the fish until they are cooled to 35°F. Then brine, refrigerated to about 15°-20°F, is pumped into the well. When the fish are all frozen and at a temperature of 20°F or lower, the brine is pumped out and used in another well on another lot of fish. Refrigeration in the coils in the well around the fish is continued until thawing is begun shortly before coming in to port. The fish are usually thawed by circulating sea water through the well.

Upon arrival at the cannery the thawed fish are placed on a conveyor belt which carries them to butchers who cut open the belly and remove the viscera. The eviscerated fish pass under sprays of water which rinse off blood and slime. The tuna are then sorted according to size and placed in large baskets or racks. The racks of tuna are placed in large box-shaped cookers, each holding 20–30 racks of fish, in which the fish are cooked with steam under pressure. Small fish (5–10 lb) are cooked at 215°-220°F 105 min, but fish weighing 100 lb or more take as long as 8 hr.

After cooking, tuna are cooled overnight in a "cooling room." The cool fish are conveyed to cleaning tables where the head is removed and the fish skinned and split. The backbone and tail are removed and the halves are split into quarters or "loins" along median lines. The red meat is cut and scraped from each piece.

The tuna is then packed into cans of various sizes. The filled cans pass under salters, then optionally under a vegetable broth feed, and finally under one or more oil feeds. Usually, either hot (180°F) soybean or corn oil is used. Either vacuum or steam flow exhaust seamers are employed to seal the cans. After sealing, the cans are washed with a detergent solution to clean the exterior of the cans.

The following indicate the usual times and temperatures for the various sizes and packs of tuna.

Can Size (Lb)	Can Dimension	Style of Pack	Usual Net Weight (Oz)	Retort Time in Minutes at 240°F	250°F
$1/4$	211 × 109	Solid	3.50	65	40
		Chunk	3.25	65	40
$1/2$	307 × 113	Solid	7.00	75	55
		Chunk	6.50	75	55
		Grated	6.00	75	55
$3/4$	303 × 312	Chunk	9.25	100	75
1	401 × 206	Solid	13.00	95	80
		Chunk	12.50	95	80
4	603 × 408	Chunk	60.00	230	190

Processing times and temperatures should be checked with can supplier or with the National Canners Association.

SOURCE: *Industrial Fishery Technology* by Maurice Stansby published by Reinhold Publishing Corp., New York, N.Y.

CANNING FRESH TUNA

Tuna are gutted and washed before delivery to the canneries. On the conveyor from the wharf to the cannery they are again washed by water sprays, then placed in baskets, belly downward, to drain off the blood and keep the meat white. They are then run on racks into large steam chambers or cookers and cooked from $2\frac{1}{2}$ to 4 hr at 212°-216°F, depending upon size and condition of the fish. The racks are then run out of the cooking chambers and the tuna is allowed to cool in an air current for at least 12 hr, or until the flesh has become firm enough to handle without breaking up. The fish are then easily skinned and beheaded and separated into four longitudinal sections. White meat and dark meat are separated, the white meat being the choice portion and commanding a higher price when canned. The strips of cooked tuna meat are cut into proper lengths to fit the cans into which they are to be packed; salt and oil are added mechanically. Cottonseed oil is commonly used, although water-packed canned tuna is becoming increasingly popular. Check processing times and temperatures with can supplier and with the National Canners Association.

SOURCE: *Marine Products of Commerce* by D. K. Tressler published by Chemical Catalog Co., New York, N.Y.

CANNING SALMON

The first step in canning salmon is dressing and cleaning of the fish by a machine known as the "iron chink." This is a complicated machine which, by a series of knives and brushes, rapidly removes heads, fins, tails, and entrails and washes the fish under jets of running fresh water. The next step is the "sliming" of the salmon which may be done either by machine or by hand. This consists of removing all of the blood, slime, loose membranes, etc., that were not removed by the "iron chink." After sliming, the dressed fish are fed into a cutting machine where rapidly revolving knives cut them into slices of the proper size to fill $\frac{1}{2}$- or 1-lb cans. The slices are then fed into automatic filling machines.

Empty cans are usually stored on the 2nd story of a cannery and are fed down a chute into the automatic filling machine which fills each can with the proper amount of fish and adds the desired amount of salt. One type of automatic filling machine cuts the fish into slices, salts the cans, and fills them at the rate of 115-125 per min. Many of the small, flat cans are filled by hand; this is particularly true of the chinook and sockeye salmon. Filled cans then pass on belts down to the "patching table," where they are either weighed automatically or inspected to verify that they contain the proper amount of fish and have no bones or skin showing at the top of the fish in the cans. From the "patching table" they pass on moving belts to the "clincher" machine where can tops are loosely crimped on cans to keep the fish intact in the cans and to keep condensation water from getting into the cans during their passage through live steam in the exhaust box. The function of the exhaust box is primarily to heat the filled cans sufficiently to drive out some of the air and insure sufficient vacuum in the can after cooling. Usually, cans are exhausted from 6 to 16 min with live steam at a temperature of 200°-210°F. The hot cans from the exhaust box pass immediately to the closing machine, or "double seamer," which rolls the tops on very firmly making the cans air-tight. From the exhaust, the cans roll into "coolers," large shallow trays made of flat, iron strips which hold several dozen cans. Several "coolers" are placed in a stack on a small car which rolls on tracks into the retorts for processing, cooking by steam under pressure. The 1-lb cans are usually processed from 80 to 90 min at 240°-245°F; the $\frac{1}{2}$-lb cans receive a process of about 70-75 min at the same temperature. After processing, the cars are rolled out of the retorts and the coolers, filled with hot cans, are then passed through a "lye wash" to remove oil. They are then washed with clean water and finally set aside on the floor of a warehouse overnight to cool.

The processing time and temperature should be checked with the supplier or with the National Canners Association.

SOURCE: *Marine Products of Commerce* by D. K. Tressler published by Chemical Catalog Co., New York, N.Y.

CANNING MACKEREL

The California method of canning mackerel consists of the following steps:
The fish are scaled, eviscerated, and head and fins are removed. The dressed fish are then put into brine, about 75° salinometer scale, until blood is extracted. They are then rinsed in fresh water and packed tightly in oval cans. The full cans are then inverted on wire mesh racks and cooked in retorts with live steam for 45 min at 3 lb pressure. After draining about 30 min, the cans are reversed, the backbones of the fish removed, and the cans repacked with cottonseed or other vegetable oil added. After exhausting the cans for about 10 min at 212°F, the cans are sealed and processed $1\frac{1}{2}$ hr at 240°F

or 2 hr at 230°F. Check processing time and temperature with can supplier or with the National Canners Association.

SOURCE: *Marine Products of Commerce* by D. K. Tressler published by Chemical Catalog Co., New York, N.Y.

CANNING SARDINES IN OIL

A considerable quantity of Maine sardines are fried after partial drying of the raw fish. The frying device used most often consists of a long iron tank containing a horizontal set of steam heating coils about 8 in. above the bottom. Water is run into the tank to within an inch or two below the coils and then sufficient vegetable oil, usually cottonseed or olive oil, is added to cover the coils and give sufficient depth of oil above coils to properly fry the fish in the wire baskets used to hold them. The temperature of the oil in the fry bath is maintained about 240°–260°F.

Sardines in oil constitute the large bulk of the Maine sardine pack, and for this purpose cottonseed oil is most commonly used. Considerable quantities of sardines, usually of the higher grades, are packed in olive oil. Sardines in oil are sometimes flavored with a bay leaf, clove, or essential oils. About 1 gal. of oil is absorbed in the frying process for each 5–6 cases of fried product. About 5–6 pt of oil are required in packing 100 small tins.

The fried sardines are packed in cans, filled with oil, and then crimped closed. They are heated in an autoclave until sterile. Consult can supplier or the National Canners Association for processing time and temperature.

SOURCE: *Marine Products of Commerce* by D. K. Tressler published by Chemical Catalog Company, New York, N.Y.

CANNING CALIFORNIA SARDINES

Canning of large sardines in California is generally distinctly different from canning the small sardine pack. Small sardines, which require great care and are much more expensive to handle, are packed in oil in 1/4-lb cans and are generally regarded as a luxury item. The large sardines are usually put up in 1/2- or 1-lb oval cans in tomato sauce.

The large sardines are brought to the canneries on the decks of fishing boats where they are washed and scaled in a revolving cylindrical sieve before being sluiced to the cannery. At the cannery, they are beheaded and eviscerated by hand. They are then held in a brine of about 70° salinometer scale for about 1 hr in the case of the larger fish. The strength of brine and length of salting period depend on the size of fish.

The fish are then dried and fried by a process similar to that used in Maine in preparing fried sardines. The fish are allowed to cool thoroughly before packing into cans. If the sardines are packed with tomato sauce, it is added at this point in processing. After filling and just before sealing, the larger cans are usually exhausted; i.e., heated by passing through a steam box. The cans are sealed and sterilized or processed in closed retorts from 1 3/4 to 2 1/4 hr at 220°F, depending upon the size of the fish. Processing time and temperature should be checked with the can supplier or with the National Canners Association.

SOURCE: *Marine Products of Commerce* by D. K. Tressler published by Chemical Catalog Co., New York, N.Y.

CANNING HERRING

Large plain or kippered herring are canned to some extent in Maine, on the Pacific Coast, and in Great Britain. Other canned herring products are put up in European countries bordering on the North Sea. Methods used are similar.

In Maine, herring running to 10 in. or more in length are used for plain canned herring. The fish are beheaded, dressed, and held in strong brine (70°–80° salinometer) for about 1 hr. They are then packed vertically in tall 1-lb cans, are steamed in retorts for 30 min at 230°F, and, after sealing hot, are processed 2 hr at 240°F. Processing time and temperature should be checked with can supplier or the National Canners Association.

SOURCE: *Marine Products of Commerce* by D. K. Tressler published by Chemical Catalog Co., New York, N.Y.

CANNING SHAD

The fresh shad are scaled, split, and dressed. After thorough cleaning they are cut in pieces transversely to fit the 1-lb tall salmon can in which they are usually packed. Cans are exhausted about 4 min and processed at 240°F for 80 min. Processing time and temperature should be checked with can supplier or with the National Canners Association.

SOURCE: *Marine Products of Commerce* by D. K. Tressler published by Chemical Catalog Co., New York, N.Y.

CANNED SALMON CAVIAR CANAPÉ SPREAD BASE

Skeins of chum-salmon eggs frozen in 30-lb berry tins are used. Thaw at room temperature. Remove skeins from tin and immerse in 95° salinometer brine (2.8 lb salt per gallon of water) for 25 min. Drain. Place the brined eggs on smoking trays which are covered with greased aluminum foil. Smoke for $2\frac{1}{2}$ hr at 115°–120°F. Remove eggs from smokehouse and allow to cool. Then put them through a hand-operated corn-mill-type grinder. Strain the resultant slurry through a fine, 16-mesh wire screen. Recovery of the strained smoked-egg liquor from the raw frozen salmon eggs averages 60%. Use the following formula for the caviar canapé spread.

Ingredients	Lb	Oz	
Smoked-egg liquor	4.5		
Salt	0.23		(or 5% by weight)
Garlic salt		$\frac{1}{4}$	
Pepper sauce		$\frac{1}{4}$	

Procedure

Add salt, garlic salt, and pepper sauce to the egg liquor and thoroughly mix ingredients. Pour into $2\frac{3}{8}$-oz jars ($1\frac{3}{4}$ in. in diam by $2\frac{3}{4}$ in. in height). The lids, with rubber gaskets, are screwed on tightly. Immerse jars in hot water bath. Process at 197°F for 1 hr. Check processing time with container supplier or the National Canners Association.

SOURCE: U.S. Bureau of Commercial Fisheries, Washington, D.C.

CANNED FISH CHOWDER

Fish chowder (or haddock chowder as it is sometimes called since this chowder is usually made with haddock) is an off-season product prepared when potatoes and fish are cheapest. Skill and experience are required, since carelessness or ignorance may result in discoloration and off-flavors. Fish used in fish chowder are usually trawler-caught haddock. The broth portion is generally made from cod heads or fish filleting trimmings, using a quality equal to those portions sold in the fresh trade. Green Mountain potatoes are a preferred variety for fish chowder since a firm-textured potato of high starch and low moisture content is required; potatoes that are smooth in shape with few and shallow eyes are also desirable. (Potatoes with low starch and high moisture content "mush up" in processing.) Potatoes should be blanched to avoid discoloration. Raw potatoes are reported to give the product a faintly unpleasant flavor. Salt pork should be of good quality and free from rancidity. Onions moderate in flavor are recommended; large onions are most economical.

Make a Fish Broth First

This is a time-consuming step in canning fish chowder. So most canners use two tanks for making the fish broth: One tank is cooking broth while the second tank is being drawn off. Enclose about 1750 lb of fillet trimmings or cod heads in cloth or cotton mesh bags and place in cooking tank with 500 gal. of water. Bring to a boil and simmer for 2 hr. Sometimes the trimmings and heads are placed directly in the water and then the solid cooked material is strained out.

Then Make the Chowder Base

Soup Ingredients	Gal.	Lb	Oz
Flour		50	
Fresh onions, diced		18	
Salt pork, diced		18	
Fish broth	56		
Water	25		
Salt		16	
White pepper			5

The haddock may be steam-cooked (as in precooking fish flakes), but some packers use raw fish cut in small chunks for can filling. Allow 2 oz of haddock per No. 1 Picnic can.

Dice onions and simmer until they are soft in an 80-gal. steam-jacketed kettle; then add diced salt pork and cook until pork is soft. Make a smooth slurry in a bakery mixer of 25 lb of the flour with 15 gal. of the water. Add 20 gal. of the fish broth to the pork-onion mixture in the kettle and bring it to a boil; then, with continuous stirring, add the slurry to the batch and bring contents of kettle back to a boil. Prepare a second batch of slurry with 25 lb of flour and 10 gal. of water. Add another 20 gal. of fish broth to the chowder base and bring contents to a boil; then, with continuous stirring, add the second batch of slurry and bring kettle contents back up to boiling. At this time, sufficient fish broth is added to bring volume up to about 80 gal. along with the salt. When contents are again heated to boiling, chowder base is drawn off to a tank at the filling machine.

Fill Cans

At the filling line, each No. 1 Picnic can is hand-filled with 2 oz haddock and 2 oz potato dice. At this time, some packers add from 0.8 to 0.9 gm of citric acid to each can as a preventive against discoloration. As cans pass under the filling machine, they are filled with a measured volume of hot broth. Filling temperature of the broth should not fall below about 165°F. If this broth temperature is maintained, cans are sealed without exhaust.

Suggested Process

For No. 1 Picnics, process time varies from 60 to 75 min at 240°F with 10 lb pressure. Check processing time and temperature with can supplier or the National Canners Association.

Water-cool the pack immediately after processing.

SOURCE: Fish and Wildlife Service, U.S. Department of the Interior, Washington, D.C.

CANNED NORWEGIAN-STYLE FISH BALLS (FISKEBOLLER)

While a portion of the domestic supply of Norwegian-style fish balls is imported from Norway, "Fiskeboller" are also packed by fish canners in the United States.

A typical formula used in the United States is given here.

Ingredients	Gal.	Lb
Cooked, ground haddock		56
Fresh whole milk	5	
Fish broth	5	
Potato flour		2
Wheat flour		1
Salt		1
Nutmeg and ginger to taste		

The haddock must be fresh, and the milk sweet and fresh. An equivalent of whole dry milk may be used in place of the fresh milk; some packers prefer using the dry milk as quality and uniformity are more easily controlled. Nutmeg and ginger are generally used in the form of essential oils (oil of nutmeg, oil of ginger).

Place whole washed and cleaned haddock in large shallow aluminum pans with perforated bottoms and steam cook for about 15 min at 240°F with 15 lb pressure, or until meat can be separated easily from skin and bones. Then grind the flakes through the $3/8$-in. plate of the grinder.

Fish broth (called for in the ingredients and to fill cans) will be needed. Follow directions for making fish broth given above for **Canned Fish Chowder.**

In a mixer, beat together the milk, fish broth, flours, and seasonings until a creamy liquid is obtained. Then add the ground haddock slowly as the mixer is operating. Continue to beat until contents are a homogeneous paste. Transfer paste to hopper of a forming machine to form small cakes of the paste. As the cakes are formed, drop them into hot water for about 10 min until cakes are "set."

The fish balls are then hand-packed into "2-ration" (squat) and "4-ration" (1-lb flat) cans. Have fish broth to fill cans hot (165°F); fill cans with broth and seal immediately.

Suggested Process

The suggested process for 2-ration cans is 75 min at 230°F; for 4-ration cans, 80 min at 230°F. Processing time and temperature should be checked with can supplier or the National Canners Association.

The pack is water-cooled immediately after processing.

SOURCE: Fish and Wildlife Service, U.S. Department of the Interior, Washington, D.C.

CANNED SALMON OR TUNA LOAF IN 12-OZ OR 3- OR 6-LB OBLONG CANS

Ingredients	Lb	Oz
Salt	15	
Prepared lemon powder[1]	1	4
Dry soluble pepper		12
Sodium nitrite		1
Salmon or tuna, boneless, skinless fillets	500	
Precooked wheat flour	50	
Ice, chopped	100	

[1] Combine powdered citric acid, 30 oz; oil of lemon, cold processed, $4^{1}/_{4}$ oz; with corn sugar, $125^{3}/_{4}$ oz.

Procedure

Premix salt with cure and flavorings. Put fillets in a meat chopper; add half the ice and chop for

5 min. Then add flavoring-cure mixture and the remaining ice and chop for 2 min more. Add flour evenly over top of the chopped mixture and run machine for 2 min more.

If an emulsifier is used: grind fillets through the $1/4$-in. plate of the grinder. Put all ingredients in a mechanical mixer and mix thoroughly. Then put product through the finest plate of an emulsifier.

To avoid product sticking to the interior of the cans, spray cans with heated edible oil (corn or cottonseed) on the conveyor filling cans. Fill product into 12-oz, or 3- or 6-lb oblong cans. Close under 27 in. vacuum.

Suggested Process

12-oz oblong cans, 1 hr 30 min at 240°F
3- and 6-lb oblong cans, 4 hr 30 min at 240°F

Check process times and temperature with can supplier or the National Canners Association.

SOURCE: Stephan L. Komarik, 4810 Ronda, Coral Gables, Florida.

CANNED FISH CAKES

For this product, use only the best quality of salt cod. The Green Mountain variety of potato is recommended. Some packers add a small amount of citric acid dissolved in water to inhibit discoloration. This can be added when ingredients are mixed. But if used, add it carefully; an excess of citric acid will result in a decidedly sour taste in the cakes.

Some formulas include onions and some fat, such as beef tallow; however, these ingredients are not generally used in the commercial canning of fish cakes.

Ingredients	Lb	Oz
Peeled, sliced, fresh potatoes	200	
Freshened, shredded salt cod	100	
Hydrogenated coconut oil	5	
White pepper		2

Freshen cod by soaking in water about 10 hr, or $1\frac{1}{2}$ hr if running water is used; then shred. Potatoes should be free of bits of skin and eyes removed after peeling; then slice about $1/4$-in. thick. Put 2 parts potatoes and 1 part cod in basket of a steam-jacketed kettle partly filled with water. Boil for 30 min; then put through $1/8$-in. plate of the grinder. Transfer to a mixer; add oil and pepper and mix thoroughly for 5 min. Convey mixture to the hopper of a filling machine and, while still hot, fill into cans. No exhaust is needed if product is hot (165°F or hotter) when cans are filled. Seal immediately.

Suggested Process.

Most of this pack is put up in 8-oz flat cans; however, some also is packed in No. 10 tins for institutional trade.

The process for 8-oz cans is usually 75 min at 240°F with 10 lb pressure; No. 10 cans require 240 min at 240°F with 10 lb pressure. Check process time and temperature with can supplier or the National Canners Association.

Water-cool the pack immediately after processing.

SOURCE: Fish and Wildlife Service, U.S. Department of the Interior, Washington, D.C.

FROZEN FISH

FREEZING MINCED-FISH BLOCKS

Preparation of Minced Fish Flesh

Pass the fish through a washer-scaler or equivalent. Head, gut, and wash fish. Pass the headed-and-gutted fish through a meat-bone separator machine: (1) On the first pass, adjust the machine to obtain bone-free minced flesh which is ready to use. (2) Increase the belt tension of the machine and pass the "waste" from the first pass-through to extract additional minced flesh from the skin and bones. This flesh may contain small pieces of bones or cartilage and should then either be passed through a flesh-strainer machine to remove bits of bone, connective tissue, etc., or passed through a food emulsifier or equivalent to reduce particles to a micro size.

As required, wash the minced flesh in ice water to remove water-soluble constituents, including blood and some fats. Washing makes the minced flesh lighter in color, blander in flavor, and increases the stability of quality during frozen storage.

Make a binder using the following ingredients with the percentage by weight of the ingredients being calculated on the weight of the minced flesh being used to prepare the frozen blocks.

Ingredients	By Weight %
Fish flesh	2
Salt	1
Sugar	1
Monosodium glutamate	0.3
Sodium tripolyphosphate	0.15
Water	Up to 5

Homogenize the binder ingredients until the mixture becomes "tacky." (National Marine Fisheries Service mixed the ingredients in a 1-gal. capacity Waring Blendor or in a silent cutter for about 2 min.) Keep temperature of the binder below 40°F.

Preparation of the Frozen Blocks

Add the binder to the minced fish flesh and mix thoroughly. In the Hobart Food Mixer, a 2–3 min blend at 50 rpm is adequate. Pack the mixture into suitable cartons for freezing and freeze in a plate freezer under pressure. The frozen blocks can then be packed into master cartons for shipping and storage. Store at 0°F or lower.

This product can be cut into portions or sticks which can be battered and breaded, then deep fried as in the formula given below for Ready-to-Heat-and-Eat Fish Sticks.

SOURCE: National Marine Fisheries Service, Seattle, Wash.

FREEZING READY-TO-HEAT-AND-EAT FISH STICKS

These are one of the most popular items in frozen food sections of groceries and supermarkets. They are dipped in batter, then in a breading mix (see formula for each following), and are fully cooked so all a consumer has to do is warm them to serving temperature. Fish sticks are cut from frozen fillet blocks and processed as described below.

Forming Fillet Blocks.—Carefully prepared boneless and skinless fillets (haddock, cod, or one of the species utilized commercially) are laid in a waxed kraft fiberboard container (some pans are used) either parallel or perpendicular to the long axis of the container. The latter (perpendicular) is claimed to minimize breakage of the sticks during processing. The thick portion of the fillet is placed adjacent to the side of the container with the thin portion to the center. The center is then built up with fillets until the desired weight is obtained. Most processors add an extra $1/4$ lb of fillets over the indicated weight to ensure against "void" formation during freezing.

Freezing Fillet Blocks.—The containers are then placed in a multiple plate freezer with spacers $3/32$ in. less in depth than the cartons of fillets. This results in a compression of the cartons when the freezer plates are closed, and the compression smooths the surfaces of the containers. Also, when the fillets freeze, they expand about 7%, thus forcing the expanding mass to fill each carton completely and to fuse together to form a single block.

Cutting the Fish Sticks.—Most shapes of fish blocks require 3 cutting operations; if blocks are only $1/2$- or $7/8$-in. thick, only 2 cutting operations are needed. However, there is much greater danger of breakage in cutting the thin blocks and for this reason they are usually prepared in thicknesses of 2 or 3 multiples of $7/8$ in.

In the first cutting operation, the block is divided by means of a bandsaw into 3 portions parallel to the long axis of the block; the second cutting operation splits these 3 portions into 6 slabs by means of either a bandsaw or gangsaw. The third cutting is done by a guillotine-type cutter which divides the slabs into individual sticks.

Coating the Sticks.—A batter mix and a breading mix are required for this step. A suggested formula for each is given here.

FROZEN FOODS DIPPING BATTER MIX

Ingredients	%
All-purpose wheat flour or a mixture of wheat and corn flours	72.30
Salt	1.00
Baking powder	1.70
Dehydrated whole egg solids	8.15
Nonfat dry milk	6.00
Hydrogenated vegetable shortening	9.00
Monosodium glutamate	1.85

Melt shortening and mix together all dry ingredients. Combine, mix thoroughly. Chill, preferably in freezer. Put through a hammermill and mix again. Store refrigerated. To use mix: Prepare batter by stirring the mix into $1\frac{1}{2}$ times its weight of water.

FROZEN FOODS BREADING MIX

Ingredients	%
All-purpose wheat flour or a mixture of wheat and corn flours	40.00
Dehydrated whole eggs	10.00
Nonfat dry milk	2.50
Salt	1.00
Fine cracker crumbs (meal)	45.85
Monosodium glutamate	0.65

Mix and sift all ingredients together.

The frozen sticks are usually given a batter-dipping and then breaded on an automatic processing line. The frozen sticks are fed onto a set of parallel bars spaced above a flat conveyor belt. The bars vibrate while the endless belt moves toward the batter tank. This vibration separates the sticks and feeds them in equidistant rows onto the metallic belt of the batter machine.

The batter in the machine is usually refrigerated to below 50°F so as to minimize bacterial growth. Batter is pumped from the bottom of the tank into a manifold extending over and about 3 in. above the conveyor belt. A steady curtain of batter falls from the manifold onto the sticks; the excess forms a small puddle around the belt and drains back into the tank. Thus, all sides of the sticks are coated. The coated sticks next pass under a blower which removes excess batter from both sticks and belt. The conveyor then moves the coated sticks to the breading equipment. The sticks—still spaced and aligned on the conveyor—then pass beneath a curtain of falling breading which covers the sticks to a depth of about $2\frac{1}{2}$ in. This procedure makes certain that all sides of the sticks are adequately coated. The coating is then pressed into the batter either by a roller or a series of ascending and descending flexible rings actuated by a rod connected to an eccentric gear. The conveyor then passes through a vibration zone which frees the sticks of most of the excess breading. The sticks are turned over in a fall to a lower belt which dislodges all remaining loose breading. This is important in order to prevent loose breading from getting into the oil in the cooker into which the sticks are next conveyed.

Cooking the Sticks.—Two different methods of frying breaded fish sticks are in common use: the batch process, and the continuous process. In the batch process, loaded trays of fish sticks are immersed in hot oil. In the continuous process, an endless belt conveys the sticks through hot oil. The fry-bath temperature is maintained between 350° and 390°F.

Cooling and Packaging the Cooked Sticks.—After frying, the fish sticks must be cooled to approximately 90°F before packaging; otherwise, if the sticks are packaged while still warm, moisture-vapor will condense as frost within the package during freezing. Cooling equipment may be a very simple plywood box equipped with a fan to blow air on the racks of trays of fish sticks, or it may be a tunnel equipped with fans and an air filter through which the sticks are slowly conveyed on a belt and cooled. The cooled sticks are conveyed to a packaging line where they are packed in moisture-vaporproof packages and heat-sealed.

Freezing.—Several types of freezing systems are in use for freezing fish sticks. These include multiple-plate freezers, simple sharp freezers, and various types of air-blast freezers.

SOURCE: *The Freezing Preservation of Foods, 4th Edition, Vol. 3* by Tressler *et al.* published by Avi Publishing Co., Westport, Conn.

FREEZING FISH FILLETS

A fillet is the piece of flesh cut away from either side of the fish along the backbone behind the visceral fin down to the tail section of the fish. If that portion of the flesh that lines the visceral cavity remains with the fillet, the fillet is called a full nape fillet. Most high quality fillets do not contain the nape. Fresh fillets are marketed with skin on or off, or as a butterfly fillet in which the fillets from both sides of the fish adhere by the upper tough skin of the belly as in whiting.

Fish such as haddock used in the manufacture of fillets are eviscerated after capture right on the fishing vessel. They are then stored in ice in the fish hold.

The processing operations involved in production of chilled and frozen fish fillets consist of washing, scaling, sorting, inspecting, filleting, skinning, brining, packaging, and weighing. In a small plant, many of these operations are performed by hand. In larger plants, equipment is available for scaling, filleting, skinning, and weighing.

In a typical fish-filleting plant, when haddock or cod are received from the fishing vessel they are first dumped into a tank of running chlorinated water in which they are washed to remove slime, blood, ice, etc. An automatic conveyor removes the fish from the wash tank and transfers them to a hinged wooden box which holds approximately 500 lb of fish. A layer of crushed ice is placed on the bottom, another is added when the box is half filled, and a final layer of crushed ice is put over the fish when the box is full. Boxes are trucked to a refrigerated room where they are held until the fish can be prepared for freezing.

Boxes of similar sizes of fish are then removed from the refrigerated room and the fish are emptied through a hinged door in the side of the box into the hopper of a scaling machine. Scales are removed and the fish are washed with sea water. From the scaler, the fish are passed through wash tanks before being conveyed to either manual filleters or filleting machines. Waste is conveyed to the reduction hopper while the fillets are conveyed to skinning machines and then to a brine tank where they are immersed for a short period in a solution of sodium chloride containing a few parts per million of sodium hypochlorite. The brined fillets drain as they are conveyed to plastic or stainless steel pans in which they are carried to packing tables where they are packaged.

Fillets for freezing are usually packed in 1-, 5-, or 10-lb packages. In the 1-lb pack, the fillets are placed into waxed chipboard cartons which are overwrapped in a suitable moisture-vaporproof material. Fillets to be packed in larger lots are wrapped in 1- or 2-lb lots with Cellophane and placed into waxed chipboard cartons. The packaged fillets are quick frozen preferably in a horizontal plate freezer which prevents the packages from bulging.

SOURCE: *The Freezing Preservation of Foods, 4th Edition, Vol. 3* by Tressler *et al.* published by Avi Publishing Co., Westport, Conn.

FILLETS OR PIECES OF BREADED FISH

Batter-dipped and breaded frozen fish fillets and bite-sized pieces are popular items in the frozen food sections of groceries and supermarkets.

Select haddock and/or flounder fillets and cut to 4-in. lengths or select ocean perch fillets of a size suitable for single servings. Prepare Frozen Foods Dipping Batter Mix as given above in the formula for **Ready-to-Heat-and-Eat Fish Sticks.** Hand dip the fillets or pieces into the batter (use stainless steel rectangular pan for this) then cover with bread crumbs, pressing bread crumbs to the fish pieces or fillets. On a production line, the hand-dipped pieces or fillets are placed on a 2-in. deep layer of bread crumbs on a plastic conveyor belt 2 ft wide by 3 ft long. As the fish move along the belt they are sprinkled with crumbs from above by an aluminum square-faced roller that uniformly presses the crumbs to the pieces or fillets. The conveyor discharges the breaded fish onto a slide grid. The crumbs remaining on the belt are chuted to a floor-level hopper of the breading machine and then automatically conveyed to a sifter and reused. The breaded fish are placed on metal trays which are roller-conveyed to the packing station where they are packed into cartons. Cartons are machine wrapped and heat-sealed with lithographed paper. Sealed cartons are placed on metal trays which are moved into a quick freezer.

SOURCE: *The Freezing Preservation of Foods, 3rd Edition, Vol. 2* by Tressler and Evers published by Avi Publishing Co., Westport, Conn.

FREEZING HALIBUT AND SALMON STEAKS

Halibut and salmon are caught mainly in the Pacific Northwest and in Alaska. After being landed, they are trimmed (heads usually removed), eviscerated, and washed thoroughly. They are frozen and stored whole, being given an ice glaze after freezing. The glazed, whole fish are withdrawn at intervals as needed and steaks (or fillets) are cut from either the hard-frozen or partially-thawed fish. The cut product is packaged, refrozen if necessary, and returned to cold storage.

Steaking the Frozen Whole Fish.—The usual starting material is dressed, head-off fish. Upon removal from frozen storage, the dorsal and the ventral fins are shaved away with a large sharp knife. The whole fish are then steaked, one at a time, with a hand saw. With the initial cut, 2–3 in. of gristle is removed at the nape of the neck. The second cut removes the belly and nape as one unit. A third cut separates this unit into two pieces. The remainder is cut into steaks 3/4 or 7/8 in. thick. The belly piece is conveyed to a scrap box.

Freezing.—The steaks—still frozen or only partially thawed—are glazed by spraying or immersing in ice water. They are then packaged, usually in waxed cartons which are overwrapped and heat-sealed usually with waxed paper. Cartons are then packed in fiberboard shipping cases which are placed in storage at 0°F.

SOURCE: *The Freezing Preservation of Foods, 4th Edition, Vol. 3* by Tressler *et al.* published by Avi Publishing Co., Westport, Conn.

FROZEN HEAT-AND-EAT FRIED FISH

A breading mix is needed to prepare these frozen fried fish. Mix and sift all the following ingredients together:

	%
All-purpose flour	40.00
Dehydrated whole eggs	10.00
Nonfat dry milk	2.50
Salt	1.00
Fine cracker crumbs	45.85
Monosodium glutamate	0.65

Procedure

Almost any species of edible fish can be used. Small fillets may be used whole. Larger fillets that are accidently broken in handling can be utilized for bite-size fried pieces. Large fillets may be cut into individual serving pieces.

Preparation of the fillets or pieces for frying is sometimes a hand-dipping operation. Dipping in plain bread crumbs may be done, if preferred; however, the breading mix given above will give a tastier product and will adhere better to the fish through the frying process and subsequent handling. Use deep fat batch fryers. Fry the fish at 375°F for 1 to 2 1/2 min depending upon the thickness, weight, and temperature of the pieces or fillets being fried. Remove from the fryer and drain to eliminate excess oil. Then cool before packaging. This can be done on shallow trays in a refrigerated cabinet or on a conveyor belt to a cooling station in the production line. Pack the cooled fish into 10- or 12-oz greaseproof packages, or into larger institutional sized containers. Check-weigh contents, overwrap and heat-seal, and load into freezer.

SOURCE: *The Freezing Preservation of Foods, 4th Edition, Vol. 2* by Tressler *et al.* published by Avi Publishing Co., Westport, Conn.

FROZEN FISH CHOWDER

Ingredients	Lb	Oz
Haddock fillets or other skinless, boneless fish, cut into 1/2-in. cubes	100	
Water	75	
Salt pork, diced	12	8
Potatoes, peeled and thinly sliced	100	
Onions, chopped	10	
Whole liquid milk	5	
Butter	1	
Salt		3
Paprika		0.5

Procedure

Using only half the water, simmer the fish for 10 min. Slowly heat salt pork in a steam-jacketed kettle for 15 min. Add potatoes, onion, and remainder of water; cover and cook for 10 min. Add the fish and cook for an additional 10 min. Melt the butter; warm the milk in a double boiler to 100°F, and homogenize the melted butter and warm milk. Add salt, paprika, and the homogenized milk to the cooked ingredients in the steam kettle and bring to a boil. Cool before packaging in suitable containers for marketing. Blast freeze.

Note: When reheating, this chowder should be diluted with half its weight of milk.

SOURCE: *The Freezing Preservation of Foods, 4th Edition, Vol. 4* by Tressler *et al.* published by Avi Publishing Co., Westport, Conn.

FROZEN FISH STEW

Ingredients	Lb	Oz
Salt pork, finely diced	3	12
Corn, frozen whole kernel	7	8
Tomatoes, canned	40	
Green baby lima beans, frozen	6	4
Onions, finely chopped	5	
Potatoes, 1/4-in. dice	7	8
Carrots, diced	3	2
Celery, diced	5	
Green pepper, diced		5
Salt		1
Pepper, black		0.5
Thyme		0.2
Cod consommé (liquid in which cod was cooked)	20	
Waxy rice flour		10
Water	25	
Cod fillets, 1-in. cubes	60	
Butter		6

Procedure

Cook cod in just enough water to cover until cubes are tender but not overcooked. Fry out salt pork in steam-jacketed kettle until golden brown. Add vegetables and water and simmer 30 min. Add enough water to rice flour to make a thin paste and run mixture through a colloid mill; add flour to batch, blend well, and cook 5–8 min to thicken. Add cod and cod consommé; mix to uniformly blend all ingredients. Package in suitable containers for freezing. Blast freeze and hold in frozen storage until marketed.

To Serve.—This product may be thawed and heated to serve as a stew without dilution. Or, it may be diluted with an equal volume of whole milk and served as a soup.

SOURCE: *The Freezing Preservation of Foods, 4th Edition, Vol. 4* by Tressler *et al.* published by Avi Publishing Co., Westport, Conn.

FROZEN TU-NOODLE

Ingredients for White Sauce	(%)
Margarine	11.2
Flour	3.7
Nonfat dry milk	84.5
Salt	0.4
Monosodium glutamate	0.2

Ingredients for Assembling

Egg noodles, cooked and drained
Tuna, canned
Sharp cheddar cheese, grated
Rolled cracker crumbs
Paprika

Procedure

Prepare white sauce: melt margarine in a steam kettle and slowly stir in flour. Continue to stir and heat to about 190°F; then add milk, salt, and monosodium glutamate and continue with stirring until sauce is thick.

Assemble: Package in 14-oz aluminum foil containers. Place 2 oz of noodles on bottom of container. Top with 1 1/2 oz of pieces of canned tuna and 1 oz grated cheese, followed with another layer of 2 oz noodles. Then 7 1/2 oz of white sauce is added to package. Rolled cracker crumbs mixed with a little paprika for color are sprinkled over top of finished package. Close package and, preferably, blast freeze.

SOURCE: *The Freezing Preservation of Foods, 4th Edition, Vol. 4* by Tressler *et al.* published by Avi Publishing Co., Westport, Conn.

FROZEN SWORDFISH au GRATIN

Ingredients	By Weight Lb	Oz	By Measure
Swordfish steaks, 3/8-in. thick	2 1/2		
Fish stock			1 qt + 1 cup
Dry white wine		3 1/2	
Salt			1 tsp
Evaporated milk	14		
Modified starch	2		(1/2 cup + 2 tbsp)
Modified cream	2 3/4		(3/4 cup + 1 tbsp)
Tobasco sauce			6 drops

Nutmeg	½ tsp + ¼ tsp
White pepper	1
Mushrooms, fresh, sliced length- wise and sautéd	4½
Parmesan cheese, grated	2 tbsp

YIELD: 6 portions consisting of 7-oz steak, ¾ oz mushrooms, and 7 oz sauce

Procedure

Combine fish stock, wine and salt. Pour over fish, cover and poach in 400°F oven for 10 min. Carefully remove fish. Bring liquid to a boil.

Slowly add evaporated milk to starch and stir until smooth; heat to 180°F stirring constantly; then add cream, Tabasco sauce, nutmeg, and pepper. Blend sauce thoroughly.

In 12 × 8 in. vacuum pouch, pack 7-oz fish steak, ¾ oz mushrooms, and 7 oz hot sauce; evenly distribute sauce over fish steaks. Heat seal. Blast freeze for 30 min.

To Serve.—Heat pouch in boiling water to cover for 6 min. Serve fish in buttered gratin dish, pouring sauce over steaks, and sprinkling with Parmesan cheese. Brown under broiler 1-2 min.

SOURCE: Cornell Hotel and Restaurant Administration Quarterly, Statler Hall, Ithaca, N.Y.

SMOKED FISH

SMOKING SALMON

Cold-smoked salmon, or just "smoked salmon" as it is known in the trade, is prepared almost exclusively from king salmon sides that have been subjected to a preliminary mild-curing, lightly-salted process. Mild-cured salmon has been used extensively for smoking in Germany, England, and the Scandinavian countries. However, the largest market is in the urban areas of the eastern part of the United States, especially in the large Jewish centers where smoked salmon or "lax" (more commonly called "lox") is part of the daily diet. Lesser amounts are smoked in the middle west and on the Pacific coast.

Before the mild-cured sides can be given the smoke cure, it is necessary to remove the excess salt. This is done by soaking or freshening the sides in a tank of running cold water for a period of 12-24 hr, depending on how long the salmon has been in brine and on the demands of the trade. After proper freshening the sides are trimmed of any rough edges and then given a final wash with a soft cloth to remove any attached foreign particles. It is customary to pile the sides on a platform for a short while before hanging in the smoke oven. This pressing or "waterhorsing" serves a dual purpose because pressure not only removes considerable moisture, but also smooths the cut surfaces of the fish, all of which makes for better appearance and quicker smoking. Some smokers eliminate this step by hand-pressing and smoothing each side as it is being hung in the oven.

The salmon sides are hung from rods placed across the smoke oven at a sufficient height above the fires to avoid danger of overheating. Hanging is done by means of a special type of steel wire hook, having one end curved to fit over a rod and the other equipped with 6 sharp prongs which penetrate the skin and flesh near the nape. Care should be exercised that the sides do not touch one another. Crowding or overloading of the oven should be avoided as it might interfere with proper air circulation.

The first fires that are kindled under the salmon should be "drying" fires in which the combustion is quite complete (i.e., those that produce "blown" smoke). All drafts and ventilators should be opened and the drying continued until all surface moisture is removed and a glossy pellicle has been formed. The time required will be from 24 to 48 hr depending upon weather conditions. This is followed by building fires which smoke heavily, in which a considerable amount of sawdust is generally used. The drafts and ventilators are almost closed so that combustion is incomplete and "distilled" smoke is produced. During this stage which takes from 1 to 3 days, depending on the local market requirements, the sides will assume a distinct smoky flavor and the color will darken. The temperature of the smoke-house should be held below 85°F. If the sides are exceptionally fat and oily, it may be necessary to keep the temperature below 80°F to prevent excessive drip. The weight loss or shrinkage from the mild-cure weight during smoking will run from 0 to 30%, depending on the length of cure and the size and quality of the sides.

After smoking, the sides are wrapped in oilproof paper and packed for shipment in boxes to a net weight of approximately 30 lb. Smoked salmon is perishable and should be stored at 33°-40°F. Storage below freezing at 0°F is not detrimental if the period of storage is not extensive. In an endeavor to broaden the market and as an aid to the retailer in merchandising smoked salmon, several fish smokers now package sliced smoked salmon in 1- and 5-lb tin cans. Although the cans are hermetically sealed, they are not heat processed and should, therefore, be stored and displayed under refrigeration.

SOURCE: *Marine Products of Commerce* by D. K. Tressler published by Chemical Catalog Co., New York, N.Y.

HARD-SMOKED SALMON

The best product can be prepared by starting with fresh or frozen salmon. By so doing, the smoker can control the preliminary salting himself and secure the maximum extraction of moisture from the flesh. The salmon are split into 2 sides, with the backbone removed. After thoroughly cleaning and washing, they are salted in barrels or tierces (some prefer dry salting) for 3–5 days. This is followed by soaking in fresh water for a few hours to remove the slight excess salt near the surface of the fish. Hard-salted salmon must be soaked 24–48 hr and difficulty is experienced in getting a uniform freshening.

After draining and "waterhorsing" (pressing) the sides are hung from rods in the smoke oven by means of hooks, similar to those used for mild-cured sides. The first fires to be kindled are of the drying type in order to remove surface moisture and form a pellicle. From 2–4 days are required, during which time dampers and louvers are kept open so as to maintain good circulation. When the sides are sufficiently dried, smoking fires are built and air circulation reduced by partially closing dampers and louvers. The length of this stage of smoking will depend on the type of product desired; it may be as long as 10 days for a really hard-dried smoked salmon with good keeping qualities. However, 4–6 days will suffice for the average markets. Temperature should not exceed 85°–90°F.

These hard-smoked sides may be packed for shipment and sold without further preparation. But, more often they are cut into strips, chunks, or slices and packed in jars or Cellophane bags as a snack item. Since this product is fairly dry and somewhat salty, it keeps quite well without refrigeration. In humid climates the growth of molds must be guarded against by use of adequate packaging materials.

SOURCE: *Marine Products of Commerce, 2nd Edition* by Tressler and Lemon published by Reinhold Publishing, Corp., New York, N.Y.

BARBECUED SABLEFISH (KIPPERED BLACK COD)

This is a smoked fish product that had its original development in the Pacific Northwest. Its popularity has increased and it is now being smoked in California and many of the larger cities in the midwest and east. It is a rich, oily fish especially relished by those who also like kippered salmon, and smoked herring.

Barbecued sablefish prepared from frozen stock is inclined to be firmer and less watery than that from fresh fish. As a result, nearly all smokers now use only frozen fish for their raw material.

The entire barbecuing process is essentially the same as that used in smoking kippered salmon. Due to the oily nature of the fish, cooking temperatures slightly lower than that used for salmon may be employed with success. The backbone is customarily not removed. Shrinkage in the smoke oven is somewhat less than with salmon, shrinkage running only 10–15%. As with kippered salmon, freezing temperatures are recommended for shipping and storage.

SOURCE: *Marine Products of Commerce, 2nd Edition* by Tressler and Lemon published by Reinhold Publishing Corp., New York, N.Y.

CANNED SMOKED SALMON SPREAD

The following ingredients are proportioned for 5 lb of ready-to-be-mixed ground smoked chum salmon with skins and bones removed:

	Oz
Water (liquid measure)	20
Melted margarine	36
Garlic salt	0.4
Gelatin (added dry)	0.4
Tomato purée (sp. gr. 1.06)	15
(Or 1 2/3 oz of dye solution may be substituted for the tomato purée)	

Procedure

Thaw the frozen, dressed chum salmon overnight at room temperature. Score the skin on either side in 6–8 places to allow salt to penetrate the flesh rapidly. Split the salmon and, if necessary, trim sides. Cut each side into 2 pieces. Immerse pieces in 95° salinometer brine (2.8 lb salt per 1 gal. water) for 1 hr 15 min. Rinse with fresh water and drain. Place on greased smoking trays and dry for 30 min in a preheated smokehouse at 130°F ± 5°; then smoke for 4½ hr at the same temperature. Cool the smoked pieces and remove skin and bones; grind flesh for a few minutes in a bowl-type food cutter. Add the spread ingredients in the order given while continuously mixing in a mechanical mixer. Blend ingredients for an additional 5 min. Pour the finished spread into ¼-lb cans (3.8 oz per can) and hermetically seal.

Suggested Process

For ¼-lb cans (3.8 oz net) 35 min at 240°F

Check process time and temperature with can supplier or the National Canners Association.

Immediately after processing, cool pack in water until cans are cool enough to handle. Stack and allow to air-dry.

SOURCE: U.S. Bureau of Commercial Fisheries, Washington, D.C.

PROCESSING KIPPERED SALMON

On the Pacific coast practically all of the kippered salmon is prepared from frozen white-meated king salmon, which on account of the color of the flesh is not in much demand. It is, however, fully the equal, in both flavor and food value, of the red-meated kings. It is not absolutely essential that the fish be first frozen, as the fresh fish may be kippered after dressing, but the latter is always a little soft when so prepared, owing to an excess of moisture, which is largely removed in freezing. Fresh salmon is available only part of the year, so it is found most convenient to freeze and store the stock and work it up when needed throughout the year.

The fish are dressed before freezing, so when thawed in cold running water, it is only necessary to split and cut them into pieces of 1 lb or less, these being about 6 in. long, or perhaps 3 in. broad, depending upon the part of the fish the piece is taken from. They are then placed in a tank of strong brine to season for several hours. They are then dipped in a harmless vegetable coloring, similar to that used by the butchers for coloring sausage; this gives the outside of the product a red color, a concession to popular prejudice.

From the coloring tank, the pieces are placed on a tray with wood frame and bottom of ½ in. sq meshed wire; care is taken that the pieces do not touch each other. The tray is then slipped into a rack which will hold a number of these, placed one above the other, and the rack is run on a track into the smokehouse.

A medium fire is kindled which dries and slightly smokes the pieces from 16 to 18 hr. When they reach a proper stage the fire is enlarged, but great care must be exercised in order to prevent their being overheated, and this is done by means of the damper at the bottom of the smokehouse and the ventilator at the top. The fish are baked in this manner from 25 to 35 min at a temperature from 250° to 275°.

When cooking is completed the cars are pulled out and the fish allowed to cool, after which each piece is wrapped in a square of parchment paper and packed in a box which holds 10 lb.

SOURCE: *Marine Products of Commerce* by D. K. Tressler published by Chemical Catalog Co., New York, N.Y.

PROCESSING KIPPERED HERRING

The kippered herring industry of England and Scotland is the most important smoked fish industry. Herring intended for kippering must be very fresh and are split as soon as they are received. The salting is effected by immersing the split fish in strong brine from 15 to 60 min. After slightly drying the herring, they are hung on square sticks by means of hooks and smoked over a hot fire for 6–16 hr. Immediately after smoking they are packed in boxes and are ready for market.

SOURCE: *Marine Products of Commerce* by D. K. Tressler published by Chemical Catalog Co., New York, N.Y.

CANNING KIPPERED HERRING

The fish are dressed and pickled in brine as for plain herring. They are next strung through the tails on nails a few inches apart on long wooden rods (approx ½ in. × ½ in. × 24 in.). The strings of herring are then hung in horizontal rows, spaced close together, on frames built in a smokehouse, one row of fish extending above the other to the top of the building and to within 6 ft of the floor. Smoke and heat are produced by a smoldering fire of birch or other hardwood. The fish are smoked for 18-24 hr which dries them and gives them the slightly smoky flavor desired. After removal from the smokehouse, the herring are packed by hand in 1-lb oval cans. The cans are then sealed without any further addition and are processed in a boiling water bath for about $2\frac{1}{2}$ hr. Check processing time and temperature with can supplier or with the National Canners Association.

SOURCE: *Marine Products of Commerce* by D. K. Tressler published by Chemical Catalog Co., New York, N.Y.

SMOKING HERRING

The first step in smoking herring is pickling of the fish in strong salt brine. Small fish are kept in brine from 24 to 36 hr, while larger ones are kept in brine for about 48 hr or until they are thoroughly "struck." The length of time fish remain in the brine vats depends to some extent upon the weather; the colder the weather the longer they are held in brine. When properly salted, herring are dipped out of the vats by dip or "wash" nets. Usually, as they are dipped out of the vats they are washed in sea water or salt brine. After washing, they are laid on stringing tables and allowed to drain. They are then strung on long, thin sticks (about $3\frac{1}{2}$ ft long, $\frac{3}{4}$ in. square) that are pointed at one end. The point of the stick is inserted through the left gill and then through the mouth with 25-35 herring strung on each stick. An experienced stringer can string from 500 to 1000 sticks a day. After stringing, the herring are dipped in a trough of sea water, then hung on rectangular frames called "herring horses." Each holds about 45 sticks (approx 1 barrel of smoked herring). The filled "herring horse" is then carried into the open air where they are left to drain and slightly dry. This preliminary drying hardens the gill covers and prevents the fish from falling off the sticks in the smokehouse. When the smokehouse has been completely filled and the herring have been given a preliminary smoking, smoking is continued for about three weeks.

"Bloaters."—Bloaters are prepared in much the same way except that the fish are salted for a longer period and then smoked lightly but at a higher temperature. Bloaters cannot be stored at room temperature but must be refrigerated.

SOURCE: *Marine Products of Commerce* by D. K. Tressler published by Chemical Catalog Co., New York, N.Y.

SMOKING HALIBUT

When halibut is prepared for smoking, the thoroughly salted fletches, or halves, are removed from the kenches, washed thoroughly, and freshened in water for about 8 hr. They are then drained for a few hours by water-horsing or compressing in regular piles. After this, the halibut are spread on flakes similar to those on which salted cod are dried. They remain on the flakes for 2 days during fair weather; but during damp weather, a much longer period is required. At night and during rainy weather, the fish are collected in small piles and covered with flake boxes. When the fletches are dry, they are cut into small pieces, from 2 to 6 pieces to the fletch depending upon the size. These are then strung on hardwood sticks or small iron or steel rods which pass through the splits or gashes cut in the fletches. The sticks or rods are then placed on bars in the smokehouse and smoked. Smoke is usually produced by burning oak chips partly covered with sawdust. The fires are kept smoking until the halibut is considered cured, which requires from 2 to 5 days. During cold weather, hot fires may be used for smoking the halibut and the smoking operation can be accomplished in less time than in warmer weather.

The yield of 100 lb of fresh halibut is about 30 lb of the smoked product.

SOURCE: *Marine Products of Commerce* by D. K. Tressler published by Chemical Catalog Co., New York, N.Y.

SMOKING HADDOCK (FINNAN HADDIE)

Haddock are eviscerated, cleaned, washed, and then split down the back from tail to head. The clean, split fish are then placed in strong brine for 1-2 hr, the exact degree of salting depends upon the size of the fish and the flavor desired. After "pickling," they are fastened to sticks from which they are suspended in the smokehouse, the napes being stretched out flat and pierced by two nails fixed in the sticks. These sticks are about 4 ft long and $1\frac{1}{2}$ in. square at the end. Three fish are usually hung from each stick. After hanging in the smokehouse to dry for a few hours, an oak fire is kindled and allowed to burn freely from 8 to 18 hr. The fire is then partially smothered in sawdust which produces a dense smoke. The smoking is continued for about 6 hr when the fires are extinguished and the fish removed to the packaging rooms. They are ready for packing in boxes for the market.

Inasmuch as the brining and smoking has only partly cured the fish, they must be held under refrigeration until sold at retail.

SOURCE: *Marine Products of Commerce* by D. K. Tressler published by Chemical Catalog Co., New York, N.Y.

FINNAN HADDIE (SCOTCH METHOD)

The first step in preparing finnan haddie is cleaning the fish by cutting off the head, splitting down the back, and eviscerating. Then in order to facilitate curing the thick muscles of the back, an extra cut is made part of the way down the back behind the back bone from the right-hand side. After washing, the fish are salted in strong brine for about 30 min. The slightly salted haddock are dried somewhat, spread open on sticks, and hung in tiers in the smokehouse. The lowest row of haddock are hung about 2 ft above the fire; but the position of the fish is changed often during smoking to obtain uniformly smoked fish. Smoking process should last from 5 to 6 hr. Smoke is produced by slowly burning a mixture of peat and sawdust. Some curers wash the slightly smoked haddock in sea water to remove any soot deposited during the smoking. The Scotch finnan haddies are marketed in barrels or boxes containing about 150 lb of fish.

SOURCE: *Marine Products of Commerce* by D. K. Tressler published by Chemical Catalog Co., New York, N.Y.

SMOKING ALEWIVES OR RIVER HERRING

In smoking sea herring, the process used in the Chesapeake Bay region is similar to that employed in Maine except that the fish are lightly smoked.

The washed, scaled river herring are put in strong brine overnight. The following morning, they are strung on herring sticks, resembling those used in New England, and rinsed in fresh water. After draining and drying for a few hours, the strings of fish are hung in a smokehouse and smoked with a dense smoke for 2-3 days. Cured in this manner, the fish will keep for about a month.

In Washington and Baltimore and a few other places, some alewives are gibbed, washed, and salted in brine for a few hours. After drying slightly, these lightly salted river herring are smoked and steamed over a hot fire for about 3 hr.

SOURCE: *Marine Products of Commerce* by D. K. Tressler published by Chemical Catalog Co., New York, N.Y.

SMOKING MACKEREL

Fresh mackerel are cured without evisceration. The fish are salted in brine for about 12 hr. After salting they are opened at the vent to let the pickle in the abdominal cavity run out. Then the fish are hung on smoke-sticks, drained, dried, and smoked for 4-5 hr. After this cold-smoking, the fires are increased and the fish are partially cooked by hot smoking for a couple of hours.

Salted mackerel are freshened, dried, and cold-smoked for 5-15 hr.

SOURCE: *Marine Products of Commerce* by D. K. Tressler published by Chemical Catalog Co., New York, N.Y.

SMOKING STURGEON

Sturgeon are ordinarily cut into chunks about 3 in. wide and weighing about 2 lb. These chunks are usually salted in brine from 6 to 16 hr, although some sturgeon is dry-salted. The salted sturgeon is washed and strung on rods, and the fish are placed in the smokehouse. They are smoked over a low fire for 1-4 hr, then the fire is increased and the sturgeon is partially cooked from 1 to 2 hr.

There are many modifications of this process, but the above is the procedure most generally used.

SOURCE: *Marine Products of Commerce* by D. K. Tressler published by Chemical Catalog Co., New York, N.Y.

SMOKING EELS

There is little uniformity in the methods followed in smoking eels in this country. One method is to clean the eels by splitting, eviscerating, and beheading. The cleaned eels are salted in strong brine for about 24 hr, and are then thoroughly washed. The fish are strung on rods and hung in a smokehouse. The eels are hot-smoked over a hot fire of corn cobs and kindling until they are nearly cooked; then the fire is partially smothered with sawdust which produces a dense smoke that soon cures the eels. The total length of time that the eels are kept in the smokehouse is about 4 hr.

In many districts the eels are neither skinned nor beheaded, and are cold-smoked for about 4 hr before being cooked over a hotter fire.

In Germany it is a common practice to cover the eels with a paste made of sugar, saltpeter, anchovies, salt, and butter before smoking in a cool smokehouse for 5–6 days.

SOURCE: *Marine Products of Commerce* by D. K. Tressler published by Chemical Catalog Co., New York, N.Y.

SMOKING CARP

First the head, viscera and fins are cut away and skin and scales are cut off in broad strips. Then the fish is cut up in transverse sections 2 or 3 in. in thickness. These steaks are placed in 90° salinometer brine for from 10–16 hr. They are then strung on long iron rods, which are dipped in fresh water to remove any undissolved salt and slime. They are then placed in a smokehouse and subjected to a gentle smoke. The dampers are then closed and the carp subjected to a smoke hot enough to cook the fish for 1–2 hr, after which the smoked fish is cooled and packed in cartons. This product must be held under refrigeration at about 32°–35°F.

SOURCE: *Canning of Fishery Products* by Cobb published by Miller Freeman Publications, San Francisco, Calif.

MISCELLANEOUS FISH DISHES, SPREADS, SALADS, LOAVES

FISH SPREADS FOR APPETIZERS, SANDWICHES

Ingredients, Their Function and Sources of Supply	Neutral Base %	Scallop Spread %	Chive Spread %	Smoked Spread %
Fish flesh (nutritional base and texture)	65.0	62.5	65.0	65.0
Oil (texture, lubricity, and carrier for surfactants)	18.0	18.0	18.0	18.0
Water (spreadability, texture)	7.25	8.0	7.25	6.6
Cornstarch (texture)	5.0	5.0	5.0	5.0
Corn syrup solids (texture and flavor)	2.0	2.0	2.0	2.0
Salt (solubilize protein, texture, and flavor)	1.1	1.1	1.2	1.2
Monosodium glutamate (flavor intensifier)	0.5	0.5	0.5	0.5
Sodium tripolyphosphate (water-holding capacity)	0.15	0.15	0.15	0.15
Potassium sorbate (mold inhibitor)	0.10	0.10	0.10	0.10
Ribotide (flavor enhancement; 1 : 1 mix of disodium inosinate and disodium guanylate) (available: Tokeda Chemical Industries, New York)	0.05	0.05	0.05	0.05
Span 80 (lipophilic surfactant) (available: Atlas Chemical Co., Wilmington, Del.)	0.035	0.075	0.075	0.075
Tween 80 (hydrophilic surfactant) (available: Atlas Chemical Co., Wilmington, Del.)	0.035	0.075	0.075	0.075
Papain (texture)	0.003	0.003	0.003	0.003
Commercial scallop flavor (No. V-1367, available: Norda Essential Oil & Chemical Co., New York)		0.4		
Sugar (flavor)		2.1		
Dimethylsulfide (shellfish flavor)		0.065		

Freeze-dried chives (flavor, color) (available:
    G. Armanino & Son, San Francisco)   0.25
Rose-pink food grade dye (color)   0.0022
Paprika (color)   0.06
Tomato paste (color)   0.25
Liquid smoke flavor (Charsol H-10, available:
    J. A. Jenks Co., or Heller & Co., San
    Francisco)   0.22
Soluble spice (No. 2700, available: J. A.
    Jenks Co., or Heller & Co., San Francisco)   0.85
Meat flavor intensifier (available: Heller &
    Co., San Francisco)   0.10

NOTE: Equivalent or similar food-grade ingredients may be substituted for any of the above ingredients. The incidental choice of the above ingredients does not constitute a product endorsement.

The Neutral Base ingredients given will produce a "cream-cheese" white spread. It may be used as the base for preparing a white product such as the Scallop Spread. The Chive Spread ingredients are indicative of a spread with contrasting reds or greens using pimiento, olive, chives, etc. The Smoked Spread given is indicative of a uniform colored product.

Procedure

Coarse Mincing.—Load the partly frozen deboned fish flesh (25°-28°F) along with all other ingredients into a Hobart vertical cutter/mixer or Hobart silent food cutter or equivalent and mince for 3–5 min to a hamburger consistency (hold final temperature below 30°F).

When large-sized additives for color or flavor, such as chives or pimiento, are used in the product, they are mixed in after the emulsification or particle-size reduction is completed. Thus, the chive ingredient in the Chive Spread is separately blended into the product after emulsification for about 1/2 min in a silent cutter or other suitable equipment in order to essentially retain the larger particle size of the chives.

Emulsification.—Gravity feed the material through a Hobart vertical microcut emulsifier or equivalent using a 0.2 mm cutter head. Pass through 2 times for maximum whiteness and minimum particle size, holding final temperature below 60°F.

In lieu of emulsification, an alternate procedure is to continue mincing in the silent cutter for an additional 10–15 min using a chilled bowl or working in a chill room.

Since the emulsifier or silent cutter does not completely reduce all the darker, fatty tissue to subvisual range, these may be apparent as trace quantities of very small light tan specks. To completely reduce these minor specks to subvisual range will require homogenization under pressure.

Packaging.—Fill product into cans, capped jars, or into aerosol or squeeze-type tubes.

Pasteurization.—Steam pasteurize the product at 183°-185°F for a period of time adequate to obtain 180°F at the center of the product for 30 min.

Storage.—Store the pasteurized product in a refrigerated chill room until ready for shipment. Product that is to be stored for over 1 month should be quick-frozen and stored at 0°F or lower.

SOURCE: U.S. Bureau of Commercial Fisheries, Washington, D.C.

FISH LOAF

Whiting or other fish can be run through a machine that removes bones and crushes the meat into a pulp. Using the pulp as a binder and larger chunks of meat for body, a loaf, cake, or sausage is formed that can be baked and sliced, like a loaf of bread. The loaf may be flavored with smoke or other seasonings.

SOURCE: *Food Engineering*, Chilton Co., Philadelphia, Penn.

FRIED FISH CAKES

Fried fish cakes are sold rather widely in delicatessens and at prepared food counters in the Atlantic coastal area. They offer possibilities for other sections of the country.

Ingredients	Lb	Oz
Potatoes, peeled and sliced	10	
Salt cod, shredded	5	
Whole eggs, beaten	8	

Butter or margarine	8
Diced onions	1
White pepper	1/4

Procedure

Soak salt cod in cold water for several hours; then shred or break into small pieces. Place in a kettle with water and heat to boiling; drain off water. Then boil fish and potatoes together until tender. Drain off cooking liquid and put both fish and potatoes through the 1/4-in. plate of the grinder. Transfer the product to a mixer, add beaten eggs, margarine, onion, and pepper; mix until a uniform mixture is obtained. (Onions may be omitted if trade prefers the fish cakes without this ingredient.)

Put the mixture through a forming machine to make cakes of the desired size and weight. Dip cakes into batter and then roll in fine bread crumbs. Fry in deep fat at 350°F until light brown.

Usually, these cakes are not packaged but are sold from refrigerated display cases held at approximately 40°F.

SOURCE: U.S. Bureau of Commercial Fisheries, Washington, D.C.

MARINATING FRIED SMALL FISH

Young herring, sardines, anchovies, or any small food fish may be preserved by frying and marinating.

The fish are cleaned, washed, and then dried for about 1 hr in the open air. After drying, they are fried in hot oil, cooled and allowed to drain. The drained, fried fish are packed in barrels, kegs, glass jars, or other containers and covered with hot, spiced vinegar containing some salt. The containers are allowed to stand for a short time before they are closed. They are then ready for shipment.

Small fish preserved in this way will keep for a long period if strong vinegar is used for preparing the pickle.

SOURCE: *Marine Products of Commerce*, 2nd Edition by Tressler and Lemon published by Reinhold Publishing Corp., New York, N.Y.

FISH SAUSAGE

Ingredients	Gm	%
Fish fillets	1000	70.40
Ice water	200	14.08
Vegetable shortening	100	7.04
Cornstarch	80	5.63
Salt	25	1.76
Sugar	7	0.49
Monosodium glutamate	3	0.21
Spices[1]	5.5	0.39
Ascorbic acid	0.05	35 (ppm)
Sodium nitrite	0.01	7 (ppm)

[1] White pepper, 2 gm; onion powder, 1 gm; nutmeg powder, 1 gm; ginger powder, 1 gm; and garlic powder, 0.5 gm.

Procedure

Store fish fillets overnight at 35°F so as to have fish well chilled at start of operation. Then cut them into about 1 1/2-in. cubes and chop in a silent cutter with all the other ingredients. Add the salt at the beginning to extract the salt-soluble proteins for binding. Then add the starch in a slurry. Spices and shortening are added in the latter part of chopping to prevent possible fat smearing. Combine several batches of the formualted sausage mixture and chop to a fine emulsion. Stuff about 250 gm of the combined sausage emulsion into polyvinylidene chloride casings of 43 mm (diam) × 270 mm (length), using a hand-operated stuffer. Seal ends of the casings with aluminum wire, using a clipping machine.

Heat sausages in a steam-jacketed kettle at near boiling temperature (207°F ± 3°). Cook for 30 min *after* the internal sausage temperature reaches 180°F. Then promptly cool in ice water until internal sausage temperature drops to 70°F. Immerse the cooled sausages in boiling water for 1 min to shrink casings in order to obtain a tight package.

This product is perishable and should be held at a storage temperature of 35°F for short storage. However, shelf-life will be extended if product is held in frozen storage of 0°F or below.

SOURCE: Food Science Department, University of Hawaii, Honolulu, Hawaii.

SALMON SALAD

Combine the following ingredients and season with salt, pepper, and fresh dill; mix just to blend (do not overmix):

	Lb	Oz
Canned salmon, flaked	5	
Boiled, diced potatoes	5	
Diced onions		12
Sour cream dressing (see below)	4	

The following ingredients and procedure will make the necessary amount of sour cream dressing for the ingredients given above:

Sour cream	6 cups
Eggs, beaten lightly	6
Vinegar	1 cup
Salt	4 tbsp

Mustard	2 tbsp
Pepper	3/4 tsp

Add eggs, vinegar, and dry ingredients to cream and mix thoroughly. Cook in a double boiler stirring constantly until the mixture thickens. Cool before making up the salad.

Alternatives

A cup of diced dill pickle is sometimes used in place of fresh dill. And sometimes 1/2 cup of fresh grated horseradish is added to the sour cream dressing; in this case, omit the fresh dill or dill pickles.

SOURCE: U.S. Bureau of Commercial Fisheries, Washington, D.C.

TUNA SALAD

Formula No. 1

Ingredients	Pt	Lb	Tsp
Canned tuna		5	
Finely diced celery	2 1/2		
Finely diced sweet pickle	1		
Mayonnaise	1 1/2		
Hydrogenated vegetable shortening		1/2	
Salt			1 1/2
Pepper			3/4
Lemons, 5			
Hard boiled, diced eggs, 12			

Flake tuna, dice celery, pickles, and eggs. Extract juice of lemons. Combine all ingredients except lemon juice. Season with salt and pepper, and sprinkle lemon juice over the whole. Combine shortening with mayonnaise, then mix with other ingredients. In some formulae one pint of diced cucumber is included. Others use sour instead of sweet pickles. Still others use capers in place of pickles. These variations are entirely a matter of taste. Package and hold at 40°F until retailed.

Formula No. 2

This is a commercial formula for tuna salad that differs widely from that given above.

Ingredients	Lb
Canned tuna	5
Boiled, diced potatoes	5
Diced dill pickles	1
French dressing	4

Flake tuna, mix with other ingredients and season. Fill salad into containers and hold at 40°F until retailed.

SOURCE: U.S. Bureau of Commercial Fisheries, Washington, D.C.

TUNA SALAD WITH TEXTURED VEGETABLE PROTEIN

Ingredients	%
Tuna (drained)	26.8
Textured vegetable protein (Mira-Tex 230-F)	3.7
Spice blend (Asmus 97T-91-69-10)	0.2
Water and liquor from drained tuna	7.5
Mayonnaise	29.8
Celery (chopped)	3.7
Sweet pickle relish	13.0
Eggs (hard cooked, chopped)	14.9
Lemon juice	0.4

Procedure

Dry blend textured vegetable protein (Mira-Tex 230-F) with spice blend and hydrate with water and tuna liquor. Mix all ingredients and blend thoroughly. Chill.

SOURCE: A. E. Staley Mfg. Co., Decatur, Ill.

SMOKED HERRING SALAD

Ingredients	Lb	Oz	Tbsp	Cup
Canned smoked herring fillets in oil		8		
Anchovy fillets		4		
Boiled potatoes	2			
Boiled beets	2			
Tart cooking apples	2			
Onion, finely chopped				1/2
Vinegar				1/4
Sugar			4	
Whipping cream				1 1/2

Procedure

Cut herring and anchovy fillets into very small cubes. Peel boiled beets and potatoes; cut into somewhat larger cubes. Pare apples and cut into smallest cubes possible. (Apples are intended to give freshness to the taste of the salad, but should not be visible as "pieces.") Mix together fish, beets, potatoes, apples, and onion. Dissolve sugar in vinegar and add to fish mixture. Toss vinegar with salad ingredients lightly so cubed ingredients do not become broken. Whip cream to consistency of thick sauce; fold into salad ingredients. (Cream must not be whipped too thick or it will curdle when mixed into salad.) Pack salad into containers, seal, and hold at a temperature of 40°F until sold.

SOURCE: U.S. Bureau of Commercial Fisheries, Washington, D.C.

GERMAN-STYLE HERRING SALAD

Ingredients	Lb	Oz
Boiled potatoes	25	
Salted cucumbers	28	
Boiled beets	20	
Salt herring	50	
Mayonnaise	10	
Ground onions	$1^1/_2$	
Horseradish, ground	$^1/_2$	
Pepper		2
Juice and oil of 3 lemons (optional)		
Paprika to taste		

Procedure

Freshen herring by soaking in a tank of water from 11 to 24 hr, depending on individual taste. Then skin, fillet, and dice fish. Dice cucumbers, beets, and potatoes and mix with herring. Mix horseradish, onions, and pepper with mayonnaise. The juice and oil of 3 lemons may be added, if desired. Fold mayonnaise mixture lightly but thoroughly into the other ingredients. Package and store at 34°–40°F.

SOURCE: U.S. Bureau of Commercial Fisheries, Washington, D.C.

ITALIAN-STYLE HERRING SALAD

Ingredients	Lb
Boiled tongue	10
Apples	6
Boiled potatoes	20
Celery	6
Carrots	10
Salted cucumber	30
Salt herring	20
Mayonnaise	6
Ground onions	$1^1/_2$
Horseradish, ground	$^1/_2$
Juice and oil of 3 lemons (optional)	
Seasonings: curry powder, mace, and pepper to taste.	

Procedure

Freshen the salt herring by soaking in water overnight. Skin and fillet, removing all bones. Dice. Chop the celery fine. Peel apples, potatoes, and carrots and cut into small dice. Dice tongue and cucumbers. Mix all these ingredients thoroughly. Blend onions, horseradish, and spices with the mayonnaise. The juice and oil of 3 lemons may also be added, if desired. Then add mayonnaise to other ingredients. Store in a cool place.

SOURCE: U.S. Bureau of Commercial Fisheries, Washington, D.C.

ALASKA-STYLE HERRING SALAD

Ingredients	Lb	Oz
Salt herring	10	
Pickled beans	2	
Sour cucumber pickles	1	
Sweet cucumber pickles	1	
Mustard pickles	1	
Apples	3	
Mayonnaise	2	
Smoked salmon	$^1/_2$	
Onion	$^1/_4$	
Capers		2

Procedure

Soak the salt herring in water for about 24 hr, changing the water 2–3 times, or the herring can be freshened in running water for 4–6 hr. Skin and fillet the herring, removing all bones; dice into small pieces. Peel and dice apples; hold diced apples under water until used to prevent discoloration. Chop finely the pickles, beans, and capers; dice the smoked salmon and grate the onion. Mix all ingredients thoroughly with the mayonnaise. Salad is best if left to stand 24 hr to blend flavors. May be garnished for serving with sliced hard boiled eggs, capers, and nut meats. Makes a good delicatessen item.

SOURCE: U.S. Bureau of Commercial Fisheries, Washington, D.C.

TUNA SOUFFLÉ

The formula given below is for the fresh-baked product for institutional food service. However, this is a product that can be frozen unbaked in aluminum foil oblong pans and marketed for retail as well as institutional trade.

Ingredients	Weight Lb	Oz	Approx Measure
Water			6 qt
Butter	3		
Nonfat dry milk	1	14	(2$^1/_2$ qt instant)
All-purpose flour	$1^1/_2$		
Salt			5 tbsp
Pepper			$^1/_2$ tsp
Cold water			$1^1/_2$ qt
Egg yolks	3		(63–64)
Canned tuna, drained and flaked	8		
Chopped onions	1		
Lemon juice		8	
Egg whites	4		(63–64)

YIELD: 96 portions approximately 3 × 3$^1/_3$ in.

Procedure

Heat butter and water in top of double boiler until butter is melted. Combine dry ingredients and add water to make a smooth paste; slowly add slurry to hot water-butter mixture, and while stirring constantly, cook until smooth and thickened.

Beat egg yolks until thick and creamy. Then stir a small portion of the thickened sauce into the yolks before adding yolks to the hot sauce. (This prevents curdling of the yolks.) Then add tuna, onions, and lemon juice; mix to distribute ingredients uniformly.

Beat egg whites until stiff but not dry. Then carefully fold whites into tuna mixture and pour into 4 counter pans (12 × 20 × 2¹⁄₄ in.) greased on bottoms only. Scale 9¹⁄₂ lb of mixture per pan. Bake at 350°F for 40 min.

SOURCE: American Dry Milk Institute, 130 N. Franklin St., Chicago, Ill.

SALMON LOAF

The formula given below is for the fresh-baked product for institutional food service. However, this is a product that can be frozen unbaked in aluminum foil loaf pans and marketed for retail as well as institutional trade.

Ingredients	Weight Lb	Oz	Approx Measure
Canned salmon	18		
Fresh bread cubes	4		(1 gal.)
Chopped onions	1	4	(2¹⁄₂ cups)
Diced celery	4	8	(3 qt)
Butter, melted		4	
Whole fresh eggs	3		(30)
Water			2 qt
Nonfat dry milk	1	8	(2¹⁄₄ qt instant)
Salt		3	
Paprika			1¹⁄₂ tsp

YIELD: 10 3-lb loaves with 10 slices per loaf (100 slices)

Procedure

Flake salmon. Put in mixer and add bread. Cook onions and celery in butter until tender and add to salmon-bread mixture.

Blend eggs lightly with whip; add water, dry milk, salt, and paprika. Blend until smooth and add to salmon mixture. Blend ingredients together until well mixed. Scale 3 lb per loaf pan and bake at 350°F for 45-50 min.

SOURCE: American Dry Milk Institute, 130 N. Franklin St., Chicago, Ill.

TUNA NOODLE CASSEROLE

The formula given below is for the fresh-baked product for institutional food service. However, this is a product that can be frozen unbaked in aluminum foil loaf pans and marketed for retail as well as institutional trade.

Ingredients	Weight Lb	Oz	Approx Measure
Noodles (dry weight)	4	2	
Salt		4¹⁄₂	
Liquid from drained mushrooms and water			7¹⁄₂ qt
Nonfat dry milk	2	4	(3¹⁄₃ qt instant)
Butter, melted	1	12	
Chopped onion		6	
Chopped celery	1	2	
Canned, sliced mushrooms (drained)	3		
Pastry flour		12	
Salt		3	
White pepper			1¹⁄₂ tsp
Canned, drained tuna	12		
Dry bread crumbs		12	
Butter, melted		8	

YIELD: 100 portions of 6 oz each

Procedure

Cook noodles in 4¹⁄₂ gal. boiling salted (4¹⁄₂ oz) water until tender; drain and rinse in cold water.

Simmer onions, celery, and mushrooms in 1 lb 12 oz of butter until celery is tender. Then pour off butter and blend with flour to make a smooth paste.

Stir dry milk into mushroom-water liquid until well blended. Then heat to 170°F but *do not boil*. Stir the butter-flour paste into the hot mixture and cook until thickened. Then add onions, celery, mushrooms, salt (3 oz), and pepper and stir to thoroughly mix ingredients. Lastly, add tuna and cooked noodles mixing just enough to obtain a uniform mixture.

Divide into 3 counter pans (12 × 20 × 2¹⁄₄ in.). Melt 8 oz of butter and mix with bread crumbs; sprinkle mixture over top of pans. Bake at 350°F for 30-35 min or until top is browned.

SOURCE: American Dry Milk Institute, 130 N. Franklin St., Chicago, Ill.

LUTEFISK

Cover the stockfish with clear cold water and allow it to soak for 4 days, being sure to change the water every day. The fish should be kept in a cool place preferably out-of-doors as the odor is objectionable to some people, but care should be taken to prevent freezing as this ruins the product. When the fish has been sufficiently soaked, cover with cold water to which has been added a solution of soda and lime; for 5 lb of fish use 2 cups of washing soda and 3–4 cups of slack lime to about 12 gal. of water. A large container such as a salting butt is used for soaking. Let the fish soak in this "lute" for 3–4 days. Pour off the solution and again soak the fish in clear cold water for at least 3 days to remove all the chemicals, changing the water every day. Keep in a cool place or the fish will spoil. The lutefisk should now have the desired consistency and flavor.

Standard Cooking Procedure

Cover fish with cold water, add salt to taste, and bring to a boil. Boil about 10 min and pour off water. The cooked lutefisk should have a white and flaky appearance. Flake and serve with melted butter or white sauce. Northern Europeans accompany their lutefisk with boiled or mashed potatoes liberally salted and peppered.

SOURCE: U.S. Bureau of Commercial Fisheries, Washington, D.C.

SHELLFISH AND MISCELLANEOUS MARINE PRODUCTS

SHRIMP

FREEZING SHRIMP

Preparation of Raw Shrimp

Upon receiving the raw shrimp at the freezing plant, heads are removed from any remaining whole shrimp. The shrimp are washed and inspected to remove defective ones. They are then graded for size. At this point, some may be iced for distribution as fresh shrimp. Those for freezing are peeled and deveined by machines. (This operation was formerly done by hand.) The peeled, deveined shrimp are discharged onto a conveyor and then on to an inspection station; shells and veins are discharged onto a waste belt.

Blast Freezing Shrimp

The raw shrimp ready for freezing are conveyed to work stations where they are placed on thin aluminum sheets. Each sheet holds approximately $2\frac{1}{2}$ lb of shrimp; they are spaced on the sheet so they do not touch one another. The loaded sheets are separated by angle irons and placed in stacks on a rolling rack which is rolled into the freezing tunnel. A temperature of from $-25°$ to $-40°F$ is recommended. This low temperature can be reached in multiple plate freezers and in blast freezers and is low enough to freeze the shrimp so rapidly that the cellular breakdown is kept at a minimum. At the discharge end of the freezing tunnel the shrimp are packaged in moisture-proof bags or cartons, size depending upon the market for which they are intended, consumer or institutional. Storage temperature should be maintained at $0°F$ and, preferably, lower at all times. At the lower storage temperature, the development of rancid flavor is minimized.

Freezing Glazed Shrimp

A large quantity of fresh shrimp are frozen in the shells and then given an ice glaze, which keeps the shrimp in excellent condition during frozen storage.

The fresh, raw shrimp are washed, inspected, graded for size, and the heads removed. They are then packed in 5-lb cold-waxed telescoping cartons. Cartons are spread out individually on portable racks, or are placed on refrigerated plates or trays. Some packing companies may not own their own freezing equipment. If so, the freezing is usually done in a local refrigerated warehouse which is equipped to freeze shrimp on a large scale. The shrimp are usually frozen at $0°$ to $-10°F$. After the shrimp are frozen, cartons are opened and the shrimp are glazed with water. In some plants, the glazing is done by brushing cold water on the top layer of shrimp, using a whitewash brush. Other plants use a spray system whereby a small amount of water is sprayed on the shrimp. Occasionally, the shrimp are glazed by immersing the entire package in cold water. The glazed shrimp are then returned to frozen storage.

Freezing Cooked Shrimp

Formerly, a large proportion of the frozen shrimp was cooked before freezing. Because cooked shrimp become somewhat tough during storage, there are fewer shrimp frozen in this manner than otherwise. (The toughening is caused in part by the denaturation of the protein.) Those which are cooked prior to freezing are, ordinarily, used within a relatively short time after freezing. Cooked shrimp intended for freezing generally are peeled before freezing; also, usually, they are not glazed as in the above process.

The customary method of cooking shrimp for freezing is to boil them for 6–8 min in an 8–10% salt brine, similar to the process employed in preparing shrimp for canning. However, in studies conducted on the effect of the concentration of salt solution and length of cooking on the flavor and tenderness of the frozen product, it was found that boiling the shrimp for 4 min in a 15% salt solution gave the best results.

In Alaska, most of the shrimp are cooked before freezing. On arrival at the plant, the whole shrimp are cooked before freezing in a tank of boiling fresh water heated by direct injection of live steam. This simplifies the picking operation. After picking and washing, the meats are usually cooked in a strong salt solution (25°–30° salinometer) for from 1 to 3 min. Another method that is used is to first dip the trays of picked meats in a saturated salt solution for about 3 min, after which the trays are allowed to drain. The trays are then placed in a steam retort and cooked without pressure for 3–4 min. The meats are then cooled after which they are put through a combination shaking and blowing machine to remove any particles of shell that may remain.

Regardless of how the shrimp are cooked, usually they are cooled in running cold water before packaging. For the institutional pack, cans may be used; for the retail trade, cartons of suitable size are used. The shrimp are then quick frozen either in an air blast or a horizontal plate freezer at −10°–−20°F.

SOURCE: *The Freezing Preservation of Foods, 4th Edition, Vols. 3 and 4* by Tressler *et al.* published by Avi Publishing Co., Westport, Conn.

CANNING SHRIMP

Shrimp are usually graded for canning size prior to delivery at the cannery. Upon arrival at the plant, the ice is separated from the shrimp which are thoroughly washed as they are conveyed into the cannery. Then they should be carefully inspected and foreign debris eliminated. The clean shrimp are then conveyed to a peeling machine equipped with oscillating rubber-covered rolls which separate the shells and the heads from the body of the shrimp. The shrimp then pass to a "scrubber" which loosens and removes any shell fragments left by the peeling machine. Next, the shrimp are conveyed to a deveining machine. In this machine, a sharp knife cuts the back muscle so that the "sand vein" can be removed by a rotating drum underneath a strong spray of water. The deveined shrimp are then cooked for about 4 min in a 10% salt solution.

After cooking, the shrimp should be passed over an inspection belt and all broken shrimp and pieces separated from the perfect ones. Then the shrimp should be hand-filled into cans, with the amount in each can weighed to make certain that the proper weight of shrimp is put into each can. This should be 64% of the weight of the water required to fill the can. The shrimp are then covered with boiling hot dilute brine, after which cans are automatically closed and immediately processed in retorts.

Suggested Process

Small cans (No. 1 Picnic, 307 × 208, and 307 × 400) require 15 min at 250°F. Larger cans and those which are dry-packed require longer processing. Consult can supplier or the National Canners Association for processing times.

FROZEN SHRIMP IN CREOLE SAUCE

Ingredients for Sauce	Gal.	Lb	Oz
Tomato purée (sp. gr. 1.035)	25		
Water	25		
Fresh chopped onions		35	
Fresh chopped green peppers		15	
Canned chopped red peppers		15	
Vegetable oil		12	
Salt		6	
Waxy maize starch		15	
Monosodium glutamate		1	
Plant protein hydrolyzate			8
Ground red pepper			2
Ground celery seeds			1/2

Procedure

Put 50 gal. of water in a steam-jacketed kettle and make a mark on a measuring stick at water level so as to gage final gallonage of sauce. Drain water. Put tomato purée in the kettle and add oil, onions, green peppers, and salt mixed with the seasonings. Add 20 gal. of water, heat to 200°F, and cook for 30 min. Make a slurry free of lumps of the starch and 5 gal. of water; with steady stirring add it to the sauce. Cook an additional 20 min, add red pepper and bring sauce volume up to 50 gal. Mix thoroughly.

Put 4 oz cooked shrimp in polyethylene Mylar bags and evenly distribute 12 oz of sauce over shrimp. Close under vacuum and prechill before transferring to a sharp freezer at −20°F.

SOURCE: Stephan L. Komarik, 4810 Ronda, Coral Gables, Florida.

FROZEN SHRIMP BISQUE

Ingredients	By Weight		Or By Measure
	Lb	Oz	
Shrimp, cooked	2¼		
Onions, chopped		7	
Celery, coarsely chopped		7	

Butter	7	
Brandy, inexpensive		⅓ cup
Water or fish stock		1 gal. + 1 cup
Salt	1	(2 tbsp)
White pepper		1 tbsp
Rice, cooked	7	
Evaporated milk	14	
Tabasco sauce		2 tsp
Modified starch	2¾	(½ cup + 2 tbsp)
Sherry wine		½ cup

YIELD: 10 portions allowing 1½ cups per portion

Procedure

Weigh out ¼ lb of the shrimp, dice and reserve for garnish. Chop remainder of the shrimp. Sauté onions and celery in butter until transparent but not brown; add shrimp and heat through. Add brandy and flame. Add water or fish stock, salt, pepper, and rice. Cover, bring to a boil, reduce heat and simmer 15 min. Purée mixture by putting it through a fine food mill. Bring mixture to a boil. Slowly add evaporated milk and Tabasco sauce to starch and stir until smooth. Add to mixture; heat to 180°F stirring constantly. Add sherry.

In 12 × 8 in. vacuum bags, put 1½ cups of bisque and add a few diced shrimp. Heat seal; blast freeze for 30 min.

SOURCE: Cornell Hotel & Restaurant Administration Quarterly, Statler Hall, Ithaca, N.Y.

FROZEN SHRIMP CREOLE

	By Weight		Or By
Ingredients	Lb	Oz	Measure
Shrimp, medium size, cooked, shelled, and deveined	2½		
Peanut oil		3½	
Salt			1 tsp
Spanish paprika			1½ tsp
Onions, coarsely chopped		7	
Instant dehydrated onion powder			1 tbsp + 1 tsp
Instant dehydrated garlic powder			2 tsp
Green pepper, cut in ½-in. squares, precooked		¼	
Italian tomatoes (canned), peeled, chopped, and seeds removed	1		
Tomato sauce	1	2	
Pimiento, ¼-in. diced		3	
Chili peppers			1 tbsp
Rice, cooked	1	14	

YIELD: 6 portions of 13 oz each

Procedure

Sauté shrimp in peanut oil over high heat for 2–3 min. Add salt, paprika, onions, instant onion and garlic powders, and green pepper. Cover and simmer 5 min. Remove shrimp. Add to the mixture the tomatoes, tomato sauce, pimiento, and chili peppers. Blend ingredients well.

In 12 × 8 in. vacuum pouch, put 6 oz shrimp; add 7 oz creole sauce, distributing it evenly over shrimp. Heat seal. Blast freeze 30 min.

SOURCE: Cornell Hotel & Restaurant Administration Quarterly, Statler Hall, Ithaca, N.Y.

FROZEN CURRIED SHRIMP

Ingredients	Lb	Oz
Frozen shrimp (medium, peeled, and deveined; may be butterfly or cut in half lengthwise)	2½	
Butter		3½
Curry powder		⅔
Salt		⅐
Dehydrated onion powder		½
Celery, finely diced		1½
Broth (made from raw shrimp shells, shrimp cooking water, fish bones, etc.)	2	
Evaporated milk		10½
Modified starch		2½
Apples, peeled, finely diced		3½
Mango chutney		1
Modified cream (Pream)		1½

Procedure

Cook shrimp 2–3 min in boiling water. Reserve the cooking water for the broth. Sauté shrimp in butter 5 min, stirring often. Add curry powder, salt, celery, onion powder and simmer covered 5 min. Remove shrimp and add fish broth. Add evaporated milk to starch slowly and stir until smooth; add to broth. Heat mixture to 180°F, stirring constantly. Add apples and chutney; stir until well blended, then add modified cream and stir until dissolved.

Package 6 oz shrimp in each vacuum pouch (12 in. × 8 in.); evenly distribute over shrimp 7 oz of sauce. Blast freeze for 30 min.

SOURCE: *The Freezing Preservation of Foods, 4th Edition, Vol. 4* by Tressler *et al.* published by Avi Publishing Co., Westport, Conn.

FROZEN SHRIMP PATTIES WITH TEXTURED VEGETABLE PROTEIN

Ingredients	%
Shrimp	68.97
Textured vegetable protein (Edi-Pro® 200)	29.56
Imitation shrimp flavor 306B (available from Knickerbocker Mills Co., Totowa, N.J.)	1.08
Salt	0.39

NOTE: Imitation shrimp flavoring may not be necessary when flavorful shrimp are used.

Procedure

1. Chop textured vegetable protein (Edi-Pro® 200) for 15 min in a silent cutter.
2. Chop shrimp with chopped textured vegetable protein, flavor, and salt in a silent cutter for 20 sec.
3. Check for proper mixing and continue chopping for 15 sec more.
4. Remove from the chopper and form patties for breading[1] using Modern Maid Batter No. 1163, Breader No. B287-D15, and Japanese Crumb No. 6071.
5. A prefry may then be accomplished in a 350°F deep fat fryer for 1 min.
6. The patties are then frozen.
7. Frozen patties may be heated to serving temperature in a 400°F oven for 15 min without prior thawing.

SOURCE: Ralston Purina Company, Checkerboard Square, St. Louis, Mo.

FLAVOR BASE FOR RICE PILAF WITH FREEZE-DRIED SHRIMP

Ingredients	%
Maggi HPP Type 3H3 powder with partially hydrogenated vegetable oil	5.00
Maggi HPP Type 245 powder with partially hydrogenated vegetable oil	5.00
Salt	20.00
Sugar	4.00
Monosodium glutamate	7.20
Soluble celery	0.50
Soluble pepper	0.30
Oleoresin paprika	1.00
Freeze-dried mushroom dice	5.00
Green pepper granules	10.00
Dehydrated sliced onions	12.00
Tomato crystals	24.00
Hydrogenated vegetable oil	6.00
	100.00

Procedure

Mix ingredients until a uniform mixture is obtained.

To Use.—Combine 35 gm of flavor base, 6 gm of freeze-dried shrimp, 140 gm (2 cups) quick cooking rice, 1 tbsp butter, and 2 cups cold water. Bring to a boil while stirring. Reduce heat, cover, and simmer 5 min.

SOURCE: Nestlé Company, Food Ingredients Division, 100 Bloomingdale Road, White Plains, N.Y.

SMOKED SHRIMP

Remove heads from freshly caught shrimp. Wash shrimp in cold fresh water. Soak shrimp in 60° salinometer brine or slightly stronger for 1 hr. Steam shrimp until they turn pink (about 20 min). Spread on screen bottom trays so that they do not touch each other. Dry the shrimp in a slightly warm smokehouse for about 1/2 hr. Smoke for 1–2 hr until the desired flavor and color are obtained. Use hickory sawdust for smoke and keep temperature low (under 100°F). Package and store at 35°F or lower.

SOURCE: *Meat Merchandizing*, St. Louis, Mo.

PICKLED SPICED SHRIMP

Formula No. 1

Ingredients for 5 lb shrimp

Water	1 gal.
Salt	1/2 cup
Distilled vinegar	1 pt
Red peppers	1 tbsp
Cloves	1/2 tbsp
Allspice	1/2 tbsp
Mustard seed	1/2 tbsp
Bay leaves	6

Use green shrimp; peel and wash them well. Make a brine of the ingredients by simmering slowly for 30 min, then bring it to the boiling point and add the shrimp. When the brine again comes to a boil, cook the shrimp for 5 min. Remove shrimp from brine and cool. Pack in sterilized jars with a bay leaf, a few fresh spices, and a slice of lemon in each jar. Fill the jars with a solution made in the proportion of 2 pt water, 1 pt distilled vinegar, and 1 tbsp sugar. Seal jars tightly and store in a cool, dark place.

[1] Use of the breading will lower the above percentages.

Formula No. 2

The pickled shrimp made by this method do not keep as long as those prepared by the above formula, but they require less labor and so are somewhat less expensive to prepare.

Using 5 lb of fresh, green, headless shrimp, wash them well but do not remove the shells. Prepare the brine ingredients as given above adding celery tops, parsley, and thyme, if desired. Boil the brine for about 45 min; then add the shrimp and boil for 10 min. Do not remove the shrimp from the liquor; allow to cool before draining liquor from shrimp. Pack in small containers with a few fresh pickling spices. Refrigerate, or hold in a cool, dark place.

SOURCE: U.S. Bureau of Commercial Fisheries, Washington, D.C.

CLAMS

PREPARING CLAMS FOR FREEZING

Practices employed in preparing clams for freezing are largely dependent on the species being frozen.

Soft Clams.—The shell stock is washed, then the clams are opened—a relatively easy job as the shells are not as tightly closed as in many other bivalves. The meats are washed, drained, and packed in containers ranging from 1-lb cartons to 1-gal. cans.

Hard Clams (Quahog).—The shells of this mollusk are tightly closed; so, in some areas of the country, to facilitate insertion of the shucking knife, the edge of the clam is drawn over a coarse rasp which removes some of the shell and makes it easier to insert the shucking knife and cut the adductor muscles. In other areas of the country, the knife is forced in between the shells near the hinge, the adductors cut, and the clam opened. Prior to being frozen, the meats are thoroughly washed before being packaged.

Surf Clams.—Shells of the surf clams do not close as tightly as the quahog and so are somewhat easier to open. Treatment after opening is, however, radically different from that given soft and hard clams. Surf clams are eviscerated by squeezing the meats which removes the stomach and other soft tissues. The eviscerated clams are then washed and, depending upon intended use, may be chopped, sliced into strips, or left whole. Meats are then packed in containers of various sizes for freezing.

Freezing

The freezing method varies with the type of container used; i.e., compression plate for rectangular 1- to 5-lb packages, and blast or shelf coil for large cans.

SOURCE: *The Freezing Preservation of Foods, 4th Edition, Vol. 3* by Tressler *et al.* published by Avi Publishing Co., Westport, Conn.

CANNING RAZOR CLAMS

Clams are first washed and then put through an automatic shucker. This consists of a long rectangular box containing a rack which is operated as a rocker. The motion of the rocker carries the clams toward the opposite end of the trough and through hot water which causes the clams to gape. The motion of the rack shakes out the meats. When the meats and shells reach the opposite end, jets of cold water are played upon the meats to cool them rapidly in order to prevent them from becoming tough. The meats are then picked off the frame and placed in large pans while the shells pass on and are dumped outdoors.

The meats are then dressed and cleaned. This is accomplished by splitting them on one side with scissors so that they are opened wide. The dark mass near the end of the siphon which contains much sand and dirt is clipped off. The cut meats are washed in a special washing machine, consisting usually of a cylindrical perforated drum which revolves half a turn in one direction and then half a turn in the opposite direction. The siphon and side walls are cut away from the washed meats and discarded, and the stomach is slit open and cleaned out. The cleaned, dressed meats are minced in a meat grinder. The ground meats are placed in the hopper of an automatic filling machine which feeds the desired quantity of clam meat into cans which pass under it on an endless belt. Some of the juice of the clams which runs out during the process is added to the filled cans. The tops of the cans are put in place and the cans are exhausted at about 210°F for about 8 min. The tops are then sealed and the cans are processed at about 220°F.

Suggested Process

1 lb cans for 90 min at 220°F
½ lb cans for 70 min at 220°F

Check process times and temperature with can supplier or the National Canners Association.

After processing, the cans are quickly cooled with streams of cold water to prevent the clam meat from becoming tough.

SOURCE: *Marine Products of Commerce* by D. K. Tressler published by Chemical Catalog Co., New York, N.Y.

CANNING CLAM EXTRACT

Clam extract finds extensive use as a food for convalescents and invalids. It is usually prepared by placing fresh clams in the shell on racks or gratings in an autoclave. The clams are steamed for about 20 min; the heat cooks the clams and causes much of the juice which they contain to run out. The liquor is collected in pans under the racks. This liquor is filtered and concentrated by boiling. The concentrated extract is put into cans which are topped, sealed and sterilized by processing in an autoclave at 240°F.

Suggested Process

1 lb cans for 1 hr at 240°F
½ lb cans for 50 min at 240°F

Check process times and temperature with can supplier or the National Canners Association.

SOURCE: *Marine Products of Commerce* by D. K. Tressler published by Chemical Catalog Co., New York, N.Y.

CANNING CLAM NECTAR

During the grinding of the meat of razor and other clams, a considerable quantity of liquid is expressed. Even though some liquor is added to each can of clams, there remains a considerable surplus of this liquor. This is canned separately and sold under the name of clam nectar.

The hot liquor is placed in 1 lb cans, sealed, and sterilized. If the liquor is cold when it is put into the cans, cans are first exhausted, then sealed and sterilized.

Suggested Process

1 lb cans for 1 hr at 240°F

Check process time and temperature with can supplier or the National Canners Association.

SOURCE: *Marine Products of Commerce* by D. K. Tressler published by Chemical Catalog Co., New York, N.Y.

MARYLAND FRIED CLAMS

The ingredients given below are for six servings and while this is not a commercial formula, it is included here because of its adaptability as an excellent frozen product. Cool the product after preparation, then package in containers suitable for freezing and freeze at −20°F.

Ingredients

Fresh-shucked soft shell clams	1 qt
Eggs, beaten	2
Milk	2 tbsp
Salt	2 tsp
Pepper	Dash
Dry bread crumbs	3 cups

Procedure

Drain clams. Combine egg, milk, and seasonings. Dip clams in egg mixture and roll in crumbs. Deep fry at 350°F for 1–2 min or until brown. Drain on absorbent paper and allow to cool before packaging for the freezer.

SOURCE: Fish and Wildlife Service, U.S. Department of the Interior, Washington, D.C.

CANNED CLAM CHOWDERS

Two types of clam chowder are canned: Manhattan (also called Rhode Island and Coney Island) and New England. The formula ingredients for New England clam chowder are generally the same in all plants; but the formula for Manhattan chowder differs with each packer.

Both soft clams and quahogs are used, the species usually dependent upon whichever is most abundant. Quahogs are preferred by some packers as the clam flavor is stronger. Potatoes used for chowder should be firm-textured, with few and shallow eyes, of regular shape, and with smooth surface. Salt pork should be fresh and free from rancidity; usually a good grade of fat brisket pork is selected. Smoked bacon is specified in some published formulas, but is not favored in practice. In packing Manhattan chowder, standard grade tomatoes in gallon cans (No. 10) are generally used. Carrots, celery, peppers, or any other vegetables are fresh and of the best market quality.

For Manhattan Chowder

One commercial formula for Manhattan chowder contains the following ingredients:

	Gal.	Lb	Oz
Fine cracker crumbs		65	
Ground salt pork		18	

Onions, diced		18	
Water	55		
Salt		16	
White pepper			5
Canned tomatoes, 24 No. 10 cans			

In making this chowder, simmer the diced onions in an 80-gal. steam-jacketed kettle until they are soft. Add the ground salt pork and sauté until salt pork is golden but not brown. Then add 15 gal. of the water and allow mixture to come to a boil. Meanwhile, put 35 lb of the cracker crumbs in a mixer with 15 gal. of the water and beat until mixture is smooth; add mixture to contents of kettle. Then prepare a second batch of cracker crumbs (30 lb) in the mixer with 10 gal. of water and beat until mixture is smooth. Before adding this mixture to kettle, first add the final amount of water (15 gal.) to the kettle and heat to 200°-212°F; when contents reach boiling, add the second batch of cracker crumb-water mixture.

When the broth has been brought to the boiling point for the fourth time, add tomatoes together with salt and pepper. The hot soup is then drawn off to the reservoir tank of a syrup filling machine such as is used in fruit canneries. The soup should be added hot in the can-filling operation.

Clam juice may be substituted for a portion of the water called for in the ingredients, but as a rule the liquid in Manhattan style chowder is water.

Potatoes are prepared while soup base is cooking. Potatoes are peeled mechanically, but eyes have to be removed by hand. Dice potatoes into 3/8-in. cubes and blanch for 1-2 min (or place in water to cover to prevent discoloration).

Wash clams thoroughly to remove as much sand as possible. In some canneries, they are then steamed sufficiently to open the shells. The siphon is removed and the whole clam is ground. Other canners use raw shucked clams removing the "stomach" or dark body mass and cutting off the siphons before grinding. This is believed to reduce the possibility of darkening.

Cans are usually lined with "C" enamel, seafood formula. Filling the cans with potato dice and clam meat is a hand operation after which sufficient hot broth is added to fill. For No. 1 Picnic cans, fill with 2 oz potato dice, 2 oz clam meat; for No. 3 cans, fill with 7½ oz of potato dice and 7½ oz clam meat. Complete can filling with hot broth and seal immediately.

Process No. 1 cans for 45-50 min at 240°F; No. 3 cans for 85-90 min at 240°F; using 10 lb pressure for either size. Check process times and temperature with can supplier or the National Canners Association.

Water cool the pack immediately after processing.

For New England Chowder

The method used for making New England style chowder follows the general outline just described, except that clam juice, previously heated to remove suspended solids, replaces at least a portion of the water, and no tomatoes are included, the only ingredients being potatoes, pork, onions, clams, juice, cereal "filler," and seasoning. Clams are added whole or only coarsely chopped. Flour is substituted for cracker crumbs. For the exact formula and method of preparing the soup, refer to the preparation of Fish Chowder in Sect. 9. The processing times vary within the range previously given for Manhattan chowder, but tend toward the upper limit. Check processing times and temperature with can supplier or the National Canners Association. This pack is also water-cooled immediately after processing.

Batch Process

In some canneries, chowder is made by the batch process with all ingredients precooked together in an 80-gal. steam-jacketed kettle. Paddles are used to stir ingredients. This method is somewhat cheaper but it is claimed that the mixing is not efficient enough to give an even blend of ingredients in the can.

SOURCE: Fish and Wildlife Service, U.S. Department of the Interior, Washington, D.C.

CANNED CLAM STEW (HOT PACK)

Ingredients	Gal.	Lb	Oz
Fresh whole milk	22		
Frozen soft clams, sliced and defrosted		103	
Butter or shortening		16	
Wheat flour		17	
Cornstarch		4	
Salt		4	6
Dry soluble pepper		1	8
Dry soluble celery salt			14
Monosodium glutamate			12
Water to make 50 gal.			

Procedure

Put milk in a steam-jacketed kettle and heat to 160°F. Add butter and flavorings. In a bakery mixer, make a slurry free of lumps with 5 gal. of water and flour and starch. Agitate sauce with a "Lightning" mixer and add slurry; raise temperature to 200°F and add clams. Discontinue use of "Lightning" mixer. Increase volume to 50 gal. with added water. Stir product gently with a paddle during final cooking; bring temperature back up to 200°F and cook 20 min.

Fill cans while stew is hot, keeping product well mixed while filling so that clams are well distributed in stew.

Suggested Process

211 × 400 cans (10$\frac{1}{2}$ oz net) 1 hr at 240°F

Check process time and temperature with can supplier or the National Canners Association.

SOURCE: Stephan L. Komarik, 4810 Ronda, Coral Gables, Florida.

FROZEN NEW ENGLAND CLAM CHOWDER

Made from Fresh Clams

Ingredients	%	Lb	Oz
Soft clams (diced) or			
quahogs (ground)	31.00	31	5.0
Potatoes, diced	10.50	11	
Water + clam liquor	45.40	46	7.0
Bacon or salt pork, diced	3.80	4	
Onions, chopped	3.80	4	8.00
Salt	0.40		4.0
Pepper	0.04		0.6
Nonfat dry milk	3.17	3	4.0
Flour, pastry type	0.74		12.0
Margarine	0.95	1	
Monosodium glutamate	0.10		1.7
Irish moss extract			
(SeaKem Type 3)	0.10		1.7

Place clam meats on coarse screen and collect liquor; also remove any shell pieces. Separate tough from tender portions and discard tough skin cover of siphon. (These may be tenderized by pressure cooking, if desired.) Open stomachs with small scissors, lay back, and remove black portions (livers) near siphon. Dice soft clams; grind quahogs.

Fry salt pork until crisp; remove solid pieces. Add chopped onions and sauté until almost tender and golden brown. Add margarine, and slowly add, while stirring constantly, the following dry ingredients mixed together: flour, monosodium glutamate, Irish moss extract, salt, and pepper. When dry ingredients are well absorbed in the fat, add dry milk gradually while stirring, adding a small amount of water if necessary. When milk appears to be well blended with fat ingredients, add a portion of clam liquor gradually, stirring until no lumps remain. Then add remainder of clam liquor and potatoes and simmer until potatoes are about half done. Then add clams and continue to simmer until potatoes are just tender (about 10 min). Strain solids out of mixture and homogenize liquid.

Packaging.—This formula gives 70 12-oz packages.

Pack in ratio of 6 oz solids and 6 oz liquid per 12-oz package.

For a Chowder Concentrate.—Use only 65% of the amount of liquid in preparing the chowder and pack 8 oz of solids with 4 oz of liquid in the container and give directions for adding a quantity of whole milk (1$\frac{1}{2}$ cups) when heating product for serving.

If the product is packaged in cartons or composite cartons, both the liquid and the solids should be cooled to 55°F before filling.

Made from Canned Clams

Ingredients	Oz
Salt pork, diced, $\frac{1}{4}$-in. cubes	8
Butter	3$\frac{1}{2}$
Yellow leeks, diced	8
Celery, diced	8
Onions, chopped	16
Salt	1
White pepper	$\frac{1}{2}$
Sachet bag: 1 medium bay leaf,	
$\frac{3}{4}$ tsp thyme, 3 cloves	
Fish stock or water	120
Potatoes, diced	32
Nonfat dry milk	3$\frac{1}{2}$
Instant potatoes	3$\frac{1}{2}$
Clams, chopped plus juice	
(No. 2 can)	20

Procedure.—Sauté salt pork in butter until transparent; add leeks, celery, and onions and sauté 5 min. Then add salt, pepper, sachet bag, and fish stock. Bring to a boil, reduce heat and simmer 15 min. Add potatoes and continue to simmer another 8 min. Bring mixture to a boil and remove sachet bag. Combine dry milk and instant potato; slowly add clams and juice, stirring to blend. Add clam-juice mixture to soup base and heat to 180°F stirring constantly. Cool to room temperature.

Packaging.—The boil-in-bag type of packaging is recommended. Pack 12 oz into each bag, heat seal, and blast freeze.

SOURCE: *The Freezing Preservation of Foods, 4th Edition, Vol. 4* by Tressler *et al.* published by Avi Publishing Co., Westport, Conn.

CANNED MANHATTAN CLAM CHOWDER

Clam chowder for canning is usually prepared from the hard or quahog clam inasmuch as this clam possesses a pronounced clam flavor. If milk is used as an ingredient in the preparation of chowder, it is necessary to add small quantities of a citrate or phosphate to prevent separation.

To make a batch of Manhattan clam chowder

using 2500 quahog clams, the following ingredients will be needed:

	Gal.	Lb	Oz
Bacon		25	
White potatoes		25	
Onions		7	
Tomatoes		25	
Chopped parsley			$^1/_4$
Thyme			$^1/_8$
Sweet marjoram			1
Salt		1	
Ground white pepper			$^1/_2$
Water	15		

Thoroughly wash shucked clams and drain; then chop. Dice potatoes and bacon. Put all ingredients in a steam-jacketed kettle, bring to a boil, and cook for 10 min. Immediately fill into cans and seal. While filling cans it is necessary to stir chowder constantly so as to keep ingredients evenly distributed in cans.

Suggested Process

Process No. 3 cans for 80 min at 250°F; 1 qt cans for 50 min at 250°F. Check process times and temperature with can supplier or the National Canners Association.

For Condensed Canned Chowder

The same amount of ingredients given above are used *except* add only half the amount of water (7$^1/_2$ gal.). Strain out the solids from the cooked batch; fill the desired weight of solid ingredients into cans; add chowder liquid to fill the interstices; close cans, seal, and process.

SOURCE: *Marine Products of Commerce* by D. K. Tressler published by Chemical Catalog Co., New York, N.Y.

FROZEN MANHATTAN CLAM CHOWDER (BATCH PROCESS)

Ingredients	%
Butter	2
Whole milk	67.52
Starch (Freezist M)	3
Potatoes	12.30
Tomato purée	8.20
Clams	4.90
Salt	1.20
Onion powder (Asmus)	0.50
White pepper (Asmus)	0.11
Paprika (Asmus)	0.11
Celery salt	0.017
Parsley (Asmus)	0.033
Thyme (Asmus)	0.08
Garlic powder (Asmus)	0.03

Procedure

Combine all ingredients and heat slowly to 190°F. Hold for 5 min at this temperature; then cool. Package in containers of desired size suitable for freezing; heat seal and freeze.

SOURCE: A. E. Staley Mfg. Co., Decatur, Ill.

FROZEN CLAM PATTIES

Ingredients	Lb	Oz
Cooked clams	250	
Stale white bread (sliced)	150	
Clam broth	100	
Fresh or frozen eggs	35	
Vegetable oil	25	
Nonfat dry milk	10	
Fresh onions	25	
Fresh celery	15	
Monosodium glutamate	2	
Plant protein hydrolyzate	1	
Lemon powder (see below)	1	
Fresh parsley	2	8
Salt	7	8

Lemon Powder Mixture[1]	Lb	Oz	Gm
Citric acid (powder)	1	12	
Cold pressed oil of lemon		4$^1/_4$	
Corn sugar	7	15$^3/_4$	
Tartrazine			2

[1] Mix sugar with Tartrazine and 10 cc of water; add citric acid and oil of lemon. Thoroughly mix ingredients.

Procedure

Chop celery and onions in $^1/_4$-in. pieces, parsley into $^1/_8$-in. pieces. If frozen eggs are used; defrost and then grind through the $^1/_2$-in. plate of the grinder.

Cook clams in their own juice with some added water; cook at 160°F until edges begin to curl. Remove clams from broth and chill in cold water; then dice into $^1/_2$-in. cubes. Also chill clam broth down to 100°F or lower.

Mix together nonfat dry milk, salt, and seasonings. Put chilled broth in a mechanical mixer and add eggs; while mixer is running add milk-seasonings mixture, then oil and bread. Let mixer run approximately 2 min. Then put mixture through the $^1/_2$-in. plate of the grinder. Regrind bread mixture with clams and vegetables; mix thoroughly.

Stuff product tightly into "Easy Peel" fibrous casings 3$^1/_4$–3$^1/_2$ in. in diameter. Cook in hot water at 180°F 1$^1/_2$–2 hr until an internal temperature of 160°F is obtained. Chill in cold water to internal temperature of 100°F. Transfer to chill room at 34°-36°F overnight for thorough chilling.

Slice patties to desired weight and peel. If desired, slices may be breaded or coated with batter and breaded. Pack slices between parchment papers in cartons suitable for freezing. Freeze at −20°F.

SOURCE: Stephan L. Komarik, 4810 Ronda, Coral Gables, Florida.

CRABS

CANNING PACIFIC CRAB MEAT

Some packers prefer to kill crabs by cutting their throats with a knife and allowing them to bleed thoroughly before cooking. However, the majority simply put them live into boiling water. This is done by dissolving 1 lb of bicarbonate of soda per 25 lb of crabs in fresh water brought to a "jumping" boil adding the live crabs. Cook for about 25 min (length of time varies somewhat with size; larger crabs require longer cooking time than smaller ones). At the end of the cooking period, remove the crabs, wash in cool water, and allow to cool.

The back shell is first removed. This is done as the body is washed under a stream of water. Meat is then removed from the crabs. Take care to see that none of it comes in contact with wood surfaces. After meat is removed from shells, wash in cold 1% brine (1 lb salt to 12½ gal. water), drain, and press to remove excess moisture. Parchment-lined cans are used for canning crab meat. (Some cans, in addition, are used that are enameled on the inside but this is not absolutely necessary.) Claw meats are packed at the bottom and top of the can with the center filled with body meat. Crimp tops loosely on cans and exhaust for about 8 min at 212°F.

Seal tops after exhausting and replace in the retort for a cook of 40 min at 15 lb pressure for ½-lb cans. Cool cans before removal from the retort. Check time and temperature of processing with either can supplier or National Canners Association.

SOURCE: *Marine Products of Commerce* by D. K. Tressler published by Chemical Catalog Co., New York, N.Y.

FREEZING BLUE CRAB MEAT

Cooking

Fresh caught crabs are dumped into circular iron baskets for cooking in vertical retorts. Cooking conditions vary considerably because of the type of equipment used, but most plants use steam at 250°F for from 3 to 20 min after temperature and pressure in the cooker are brought up to the desired level. A few plants use boiling water for 15-20 min. Many processors deback the cooked crabs, wash, and refrigerate them overnight before picking the meat, a practice that tends to increase the meat yield.

Meat Removal

The meat is picked by hand. It is sorted into three categories: (1) The "lump" meat which is the large muscle controlling the swimming legs and is the premium product. (2) The "regular" or flake meat which is the remainder of the muscles from the body and is second in value. (3) "Claw meat" which is the lowest in price. About ½ of the meat yield is flake, about ¼ is lump, and ¼ is claw meat.

Most of the blue crab meat is packed in hermetically-sealed 1-lb cans and is sold in the fresh chilled form. To extend the marketing period for the chilled product, a heat pasteurization process was developed and has been used successfully for 1-lb sealed cans which are stored and distributed at 32°F or as near that temperature as practicable.

Blue crab meat does not freeze and store well; therefore, only a relatively small volume of frozen meat is produced. This is produced mostly for institutional use and for later processing into crab specialties. For these purposes, it is frozen in 5-lb cans or plastic bags. A small amount is packaged in 12-oz cartons and frozen for retail sale.

SOURCE: *The Freezing Preservation of Foods, 4th Edition, Vol. 3* by Tressler *et al.* published by Avi Publishing Co., Westport, Conn.

FREEZING SOFT-SHELL CRABS

Soft-shell crabs have been a popular frozen item for many years, a product common only in the blue crab industry. A soft-shell crab is one that has just molted. They are obtained for commercial purposes by holding hard-shell crabs in floats until molting occurs. Within a few hours after molting the crabs are removed from the water and are graded for size. Then they may be held in cool storage for 2–3 days before processing, until sufficient of the crabs have molted to start processing. They are then killed, eviscerated, washed, wrapped individually in parchment, packed 1 or 2 dozen to a carton, and frozen.

SOURCE: *The Freezing Preservation of Foods, 4th Edition, Vol. 3* by Tressler *et al.* published by Avi Publishing Co., Westport, Conn.

FREEZING KING CRAB MEAT

The crab is butchered by grasping the legs and striking the bottom of the shell sharply against a dull bladed knife. This operation separates the carapace and viscera from the legs, claws, and shoulders. Legs, claws, and shoulders are immediately placed on a continuous conveyor which conveys them through boiling water (some processors use fresh water for this, others use sea water). The sections are held in the cooker long enough to cook them thoroughly. On the Wakefield ship, Akutan, the cooked sections are automatically ejected into a stainless steel tube 22 in. in diameter and 42 ft long through which cold sea water is pumped continuously. This cools the sections to approximately 45°F and conveys them to the head of the processing line.

After cooking and cooling, the legs are separated and graded into those from which the meat will be removed and those which will be packed as king crab legs in the shell. From this point on, two separate and distinct procedures are used in packaging and freezing.

When sections are to be packed in the shell, they are degilled, scrubbed, the barnacles are removed, and they are packed in metal pans and placed in a blast freezer. From the blast freezer, the sections are removed and taken to a glazing station where the legs or other sections are dipped in cold fresh water to glaze them. They are then packed in corrugated fiberboard containers and placed in low-temperature storage to await shipment.

The legs from which meat is to be extracted are cut into shorter pieces. These are placed on a flat conveyor belt which carries them to meat extractors or "wringers." These wringers are constructed much like a laundry wringer. They crush the shell and squeeze out the meat which drops on the feeding side of the wringer into a trough which conveys it by water to a packing table. There it is packed into lined metal trays which hold 15 lb of meat. The 15-lb blocks are frozen either in a plate freezer or in an air blast freezer. When frozen, the blocks are given an ice glaze and packed into cases for cold storage prior to shipment. The 15-lb blocks are of 2 shapes: some are 11 × 15 × 3 in., others are 5 × 3 × 33 in.

When the glazed blocks are prepared for retail sale, they are cut with a saw and packaged in 6-, 8-, 12-, or twin 8-oz consumer packages. In addition, some are cut into institutional packs of 1, 2½, or 5 lb. Blocks which are frozen in the 11 × 15 × 3 in. dimension are first cut into three 11 × 5 × 3 in. blocks and then cut again to yield portions 3 × 5 in. by the thickness required to produce 6-, 8-, or 12-oz portions. (Blocks frozen in Alaska are about 10 oz in weight over the 15 lb to make up for losses due to desiccation and the "sawdust" lost when blocks are cut into sizes for retail cartons.) The frozen portions of the blocks are placed in retail cardboard cartons which are then heat-sealed in a waxed overwrap.

A special "fancy" or "fry leg" pack is also produced. This is made up of the meros piece only and is packed in 3½-lb units by dividing the standard 15-lb tray into 4 separate sections and lining each section with a waxed carton.

SOURCE: *The Freezing Preservation of Foods, 4th Edition, Vol. 4* by Tressler *et al.* published by Avi Publishing Co., Westport, Conn.

FREEZING KING CRAB LEGS IN THE SHELL

King crab legs are cooked in the shell, then sorted for freezing. Legs having clean bright-colored shells and a proper meat fill are washed, trimmed, packed into trays or cartons, and blast frozen. The frozen legs are then given an ice glaze and packed into 10- or 15-lb cartons. In later processing, the legs may be split into ready-to-cook portions, reglazed, and packaged for retail sale. Much of the frozen king crab in the shell goes to restaurants or to markets where it is thawed just before use or sale. For special seafood displays it is common to freeze the whole crab, eviscerated, with the carapace in place.

King crab meat frozen in the shell retains more of the flavor of the fresh cooked king crab than does the meat frozen in the block. Storage life of king crab frozen in the shell and well protected from dehydration is 6 months or more at $0°$ to $-10°F$.

SOURCE: *The Freezing Preservation of Foods, 4th Edition, Vol. 3* by Tressler *et al.* published by Avi Publishing Co., Westport, Conn.

FREEZING DUNGENESS CRAB IN THE SHELL

Owing to the market demand for chilled fresh or thawed crab in the shell, these items comprise the larger part of the frozen Dungeness crab production.

For freezing, the crabs are cooked whole and eviscerated. They are prepared both for institutional and retail sale. Both brine freezing and blast freezing are used for freezing the whole cooked crabs. For brine freezing, the crabs are placed in metal trays or baskets and lowered into circulating brine of $88°$ salinometer at $0°-5°F$ for up to 45 min, then are removed and dipped into fresh cold water to remove excess brine and provide a light ice glaze. The frozen whole crabs are packed in flexible film bags or in shallow cartons for storage and distribution.

Frozen Dungeness crab meat stores well only if protected against dehydration and oxidation by packaging in suitably sealed containers and stored at $-10°F$ or lower. Under these conditions it stores well for 6 months.

SOURCE: *The Freezing Preservation of Foods, 4th Edition, Vol. 3* by Tressler *et al.* published by Avi Publishing Co., Westport, Conn.

FREEZING DUNGENESS CRAB MEAT

Cooking

Both whole crabs and butchered crab sections are cooked. The crabs are butchered by use of a fixed iron blade. The carapace is removed and the crab is eviscerated, split into halves, washed, and conveyed to the cooker. The halves or sections are cooked in boiling water for 10–15 min in stainless batch or continuous cookers. If whole (uneviscerated) crabs are cooked, cooking time is longer, about 20–25 min. The cooked crabs, halves, or sections are cooled in water and then dumped onto a stainless steel table for meat removal.

Meat Removal and Prefreezing Treatment

About half of the crab is body meat and half leg meat. Legs and body sections are separated and meat is removed separately. This is a hand operation. They are shaken vigorously against the side of an aluminum or stainless steel pan to dislodge the meat. The leg meat and body meat are washed separately in a strong salt brine (about $97°$ salinometer, i.e., 97% saturated salt) to remove bits of shell from the meat. The meat floats to the top of the tank and is conveyed out of the tank where it is immediately inspected, and then washed with cold water sprays to remove excess salt. Some processors dip the meat into a solution of citric acid or sodium benzoate to improve keeping quality.

Packing and Freezing

Body and leg meats are weighed separately and packed in about equal proportion in No. 10 C-enamel cans holding 5 lb net weight of drained crab meat. Number 2 cans, holding 1 lb, are also packed, but in smaller volume. The cans are sealed under a low vacuum, frozen in a sharp or a blast freezer, and stored at $0°$ to $-10°F$.

For retail sale, the meat is usually thawed and repacked into trays or cartons for display as fresh, chilled crab meat. The thawed meat should be used within a few days.

SOURCE: *The Freezing Preservation of Foods, 4th Edition, Vol. 3* by Tressler *et al.* published by Avi Publishing Co., Westport, Conn.

FROZEN CRAB CAKES

Ingredients	Lb	Oz		Lb	Oz
Nonfat dry milk		5	Hydrogenated vegetable shortening	1	4
Water	4		All-purpose wheat flour	1	
			Whole egg or yolk solids		$1^3/_4$
			Dry mustard		$^3/_4$
			Salt		2

Dehydrated onion powder		$^1/_4$
Cracker crumbs		10
Dehydrated parsley		$^1/_2$
Monosodium glutamate		$^1/_4$
Crab meat		5

Procedure

Place dry milk and water in a stock pot and stir until powder is dissolved. Melt shortening in a steam-jacketed kettle equipped with a variable speed stirrer; slowly blend in flour with continuous agitation. Then stir in all but about 1 pt of the water-milk mixture. Make a thin paste of this reserved milk mixture by mixing with the egg solids and, to avoid curdling, stir in also about 1 pt of the warm sauce mixture stirring until smooth; then add to the main lot of warm sauce in the kettle. Heat sauce to 180°F. Stir in with thorough mixing the remaining ingredients, except the lemon juice, and heat mixture to 160°F before lemon juice is added. Refrigerate product and cool to 60°F or lower. Then form into 2-oz cakes. Coat cakes first in dipping batter, then in breading or cracker crumbs and deep fry at 365°F until golden brown. The fried cakes are cooled, packaged, overwrapped, and frozen on trays placed on racks in air-blast freezer at −10°F.

SOURCE: *The Freezing Preservation of Foods, 4th Edition, Vol. 4* by Tressler *et al.* published by Avi Publishing Co., Westport, Conn.

FROZEN DEVILED CRABS

Ingredients	Lb	Oz
Whole fluid milk	6	13
Nonfat dry milk		6
Waxy maize starch		12.5
Hydrogenated vegetable shortening	2	4
Dry mustard		1
Worcestershire sauce		3
Cayenne pepper		$^1/_{30}$
Dehydrated parsley		1
Salt		3
Chopped green peppers		10
Monosodium glutamate		1
Dehydrated egg yolk		8
Lemon juice		2
Blue crab meat	6	

YIELD: 100 aluminum foil crab "shells" of $3^1/_4$ oz each

Procedure

Put 6 lb of the whole milk in a 6-qt aluminum or stainless steel pan or bowl and, while agitating with a high speed electric mixer, add dry milk; continue agitation until milk is completely dissolved. Melt shortening in a steam-jacketed kettle equipped with a variable speed agitator. Stir in the starch and blend until smooth and temperature is raised to 180°F. Slowly stir milk into the fat mixture and bring temperature back up to 180°F.

Place egg yolk in an 8-qt bowl of Hobart mixer; start the mixer and add remaining whole milk (13 oz) slowly; stir until smooth after each addition of milk. When all the milk has been added, a small portion of the hot milk mixture is blended into the egg yolk mixture; continue blending in hot milk mixture until half of it has been added. Then transfer entire contents of mixer bowl to the hot milk mixture in the steam-jacketed kettle which has been kept at 180°F; add in portions while stirring until both mixtures are homogeneous and bring temperature back up to 180°F. Add remaining ingredients (adding the crab last) while continuing to slowly stir until temperature is brought up to 160°F. Then cool, either by running cool water through the jacket of the kettle or by placing the mixture in shallow pans and floating them first in cold water, then setting them in crushed ice. If preliminary cooling is effected through the jacket of the kettle, final cooling to 50°F can be effected by transferring the deviled crab from the kettle to smaller, shallow pans and packing in crushed ice or placing in refrigeration.

Packaging

Crab "shells" are available formed from aluminum foil for individual servings of frozen deviled crabs. Fill shells with $3^1/_4$ oz of the crab mixture and sprinkle top with bread crumbs which have been mixed with hydrogenated vegetable shortening (5 oz crumbs: 1 oz shortening). The crab mixture may also be filled into pastry shells which have been fried in deep fat for 10 sec at 375°F. If desired, each deviled crab may be packaged in a transparent moisture-proof envelop, heat-sealed, and then cartoned. Or, they may be packed in shallow cartons, one layer to a carton, and overwrapped with heat-sealing moisture-proof wrapping. Blast freeze, and hold in frozen storage until marketed.

SOURCE: *The Freezing Preservation of Foods, 4th Edition, Vol. 4* by Tressler *et al.* published by Avi Publishing Co., Westport, Conn.

FROZEN CRAB CAKES

The product is somewhat similar in composition to that used in deviled crabs. However, it usually is less highly seasoned. The following formula will produce 100 2-oz crab cakes.

Ingredients	Lb	Oz
Water	4	
Instant nonfat dry milk		5
Hydrogenated vegetable shortening	1	4
All-purpose wheat flour	1	
Whole egg or yolk solids		1¾
Dry mustard		¾
Salt		2
Dehydrated onion powder		¼
Crab meat	5	
Dehydrated parsley		½
Cracker crumbs		10
Fresh lemon juice		1¾
Monosodium glutamate		¼

Procedure

The instant dry milk is stirred into a portion of the water in a stock pot. The hydrogenated vegetable shortening is melted in a steam-jacketed kettle, equipped with a variable speed stirrer, and the flour slowly blended in, with continuous agitation. Then a sauce is made by stirring in all but about a pint of the water. The remaining water is used to make a thin paste of the egg yolk. About a pint of the warm sauce mixture is stirred into the yolk solution and stirring is continued until the product is smooth, then it is added to the main lot of warm sauce, and heated to 180°F. The crab meat and remaining ingredients, except for the lemon juice, are stirred in with thorough mixing. The mixture is heated to 160°F then the lemon juice is added. The product is cooled in a refrigerator to 60°F or lower. It is then formed into 2-oz cakes which are dipped first in batter, then in cracker crumbs or breading, and fried in deep fat at 365°F until golden brown. The cakes are cooled, packaged, overwrapped, and frozen on trays placed on racks in an airblast freezer at −10°F.

SOURCE: *The Freezing Preservation of Foods, 4th Edition, Vol. 4* by Tressler *et al.* published by Avi Publishing Co., Westport, Conn.

FROZEN DEVILED CRAB PASTRIES

Ingredients	Lb	Oz
Whole fluid milk	6	13
Nonfat dry milk		6
Waxy maize starch		12½
Hydrogenated vegetable shortening	2	4
Dry mustard		1
Worcestershire sauce		3
Cayenne pepper		1/30
Dehydrated parsley		1
Salt		3
Green peppers, chopped		10
Monosodium glutamate		1
Dehydrated egg yolk solids		8

	Lb	Oz
Lemon juice		2
Blue crab meat, shelled	6	
Pastry tartlette shells, or patty shells: 100		
Bread crumbs moistened with vegetable shortening: ratio 5:1 oz		
YIELD: 100		

Procedure

Place the 6-lb portion of fluid milk in 6-qt bowl of electric mixer; agitate at high speed while slowly adding nonfat dry milk; continue agitating until dry milk is completely dissolved. Melt shortening in a steam-jacketed kettle equipped with a variable speed agitator. Stir in the starch and continue stirring until smooth; then heat to 180°F. While stirring, add milk slowly; and bring the mixture back up to 180°F.

Place egg yolk solids in 8-qt bowl of mixer and slowly mix in the remaining 13-oz portion of fluid milk. To this egg yolk-milk mixture, slowly mix in a small portion of the hot milk-shortening mixture to prevent curdling when the cooler yolk-milk mixture is added to the hot milk-shortening mixture. Combine the two mixtures in the steam-jacketed kettle, slowly adding the cold mixture to the hot mixture while stirring until mixtures are homogeneous and temperature is brought back up to 180°F. Add the remaining ingredients, adding the crab meat last. Continue mixing slowly until temperature reaches 160°F. Then cool.

Partial cooling may be done either by running cold water through the jacket of the kettle or floating pans of the mixture in cold water; with final cooling effected by placing mixture in aluminum pans packed in crushed ice or placing them (covered) in a large refrigerator.

The tartlette pastry shells are baked and cooled. Or, if patty shells are used, they may be either baked or deep fried (375°F, 15–30 sec) and cooled before use. Fill 3¼ oz of crab mixture into each shell. Sprinkle top with moistened bread crumbs.

Place each deviled crab pastry in separate transparent moisture-proof envelops and heat seal. Then pack in shallow cartons, one layer deep. Freeze at −20°F or below. After pastries are frozen, pack in fiberboard shipping containers for storage.

SOURCE: *The Freezing Preservation of Foods, 4th Edition, Vol. 4* by Tressler *et al.* published by Avi Publishing Co., Westport, Conn.

FROZEN CRAB IMPERIAL

Prepare White Sauce

Ingredients	Lb	Oz
Dehydrated egg yolk		2
Hydrogenated vegetable shortening		8½

All-purpose flour		7½
Salt		½
Nonfat dry milk		3½
Water	5	8

Procedure

Melt shortening in a steam-jacketed kettle; add flour while stirring and continue to stir until mixture is smooth. Dissolve dry milk in water and slowly stir into fat-flour mixture. Cook until mixture is thick and smooth, stirring continuously. Cool sauce to 140°F then add a small portion of it to the egg yolk solids, stirring until mixture is smooth. Stir the egg yolk mixture into the main lot of sauce. With slow heating, continue cooking and stirring until cream sauce is smooth and near the boiling point. Blend in salt and cool sauce.

Prepare Crab

Ingredients	Lb	Oz
Chopped green peppers, blanched		14½
Onion powder		½
Paprika		¼
Salt		2
Lemon juice		7
Monosodium glutamate		¾
White sauce (or an emulsified salad dressing may be used)	6	14
Crab meat (lump)	12	14

YIELD: 100 3¼-oz portions

To the white sauce (or salad dressing) add all ingredients except crab meat; mix until uniformly blended; then carefully fold in crab meat with just sufficient mixing to obtain a uniform product.

Package and Freeze

Aluminum foil "crab shells" are used for this product, portioning 3¼ oz to each. Sprinkle tops with cracker crumbs which have been mixed with hydrogenated vegetable shortening (5 oz crumbs: 1 oz shortening). If desired, each crab serving may be packaged in a transparent moisture-proof envelope, heat-sealed, and then cartoned. Or, they may be packed in shallow cartons, one layer to a carton, and over-wrapped with heat-sealing, moisture-proof wrapping. Blast freeze, and hold in frozen storage until marketed.

SOURCE: *The Freezing Preservation of Foods, 4th Edition, Vol. 4,* by Tressler *et al.* published by Avi Publishing Co., Westport, Conn.

CHESAPEAKE BAY CRAB IMPERIAL

The ingredients given below are for six servings of a ready-to-serve product and while this is not a commercial formula, it is included here because of its adaptability as an excellent frozen product. Prepare the crab mixture, portion the mixture into aluminum foil shells for freezing, and package in containers suitable for freezing. Freeze at −20°F.

Ingredients

Back-fin blue crab meat	2 lb
Freeze-stable mayonnaise or salad dressing	½ cup
Chopped pimiento	2 tsp
Salt	1 tsp
Worcestershire sauce	1 tsp
Tabasco sauce	6 drops
Freeze-stable mayonnaise or salad dressing	2 tbsp
Paprika	For garnish

Procedure

Remove any bits of shell or cartilage from crab meat. Combine mayonnaise, pimiento, salt, Worcestershire and Tabasco sauces. Add to crab meat and mix lightly. Portion into aluminum foil freezing shells and top with about 1 tsp of mayonnaise or salad dressing; sprinkle with paprika.

To Use.—Product need not be thawed prior to baking. Bake in a moderate oven (350°F) for 20–30 min until brown.

SOURCE: Fish and Wildlife Service, U.S. Department of the Interior, Washington, D.C.

FROZEN CRAB COCKTAIL BALLS

Ingredients	%
Crab meat, finely chopped	52.60
Cracker meal, rolled fine	13.30
Hydrogenated vegetable shortening	10.00
Blanched parsley, chopped fine	4.30
Whole egg solids	1.60
Salt	1.00
Monosodium glutamate	0.20
Dehydrated onion powder	0.16
Dehydrated garlic powder	0.08
Worcestershire sauce	0.03
Water	16.73

Procedure

Mix all dry ingredients together. Mix Worcestershire sauce with water and stir into dry mixture. When a homogeneous mixture has been obtained, press into small, ⅙-oz balls. First dip balls into batter, then in breading mix, and deep fry at 370°–375°F until golden brown. Drain, cool, package, and freeze.

SOURCE: *The Freezing Preservation of Foods, 4th Edition, Vol. 4* by Tressler *et al.* published by Avi Publishing Co., Westport, Conn.

FROZEN CRAB PATTIES

Ingredients and procedure are identical with that given above in this section on clams for **Frozen Clam Patties** except that cooked and diced crab meat and crab meat broth are substituted for the clam ingredients.

SOURCE: Stephan L. Komarik, 4810 Ronda, Coral Gables, Florida.

FROZEN CRABBURGERS

Ingredients	Lb	Oz
Cooked crab meat	26	
Cooked codfish	24	
Stale white bread (sliced)	29	
Water	21	
Fresh or frozen whole eggs	7	
Vegetable shortening or oil	5	
Nonfat dry milk	2	
Fresh or dehydrated minced onion	5	
Chopped celery	1	6
Chopped parsley		5
Chopped green pepper	1	7
Salt	2	4
Dry soluble pepper	2	
Monosodium glutamate	2	

Procedure

Cook crab meat and codfish approximately 15 min in simmering water (200°F). Transfer to silent cutter and run machine until piece size is reduced to approximately 1/2 in.

Clean vegetables and transfer to silent cutter. Chop to approximately 1/4-in. pieces.

If dehydrated onion is used, rehydrate in water: 1 part minced onion, 7 parts water.

If frozen eggs are used, put container in warm water until frozen block can be removed from container. Then cut into small pieces with a cleaver and grind through the 1 1/2-in. plate of the grinder.

Mix salt, seasonings, and nonfat dry milk. Mix water with eggs (do not whip). Put bread in a mechanical mixer; add water-egg mixture, seafood, and vegetables. Start machine and add evenly the salt-seasoning mixture; then pour melted shortening or oil over the contents and mix until all ingredients are thoroughly distributed (approximately 1-2 min). Transfer mixture to grinder and grind through the 1-in. plate.

Stuff mixture tightly into Easy Peel fibrous casings 3 1/4-3 1/2 in. in diameter. Cook product 1 1/2-2 hr in hot water at 180°F until an internal temperature of 160°F is reached. Chill product in cold water until internal temperature drops to 100°F and transfer to cooler (34°F) for thorough chilling overnight.

Slice crabburgers to desired weight and peel. If desired, slices may be breaded or coated with batter and breaded. Pack slices between parchment papers in cartons suitable for freezing. Freeze at -20°F.

SOURCE: Stephan L. Komarik, 4810 Ronda, Coral Gables, Florida.

OYSTERS

FREEZING OYSTERS

Oysters are unloaded from the dredges onto conveyors that carry the shell stock to a cylindrical washer where the mud is removed by sprays of water. They are then conveyed to shucking benches.

Shucking.—The shuckers stand at a long bench. In front of each is a small anvil-like iron on which he rests the oyster while he breaks a small piece from the edge of the shell with a hammer. A special knife is then inserted between the shells, the adductor muscle is cut free from its attachment to the shell, the halves are separated, and the meat is removed. In many plants the shucker sorts oyster meats by size into 2 or 3 containers. In others, sorting is done mechanically. The table below shows the count per gallon for the various size categories of fresh and frozen Eastern and Pacific oysters. The Olympia oysters are uniformly small averaging about 1600 meats per gallon and are not ordinarily sorted by size.

Washing, Culling, and Blowing.—Shucked oyster meats may be dumped on a washing table and given a preliminary rinse with a hand-held spray while the operator culls out large pieces of shell and torn or discolored oysters. Oyster meats then usually go to a blowing tank where they are violently agitated by compressed air from a perforated pipe in the bottom of the tank. This process serves to remove sand, silt, and shell fragments. It may also, unless controlled carefully, serve to reduce quality as oyster meats will absorb water readily.

Freezing.—The freezing method should conform to accepted commercial practice for the type of package used, such as compression plate for meats packed in waxed cartons and overwrapped, and blast tunnels for meats packed in cans or for those frozen individually. Freezing rates should be as fast as practicable, and storage temperatures should be as low as possible. In no case should temperature exceed 0°F. Although frozen oyster meats may remain in good condition for 9 months or even longer if prepared from freshly harvested and shucked shell stock and stored at –20°F in airtight and moisture-vaporproof containers, it would be unwise for the processor to plan on a shelf-life in excess of 6 months as raw material quality and storage conditions will vary greatly.

CLASSES AND SIZES OF FRESH AND FROZEN OYSTERS

Class	Size (Counts)	Type I—Fresh			Type II—Frozen
		Count per Gal.	Count per Quart		Count per 6 Lb
			Largest[1]	Smallest[2]	
I—Eastern or Gulf (*Crassostrea virginica*)	Extra large	160[3]	—	44	Not more than 113
	Large (extra selects)	161–210	36	58	114–148
	Medium (selects)	211–300	46	83	149–212
	Small (standards)	301–500	68	138	213–352
	Very small	Over 500	112	—	353 and over
II—Pacific (*Crassostrea gigas*)[3]	Large	Not more than 64	—	—	Not more than 45
	Medium	65–96	—	—	46–68
	Small	97–144	—	—	69–101
	Extra small	More than 144	—	—	102 and over

SOURCE: Federal specification—Oysters, Fresh (Chilled) and Frozen: Shucked.
[1] Least count.
[2] Maximum count.
[3] Largest oyster shall be not more than twice the weight of the smallest oyster within each size category.

SOURCE: *The Freezing Preservation of Foods*, 4th Edition, Vol. 3 by Tressler *et al.* published by Avi Publishing Co., Westport, Conn.

CANNING OYSTERS

At most of the large canneries, oysters are unloaded directly into latticed iron cars 10–12 ft long. These cars are pushed—sometimes 3 at a time—into a large steaming room or "steamer" and the oysters are steamed 3–10 min or until killed. The cars are then pushed on through the "steamer" into the opening room. Steaming opens the shells, so it is comparatively easy work to remove the meats with the usual oyster knife. This is done directly into perforated buckets from the cars in which they were steamed. The meats are then washed and packed by weight into cans varying in size from 3 to 10 oz. By an endless belt, the filled cans are conveyed to capping machines. After being capped, the cans are conveyed in large iron baskets to the retort where they are steamed at a high temperature until they are sterile. (Consult can supplier or the National Canners Association for processing time and temperature.) They are then cooled in running water. The final step is labeling and packing in boxes when they are ready for shipment.

SOURCE: *Marine Products of Commerce* by D. K. Tressler published by Chemical Catalog Co., New York, N.Y.

FROZEN OYSTER STEW

Ingredients	%	Lb	Oz
Fresh oyster meats, drained	30.00	28	2
Water, including oyster liquor	58.35	55	
Nonfat dry milk	6.90	6	9.2
Butter or margarine	4.20	4	
Salt	0.30		5
Irish moss extract (SeaKem Type 3)	0.10		1.5
Monosodium glutamate	0.10		1.5
Paprika	0.03		0.5
White pepper	0.02		0.3

Prepare Base

Melt margarine (or butter) in steam-jacketed kettle. Mix together dry milk and other dry ingredients and, while stirring constantly, add to melted fat in kettle and blend until mixture is homogeneous, adding water as needed. Then add remainder of water, increase heat and continue stirring until base comes to a simmer. Draw off and keep hot. To avoid fat separation and surface scum, homogenize base at this point.

Prepare Oysters

Place shucked oysters on coarse screen and collect liquor. Also remove any pieces of shell. Heat oysters in their own liquor for about 5 min until the edges begin to curl.

Package

Strain hot oyster liquor into hot milk base. Pack 8–12 oysters (depending upon size) volumetrically into containers and cover with hot milk base. If packaged in cartons or composite cartons, both oysters and milk base should be cooled to about 55°F before filling. If an oyster stew concentrate is desired, use half as much water in the milk base and pack double the amount of oysters per package (3–3.5 oz) and only 9 oz of milk base and give label instructions to add a quantity (1½ cups) of whole milk when heating before serving.

It is important to have the same quantity of oysters in each package or can of stew. At Campbell Soup Company this is accomplished by automatic multispout rotating machines that operate on a volumetric principle. From an open front, stainless steel bin the oysters drop into pockets of the rotating multispout dispenser and drop from each pocket into a can on a conveyor below. Then the can is conveyed to the liquid filler. With this system of filling only the seasoned milk is heated prior to filling; the contact of the hot milk on the oysters cooks them sufficiently.

SOURCE: *The Freezing Preservation of Foods, 4th Edition, Vol. 4* by Tressler *et al.* published by Avi Publishing Co., Westport, Conn.

CHESAPEAKE BAY OYSTER STEW

The ingredients given below are for six servings of a ready-to-serve product and while this is not a commercial formula, it is included here because of its adaptability as an excellent frozen product. Cool the product after preparation, then package in containers suitable for freezing and freeze at −20°F.

Ingredients

Fresh-shucked oysters	12 oz (1 can)
Fresh whole milk	1 qt
Butter or margarine	¼ cup
Salt	1½ tsp
Pepper	Dash
Paprika	For garnish

Procedure

Cook oysters in oyster liquor for 3 min or until the edges begin to curl. Add remaining ingredients (except paprika for garnish). Heat stew to serving temperature and garnish with paprika.

SOURCE: Fish and Wildlife Service, U.S. Department of the Interior, Washington, D.C.

FROZEN OYSTER PATTIES

Ingredients and procedure are identical with that given above in this section on clams for **Frozen Clam Patties** except that cooked and diced oysters and oyster broth are substituted for the clam ingredients.

SOURCE: Stephan L. Komarik, 4810 Ronda, Coral Gables, Florida.

VIRGINIA PICKLED OYSTERS

Formula No. 1

Ingredients	Qt	Pt	Tbsp
Shucked oysters	4		
Oyster liquor		3	
Distilled vinegar		1	
White wine, dry		1	
Onion, ground			2
Garlic cloves, crushed			2
Bay leaves, crushed			2
Parsley stems, chopped			1
Fennel, crushed			1
Allspice, crushed			1
Black peppers, crushed			1
Cloves, crushed			1
Cinnamon stick, crushed			1
Mace, crushed			¼
Thyme, crushed			¼

Remove oysters from liquor. Strain liquor and add sufficient salted water to make 3 pt. Simmer liquor gently over low heat. When it is near the boiling point, add oysters (a few at a time); cook until fringe curls, remove, and set aside to cool. Make a sauce of the cooking liquor, vinegar, wine, and spice and flavoring ingredients; simmer for 30–45 min; cool and strain. Pack oysters in glass jars with a bay leaf, slice of lemon, and a few fresh spices in each jar; fill jars with strained sauce; seal immediately. Store in cool, dark place for 10–14 days. They are then ready for use.

Formula No. 2

Ingredients	Qt	Oz
Shucked oysters	4	
Oyster liquor	2	
Vinegar	1	
Cloves		0.5
Allspice, whole		0.5
Black pepper, whole		0.5
Mace		(1 blade)

Blanch oysters in their own liquor until fringe curls. Remove oysters, cool. Bring the oyster liquor to the boiling point, then set aside to cool. Cook together vinegar and spices over low heat for 5 min. Strain vinegar to remove spices. Combine the oyster liquor and spiced vinegar; cool. Pack the oysters in glass jars with a bay leaf and thin slice of lemon in each jar. Fill containers with the cool sauce; seal immediately. Store under refrigeration.

SOURCE: U.S. Bureau of Commercial Fisheries, Washington, D.C.

LOBSTERS

FREEZING WHOLE RAW LOBSTERS

If raw, whole lobsters are frozen and later cooked, there is difficulty in the meat sticking to the shell of the cooked lobster. This can be overcome if the whole lobsters are immersed in boiling water for a short period and then cooled before freezing. The heating period in the boiling water should only be of sufficient duration to cook the meat next to the shell but not the meat below the surface. Immersion in boiling water for $1\frac{1}{2}$ min is sufficient for a 1-lb lobster.

SOURCE: *The Freezing Preservation of Foods, 4th Edition, Vol. 3* by Tressler *et al.* published by Avi Publishing Co., Westport, Conn.

FREEZING SPINY LOBSTERS

Preparation for freezing spiny lobsters consists of breaking the tail from the body and removing the intestine. The tail is about $\frac{1}{3}$ of the weight of the lobster and is about $\frac{2}{3}$ meat. The tails are thoroughly washed and sorted for freezing into 4 sizes, from 6 to 16 oz each.

The raw tails may be frozen individually if intended for retail sale; or they may be frozen in blocks protected with an ice glaze and then packed in waxed cartons if intended for institutional sale.

Frozen lobster tails store well if they are protected from dehydration and are stored at $-10°$F or lower.

SOURCE: *The Freezing Preservation of Foods, 4th Edition, Vol. 3* by Tressler *et al.* published by Avi Publishing Co., Westport, Conn.

CANNING LOBSTER

The first step in canning lobster is boiling. Live lobsters are usually placed in an iron framework basket and lowered by means of a small derrick into rapidly boiling water. These are usually rectangular wooden tanks lined with zinc and equipped with a cover; they are heated by steam which is passed into the water through perforated pipes in the bottom of the tank. About 3% of salt is usually added to the water used to boil the lobsters. They are boiled for 20–30 min and then cooled in a cold salt solution. When they are cool enough to handle, claws and tails are broken off, the body shell is opened and stomach, liver and corral removed and the body is taken out of the shell. The claws are cracked and the meat is removed whole, if possible. The "arms" are split lengthwise and the meat removed with a fork. Tails are split and the intestine is pulled out.

Lobster meat is usually packed in No. 1 cans lined with parchment paper to prevent the meat from coming in direct contact with the tin which would cause discoloration of the meat. In filling the cans, tails are usually placed in the bottom with the arm meat and claws on top. Salt is added, either dry or as a brine. Occasionally, the lobster is flavored with pepper, bay leaves, and cloves.

Can tops are crimped on and the cans are exhausted in a steam box for about 10 min, after which they are vented and sealed. They are then processed in a retort for 30 min at a temperature of 250°F after which they are cooled in cold water. Cans are then ready for cleaning, labeling, cartoning, and storage until they are marketed. Processing time and temperature should be checked with can supplier or with the National Canners Association.

SOURCE: *Marine Products of Commerce* by D. K. Tressler published by Chemical Catalog Co., New York, N.Y.

FROZEN LOBSTER CHOWDER

Ingredients	Lb	Oz
Lobster meat, diced	25	
Salt pork, diced	6	4.0
Celery, diced	1	8.0
Potatoes, diced	25	
Carrots, diced	6	
Onions, diced	12	8.0
Parsley, chopped		2.0
Chicken stock	100	
Tomatoes	31	4.0
Rice, cooked	4	
Poultry seasoning		0.2
Waxy maize or waxy rice flour	1	8.0
Milk	50	
Butter, softened	1	

YIELD: Approximately 264 lb of finished product

Procedure

Fry out salt pork in steam-jacketed kettle. Add diced vegetables and sauté lightly. Add chicken stock and poultry seasoning; simmer until vegetables are tender. Add lobster meat; simmer 15 min. Add tomatoes and cooked rice. Using mixer, blend starch with milk and add to chowder mixture stirring constantly. Finally, beat in softened butter.

May be packaged in family- or institutional-sized cartons. Heat-seal and quick freeze.

To serve: Warm to serving temperature without dilution.

SOURCE: *The Freezing Preservation of Foods*, 4th Edition, *Vol. 4* by Tressler *et al.* published by Avi Publishing Co., Westport, Conn.

FROZEN LOBSTER NEWBURG

Ingredients	Lb	Oz
Cooked lobster meat	15	
Butter	2	8
Waxy maize or waxy rice starch		6
Egg yolk solids	1	2
Nonfat dry milk	2	
Salt		3
Monosodium glutamate		1.5
Paprika		1.5
Red pepper, ground		1.5
Nutmeg, ground		1
Water	16	
Sherry	1	8

Procedure

Dice the boiled lobster meat and sauté in melted butter for 3–5 min in a steam-jacketed kettle. Make a cream sauce using the water, starch, dry milk, and egg yolk solids. With slow stirring and heating, add cream sauce to the sautéed lobster meat. Slowly bring mixture to boiling and simmer for 3 min. Cool to about 100°F. Then add the sherry.

Package in suitable size freezing containers and blast freeze.

SOURCE: *The Freezing Preservation of Foods*, 4th Edition, *Vol. 4* by Tressler *et al.* published by Avi Publishing Co., Westport, Conn.

FROZEN LOBSTER BISQUE (BATCH PROCESS)

Ingredients	%
Starch (Freezist)	3.00
Rendered chicken fat	2.00
Whole milk	68.80
Ground fresh lobster meat	25.00
Salt	1.00
Black pepper (Asmus)	0.10
Powdered onion (Asmus)	0.10
(Other seasoning to suit)	

Procedure

Combine ingredients. Heat slowly to 190°F and hold for 5 min at this temperature. Cool and package.

SOURCE: A. E. Staley Mfg. Co., Decatur, Ill.

MISCELLANEOUS MARINE PRODUCTS

FREEZING SEA SCALLOPS

Scallops cannot close their shells tightly and therefore die if kept out of water. All sea scallops are shucked aboard the vessel. Bay scallops and most calico scallops, however, are landed in the shell and shucked at shore plants.

Shucking and Washing

Only the adductor muscle, or eye, of the scallop is saved; the viscera and shells are discarded. A special knife is used to separate the shells and cut the meat free. Seemingly, a steady stream of shells arc overboard from the hands of an experienced shucker. As the pail in front of each shucker is filled with meats, it is dumped into a washing tank where the meats are washed with seawater.

Bagging and Icing

At least once every 6-hr watch, and sometimes more often, the scallops are removed from the wash tank and put in cotton bags that hold approximately 35 lb of meats. The bags are put down in the hold and iced; particular care is taken to see that bags are separated from each other by a layer of ice to speed up cooling and thus retard spoilage.

Freezing and Storing

As the bags of scallop meats are unloaded from the vessel, they may go directly to the processing line, or they may be iced in barrels if they are to be held overnight or longer or if they are to be shipped to another point for processing.

In the processing line, the meats are dumped into a wash tank, then roused briefly, either mechanically or by hand, before being conveyed to the cutting-packing table. Here the large meats are cut into bite-sized pieces and then (1) packed in 1-lb waxed cartons, overwrapped with waxed paper, and frozen in plate freezers; (2) packed in plastic pouches holding 8–16 oz and frozen in plate or blast freezers; or (3) individually frozen in plate or (preferably) blast freezers, glazed, and packed in pouches or window-type cartons.

SOURCE: *The Freezing Preservation of Foods, 4th Edition, Vol. 3* by Tressler *et al.* published by Avi Publishing Co., Westport, Conn.

FROZEN SEAFOOD CROQUETTES

Ingredients	Lb	Oz	Gm
Cooked shellfish meat or fish fillets	230		
Fish or shellfish broth	190		
Olive or vegetable oil	2		
Precooked wheat flour	35		
Salt	7		
Monosodium glutamate	2		
Plant protein hydrolyzate	1		
Lemon powder (see below)		10	
Onion powder		12	
Garlic powder		$^1/_4$	
Dry soluble pepper		2	
Ground celery seeds		$^1/_2$	

Lemon Powder Mix[1]	Lb	Oz	Gm
Citric acid (powder)	1	12	
Cold pressed oil of lemon		$4^1/_2$	
Corn sugar	7	$15^3/_4$	
Tartrazine			2

[1] Mix sugar with tartrazine and 10 cc of water; add citric acid and oil of lemon. Thoroughly mix ingredients.

Procedure

Have both the seafood and broth well chilled at start of procedure.

Grind shellfish meats or fish fillets through the $^1/_4$-in. plate of the grinder (or this may be done in a chopper and chopped to the same size). Put well-chilled broth in a mechanical mixer; add seasonings and flavorings previously mixed with salt; then add oil and slowly add the flour. Let machine run until the paste is smooth and without lumps. Reduce mixer speed to slow and add ground or chopped seafood. Run mixer until all ingredients are uniformly distributed. Transfer mixture to cooler and chill to 34°–36°F for easier forming into croquettes. Then form product in a forming machine into desired size and shape. Coat with breading mix or finely-crushed potato chips. Package in cartons suitable for freezing and freeze at −20°F.

To Serve

This product need not be defrosted prior to cooking. Immerse in deep fat at 350°F and fry until brown with an internal temperature of 180°F. Drain and serve with cream or mushroom sauce.

SOURCE: Stephan L. Komarik, 4810 Ronda, Coral Gables, Florida.

CRAYFISH BISQUE

This specialty product is canned commercially in Louisianna and Mississippi and is sold by grocers dealing principally in fancy foods. The formula below is an adaptation of the kitchen procedure. Each packer uses a secret formula, usually based on a family recipe. But the following is typical.

Ingredients

Fresh-water crayfish	10 lb
Onions	6 large
Butter	6 oz
Olive oil	$1/2$ cup
Garlic cloves	2
Minced parsley	1 tsp
Black pepper	$1/16$ oz
Dried bread	6 slices
Flour	4 oz
Canned tomatoes	1 No. 1 can
Canned chicken consommé	1 No. 2 can
Water	3 qt
Bay leaves	2
Cloves	4
Cayenne and thyme	a dash of each

Prepare the Crayfish

Purge the crayfish in a $30°$ salinometer brine for 15 min. Then wash thoroughly and clean the shells with a brush. Boil the crayfish in water until they are red, or about 5 min. Remove and clean the heads; peel the tails and set aside the meat; crack claws with a hammer. Then put heads, claws, and shells back into the water to simmer. Strain and reserve cooking liquid.

Prepare a Dressing

Mince onions fine and cook in 2 oz of the butter until soft but not yellow. Soak bread in water and then squeeze out the water. Mix bread thoroughly with onions and cook over low heat for 10 min. Chop fine the meat from the tails and add to the bread-onion mixture along with black pepper, garlic minced fine, and chopped parsley. Stir mixture together well and cook for about 10 min; salt to taste.

Prepare the Bisque

Blend remainder of the butter with flour until the mass is smooth and cook over low heat until the mixture is browned. Then gradually add tomatoes, the strained cooking liquid, consommé, bay leaves, cloves, cayenne, and thyme. Simmer the bisque slowly for about 20 min.

While the bisque is simmering, fill about $3/4$ of the head shells with the dressing and fry them in olive oil for 3–5 min.

Fill and Process

About 12 of the stuffed head shells are filled into each No. 1 picnic can (211 × 400), allowing about 4 oz by weight. The cans are then filled with hot bisque and sealed immediately.

Accurate processing data are not available, but it is understood that a process of approximately 45 min at $240°F$ (10 lb pressure) is used and that the pack is water cooled. The usual declared weight is $10^1/2$ oz.

Process time and temperature should be checked with the can supplier or the National Canners Association.

SOURCE: Fish and Wildlife Service, U.S. Department of the Interior, Washington, D.C.

CANNING MUSSELS

Canned mussels possess an attractive appearance and pleasing taste. They do not shrivel when canned as do oysters, but remain tender and retain their full flavor.

As soon as the collecting boats deliver the fresh mussels, they are picked over rapidly by hand to eliminate any dead or unhealthy ones and to discard the coarse adhering debris. They then go into a cleaning apparatus for vigorous scrubbing and are rinsed off with clean, fresh water. They are then placed in a steam chest and subjected to live steam for 5–10 min or until the shells begin to open. They are removed from the chest and transferred to shallow pans to cool. The natural liquor which has collected in the chest is reserved in a separate container for use later. As soon as the mussels are cool enough to handle they are shucked and the "horny beard" removed. The liquor that is collected from shucking is also reserved and added to that from steaming the mussels. The liquor is filtered through a fine mesh cloth. The mussel meats are packed in glass containers. The filtered liquor, to which 2 oz of salt is added per gallon of liquor, is brought to a boil and the containers are filled and sealed. To ensure complete sterilization, the sealed containers are placed in an autoclave and subjected to 5 lb pressure for 15 min, after which they are allowed to cool down slowly. When container temperature has fallen to about $100°F$, they are removed and allowed to stand at room temperature until cleaned, labeled, and cartoned for storage and/or marketing.

Processing time and temperature should be checked with the can supplier or with the National Canners Association.

SOURCE: *Marine Products of Commerce* by D. K. Tressler published by Chemical Catalog Co., New York, N.Y.

PICKLING MUSSELS

Pickling is the most common way of preserving mussels. Wash the mussels in their shells, then steam until shells open. Remove meats from shells and pull off beards. Place mussel meats in bowl and cover with spiced vinegar. Spiced vinegar can be a mixture of vinegar, onions, black pepper, cloves, salt, allspice, olive oil, garlic, etc. Refrigerate. When prepared in this way, the pickled mussels will keep for 1–2 weeks.

SOURCE: *Marine Products of Commerce* by D. K. Tressler published by Chemical Catalog Co., New York, N.Y.

PICKLED MUSSELS

This formula may also be used to pickle clams or oysters.

Scrub the shells well. Steam just enough to open shells. Save the cooking liquor. Remove the meats from shells, cutting out the byssus or beard. Cool meats and liquor separately. Pack meats in sterilized glass jars adding a bay leaf, a few whole cloves, and a thin slice of lemon to each jar. Strain the liquor and to each quart of liquor add the following ingredients:

Distilled vinegar (white wine or wine vinegar may be used if preferred)	$1/2$ pt
Allspice	$1/2$ tbsp
Cloves	$1/2$ tbsp
Red pepper	$1/2$ tbsp
Cracked whole mace	$1/4$ tsp

Simmer ingredients in liquor for 45 min; cool; pour into jars containing meats and spices; seal. Store in a cool, dark place. (Pickled mussels and oysters turn dark if exposed to the light.) The product will be ready for use in about two weeks.

SOURCE: U.S. Bureau of Commercial Fisheries, Washington, D.C.

CANNED PICKLED MUSSELS

After washing, steaming and removing the mussels from the shell, the beards are pulled off. The liquor formed during the steaming process is mixed with spiced vinegar. For each quart of natural liquor the following ingredients are added: 1 pt vinegar, $1/2$ oz cinnamon, $1/4$ oz cloves, $1/4$ oz salt, and 1 small red pepper. This liquor-vinegar mixture is simmered for 15 min and is then poured over the meats and left to stand for 24 hr. The meats are then removed from the spiced liquor and are packed in glass containers. The liquor is filtered, heated to boiling, and poured over the meats in the containers to fill. The containers are sealed and heated in an autoclave with 5 lb pressure for 15 min. Processing time and temperature

should be checked with the container supplier or with the National Canners Association.

SOURCE: *Marine Products of Commerce* by D. K. Tressler published by Chemical Catalog Co., New York, N.Y.

PREPARING ABALONE STEAKS

Abalones are taken in considerable quantities in California and Mexican waters. The large central muscle, which is the foot of the mollusk, is cut from the visceral mass and then cut into slices which are used as steaks or minced for chowder. When used as steaks, the slices are pounded to obtain a more tender texture.

SOURCE: *Industrial Fishery Technology* by Stansby published by Reinhold Publishing Corp., New York, N.Y.

FROZEN BATTER-DIPPED ABALONE PATTIES

Pieces of abalone trimmings are used for these patties. The trimmings are first minced in a mechanical meat grinder. Then the ground meat is forced under pressure into a metal tube 24 in. long and 3 in. in diameter. The "cores" made in this manner are stacked in a freezer. After freezing, the meat is released in a solid frozen "loaf" by running water over the core. The frozen core is then sliced into $1/4$-in. rounds. These thin patties are then dipped into a batter and then into fine cracker crumbs. They are usually packed 4 to a Cellophane bag and then put into cartons for freezing. They should be quick frozen at $0°F$ or below. For storage or shipment, 12 or 24 of the cartons are packed in each shipping container.

SOURCE: *The Freezing Preservation of Foods*, 4th Edition, Vol. 4 by Tressler et al. published by Avi Publishing Co., Westport, Conn.

FRESH-GRAIN RUSSIAN CAVIAR

Fresh-grain caviar is prepared in Russia from the full roe of the female sturgeon. After killing, the fish is placed on a coarse mesh screen spread across a wooden tub. The roe is removed by splitting the belly of the sturgeon with a sharp knife. The roe is then gently rubbed through the screen with the palm of the hand. This separates the eggs from the binding tissue and they drop into the tub below. After a portion of the eggs have been collected in the tub, they are transferred to a bucket and the process is repeated. Considerable care must be taken in rubbing the eggs through the screen since bruising them results in very poor caviar.

When all of the eggs have been collected, they are put into a tub and dry salt is added in the proportion of 1 lb to 9 lb of roe. (In early spring or late fall, the proportion of salt is changed to 1 part salt to 36 parts roe.) The salt is mixed with the roe thoroughly and gently with a wooden paddle for 5-8 min. The eggs are then placed on a fine mesh screen to drain.

After the pickle or brine is drained, the caviar is packed in tin, glass, or porcelain containers equipped with tight-fitting covers. It is then ready to eat or store under refrigeration at about 41°-46.5°F. When removed from refrigeration, it must be eaten immediately as it will not keep. Caviar cannot be pasteurized or processed without change in flavor.

SOURCE: *Marine Products of Commerce*, *2nd Edition* by Tressler and Lemon published by Reinhold Publishing Corp., New York, N.Y.

PICKLED GRAINY CAVIAR

This type of caviar, prepared for export from the U.S.S.R., is the pickled grainy variety. The eggs are first put through a screen, the same as for fresh caviar, and a saturated salt brine pickle is poured over the roe in the tub. The mixture is stirred until the individual eggs make a slight "bumping" noise. (An experienced operator can judge when the caviar is finished by squeezing individual eggs between his thumb and forefinger.) The eggs are then drained on a screen and are ready for packing in containers similar to those used for fresh caviar.

Salt imparts a sharper taste and a graininess to the pickled grainy caviar and enables it to be stored at a slightly higher temperature than fresh caviar.

Another method is similar, except that the eggs are pickled longer. Usually, they are pickled so hard that they cannot be crushed with the fingers. The eggs are drained, put into cotton bags, and placed in a press. Excess liquid is squeezed out of the caviar and it becomes a cake which may be sliced. Caviar in this form is considered a delicacy. The cakes are wrapped in oiled paper to prevent drying and stored in a cool room at a temperature of about 46.5°F.

SOURCE: *Marine Products of Commerce*, *2nd Edition* by Tressler and Lemon published by Reinhold Publishing Corp., New York, N.Y.

PASTEURIZED CAVIAR

Caviar, in the strictest sense of the word, is the prepared roe of various species of sturgeon. Recently, however, roe of various other species of fish has been used for making caviar since the supply of sturgeon roe has diminished to the point where it is entirely inadequate to meet the demand. Other species of fish whose roe are sometimes used for making caviar include spoonbill cat or paddlefish, whitefish, salmon, lake herring, carp, and cod.

Preparation of the Roe.—Immediately after its removal from the fish, sturgeon roe is placed on a 4-mesh sieve over a large mixing tub. The roe is rubbed back and forth on the sieve until the eggs pass through, leaving behind membranes and connective tissue. About 1 lb of Luneburg salt (or ½ lb American dairy salt) is sifted over each 12 lb of eggs. Luneburg salt is a German salt that has a flavor which is particularly complementary to caviar. Immediately after the addition of the salt, the mass is thoroughly mixed. At first the mass is sticky, but enough water is soon extracted from the sturgeon eggs to dissolve the salt and form a brine. Mixing is continued for 5-8 min, after which the mixture is allowed to stand 10 min longer. The eggs are then poured into sieves, having a capacity for 8-10 lb of caviar, and are allowed to drain for about 1 hr. The eggs are poured into kegs and shipped to a canning factory where they are placed in cans or jars, sealed, and pasteurized.

Pasteurization.—Pasteurization is effected by immersion of the cans or jars of caviar in a hot-water bath at 155°-160°F for 30, 45, and 60 min for 1-, 2-, and 4-oz containers, respectively. This treatment makes it possible to store caviar at temperatures as high as 60°F for several months without off-flavors or decomposition resulting.

SOURCE: *Marine Products of Commerce*, *2nd Edition* by Tressler and Lemon published by Reinhold Publishing Corp., New York, N.Y.

DRIED MULLET ROES

Mullet roes are dried along the southeastern coast of the United States from North Carolina to Florida.

The unbroken roe bags containing the mullet roe are placed in tubs where they are either sprinkled with salt or soaked with brine. About 5 qt of salt are added to each 100 lb of eggs. Too much salt will cause the egg sacks to break. After the roe sacks have remained in the salt or brine for 10-12 hr, they are drained and spread on boards in the sun to dry. They are taken in each night to prevent their becoming wet by dew. During fair weather the drying process requires about a week. The finished product varies in color from a yellowish brown to a dark red.

When the drying process is completed, the roe may be dipped in a mixture of melted beeswax and paraffin and held for a considerable period of time at room temperature. It can be kept for much longer periods if held under refrigerations at 40°-50°F. The mixture of 50% beeswax and 50%

paraffin prevents further loss of moisture in the preserved roe.

SOURCE: *Marine Products of Commerce, 2nd Edition* by Tressler and Lemon published by Reinhold Publishing Corp., New York, N.Y.

FREEZING SEA URCHIN ROE

The sea urchins are brought to the processing plant where workers crack the shells with a knife and mallet. The internal parts, including the five gonadal sections, are then removed with a spatula. The roe and other internal parts are then placed on a wire mesh screen and quickly rinsed in salt water to remove most of the extraneous material. The final cleaning process, that of removing the intestinal mesentaries attached to the roe, is done with tweezers. A minimum of salt water is used to rinse the roe. The cleaned roe is drained, then packed in compartmentalized plastic trays, and frozen. Because color is an important factor in the grading of roe, only those of similar color are packed in a tray. A bright yellow color is preferred, but roe with an orange color is also acceptable. Brown roe is discarded or used in secondary products to a buyer.

SOURCE: National Marine Fisheries Service, Washington, D.C.

FREEZING TURTLE MEAT

A 10-lb snapper can be made ready for freezing (or cooking) in 5–10 min; and an 8-lb snapper will provide enough stew meat to serve 50. The flesh of turtles may be broiled and roasted as well as stewed.

The first step in dressing a turtle is to remove the head. A snapper can be teased into grasping a stick in order to sever the head; other species may be forced to protrude their necks by applying foot pressure to the back or upper part of the back. When the head is well stretched forward, the neck can be severed from the body. The turtle is then turned on its back and a sharp knife is run around the junction of shell and skin. This makes it possible to pull back the skin from the legs and disjoint the legs. The lower shell (plastron) is removed by cutting the bridges which connect the top and bottom shells. In the snapper or soft shell turtles, these bridges are soft cartilage and may be cut with a sharp knife. A hatchet or saw is useful when skinning a terrapin. A sharp knife is inserted under the lower shell and lifted up to remove it. The entrails may now be removed easily and the four quarters of edible meat may be taken from the upper shell (carapace). It is worth the effort to remove the tenderloin also; to do this, cut the ribs in the carapace with a hatchet.

Turtle meat is packaged and frozen in the same manner as beef. Snapping turtle meat is commercially frozen in 12-oz retail, and $2\frac{1}{2}$- and 10-lb bulk packages for institutional trade.

Green sea turtle meat may also be frozen. They are large enough to yield many "steaks" and much other meat for stews.

SOURCE: *The Freezing Preservation of Foods, 3rd Edition, Vol. 1* by Tressler and Evers published by Avi Publishing Co., Westport, Conn.

CANNED TERRAPIN STEW

The salt-water or diamond-back terrapin (*Malaclemmys palustris*) is the most highly prized of the edible turtles in the United States.

Diamond-back terrapin is canned in Maryland and at one time small amounts were packed in Georgia. Some terrapin is still canned in Louisiana, utilizing the fresh-water species. Though packed commercially, canned terrapin is not an important product. However, the following formula for Canned Terrapin Stew is a gourmet item.

Ingredients

Terrapin	24
Butter	10 lb
Hard boiled egg yolks	6 doz
Sherry wine	12 pt

Wash the terrapin and plunge them live into salted boiling water; cook until toenails and outer skin come off readily when they are removed. Then put them in fresh salted boiling water and cook until the legs are quite tender. Reserve this liquor in which the terrapin were cooked. Clean the cooked terrapin the same as snappers except that the small intestines and liver are saved and cut into very small pieces. Dice the meat ($\frac{1}{4}$-in. cubes). Then put the meat, intestines and liver, and cooking liquor in a kettle together with the butter. Bring the mixture just to a boil. Mash and cream the egg yolks with the sherry and add to the kettle contents. The product is ready for filling into cans.

Suggested Process

No. 1 cans are processed for 50 min at 250°F under 15 lb pressure. Check process time and temperature with can supplier or the National Canners Association.

SOURCE: Fish and Wildlife Service, U.S. Department of the Interior, Washington, D.C.

CANNED SNAPPING TURTLE STEW

"Snapper Stew" is canned in small quantities. No standard formula is used, but that given below is typical. It is a formula used in Louisiana for Ragout de Tortue a la Bourgeoise.

Ingredients	Pt	Lb	Oz
Snapper meat		20	
Minced onions		1	
Flour			$1/2$
Lard or olive oil			$1/2$
Bay leaves			$1/8$
Water	5		
Madeira wine	$1/2$		
Minced garlic			$1/8$
Thyme			$1/8$
Salt to taste			

Procedure

Dice meat into cubes about 1-in. square. Cook onions with the lard or olive oil and garlic until onions are yellow. Then add flour slowly while stirring. Add the meat and braise lightly; then add water slowly while stirring. When the stew approaches the boiling point, add wine and seasonings and mix well. Keep the mixture hot and stir well while filling into cans. Fill into No. 1 picnics and seal immediately without exhaust or vacuum seal.

Suggested Process

Process No. 1 picnic cans for 45–50 min at 240°F under 10 lb pressure. Check process time and temperature with can supplier or the National Canners Association.

Water-cool pack in tanks immediately after processing.

SOURCE: Fish and Wildlife Service, U.S. Department of the Interior, Washington, D.C.

PREPARATION OF AGAR-AGAR

The species of algae which may be used for the manufacture of agar that are found in sufficient quantities on the California coast to be of commercial importance are the following: *Gelidium corneum*, *G. cartilagineum*, *Gracilaria confervoides*, *Eucheuma spinosum*, and various species of *Tenax* and *Gigarteneae*.

The red seaweed is collected from water up to eight fathoms in depth by men in boats. When the weed is brought ashore it is partially dried and transported to a factory.

The first step in the manufacturing process is the bleaching treatment. The seaweed is spread out in the sun and washed with a whirling spray of water. The colorless seaweed is then placed in a large tank where it is steamed until it is in solution. When

this is accomplished, the solution is run into a settling tank where it is permitted to stand until all the suspended matter contained in the solution has settled. The clarified agar solution is then siphoned off and run into frames where it is allowed to gel. The blocks of jelly are cut with wire into strips about 12 in. long and $1/4$ in. wide. These are placed on canvas frames and carried into the freezing room where the agar jelly is frozen at a temperature of about 14°F. When frozen, they are taken out of the freezing room into the sun which melts the frozen strips. As the jelly melts the water runs out leaving a very porous strip which quickly dries in the sun. The dried strips are tied into 1-lb bundles and are ready for market.

SOURCE: *Marine Products of Commerce* by D. K. Tressler published by Chemical Catalog Company, New York, N.Y.

DRIED SHARK FINS

Shark fins are commonly used by Orientals, particularly the Chinese, in making soup. Though classed as either white fins or black fins, none is either perfectly white or perfectly black. They are divided into several groups of different values, depending upon color, size, and variety. The chief commercial classes of fins are the following: white spotted fin (Chinese *boon leong sit*) graded into large and small white fins; large white fin (*chu sit*); small white fin (*peh sit* and *khiam sit*); large black fin (*tua sit*); small black fin (*oh sit* and *seow oh sit*); and small black-tipped fin (*oh ku sit*). In preparing fins for market, they are merely cut from the shark, are well salted or dusted with lime, and dried in the sun.

SOURCE: *Marine Products of Commerce*, 2nd Edition by Tressler and Lemon published by Reinhold Publishing Corp., New York, N.Y.

SHARK-FLESH PASTE

The Japanese prepare an especially tasty dish from shark and dogfish flesh called shark-flesh paste. The flesh is freed from skin and bones and cut into shreds which are pounded with a wooden pestle in a wooden or stone mortar until the shreds are reduced to paste. During the pounding a little salt and various other condiments are added (the practice varies in different parts of the islands). The paste is made into rolls upon a board, much as home churned butter might be handled. Then the rolls are steamed over boiling water for 20 min in a closed oven. The product is white and has an attractive appearance. It will keep for several days, even in summer.

SOURCE: *Marine Products of Commerce*, 2nd Edition by Tressler and Lemon published by Reinhold Publishing Corp., New York, N.Y.

Addendum

Following is a list of patents issued to Stephan L. Komarik, all assigned to Griffith Laboratories, Inc., Chicago, Illinois:

Apparatus for Canning Meat, U.S. Pat. 2,181,945, Dec. 5, 1939.
Manufacture of Dried Beef, U.S. Pat, 2,224,397, Dec. 10, 1940.
Process for Canned Meat, U.S. Pat. 2,224,398, Dec. 10, 1940.
Production of Canned Ham, U.S. Pat. 2,224,399, Dec. 10, 1940.
Spread Comprising Animal Body Fat, U.S. Pat. 2,288,244, June 30, 1942.
Production of Canned Meats for Storage, U.S. Pat. 2,305,479, Dec. 15, 1942.
Production of Canned Meats for Storage, U.S. Pat. 2,305,480, Dec. 15, 1942.
Canned Meat and Meat Products, U.S. Pat. 2,331,467, Oct. 12, 1943.
Curing Process for Bacon, U.S. Pat. 2,553,533, May 15, 1951.
Production of Meat Products, U.S. Pat. 2,634,211, Apr. 7, 1953.
Manufacture of Conditioning Compound for Ground Meat Products, U.S. Pat. 2,634,212, Apr. 7, 1953.
Perforating process for animal Pieces, U.S. Pat. 2,688,151, Sept. 7, 1954.
Meat Curing Process, U.S. Pat. 2,688,555, Sept. 7, 1954.
Meat Curing Process, U.S. Pat. 2,688,556, Sept. 7, 1954.
Method of Canning Pork Bellies, U.S. Pat. 2,854,342, Sept. 30, 1958.
Production of Meat Emulsion and Products, U.S. Pat. 2,982,115, July 11, 1961.
Meat Curing Process, U.S. Pat. 2,902,369, Sept. 1, 1959.
Method of Improving Tenderness of Meat and Composition Thereof, U.S. Pat. 3,147,123, Sept. 1, 1964.
Means for Shaping Articles Such as Meat Products, U.S. Pat. 3,202,085, Aug. 24, 1965.
Production of Integrated Meat Products, U.S. Pat. 3,238,046, Mar. 1, 1966.
Curing Emulsified Meat Products, U.S. Pat. 3,391,006, July 2, 1968.
Method of Emulsifying and Curing Meat Products, U.S. Pat. 3,391,007, July 2, 1968.
Production of Cured Whole Meat, U.S. Pat. 3,526,521, Sept. 1, 1970.
Meat Curing Process, Can. Pat. 527,627, July 10, 1956.
Meat Curing Process, Can. Pat. 527,628, July 10, 1956.
Perforating Process of Animal Pieces to be Cured, Can. Pat. 527,629, July 10, 1956.
Curing Process for Bacon, Can. Pat. 561,749, Aug. 12, 1958.
Production of Meat Emulsion, Can. Pat. 694,680, Sept. 22, 1964.
Method and Means for Shaping Articles Such as Meat Products, Can. Pat. 725,917, Jan. 18, 1966.
Production of Integrated Meat Products, Can. Pat. 754,500, Mar. 14, 1967.
Treating Meat, Can. Pat. 792,201, Aug. 13, 1968.
Method of Processing Meat, Can. Pat. 1,056,078, Febr. 1, 1967.
Production of Meat Emulsion, Australia Pat. 242,880, Jan. 17, 1963.

Index

NOTES

NOTES

NOTES

NOTES

NOTES

NOTES

NOTES

NOTES

NOTES

NOTES